Library of
Davidson College

North American and Western European Economic Policies

OTHER INTERNATIONAL ECONOMIC ASSOCIATION PUBLICATIONS

THE THEORY OF WAGE DETERMINATION
THE ECONOMIC CONSEQUENCES OF THE SIZE OF NATIONS
THE THEORY OF CAPITAL
THE ECONOMICS OF TAKE-OFF INTO SUSTAINED GROWTH
INTERNATIONAL TRADE THEORY IN A DEVELOPING WORLD
ECONOMIC DEVELOPMENT WITH SPECIAL REFERENCE TO EAST ASIA
ECONOMIC DEVELOPMENT FOR AFRICA SOUTH OF THE SAHARA
THE THEORY OF INTEREST RATES
THE ECONOMICS OF EDUCATION
PROBLEMS IN ECONOMIC DEVELOPMENT
ACTIVITY ANALYSIS IN THE THEORY OF GROWTH AND PLANNING
THE ECONOMIC PROBLEMS OF HOUSING
CAPITAL MOVEMENTS AND ECONOMIC DEVELOPMENT
PRICE FORMATION IN VARIOUS ECONOMIES
THE DISTRIBUTION OF NATIONAL INCOME
ECONOMIC DEVELOPMENT FOR EASTERN EUROPE
RISK AND UNCERTAINTY
ECONOMIC PROBLEMS OF AGRICULTURE IN INDUSTRIAL SOCIETIES
INTERNATIONAL ECONOMIC RELATIONS
BACKWARD AREAS IN ADVANCED COUNTRIES
PUBLIC ECONOMICS
ECONOMIC DEVELOPMENT IN SOUTH ASIA

CLASSICS IN THE THEORY OF PUBLIC FINANCE

North American and Western European Economic Policies

Proceedings of a Conference held by the
International Economic Association

EDITED BY
CHARLES P. KINDLEBERGER
AND
ANDREW SHONFIELD

MACMILLAN
ST MARTIN'S PRESS

© The International Economic Association 1971

All rights reserved. No part of this publication may be reproduced or transmitted, in any form or by any means, without permission.

First published 1971 by
MACMILLAN AND CO LTD
London and Basingstoke
Associated companies in New York Toronto
Dublin Melbourne Johannesburg and Madras

SBN 333 12163 5 (hard cover)

Library of Congress catalog card no. 75–144220

Printed in Great Britain by
R. & R. CLARK LTD
Edinburgh

Contents

Acknowledgements	vii
List of Participants	ix
Introduction Charles P. Kindleberger and Andrew Shonfield	xi

PART ONE: THE ESSENTIAL AIMS OF ECONOMIC POLICIES

1	The Determinants of United States Foreign Economic Policy *Henry C. Wallich*	3
	Discussion	17
2	Canada in an Interdependent North Atlantic Economy *H. C. Eastman*	31
	Discussion	48
3	Repercussions of the Economic Policy of the United States on the Policies of the Countries of the European Economic Community *M. Albert*	57
	Discussion	75
4	United Kingdom External Economic Policy *Samuel Brittan*	87
5	International Economic Policies of a Nordic Group *Nils Lundgren*	103
	Discussion of Chapters 4 and 5	124
6	Portuguese Economic Development in the Presence of the Post-war Foreign Policies of the United States *A. M. Pinto Barbosa*	140
	Discussion	159

PART TWO: CONFLICTS OF INTEREST IN TRADE, CAPITAL FLOWS AND MONETARY POLICY

7	North Atlantic Trade and Payments *Angus Maddison*	163
	Discussion	172
8	Economic Relations between European Socialist Countries and Capitalist Countries of Europe and North America *K. Plotnikov*	180
	Discussion	187
9	Towards an International Capital Market? *Richard N. Cooper*	192

10	European Capital Markets and Financial Intermediation by the United States *Alexandre Lamfalussy*	209
	Discussion of Chapters 9 and 10	223
11	Monetary Relations between Europe and America *Robert A. Mundell*	237
12	The Problems of International Monetary Arrangements *Gabriel Ferras*	256
	Discussion of Chapters 11 and 12	270

PART THREE: CONFLICTS OF INTEREST IN AGRICULTURAL AND INDUSTRIAL POLICIES

13	Mutual Repercussions of Western European and North American Agricultural Policies *D. R. Campbell*	283
14	The Common Agricultural Policy of the European Economic Community and North American Exports *Luc Fauvel*	298
15	The Mutual Impact of North American and Western European Agricultural Policies *John Ashton*	321
	Discussion of Chapters 13, 14 and 15	337
16	American Influence on Industrial Policy in Western Europe since the Second World War *Jacques R. Houssiaux*	351
17	United States Foreign Investment and the Technological Gap *John H. Dunning*	364
	Discussion of Chapters 16 and 17	407

PART FOUR: CONFLICTS OF INTEREST IN MIGRATION POLICIES

18	Transatlantic and North American International Migration *Anthony Scott*	425
19	Intra-European Migration of Labour and Migration of High-level Manpower from Europe to North America *H. Rieben*	452
	Discussion of Chapters 18 and 19	478

PART FIVE: THE SEARCH FOR SOLUTIONS

20	Optimal Economic Interdependence *Charles P. Kindleberger*	491
	Discussion	503
21	Regionalism in International Trade *Andrew Shonfield*	518
	Discussion	535
	Index	547

Acknowledgments

The International Economic Association wishes to express its gratitude to the three bodies whose financial support made possible the organisation of this conference and the publication of this volume – the Ford Foundation, the Sociedade Portuguesa de Siencias Economicas, and UNESCO. The Association is also deeply indebted to Rector M. B. Amzalak, President of the Portuguese Economic Association, to Professor A. M. Pinto Barbosa, Governor of the Bank of Portugal, to Professor Manuel Jacinto Nunes, Vice-Governor, and to Dr José de Mello, for the help which made it possible for the meeting to be held in the very agreeable surroundings of the Alvor Praïa Hotel, Algarve.

All participants in the conference will share our deep regret at the tragic death in an automobile accident soon after the conference of Professor Houssiaux, who both as writer of one of the papers and as a protagonist in many of our discussions took a central part in our work. The paper that we here print must have been one of his last contributions to economic studies.

List of Participants

Mr M. Albert, Direction Générale des Affaires Économiques, Commission des Communautés Européennes, Brussels
Professor M. B. Amzalak, The Technical University of Lisbon, Portugal
Professor J. Ashton, University of Newcastle upon Tyne, United Kingdom
Professor A. M. Pinto Barbosa, Technical University of Lisbon, Portugal
Mr S. Brittan, *Financial Times*, London, United Kingdom
Professor D. R. Campbell, University of Toronto, Canada
Professor R. N. Cooper, Economic Growth Center, Yale University, New Haven, United States
Professor J. H. Dunning, University of Reading, United Kingdom
Professor H. C. Eastman, University of Toronto, Canada
Professor L. Fauvel, Université de Paris, France
Mr Gabriel Ferras, Bank for International Settlements, Basle, Switzerland
Professor D. C. Hague, Manchester Business School, United Kingdom
Professor Sir John Hicks, All Souls College, Oxford, United Kingdom
Professor J. Houssiaux, Université de Nancy, France
Professor L. Izzo, Università di Siena, Italy
Professor E. James, Université de Paris, France
Professor T. S. Khachaturov, Academy of Sciences of the U.S.S.R., Moscow, U.S.S.R.
Professor C. P. Kindleberger, Massachusetts Institute of Technology, Cambridge, United States
Mr A. Lamfalussy, Banque de Bruxelles, Belgium
Professor I. A. Lebedev, Institute of World Economy and International Relations, Moscow, U.S.S.R.
Professor E. Lundberg, University of Stockholm, Sweden
Mr N. Lundgren, Institute for International Economic Studies, Stockholm, Sweden
Mr Angus Maddison, Paris, France
Professor Jean Marchal, Université de Paris, France
Mme André Marchal, Paris, France
Dr Jorge de Mello, Lisbon, Portugal
Professor M. A. G. van Meerhaeghe, University of Ghent, Belgium
Professor R. A. Mundell, University of Chicago, United States
Professor M. J. Nunes, Technical University of Lisbon, Portugal
Professor D. Patinkin, The Hebrew University, Jerusalem, Israel
Professor E. S. Phelps, Wharton School of Finance and Commerce, University of Pennsylvania, United States
Professor K. N. Plotnikov, Academy of Sciences of the U.S.S.R., Moscow, U.S.S.R.
Professor P. Nørregaard Rasmussen, University of Copenhagen, Denmark
Professor H. Rieben, Centre de Recherche Européenne, Lausanne, Switzerland
Professor Austin Robinson, University of Cambridge, United Kingdom
Professor A. D. Scott, University of British Columbia, Vancouver, Canada
Professor F. M. A. dd Seabra, Oporto University, Portugal
Mr A. Shonfield, Social Sciences Research Council, London
Professor O. Šik, Academy of Science, Prague, Czechoslovakia
Professor Egon Sohmen, University of Heidelberg, West Germany
Professor S. Z. Tolpekin, Association of Soviet Economic Scientific Institutions, Moscow
Professor M. A. G. van Meerhaeghe, University of Ghent, Belgium
Professor H. C. Wallich, Yale University, United States

x   *List of Participants*

Observers

Mr F. O. Grogan, University of Newcastle upon Tyne, United Kingdom
Ursula K. Hicks, Fellow Emeritus, Linacre College, Oxford, United Kingdom
Mr E. Merigó, O.E.C.D., Paris
Dr Bernard Molitor, Commission des Communautés Européennes, Brussels
Dr J. J. de A. Soares, Technical University, Lisbon, Portugal
Professor Noboru Yamamoto, Keio University, Tokyo, Japan

Programme Committee

Professor Austin Robinson
Professor C. P. Kindleberger
Mr A. Shonfield
Mr A. Lamfalussy

Introduction

Charles P. Kindleberger and Andrew Shonfield

I. THE ISSUES

In contrast with domestic economic policies, or with the international economic relations between developed and less developed countries, the economic relations among developed countries may be thought to pose few controversial issues. Discussion of the 'Mutual Repercussions of North American and Western European Economic Policies' at the International Economic Association Conference at Alvor in the Algarve, Portugal, from 28 August to 4 September 1969 proved otherwise. The debate ranged over a wide number of issues, partly technical questions of economic analysis, although a surprising number of them were political – and its tone was sharp. The Conference ended with no emerging consensus whether international economic institutions functioned in a symmetrical way or were dominated by the power of the United States; or whether economic policy should be designed co-operatively for cosmopolitan or separately for national ends.

The problem was approached in a variety of ways. In functional terms, trade and commercial policy came first, with a separate rubric for the special problems posed by trade and integration in agriculture, then factor movements, with the usual subject of capital movements enlarged by attention to labour migration. The relatively recent topic of international business posed questions of international technological transfer and industrial organisation. Not least among the functional questions were international payments and monetary arrangements.

A dimension separate from the function was the geographic. Here papers covered both North Atlantic questions dealing with the relations between Western Europe and North America, and those within the separate geographical components. Transatlantic topics, moreover, varied in scope, sometimes concerning the entire continent on each side, as in Maddison's discussion of trade; sometimes a single country, as in the impact of the United States on Portugal's development, discussed by Pinto Barbosa; sometimes North America with the various groups in Europe. Within the continents, papers dealt with Canadian trade with the United States and especially with the functional integration in a single commodity represented by the automobile agreement (Eastman); or with the special problems faced by the European Economic Community (Albert), the European Free Trade Area and the embryonic Scandinavian

Economic Union, called Nordek (Lundgren). The extreme complexity of the geographic relationships can be illustrated by the suggestion put forward during the Conference that the economic integration of Europe, or at least of the E.E.C., was advanced by United States business, the Euro-dollar market and Mediterranean labour. Not being rooted in any particular European country, United States firms were more mobile and readier to move in economic space than their Common Market competitors, and hence more effective in producing single markets for goods and labour. The Euro-dollar market brought together existing local markets for money and capital by stimulating movements of funds between the separate countries, and also created a neutral, outside market to perform the function of mediating between them.

Perhaps the most fundamental question on which it proved impossible to reach consensus was the extent to which cosmopolitan solutions of the sort represented by *laissez-faire* were fundamentally policies in the interest of a single dominant (or once dominant) country, such as the United States. Free trade, in Bismarck's eyes, was the aggressive, self-serving policy of the strong. *Laissez-faire* in trade, capital movements, labour migration and the regulation of international business – not to mention the dollar standard in international payments – may be put forward by the United States as public goods for world use, but are scepticllay regarded by many Europeans, as well as by less developed countries, as private United States goods. Wallich's paper discussing United States policies made a contrary point: in finance for collective defence, and initially in aid to less developed countries, the United States has been forced by bargaining strategy to assume the lion's share of the burden of producing the collective good. But in bilateral monopoly, a non-zero-sum, collective-bargaining game, the task of arriving at a 'fair' distribution of costs and benefits is virtually an impossible one.

Conflict in the discussion ran not only between the economic and the political, but between the short- and the long-run in each area. This was amply illustrated in the papers of Ashton, Campbell and Fauvel on agricultural issues. In the short run export more; in the long, move resources out of the sector; but which country bears the burden of moving first? Rieben and Scott on migration made clear that the brain drain may not be a social problem in the long run, when a man earns and consumes his marginal product with no external effects on his old or new compatriots. In the short run, however, the haemorrhaging of skilled and professional workers from a country can be painful, leaving it, and complementary factors of production, poorer for lack of managers, engineers, scientists, doctors. Cooper, backed in the discussion by Lundberg and Sir John Hicks, made an analogous point about capital movements: with perfect markets and no political factors to distort rational economic choice, they would concede that *laissez-faire* provides the optimum

Introduction xiii

solution in the long run to move savings from countries where they are abundant relative to investment opportunities to those where they are scarce; in the short run, the danger is that freedom will permit or induce movements from capital-poor to capital-rich countries, or deprive complementary factors of capital needed for national growth plans.

The several intersecting dimensions of the discussion – North America/Western Europe, economic/political, short-run/long-run – were perhaps most intricately intertwined in the question of payments and money. Many of the questions were technical: the existence and importance of international financial intermediation, on which Lamfalussy was sceptical; the relative merits of Special Drawing Rights and a rise in the price of gold, in which Ferras defended the latter; the role of forward markets in providing hedging sufficient to sustain trade under a system of flexible exchange rates, debated between Kindleberger and Sohmen; plus the perennial fixed versus flexible exchange rates in which Mundell led the adherents of fixed rates, and Brittan the ranks of floaters.

II. ASYMMETRY BETWEEN THE UNITED STATES AND THE REST

The more basic issue, however, was whether Europe and the world were on the dollar standard, like it or not. The Euro-dollar and Euro-bond markets take both the dollar and world capital markets out of the jurisdiction of the United States, and depoliticise the issue to some extent. The United States and Canada, along with European nation-states, have lost the power to control resources within their boundaries because of the greater mobility not only of goods, but also of professional and highly skilled labour, finance capital, and industrial capital under the command of international corporations. The world economy these developments foreshadow is not yet clearly delineated or understood. If the economic strength of the United States declines drastically, and that of some other country such as Western Germany rises, significant change may occur. At the moment, however, it is a dollar world, just as 1913 was a sterling world. In the view of some American economists (among whom the American author of this Introduction is numbered), this produces certain asymmetries in financial relationships which are an inherent part of the present system. Put baldly and with some exaggeration, these are:

> (1) The dollar is the world medium of exchange, unit of account, store of value, standard of deferred payment. It is the vehicle currency through which French francs are transferred into Deutschmarks, for example, and lire into Danish kroner. No other currency performs a similar role on a similar scale.

(2) If the dollar is a world money, the United States is a bank and not a firm as other countries are. The difference between a firm and a bank, of course, is that the liabilities of the former are expected to be paid off at regular intervals, while those of the latter are passed from hand to hand as money, and tend to be permanent in fact, despite being 'demand' in form. A special role midway between a firm and a bank is given to the United Kingdom which is a firm vis-à-vis Europe and North America, but a bank in the sterling area. To the extent that a country is a bank and not a firm, its balance of payments must be viewed from a different perspective, with equilibrium, deficits and surpluses measured on a different basis.

(3) The dollar is a money's money, a numéraire for foreign exchanges, and cannot be regarded as other currencies. It cannot float, except as other currencies float against it, and its value is the reciprocal of the value of all other currencies, not its price in one.

(4) The United States can change the value of gold, but not the price of the dollar. Other countries can readily change the value of their currencies against the dollar, but not the price of gold.

(5) United States long-term lending prior to the Voluntary Credit Restraint Program of February 1965 and the Mandatory Restraint Program of January 1968 was matched by increases in European dollar deposits in New York. This represented international financial intermediation by the United States in Europe in exchange for the spread between long- and short-term rates. This intermediation is a normal economic function which enables borrowers to get cheaper credit and lenders more liquid assets.

(6) Changes in United States interest rates change the level of world rates, but not the interest-differential between New York and other financial centres. Other central banks can change the interest-differential of their leading financial centre, but not, acting individually, the level of world interest rates.

There is no agreement that the system in fact has these asymmetries running between the United States and the dollar and Western Europe and its moneys. In differing degree, many American economists regard these as objective statements of fact; European economists largely view them as subjective claims by the United States to preferred treatment. It is difficult to devise objective tests of their validity. It is simple, however, to measure the intensity of the negative reaction in Europe, which was at its highest in France under President de Gaulle, and scales down to moderate amounts in Belgium and Italy, despite Lamfalussy's particular criticism of the international financial intermediation thesis. What is difficult to sort out is how much of the reaction against the total view is

Introduction

objection to the economic analysis, and how much objection to the political dependence of Europe implicit in the asymmetrical or hierarchical relationship.

While the possible asymmetry between the United States and Western Europe (plus much of the rest of the world) is sharpest in international payments and monetary relationships, it is not altogether absent from trade and international business. Further tariff reductions depend critically on United States leadership: a new initiative can come only, like the Kennedy Round, from that country. If that country slips back into protectionism, much of the rest of the world is likely to follow. Heightened world concern over the penetration of national economies by international companies is focused almost exclusively on companies of American parentage. The Canadians long maintained a Dutch-owned bank without formulating a policy against foreign ownership of banks until an American bank undertook to acquire it. Unilever, Shell, Philips, Nestlé, B.A.S.F., Pechiney, Brown Boveri, Massey-Ferguson, do not excite the resistance, antipathy, excitement aroused by Procter and Gamble, Esso, Westinghouse, Coca-Cola, DuPont, General Motors, International Harvester.

Attention to North Atlantic economic relations, and the debate over whether these are symmetrical or dominated by North America, and specifically the United States, by no means diverted attention from the many specific problems affecting economic organisation within North America, and especially within Europe. The topics are, to be sure, organically related in more than one way. External factors and institutions can assist in the integration of European goods and factor markets, as noted above.

III. EUROPEAN REGIONALISTS v. AMERICAN COSMOPOLITANS

But the drive to establish restricted regional organisations in Europe may also impede the advance towards a 'one world' economic system. The argument between the European regionalists and the American cosmopolitans tended to be presented by the latter in terms of a straightforward trade-off between the optimisation of world-wide economic welfare, through the achievement of the maximum feasible mobility of factors, and the fulfilment of certain non-economic objectives dear to European sentiment. If the latter included, as it seemed to do, a certain parochial hostility to American business and to other manifestations of American economic and technological prowess, then the Europeans would just have to decide how much the satisfaction of these feelings was worth to them in terms of economic welfare forgone. The expectations seemed to be that although the Europeans liked to complain about American predominance, when it came to the point of actual choice they would plump for the continuance of something pretty like the *status quo*, rather than give up the very solid gains which they derived from an increasingly liberal world economic system.

There are, however, dangers to the established system of liberal commercial practice governing trade in industrial goods between the advanced countries that may arise from the freeing of the international capital market. Cooper, in elaboration of the argument noted above, contended that the probabilities of disturbance to any individual nation's balance of payments will be greatly increased by this process, unless there is (*a*) effective machinery in place to ensure co-ordinated monetary and fiscal policies among the countries of the North Atlantic area, and (*b*) an agreed method for ensuring more frequent, small alterations in exchange-rate parities. Without these major reforms, the likelihood is that the industrial nations will revert to some of their old trigger-happy ways of defending their balances of payments by trade restrictions of one kind or another. Since Cooper's desiderata for a reformed international system capable of accommodating the free flow of capital amount to a pretty tall order, his concluding warning that if they were not fulfilled, 'high international mobility of capital may well leave us with a third- or fourth-best world', had an ominous ring.

Members of the American cosmopolitan school tended to the answer that if this was indeed going to be the outcome, then there was precious little that national economic policy or national institutions would in fact be able to do about it. There was, they alleged, an irreversible tendency for factors of production to move from place to place with increasing freedom. It was even claimed that national governments were no longer able in practice to interfere seriously with the movement of factors among advanced industrial countries; whatever they were still able to do to control their external trading accounts, the capital account was already beyond them. It might be added that since these two elements in the external accounts cannot be kept rigidly separate in practice, the implication of this view was that the ability of individual nations to control the behaviour of their current accounts was very shaky too.

But the evidence of the bankers with direct experience of operating in the international capital market at the European end suggested that governments were by no means ineffective, at any rate in the short term, in getting their wishes obeyed. The concentration of financial activity in the hands of a very few banks in the typical European country, coupled with the dependence of these financial institutions on the goodwill of the national central bank, tended to make them highly responsive to pressures exerted by governments. Indeed there was evidence from several European countries that the national authorities were beginning to assert their control over their domestic banks' operations in the Euro-dollar market, and succeeding in doing so with remarkably little trouble. Was this another case where the institutional differences between the United States and Europe, with the power over external capital movements far more diffused in the United States financial system than it was in Europe, caused the two sides of the Atlantic to form different pictures of the world? Perhaps. But on the other hand it might be that the American cosmopolitans, basing their predictions on American experience, were in a better position than the Europeans to foresee the likely structure of the future international financial system. Like de Tocqueville's America, it might be a clearer guide to the future society of Western Europe than what the Europeans could see under their own noses. That raised the question whether a completely free international capital market among the industrial countries was so obviously advantageous to their peoples as to overcome the desire of individual nations to maintain control over their own affairs. In practice the wishes of the ordinary citizens responsible for voting governments into power might well conflict with the objectives of the small class of persons and institutions responsible for guiding the flow of substantial amounts of capital across national frontiers. In the last resort the freedom of the capital-owning class would put a curb on the ability of governments to promote domestic welfare policies of their own choosing. Other things being equal, nations would compete for international capital by progressively lowering taxes on investment income. The less public welfare the better. Was this, some of the European economists asked, a covert attempt to hobble the modern welfare state – to halt the process which, they believed, had significantly improved the condition of Western societies during the period since the Second World War?

This argument, like so many others in the field of international economic relations, developed heavily political overtones. In the end, as Kindleberger showed, the cosmopolitan position in the economic debate depended on a political judgement about the readiness of the advanced industrial nations to accept new international institutions which would express their common purposes. These institutions would have to be more than conventional judicial bodies applying broad general principles; they would, for example in their dealings with the international corporation, have to address themselves 'to separate cases, since in the anti-trust field small differences in fact lead to different decisions'.

But are the likely differences which international institutions will be called upon to settle going to be mainly about questions of 'fact'? Will there not be many cases where, with the facts firmly established, the essential decision to be made will depend on political judgement? If so, activities like anti-trust conducted on an international scale would require a high degree of international political consensus. It was indeed the sense of the difficulty of achieving this which led some to argue in favour of the establishment of regional groupings acting as intermediaries between the nation-state and the world-wide community. The regional organisations might not see themselves in this light; indeed they would be likely to be tempted into the making of bargains between member countries which were disadvantageous to outsiders. However, it was pointed out that this was a challenge which the international community could, and should, take up – as it had done with the European Economic Community in the Kennedy Round. The experience with the E.E.C. in the 1960s suggested that the presence of a regional bloc actively engaged in integrating a growing range of its economic activities sometimes acted as a powerful stimulus forcing the pace of wider international collaboration. It was not claimed that the dynamics of regionalism would necessarily work in this way; the outcome plainly depended on the ability of those outside the regional blocs to reach a large measure of agreement on their common interests. The strengthening of international institutions such as GATT and the I.M.F. was thus not an alternative, but complementary to the growth of regional economic organisations.

The regional bloc to be effective must be so constituted as to make it relatively easy for its members to strike bargains with one another. This means not only that they must have a large number of interests in common but also that national attitudes, social and political assumptions, styles of conducting business, must be very much alike. It was on this basis that Lundgren argued for the establishment of Nordek as a tightly-knit group of Scandinavian countries, to replace EFTA. Once the Scandinavians had shed their present EFTA partners, and Britain in particular, they would, he argued, become a much more effective unit in bargaining about wider international economic relations both with the United States and the E.E.C. On this showing Britain would be the odd man out in the Atlantic context, much as Japan is in the Pacific. How far out, it was argued, would be determined by Britain's economic performance. It if continued as weak as in the 1960s, it was suggested, Britain would not readily find a place in any European regional grouping.

It was not in any case felt that Britain's economic performance would be significantly affected one way or another if it were admitted to the European Economic Community in the 1970s. Indeed anxieties were expressed by some that membership of E.E.C. might inhibit British freedom to choose appropriate policies to cope with its own balance of payments problem. Reasons were advanced by Brittan for believing that the 1967 devaluation of the pound combined with the other economic policy measures which had belatedly followed were successfully bringing this problem under control. But there were widely-felt doubts about whether, in spite of the prospect of external surpluses in the short run, the phenomenon of persistently slow economic growth, by comparison with other advanced industrial countries, which was believed to be the ultimate source of the intermittent external payments deficits of recent

Introduction xix

years, had been overcome. To remedy this, it seemed, would require a substantial further shift in resources out of consumption, this time into industrial investment. The outcome would depend on whether Brittan was right in his view that a successful shift of this kind was quite likely to take place gradually without undue strain during the period ahead – or whether it was more plausible to conclude that a more drastic transfer of resources over a shorter period was required to bring about the required change in the tempo of British economic growth.

IV. AGRICULTURE AND MONETARY POLICY

In general the debate was less concerned with the possible composition of alternative regional groupings than with the prospective evolution of the *modus operandi* of those already in existence. It concentrated in particular on the structural characteristics of the E.E.C. and on the way in which these were likely to influence international relations during the 1970s in two key areas – monetary policy and trade in agricultural produce. The E.E.C. had been curiously ineffective in the former; the ideas and the initiatives have largely come from other countries, and where E.E.C. members have played an important role in the formulation of monetary policy it has been as individual countries rather than as a group. By contrast E.E.C. policy in the agricultural field has been extremely ambitious, demanding rigid discipline on the part of member countries in support of defined objectives. The managed market in agriculture has been a dominant factor in international trade in non-industrial products during the 1960s.

The general feeling was that this situation was likely to continue during the 1970s. The E.E.C. had devised a most effective instrument for diverting export trade from outsiders to members of the Community. Fauvel argued, however, that the diversion had still left room for a very substantial increase in United States agricultural exports to the E.E.C. The system of agricultural levies forced exporters outside the Community to compete by means of the quality of their products rather than the price. Thus the Europeans continued to buy large quantities of hard wheat from North America, in spite of the fact that the Community had moved from being a wheat-deficit area to a wheat-surplus area by the late 1960s. Western Europe's deficiency in protein production also provided the United States with a number of useful export outlets for its agricultural produce. Where E.E.C. methods of trading probably hurt most was when it appeared as an exporter selling heavily subsidised agricultural products in third markets, against the competition of traditional low-cost producers. It was difficult to deny that this was both an especially disruptive and extremely expensive way of protecting the European farmer's livelihood.

Introduction

If the aim of the Common Agricultural Policy was to transfer income from the urban to the rural population, the results, as Campbell indicated, have been both inequitable and inefficient. If it was to allow trade in agricultural produce to move freely across national frontiers, then the method chosen – a system of Community-wide minimum prices fixed at a high enough level to keep the inefficient farmers in business – seemed to be the negation of the principle of comparative advantage. It was suggested that the two objectives, of welfare and of freer trade, might usefully be separated from one another and the method that could best be employed to fulfil each of them considered on its own. The events following the devaluation of the French franc in the summer of 1969 suggested some lessons on this score. France had found it expedient not to pass on to its farmers the full benefit of the higher domestic prices resulting from the export of agricultural produce at the minimum Community price levels fixed in units of account. Instead it had decided to draw off some of this additional income by imposing export taxes on these products when they were sold to other Community countries. In this case part of the subsidy to French farmers represented by the high minimum prices was reduced by national fiscal devices. It was against the spirit of the Common Agricultural Policy, whose objective was to manage all agricultural taxes and subsidies through a single fund operating uniform rules throughout the Community, and France had had to obtain special permission for this waiver of the rules, which was granted for a limited period of time. The subsequent German revaluation of the Deutschmark presented similar problems in regard to the subsidy payments to German farmers, only in a reverse sense. It too was met by introducing a separate national element into the management of the agricultural subsidy scheme. In both cases the outcome suggested that the Community might find some convenience in placing part of the responsibility for the welfare element in its programme, at least temporarily, on the individual national governments concerned.

However, the notion that an element of national fiscal management of agriculture might be generalised throughout the Community was, perhaps not surprisingly, strongly resisted by Continental economists most directly concerned with the day-to-day affairs of the E.E.C. Any admission of retreat from the doctrine of the common financial pool handling all the fiscal income and outgo of the Community's agriculture was evidently regarded as a serious fall from grace. When insiders felt so strongly about what they regarded as a point of principle, it was not for those outside the Community to attempt to persuade them otherwise. But the outsiders did point out that there was, in the not so long run, an unavoidable choice between the objective of securing a more efficient allocation of resources in agriculture through free intra-Community trade and the welfare objective pursued by fixing minimum prices high enough to keep the marginal producing unit permanently in business.

The one source of hope that could be identified for the future of a more rational system of European agriculture came from the evidence of the mass withdrawal from rural occupations. European industrial prosperity and the growth of all kinds of urban employment opportunities should in the long run go far to eliminate the welfare problem of peasant families with low incomes. The North American experience of mass migration of the rural poor is by now familiar. What is less well known is the fact that in France during the 1960s the farm labour force was, as Campbell pointed out, declining even faster than it was in Canada. In the six years 1962–8 the total was reduced by more than one-fifth. In the light of such figures as these Campbell's final warning comment on the process of agricultural adaptation in the North Atlantic area as a whole acquired additional force. 'A more rapid rate of structural change might have been detrimental not only to individuals but to nations.' The moral seems to be that economists ought sometimes to restrain their impatience even in the face of something that is clearly a piece of economic nonsense.

That, however, still leaves unsolved the problems of living with the particular system of economic management and adaptation which the E.E.C. has chosen for itself. It is a notably rigid system. The effect of an agricultural policy built around a set of highly negotiated minimum commodity prices, calculated in dollars, has been to impede the process of exchange-rate adjustment inside the European Common Market. Indeed it has been the avowed aim of much of E.E.C. policy-making to reduce the capacity of individual member countries to adjust to changing economic circumstances, while at the same time exposing them to the risks of ever greater economic pressures from their neighbours. The cushioning devices are progressively removed, so that the six nations are ultimately left to take the shocks of any sudden movement coming from one another body to body. Albert makes the point in his paper that by now a decision to change the level of budgetary expenditure in Germany produces almost as large a consequential movement in the French national product as in the German. 'It has become a matter of the greatest importance', he says, 'for each of the Six to make sure that its own economic and financial equilibrium is not disturbed by the policies of the others.'

V. POLITICS AND ECONOMICS

The moral that Albert drew from this situation was the familiar one that effective integration of the European Community will have to be pursued with more urgency than ever before. This might almost be called the 'Monnet effect': first create the crisis by removing the possibility of separate action, then offer to solve it by new forms of common action.

This is a formula for living dangerously, but it cannot be faulted on that account. It undoubtedly has some major successes to its credit. However, it is possible that at some stage a set of economic problems will arise which will require for their joint management by the E.E.C. countries a significantly higher degree of political integration than they are capable of achieving at that point in time. Indeed it is clear in retrospect that the assumption commonly made in the middle 1960s that the E.E.C. countries had reached a tacit agreement (largely as a result of the establishment of the Common Agricultural Policy) to maintain a permanently fixed relationship between the dollar values of their currencies, implied a far higher degree of co-ordination of monetary policy than was politically feasible either then or since that time. By helping to impede the adjustment of currency parities, on the ground that such an act would be anti-Communitarian, the cause of European integration was not advanced at all. The cause of international monetary disorder was.

The example prompts a more general question. In circumstances where the Six are not prepared to respond promptly to the "Monnet effect' as applied to some particular aspect of economic policy, must one conclude, like Cooper in the context of a world-wide system, quoted above, that the Community will tend to opt for a 'third- or fourth-best world'? Cooper's conclusion seems to be pertinent in this case too – that a modest assertion of national separateness would at least increase the chances of attaining a 'second-best world'.

The characteristic features of international economic organisations can be categorised in terms of the limitations which they impose on the range of techniques available for use by governments to adjust to the unforeseen or the undesired event. The world-wide organisations on the whole circumscribe lightly; the regional ones tend to be stricter. But there is no invariable rule about this. All that one can say is that among the developed countries, which are the subject of the present volume, regional organisations seem to be more readily able to restrict the number of economic policy options open to sovereign states, in regard to actions that are uncomfortable for their neighbours, than world-wide organisations. It might seem then that European integration in its various contemplated forms – customs unions, loose or tight, with or without the inclusion of agriculture; economic unions with freedom of factor movement and harmonisation; monetary unions with fixed exchange rates; and most obviously political unions – are all alternatives, more or less deliberately chosen, to a wider world integration. The proponents of regionalism maintain on the other hand that without this goad the process of international collaboration on a world-wide scale would not proceed nearly so far or so fast. The challenge of the regional blocs can only be met by the invention of more effective supra-regional devices. It could be that the variety of contending forms of organisation of the world economy –

Introduction xxiii

regional groupings, functional groups like the North Atlantic developed states and the less developed countries with their organisations – each have their place and appropriate role in a system which can accommodate a wide spectrum of organisational styles.

The major question for economic policy-makers on both sides of the Atlantic remains, however, how far their decisions should be guided by national interests and motives or by more cosmopolitan considerations. In the world of Adam Smith and no externalities or public goods, each country is never so innocently engaged as when it is looking out for its own interests. In the real world, Adam Smith notwithstanding, there are plenty of occasions when the national and general interests do – or appear to – diverge. It may be argued by some that the appearance of divergence is primarily due to differences in the way in which individual countries perceive long-term and short-term advantages, so that the trade-off which each makes among a set of common objectives varies. On this view the underlying harmony between the particular and the general is still present, at any rate in large measure; different notions of optimisation are due chiefly to false perceptions of reality. But the evidence suggests that at least in some matters there are genuinely different interests pursued by different types of state. If one had a developed typology of states one could foresee, as for instance by the identification of the group of nations which conducted the Kennedy Round, when compromise and collaboration was going to be easy. However, in other cases, where for instance the determining characteristics of the type are the sheer size of its national product or the combination of political and economic influence that it can exert over client states, international negotiation, even when guided on both sides by the most rational kind of game theory, may not produce a satisfactory or even determinate answer. The possibilities of blackmail by weak, irresponsible countries of large, powerful ones which are known to have a highly developed sense of responsibility is a commonplace of post-war international relations. It applies in the economic sphere as well as in the political, and leaves some countries feeling that they are made to bear an undue share of the burden of maintaining the international system in good repair.

What can hardly be doubted, however, is the pressure of economic events – lower costs of transport, communication, wider horizons scanned by businessmen, investors, professional men and workers – in the direction of requiring cosmopolitan economic policies and reducing the capacity of the single country to put its monetary, tariff, manpower, etc., policies into effect. With increasing mobility of labour and capital, and internationalisation of economic horizons scanned, Scott raises the question of how a 'country' is defined in the world into which we are moving. The political problems are thorny. It is difficult to distinguish leadership from domination, and respect for sovereignty from the blackmail of the United

States, United Kingdom, Germany and France by Andorra, Liechtenstein, Luxembourg and Monaco. Particular puzzles are presented by the need to separate the 'force des choses' from the 'force des hommes'. At minimum in the determination of economic policies, economics and politics will remain inextricably intertwined.

Part 1

The Essential Aims of Economic Policies

1 The Determinants of United States Foreign Economic Policy

Henry C. Wallich
YALE UNIVERSITY

I. INTRODUCTORY

It has been said that the United States is important to the world; the world is not particularly important to the United States. This is the simple consequence of the United States being a large and rich country. Its ramifications go far to determine United States policies. They also determine the automatic responses of the United States economy to the rest of the world, quite aside from discretionary policy decisions.

The American economy accounts for 16 per cent of the world's trade (excluding Soviet Area countries) and 42 per cent of the world's G.N.P. Trade equals 4 per cent of United States G.N.P. These data give a – far from complete – measure of the weight of the United States in the world economy, and of the foreign sector in the American economy.

It is particularly appropriate to discuss United States economic policy interaction with Western Europe in terms of these structural determinants, because Western Europe may eventually end up in a similar condition. As the E.E.C. coalesces and expands, it will become another large unit similar in some respects to the United States. Many of the implications that structural determinants today have for the United States will then follow also for Western Europe.

In this paper, I shall draw on these properties of the American economy to attempt to explain:

(1) patterns of automatic behaviour in international economic relations; and
(2) patterns of international economic policy.

The empirical side of the argument will at best be illustrative. Particularly as regards policy behaviour, it will have to be recognized that influences other than those emanating from economic structure may be operative, and that at times a country may simply be unresponsive to what seems the self-interest dictated by its economic structure.

II. THE UNITED STATES IN THE WORLD ECONOMY

The large share in world trade raises the question, first of all, of monopolistic exploitation. By raising its prices and restricting its supplies and purchases, through appropriate tariffs for instance, a country with a dominant position could improve its terms of trade. Nevertheless, the United States share in world trade is large without being dominant. It exceeds by only 6 percentage points that of the next country, Germany. In terms of an industry, 16 per cent would not be construed as conveying decisive market power, nor would an industry where the top three firms (United States, Germany, United Kingdom) held one-third of the market be regarded as more than moderately concentrated.

In particular industries, the picture is of course different. The United States share runs from a very minute fraction in some to 100 per cent in numerous highly differentiated products. But in any event it is fairly obvious that the United States as a nation has not deliberately sought to exploit its oligopolistic market position to improve its terms of trade. Its anti-trust policies, moreover, have made it more difficult for individual firms to exploit their particular position in world markets as well as at home. The recent tendency towards an overvaluation of the dollar, to be sure, may have had the effect of improving United States terms of trade. It is not difficult to believe that this has been a wholly unintended by-product of an unwanted situation and that, in ordinary American judgement, overvaluation of the dollar is undesirable.

But if the United States does not maximise oligopolistically via price, it nevertheless has 'market power' in the broadest sense of the word and uses it. More succinctly, the United States is in a position to influence the state of the world and to benefit – and be hurt – by its own actions. Most other countries are in a position analogous to that of atomistic competitors. They can do as they please – within limits – without hope or fear of repercussions. They cannot, by their own efforts, influence the state of the world enough to benefit. The United States is large enough to capture a significant part of the externalities it creates. Its impact on the level of world activity, world interest rates, world prices, the progress of developing countries, the freedom of trade and capital movements, are all externalities, in a sense public goods. This influence results partly from the United States large share in trade but also, of course, from its position as a lender as well as a political leader.

The creation of externalities usually has a cost. The United States rationally should carry the activity to the point where its costs stand in appropriate relation to its share in the benefits it creates. The same rule applied to small countries implies that they should contribute nothing. They should aim at a free ride at the expense of the United States. The case is analogous to that of an oligopolistic industry in which the largest firm holds an umbrella over the industry.

The United States is of course far from accepting the logic of the situation. In its many international enterprises – I.M.F., the development financing institutions, GATT, NATO and many others – it has taken the attitude that everybody ought to bear his fair share of the cost. A conflict thus arises. One must assume that the result of the 'fair shares' principle has been for the United States to do less and many smaller countries to do more than was in their strict interest. On balance one may suspect – but this is purely a guess – that more was accomplished towards improving the state of the world by proceeding on a fair shares basis than could have been accomplished if all had proceeded on the basis of their properly calculated self-interest.

The distribution of successes and failures, on the part of the United States, in obtaining acceptance for the fair shares principle suggests another rule at work. The United States has been relatively successful in obtaining co-operation with respect to the I.M.F. and GATT, relatively unsuccessful with respect to development financing on soft terms and NATO. The casual principle underlying this distribution seems to be that 'love' is a public good, 'fear' a private one. It will be observed that the United States has scored successes in areas in which non-contribution, non-co-operation, or disruption can be effectively penalised. The I.M.F. can refuse credit to bad borrowers, impose the scarce currency clause on bad creditors; GATT can authorise retaliation. There are no comparable penalties for not making soft loans or grants, for not putting up the promised number of NATO divisions, to say nothing of compliance with United States-sponsored restraints on East–West trade. In these areas, 'love', a general improvement of the state of the world, is the sole incentive, and it does not pull very hard.

A far more speculative analysis of the bargaining relation and mutual constraints between the United States and Western Europe rests on the distinction between long-run and short-run goal trade-offs. In the short run, pronounced conflicts exist between alternative goals of the same transactor as well as between identical goals of competing transactors. In the long run, these conflicts diminish and tend to be replaced by harmony of interests. Thus, in the short run, price stability and full employment can be traded off. In the long run, after inflation becomes fully discounted, that opportunity diminishes. In the short run, the income of household A or country X can be increased by reducing that of household B or country Y and perhaps in no other way. In the long run, this type of gain becomes small relative to gains in their aggregate incomes that are open to them if they co-operate.

There is a wide range of conflicts that, if left unresolved, or resolved to the strong dissatisfaction of one of the parties, will reduce the prospects of future co-operation and the benefits therefrom to both parties. Each party then faces a trade-off between favourable resolution of the short-run conflict and long-run gains from co-operation and harmony. If the parties differ in their degree of time preference, this will predispose the party with high time preference to insist on having its way in the short run, at the expense of the future, and the party with low time preference to yield immediate gains in order to increase future benefits.

It could be argued that the United States has a higher rate of time preference than the Western European countries. Certainly this seems to be the view of European politicians and negotiators who have observed rapid switches in United States interest, from post-war reconstruction to containment of the Soviets, to aid to developing countries, to international monetary reform. European scepticism with respect to these successive United States urgencies, and occasional harsh words about 'American hysteria', may reflect a low rate of time preference in the solution of problems. It may also reflect simply the bargaining attitude of the near-atomistic transactor hoping for a free ride. To the extent that there is substance to the hypothesis of a difference in time preference, the consequences are beneficial to the United States. It tends to get its way in the short run, and benefits from the maintenance of long-run co-operation and harmony which is aided by European short-run concessions.

III. THE SMALL FOREIGN SECTOR

We still need to examine the implications of the low trade/income ratio in the United States. They are essentially twofold:
 (1) foreign affairs carry little weight in United States domestic policy making; and
 (2) the United States is potentially even more important in the world as a lender than as a trader.

The United States is not altogether dissimilar to a few other countries in the size of its foreign trade. Germany, Japan, Canada and the United Kingdom are broadly comparable, and the first two are narrowing the gap. But the United States is altogether unique in that its absolutely large foreign trade amounts to so little domestically. Other countries experience a strong discipline emanating from their foreign interests. The United States, in purely economic terms, does not. However this fact is expressed – in terms of propensity to isolationism, or the relation of tail and dog, or an optimum currency area – it is always true that the United States has less reason than most countries to make domestic sacrifices proportionate to its G.N.P. in order to achieve international economic objectives.

This remains broadly true when we consider the commodity structure of United States trade. United States resources are so well diversified that there are few commodities that it *must* import. In the case of some extreme catastrophe befalling world trade, the United States almost certainly will always be able to earn enough foreign exchange to pay for the coffee, bananas, and some critical minerals that it needs.

Never since the days of the 1933 World Economic Conference has the

United States taken advantage of the bargaining power that this condition gives it. The United States has been surprisingly internationalist, perhaps irrationally so. Its ability to influence world affairs, analysed above, may have pulled it in that direction. Power demands exercise. Should the development and expansion of the E.E.C. limit that ability, the United States conceivably might turn in the inward direction towards which its structure seems to predispose it.

The importance of the United States as an international lender and investor derives from its large flow of savings and its high capital/labour ratio which presumably tends to depress the return on domestic investment. In relative terms, the United States is not a high saving country. Its gross saving/G.N.P. ratio is of the order of 17 per cent, contrasted with ratios of over 25 per cent in Germany and as much as 40 per cent in Japan. Nevertheless, when a large number of high-income households and corporations save at relatively low rates, the aggregate flow is still substantial. The United States, moreover, also refinances some of its international investment with countries that transfer capital to the United States. In time, its foreign investment interests may give the United States a bigger stake in the world than its trade interests. Policy constraints and conflicts in this area will be examined subsequently.

IV. BALANCE OF PAYMENTS ADJUSTMENT

Payments imbalances, and particularly the payments deficit of the United States that began in 1958, have generated strong policy constraints and conflicts. Most of the considerations here – as in the rest of the paper – are familiar ground. All that is needed is to place them in the context of these constraints and conflicts.

Payments imbalances must be financed or adjusted. Either involves costs. One way of approaching the problem is to try to minimise aggregate costs. If other things – unemployment, inflation, various frictions – are equal, a short adjustment period will be better than a long one. Richard Cooper has shown that co-ordination of policies directed towards domestic and international objectives minimises the adjustment period. If it also minimises the range of the intervening fluctuations, the costs of imbalance will be further reduced.[1]

Minimisation of joint costs may not be attractive to the participants, however, if each side thinks it can shift a larger share of the burden to the other. The two sides, moreover, may not agree on the relative costs of the different burdens they must bear, e.g. inflation and unemployment. The following aspects may help to clarify – though not necessarily to settle –

---

[1] Richard N. Cooper, 'Macroeconomic Policy Adjustment in Interdependent Economies', *Quarterly Journal of Economics* (Feb 1969).

the issues that have arisen between the United States and Western Europe, principally the E.E.C.:

(1) Financing of a deficit can proceed with and without adjustment. If the European countries, having a surplus, succeed in fully compensating its expansive effects while the United States compensates the contractive effects of its deficit, that deficit can continue indefinitely. The United States has tended to view a situation of this kind as simply a monetary phenomenon. The Europeans have tended to stress the transfer of real resources. Europeans, moreover, seem to have drawn a distinction, immaterial with respect to the real resource transfer, between deficits financed with gold and deficits financed with dollars.

(2) The amount of financing available determines the distribution of the burden of adjustment. Typically, the burden has taken the asymmetrical form of unemployment in the deficit countries and inflation in the surplus countries. The more financing has been available, the less unemployment has had to be accepted by the deficit countries and the more inflation by the surplus countries. As it happens, historical traumata have made the United States and the United Kingdom particularly sensitive to unemployment and, among Western Europeans, the Federal Republic of Germany particularly sensitive to inflation. In the recent imbalance, each side thus has had to bear the burden it particularly dislikes.

(3) Only the side undergoing inflation contributes permanently to adjustment. The side undergoing unemployment, reducing imports without reducing prices, on the whole contributes only temporarily. Qualifications attach to the latter statement in so far as unemployment affects capital movements, investment, and the rate of growth, and to the extent that a stable Phillips curve relating prices and unemployment can be presumed to exist.

(4) Confronted with European complaints about imported inflation, American policy-makers have tended to argue that the Europeans are responsible for their own predicament since by appropriate monetary policy they could have neutralised the inflationary impulse. European policy-makers confronted with American demands for a fair sharing of the burden of adjustment have tended to argue that countries suffering a payments deficit are guilty of loose policies and should put their house in order.

(5) Something can be said for making the division of the burden of financing and adjustment dependent on the presence of a 'dilemma situation', i.e. a conflict between internal and external goals. Presence of a dilemma, e.g. deficit and unemployment, or surplus and inflation, means that a heavy sacrifice is imposed upon a country in requiring it to adjust its balance of payments. Absence of a dilemma, e.g. deficit and inflation, or surplus and unemployment, implies that the country has a motive, for domestic reasons, to take the actions that will also improve its balance of payments. More can be asked of it under those circumstances.

(6) Imported inflation or deflation normally creates a dilemma. Dilemmas are therefore particularly likely to occur in countries where the foreign sector is large relative to G.N.P. In countries like the United States, where the foreign sector is relatively small, exogenous fluctuations in G.N.P. are unlikely. Endogenous fluctuations, if they start from internal and external equilibrium, will not create a dilemma. However, if an external imbalance exists when an endogenous fluctuation begins, a dilemma is as likely as not to arise. During the long deficit period of the United States, dilemma situations have existed throughout except in periods of overheating. Thus the fact that its structure predisposes the United States towards endogenous fluctuations does not preclude the appearance of dilemmas and does not argue strongly for a one-sided shifting of the burden of adjustment towards the United States.

(7) Automatic impulses towards balance of payments adjustment work less well and their operation is slower in the United States than elsewhere. The income mechanism works more slowly, because the United States, with its relatively low propensities to save and to pay taxes and its absolutely low propensity to import, has a higher multiplier than most other countries. The price mechanism also can be expected to work slowly. The reason is that while the low propensity to import and the diversified structure of production no doubt enhance the international elasticity of substitution, short-run elasticities are probably quite low relative to long-run, owing to the imperfect knowledge of foreign markets and sources of supply natural to a large country.

(8) Discretionary action to end a deficit is less likely to be taken by the United States because of the high cost of achieving balance via income restriction, given the low propensity to import, and because this low propensity also prevents international financial considerations from gaining much weight in American politics. For these reasons and others still to be discussed, the example of numerous countries that achieved quick balance of payments adjustment after suffering a deficit – France, Italy, Germany, Japan – is not clearly applicable to the United States.

(9) Both the United States and Western Europe have followed mildly mercantilist policies in subsidising exports via tax policy, credit policy, and promotional devices, while restricting imports by tariffs, non-tariff restrictions, and governmental purchasing policies. Taking into account massive European border taxes, the common agricultural policy (C.A.P.) of the E.E.C. countries, export, credit insurance, aids to tourism, and sometimes complete preclusion of government purchases from abroad, it is probably true that the United States has had the worst of this competition.

(10) Inability to make flexible use of fiscal policy to curb domestic overexpansion has led to an excessive use of monetary policy for inflation control on both sides of the Atlantic. The induced capital flows have at

times frustrated the purposes of the authorities. They have also led to competitive or protective escalation of interest rates which in some cases has precluded what would have been a desirable level for domestic purposes. The net result for the time being has been to make United States monetary policy a very preponderant determinant of world interest rates, a condition that is certainly questionable when United States interest rates in turn are strongly affected by inflation.

(11) Countries are likely to have inconsistent balance of payments objectives. In relations between the United States and Western Europe the main sources of these inconsistencies have been:

(a) Deficit countries have had to consider their overall position; surplus countries may have preferred to ignore capital imports and to focus on the current account.

(b) The United States liquidity balance overstates aggregate world deficits so long as private foreigners accumulate dollars.

(c) Statement of United States and United Kingdom reserves on a gross basis makes world reserves dependent on surpluses and deficits of these reserve countries.

(d) Demand for reserves probably has exceeded supply in acceptable forms, i.e. in forms other than reserve currencies.

(e) Countries may have structural objectives concerning their balance of payments, e.g. the desire for a current account surplus, as a stimulus, as insurance, or to finance some non-current expenditure.

(12) The low weight of the foreign sector in the United States, together with the reserve role of the dollar, tends to push the United States into an 'nth country' role, i.e. to enable other countries to make their balance of payments objectives prevail over those of the United States. If the sum of the objectives of other countries adds up to a surplus, as seems to have been the case in recent years, the United States tends to inherit the residual deficit.

V. RESERVE CURRENCY PROBLEMS

The dollar serves as official reserve currency, as a vehicle currency for private trading and lending, and as an intervention currency in national exchange markets. Some of the policy constraints that the United States and the countries of Western Europe have imposed upon each other have resulted from those international functions. It must be borne in mind, however, that some of the phenomena seemingly connected with the special roles of the dollar may simply mean that the United States is a large and important country. They might persist in some degree even if critics of the system ostensibly were to achieve their objective of making the dollar 'just like any other currency'.

(1) The gold exchange standard has given the United States some

flexibility in financing its payments deficit. 'Liability adjustment' in lieu of 'asset adjustment' has allowed some stretching of reserves. Whether the low balance of payments discipline of the United States about which some European countries have complained reflects more fundamentally the reserve role of the dollar or the low domestic weight of the United States foreign sector is debatable. At any rate, the over-use by the United States of its special facility and the ensuing attempt to discipline the United States by gold withdrawals have meant bitterness if not a very effective policy constraint.

(2) The unsystematic creation of reserves under the gold exchange standard has led to criticism of the system. United States deficits create, United States surpluses extinguish dollar reserves. To the extent, however, that the United States balance of payments is in fact the residual of all other countries' balances, the criticism is inappropriate. The system then generates precisely the volume of reserves that the world in the aggregate demands. In all probability, United States deficits have gone beyond that. But the fact noted earlier, that countries were willing to hold in gold reserves they were not willing to hold in dollars, suggests that dissatisfaction was not with the volume of reserves *per se*.

(3) Even after United States official liabilities had in effect ceased to grow – in 1964 – their large volume constituted an overhang that gave rise to the 'problem of confidence'. Suggestions have been made for funding the overhang. The United States so far has resisted these, as being a polite means of limiting and ultimately threatening to end the reserve role of the dollar.

(4) The role of the dollar as an intervention currency deprives the United States of control over its own exchange rate. Although national parities are defined in gold, all countries but the United States meet their obligation to maintain these parities by operating in dollars. Thus, the United States determines the price of gold, other countries determine the exchange rates of the dollar. If the United States were to devalue by raising the price of gold, few if any exchange rates might change in consequence. To be sure, the role of the United States in world trade might produce a result somewhat similar in principle even if currencies were not pegged to the dollar, but probably not to the same degree. This is the counterpart to the frequently made statement that, as a reserve currency, the dollar *must* never be devalued. As an intervention currency, it hardly *can* be devalued.

(5) The intervention currency role exposes the dollar to progressive overvaluation. Occasional rate realignments, always with respect to the dollar and beginning in 1949, have been predominantly downwards. Upward revaluations have been fewer and for smaller amounts. If the world were to shift to a wider band or a crawling peg or both, the chances are that the same tendency would appear more continuously. Provisions to

eliminate central bank intervention in rate movements would help. But they could hardly preclude the many indirect techniques that could be employed. On the other hand, if under some limited flexibility scheme the dollar should nevertheless float or crawl downward continuously and predictably, demand for it from official and private holders might diminish.

(6) The constraints and conflicts noted suggest that both sides might be better off under alternative arrangements. Reserve creation is already being systematised by Special Drawing Rights. The United States, under pressure, has promised to limit if not eliminate the deficits that have fed dollars into world reserves. Proposals for consolidating existing dollar reserves abound. No good ideas seem to exist as to how the dollar could be displaced as an intervention currency. This is particularly important because the ability of the E.E.C. countries to move as a bloc in any system of limited or unlimited flexibility depends on there being available some common unit to which the Six could peg.

VI. CONSTRAINTS AND CONFLICTS ARISING FROM UNITED STATES FOREIGN INVESTMENT

The rapid growth of United States foreign investment and, until recently, foreign lending, makes conflicts and constraints in this area increasingly probable. But since national objectives on both sides are poorly defined and internally conflicting, the nature of the confrontations is less clear than in other areas.

(1) The United States Government views foreign direct investment detachedly, as on the whole and in the long run probably a good thing. Very few policy thinkers at any level probably harbour the imperialistic or Machiavellian designs foreigners sometimes surmise to be behind the private thrust of American corporations. In the short run, the United States Government views foreign investment with alarm, as threatening the balance of payments through capital outlays and displaced exports.

(2) Western European governments are aware of the benefits of United States direct investment in general but question many particular aspects. Fear that action to keep out some applicant would cause the application to be shifted elsewhere in the E.E.C. has hampered restraining action by individual countries. Concerted action has not materialised. Creation of the E.E.C. presumably has by itself increased the pull of the area upon American capital.

(3) Some issues arise from competing claims of sovereignty. The United States Government claims the right to regulate foreign subsidiaries in certain respects not consistent with host-country law, such as behaviour with respect to the anti-trust laws and Trading with the Enemy Act. The United States Government also seeks to subject foreign corporations raising capital or allowing their securities to be traded in the United

States to some forms of S.E.C. disclosure requirements. It has tried – without success – to tax the parents on the undistributed income of their subsidiaries.

(4) Sovereignty, or security interests, or other major considerations transcending ordinary economic rivalry, are involved where United States subsidiaries acquire a large share of sensitive industries or pre-empt or drain away management, research, and brains.

(5) United States Government action against foreign investment, designed to reduce its immediate balance of payments impact, has encountered a characteristically ambivalent response. Anything done to strengthen the dollar tends to be well received in the E.E.C. But the Interest Equalisation Tax, as well as the voluntary and later partly mandatory controls over corporations and financial institutions, have brought pressure upon European capital markets, and this has hurt.

(6) The economic wisdom of helping the United States to play a role as financial intermediary has been questioned on the Western European side. American firms have built or bought high-yielding direct investments in Europe and in developing countries. European central banks and private dollar holders have helped finance this by holding low-yielding short-term dollar assets. 'Liquidity preference' of this sort is expensive.

(7) European critics have charged that overvaluation of the dollar is partly responsible for some of this direct investment which it allegedly has both stimulated and facilitated. This comment contrasts with views expressed in connection with trade, where undervaluation of E.E.C. currencies has rarely been alleged. The view that devaluation of the dollar would reduce foreign investment is plausible where the investing firm has only limited resources available. Otherwise, the volume of investment should remain unaffected, since devaluation would not alter the rate of return.

(8) Gradual decline of European rates of growth and rates of return has reduced foreign investment incentives for United States firms. Meanwhile, European investment in stocks of the parent companies, directly or via mutual funds, has increased. Both facts should help to defuse issues in this area.

VII. COMMERCIAL POLICY, RESOURCE ENDOWMENT, AND COMPARATIVE ADVANTAGE

Plans for the E.E.C. were made, and United States support secured, at a time when the United States was unconcerned about its balance of payments. Had the latter problem been correctly assessed, the United States would no doubt have requested consideration of its interests on a number of points that have become troublesome and can only be negotiated at the cost of expensive concessions, if at all.

United States commercial policy, like anti-trust policy, is an area where the President can acquire mostly enemies. That both policies have carried so much weight and, particularly in the case of commercial policy, have even attracted a modicum of Presidential support, is testimony to what economists can achieve when they are agreed.

(1) *Commercial Policy*

United States trade relations with Western Europe have given rise to two kinds of problems: those related to trade between the United States and Western European countries, and those related to United States trade with third countries with which the United Kingdom or the E.E.C. have maintained preferential arrangements:

(*a*) Having accepted discrimination by the E.E.C., the United States has seen its interest in bargaining down the Common Market tariff wall. The Common Market countries, which regard the common tariff as the main bond of their union until others can come into being, have had a non-economic motive to hang back.

(*b*) Because of the payments deficit, the United States has had to bargain much more intensively in the Kennedy Round than previously. The Reciprocal Trade legislation was promoted domestically on the grounds that it would help improve the balance of payments. Research by Bela Balassa has since shown that, if anything, the United States balance of payments stands to suffer from reciprocal cuts of the Kennedy Round type.[1]

(*c*) Diminishing competitiveness and rising imports have produced numerous demands for quota protection in the United States. Meanwhile, an essential element of the Kennedy Round, the American Selling Price legislation, has not been implemented. Both factors have made it difficult to approach discussion of reduction of non-tariff barriers, which presumably should be the next order of business.

(*d*) While the United Kingdom's Commonwealth Preference arrangements, once a major thorn in the flesh of United States commercial policy, have become increasingly less important, the preferences given by the E.E.C. to African countries have become more so. European preferences for African products hurt many Latin American countries. African preference for E.E.C. products hurts the United States directly. The latter preference also interferes with consideration of general preference schemes for the developing countries. The United States can hardly be expected to extend preference to countries discriminating against it.

---

[1] Bela Balassa, 'Trade Liberalization and the Kennedy Round', *Review of Economics and Statistics* (May 1967).

(2) *Resource Endowment and Comparative Advantage*

The problems connected with resource endowment and comparative advantage have ranged from the very practical, such as the Common Agricultural Policy (C.A.P.), to the highly theoretical, such as the Leontieff paradox:

(*a*) The highly protectionist shape of the C.A.P. could not have been foreseen when the Treaty of Rome was being negotiated. The very substantial loss of farm exports that it threatens to inflict on the United States is a major political as well as balance of payments factor. It is sometimes argued that European agriculture has ahead of it a productivity explosion similar to that which occurred in the United States after 1940. Hence, it is concluded, the United States is bound to lose its European markets for farm products anyhow and might as well stop protesting against the C.A.P. A closer examination of the comparative structure of European and American agriculture and their differential use of labour, capital, and land makes that hypothesis highly questionable.

(*b*) The surprising finding of Wassily Leontieff that United States exports are more labour-intensive than the (United States-produced) goods displaced by United States imports, has received various – not altogether satisfactory – explanations. The generally-accepted view that a large part of United States exports is research-intensive, and that the United States must run hard in developing new products in order to stand still, does not really explain why research-intensive products should be labour-intensive. The 'product cycle' theory of Ray Vernon focuses on new products regardless of their research intensity. It assumes that these new products tend to be developed in the United States, owing to high per capita income and high labour cost, and that in the course of acquiring mass world markets the firms controlling them shift from United States production to production abroad while also mechanising the process and making it more capital-intensive. In that case, production abroad of these products would be more capital-intensive than initial production in and exports from the United States. The question remains as to how wide a range of products is susceptible to this cycle.

VIII. CONCLUDING REMARKS

An attempt was made in the early pages of this paper to explain the automatic as well as the policy behaviour of the American economy in terms of its size and per capita income. The E.E.C. is on its way to becoming a comparable unit. If it is joined by the United Kingdom and perhaps other countries, and if it achieves some degree of unity in external policies, its automatic and quite likely its policy responses will become similar to those of the United States. Some reactions of this kind are already observable – for instance, the effort to discipline the United States in balance of payments matters.

For the time being, the individual E.E.C. countries are still more sensitive to their individual balances of payments, including that with the rest of the E.E.C., than to the external balance of the area. Political cohesion may be needed before this can be overcome. Eventually, however, one must assume that the ratio of trade to G.N.P. will become small in the E.E.C., although not so small as it is in the United States. Internal considerations will then predominate, as they do in the United States. Balance of payments adjustment will be slower in the automatic sense and less worth while in the policy sense. Meanwhile the E.E.C., if it acts as a unit, will have acquired considerable power to influence the rest of the world, including the United States.

The most difficult evolution will be in the area of policy thinking. Having been accustomed to think atomistically, to respond to the world defensively and in terms mainly of its direct self-interest, will the E.E.C. make the transition to the role of oligopolist who can benefit by influencing the state of the world? Assuming it does, will it emphasise the potential of this role for improving its terms of trade, to the detriment of the rest? Or will it see its advantage mainly in improving the state of the world and so doing well by doing good? How will the United States and the E.E.C. respond to their approximate roles as duopolists and perhaps optimum currency areas? The experience of the United States in a similar role gives some clues, but they are not conclusive.

Discussion of the Paper by Professor Wallich

Professor Robinson, in the chair, said that during the first four sessions of the Round Table it was intended to find possible areas of conflict between the interests of North America and of Europe. It was necessary to get the interests of each area clear, as seen by its inhabitants. Professor Wallich would talk about the interests of the United States. Professor Robinson said that, as Chairman of the Programme Committee, he had deliberately asked another American participant to comment on this paper in order to try to make it as clear as possible what were the interests of the United States. The same would be done in the following session for Canada, and later papers and their discussions would deal similarly with the areas of Europe.

Professor Kindleberger said that the paper was a curious one. Instead of looking at the determinants of American policy, it looked at the interaction of American economic foreign policy with that of the E.E.C. He was particularly interested in the discussion of game and bargaining theory in international foreign policy, and how far a given national policy was a private and a public good. He did not know whether many participants had seen a book by Russet on the economic theory of international relations which dealt with the issue formally. The idea went back a long way, to the point where Bismarck had commented that the United Kingdom pretended that its foreign policy was a public good but really pursued narrow national interests.

The bargaining approach seemed to suggest that the United States followed policies of love, while other countries were more concerned with policies of fear. Professor Kindleberger found this interesting and suggestive, but he was not persuaded. For example, he thought of NATO and France where the French had been unwilling to accept the price of a policy of fear. It might be a fruitful notion when bargaining and game theory had gone farther. There was too much indeterminancy at present, but he thought it all worth thought and discussion. He wondered, for example, how far the United States had been a 'sucker', paying too many of the costs relative to the benefits.

Professor Wallich went on to look at time-preference concepts and therefore at the short-run versus the long-run. Professor Kindleberger said he could not understand the notion that the United States had a shorter time preference than the rest of the world. In fact, he thought that it was frequent changes of policy which made the American economy appear to have a shorter time horizon, but most of the policies concerned were public policies.

He had in mind, for example, the policy of European reconstruction, and the containment of the East. He agreed that shifts in American policy had been frequent and this made her policies seem short-run. He thought it was true that the United States was nationalist in monetary reform and this issue might well reflect private rather than public concern. The other policies quoted were public, however, and covered long time periods. Moreover, the Americans felt that the rest of the world did not pay a big enough share. On other issues, for example, the Kennedy Round, the United States allowed discrimination against themselves. On international economic policy with, say, Japan, the United States was more willing to remove discrimination against Japan, with a long time horizon and without reciprocity. This was contrary to Bismarck's view of the United Kingdom.

Beyond this, Professor Wallich went on to make many suggestive remarks, but there were no big themes. Professor Kindleberger did not agree that the higher multiplier of the United States worked slowly. Nor did he think that Professor Wallich took a clear position on the costs and benefits of being a reserve country. He thought that the development of the New York money market and the Eurodollar market were useful ways of making capital available to Europe.

On commercial policy, not enough attention had perhaps been given to the fact that the world of tariffs and quotas was over. In the past no one had worried about increasing tariffs against an unknown country, over the horizon. But the world was now too small for tariff changes to be made so easily. Professor Kindleberger suggested that free trade was here to stay!

Professor Kindleberger was surprised that there was no discussion in the paper the swing from foreign to domestic problems in the United States. The United States was peculiar in being a large country but having a small amount of foreign trade. She had tried to correct the protection of the inter-war period, but was now facing domestic problems like colour, students and depressed areas. A country with the time preference that Professor Wallich attributed to it would turn to domestic rather than international problems. This danger ought to be a major concern. Professor Kindleberger predicted that, as in tariffs, while a declining American interest in foreign problems was likely, there would be no inward turning. He expected more discussion in the Conference of the ebb and flow of domestic versus foreign problems.

Professor Wallich said that for lack of time he would simply have to either agree or disagree with much of this, and was afraid that there was much of the latter. There was, however, one point where he was either right or wrong, and this was over the multiplier. He had said that a lower multiplier meant that a larger part of the increase in income would take place in the first and second time periods. With a higher multiplier, a smaller percentage of the adjustment would take place in the earlier periods.

Professor Patinkin disputed this. He suggested that while it was true that a greater *proportion* of a multiplier effect would take place in early periods, what mattered was the absolute size of the effect. For example, if the multiplier were 2 and an injection of $1 billion were put into the economy, then there would be an increase in absolute income of $0·5 billion in the first period. If, however, the multiplier were 10 (with the same marginal propensity to import), then the increase in the first period would be $0·9 billion. This might not be as big a percentage of the final increase in income, but it was a bigger absolute amount.

Professor Hague said that he was interested in what Professor Wallich had said about the role of oligopolistic industries in various countries. Research in Manchester was looking at the response of United Kingdom firms to devaluation, and a large number of the firms being studied were oligopolistic. They were faced by oligopolists in overseas markets. This unfortunately raised a topic about which we knew very little – bilateral oligopoly. He thought that the benefit from the research would be that in the end it would be possible to show those making policy in Whitehall that pure competition did not reign throughout the world. At the same time, the research was showing that firms did use oligopolistic power in these circumstances. He would therefore like to throw a little doubt on Professor Wallich's belief that American firms had not used their oligopoly power to the full. American businessmen knew how to defend their own interests at least as well as anyone else, and he would be surprised if oligopoly power were not being used quite widely.

Professor Lundberg said an important issue was that the Americans were now becoming more involved in their own domestic problems. Yet, Professor Kindleberger said that free trade had come to stay. He wondered if this was true. If the Americans became more involved in domestic problems, did this not mean that there would be a risk of more protectionism? There were economists who thought they had discovered how little was to be gained from foreign trade and he wondered whether Professor Kindleberger would like to expand his remarks.

Professor Kindleberger said that the Americans' biggest problem was that of employment for Negroes. They were concerned about inflation, yet their Phillips curve had many young Negroes on it. Therefore, the Americans were more prone to suffer inflation, because they feared race riots. But did this mean that America would keep out goods from, say Hong Kong? What was necessary was to give Negroes jobs similar to those given to white youths. Protectionism against Hong Kong would not help there. Young Negroes wanted jobs at the going wage – not at Hong Kong wages. This was not to say that the Americans would not try to keep out cheap cloth, but he thought that those who tried would fail. Oil had now lost support in Texas and Northern Senators were moving to work for increased imports and lower oil prices. More and more, he thought that the general interest would prevail over the particular.

Mr Shonfield said that Professor Kindleberger was very persuasive in arguing about industries and firms. But there was a more general problem. This concerned welfare. If the American government insisted that firms should employ a larger proportion of black people, this implied in present circumstances employing a higher proportion of less-educated people. There would then be a tendency to see the problem as requiring something less than exposure of the American economy to international competition. The real argument was surely about the way such policy decisions were going to be made. The overall American preoccupation with the welfare aspects of economic policy must surely have an important international dimension during the next twenty years.

Professor Robinson said he would like to embroider what Mr Schonfield had said. All countries were continuously needing to make structural adaptation to change, and all tried to shuffle off this problem by holding back the decline of declining industries. Were those who looked at the American problem as an overall one so sure that America looked at the growing and gaining industries rather than at pressures from industries suffering from this structural adaptation? What were the main areas of structural change, and what was being done actively to hold back these declines? Where was the conflict of interest between America and Europe emerging?

Professor Wallich said that an important question was that if a country began to identify its interest with the stagnant rather than the growing industries, then it was in for slow growth. As a broad generalisation, contracting industries did attract more than their fair share of support. For example, farmers in the United States had done so. In the same way, American railroads had attracted support. He would regard this as a minor phenomenon. It was a universal problem, but not one dominating the policies of the United States. The structure of competition, in what was after all an entrepreneurial economy, favoured growing industries. The freedom of capital markets helped to channel resources into high technology industries. Their share of the G.N.P. therefore rose. In transport, for example, there was less support for the railroads than for the airlines. He would be surprised if support for declining industries was a dominating feature.

Professor Robinson said the problem was that contracting industries were often modern industries – for example, the aircraft industry in many countries.

Professor Eastman wanted to compare the position today with that in 1962 when the United States Government had argued that an increase in international competition would improve her balance of payments. It was now easy for industries with decreasing comparative advantage to justify their claims for protection, by appealing to the balance of payments situation. How far into the future could one see American policy remaining liberal?

Professor Wallich wished that it were true that we were moving into a more liberal trade period. The basic trends in the American economy could rarely be seen for more than three years. He did not think that the trend to more liberal trade was continuing in the United States. It was true that this had gone on for thirty years, but it had perpetually gained strength from quite different sources. In the present situation, the position depended on the balance of payments, with more than the usual number of industries sensitive to foreign competition. If one looked at present negotiations for export quotas on other countries' textiles, and at the number of quota bills which could come before the Senate, it was surprising how little new protection there had been so far. But as unemployment rose from 3·5 per cent to 4·5 per cent, all the bills might well descend upon us.

Professor Kindleberger said he took strong exception to these views on the balance of payments. The United States had had its biggest 'deficit' in history in the second quarter of 1969 and the White House ignored it. He thought it unfortunate that President Kennedy had said that the two big problems of the age were (1) the nuclear bomb and (2) the balance of payments of the United States. More interest was being given to how to get Japan to open her economy to trade than to worry over increasing steel imports.

Mr Brittan thought that Professor Kindleberger was too quick to assume that the balance of payments was not an important determinant of what the Americans did. In the last year or so the basic deficit had been covered by an inflow of funds because of the world interest-rate structure. Only when Americans had eliminated the basic deficit with a more normal pattern of interest rates, and no flow of private funds to bridge the gap, would he feel happy about Professor Kindleberger's assertions.

Mr Ferras said he would disagree with Professor Kindleberger on recent experience. The dollar situation had been stabilised by artificial and temporary factors.

To Professor Wallich, Mr Ferras suggested that there was a contradiction in what had been said in the paper and what had been said during the morning. In the paper, Professor Wallich stressed that American policy was internationist; but on a specific point he suggested that because of the small role of foreign trade in the United States economy, external considerations had little influence.

Professor Wallich said he would argue that in the past the United States had made big sacrifices to bring the balance of payments into line. Up to 1965, he thought these sacrifices necessary. Since then, partly because of circumstances under nobody's control, it had been hard to work out American salvation through deflation, unemployment, sweating-it-out, etc. Mr Ferras deplored accepting this imbalance – so far this had been done by capital inflow plus some inflation in the United States – but there came a point where other countries might have to ask themselves if they wanted to adjust. Professor Wallich did not suggest a Roman solution – that solution implied confronting the rest of the world with the alternative of accumulating dollars or revaluing. He thought, on the contrary, the United States had responsibilities, but they were not unlimited. For instance, the United States could not be expected to go back to 7 per cent unemployment.

Mr Schonfield said that to suggest that there was no link between the balance of payments and tariffs seemed very surprising. He would not look at the last quarter-century, but at the last hundred years. If one took the United Kingdom economy in the 1920s, one found that there was free trade despite a poor balance of payments situation. He would like to contrast the United States in the same period, which had a strong balance of payments and yet where the slightest breath of wind would set Congress rushing for tariffs. He was not suggesting a new rule that there was an inverse correlation between the state of the balance of payments and protectionism, or even that the United Kingdom was very stupid. He was simply suggesting that the forces leading to an open or closed economy were not to be seen as a question of how bad the balance of payments had been for how long. To say that if the balance of payments were bad enough for long enough corrective measures would be taken, was hardly a significant remark. What impressed him was the way that ideology came to dominate policy. He wondered whether the United States would continue to cling so hard to its current ideology on international trade. Looking at its history, one could reasonably assert that for the United States the moment of greatest strength was also the moment of greatest protectionism – the opposite of the British case.

Professor van Meerhaeghe, referring to what Professor Wallich said on p. 10 of his paper, did not believe that the price mechanism worked better in adjusting the balance of payments in Europe than in the United States.

Professor Wallich replied that short-run elasticities were lower than long-run ones and that in the United States' foreign trade the difference was very big because of foreign markets. The opportunities these could offer would not at once be known. But if, for example, Holland devalued, German housewives would cross the frontier to buy butter.

Professor van Meerhaeghe argued that this did not necessarily happen. Prices were maintained when the Netherlands and Germany had revalued.

Professor Wallich said that if there was not a competitive system, then things would obviously look a little different.

Professor van Meerhaeghe said this was why he had challenged the remark.

Professor Wallich noted that all countries in Europe had achieved successful devaluations since the war.

Professor Lundberg wondered how anyone knew what would be the effect of devaluation in America, because the Americans had never devalued. The appreciations of other currencies had also been small compared with the total position of the dollar.

Professor Wallich said he wanted to plead guilty. He had been going mainly on the basis of introspection. However, the devaluations of 1949 in the rest of the world seemed to have caused most of the trouble in the United States since 1957. Without them, he doubted whether the United States would now have balance of payments difficulties.

Professor Izzo suggested that in looking at the American and British positions one should not look simply at the overall balance of payments, but at the current and capital accounts separately. If one looked at the American current account, one found that only in 1958 and 1968 had there been deficits. However, it seemed that the current account of the United States balance of payments was deteriorating, while that of the United Kingdom had been negative for many years, and it was possible that a deficit on the current account was to become a permanent feature of both the American and British balance of payments. A deficit on current account implied transfers of real resources from surplus countries, and he wondered whether one could consider as satisfactory a situation in which there were transfers of real resources from countries like Italy or Japan to the United Kingdom or the United States. Furthermore, he wondered whether one could consider satisfactory a situation in which capital exports and unilateral transfers from the United States were larger than the American current account surplus. This situation implied that countries which were net importers of United States capital and/or receiving foreign aid from the United States were using real resources supplied by countries having a surplus with America on current account. For example, in 1968 capital exports and unilateral transfers from the United States to the rest of the world amounted to $10 billion. The real resources supplied by the United States to the rest of the world were practically nil, while those supplied by Germany, Japan and Italy amounted to $7 billion.

Professor Kindleberger pointed out that how quickly the Americans responded to price effects was shown by how fast the current surplus collapsed in 1968. There was a big gap each year between the amounts the Americans transferred, in terms of financial and real resources. The issue we were discussing was largely a financial, not a resource question. He suggested that the 1949 devaluation had not hit American exports, even in 1964; he therefore could not see how it could be relevant.

Professor Lundberg wanted to suggest some concrete problems. Professor Wallich had said that the Americans carried out an anti-inflationary policy using crude monetary measures. This was a kind of isolationism. The United States had curbed the capital outflow through higher interest rates and had been pushed further than would have been desired, given the American welfare functions. Could we look at this as an example of American policy and at its repercussion on Europe, which not all European countries favoured?

Professor Wallich said that the United States had found it harder than expected to hold down bank credit. The rate of interest had been surprisingly high. This went with an increasing deficit on liquidity account. There had been no internal/external conflict. If there *had* been a dilemma, and if the United States had pursued solely its own domestic interests, there might well have been criticism from abroad. His model of a situation where domestic and external interests conflicted could then have been used.

When it did something which was in *everyone's* interest, he wondered why the United States was criticised. He recognised that the measures taken were painful

– and that they hit other people's capital markets – but what were the alternatives? If fiscal policy had been used there would have been domestic benefits, but not much gain for the balance of payments. In analytical terms, using monetary policy seemed very close to the optimal thing to do. What could the United States do to improve its balance which did not hurt someone? The answer was that everyone lived off the American balance of payments deficit. The United States' deficit was a thing that the world wanted. This was why he had referred to the United States as the nth country, running a residual deficit.

Professor Plotnikov said we had been discussing a number of problems but he thought that the problem of foreign trade should also be discussed. He wondered whether the Conference had not underestimated the importance of trade for the American economy. What did Professor Wallich think about this? Professor Plotnikov thought that Americans underrated the prospects of increasing American foreign trade, especially with Eastern countries.

Professor Wallich said that at the level of dealings between American firms and the authorities of socialist countries, it was a question of how one could organise this trade. At the level of the economy, it was a question of how in the long run it would be balanced or financed multilaterally. The latter was the basic issue to an economist. One way (and American firms did want this kind of trade) was to take gold. However, if goods were to be taken, what could the United States take? It was not possible to increase imports of oil. Nor could it take natural gas by pipeline. He suggested that the product range was limited.

Professor Lundberg wondered whether part of the answer was to make the rouble as easily transferable as the dollar.

Professor Wallich said that, in the West, trade depended on price. But would Russia be prepared to import, for example, cheaper cars or machine-tools? Would not such imports conflict with the Plan? A flow might begin whenever there were bottlenecks in the East, but then trade would be spasmodic. This was not a sound basis for trade.

Professor Rasmussen said he did not understand how what Professor Wallich had said fitted in with the idea of comparative advantage. This must exist between America and Russia just as it did between the United Kingdom and Portugal.

Professor Plotnikov referred to the problem of comparative prices and the consistency of demand in trade with the U.S.S.R. He said that the U.S.S.R. traded both with socialist and capitalist countries at world prices. If trade with the United States became great, and the Soviet Union could rely confidently on deliveries, then Soviet demand would cease to be spasmodic.

Mr Maddison said the paper did not take a serious enough view of the American balance of payments problem and its policy implications. In the last few years, American aid had been tied, and this had reduced its efficiency. Its volume was now being cut. The position had been temporarily stabilised by large short-run capital flows from Europe to the United States, but European countries were unlikely to tolerate a flow on this scale for any lengthy period. On the trade side, American policy remained liberal, though less liberal than it might have been.

Mr Maddison did not see why Professor Wallich rejected the possibility of a reduction in the gold value of the dollar, and did not agree that all other countries would follow if the United States were to devalue by raising the price of gold. If one or two exchange rates changed vis-à-vis the dollar, the world payments position would be much better. For example, the Italian and Swiss rates might be altered. If the Italians and Swiss moved, then the Germans might be encouraged to make the change they should have made before. Professor Wallich appeared to believe that exchange-rate changes made little difference to trade, but who would doubt that German revaluation would not slow down exports of German cars?

Professor James said he had heard it suggested that the world as a whole was satisfied with the American balance of payments deficit. There seemed to be some illusions abroad. These might not be obvious while we were studying the commercial balance of the United States with the rest of the world. In financial terms, the world was not so satisfied with an enduring American deficit. He agreed with Mr Maddison that the Conference had not taken up the real problem – that of relations between the American economy and the rest of the world. The world was not satisfied with what the Americans were doing, and if the Americans had not yet taken adequate measures, they must begin to act now. Then one could say that American policy was internationalist in its intention.

Professor Yamamoto said that during a recent trade conference between American and Japan in Tokyo, the Americans had increased protection against Japan. There were now many advocates of NAFTA among North Atlantic countries, and in Japan there were increasing numbers of people advocating PAFTA – Pacific and Asian Free Trade Area among five advanced countries in this region. He wondered which Professor Wallich thought more likely. Years ago it had been argued that if the Asians wanted to create a unit for co-operation, there would be three stages: first, the stage of co-operation; second, the stage of co-ordination; and third, the stage of integration. For Asian countries, it was argued that the need was to promote more mutual co-operation in order to reach the next stage, of co-ordination, in the near future. The stage of integration would be a future, ultimate goal. For Europe, perhaps this step would be easier than for Asia.

Professor Phelps was puzzled by frequent references to American balance of payments problems. He was surprised that not more had been said about the fact that the world was on the dollar standard. The real value of dollars held abroad was largely independent of American fiscal and monetary policy. Proper accounting of the American balance of payments surplus would need to take account of the fall in the real value of the dollar. The surplus, thus measured, of the rest of the world with the United States, did not depend much on America, because the real value of the dollar and the volume of world trade did not. What America did control was its own rate of inflation and to some extent that of the world. Professor Phelps felt that the American inflation would be welcomed by many countries, for example in Latin America.

Professor Wallich said that Professor Phelps had answered Mr Maddison. He himself was increasingly moving to take the Phelps view. So long as the payments problem in America had not been too difficult, it was worth the sacrifices that had been made. Now it was much more difficult – and curing it would require carrying an adjustment burden for several years. He was not sure that this degree of sacrifice was worth while. As for the benefits from a rise in the price of gold, he was sorry to see economists, of all people, wanting to increase its price. Aside from the question of who benefited, the world was moving from commodity money through paper money to computerised money. He did not see why we should want to go back to gold. As to what would happen if the United States were to change the price of gold, he thought everyone would move with the United States. He could therefore see little hope of an adequate realignment of exchange rates after a rise in the price of gold.

Professor Wallich said one had to distinguish two things. First, there was the increase in the price of gold required to realign exchange rates. A small rise in the price would be sufficient if America moved alone. The second proposition was a doubling or trebling of the price of gold in order to engineer a large increase in reserves. The two need not go together. The emphasis on creating reserves was not relevant in the context of realignment.

To Professor James, Professor Wallich said he had not meant to argue that the rest of the world liked the American deficit in its financial aspects. The world liked it in the sense that when one added together the current account objectives of the $n - 1$ countries, these countries seemed to want overall surplus. Therefore, the nth country must have a deficit. If one could get a current account surplus for the $n - 1$ countries by higher gold production, the world would probably prefer this. On the subject of monetary reform, he thought the United States deserved credit for not trying to impose a dollar standard because every dollar of S.D.R.s created, displaced approximately 1 dollar in the rest of the world's reserves. Some said that the United States should give up trying to limit the dollar outflow, and simply hand out dollars. But the world would not see this as a satisfactory solution. The United States was accommodating this worldwide reaction. The United States was trying to supply liquidity in dollars and in S.D.R.s in the desired proportion.

To Professor Yamamoto, Professor Wallich said that he thought the prospect for a new trade area including the United States was minimal. Such an agreement was a treaty and this meant that the measure would have to go through the Senate. He could not see such a Bill being passed at present or in the foreseeable future. At the same time, regional groupings without the United States seemed likely to raise serious problems. Two hundred years ago, to be sure, Americans had set up a customs union to give its members advantages relative to the rest of the world. Now others wanted to do this, notably the E.E.C. This discriminated against American exports; even so the United States had favoured the E.E.C. because commercial and economic integration was a starting point for political integration. America was now suffering from discrimination from the E.E.C., yet it had not reaped any of the benefits of European political unity. He would therefore be surprised if the United States should be happy about the creation of similar new groupings, without clear pay-offs in terms of political integration. For example, he could not see a Pacific Free Trade Area coming into being. All such groupings had a clear cost of the U.S.A.

To Professor Phelps, he said it was perhaps too strong to say that the world was on a dollar standard or that the level of reserves depended on the demand of other countries for reserves. This was analytically true – the amount held in equilibrium must be the amount demanded. But there was certainly a cost to other countries if they adjusted at a fixed rate, and it was not easy for them to revalue. Hence they might not be in equilibrium, and the supply of reserves might not be the amount demanded. However, it was useful to have the point put analytically as Professor Phelps had done.

Dr Molitor pointed out that there was a somewhat ambiguous attitude in Europe to the economic policy of the United States. On one hand, the European countries insisted that the United States should eliminate its balance of payments deficit; on the other hand, they were frequently worried if they could not continue to run comfortable surpluses on their own. In fact, an improvement in the United States balance of payments would mean a substantial reduction of the European surpluses. Similarly, complaints by Europeans about the effects of a restrictive policy in the United States on their own economies did not seem justified, since the European countries had shown themselves in favour of such a policy.

Dr Molitor thought that the policy-mix in the United States was not always appropriate. As the procedure for changing direct taxation was particularly lengthy, the emphasis had to be on monetary policy. Moreover, within this field, stress was put on interest rates rather than liquidity. In both fields, however, substantial progress has been made since July 1968. If, because of lasting inflationary pressure and the present disequilibrium in the United States balance of payments, a restrictive monetary policy had to be accepted by the Europeans, some of the negative effects on European economies could be eliminated by changing the way in which American policy was implemented. For instance, minimum reserve requirements could be introduced for funds borrowed by American banks on the Euro-dollar market, or Regulation Q could be adapted. Dr Molitor referred also to the quantitative restrictions applied in France, the Netherlands, Belgium and Switzerland.

Professor Wallich said these were detailed comments which needed an answer. It was true that American monetary policy had been too expansive, but it had been based on wrong forecasts of the effectiveness of fiscal policy. That the techniques of monetary policy were objectionable, could less readily be accepted. The measures that Dr Molitor wanted were satisfactory for countries with rudimentary monetary mechanisms and where credit restriction could be used. One would want to avoid these in other countries. For example, credit quotas on 14,000 banks would be regarded as retrograde and difficult to apply. The free market was better. In the United States, if one curbed the banking system in this way, borrowers would be driven to financial intermediaries, Euro-dollars, etc.

Professor Wallich was a little surprised that anyone should separate liquidity and the rate of interest. It was true that the real rate of interest in inflation was low, but he questioned the Brussels Commission Report, ten years old, which treated interest rates and liquidity as though the two were scarcely linked. He preferred to draw less of a distinction between liquidity and interest-rate policies. A sensible policy would let the money supply grow at a reduced rate: if this did work, then as a last resort, one could use a direct control of lending.

Mr Shonfield went back to the issue which Professor Wallich had closed by suggesting it was impossible for the United States to do anything about its deficit. He might simply be expressing a temperamental dislike of the situation, but he would try to be rational.

First, Professor Wallich said that few or no countries would follow if the United States raised the dollar price of gold. Mr Shonfield assumed that his argument was that none would do so. In 1961, Holland and Germany did revalue against the dollar. This might not have been a big revaluation, but the

German story was not yet at an end. Professor Wallich had thus made a major proposition about non-revaluation which was not proven.

He would like to go on to the other major proposition – that we faced, for ever, a deterioration of the American balance of payments. Others might devalue, but the Americans never would devalue. The American cost/price position was to face unending deterioration. The consequence was that there would be a transfer of real resources to the United States. Mr Shonfield would not say what the Europeans might do; he just wanted to look at what the Americans themselves might be induced to do. Professor Wallich said the dollar could not be devalued because the world would not let it be. Say this was true so far as the current account was concerned; there might still be ways of operating on capital account by means of control. The result might then be that dollars on capital account were in fact devalued; there would be two exchange rates. It was perfectly possible for America, or indeed any other country, to distinguish the various items in its external accounts. This would need new institutional devices, which the Americans would not like. But it was an example of the kind of measure that the Americans *could* take, and might well take, in these circumstances.

Professor Izzo thought that too much attention had been given in the last two or three years to looking at American inflation. The idea had been propagated that Europe thought that America exported inflation; on the other hand, some people in America thought that the international monetary system was pushing reserve currency countries towards a liquidity deficit or that the increase in the short-term liability position of the United States was caused by the high liquidity preference of the European wealth holders. He could not agree with these opinions. If one looked at the events of the past decade, one could not say that America had exported inflation. From 1958 to 1961, only in Germany and Holland was the surplus in the current account of the balance of payments as a percentage of the G.N.P. larger than the increase of prices, implying that the rate of growth of internal monetary demand was lower than that of the production of goods. However, it was difficult to say whether this resulted from a deliberate policy pursued by the authorities to check inflationary impulses coming from abroad.

From 1962, price movements and movements of the extenal accounts of the European economies took place while growth of production was satisfactory, the level of employment was high and there were large increases of productivity. On the available evidence, one could say that internal demand was kept at a level sufficiently high to absorb the increase of supply, to allow an increase in the domestic uses of national products and to increase the rate of inflation. If the latter was determined principally by external demand it would have probably led to an increase in the profit margins; however, it happened that price increases were larger when they took place in conjunction with an increase in the share of wages and a worsening in the current account of the balance of payments. On the other hand, one could not say that the United States and United Kingdom balance of payments deficits had been demanded by European countries. If this proposition was true, the implication was that the European authorities were aiming at a surplus on the current account of the balance of payments. However, from 1962 the latter was very small, while the level of employment was high and price increases were larger than in the past. One could not say that the short-term liability position of the United States was caused by the high liquidity preference of the European wealth holders, as it was well known that European and American authorities had tried to influence the magnitude and the maturity structure of the international flow of funds across the Atlantic.

Professor Rasmussen said Professor Wallich argued that America was the *n*th country – unable to do anything itself. He wondered whether the reserve position and the small percentage of foreign trade in the United States *really* made the position as bad as this.

Professor James said that it was now agreed that the American deficit did help, the rest of the world. Nevertheless, he would like to suggest that, in a philosophical sense, to seek equilibrium was not enough. Equilibrium meant two things. It meant reaching a stable position; but it also meant accepting the sacrifices this implied. It was important to distinguish the two.

Professor Patinkin said that we had spent the morning listening to predictions of the inevitability of an American balance of payments deficit. He would just like to add a little historical perspective. If, twenty years ago, a similar conference of economists had been held there would have been equally fervent predictions of the inevitability of the dollar shortage.

Professor Wallich said that he had been asked whether the United States could not restrict capital exports. Presumably the United States ought to export capital because of a lower marginal efficiency of capital in the United States. This view was to some extent disputed in the United States where some people saw no reason why America should not become a capital importer. This worried him because of the effect on the development of other countries, but it was certainly a possible answer.

If the United States did restrict capital exports, there would be a significant misallocation of resources. It might be better to keep down American commodity and invisible imports. If the United States ever did run out of means to finance its deficit, it would face having to take one or other of these measures. So long as other countries would accept dollars, the United States was under no strong compulsion to do so. If other countries were either to control capital movements or to revalue, the United States would get into equilibrium. But the United States could do little to encourage this. He could not see a large country revaluing at the mere insistence of the United States. Even if Germany were to revalue, it would be because she herself wished to do so. To Professor Rasmussen, Professor Wallich said that both factors were relevant though he agreed that neither was compelling.

ADDENDA

In the course of the discussion on Professor Wallich's paper, Professor Cooper called in question certain of Professor Wallich's conclusions. A note by Professor Cooper and a rejoinder by Professor Sohmen, defending Professor Wallich, are here printed.

1. Note by Professor Cooper
Proof of Faster Response of Open Economies to Payments Imbalances

Consider an economy governed by the following relationships:

$$Y_t = E_t + X_t - M_t \qquad X_0 = M_0$$
$$E_t = eY_{t-1} \qquad m = M_0/Y_0$$
$$M_t = mY_{t-1} \qquad X_t = X_1 < X_0 \text{ for } t > 0$$

where Y = national product, E = national expenditure, X = exports, M = imports, and e and m are the marginal (and average) propensities to spend and to import out of additional income, respectively. If follows that

$$Y_t = (e-m)Y_{t-1} + X_1 = (e-m)^t Y_0 + \frac{1-(e-m)^t}{h+m} X_1,$$

and therefore that $T_t \equiv \dfrac{M_t}{X_1} = m\left[(e-m)^{t-1}\dfrac{Y_0}{X_1} + \dfrac{1-(e-m)^{t-1}}{h+m}\right]$,

where $h = 1-e$, the marginal propensity not to spend, and T_t is the ratio of imports to exports at time t.

To compare two or more economies governed by these relationships requires that the disturbance, a fall in exports from X_0 to X_1, be made comparable. Two possible assumptions regarding comparability are that (i) the fall in exports is proportional to national product and (ii) the fall in exports is proportional to the initial level of trade. In symbols,

(i) $\dfrac{\Delta X}{Y_0} = k_1$, \qquad (ii) $\dfrac{\Delta X}{M_0} = k_2$,

where $\Delta X = X_0 - X_1$ and k_1 and k_2 are constant.

If $h = 0$, necessary on the assumptions here for initial equilibrium, then

$$T_t = 1 + (1-m)^{t-1}\left[m\frac{Y_0}{X_1} - 1\right].$$

Under (i), this becomes $T_t = 1 + (1-m)^{t-1}\left[\dfrac{k_1}{m-k_1}\right]$, since $\dfrac{X_1}{Y_0} = m - k_1$,

so $\dfrac{\partial T_t}{\partial m} = -(t-1)(1-m)^{t-2}\left[\dfrac{k_1}{m-k_1}\right] - (1-m)^{t-1}\dfrac{k_1}{(m-k_1)^2} < 0.$

Under (ii), $T_t = 1 + (1-m)^{t-1}\left[\dfrac{k_2}{1-k_2}\right]$, since $\dfrac{X_1}{Y_0} = m(1-k_2)$,

so $\dfrac{\partial T_t}{\partial m} = -(t-1)(1-m)^{t-2}\left[\dfrac{k_2}{1-k_2}\right] < 0.$

Under either assumption, therefore, a larger marginal propensity to import (m) will result in more rapid convergence to the new trade equilibrium. This is true despite the fact that under assumption (i) the proportionate decline in income ultimately required to restore trade balance is *inversely* related to m: $\Delta Y/Y_0 = -\dfrac{k_1}{m}$. (Under (ii) the proportionate decline in income required to restore balance is k_2, independent of m.).

If $h \neq 0$ (initial equilibrium being assured by introducing an autonomous component to domestic expenditure), higher m will still lead to more rapid convergence towards the new equilibrium, as can be seen by differentiating T_t/T_∞

with respect to m. But the analysis is complicated in this case by the fact that income changes alone will not restore trade balance, and that the extent of that failure will depend both upon h and upon m.

2. Note by Professor Sohmen

This note proves the statement in the text that higher multipliers mean longer periods of balance of payments adjustment. Another proof of that proposition, which was challenged in the discussion, is provided in the addendum submitted by Richard N. Cooper (see above).

Wanted: The income adjustment during a given period as a fraction of the total adjustment, in response to a balance of payment disequilibrium.

(1) Total income adjustment $= \dfrac{1}{1-MPC} = m,\ m \geqslant 1$.

(2) Adjustment in 2 multiplier periods $= 1 + MPC$.

(3) $Q_2 = \dfrac{2 \text{ periods adjustment}}{\text{Total adjustment}} = \dfrac{(1+MPC)/1}{1-MPC} = 1 - MPC^2$

(4) From (1) $MPC = 1 - \dfrac{1}{m}$.

Substituting in (3):

(5) $Q_2 = 1 - \left(1 - \dfrac{1}{m}\right)^2 = \dfrac{2}{m} - \dfrac{1}{m^2}$.

(6) $\dfrac{dQ}{dm} = \dfrac{-2}{m^2} + \dfrac{2}{m^3} = 0;\ \dfrac{2}{m^2} = \dfrac{2}{m^3}$, max at $m = 1$.

The proportion of total income adjustment reaches its peak, at unity, when the multiplier equals unity.

m = multiplier
MPC = marginal propensity to consume
Q_i = proportion of total adjustment during i periods.

2 Canada in an Interdependent North Atlantic Economy

H. C. Eastman
UNIVERSITY OF TORONTO

I. INTRODUCTORY

Recent years have witnessed a regular epidemic of publications on economic interdependence. This has followed the increased mobility of capital and factors of production as well as goods between advanced countries. We are told that when stout Cortez first upon a peak in Darien stood, he gazed about him with wild surmise. However, the sight of the wide Pacific was doubtless somewhat less novel to the natives of the area. Canadians may feel a little like these aborigines when interdependence is discussed, for the Canadian economy has long been unusually open.

The Canadian economy is open in the sense that exports, as a percentage of G.N.P., are nearly 25 per cent, and that a very large part of domestic production is in direct competition with imports. It is also open because the country relied for its growth on foreign supplies of factors of production to an unusual extent. For many years, Canada has drawn labour from Europe and capital from the United States.

Canadian population has grown by 250 per cent since 1900, or by 19·1 million people of whom 4·7 million were contributed by net immigration. In this period, population growth in Western Europe was 50 per cent; in the United States, it was 150 per cent. The use of foreign capital resources as a percentage of net capital formation has varied widely from year to year with changing conditions, but has chiefly ranged between 20 and 35 per cent since 1926.

The Canadian economy has necessarily been strongly influenced by changing conditions abroad. Its small size relative to Europe and the United States has meant that the relationships have been more of dependence than of interdependence. Deliberate co-ordination of policies has varied in extent and importance not within the evolution of a closely tied international economy, but with fluctuating degrees of interference by foreign governments with the price system. Thus wartime and the recent period of special United States balance of payments measures have given rise to especially active Canadian participation in international consultation and co-operation in economic policy.

This paper will discuss, first, factor supplies as a basis of comparative advantage and as an explanation of the pattern of Canada's trade; second,

Canadian policies designed to affect the size and efficiency of the Canadian economy, and their consequences; and lastly, the co-ordination of Canadian with foreign policies.

II. FACTOR SUPPLIES AND THE PATTERN OF CANADIAN TRADE

About 70 per cent of Canadian trade is with the United States, and 7 or 8 per cent with each of the United Kingdom and the rest of Western Europe. The composition on the export side is untypical of an industrialised country, being largely composed of food and of raw and processed materials. Highly manufactured end-products constitute well below 20 per cent and have increased very rapidly recently. Canada's share of world trade, over 5 per cent, is now about one-quarter greater than in the inter-war period. This has been accomplished by maintaining the Canadian share of the relatively declining world trade in food, and by increasing markedly its share both of relatively declining world trade in raw materials and of trade in processed materials. The proportion of world trade consisting of raw materials is now about one-half as large as it was twenty years ago, but raw materials remain at 28 or 30 per cent of total Canadian exports. Canadian fuel exports have increased very greatly.[1]

On the side of imports, highly manufactured end-products are the dominant type of imports and industrial materials constitute about 30 per cent of total Canadian imports. Factor proportions, especially the availability of natural resources, and the size of the economy explain the pattern of trade. A study by the Economic Council of Canada developed data[2] to compare with those for the United States and Europe in E. F. Denison's *Why Growth Rates Differ*.[3]

In 1960, the amount of capital other than education per employed person was very similar in Canada and the United States, and over twice the level in Western Europe. However, the high level in Canada was owing chiefly to non-residential construction and inventories, doubtless made necessary by climate and long distances. The amount of machinery and equipment per person was similar to the United States in agriculture and manufacturing, but much less in other enterprises, so that the average level was 80 per cent of the United States. The amount of agricultural land per person was estimated to be twice the United States level and of

---

[1] See D. W. Slater, *World Trade and Economic Growth: Trends and Prospects with Applications to Canada* (Toronto: University of Toronto Press, 1968); B. W. Wilkinson, *Canada's International Trade: An Analysis of Recent Trends and Patterns* (Montreal: Private Planning Association, 1968).

[2] Dorothy Walters, *Canadian Income Levels and Growth: An International Perspective* (Ottawa: Economic Council of Canada, Staff Study No. 23, 1968).

[3] E. F. Denison and Jean-Pierre Poullier, *Why Growth Rates Differ: Post War Experience in Nine Western Countries* (Washington: Brookings Institution, 1967).

mineral resources 170 per cent, whereas the European levels are given by Denison as 16 and 26 per cent of the United States level respectively. Educational investment per capita in the Canadian labour force was estimated to be 93 per cent of the United States level or about equal to that of north-west Europe.[1]

Factor endowments can be shown to form the principal influence on the pattern of Canadian trade. Canadian exports are largely based on natural resources. Approximately 35 per cent of total Canadian exports are of crude materials produced in farms, mines and forests. We have noted already that Canada was land and resource intensive relative to the United States and Europe. But a substantial amount of exports of manufactured products are also based on the richness of Canadian resources.

An examination of the Canadian input–output tables gives results evocative of Leontieff's famous paradox. A million dollars worth of Canadian exports required more capital and less labour to produce than a million dollars of import-competing production.[2] This was true of trade with the capital-rich United States as well as of total trade. Professor Wilkinson[3] has made a much more detailed study including four factors: labour, human capital measured by the height of wages and salaries, physical capital, and natural resources. Canadian manufacturing industries that export use physical capital more intensively than does manufacturing in general and more intensively than does import-competing production (as already discovered). They are also more intensive in human capital, znd they are markedly intensive in natural resources. A natural resource

[1] Differences in factor proportions, tariffs on imports, transportation costs and a separate currency have combined to make for a marked difference in relative factor prices between Canada and the United States. In 1965, average hourly earnings in manufacturing in Canada were 81 per cent of the United States level, machinery, equipment and materials prices were between 120 and 126 per cent of United States prices and bond yields were 23 per cent higher. D. J. Daly, B. A. Keys, E. J. Spence, *Scale and Specialization in Canadian Manufacturing* (Ottawa, Economic Council of Canada, Staff Study No. 21, 1968).

The measured differences in factor endowments explain very little of differences in income per capita in either the Denison or the Economic Council of Canada study. Vast differences in output per unit of input must then be explained chiefly by differences in organisation and production. Observers typically attribute to the Canadian and to foreign tariffs a major role in reducing the efficiency of Canada production. See H. C. Eastman and S. Stykolt, *The Tariff and Competition in Canada* (Toronto: Macmillan Company of Canada, 1967); 'A Model for the Study of Protected Oligopolies', *Economic Journal* (1960); H. E. English, *Industrial Structure in Canada's International Competitive Position* (Montreal: Private Planning Association, 1964); D. H. Fullerton and H. A. Hampson, *Canadian Secondary Manufacturing Industry* (Ottawa: Queen's Printer, 1957); R. J. Wonnacott and Paul Wonnacott, *Free Trade between the United States and Canada: The Potential Economic Effects* (Cambridge, Mass.: Harvard University Press, 1967); Wilkinson, op cit.

[2] D. Wahl, 'Capital and Labour Requirements in Canada's Foreign Trade', *Canadian Journal of Economics and Political Science*, XXVII 3 (Aug 1961).

[3] Op. cit.

intensive manufacturing industry is defined as one in which 50 per cent or more of the total value of material inputs is from the primary sector. It then turns out that manufacturing based on natural resources contributes two-thirds of total Canadian exports of manufactures, though it constitutes only one-quarter of the total manufacturing sector in Canada.

The remaining and very rapidly growing Canadian exports are chiefly of highly manufactured products, such as automobiles, machinery, aircraft and electrical apparatus. Wages and salaries are well above the average for all manufacturing in these industries. This indicates relatively high skill levels or human capital intensity in industries that are not intensive in physical capital. Wilkinson believes that exports of human capital-intensive products to the United States, which is relatively better endowed than Canada in human capital, reflects the role of innovation and technical change in successful international competition. In any event, increasing international trade in highly manufactured products between industrialised countries is a general phenomenon in which Canada is sharing.

III. POLICIES TO INCREASE THE SIZE AND EFFICIENCY OF THE CANADIAN ECONOMY

It is always something of a relief when the facts correspond with the general theoretical preconceptions so that we are spared explaining away divergences from the Heckscher–Ohlin model, and turn to questions of policy after the observation that Canadian experience indicates *a priori* concern with the composition of trade which may often be misplaced. Raw and processed materials form a declining proportion of world trade and the terms of trade have turned against them during the past fifteen years. Yet Canadian export trade, which is heavily concentrated on them, has had a satisfactory performance. Efficient use of resources depends on the response to comparative advantage and not on whether relative prices were yet more favourable in some earlier years.

As has already been noted, supplies of factors of production in the Canadian economy have not been entirely accumulated domestically. Labour and capital continue to be attracted from abroad by high yields in resource-based industries which are internationally competitive, and in most cases export a large proportion of this output.

Imported factors of production also are employed in import-competing and domestic sectors of the economy, the growth of which has traditionally been encouraged by governmental policy. Since the French colonial period, governments have continuously encouraged the growth in the total size of the Canadian economy. In the first period, this concern with growth was based on considerations of military defence. Subsequently the issue was the settlement of the Prairies from Central Canada to occupy the area effectively in advance of American encroachment. Later yet, the goal became the creation of a larger domestic economy to make possible large-scale production and lower average costs in manufacturing.

The chief instruments to increase the size of the Canadian economy have been the tariff and immigration policy.[1] The tariff has induced the substitution of manufacturing in Canada for imports. Higher prices for import-competing goods led to an inflow of capital, management talents and technology to establish production in Canada, and this, in turn, increased the demand for labour, causing an influx of labour from Europe attracted by job opportunities and a higher standard of living.

While achieving the goal of increasing the size of the economy, these policies have had some unwelcome by-products. One is that protected manufacturing industry in Canada has tended to be in plants of inefficiently small scale. Interdependent competing firms tend to overcrowd the market producing at prices and costs at the import-competing level. Many of these firms are financed from abroad owing to a high level of demand for capital, and many are owned abroad, since their origin is the transfer of foreign production to Canada. Thus the tariff has also tended to raise the level of foreign control of Canadian manufacturing industry.

The relatively high cost of much Canadian manufacturing has made for real wages lower than in the United States, which has long been accessible to immigrants from Canada, so that the combination of Canadian policies has also tended to cause a replacement in Canada of Canadian-born workers emigrating to the United States by workers of European origin, each group attracted by the high wages in the country of destination relative to their country of origin.

The pattern of Canadian trade and production is also affected by the tariff policies of other countries. Foreign tariffs reduce the size of markets available to Canadian manufacturers, increase their interdependence and tend to reduce their scale of operations. The structure of foreign tariffs also tends to shift processing of Canadian materials to the foreign country. The theory of effective protection is another recent discovery of economists who have systematised what businessmen and officials have realised since tariffs were invented. To some extent Canadian resource policies have attempted to offset the effect of the typical structure of foreign tariffs in advanced countries that shift processing away from Canada.

The usually higher rates of duty on processed than on raw materials give the well-known result of escalating rates of effective protection with increasing processing which induces location of processing in the country in which final consumption occurs. Seventy years ago, Quebec and Ontario prohibited pulpwood exports and forced the establishment of the newsprint industry in Canada. This then led United States newspaper

[1] See J. H. Dales, *The Protective Tariff in Canadian Development* (Toronto: University of Toronto Press, 1967).

publishers to press successfully for the removal of the United States tariff on newsprint. In 1969 Ontario announced a policy of gradually requiring ores mined in the province to be smelted in Canada. This is expected to shift smelting of such metals as nickel to Canada. Various restrictions on the export of electric power and possible future policies with respect to water also have the same effect of keeping down the price of resources in Canada and offsetting to some extent the discriminatory effect that foreign tariffs have on stages of manufacture. In other words, such hindrances to exports increase the efficiency of location of processing but, at the same time, make a transfer in the low price of materials from Canada to the importing countries which have a high rate of effective protection on processed products.[1] In the long run they may lead to the removal of foreign tariffs if Canada is an important source of the processed material because the tariffs raise the costs of users of these materials abroad.

The Canadian tariff today is similar to those of other countries with high per capita incomes in giving the highest rates of protection to commodities produced with relatively unskilled labour. Nominal rates in excess of 20 per cent will still exist after the Kennedy Round reductions for some textiles and footwear. Average rates of duty, both nominal and effective, are relatively high and fall between the higher United Kingdom and the lower United States rates in the usual ranking by country.[2]

In recent years, a realisation has become more widespread that tariffs are in large part responsible for the small scale of plant and high costs of manufacturing in Canada. Whereas earlier free-trade sentiment was based entirely on lowering costs and finding international markets for Canada's great export industries, it is now partly also based on a desire for greater efficiency in Canadian manufacturing industry. Lower Canadian tariffs allow imports to push down Canadian costs and prices and force a more efficient organisation of production. Lower foreign tariffs induce a better allocation of resources in Canada by opening wider markets in which the interdependence of firms is lessened and economies of large plant scale can be exploited.

Canadian policy since the treaty with the United States in 1936 has favoured reciprocal non-discriminatory tariff reductions, resulting from bilateral, and since 1947 multilateral negotiations. The unequal power of

---

[1] H. G. Johnson, 'Implications of Free or Freer Trade for the Harmonization of other Policies', in *Harmonization of National Economic Policies – under Free Trade* (Toronto: University of Toronto Press, 1968) and 'Harmonization of Economic Policies under Free Trading Arrangements: Issues for Canada', *Journal of Canadian Studies* (1969).

[2] J. R. Melvin and B. W. Wilkinson, *Effective Protection in the Canadian Economy* (Ottawa: Economic Council of Canada, Special Study No. 9 1968); B. Balassa, 'Tariff Protection in Industrial Countries: An Evaluation', *Journal of Political Economy* (Dec 1965).

Canada relative to the United States and Europe enhances the value of multilateralism to Canada. Close economic ties are accepted because of their economic benefit, not as a means of furthering a political association as may be the case for economic arrangements between some other countries. The political cost of co-operative economic measures is least when dependence on any particular other nation is diluted in a multilateral context.

Despite a general attitude favourable to multilateral tariff reductions, Canada did not take a place at the forefront in the Kennedy Round negotiations, and the results for Canada can be thought of as a success in old-fashioned terms which see foreign reductions as a gain and cuts in a country's own tariffs as a loss. In terms of today's awareness of the burden of a country's own tariff in raising costs of production through small-scale production in a small domestic market in Canada, the results were disappointing.

One of the inhibiting influences on a bolder Canadian tariff position in multilateral negotiations is the unusually conjectural nature of possible results stemming from the composition of Canadian trade. Canadian exports are largely raw and processed materials on which present foreign rates of duty are low and for which the elasticity of demand may be relatively small. Imports are chiefly of highly protected manufactured goods. If Canada and other countries abolished tariffs, exports and export prices would rise very little relative to the value of imports, and the balance of payments would deteriorate unless a major change in the structure of Canadian secondary manufacturing lowered costs and encouraged exports and the substitution of imports by domestic production. Professor Balassa estimated that an Atlantic free-trade area including Japan would increase trade in manufactured goods by 24 to 27 per cent, and in industrial materials by only 2·2 per cent. Canadian exports would increase by less than 6 per cent, and imports by more than 18 per cent. This would have caused a deterioration in the Canadian balance of payments of $600 million in 1960 that would have required a devaluation of perhaps 5 per cent to correct.[1]

IV. THE CANADA–UNITED STATES AUTOMOTIVE AGREEMENT

The developing concern in Canada as elsewhere with achieving productive efficiency through freer trading arrangements has recently led to a major departure from multilateral practice. The Canada–United States automotive agreement[2] falls in the traditional path of promoting exports and

---

[1] B. Balassa, *Trade Liberalism among Industrial Countries* (New York: McGraw-Hill Book Company, 1967).

[2] An Agreement Concerning Automotive Products between the Government of Canada and the Government of the United States of America, 16 January 1965.

the more recent one of stimulating the rationalisation of domestic production. It also contains provisions stimulating the growth of the manufacturing sector and hence the total size of the Canadian economy which is also a traditional goal. However, the arrangement is effectively bilateral with the United States, and gives very great power to the United States Government, as the arrangement is renegotiated periodically. It also gives some United States trade unions a direct interest in Canadian labour costs and wage levels, and has already increased foreign interference from that quarter.

The automotive agreement has resulted in an immense increase in trade between the United States and Canada in vehicles and parts, in a markedly lessened Canadian trade deficit in these items and in very substantial gains in efficiency in the Canadian industry. The essential elements of this arrangement are that automotive vehicle assemblers in Canada were given the privilege of importing cars and parts free of duty chiefly on the condition, firstly, that they maintain the 1964 rate of assembly relative to sales of vehicles in Canada, and the absolute Canadian value added in each vehicle assembled in Canada, and, secondly, that value added to production in Canada increase by a lump sum of $260 million, plus 60 per cent of any increase in the sale of vehicles in Canada and of Canadian parts.[1] The privilege of importing vehicles and parts free of duty is given only to firms assembling in Canada, so that Canadian car prices can exceed those abroad, and in fact do exceed identical models in the United States by about 4 per cent net of taxes. This is a decreased differential. Before this scheme, the differential was 9 per cent. This reduction reflects the probable substantial decrease in costs brought about by marked modernisation and specialisation and a marginal shift of the North American industry into Canada.[2] The advocates of the arrangement hope that its dynamic effects in increasing productivity in Canada will lead to a state in which the inherent comparative advantage of the Canadian industry is realised and the industry can grow satisfactorily at free-trade prices. The arrangement would then wither away.

The automotive arrangement is quite an ingenious scheme. It belongs to the genus of arrangements for protection through domestic content requirements. It induces international specialisation in the assembly of

[1] See especially Paul Wonnacott and R. J. Wonnacott, 'The Automotive Agreement of 1965', *Canadian Journal of Economics and Political Science* (1967) and Paul Wonnacott, *The U.S.–Canadian Automobile Agreement of 1965: The Early Effects* (Working Paper Series, Bureau of Business and Economic Research, University of Maryland, 1968).

[2] Canadian imports from the United States increased from about $700 million in 1964 to $1,900 million in 1967 and exports from $100 million in 1964 to $1,500 million. Thus the deficit decreased from $600 million to $400 million. These are approximate figures only based on inconsistent estimates from official Canadian and United States publications.

different types or models of vehicles, and in the manufacture of parts or components. Thus production in Canada is in processes in which it has the greatest advantage or least disadvantage. At the same time the provisions of the scheme protect the industry in Canada from the chill winds of international competition through the subsidy that is the higher Canadian than United States car prices accompanied by tariff-free trade in vehicles and parts. Thus an automotive industry of a size perhaps exceeding the free-trade size is maintained in Canada while the inefficiencies in industrial organisation that usually accompany the small market size created by tariffs are minimised. It might be that increased efficiency would lower costs to internationally competitive levels, in which case industry regional free trade would result. But even without diseconomies of scale, a country may have a comparative disadvantage in that industry because of unfavourable factor prices or some other reason. The automotive agreement did not create free trade, but it might provide a controlled movement to it. That is certainly the intention of the United States Government.

Once the decision is taken to protect a suitably structured local industry, namely one composed of firms with close international connections, the Canadian–United States automotive arrangement provides a technically efficient and flexible instrument.[1] It is to be expected that similar arrangements will grow between other pairs of countries. Already another exists between Fiat in Italy and her affiliate in Yugoslavia.[2]

The automotive arrangement has another aspect of special interest to students of economic interdependence. It constitutes a departure from a Canadian policy of substantive multilateralism. This is a case in which prospective gains in productivity and real income led to a policy greatly increasing the dependence of the Canadian economy on United States decisions. The integration of Canadian with United States automobile production is comparable with that under free trade, but the agreement is more precarious than free trade as it is based on less general principle: it applies to a particular industry and involves effective subsidies to

---

[1] At one time, a great deal of interest existed in Canada in extending the scheme to other industries, but the accompanying investigations did not lead to other arrangements for two principal reasons. One was that few other manufacturing industries were composed exclusively of foreign-owned assemblers. In an industry with both foreign and Canadian firms, a scheme such as the automotive arrangement would put the Canadian firms without foreign affiliation in a very weak competitive position. The other was the marked lack of enthusiasm by the United States Government for a type of arrangement that has been thought by some influential groups to have been on balance disadvantageous to the United States industry. United States manufacturing efficiency has not increased as scale was already large in that country and a good deal of investment had taken place in Canada which might otherwise have occurred in the United States.

[2] Jack Baranson, 'Integrated Automobiles for Latin America?', *Finance and Development* (1968).

Canadian operations. If it were not that United States firms profited from Canadian operations, the agreement might well not survive in Washington.

Any major change in the agreement would have much greater proportionate effects on the size and in the structure of the Canadian than the United States industry. The Canadian industry was reorganised and expanded to achieve economies of scale through specialisation as a result of the agreement, whereas the United States industry, efficient already, was not. Hence the dependence of Canada on United States decisions has risen, but that of the United States has increased relatively little. The increased dependence of Canada has elicited little public debate, but would undoubtedly become a factor in the extension of this type of agreement to other industries.

Another aspect of Canadian integration with the United States economy in this respect is that the industry is organised by the United Automobile Workers in the two countries and the power centre for both unions is in the United States. The United States union fears the transfer of a portion of the industry to Canada attracted largely by lower labour costs.[1] Whereas previously wage negotiations were quite separate in the two countries, they are very closely related now. The period during which labour contracts were in effect with the same company in the two countries overlapped in the past; they coincide now. A single contract between the U.A.W. and Chrysler now covers workers in both countries. The consequence has been a very rapid rise in Canadian automotive wages to the advantage of present U.A.W. members in both countries, but to the disadvantage of Canadian labour in general, and of the efficiency of the international structure of the industry.

The relative rise in automotive workers' wages in Canada is rendered possible by the protection given the price of vehicles in Canada by the provisions of the automobile agreement. If Canadian firms were obliged by free trade to reduce prices to the United States level, the resistance to wage increases in Canada would necessarily be greater. The arrangement has thus created closer economic ties with the United States, increased the dependence of Canadian policy on the United States, and introduced a substantial distorting effect in internal relative wages.

The automobile agreement has had some impact on European manufacturers, one of which, Volvo, had begun assembling in Canada in 1961 and two of which, Renault and Peugeot, have entered since the agreement. These firms benefit from the agreement because they import parts free of duty, so long as they maintain a certain level of Canadian value added in vehicles assembled in Canada, whereas, if the vehicles were imported, they would be subject to $17\frac{1}{2}$ per cent duty (15 per cent after the Kennedy Round). They do not gain from specialisation, economies

[1] R. J. and Paul Wonnacott, op. cit.

of scale and exchange of parts and vehicles internationally as do the subsidiaries of United States manufacturers. The costs of assembling European cars in Canada are believed to exceed those in Europe, so that the Canadian plants do not export. Thus, the only reason for assembling in Canada is the Canadian tariff, and should the tariff be lowered, that assembly will doubtless cease as Peugeot's already has.

British cars enter Canada free of duty. The automobile agreement has not affected the competitive position of British cars very greatly because they are closer substitutes for other European cars than for North American cars and the prices of European cars have not been reduced significantly because of the agreement. However, the Canadian automobile industry is changing rapidly in structure. If the automobile agreement results in an international competitive Canadian automotive industry, this will inevitably lead to formal industry free trade with the United States. Under these circumstances, the most favoured nation principle and the expendability of the Canadian tariff as a protective device for the Canadian industry will lead to its abolition. This will cause a marked deterioration in the competitive position of United Kingdom cars in the Canadian market relative to other European producers.

V. TRADE POLICY IN OTHER COMMODITIES

It is with trade in certain agricultural commodities that Canadian policy-makers are principally concerned with European practices. A large proportion of our high-quality wheat exports are bought in the United Kingdom and north-west Europe, where variable import levies, or their equivalent, give exporting countries an inducement to set high prices. High wheat prices and the farm economy's failure to distinguish between average and marginal revenue lead to overproduction of wheat relative to feed grains for which the import market in Western Europe has been very strong. Growing barriers to imports of other agricultural commodities such as cheese in the United Kingdom also pose special problems for which Canadian policy has no short-term solution. The longer-term prospect for a more rational pattern of trade in agriculture depends on the international negotiability of domestic policies for agriculture. That these were becoming negotiable was apparent during the Kennedy Round.

The Canadian tariff attracted manufacturing industry to Canada, but contributed to its inefficiently small plant scale for which solutions, such as the automobile agreement, raised the influence of foreign policies and economic developments on Canada. The attraction of foreign capital to Canada by high yields owing to abundant natural resources or to the growth of secondary manufacturing aided the growth in size of the Canadian economy, and also gave rise to increased dependence on foreign policies and developments. The conduit for such foreign influence is in part the foreign ownership of Canadian industry, and in part the close integration of the Canadian with foreign capital markets.

VI. THE CO-ORDINATION OF CANADIAN AND FOREIGN POLICIES

Canada is notably open to investment owned or controlled by non-residents in accordance with its long-lasting policy of using foreign resources for growth.[1] The high level of foreign ownership and control of Canadian industry and the increasing concentration of control in one country, the United States, has given rise to quite general disquiet that this phenomenon threatens Canadian independence. The presence in Canada of a large number of United States-owned firms has clearly increased the influence of the United States Government through the extra-territorial application of American legislation[2] and through guideline

[1] No restrictions apply to foreign investors that do not apply to Canadians, except with respect to the ownership of financial institutions and media of communications. There are very modest withholding tax measures to encourage foreign purchase of bonds rather than equity and to encourage minority participation of at least 25 per cent by Canadians in firms controlled by foreigners. In 1965, the last year for which data are available, foreign long-term investment in Canada was $30 billion. Of this, $17 billion was in the form of direct investment, of which United States investors owned $14 billion, United Kingdom investors $2 billion, and other Europeans a total of $1·1 billion with the Netherlands, Belgium, Switzerland, France, and Germany participating in that rank. The Canadian long-term investment abroad was $8 billion, of which $4 billion was direct investment, and that was held half in the United States, a quarter in Europe, chiefly in the United Kingdom, and the rest principally in the Caribbean and Latin America. Thus Canada was a net debtor on long-term capital account of $22 billion, and foreign direct investment in Canada exceeded Canadian direct investment abroad by $13 billion. In that year, national income was $39 billion, and international indebtedness as a proportion of income was much below the level of the interwar period, though it had risen very rapidly since a low in 1949. The composition of debt had also shifted from bonds to equity and from the United Kingdom to the United States. Foreign ownership of manufacturing industry has increased from 38 per cent in 1926 to 55 per cent in 1965. In mining it has increased from 37 per cent to 62 per cent. About three-quarters of petroleum and natural gas investment is owned abroad. Foreign investment was concentrated in particular industries and also the larger firms and the proportion of industries controlled abroad tended to exceed ownership where the latter was high. *The Canadian Balance of International Payments*, Third Quarter 1968 (Ottawa: Dominion Bureau of Statistics, Dec 1968).

[2] The United States legislation with most frequent extra-territorial application are the Export Control Act, which controls United States exports and the re-export from third countries of goods containing United States components or technical data, and the Foreign Assets Control Regulations under the Trading with the Enemy Act, which prohibits United States firms from trading with China, North Korea, North Vietnam, and Cuba. The effect of the Export Control Act on Canada is not a function of the presence of United States subsidiaries in Canada, for many Canadian exports would in any event contain United States components. Firms that are not subsidiaries of United States corporations in many countries have been obliged to curtail exports to

pressure on United States parent firms with subsidiaries in Canada. It must be recognised that the United States Government has done much to reduce or eliminate the impact of these policies on Canada.

Canadian policy itself has responded to some of these United States measures. Canada is the only country to which American exports are exempted from the Export Control Act by the United States, but in exchange Canada regulates her own exports to Communist countries to prevent unauthorised re-exports of United States origin.

This type of co-ordination of Canadian with United States policy implies that, in the view of the Canadian Government, the exemption from the costs imposed by United States export controls on the vast amount of trade with their country is worth the price that is the application of Canadian controls on trade with Communist countries to check re-exports of some United States goods. Though the Canadian Government may not share the view of the United States about some types of trade, the legitimacy of United States control over the destination of its own exports is unchallenged.

In contrast, a direct threat to Canadian sovereignty and a conflict of national interest does exist in the application of the United States Foreign Assets Control Regulations to firms in Canada that are subsidiaries through pressure on parent firms in the United States. This practice invalidates the claims of the political neutrality of business decisions on which toleration of foreign ownership is largely based. This Trojan horse has not yet caused damage despite a divergence of Canadian and United States policies with respect to exports to the designated countries, because consultation between the governments is institutionalised and specific exemptions are obtained by Canada on a case by case basis. However, serious difficulties may well arise in future if policies diverge more and the relevant industries contain too little Canadian capacity not owned in the United States to fill the orders involved. In such circumstances, failure to withdraw official American claims to regulate the practices of business firms in Canada would obviously lead to a fundamental re-evaluation of the position of such firms.

The interdependence in this same sense of conflict of interest rather than a co-ordinated movement towards a common goal briefly arose from United States guidelines for the behaviour of subsidiaries in Canada as elsewhere. In 1965, the United States Government issued directives to

---

Communist countries. But the Foreign Assets Control Regulations only apply to Canada because of the existence there of United States subsidiaries over which the United States Government explicitly claims jurisdiction by holding criminally responsible for their activities the shareholders and directors of the United States parent firm. See *Foreign Ownership and the Structure of Canadian Industry*, Report of the Task Force on the Structure of Canadian Industry (Ottawa: Privy Council Office, Jan 1968).

American firms limiting direct investment abroad and directing them to repatriate earnings and increase their purchases from American sources. The Canadian Government responded by establishing surveillance and issuing guidelines of its own on good corporate behaviour in an attempt to ensure that the United States measures to push on to firms abroad some of the cost of coping with United States balance of payments problems did not in fact succeed in Canada. Running down balances in Canada and redirecting purchases from lower-cost to United States sources would have raised interest rates and reduced efficiency. It appears that very little of this took place, if any. When the guidelines were made into regulations in 1968, Canada was exempted from them. No estimate of the effect of 'voluntary' restraints on capital exports to Canada exists, but their importance could easily be overemphasised, because capital could be imported by the alternative route of selling securities in the United States as Canada was exempt from the Interest Equalisation Tax.

United States restraints on the behaviour of subsidiaries of American firms in other countries for balance of payments purposes is the most recent United States interference with its trade and payments. But Canada was also exempted from the application of earlier regulations in exchange for the harmonisation of Canadian with United States policies necessary to prevent leakages from United States controls through Canada. The United States measures of control began with tying aid and military trade procurement in 1958, and continued with the increase in short-term interest rates in 1960, with control of long-term portfolio capital by the Interest Equalisation Tax in 1963, and with guidelines for direct investment already discussed and for short-term capital flows in 1965.

Canada had been importing capital chiefly from the United States at the rate of over $1 billion a year for some years when the Interest Equalisation Tax was applied. European capital markets were much too small to provide a substitute source of funds, so that the effect of the tax was likely to raise the rate of interest in Canada by the amount of the tax. Canadian authorities argued that the flow of capital to Canada did not, in any event, weaken the United States balance of payments because Canada held its reserve in United States dollars and did not wish to accumulate them. New issues of Canadian securities were then exempted by the United States authorities from the tax in return for an undertaking not to increase the level of Canadian foreign exchange reserves.

Another aspect of United States controls over movements of capital was the guidelines over short-term capital flows. Canadian banks' long-established agencies in New York and branches in Europe were important in the Euro-dollar market from the earliest days. During the 1960s, Canadian banks were net lenders in Europe of deposits obtained in New York or in United States dollar deposits in Canada. A marked change came with the United States 'voluntary restraint' programme in 1965.

This was in part owing to the co-ordination of Canadian with United States policy when the Minister of Finance requested Canadian banks not to decrease their net asset position vis-à-vis United States residents below the level of the end of 1964[1] and limited the extent to which United States funds could flow to Europe through Canada.[2]

The consequence of the ceiling on Canadian exchange reserves combined with a fixed exchange rate and multilateral agreements restricting the use of tariffs and foreign exchange control measures was to reduce the already slight Canadian ability to pursue a monetary policy different from the American. The elasticity of supply of capital to Canada is high, and attempts to raise the rate of interest relative to abroad as price increases in Canada exceeded those in the United States owing to an undervalued rate of exchange, were frustrated by the consequent upward pressure on the reserves.

The logic of obtaining for Canada a special position within United States balance of payments controls is best evaluated in terms of the theory of policy harmonisation. This is related to the closeness of economic ties of Canada with the United States on the one hand, and with Europe on the other.

An unrestricted market for capital within North America, but in which one country, the United States, erects barriers to the flow of capital to Europe, naturally requires the establishment of the same barriers by the other country, Canada, to avoid the deflection of capital.

The question arises of the costs and benefits of such policy harmonisation as against other possible arrangements. In general, the effect of the controls on capital movements should be measured in relation to a non-discriminatory policy which in this case would be a rise in interest rates in the United States to curb the outflow of capital and check the weakness in her balance of payments.[3] In contrast to higher United States interest rates, controls would reduce the European share of total United States investment. In other words, the costs of the controls is the inefficiency in the allocation of investment consisting of the choice at the margin of relatively low-yield investment in the United States rather than higher-yielding investment in Europe. The question here is that of the probable effect on efficiency of the exemption of Canada from the controls.

[1] Bank of Canada, *Annual Report of the Governor to the Minister of Finance* (1965).

[2] Another influence in 1965 was the difficulty experienced by United States firms in Canada in borrowing in the United States. This increased the demand for funds in Canada with a result that Canadian banks repatriated Euro-dollar loans and borrowed in Europe so as to cause an inflow of short-term funds of $1 billion. However, the special need for funds of 1965 gave way to a more normal position as Canada became exempted from the guidelines. Canadian banks again loaned in Europe as Euro-dollar rates rose, but under new restrictions.

[3] See H. G. Johnson, 'Implications of Free or Freer Trade for the Harmonization of Other Policies', op. cit.

If Canada were not exempted, United States investment in Canada would be reduced relative to investment in the United States, as in the European case. With the exemption, investment in Canada does not decline relative to investment in the United States. This is a relationship that would also have held if the United States had raised the rate of interest, because rates in Canada would have moved in close harmony owing to the extremely close ties of the Canadian and United States capital markets. Thus an exemption from the United States controls brings a result more similar to that of an efficiently allocative non-discriminatory United States policy than non-exemption. The element of distortion with exemption is over-investment of United States capital in Canada (as in the United States) in relation to Europe. Given the great reliance of Canada on the United States capital market, this element of distortion undoubtedly reduces efficiency less than the decreased supply of capital that would be implied by the application of the Interest Equalisation Tax and related measures to Canada. Thus, in terms of allocative efficiency for North American capital, exemption is clearly the best policy in a second-best situation.[1] From a purely national standpoint, the desirability of exemption is even clearer. The more cheaply capital can be borrowed abroad, the higher are the returns to the other factors of production at home.

A characteristic of Canadian policy distinguished from that of most other countries is a concern with the state, not of the overall balance of payments, but of the current account. When Canadians speak of a surplus or deficit balance of payments, they refer to the current account, and the implication is usually that the deficit should be closed. The level of reserves is important, of course, but the primary goal is the balance on current account.

The focus on current account is in part owing to the general understanding of the principle that there is no such thing as a free lunch, and that what is not earned by exports today must be repaid with interest tomorrow. The current account is watched to see the extent to which Canada relies on foreign saving. In part, the current balance is also thought to be significant because, in a situation of high mobility of capital, it determines the level of the interest rate in Canada relative to abroad. This mobility of capital means that maintaining international liquidity is normally no problem as Canada can attract short-term capital very easily. It also means that, hamstrung as Canadian policy is by a fixed rate of foreign exchange, the rate of interest which is determined by the balance of payments may be inappropriate to other policy goals. Fiscal and

---

[1] Controls on the outflow of funds from Canada to Europe to prevent the rerouting of United States funds through Canada involve some cost in forgoing opportunities for profit. But these opportunities are in part created by United States controls themselves which permit low rates of interest in New York, and would not be as attractive were the controls replaced by tighter money in the United States.

monetary policy must be combined to yield the particular rate of interest that achieves equilibrium in the balance of payments as well as the appropriate level of domestic demand. That poses two problems, one technical and the other economic. The technical problem is that of adjusting government expenditures and taxes on the one hand, and the rate of increase in the money supply on the other, so as to reach these two goals in a country with substantial fiscal decentralisation, and in which the federal and provincial governments quarrel over tax resources and fields of expenditures. The economic problem resides in that the combination of the rate of interest, and of the mix of fiscal and monetary policy that keep equilibrium in the international accounts, together with an appropriate level of domestic demand, may fail to meet the needs of other policy goals such as growth, price stability, or the desired size of the government sector.

A focus on the balance on current account is idiosyncratic. Concentration on a single measure that reflects long-term capital movements, portfolio and direct, movements of financial capital, and international competitiveness is not strictly scientific. A mixture of considerations are involved, including the political consequences of foreign ownership, the wisdom of accumulating large external long-term debt, and difficulties of adjusting national policy to changing external conditions.

These problems have arisen in such size in the Canadian experience because of the long-standing openness of her economy in the sense of a setting highly dependent on foreign conditions and policies owing to the very high external elasticities of demand and supply for goods, capital and labour. As the North Atlantic world becomes more open, the same concerns in other countries may lead to a similar use of the balance of current account as a summary guide for policy.

Discussion of the Paper by Professor Eastman

Professor Scott said that much of the basic research on Canada's international position had been done by Professor Eastman. His first theme in this paper was that Canada's was a very open economy, so that comparative advantage and factor supply position were important. Both present comparative advantages and the tariff policies of other countries led to highly capital-intensive activities, to a heavy draft on Canada's domestic savings and to big foreign investment – especially from the United States.

There was some confusion on p. 34. A great deal of the investment was in 'raw materials' (natural resources) leading to highly human capital-intensive activities – in terms of relative wage and salary levels. The industries in question included iron and petrol – not surprisingly leading to a high level of educational requirement. Innovation need play no role – the mix explained all. The paper also emphasised the unimportance of the trend in the terms of trade for current policies. Up to p. 34, then, the findings of the paper were about what one would expect.

Professor Eastman's contribution was to stress that factor endowments were *not* a fact of life. Labour and capital were both highly mobile. To talk of comparative advantage as though land, labour and capital were all permanently *in* Canada mistook the Canadian tariff policy. This was intended not just to protect indigenous workers – it was aimed more at attracting and holding other factors of production. Therefore, from p. 35 onwards, there was not much on structure alone but much about size and structure. Size itself was an aim and a consequence of policy instruments.

Apart from the consequences of tariff policy and of employment creation, two issues for general policy had emerged. There was inefficiency behind the tariff wall – especially in consumer-goods industries; and there was oligopoly in these protected manufacturing industries. Second, there was large-scale foreign ownership, a subject of great concern to both electorate and government. Much Canadian interference with international trade was a response to pressure to protect processing of Canadian raw materials. For example, there were both subsidies and an absolute prohibition on the export of some raw materials, in order to ensure further processing in Canada. Part of the cost was often pushed on to the United States (and later the Japanese) taxpayer rather than the Canadian consumer.

What had happened to the level of Canadian protection? Nominal rates (defined as tariff revenue relatively to the volume of duty-paying imports) were falling. They were at a higher level than in the United States, but falling at roughly the same rate.

In a hypothetical free-trade regime in the North Atlantic, Professor Balassa had argued that Canadian exports would not rise very much, while imports would rise with income. This had long been a widely accepted view on the effect of free trade in Canada. But it was a short-run view. In the longer run, secondary manufacturing would adjust and grow with tariff protection in the interests of international firms. Hence the balance of payments situation would not be so adverse as in the short run.

For a Canadian, these matters were more interesting than the famous automotive agreement which was well reviewed after p. 37. Though Professor Eastman called this a substitute for multilateral free trade, it did depend on tariffs in the two countries, for there was no free trade in automobile products as there was in farm machinery. The ultimate impact depended on the safeguards for making sure that 'enough' production located in Canada. Under the agreement, all Canadian cars *could not* be made in the United States. Some assurance had been given to Ontario by such studies as the Wonnacotts', which suggested that, even under free trade, automobile production would continue in Canada. Yet, in the western provinces, the newer Japanese cars currently outsold everyone else.

While Professor Eastman's paper dealt very well with balance of payments policy and its connection to the rate of interest, it made little reference to Canada's difficulties of dealing with inflation independently. Inflation was not surprising, with fixed exchange rates and with 25 per cent of imports coming from the United States. In such circumstances, Canada alone could not do very much to stabilise prices. Price and wage controls had been widely suggested; but the trade unions only wanted one level of real wages for the United States and Canada. Recently, an attempt had been made to reduce expenditure by fiscal policy – by cuts in government spending. It was thought that the main effects fell on imports or on employment, but not on prices.

Canada's was an open economy next to the United States, which therefore found sources of friction from small changes in structure. For example, there was a different demography. The post-war baby boom had come later than in the United States, so that at present the demand for houses was almost insatiable in Canada, while quite 'normal' in the United States. Demographic factors also led to different kinds of policy over the desired rate of immigration from Europe and over the level of government expenditure for social purposes – a whole body of quasi-economic policy questions.

Finally, Europeans should remember that a multitude of semi-technical, semi-economic policy questions were shared by the two countries and were settled jointly (if not with equal enthusiasm or power). There was almost complete jointness, similarity or unanimity in policy concerning fisheries, patents, education, the taxation of individuals and so forth. Almost all of these were matters of agreement – usually Canada accepted the American policy; sometimes they were co-ordinated or determined together.

In his able survey, Professor Eastman had looked mainly at the economic structure and trends of Canada. Another paper might have looked more at the national and international problems of the cycle – at the transmission of economic fluctuations across the frontier.

Professor Eastman suggested that his paper had been excessively elliptical on two major points. First, he had shown that Canada's economic integration with the United States was growing, though there had been no overall decision of principle on this question. A formal bilateral free-trade agreement with the United States was politically unattractive to Canada, and a North Atlantic Free Trade Area (minus the E.E.C.) was unattractive to the United States. Most Canadian trade was with the United States so that the best hope for lowered barriers to Canadian trade, without excessive diversion, was a new round of GATT negotiations. Alternatively, one could envisage multilateral agreements sector by sector.

Second, Professor Eastman pointed to a model underlying what he had written on macro-economic policy and capital flows. He had assumed perfectly elastic international capital flows and an entire dependence of Canadian on foreign interest rates. The conditions that had been attached to the exemptions from United States controls over capital flows had made it impossible for Canada to use monetary policy to change her interest rates appreciably. Under these conditions, the supply of money affected only the volume of reserves, not interest rates. The effect of monetary policy on interest rates at any time, in the Canadian setting, could easily be overstated.

Stabilisation of income then became wholly a consequence of fiscal policy. But one had to recognise that the goal of stabilisation was only one of many guiding fiscal policy, especially in a federal context. The large number of goals thus set for fiscal policy, and considerations of efficiency, meant that part of the burden of stabilisation should be borne by flexibility in the rate of exchange.

Professor Robinson said he wanted to ask a few questions. The primary concern of the Conference was with relationships between the two sides of the Atlantic. He agreed that one could not look at Canadian experience without also looking at the United States, but the paper was a little too much concerned with relationships on the North American side of the Atlantic. What about relationships between Canada and Europe? He wanted to know a little more about agricultural problems. If one went back fifty years, to before 1914, he thought that Canada would be seen to be much more part of the European economy. He did not know what Canada's trade balance with Europe then was, but with the United Kingdom it was close to zero. Large investments had been made in Canada in railways, etc. Invisible imports were required from the United Kingdom which just about balanced the balance of payments. Between 1914 and 1918, Britain had disposed of investments and suffered inflation. At the same time, Canada relied much more on the American economy. Thus there emerged the triangle of the North American trade – with the United Kingdom buying from Canada but paying in United States dollars; for it was in America that Canada wanted to buy. This separated Canada from the European economy.

His main question was this. It was easier to think of the United States and Canada as the most underused agricultural area in a world needing more foodstuffs. These foodstuffs were not needed in Europe but in Asia. Perhaps one repercussion of the development of agriculture in Europe had been a fall in demand from Europe for Canadian foodstuffs. How could we re-create a world where the agricultural potential of North America was available again for the rest of the world? Perhaps we needed a trade through which Asia had closer links with Canada and the United States – following the Australian example. Japan was now Australia's largest source of manufactures and her biggest buyer of raw materials. What would be the effect of European development on Canadian agriculture?

Professor Ashton said he knew the Conference was going on to discuss agriculture, but he was surprised Professor Eastman had eschewed the subject. He thought Professor Eastman displayed undue optimism when he said that the international agricultural negotiations had been spurred on by the Kennedy Round. This was not true. There had been no really effective outcome from the discussions of agricultural trade policy in those negotiations. There was now, in effect, an *impasse* on both sides of the Atlantic, showing the tail of agricultural policies wagging the dog of economic policies.

Professor Eastman said he had ignored agriculture, but he thought that the evolution of agricultural trade policy centred on the question of how to absorb cereal production from the Canadian West. Unless there was more demand from Europe, it would be necessary to feed grain to animals for export to the United States. Japan was a major wheat market. As for markets in Russia and China in the future, he thought it unlikely that they would become of such importance as to permit a shift in emphasis from trade in agricultural products with the United States.

Professor Campbell explained that major cereal exports had been made to India and Pakistan, but these were now experimenting with new varieties of wheat and rice which reduced the market for Canadian produce. Professor Eastman had summarised well the position about the Prairies. These were producing about as much wheat as they could, and now held about half of all wheat stocks held by exporters. It was necessary to export more livestock to the United States. Professor Eastman had also covered adequately the questions of tariffs and of restrictions on capital flows. Perhaps not enough emphasis had been put on export subsidies and on taxation, apart from tariffs.

Mr Shonfield wanted to turn to the important issue of the current account of the balance of payments. He wondered how special Canada was in looking particularly at the current account of the balance of payments. How were other countries different? There was a more fundamental question. Canada was surely not solely guided by the current account balance. The United States had exported about $1 billion worth of capital per annum to Canada. Canada had set a limit to the current account deficit – saying $1 billion is all right but not $2 billion. Professor Eastman had said that a current balance deficit was not a free lunch, but what did this mean? It was a paradox to say that Canada was 'concerned' in the sense of wanting equilibrium on current account. It could be confident that its big deficit would be covered by capital movements. It had a big neighbour with virtually no economic frontier between, and this gave unusual room for movement. The Canadian case was different from that of the rest of the Atlantic community.

Professor Eastman replied that there was increasing similarity between many economies in the dependence of the home on the foreign rate of interest owing to the ease of capital flows. The only instrument for dealing with a current account deficit – with a stable exchange rate – was fiscal policy, apart from controls. In some papers, there seemed to be a dichotomy between exchange-rate alterations to separate economies, and policy co-ordination to bring them together. In terms of Canadian experience, he saw exchange-rate flexibility as an alternative to controls, rather than to a closer meshing of policy.

Mr Shonfield said he took the point. Canada had been robbed of the rate of interest weapon. But the same was true of the United Kingdom. There was a chronic balance of payments on current account. Was it not a feature of a country with continuing current account deficits, that it had to use the rate of interest to make up the difference? Some countries planned to have a deficit, others – like the United Kingdom – just had one.

Professor Eastman said it was less a question of having a deficit than of the existence of close links with the United States capital market.

Professor Kindleberger said that Germany was linked to New York too, and clearly a German deficit had nothing to do with this.

Mr Shonfield insisted that the fact that the rate of interest was similar in various centres was not the point. It was whether one could use the rate of interest as a monetary weapon. Then the argument was not peculiar to Canada.

Professor Kindleberger said that he agreed.

M. Houssiaux understood that short-term economic relations between America and Canada were decisive for Canada. On long-term growth, Canada had evolved differently from the United States. Because of the stress on raw material supplies in her trade, she needed to use successive staple resources. In the short run, this fact made growth in Canada dependent on cyclical patterns in the United States. In the long run, the staple goods theory explained why Canadian growth did not imply, until recently, a high degree of diversification towards manufactured products.

Owing to these peculiar conditions, and to the differences in population movements in Canada and the United States, it was difficult to say that economic policy in the two countries could be reconciled in either the short or the long term.

Professor Marchal said he understood that the automotive agreement gave Canadian firms the opportunity to import cars and spares in proportion to the level of imports in 1964. An economist would say two things. First, Canadian negotiators were looking at productivity and prices on both sides of the frontier. They were concerned with increasing specialisation and economies of scale. Professor Eastman had concluded that the differential between Canadian and American prices of cars had fallen from 9 to 4 per cent. This reduction had been due to a fall in the difference of production costs. It was the result of greater specialisation and increased output.

On the other hand, Canadians had had to accept that their dependence on the American economy had been increased. Production and wage decisions had to be made by a single trade union. Thus wages in Canadian automobile factories were being distorted by comparison with the rest of the economy. This seemed to cancel out some of the benefits of productivity. Perhaps Professor Eastman should modify his favourable opinion of the agreement.

Professor Kindleberger noted that Professor Eastman had referred to 'a trade deficit in automobiles'. Was this a useful concept? There had been a talk in the United States recently about the 'tourist gap'. He found this a very offensive expression. For example, the Algarve would suffer if all countries tried to balance their tourist accounts with Portugal. There was nothing to be gained from trying to balance accounts in one commodity.

Professor Eastman agreed that it was absurd to balance trade for one good. The significance of talking about automobiles in this way was that the automobile agreement reflected the rates of growth of output in the two countries. Since there was negotiation every three years, and conflicting interests in these negotiations, the course of bilateral trade in this commodity was a result of the negotiations.

With respect to wages, he thought, though he had no real knowledge, that the United Automobile Workers in America were worried about the shift of output to Canada, and tried to solve their problems by raising wages to the same level in Canada as in the United States.

To Professor Marchal, Professor Eastman said that he foresaw trouble in the next few years. The United States Government had gone into the agreement on the basis that it would lead to continental free trade. Canadian officials did not talk of this goal without apprehension. Therefore, unless prices were equalised and all restrictions removed, renegotiation of the whole agreement might be necessary. This interdependence was coming to create more and more an international currency area that would reduce the effect of exchange-rate changes in the future.

To Professor Houssiaux, Professor Eastman said there had been an historical reorientation of Canadian exports from Europe to the United States. The exploitation of Canada's new frontier did depend on American demand. The dependence of Canadian on American economic cycles was reflected in the virtual coincidence of peaks and troughs in the two countries. As for the development of secondary manufacture in Canada, lower labour costs provided a sound basis for such developments. Some interesting studies of the competitiveness of various Canadian products had been made, especially by the Wonnacotts, but the results so far were not definitive.

Professor Izzo spoke about the rate of interest policy. He said that many people favoured freedom of capital flows, but the case for the latter rested on the fact that monetary and fiscal policy in each country would be geared to induce foreign capital owners to supply an amount of capital equal to the deficit on current account of the balance of payments. This implied that domestic investment and saving rates should be such as to ensure a level of interest rates at which inflows of foreign capital matched the deficit on current account. He said that there was no presumption that this mechanism was superior to direct control of capital flows. Furthermore, these were probably determined by the expectation of private net income, and the relation between the latter and social income was influenced by taxation and other public policies. Consequently, he thought that there was no *a priori* reason to believe that freedom of capital movements would imply a more efficient allocation of international resources than direct controls over capital flows.

Mr Maddison said that Professor Eastman had argued that Canadian policy was hamstrung by fixed exchange rates but that flexible rates might conflict with other policy goals. He doubted whether this was true. Canada could have grown faster if it had been less tied to the United States in the 1950s, but at that time it did not exploit the policy options available with floating rates. In the 1960s, Canada had not suffered from its close links with the United States.

He wondered how responsive the capital inflow was to exchange-rate changes. He thought that United States investment in Canada was largely independent of the exchange rate. If Canada did move to a floating exchange rate, it was important to begin at a time when appreciation would be the immediate result.

Professor Eastman replied that his own view was that the rates of return did lead to the efficient allocation of resources in North America. He expected private investment flows to go into assets with the highest yield. It was true that monetary policy did not affect real capital flows between the two countries, because it did not affect the rate of interest and income significantly. Therefore its role was to keep financial flows equal to real flows. The efficient allocation of resources would require government expenditure giving roughly the same marginal efficiency of capital as private at full employment. If this did not happen, then the real capital inflow was wrong and the exchange rate should be changed.

Professor Eastman agreed with Mr Maddison that Canada had had an undervalued dollar. Up to about two or three years previously, price increases had been greater than in the United States, despite a lower level of demand and employment. Probably the devaluation of 1962 had been too great. The single greatest argument against a floating rate was that politicians had proved unable to keep their hands off it.

Professor Scott returned to what Professor Robinson had said about agriculture. There was clearly a large gulf between the Malthusian forecasters and those who said that the market for North American foodstuffs was not expanding. The forecasts of 1955 were best summarised by the following figures. Canadian exports of food had then been expected ro rise by 2·2 per cent; in fact they had risen by 4·7 per cent. There had been the same kind of underestimation in earlier figures for Canada's share of total world exports and of exports of food. He would point out that during recent years there had been large exports of grain to China and Russia and these might not be repeated. But, on balance, the Malthusians had made the better predictions.

Professor Robinson did not wish to deny any of this. In some degree, a conference of this kind had to look at what seemed desirable as well as at what was. He wondered whether the world structure was not a good deal less desirable many people often thought it to be.

Professor Kindleberger wondered whether one did not need to integrate the parts, as well as the whole, of capital markets. There had been suggestions that the Canadians should buy out all United States investments in Canada in exchange for Canadian holdings of United States securities and a large new debt. This idea was rejected by Canadians who wanted to retain United States equities gross. The point was that integration should take place at all levels, and this would give individuals the opportunity to invest in both countries. Portfolios in both countries might then turn out to contain 10 per cent Canadian and 90 per cent United States assets. On whether this was desirable or not, economic and political views would differ. He wondered whether Professor Eastman was an economist or politician on this question.

Mr Grogan said Mr Shonfield had queried what experience in other countries might have been. The post-war period in Australia had been marked by cyclical fluctuations in economic activity whose repercussions on imports and on the balance of payments were complicated by movements in prices of exports and imports. For the period from 1948–9 to 1963–4, there was a deficit on current account in eleven years out of the sixteen. For the whole period, the deficit totalled £1,772 million. This gap was bridged by a capital inflow which, in fact, was sufficient to allow some building up of reserves. Mr Grogan doubted whether this capital had been attracted by high interest rates; rather, he thought, it was a response to profitable investment opportunities. The recent mineral discoveries in Australia would in due course increase exports; meanwhile the cost of their development contained a foreign exchange component which, presumably, was being covered by overseas investment.

Professor Rieben said that Canada had a strong competitive position in minerals, petroleum and electricity. He wondered whether there was an agreement with the United States over steel and aluminium like that over automobiles. He also wondered whether rates of interest and wages were co-ordinated. Were there the same levels of added value in the two countries?

In the United States, a general agreement had been made between steel exporters in Japan on the one hand and in Europe and North America on the other. This was intended to regulate the rate of growth of steel output. It was intended to keep down investment in the United States and so keep down American prices. Was there an agreement between the United States and Canada? He thought that if there was an agreement between countries which were close to each other, with such vast quantities involved, there would be a problem.

He thought there was a huge potential in agriculture; that Canada like Australia also had a huge future potential for producing raw materials. What strategy was being evolved in respect of these issues?

A few days ago, Reynolds and Kaiser had sought to increase the price of aluminium ingots. Alcan had refused to follow because it did not want the domestic price of aluminium to be above the world market price. He wondered whether something similar would happen with steel.

Professor Eastman explained that the automobile agreement was the only industry agreement. The steel industry was almost entirely under Canadian ownership and was chiefly a domestic industry with net imports in the past. Recently, it had changed to make small net exports. Aluminium was an export industry facing difficulties abroad, one of the most significant of which was recent heavy British subsidisation of new domestic production.

Professor Scott said he would like to make a few comments on Professor Rieben's query. Canada did have vast resources of iron ore, but she still imported coal, and steel was mainly a *domestic* industry. He did not foresee any very great expansion, and there was not much connection of the kind Professor Rieben had suggested.

In aluminium there was a sort of international cartel, with disagreements between the participants. The pressure to locate in producing countries was there, but coal-smelted aluminium was economic and it was now seen that location near the market (as that was often where the coal was) had its attractions.

Mr Shonfield returned to the dependence of Canada on the United States foreshadowing the same for other parts of the world. How far was this a special relationship? He wanted to be forgiven for 'worrying' the point. One important factor was that current and capital elements in the balance of payments were not independent. The current account deficit was a dependent variable related to the level of foreign investment in Canada. This was apparently not exceptional because the same happened in Australia. There were large imports of capital goods *because* foreign investment was high. Professor Eastman's argument was very short-run; Professor Grogan's was long-run. Perhaps this was why Professor Eastman had emphasised the particular dependence on the United States.

Professor Eastman agreed that this was part of the difference. He had ignored cyclical elements. It was true that the deficit sprang in part from imports of capital and consumer goods bought in times of prosperity. At any given moment, the size of the current account deficit or surplus depended on the level of activity and the exchange rate. The rate of interest could not be changed significantly and monetary policy either attracted or repelled foreign funds. In the last year, the problem had been to keep capital out.

He thought that what had happened in the North Atlantic foreshadowed less what might happen in the rest of the world than it did five years ago when capital was less mobile outside the United States and Canada. Capital markets were now much more unified.

To Professor Kindleberger, Professor Eastman said it was essential for the competitiveness and efficiency of Canadian industry that it should have a large range of investment opportunities in Canada. It was true that legal restrictions existed, requiring that some types of financial institutions be Canadian-owned, but he did not see this as a sound basis for the growth of the community. This should rest rather on competitiveness in international terms. For that, he wanted to see free access to the New York capital market.

Professor Robinson had commented on changing relations between Europe and Canada. He ought to have commented on the historical importance of London as the intermediary for the channelling of capital to Canada. Today, the connection was predominantly with New York, but British and other financial institutions also provided finance through New York, so that, though less important and direct, the connection with London was still there.

3 Repercussions of the Economic Policy of the United States on the Policies of the Countries of the European Economic Community[1]

M. Albert
DIRECTION GÉNÉRALE DES AFFAIRES ÉCONOMIQUES,
COMMISSION DES COMMUNAUTÉS EUROPÉENNES, BRUSSELS

I. INTRODUCTORY

The topic to be discussed in the first four sessions of this Round Table is the mutual repercussions between the economic policies of North America and Western Europe. The organisers of the meeting have rightly split up this general subject into four symmetrical parts, so that the paper which follows is concerned with the repercussions of the economic policy of the United States on the economic policies of the countries of the European Economic Community (E.E.C.). But this subject itself is further subdivided into six questions. These are not of equal scope and they cannot all be discussed in a few pages.

As an official of the Common Market, my middle name is compromise, and on this occasion I propose to adopt a compromise by which I shall take up three main points within the subject assigned to me. They concern respectively:

(a) Complementarity and competitiveness as between the E.E.C. and North America.
(b) An attempt to summarise the economic and commercial policies of the European Economic Community.
(c) Some considerations regarding the possible influences, or indeed constraints, exercised or imposed by United States economic policies on those of the Six and of the Community itself.

II. COMPLEMENTARITY AND COMPETITIVENESS

Three questions have to be answered: How far are the resource endowments of Europe complementary to those of North America? How far are they competitive? Where do the comparative advantages of Europe[2] lie?

---
[1] Translated by Elizabeth Henderson.
[2] For purposes of simplification, or perhaps in anticipation of the future, the word 'Europe' is here used as a synonym for European Economic Community.

The three questions are interrelated. International specialisation of labour tends to create complementarities among different economies; to the extent that the latter are thereby integrated into international trade they can no longer be competitive in all fields. The competitiveness of each individual economy is then determined by comparative advantages, in the broadest sense of the word.

(1) *Complementarity*

Although I do not have much leisure to read works on theoretical economics, I get the impression that the concept of economic complementarity no longer occupies the position it used to in the literature. In any case, it seems to me to have changed its meaning.

The concept goes back to the time when England was the world's workshop, and it traditionally refers to the complementary structure of production and of the trade flows between industrialised countries on the one hand and underdeveloped countries on the other. The latter produced mainly raw materials and agricultural commodities, and bought manufactures from the industrial countries. This situation has not radically changed, but a new factor has been added to it. Until about 1950, the volume of trade between industrial and underdeveloped countries increased at roughly the same rate as did world trade as a whole. Since then, for the last twenty years or so, trade between industrial countries has been expanding much faster.

This circumstance is influencing some of the concepts which govern economic policy. Until not long ago a country was regarded as fulfilling the optimum conditions of development when it owned both raw material resources and an industry capable of transforming them. The American economy was the best possible example. About fifteen years ago, on the eve of the negotiations that led to the Treaty of Rome and at a time teeming with projects of such charming and now forgotten names as 'Francital', 'Fritalux', etc., it was often thought that a customs union between France and Germany would be much more fruitful than one between France and Italy, because the economies of the latter two countries were far less complementary.

Today, things look different. Far from being a source of wealth in all cases, the possession of raw materials can as often as not be a handicap. The recent history of coal in Europe is a case in point. By contrast, countries like Japan and Italy are characteristic examples of economies the extremely fast development of which rests on genuine specialisation of labour on the world scale and in accordance with each people's own peculiar talents.

Furthermore, we are witnessing, nowadays, a diversification in the forms of international trade, and this forces us to add a new dimension to the old theory according to which the proportion of raw material exports in a country's foreign trade is a measure of that country's degree of development. In 1967, agricultural commodities, raw materials and fuel and power accounted for 30·1 per cent of the exports of the United States but for only 14·5 per cent of those of the E.E.C. (source: O.E.C.D.). At the same time, exports of industrial products and the transfer of knowledge and know-how in the broadest sense are steadily increasing. It is, therefore, not so much the structure of their respective exports and imports that makes for complementarity between the United States and the E.E.C., but two new important elements, to wit:

(a) the growing export surplus of the United States in its exchange of patents and licences[1] with Western Europe, a surplus that more than quadrupled between 1956 and 1968 from $103 million to $454 million;

(b) the growth of direct investment in Europe on the part of American corporations, which is becoming a more and more specific and intangible matter connected with the excess entrepreneurial capacity of the United States.

The first of these elements has to do with American superiority in innovation, the second with the so-called management gap.

It seems we are approaching a situation in which Europe tends to specialise on industrial activities of a semi-traditional kind, whereas America is taking the lead in pioneering activities, with a high content of research, technology and sales promotion. This view cannot be conclusively proved on the basis of available statistics. Nevertheless some figures in support of the argument will be quoted later under the heading 'Comparative Advantages'. For the moment, let us take two names and think what they stand for – I.B.M. and Volkswagen – and let us note that they seem to confirm the Leontieff paradox, according to which the United States is more efficient in labour-intensive activities.[2]

More precisely, we might say that the United States has a permanent surplus in innovation and entrepreneurial capacity. Europe, on the other hand, suffers from organisational deficiencies of various kinds which prevent a satisfactory combination of its factors of production. So Europe ends up with apparent surpluses; witness especially the brain drain and

---

[1] Source: O.E.C.D. The accuracy of any figures in this field has to be taken with a grain of salt. Certainly, the transfers officially accounted for fall far short of those that actually take place, and the American surplus must, therefore, in reality be much bigger. This is a fact of wide implications, for we have reached an era where only one raw material will really be decisive for economic development, and that is the 'grey matter' of the human brain.

[2] Is this really so paradoxical? It is a fact that new industries (electronics, data processing, the aerospace industry, etc.) are labour-intensive at least for some time, even if later they tend to be more highly automated. The very word labour, incidentally, is changing its meaning, for it is increasingly coming to mean highly skilled personnel.

the growth of European financial resources either poured into the Eurodollar market or used to purchase American stocks and shares.

International complementarity has always meant a certain grading of economies. This still seems to be so on the basis of new elements which to a large extent determine the competitive relations between the United States and the Community.

(2) Competitiveness

The notion of external competitiveness is much in evidence in current economic literature in Europe. It is indeed debated with passion, especially in a country like France. This can be explained by the misgivings with which many Europeans regard the structural developments briefly mentioned above. Yet it is a subject on which little is known. This is why the E.E.C. Commission decided in 1968 to ask a group of experts under the chairmanship of Pierre Uri to undertake a comprehensive study of the problem. This study is not due to be completed until the end of the year, and I do not wish to anticipate its results. I would just like to suggest that there are several possible concepts of competitiveness.

In the narrow sense, competitiveness may be understood in terms of the equilibrium conditions of the balance of payments. In principle, there always exists a rate of exchange such that any economy can balance its foreign trade. Similarly, equilibrium can always be obtained if only wages are low enough. And equilibrium can be promoted by means of various protectionist policies or export aids.

Without wishing to get involved in the tricky question of exchange-rate adjustments – in respect to which, incidentally, the member countries of the E.E.C. find themselves in very unequal situations – we may recall that according to E. F. Denison's estimates the average income of the European worker is only 59 per cent of that of the American worker. This is the key to Europe's 'competitiveness' in this sense, allowing for the relative productivity per worker. If, therefore, the E.E.C.'s current balance of payments has on the whole been in surplus for the last ten years, this was so thanks to conditions of which some, at any rate, are not particularly favourable.

There is another definition of competitiveness, broader and less precise, but probably more meaningful. In the words of Pierre Uri: 'An economy is really competitive only when it can hold its own against competition from other producers not only on its own market but also on their own and on other markets, and still meet a number of other conditions which make up the essential aims of all economic policy.'

The first of these conditions is that equilibrium should be obtained with a minimum of protection. From this point of view, the successive reductions of the common external tariff, which was not very protectionist even to begin with, are a positive point for the Community. The second condition is full employment combined with a rising standard of living. On this point the Community has done well enough on the whole. The third condition is to take the biggest possible part in developing types of production best adapted to the most dynamic sectors of world demand. In this matter there have been great divergences among the Six, and these are largely responsible for the current misgivings. The Common Market has failed to organise itself in such a way as to take full advantage of the economies of scale for which it is meant to make room, and this applies more especially to sectors with advanced technology and those where government departments are often the chief buyers. By continuing to give preference to products made by their own domestic industries, governments end up by depriving member countries of productivity gains precisely in fields where more open competition would lead to the biggest gains. It has rightly been said that there is as yet no Common Market for most of the spearhead products. While all governments keep spending more and more on technology, this does not, in the E.E.C., contribute as much as it should to better resource allocation.

Finally, a competitive economy must continuously adapt itself to the international division of labour by allowing traditional activities to shift to the less developed countries. In this matter the Community has proved to be not nearly bold enough, with the result that mounting funds are needed for government schemes designed to support declining activities, like agriculture or coal mining.

In addition there are the shifts which do take place in new sectors, and in conditions which, as suggested above, are not always very favourable. The combined result is that the economy of the Community is somehow both top-heavy and bottom-heavy, but loses strength in the middle, in its main body.

To be sure, these few observations do not add up to a full appraisal of the E.E.C.'s competitiveness in relation to the United States. They do suggest, though, that the E.E.C. is less competitive than might seem at first sight from the balance of payments alone. One of the most meaningful indicators in this respect is perhaps the remarkable growth of direct investment in Europe on the part of American corporations, which seems to suggest that many, if not all, of Europe's industries lag behind those of the United States.

(3) *Comparative Advantages*

The classical analysis of comparative advantages does not seem to offer an adequate explanation of complementarity and competitiveness as between the United States and the E.E.C. The parameters by which both are determined are expressed in units of national currencies and subsequently converted into common units on the basis of exchange parities which do not necessarily correspond to the real purchasing power of the currencies concerned. Furthermore, the combination of cost elements may vary from one country or one sector to another.

There has been no full-scale investigation in this field since the N.I.C.B. study[1] as far back as 1958–61. At that time, sectorial analysis based on a study of the comparative costs of American parent corporations and their affiliates abroad showed lower average cost in Europe for three main sectors: stone, clay and glass; instruments and similar articles; metal manufactures. The United States, on the other hand, had the advantage in such fields as transport equipment, electrical machinery and the rubber industry. An analysis of the structure of exports at the same date showed the United States to have a relatively high comparative advantage in the sectors mentioned plus machinery, and also in paper and food.

The most striking feature of developments in the last ten years is that wage costs increased more in the E.E.C. than in the United States (see Table 3.1). Over the same period, trade between the Community and the United States increased at an above-average rate. Between 1958 and 1967, the share of imports from the United States in total E.E.C. imports rose from 17 to 19 per cent, and the share of exports to the United States in total E.E.C. exports from 10 to 14 per cent. The composition of these trade flows underwent great change. In 1958, 60 per cent of E.E.C. imports from the United States were primary products, which in 1967 accounted for only 40 per cent, while the rest was manufactures. The highest rates of increase were registered in chemicals (135 per cent), other manufactures (179 per cent), machines and transport equipment (210 per cent). The United States established an advantage during that period especially for technically highly advanced machinery and for aircraft.

The structure of E.E.C. exports did indeed continue to improve (90 per cent manufactures in 1967), but the share of chemicals declined from 6·4 per cent in 1958 to 5·4 per cent in 1967 (largely as a result of the American selling price). The share of machines and transport vehicles in total E.E.C. exports increased from 31 to 37 per cent during the same period, but thanks largely to automobiles and small domestic appliances. Among other manufactures, exports that rose most were those of steel products, clothing and footwear.

There are a number of indicators, therefore, which suggest that Europe is tending to specialise on industries of a relatively traditional kind, while the Americans have the advantage in new industries. The structure of German exports to the United States is characteristic; automobiles account for 33 per cent of them, and steel for 18 per cent.

This observation brings us back to the old question of resource allocation as between the traditional and the new sectors of the economy. It also calls for an analysis of comparative advantages covering such

[1] Theodore R. Gates and Fabian Linden, *Costs and Competition* (N.I.C.B., Studies in Business Economics No. 73, 1961).

TABLE 3.1.
LABOUR COST[1] PER UNIT OF GROSS VALUE ADDED[2] IN INDUSTRY[3]

		1959	1960	1961	1962	1963	1964	1965	1966	1967	1968
West Germany	(a)	100·5	104·0	114·9	122·9	126·4	128·5	132·6	137·8	136·7	135·5
	(b)	0·5	3·5	10·5	7·0	2·9	1·7	3·2	3·9	-0·8	-1
France	(a)	86·3	89·8	95·2	98·4	105·1	108·9	112·0	114·3	116·7	124·5
	(b)	-13·7	4·0	6·0	3·4	6·9	3·4	2·9	2·0	2·1	5·5
Italy	(a)	97·1	100·2	104·6	113·4	131·7	142·3	137·8	135·7	142·6	144
	(b)	-2·9	3·2	4·4	8·4	16·1	8·1	-3·1	-1·6	5·1	1
Netherlands	(a)	96·7	97·7	107·5	113·1	121·0	129·0	136·9	145·4	144·5	141
	(b)	-3·3	1·1	10·0	5·2	7·0	6·6	6·1	6·2	-0·6	-2·5
Belgium	(a)	93·0	91·4	91·8	93·1	95·4	99·4	103·3	106·4	107·3	108
	(b)	-7·0	-1·7	0·4	1·4	2·5	4·1	3·9	3·0	0·8	0·5
United States	(a)	99·6	101·8	102·5	102·0	102·1	102·3	102·5	106·3	111·1	115
	(b)	-0·4	2·1	0·7	-0·4	0·1	0·3	0·2	3·7	4·5	3·5
United Kingdom	(a)	98·7	99·4	104·9	108·4	108·1	109·8	116·1	121·5	121·9	108·5
	(b)	-1·3	0·7	5·6	3·3	-0·3	1·6	5·7	4·6	0·4	-11

(a) 1958 = 100.
(b) Percentage increase at constant prices over previous year.
[1] Allowing for changes in exchange rates.
[2] At constant prices.
[3] Including building and construction.

additional aspects as the size of firms, their financial structure, rate of returns and management methods, the conditions of the introduction of innovations in the economy, the part of government in intensifying competition, and similar considerations.

II. ECONOMIC AND COMMERCIAL POLICIES

The general aspects of the economic and commercial policies of the Six are laid down in the Treaty of Rome. The very idea of the Common Market is probably the best possible example of the influence of the American model on Europe. What the founders of the Community most wanted to achieve was a large market comparable to that of the United States. But economic policies have so far been unified only to very varying degrees and often not nearly enough.

(1) *Commercial Policy*

The general philosophy of the Community's commercial policy rests on the simple idea that in our days protectionism is more and more coming to be an obstacle to development, especially in small and medium-sized countries. This is why Article 110 of the Treaty of Rome declares: 'By establishing a customs union between themselves Member States aim to contribute, in the common interest, to the harmonious development of world trade, the progressive abolition of restrictions on international trade and the lowering of customs barriers.' Here again we detect the influence of the liberal approach constantly upheld by the United States, especially since 1945, and which indeed was put into effect by the Community.

The common external tariff of the E.E.C. is much lower than the import tariffs of the world's other major economic powers. Its average level is 11·7 per cent compared with 17·8 per cent in the United States, 18·4 per cent in the United Kingdom and about 25 per cent in Japan. The Kennedy Round will bring the rate of external protection for the Six down to about 8 per cent. Unlike that of the United States tariff, moreover, the profile of the common external tariff is relatively flat, which further reduces its protectionist effect.

It may be maintained, therefore, that the Community has made a major contribution to the liberal trend in international trade. And it should be stressed that this contribution comes from the Community as such, for it is quite clear that if the Common Market had not been set up, it would have been impossible to get overall reductions of the same size from the individual countries of Europe. Only agriculture is an exception to this general rule.

The Treaty of Rome, in Article 111, provides that 'Member States shall co-ordinate their commercial relations with third countries so as to bring about, by the end of the transitional period (that is, the beginning of 1970), the conditions necessary for putting into effect a common policy in the field of external trade'. Notwithstanding the efforts made in this direction, however, there has unfortunately been some delay in creating the prior conditions for the establishment of a common commercial policy, especially as regards the relations of member nations with the communist countries and the developing countries. It may be hoped that work now in hand will make the Community's liberal policy more effective especially in relation to developing countries.

But the member countries watch with some apprehension a certain change which is taking place not so much, perhaps, in the theory but certainly in the actual attitude of the United States in this matter. For more than twenty years the United States have been the champion of a liberal conception of international trade. It is no exaggeration to say that the countries of the Community were their best disciples. But we may ask whether we are not now witnessing a reappraisal of American policy, which may well prove agonising for the Europeans. While the Six are becoming increasingly aware of the need to stop the often undue protection still enjoyed by certain traditional branches of European industry, they see to their amazement that protectionist tendencies are gaining ground in the United States, especially in such fields as steel and textiles.

Leaving aside the question of the validity of certain arguments at present put forward by the new administration in the United States, especially as regards refund of indirect taxes on exports, it seems likely that if the United States used these arguments to cut down on imports from the Community, the latter would be bound to react. There would then be a danger of a new shrinkage of international trade in the 1970s, as there was in the 1930s. Similarly, the very liberal attitude adopted by European countries as regards foreign investment and the outflow of capital to the Euro-dollar market might well become somewhat stiffer.

(2) *Economic Policy*

In the field of economic policy, too, the influence of the ideas dominating the United States is much in evidence. A characteristic example can be found in the recent history of the old dispute which in Europe has been raging between the planners and the champions of free enterprise and the market economy. This dispute has long been so violent that for many years it was quite impossible in Common Market meetings to talk seriously about such questions as medium-term economic projections sectorial policies or even public finance planning. But gradually the debate lost its doctrinal character and shifted into more practical ground. As a result, there has been a highly fruitful meeting of minds.

On the one side, France has slowly been retreating from the position it held so long, namely, that all member countries should adopt the relatively detailed French system of planning, which gives the government wide powers of intervention in different sectors. On the contrary, France has recently been trying to fit its own five-year plans into a pattern of increasing openness to the outside world.

Germany, in its turn, while remaining firmly wedded to the principles of the *Soziale Markwirtschaft*, in 1967 adopted a system of public finance planning which is considered as a model in the Community. In this context, the Germans have come to see how important are medium-term economic projections.

Not only has Europe been applying American ideas in organising economic life (policy on competition, on mobility of the factors of production, modern management methods, etc.), but the American example is also at the root of the frame of reference adopted in Europe, especially in such matters as education policy, the relations between industries and the universities, and a better awareness on the part of government of its responsibilities towards workers and firms.

Two passages from the second medium-term economic programme[1] may be quoted in this context:

> In the past, structural intervention by government has not always been satisfactory. Ill informed about the dangers of developments in this or that sector, government was led, most often with the praiseworthy purpose of protecting the workers against the threat of losing their jobs, to intervene unexpectedly from case to case; the common feature of these interventions was that they sheltered uncompetitive firms against competition and its punishments. The mushrooming of such interventions allowed the survival of often obsolete patterns of organisation, techniques and management methods, and eventually impeded the adjustment of whole sectors to the requirements of technical progress, thus prejudicing the growth of productivity in the system as a whole and the possible improvement in the average standard of living. In many cases, furthermore, the workers on whose behalf the government had intervened, had to accept modest wages while not escaping the possibility of losing their jobs in the end. Finally, the public funds used for these interventions became unavailable for more productive uses.

> Important as it is to improve the workers' protection against the risks inherent in economic development, it is equally important to shift responsibility back to where it belongs, to firms. It is the business not of government but of companies freely to take whatever decisions may be necessary to enable them not only to adapt themselves to the requirements of competition, but to gain a foothold on new, expanding markets,

[1] Approved by the Council of Ministers in December 1968. Ref. COM (68) 148 final.

thanks to their flexible organisation, cost reductions, the quality of their output and their innovating capacity.

All this does not mean, of course, that the economic policy of the E.E.C. countries tends to align itself to that of the United States. In some cases this is simply not possible, whatever one's wishes. While, for instance, everyone is agreed on the need for more occupational mobility, it is most unlikely that Europe will ever have a geographical mobility of labour comparable to that of the United States. It would not even be a good thing. The United States forms an enormous, almost homogeneous area where the workers, descended from immigrants, move very readily and are often almost indifferent to the choice of region. In Europe, by contrast, centuries of national history, the diversity of languages and customs, most people's attachment to familiar landscapes and strictly localised personal relationships have all created a situation in which it is better not to shift people in general to industries, but to pursue regional policies designed to shift industries to where the people live. The problem of the standard of living of the people of Sicily cannot be solved by organising a massive migration of Sicilians to northern Europe, except at the risk of very grave social hardship.

In any event, even if the customs union is a fact in the Common Market, there still remains much to do to arrive at free competition and free movement not only for products but for factors of production. For various reasons the economic policies of member nations are still widely divergent in spite of all the numerous procedures of confrontation, alignment, etc., which have been set up. As regards prices, for instance, Germany and Italy want the Community to become a 'bloc of stability'. These two countries have been making every possible effort these last few years to achieve this result for themselves, and seem determined to stick to the same attitude in the future. France and the Benelux countries are inclined to think that it is better to follow by and large the trend of international prices, which means, in effect, alignment on the United States.

Similarly, as regards policies on research and development, it can be seen that the structure of expenditures in France (and, for that matter, in the United Kingdom) is closely modelled on the United States. These two countries have been trying to finance with modest means an ambitious policy in such fields as atomic energy, electronics, and the aircraft and space industries. The other countries of the Community, on the other hand, have set themselves less ambitious aims, rather like Japan, and according to O.E.C.D. studies on the technological gap their policy is probably more effective.

The major problem of the Common Market today, if the customs union is not to fall to pieces, is to achieve effective co-ordination of general economic policies. This certainly presupposes a reinforcement of the mechanism of decision-making in the Community, which is now terribly handicapped by the unanimity rule (which gives each member state a veto right), and it also means basing decisions on macro-economic financial mechanisms designed to make room for harmonisation of policies and trends.

The customs union has made considerable inroads into the powers of member governments and into the efficiency of the measures which they can still take individually in matters of general economic policy. The void so created must be filled by a new and stronger decision-making power at Community level, even if this means redefining certain sectorial functions of not necessarily major importance now within the competence of the Community.

Finally, however divergent the economic policies of the Six may be, they have in common certain features which set them sharply apart from the economic policy of the United States.

First of all, it is surely a permanent feature of the economic policies of the Six that they give priority to full employment and growth. Admittedly the United States followed a similar line between 1961 and 1968, but it is by no means certain at this stage whether this is an irreversible choice. The ideas of Keynes and Beveridge have definitely made a stronger mark on Europe than on the United States – witness, for instance, the role of social security east and west of the Atlantic.

Secondly, the Six have for ten years continuously been piling up currency reserves. Between 1958 and 1967, the gross monetary reserves[1] of the six Common Market countries more than doubled, rising from $12,000 million to $26,000 million, while the total reserves of all the countries members of the International Monetary Fund increased by only 27 per cent and those of the United States fell by one-third. Throughout this period the Community as a whole nearly always had a balance of payments surplus. Understandably enough, there are some who hold this policy of reserve accumulation to be against the general interest. No doubt, this policy can to a large extent be explained in terms of the member countries being anxious to offset by higher reserves some of the additional risks they incur by abandoning protection not only within the Community, but also vis-à-vis non-member countries. We all know the theory of Mrs Machlup's clothes: a central bank is like a lady who, come spring, desires to acquire some new dresses regardless of how many she already owns. There certainly is something to this theory. But it is not enough to account for the common attitude adopted by all the Common Market countries throughout the last ten years.

Another point worth mentioning is that the concept of business enterprise is rather different in Europe and in the United States. On this side

[1] As defined by the International Monetary Fund (*International Financial Statistics*, Apr 1968).

of the Atlantic it is commonly accepted that employers, while not having the paternalistic functions they have in Japan, do have certain social responsibilities in relation to their workers. A few years ago, *Business International* published a list of 92 factors governing the location choice of American investments abroad. One of them was described as 'freedom to hire and fire'. Now, this is a pun somewhat shocking to European ears. In more positive terms, one might mention certain ideas which are gaining ground in Europe, like joint management in Germany, or the participation of employees in the definition of general company policies in France and the Netherlands, as well as a number of attempts in the Netherlands, France, Belgium and Germany to make incomes policy effective by the concerted action of trade unions, employers' federations and government.

Finally, it may not be out of order to state that Europeans are watching with some apprehension how the problems of the American civilisation are being acerbated today – I have in mind racial disorders, unrest among the young, urban problems and the like. These problems may come to diminish the attraction which the United States economic system exercises on Europe.

III. INFLUENCES AND CONSTRAINTS EMANATING FROM UNITED STATES ECONOMIC POLICIES

Casting one's eyes back over the last quarter of a century, it is at once obvious how drastic a change has taken place since then in the relations between the United States and the European countries. In 1945, a Europe devastated by war depended on American aid not only for reconstruction, but for the very survival of its peoples. The United States was in a position then to establish its hegemony in Europe, and the remarkable thing is that, instead of abusing their power, the Americans made such great efforts to contribute to the recovery of the European nations and to urge them to form a union such as to make of them a world power on the modern scale. In building up the Common Market, the Six made themselves economically more independent of the United States, thanks especially to the strikingly fast growth of intra-Community trade. But if we look at the most recent developments, we shall see that behind this more and more patent independence a new state of dependence has been developing, especially in monetary matters. This rests on mechanisms such that generally speaking it is no longer the United States which helps Europe, but rather the other way round.

(1) *Intra-Community Trade*

During the years 1958 to 1968, trade among the members of the E.E.C. grew on the average twice as fast as the Community's trade with non-members, even though the latter in its turn has been expanding at a particularly high rate. As a result, the economic interdependence of the Common Market countries has greatly increased. Stephen A. Resnick of the M.I.T., in his book *An Empirical Study of Economic Policy in the Common Market*, estimates that every 5 per cent increase in public expenditure in Germany causes G.N.P. to grow by 1·64 per cent in Germany and by 1·53 per cent in France.[1] It follows that the economic policy of any one country in the Common Market may have almost as much effect upon another member country as upon itself.

Two general consequences follow:

(a) It has become a matter of the greatest importance for each of the Six to make sure that its own economic and financial equilibrium is not disturbed by the policies of the others. What is needed to this end is genuine co-ordination of economic policies within the Community. This does not exist. In the absence of such co-ordination, each of the countries concerned is forced to protect itself against such disturbances as might come to it as a result of what the others do. One of the chief means of protection is to accumulate as much reserves as possible. A relatively small country where foreign trade represents a high proportion of G.N.P. cannot afford an external deficit. Their inability to run an external deficit imposes on most member countries increasingly strict constraints, which derive more especially from the relative increase in liquid assets in relation to G.N.P., from the *de jure* or *de facto* freedom of capital movements, and from the extraordinarily fast expansion of intra-Community trade (which is growing twice or three times as fast as G.N.P.).

(b) The American economy has been in continuous expansion since 1960, and hence it is hard to know to what extent the Community is still sensitive to the spontaneous influences of the American business cycle. Until 1960, and especially at the time of the 1958 recession, the countries of the Community were strongly affected by the influence of cyclical conditions in the United States. Mr Trudeau, the Canadian Prime Minister, said recently that it is hard to sleep well with an elephant as a bedfellow. Europe has never been quite in that situation, but it has been rather apt to catch a cold when America has sneezed.

If, as may be surmised, American business conditions nowadays have less direct influence on the Community, the latter is still subject to their indirect effects via the developing countries, whose purchases from Europe diminish whenever the United States cuts down on its own raw material imports.

[1] Even if the figures are open to discussion, the facts of which they are symptomatic are real enough. This is confirmed by certain staff studies recently undertaken by the E.E.C. Commission.

To the extent that the countries of the E.E.C. trade more among themselves, they normally tend to become somewhat less susceptible to the direct influences of American cyclical conditions. However, the characteristic weakness of decision-making capacity in the Common Market leaves its members far from taking full advantage of their union. The main beneficiaries of the opening of frontiers among the Six have probably been American corporations, which feel at ease in a large economic space. For the rest, it is no doubt right to say that the fast expansion of direct investment by American corporations in the E.E.C.[1] owes something at least to the attitude of European governments, which have been outdoing each other in an effort to attract to their country the most mobile investments and those which go into activities with the best future prospects, which means as often as not investments by American corporations. It is no exaggeration to say that the Community today offers strong incentives for such investments.

(2) *The Dollar as a Reserve Currency*

But more than anything else it is the working of the monetary mechanisms which places Europe in a position of dependence vis-à-vis the United States.

For many years the United States balance of payments has regularly been in deficit. We need not here go into the question whose fault it is. Just as in any family quarrel both sides are usually to blame, so it is hard to say which of the two partners is more at fault, the one who regularly runs a surplus or the one in deficit.

Be that as it may, the point to stress is that in the course of recent years the Community has rendered monetary aid to the United States on a very large scale, through such well-known devices as advance repayment of debts, swaps, Roosa bonds, agreement to the two-tier gold market, and so on.

Strange to say, with all the enormous possibilities implied in the ownership of the greatest reserve stock in the world, the countries of the Community have not only done nothing to set up a common monetary system, but have both strengthened the role of the dollar as a reserve currency and tended to integrate themselves more and more firmly into the 'dollar area'.

This has happened mainly because the money and capital markets of the Community have only scant direct relations with each other. They are connected mainly via the dollar. One of the reasons for this is that the range within which the exchange rates of the E.E.C. currencies fluctuate against each other is much wider than that within which each

---

[1] Direct investments by American corporations in the E.E.C. increased by 199·5 per cent between 1950 and 1958, and by 297·4 per cent between 1958 and 1966. The share of the E.E.C. in the whole of these investments abroad rose from 18·8 per cent in 1964 to 23·1 per cent in 1967 (source: *Survey of Current Business*).

varies against the dollar. Thus we get this paradoxical situation: the Common Market has been set up in order to facilitate all transactions among the Six; the growth of intra-Community trade shows that this aim has partly been achieved so far as goods are concerned; but in the field of capital movements there still is an exchange system which constitutes a powerful limiting factor on currency transactions within the Community. It may well be that this situation has indirectly contributed to strengthening the power of the dollar.

To be sure, there was a moment early in 1968 when it might have been thought that the prophecies of Cassandra were about to come true. Confidence in the dollar seemed shaken. But the situation was soon steadied and then redressed. If the American Government subsequently had to adopt a stricter policy in order to equilibrate the balance of payments, this was probably not so much because of external constraints as for domestic reasons. Be that as it may, this policy became the occasion of a new type of influence exercised by the United States on the monetary policies of the Six, and of new constraints upon them.

(3) *Money and the Sovereignty of the European Countries*

In fact, two radical changes took place from 1968 on. Before then, the dollar had shown some signs of weakness in relation to European currencies, largely because of the bellicose attitude of the French government. Since 1968, by contrast, it is certain European countries, including France, Belgium and the Netherlands, which have asked the United States to activate their swap lines. More than ever the solution adopted with regard to the monetary relations between the United States and Europe is the 'Roman solution' to which, quoting a third source, Professor Machlup referred in a recent statement.[1]

The restrictive policy adopted by the United States came too late and was harsh in form. This is why balance is today returning to the United States external payments in conditions which could be dangerous for Europe, especially if there should be some signs of recession there.

The Johnson programme of January 1968 revealed the true situation of the two parties concerned. The complete stoppage of capital outflows to the Community for direct investments has done nothing to slow down these investments, which easily found finance funds either on the spot or by increased recourse to the resources of the Euro-bond market. It is odd that Article 58 of the Treaty of Rome should treat as belonging to the Community any firms or companies fully owned by foreign interests, which remain subject to their own governments' rulings even if these imply action directly running counter to the interests of the European host country.

[1] Hearing before the Subcommittee on International Exchange and Payments, 9 September 1968.

The 10 per cent surcharge on income tax payable by individuals and corporations introduced by the United States in July 1968 did not reduce consumption expenditure to the expected extent. Hence the credit restrictions adopted at the end of 1968. One of these restrictive measures has a feature which deserves special mention: the reserve requirement does not apply to such funds as may be borrowed on the Euro-dollar market (that is, the dollar deposits of banking subsidiaries abroad with their parent bank). As a result, the liabilities of the major American commercial banks to their affiliates abroad rose very considerably – from $7,000 million in December 1968 to $9,200 million in March 1969. Admittedly, these borrowings amount to only about 4 per cent of total deposits, but they

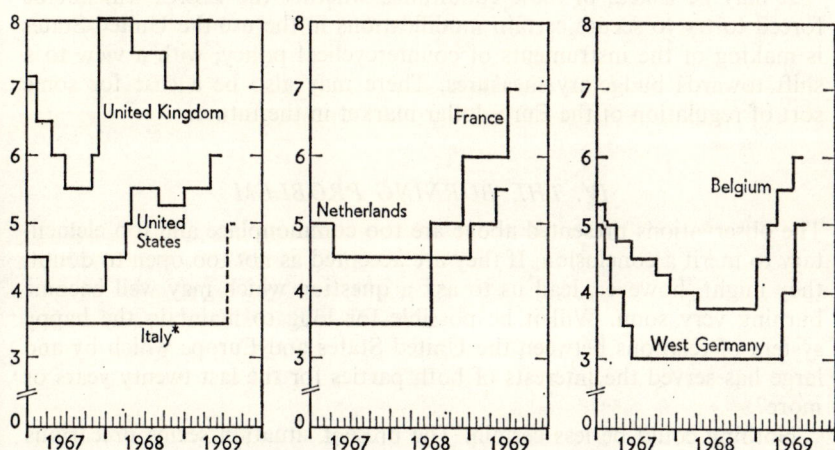

FIG. 3.1 Rates of discount at the banks of the countries of the E.E.C., the United States and the United Kingdom.

(*Increase in Italy due to become operative on 1 July, relating to certain rediscounting operations in excess of a certain total).

were enough to force Euro-dollar rates up very steeply indeed, with rates for three-month money climbing from 6·3 per cent at the end of September 1968 to about 12·5 per cent in mid-June 1969.

The countries of the E.E.C., each with its own specific needs as regards both domestic monetary affairs and external payments, reacted each in its own individual way to the rise in interest rates in the United States and on the Euro-dollar market. All of them, however, appreciably raised their discount rate in recent months.[1] These rises were certainly appropriate in a boom climate, not to speak of inflationary pressures. But without any doubt at all they also fulfilled the purpose of following the

[1] In the case of Italy, the central bank relies largely on special devices of its own and the discount rate plays a very minor part.

United States discount rate, which all European countries except Germany[1] nowadays need to do very closely (see Fig. 3.1).

Even if the Six had been in a recession, several of them would probably still have had to let their interest rates rise to some extent. This tends to show that the choice of measures to be used in their policy mix is today strongly subject to the influences of American economic policy. In the final outcome, the influence of decisions taken on the other side of the Atlantic in response to a situation peculiar to the United States is stronger than that of the action of certain European governments with respect to their own economy. Except for Germany, the monetary sovereignty of European nations is tending to become illusory.

It may be asked, in these conditions, whether the E.E.C. will not be forced to try to secure certain modifications in the use the United States is making of the instruments of countercyclical policy, with a view to a shift towards budgetary measures. There may also be a case for some sort of regulation of the Euro-dollar market in the future.

IV. THE BURNING PROBLEM

The observations presented above are too commonplace and too elementary to merit a conclusion. If they are accepted as not too open to doubt, they might, however, lead us to ask a question which may well become burning very soon. Will it be possible for long to maintain the happy system of relations between the United States and Europe which by and large has served the interests of both parties for the last twenty years or more?

Nothing could be less certain. The present situation seems precarious indeed in the light of the factors of disruption which have been in evidence within the Common Market for the last year, of the new protectionist tendencies emerging in the United States and of the extreme instability of a monetary system which today puts an almost intolerable strain on interest rates and threatens tomorrow to become a major factor of economic disturbance.

This is an enormous problem, which for the moment generates mostly academic debate, but which may soon take on a highly practical character and may lead to solutions held to be as unsatisfactory on this side of the Atlantic as on the other.

[1] In the opposite case, if the American rates were low, Germany would still need to lower its own discount rate to forestall excessive capital inflows.

Discussion of the Paper by M. Albert

Professor Houssiaux identified a number of issues raised in the paper. First, there was the existence of comparative advantages between North America and Europe. Were these evolving before the Common Market came into existence and if so, in what sense? M. Albert had showed the way in which wage costs moved and how the structure of trade altered.

Second, M. Albert looked at the economic policy of the E.E.C. He took the view of liberal economists, who had originally conceived this in terms of an external tariff and a common agricultural policy. Professor Houssiaux suggested that, without the Common Market, Europe would probably have moved back to greater protection. Therefore the Common Market had helped, so far, to maintain a liberal attitude.

Third, there was the question of what would happen to American policy. Since America had balance of payments problems and other problems of commercial policy, some people foresaw a return to the 1930s. There might be renewed protectionism in America against Europe. He wondered whether this would show up in sectoral trade negotiations, or whether America would take particular trading partners and develop trade with them.

Fourth, the paper looked at the economic policy of the E.E.C. One question was, who had the better control over aggregate demand, the United States or Europe? In the period from 1960 to now, how far had the improvement of economic techniques for sustaining growth been the result of the E.E.C. For instance, some observers thought that public finance in France had imitated what was going on in Germany and Sweden.

Fifth, again looking at the E.E.C., there was a question of the co-ordination of economic policy within the Community. Could this be run on national grounds? What would happen if economic development in various countries diverged? A 'void' had been created here and the E.E.C. had been slow in creating a central decision-taking body.

Sixth, there was the role of the United States economic system in improving economic performance. M. Albert treated this at length. Professor Houssiaux wondered whether the system, as a model, really had any importance. Had Europe abandoned it? He wondered what impartial observers, like economists from Eastern European countries, would think.

Seventh, there was the comparison between the American model and E.E.C. policy. M. Albert had tried to find specific elements in a European economic policy model. He put the accent first on employment and growth, second on public goods. Policies in these fields seemed effective compared with what went on in other countries – for example, Japan, where social elements were not given the same emphasis.

Eighth, Professor Houssiaux wondered what was the true influence of the United States on Europe. M. Albert thought that America had not influenced the E.E.C. very much. We needed to know how far the United States policy-mix did affect Europe. The best policy-mix might be concerned with fiscal and monetary impulses, etc. But we had no econometric model aimed at selecting a policy-mix for the European countries. For instance, we largely ignored the size of the policy multiplier. Again, it was difficult to measure and to assess what would be the best European policy-mix.

Ninth, Professor Houssiaux wondered how one could avoid the bad effects of American policies which were needed domestically. For example, there had been the policy changes by President Johnson in January 1968 on balance of payments; there was the effect in Europe of American anti-trust policy. Some people did pretend that anti-trust policy had had positive effects on American direct investment in Europe, great enough to compensate for the Johnson policy. In any study of the expected effects of economic policy decisions, we should introduce the impact on other countries, as well as direct domestic influences.

The tenth point was about the future of the E.E.C. Here again one had a problem of unilateral decisions. What kind of solidarity could we detect within the Common Market? So far as individual countries were concerned, each of them had designed national policies, and each country had its own appreciation of the policies needed for the E.E.C. as a whole. Something had to be done, but probably not through definitive legal rules.

Professor van Meerhaeghe said that on p. 66 of his paper, M. Albert suggested that the Common Market was perhaps the best example that one could find of the influence of American example on the countries of Europe. Was this not too categoric a statement? Several criticisms could be made of the text which supported this statement. Professor van Meerhaeghe was not convinced, for example, by the discussion on p. 64 of average rates of protection. There were multiple rates on a number of products, especially agricultural ones. On economic policy, M. Albert said that, in Europe, one accepted American concepts for better or worse – for example, on competition. Yet there was a fundamental difference between the competition policy applied by the United States and the policy – so far as one could speak of a policy – applied by the E.E.C. On p. 69, M. Albert spoke of rapprochement between ideas on general policy towards trade unions, etc. This was only an ideal, and he doubted whether it applied in many countries. As for prices, which were mentioned on p. 68, France perhaps had an individual experience here. There was no doubt that both France and Belgium were seeking price stability. They had not achieved it, not because they had not tried, but because the political will was lacking. In all E.E.C. countries, the internal price level was controlled. But with exports, from France for example, one could ask very much more than for goods sold within the E.E.C. itself.

M. Albert said that so far as the idea of the Common Market was concerned, he thought that America wanted the Common Market to be set up as a stage in the construction of a United States of Europe. It was not by accident that one spoke of the United States of America and the United States of Europe. Dr Hallstein, for example, had talked of the large economic space of Europe and had quoted the example and success of the United States. Professor Albert said that perhaps he had put the point too briefly in his paper, but he stood by what he had said. On variable rates of protection, he admitted that with agricultural products or products derived from agricultural products, there were different rates. There was no *ad valorem* duty, but the levy based on the difference between the world price and the internal price.

M. Albert pointed out that the concept of an incomes policy could be interpreted differently in different countries. It could be a wages policy, as the trade unions would say. They saw any binding policy as undesirable. All early experiments had failed, especially since the Dutch experiment collapsed in 1954. In the more recent period, there had been an incomes policy in Germany. There were contractual procedures based on a series of measures, especially public finance ones organised through the stabilisation law. Federal Germany, therefore, did seem to have an incomes policy. A good deal of progress had been made since 1969.

Those responsible for the economic policy of the E.E.C. thought one could have an incomes policy and that this could be seen as synthetic. Different aspects of public policy on industry and in the development of public finance – expenditure, taxation and transfers – could all lead to the harmonious evolution of different types of income. This was not a policy of direct control over income, though wages policy could be. Other kinds of payments could also be restrained. It was hard to have an incomes policy *stricto sensu*, but one could have something very similar.

Prices raised a delicate point. M. Albert in his paper had said that Germany and Italy wanted the Community to become a bloc of stability. At the same time, he had said that France and Benelux would rather that the Community followed the international trend of prices – that was to say, prices in the United States. One would not find this set out in ministers' speeches, for they could not prejudge changes in exchange rates or rates of inflation. France, in the Fifth Plan, foresaw an increase in prices of less than 2 per cent per annum, whereas the actual rise had been one of about 4 per cent. However, those responsible for economic policy in the E.E.C. could be divided into two different schools. The Germans and Italians thought that the E.E.C. should be this bloc of stability. He agreed that expectations were different in different countries, for example in Benelux. The German and Dutch points of view were strongly opposed to the French one. France allowed relatively more inflation, not because she saw this as good, but because she could do nothing else.

Mr Brittan said that to him an outstanding feature of M. Albert's paper was the discussion of macro-economic behaviour in the member countries of the E.E.C. Movements of prices and the competitive positions of member countries were often nearer to those of third countries than to fellow E.E.C. members. Germany tended to have an undervalued currency; the franc tended to become overvalued. Other countries came in between; and one could argue where. He did not see how the E.E.C. could possibly work successfully if it kept the fixed exchange rates so dear to the Commission. How would the E.E.C. react if the United States adopted the 'Roman' solution to its difficulties mentioned by Professor Wallich? (So far the United States approach had been what one might call a Roman republican one – but there were fears that it could become a Roman imperial solution!) Italy and the Benelux countries might well peg their currencies to the dollar. In the long run, the mark would float upwards; the franc would drift downwards. He did not see how there could possibly be a common E.E.C. response to these problems. The Commission wanted greater co-ordination of monetary policy, but the difficulties were glossed over.

The problems of co-ordination were peculiar ones. Given different structures and traditions, an equal degree of toughness in fiscal and monetary policy could lead to a different degree of inflation and of unemployment in different countries; and the differences would be aggravated if the United Kingdom joined. Was it realistic for the E.E.C. to suggest that there should be higher unemployment in

France and the United Kingdom than in Germany? A more fundamental point was that even if one felt that a very comprehensive scheme of co-ordination was ideal, he doubted whether half-hearted co-ordination could even be a second-best. He thought that the E.E.C. was in a needless mess because it insisted on an excessive degree of co-ordination, having started from the wrong assumptions. It was not just a problem of federalist sentiment. Post-war Europe had little experience of countries with different levels of wages, different social services, etc., adjusting through the price mechanism.

There was also a much too simple identification of the *results* of what would be a far-reaching economic union, with the *means* of achieving them. If one were starting today, the idea of common behaviour of price levels and exchange rates would be seen as the end-product of many years of evolution, rather than something to be achieved in a few years. He was not trying to job backwards, but made his point because of the current crisis in the affairs of the E.E.C. If one were beginning today, one would look for an industrial free-trade area with some *ad hoc* bargains on agriculture designed to give what assistance one could to what was, after all, a declining industry. One would also want a stronger mechanism for assuring co-operation in defence, foreign policy, etc. One would see that a community which could not agree on, for example, defence policy would be unable to harmonise its social services, including taxes, and achieve a common price level.

Professor Izzo commented on incomes policy. He did not see how one could have incomes policy without direct price controls. One might control wages – but not profits or rent. There were big differences in the proportion of income going to wages, profits and rents between E.E.C. countries. Must the wage level rise in line with productivity? If so, then one would have a different distribution of wages, profits and rents in different countries. Was this ideal?

M. Ferras noted that M. Albert had said that E.E.C. countries had tended to become integrated into the dollar zone, but the paper suggested that this was a result of historical fatalism. In fact, it depended on decisions, each of which had been taken in an isolated fashion. Each European country had a positive view on what should happen. Yet, one way or another, European countries had been asked to finance the United States balance of payments deficit. It was a mistake to see what they had done as purely passive.

There was the same lack of co-ordination in discussions on the evolution of the future monetary system. There was no common E.E.C. philosophy.

Mr Lamfalussy thought that Europe was on a dollar standard for several reasons. First of all, international rates of interest were in line; European rates of interest had to alter with those of the United States. Second, there was little speculation against the dollar when, as now, the balance of payments in the United States was unfavourable. He thought, for example, of the buying of United States securities by Europeans. Third, it was possible to put dollar obligations on the European markets. Rates of interest had recently been 3–4 per cent above those on mark securities. He agreed that there had been unusual conditions recently, but nevertheless what happened was tied to the dollar.

He wondered why this was. Why had Europe effectively been integrated into the dollar zone? Why did one not have an 'imperial' solution? He thought there was a lack of coherence in European policies and regarded the reasons for this as quite fundamental.

Professor Sohmen said that there were two radically different conceptions of 'integration'. First, it was seen as a set of administrative policies – as co-ordination from above. Second, it was seen as the creation of a genuine 'common market', with a free flow of goods and services. He thought that somewhat too much emphasis had usually been put on the first conception of integration; yet so far the second had been vastly more successful in the E.E.C. For example, many considered E.E.C. agricultural policies as the showpiece of European integration. Common prices were imposed from above. But after the first sign of stress – after the French devaluation – there was no longer a common agricultural market. Agricultural prices in France were now about 11 per cent lower than in the rest of the E.E.C.

M. Albert had said that incomes policy had been successful in Germany. This was perhaps more of a tribute to the public relations policies of the German government than to anything else. There was a good deal of talk on incomes policy ('concerted action') in Germany, and the Economic Ministry had treated it as a major objective. However, the Government did little, beyond organising round table discussions with trade unions and employers' organisations. The policy appeared to have succeeded primarily because the trade unions had shown remarkable restraint. But this was by no means a novelty in Germany and could not be attributed to any new policy.

As far as prices were concerned, incomes policy had been a complete failure in getting either the Government or employers to do for prices what had been done for wages. Prices continuously rose as a consequence of Germany's refusal to revalue. Wages had lagged, but profits had increased spectacularly in recent years. As long as the Deutschmark was not revalued – and chances were slim – wages would simply follow behind rising prices.

On the stabilisation law, which was often seen as a significant advance, again public relations rather than genuine accomplishments could have given the impression that outsiders had. The law mostly limited itself to regulating the jurisdiction of the federal and Land governments in financial matters. Failure to revalue was an indication that the Government paid little attention to the stabilisation law. Stability could not be pursued with a constant parity for the Deutschmark. The law had obviously made little difference.

Professor James said that M. Albert had spoken of the technical and managerial gap between Europe and the United States. It was interesting that, on p. 60 of the paper, M. Albert put ideas about competition in a new way. It was right to say that for a competitive economy several conditions had to be fulfilled. These were: (1) low tariffs; (2) full employment; (3) the development of new, dynamic industries; (4) the transfer of traditional industries to underdeveloped areas.

In the E.E.C., the success of the first two had been assured. But there had been less success with the last two. He wondered whether one could use a further tool of analysis, which was glossed over in the paper. He did not think that one could look at relations between E.E.C. countries with the traditional analysis. For analysing relationships between Europe and the United States, he thought another tool was needed – the idea of domination. No one had spoken of this at the Conference yet, but it was necessary to do so. Domination was usually seen as moral or political; he thought it was economic and must be considered.

On some more detailed points, he regretted that his death had deprived us of the knowledge of André Marchal, who knew many of these problems well. On p. 59, M. Albert spoke of the transfer to underdeveloped areas of traditional industries, and argued that this was not necessarily good because these industries would themselves decline. He wondered whether we could have more information about this. He thought that when underdeveloped countries abandoned the production of raw materials and moved to more sophisticated activities, they gained something.

On p. 67, M. Albert had said that Europe had a lower mobility of labour than the United States, and concluded pessimistically that, in Europe, labour mobility would have to be ensured by transplanting industry to where there was available labour. Yet, also on p. 67, M. Albert said, in a remark about the standard of living in Sicily, that the problem would not be solved by massive migration to the north. Professor James thought that the paper by Professor Pinto Barbosa on Portugal showed that it was possible to change the standard of living by organising large-scale immigration to the countries of northern Europe.

Replying to the debate, *M. Albert* said he would look first at a number of detailed questions. On domination, he thought everyone was inclined, in writing papers of this sort, to appear to be polite and academic. One did not say quite what one felt. Even so, he did not think that the idea of the domination of Europe by the United States reflected reality. Such domination was less based on moral than on physical phenomena. The power of the United States was greater and the United States was the principle centre of its own civilisation. Its influence inevitably radiated out to all of us.

On p. 59, he did not think he had said anything which denied that developing countries benefited if they established declining industries from advanced countries. Indisputably, it was hard in Europe to imagine that whole industrial sectors would move to underdeveloped areas. For example, in shipbuilding, it was unanimously thought in the E.E.C. that all countries needed a shipbuilding industry (except Luxembourg!). Yet the United States did not have a shipbuilding industry. There was an element of folklore in this, but the abandonment of shipbuilding would be a desirable change. Similarly, five years ago it was thought necessary for the United Kingdom to allow a good deal of textile production to move to Asia. More recently, a report on European textiles was also very pessimistic. We would have to take a much more liberal view of many issues of this kind.

So far as the transfer of Sicilians to northern Europe was concerned, he agreed that this would give them a higher standard of living – but at what cost? It would split up families, and so on. We did not want to create ghettos in the E.E.C.

On the views of Professors Izzo and Sohmen on wages policy, M. Albert said that he had only looked at the main tendencies. First, he saw a broad but diffuse view developing in various countries. Second, it was agreed that incomes policy must cover all kinds of income. Third, it was accepted that criteria for the increase of productivity were not sufficient to allow us to say what should happen to wages.

All current predictions showed private investment rising more rapidly than national income, so that a fall in public investment or consumption was needed. So far as Germany and the public relations of its Government was concerned, he agreed that these were excellent. Nevertheless, the state of mind in German trade unions was based on the conviction that if there was an increase in money wages beyond some level, the rise in real wages would be slowed down.

Dr Molitor stressed the need for more 'concerted action' between the governments and the different social groups on national macro-economic policy and particularly on public finance. Incomes policy in this sense could be quite successful; on the other hand, a wage–price policy used only to eliminate existing inflationary pressure would not be effective in most cases. Incomes policy should not be applied only to an overheated economy but also during a recession. It should be used both to keep down the growth of consumption and sometimes also to stimulate it, for instance by tax reductions. It should also take into account general social issues, such as encouraging professional training, applying the same kind of treatment to blue- and white-collar workers in respect of social benefits, providing a way of increasing the savings of private households and arranging generally for a more balanced distribution of wealth in the economy. In this respect, the policies pursued recently in Germany might be worth studying more closely.

M. Albert said that Mr Brittan had emphasised divergencies between different countries and he wondered if one could then have a real co-ordination of economic policies. M. Albert said that his paper had described rather than explained. It was true that he had not explained why, despite agreement on monetary policy, European countries had failed to look at basic issues. Professor Sohmen had referred to recent events, like the French devaluation. Progress had been made before this and showed that there was a link between a number of factors. One clearly had to reconcile synthesis and divergence.

He was unable to offer a synthetic explanation himself. He thought the first point to look at was the contrast between the way that the E.E.C. had worked in two areas. First, the E.E.C. was a customs union with a common external tariff which had been altered during the Kennedy Round negotiations. He saw this as a success. In 1957, for example, one country had given instructions to its representatives negotiating the Rome Treaty that it would be impossible to reach a customs union in five years and that safeguards were therefore needed.

Second, there was the common agricultural policy. A lot had been done here, and he thought that what had happened showed that these two elements were part of an immense package deal between the various countries. The Germans and Benelux wanted the Common Market. France was much more interested in the common agricultural policy – this was her principal aim. Each country could therefore compromise usefully. It was true that on the macro-economic plane nothing much had been done. It was also true that ministers could take decisions about competition policy but had not done so.

One problem about the E.E.C. was that its members often treated their partners as adversaries. This clearly led us back to game theory. It would be enough, perhaps, to give an example of the way French policy had affected other countries' policies in recent years. Germany was the main monetary power. Germany was therefore now taking a more independent monetary policy. France, being weaker, was seeking support from other countries, having previously taken an independent line. Similarly, in recent negotiations over atomic energy, France had been seeking American support against its E.E.C. partners, The E.E.C. was therefore developing in an ambiguous atmosphere. For example, with colour television, one had the paradox that the system being used cut the E.E.C. into two parts. Yet this was an industry where the economies of scale were big and a large market ought to be important.

On the other hand, a great deal had been said about agriculture, where the Common Market had little to offer in the way of economies of scale. It was true that there had been a certain amount of agricultural specialisation but he thought the global gains had been very small. The natural tendency of any common market was to develop natural economic problems, but little had been done to solve these. The main achievements so far had been sectoral.

Professor Rieben said that both the paper by M. Albert and that by Professor Dunning pointed to the development of sophisticated industries in the Common Market by American firms. Professor Dunning said that this was the way in which advanced technology was being brought to Europe. In some industries this move was being resisted, for example by Fiat. He wondered whether Professor Houssiaux and M. Albert could take the starting point of the policy for competition in the Rome Treaty. This was intended to moderate the power of cartels. Was it not now necessary to strengthen industrial groups to make them large enough to resist the advent of American firms?

Professor Rieben felt that one difficulty in studying intra-European integration was that of comparing wages in Europe. It seemed that at present the average wage of a European worker was 55 to 60 per cent of that in the United States. We knew that in recent years what had happened in America was that there had been a slower rise in real wages than in Europe, though this was not true in one or two countries. He thought the same reasoning could be used as for Canada. In America, he thought that the power of American trade unions was equal to or greater than that in Europe. The advent of American firms seemed likely to increase wages in American firms above the level of their European competitors. The tendency in Europe would therefore be to equate European and American wages. In 1959 when there had been a great increase in American steel wages, there had been strikes in countries like Belgium. Professor Rieben saw this as an irreversible change. He thought there would be a regrouping of European industry. M. Albert raised a lot of these questions but did not solve them. The American strategy was not simply to exploit advanced technology with new wage structures; it was using specialist personnel consultants to recruit effective managers. Europe was doing very little about this problem, while American industry was importing up to fifty top managers a week into Europe. This was clearly a good way of transmitting American management practices to Europe. It was one of the ways in which small European firms could become bigger.

Coming back to what M. Albert had said about the need for a United States of Europe, Professor Wallich had said earlier that the United States had considered the case for the European Economic Community to rest less on its economic effects than on the long-run move toward political unity. What was now needed was a breakthrough in the sphere of sophisticated products and there was a need to look at the trend here.

Mr Shonfield wondered whether Professor Rieben had misread Table 3.1. The table was concerned with unit labour costs, not with comparative real wage levels.

Dr Molitor recalled that Mr Brittan had said that there was no chance of the

E.E.C. working with fixed exchange rates, given the different behaviour of the different economies. He doubted this and underlined the fact that the Treaty of Rome not only had economic but also political objectives. Dr Molitor pointed out that the co-ordination of economic policy was more difficult to realise than was a common policy based on a common political structure. For example, if Italy were divided into a northern and a southern state, each with its own political structure and currency, the chances of a successful co-ordination of the economic policies of the two states would seem very limited. In fact, the successful operation of an economic union requires a political willingness of all member states to harmonise their targets, to co-ordinate their policies and to submit to common rules.

Professor Kindleberger said that he argued in his own paper that one market implied one price, one price implied one money, and one money implied one monetary policy. This was the starting point, and what was needed was to intensify this policy for the E.E.C. It was paradoxical to want a common agricultural policy and not to organise a common monetary policy.

Mr Lamfalussy said he had mixed feelings on this issue. He would like Mr Brittan to be wrong, but thought he was right. There was a fundamental illusion about what kind of economic policy was needed in order to avoid difficulties because different countries developed in different ways. Differences of economic evolution resulted from different individual histories. In the past five years, it had been quite clear that there was potential disequilibrium in the French economy. Specifically, the French problem was one of increasing wages. The problem in Italy was how to export continually. In Belgium, there was a problem of portfolio investment and of import taxes. In Germany, the problem was disinflation, which Germany solved by sending back labour to the countries from which it came. One had to harmonise different degrees of inflation. Mr Lamfalussy suggested what was needed was a leap to complete economic integration. One needed a complete union or some other kind of unity. Perhaps this would need an external shock to bring it about.

Professor Sohmen agreed with Mr Brittan. He would like to use the Molitor example. He thought Dr Molitor's argument reversed cause and effect when he said that a common policy needed one money. What could be said was that one could not have a common money unless one did have a common policy. If one tried to have a single money without centralisation of policy, one would inevitably run into trouble.

Mr Merigó thought that Italy provided a good example of the difficulties involved when regions in very different stages of economic development had a common currency. These difficulties had been mitigated in the case of Italy by huge fiscal transfers from North to South. But a world of permanently fixed foreign exchange parities, without fiscal transfers, was very difficult to envisage.

Mr Brittan said that Professor Sohmen and Mr Lamfalussy had defended him successfully. It was interesting that we had reached a point where a lot depended on how one analysed Italian experience. If Italy were being unified now, would one want a common monetary system? Perhaps there would be some advantages in having two currencies and two trade union movements. It might help the South to provide an incentive to development if the southern lira were at a discount and if the trade union movements were separate. Whatever might be the optimal solution, if there *were* two governments, with a *confederate* body in Rome trying to harmonise monetary policies instead of adjusting exchange rates, how much success would this body have?

Professor Lebedev said he had found the introduction by Professor Houssiaux interesting. Being Russian economists, this had now become a 'directive' for them. He would not look at all ten points, just the tenth, on the future of the E.E.C. and the possibility of its development. Perhaps economists in the Soviet Union were particularly obsessed with the future, but he was sure that other people would be interested in it too. While he did not expect M. Albert to be a soothsayer, he would appreciate it if he would say a little about the tendencies for the future as he saw them.

Professor Yamamoto thought that several new facts had emerged during the discussion. He had earlier mentioned the three stages of integration. So far as the E.E.C. was concerned, this had encouraged intra-E.E.C. trade. There was a limit to how far trade between industrial countries could develop, and he thought we now needed to consider how the world market for advanced products would develop. This meant that there would be a limit to the further development of the so-called horizontal pattern of trade among advanced countries. They should try to develop a vertical pattern of trade instead.

All countries faced this problem, and M. Albert mentioned it on p. 59 of his paper. He wondered whether M. Albert meant that the E.E.C. should liberalise trade between underdeveloped countries and third countries like Japan and the United States. The E.E.C. had preferential treatment for African countries, and he wondered whether M. Albert meant that this liberalisation should be extended to third countries as well.

Professor Izzo agreed that the Italian Government did spend money on the South, but these funds were often used to buy consumption and investment goods produced by firms established in the North. Therefore one could not actually say which part of the country benefited most from the public expenditure on the South.

He was worried about what Mr Brittan had said about flexible exchange rates between the dollar and single European currencies. The United States was in a position to attract a good deal of foreign capital because of the investment opportunities there and its interest-rate policy. In these conditions, greater exchange flexibility would have paradoxical effects. Foreign capital flowing to the United States would tend to determine the rate of increase of the exchange rate between the dollar and the European currency, thereby weakening the competitive position of the United States. Consequently the contribution of real resources flowing from the United States to the rest of the world would decrease or become negative, and the dominant position of the United States in determining the distribution of real resources in the world would increase. These resources would have to be made available by those countries which needed to finance capital exports to the United States, and these countries could be compelled to generate funds through exchange-rate depreciation. This would increase their surpluses on current account.

Professor Houssiaux said that Mr Brittan and Mr Lamfalussy had made an important basic point. As Mr Lamfalussy had said, he was in favour of a maximalist policy for European integration. It would be difficult to get the leap that Mr Lamfalussy wanted, and Mr Brittan had suggested that a minimalist policy would have to be accepted. He thought there were some factors working in favour of co-ordination, for example in sectors like textiles. Here the pressures were multiple, so that co-ordination had a more important role than was supposed. Professor Houssiaux said that there were some areas where the behaviour of economic agents in Europe had been altered by the formation of the E.E.C. – for example through the introduction of the added-value tax, or changes in tastes and knowledge. Even on monetary policy, the system had developed since 1964 into informal understanding, and this was helping to begin the 'leap'.

M. Albert replied to the discussion. He said it had been suggested in a previous session that if the meeting had taken place twenty years earlier everyone would have been talking about the dollar shortage. Five years ago, everyone would have said that the E.E.C. was developing steadily towards a United States of Europe, and that devaluation in any one country was unthinkable, given the existence of a common agricultural policy. A few years ago, he had worked in the European Bank for Investment. This never lent the currency of the country which was carrying out the investment and therefore exchange guarantees were needed. In 1965 hardly any bankers had thought there was any danger of changes in exchange rates. It was useless to go back and say there had been no change in the E.E.C. in recent years.

He wondered why there was no common E.E.C. monetary policy. A common policy did need one common money, and one exchange rate. Observation showed that there were two kinds of period. In 1961–6 the way in which prices had risen in the various countries was very similar. Prices in both France and Germany had risen by about 3·4 per cent. In Germany, this was a consequence of the building of the Berlin Wall and the end of immigration. France, on her part, had been able to pursue a rigid monetary policy. Since 1966, the way things had developed had been very different. Exchange-rate changes had therefore become necessary.

If one took a long period of time, it seemed that it was happy chances which had led to the co-ordination of economic policy. The inflation of 1964–5 in Germany had led to some changes. Again, the E.E.C. was animated by a functionalist philosophy. It minimised the importance of politics and maximised the weight of historical materialism. The unity of Europe was in the logic of things; reason lay at the heart of economic development.

In the second period, arbitrary policy changes had played a bigger role. It was true that, as Mr Brittan and Mr Lamfalussy said, events were running against functionalism. We were faced with different structures, different rates of development and different policies. Given this, one could see why there was a conflict over a common economic policy and a common money. Some people were more interested in the first, others in the second. He thought that the chances for political co-ordination were very small now, largely because this was a general and long-run problem, while sacrifices were required immediately. An example of this was the ineffectiveness of pressures to get the Germans to inflate. This would put pressure on the German Government, and would have electoral consequences. He therefore agreed with Professor Houssiaux that what was being done was to undertake modest, psychological action on economic arrangements in Europe; but this was not useless.

Replying to Mr Merigó, M. Albert said that to compensate for the fact that the co-ordination of economic policy required painful economic sacrifices, he ought to point to the fact that there were some benefits as well. He thought that one could reconstruct the E.E.C. in the light of current experience. There would be different constraints. The agricultural budget would be the main element and there were no macro-economic ways of cancelling out the sacrifices resulting from co-ordination of policy. In Italy there were bigger structural differences than in the remaining countries of the E.E.C. An improvement in the communal decision-taking process for Italy would have big effects. Unless there were built-in stabilisers, it was important to have effective co-ordination of policy. Therefore a common view on monetary policy required, first, an improvement in decision-taking methods. One needed a mechanism to cancel problems. Given this, the E.E.C. could develop successfully.

No doubt the position in the E.E.C. at the moment gave an unfavourable impression to those outside it, especially in the United States. This was mainly a result of the protectionist agricultural policy. But given the abnormal and difficult nature of the problem, there was a danger that one would underrate the positive nature of what was being done elsewhere in the E.E.C. Without it, there was a danger that the United States would gain a monopoly position in the world. However, the United States was not monopolistic in its economics or its philosophy. Its profound philosophy was one of competition, and he felt it would welcome the development of a competitor in the E.E.C.

4 United Kingdom External Economic Policy

Samuel Brittan
THE FINANCIAL TIMES, LONDON

I. OBJECTIVES

The objectives of British economic policy have rarely been set out by official spokesmen in any but a very short-term sense. For a comprehensive statement one would have to go back to the Radcliffe Report on the Monetary System which came out as long ago as 1959, and was in no sense an official government pronouncement. Even the ambitious, but quickly jettisoned, National Plan of 1965 confined its objectives to numerical targets and had no comprehensive statement of aims.

Nevertheless such aims have existed, at least implicitly. The ones most relevant to external economic policy may be listed as follows:

(1) To attain a surplus on the basic balance of payments on current and long-term capital account.
(2) To maximise the propensity of overseas residents to hold sterling.
(3) To maintain 'full employment'.
(4) To attain as steady and as rapid a rate of growth as can be combined with the other objectives.
(5) To encourage the liberalisation of world trade.

The list is confined to objectives which have direct relevance to external economic policy. Thus, there is no mention of regional objectives or the distribution of income. Nor is there any reference to the structural changes in domestic industry which are bound to accompany any attempt to reach these objectives.

Even the list as it stands must promote ironical reflections. For it could equally read (with the possible exception of (3)) as a list of the main failures of British policy in the 1960s. This is not entirely surprising. Policy discussions tend to centre on matters which are believed to have gone wrong, while the listing of successes is reserved for electoral utterances and ceremonial occasions.

II. SPECIAL FEATURES

There are two striking differences between the aims just mentioned and the corresponding lists that might be compiled for other advanced Western nations. The first is the absence of any explicit reference to price stability, or anything approaching it, as a goal. There have been ritual references on numerous occasions. But in fact the United Kingdom financial authorities have been mainly interested in the movement of British *costs, relative to other nations*, from the point of view of the country's international competitive position. This concern is so predominant that ministers and officials rarely find occasion to ask themselves how much weight they would give price stability *per se*, if the external constraints were lifted.

The second striking difference is the objective of encouraging the holding of the country's currency abroad. This need arose in the first place from the large unfunded sterling balances with which the United Kingdom emerged after the war. As these wartime balances were drawn down, others accumulated. But up to the middle 1960s there was very little change in the total net sterling liabilities (excluding central bank assistance) which fluctuated around a level of a little above £3,000 million. Thus, in contrast to the dollar, there was no net increase in the holding of sterling for reserve and trading purposes.

Britain's vulnerability arose from the low level of gold and foreign exchange reserves, which rarely rose above £1,000 million, in relation to these liabilities. At times there has been a degree of substitutability between the two aims of strengthening overseas confidence in sterling and running a payments surplus. Ideally the authorities would have liked to increase the British reserves by a series of payments surpluses; but in their absence the willingness of sterling holders to keep their funds in London has sometimes served as a second best. (A Foreign Office brief is even said to have spoken of the danger of the sterling balances 'falling into enemy hands'.)

III. DEMAND MANAGEMENT

Much the most important single economic weapon has been demand management. In the short term demand restraints have affected the balance of payments mainly through their temporary effect on the import bill and imported stocks in particular. Governments have hoped that there would be sufficient correlation between domestic overheating and payments difficulties to bring a very rough harmony between external and internal needs. Despite the very obvious disharmonies of the 1960s, the official hope still is that after the 1967 devaluation and any ensuing currency changes, deficits can be prevented in a normal year if demand is prevented from pressing too hard against capacity.

Demand policy has also had a long-run aspect, which has been to manage the economy at an average pressure of demand high enough to preserve reasonably full employment, but low enough to prevent British costs from rising faster than those of other countries. In practical terms the aim has been to maintain the unemployment rate at about 2 per cent, or in recent years slightly above.

Incomes policy has usually been conceived as an adjunct – either as a reinforcement to the Phillips curve approach, or as a way of shifting the Phillips curve – so that any particular target for money costs can be achieved at a smaller sacrifice in employment. The results have been disappointing. During the heyday of incomes policy the Phillips curve even moved in an unfavourable direction. In any event, the difficulties and unpopularity of enforcement proved so great that by 1969 incomes policy was playing only a minor role in the policy armoury. A vast institutional apparatus remains and official propaganda for restraint is likely to continue; but the main weight has shifted back to overall demand management.

It should be clear even from this very brief summary that demand management has had to bear a quite extraordinary share of the policy burden; and the load has often been greater than it could reasonably be expected to bear. It happens to be the case that until around the winter of 1968–9, demand management was mainly a matter of fiscal policy, with monetary policy playing an essentially passive and supporting role. Fiscal policy itself tended to be based on the assumption of a constant marginal savings ratio – an assumption that neglected 'permanent income' effects and the influence of expectations on consumer behaviour.

For these and a great many other reasons, demand management was not always very successful in achieving the domestic results desired by the authorities. But this is not the main point I am making in saying that demand management had to carry an excessive load. Much more important is the fact that the level of demand required for extreme equilibrium was not always consistent with that required by internal considerations. This reflected both the underlying weakness of the balance of payments and the low level of reserves, which gave insufficient cushion against both bad luck and mistakes of management.

Basically, the load on demand management was too great because policy-makers lacked an external regulator. From the middle 1950s onwards trade restrictions were no longer used as a balance of payments weapon; and with a fixed exchange rate, no other regulator was put into place. Some might argue that the authorities could have escaped their dilemma by assigning external stability to monetary policy and internal stability to fiscal policy. But as Professor Harry Johnson has pointed out, varying the monetary–fiscal mix is not a genuine adjustment system.[1] A deficit country that succeeds by high interest-rate policy in attracting overseas capital to cover the gap will pile up debts; and the current deficit will actually be swollen on interest and profit account; thus driving the

[1] *Theoretical Problems of the International Monetary System*, reprinted in *International Finance*, ed. R. N. Cooper (Penguin Books, 1969).

authorities to even further fiscal expansion and monetary contractions. In the British case, moreover, a large part of the funds which arrived whenever interest rates were raised was of a volatile short-term nature, which quickly took fright and left once it became clear that the balance of payments was in current deficit.

The one responsibility that the official British demand managers have been anxious to disclaim is responsibility for long-term growth. The main effect of demand regulation, the British financial authorities insist, is to vary the proportion of productive capacity in use; the growth of productive capacity is in their view determined by quite other forces.[1] They would probably concede that it is marginally better if the growth of demand can be steady rather than erratic. But because of the difficulties with sterling this desire had to take a back seat.

IV. TRADE PHILOSOPHY

British Governments have also been strongly committed to multilateral trade liberalisation, symbolised by the successive rounds of GATT negotiation. A parallel on the financial side has been strong support for new forms of international liquidity, and the United Kingdom has stood shoulder to shoulder with the United States in pressing for the maximum generosity in both amounts and conditions.

The precarious balance of payments has precluded any experiments with unilateral tariff-cutting and the United Kingdom market remains fairly highly protected by international standards. Even after the Kennedy Round talks have been completed, British tariffs are likely to average around 9 per cent in nominal terms and 16 per cent as effective rates on value added. The corresponding figures in both the United States and the E.E.C. are likely to be around $6\frac{1}{2}$–7 per cent and a nominal 11–$11\frac{1}{2}$ per cent effective rates.

The United Kingdom also has a much broader dispersion around the average than either the E.E.C. or the United States. Protection is, it is true, diluted by Commonwealth and EFTA preferences. But these preferential areas are not a very strong source of competition compared to the internal competition provided by the United States and E.E.C. trading areas.

On the other hand, fears of spreading a bad example which would slow down the growth of world trade, coupled with administrative inertia and a deep-seated belief in sticking to the rules, have made British Governments extremely reluctant to tackle payments deficits by direct controls on imports. Measures such as the import surcharge of 1964–6 were

---

[1] The most authoritative statement of British official thinking on the subject can be found in Sir William Armstrong's Stamp Memorial Lecture, *Some Practical Problems in Demand Management* (Athlone Press, 1969).

imposed late in the day and quickly lifted. Similar considerations have made Governments very sparing of special aids to exporters.

Yet side by side with these traditional constraints, a whole apparatus of back-door protectionism, and to a lesser extent export stimulation, has grown up under the label of 'industrial policy'. State aid has been provided for computers and aluminium smelters. Bodies such as the I.R.C., backed with state funds, have concentrated on mergers which might fight off imports or promote exports. Investment incentives and indirect taxation have been elaborately distorted in the hope of providing some differential for exporting industries. Policy against restrictive business practices can be relaxed to help ward off international competition. Indeed a vested interest has developed in such policies in new organisations largely outside both the established Civil Service and the liberal economic tradition.

It is still extraordinarily difficult to evaluate these tendencies, especially as valuable measures of industrial reorganisation and back-door protection have been inextricably mixed together. The fact that such back-door measures were much too slow-acting to have any perceptible effect on the balance of payments by the time of the 1967 devaluation should not make one underestimate their possible long-term impact; and a different Government might even intensify them in some respects and rely even less than the present one on price mechanism solutions.

For the traditional liberal trade philosophy the establishment of the European Economic Community was an unmitigated embarrassment. The first response, the abortive Maudling Free Trade Area of 1958, was an attempt to preserve as much of the traditional approach as possible while sharing in the European tariff cuts; and EFTA was its vestigial remnant. Subsequent attempts to join the E.E.C. were regarded in Whitehall as foreign policy ventures, and played a surprisingly small role in the calculations of the economic departments. In so far as there was an economic motive it could be summed up under the crude slogan 'If you can't beat 'em, join 'em'.

Whatever the ultimate structural benefits, the balance of payments consequences of joining the E.E.C. would be undoubtedly adverse, and adverse by an unpredictable amount, which would create difficulties for any Community that attempted to maintain rigid exchange rates. The fact that a looser association with more of the features of a free-trade area would suit Britain and other peripheral countries better, is likely to emerge sooner or later in any negotiations.

V. STERLING'S DIFFICULTIES

Not even the greatest enthusiasts for E.E.C. membership would attribute Britain's difficulties over the last decade to her exclusion from the Community. Two rival candidates for blame are the balance of payments and the international position of sterling. The evidence suggests that both have contributed.

In the five years 1964–8, total overseas official financing from the I.M.F., central banks, other foreign sources and United Kingdom reserves amounted to £3,600 million. The official settlements deficit which it reflected was made up as follows:

TABLE 4.1

OVERSEAS SETTLEMENTS DEFICITS, 1964–8

	April 1969 Financial Statement	September 1969 Pink Book
	(£m. Rounded)	
(1) Current account deficit	1,300	900
(2) Private investment, net outflow	500	600
(3) Official long-term capital outflow (net)	300	300
(4) Increase in gross sterling claims	700	700
(5) Reduction in gross sterling liabilities	500	500
(6) Other short-term outflows	300	600
	£3,600	3,600

The drastic revisions of the official figures as a result of the startling discovery of unrecorded exports and other errors are shown by the contrast between the two columns of Table 4.1. The current deficit is now believed to have accounted for some £900 million of the £3,600 million outflow, instead of the £1,300 million originally believed; and the 'basic' deficit, on current and long-term capital account combined, is now believed to have accounted for £1,800 million instead of £2,100 million. Indeed, official statisticians are suggesting a further adjustment to the capital account (not incorporated into the 1969 Pink Book estimates) to allow for overseas investment financed by Euro-dollar borrowing from United Kingdom banks, which makes no call on the reserves. Adjusted in this way, the basic deficit for 1964–8 would be reduced still further to £1,600 million, the greater part of this latter adjustment coming in 1968 after devaluation.

Items (5) and (6) in Table 4.1 represent 'confidence' outflows of funds, mostly from outside the sterling area, and partly taking the form of 'leads and lags'. They would undoubtedly have been less had the true basic figures been known. But even on the new and revised basis, Tables 4.1 and 4.2 show that the United Kingdom was still in fundamental disequilibrium in 1964–8.

Indeed, the statistical record understates the true disequilibrium, as imports were artificially held down in 1964–8 by an increase in the margin of unused capacity which could hardly have continued indefinitely, as well as by the surcharge of 1964–6. Moreover, the increase in gross sterling

TABLE 4.2
UNITED KINGDOM BALANCE OF PAYMENTS, 1962-9
1969 Pink Book estimates
(£m.)

Current Account	1964	1965	1966	1967	1968	1969*
(1) Imports f.o.b.	−5,003	−5,042	−5,211	−5,574	−6,801	−3,513
(2) Exports	+4,466	+4,777	+5,108	+5,026	+6,103	+3,283
(3) Payments for United States military aircraft	−2	−12	−41	−98	−109	−48
(3a) Allowance for net under-recording of exports	+20	+40	+60	+80	+130	+70
(4) Visible balance (goods)	−519	−237	−84	−566	−677	−208
(5) Official grants (net)(defence and aid)	−163	−177	−180	−188	−178	+301
(6) Other invisibles	+301	+364	+328	+471	+590	
(7) Total current account	−381	−50	+64	−283	−265	+93
Current and long-term capital account						
(1) Current account	−381	−50	+64	−283	−265	+93
(2) Private investment (net)	−247	−117	−32	−77	−163	+31
(3) Official long-term capital (net)	−116	−85	−80	−57	+21	−76
(4) Balance of current and long-term capital transactions	−744	−252	−48	−417	−407	+48

*Seasonally adjusted.

claims of £700 million shown in item (4) of Table 4.1 is mostly net new export credit and should be added to the basic deficit as far as effects on the reserves are concerned.

VI. THE RESPONSE TO CRISIS

Orthodox policy was most easily overthrown in the case of overseas investment, where there had never been a full commitment to liberalisation; and severe restrictions were imposed in 1965 and subsequently intensified. The ambivalent response on the trade side has already been mentioned. There are also elements of ambivalence in British attitudes to the October 1968 Basle arrangements for sterling.

The Basle arrangements have two parts. There is a $2,000 million standby for the B.I.S. available up to 1971, and repayable over 1974–8, to finance any rundown of sterling area balances. In addition the United Kingdom has guaranteed the dollar value of the bulk of each sterling country's official balances, in exchange for an undertaking to maintain approximately the 1968 proportion of sterling in its total reserves.

While the new arrangements have been interpreted at a political level as reducing the reserve currency role of sterling, the official White Paper talks of 'giving greater stability to the sterling system', and there are even hopes of attracting more balances to London. As a result of the dollar guarantee Britain can to some extent have it both ways. The risks involved in the reserve currency function of sterling have been taken over by the dollar. The United Kingdom will in future be vulnerable only if sterling area countries either disbelieve the guarantee, or desire to convert their reserves into gold or European correncies via the dollar – a transaction to which the United States would be most unlikely to agree on any scale.

The price that Britain has to pay is (*a*) an increase in the *sterling* value of interest payments in the event of a further devaluation of the pound against the dollar, and (*b*) the payment of a normal interest rate on the balances that makes no allowance for the dollar guarantee. Critics have asked whether the United Kingdom is not paying twice over and have wondered if item (*b*) would have been necessary had the negotiations taken place in a calmer atmosphere.

When the present arrangements lapse in 1971–3, a choice will have to be made among alternatives. Should by any chance the pound be in a strong phase, there will undoubtedly be a strong Bank of England school of thought in favour of returning gradually to the old sterling area system without guarantees or standbys. At the other extreme, if S.D.R.s are in successful operation, there will be no lack of schemes for issuing these units either to sterling area countries or to the United Kingdom. But as always in such situations, the best single bet is the renewal of the present arrangements for a further term.

The area in which British Governments have been most reluctant to move has of course been the sterling parity. The 1967 devaluation from $2.80 to $2.40 to the £ was not a freely chosen policy, but the end-product of a three- or six-year attempt to defend the previous rate. There is still a great danger that if a choice has to be made between abandoning another sterling parity or jettisoning liberal trade policies, the latter will be chosen for sacrifice.

The old objections to exchange depreciation, apart from the normal political and emotional ones, included the fear that it would lead to a rush out of sterling by overseas holders. There was also the fear that it would trigger off a run on the dollar. The Basle arrangements and the recent rundown of the private balances of non-sterling countries have reduced the force of the sterling balance arguments. The two-tier gold system has also eliminated the risk of an old-fashioned run out of the dollar into gold by private holders – although a round of devaluations which left the dollar overvalued in relation to other currencies could still embarrass the Americans. These well-known objections have now been partially replaced by fear of the 'J-curve'. This refers to the period immediately after a devaluation when the effect on the trade balance is likely to be perverse even if the long-run elasticities are favourable.

Contingency plans for a floating rate exist, but only as an emergency device for meeting a currency crisis so severe that the authorities could not or would not want to meet it by borrowing. The great official fear about a floating pound is that in the transitional period, while the current balance is deteriorating, the rate would be entirely dependent on stabilising speculation. If the market took a pessimistic view and import prices rose severely at a time when inflationary expectations were very high, there would, it is feared, be a risk of a cumulative cycle of cost inflation and exchange depreciation on almost Latin American scale. To offset such cost-inflationary forces by financial policy might require very severe unemployment if it were manageable at all.

Such risks would indeed exist if the pound were floated at the wrong time without very careful internal preparation. The right time to do it is when considerable excess capacity exists, when inflationary expectations are not historically high and when – as is likely in such a period – the statistical balance of payments is better than its underlying level. But it is in just such periods that Governments are most anxious to persuade themselves that their existing policies are 'working' and that there is no need for leaps in the dark.

VII. ELASTICITY PESSIMISM

The ultimate fear that haunts British policy-makers is that both income and price elasticities may be unfavourable. Houthakker and Magee have estimated that the income elasticity of demand for British exports in world markets (weighted by their 1958 share of British exports) was 0·86 in the period 1951–66, while the United Kingdom's own income elasticity of demand for imports was 1·66, a ratio of 1:2.[1]

A quick look at a more recent period up to the 1967 devaluation is interesting. In the nine years up to 1967, world trade increased by nearly two-thirds in volume terms, while British exports increased by about one-third. During these years the British G.D.P. increased by nearly a third while import volume increased by well over half. In the same period the N.I.E.S.R. index suggests that British export prices for manufactures rose by 18 per cent compared with 10 per cent for industrial countries as a whole.

Houthakker's income elasticities would, of course, appear rather different if more weight were given to price (and profitability). If relative price changes have their full effects after long time lags, their influence may easily be underestimated in a statistical study. Another qualification is that if the non-price attractions of British goods (delivery, salesmanship, etc.) have been declining in relation to those of competitor countries, the size of this effect would surely be related to time and the absolute level of world incomes, rather than to their rate of growth. But whatever one's reservations about the form of these relationships, there probably was a tendency for non-price competitiveness to decline in large parts of the post-war period.

This would matter less if price elasticity were high and British Governments were prepared to change exchange rates. But post-devaluation delays and disappointments have raised many questions here. There is no need to postulate perverse elasticities or long-run kinked demand curves in export markets. Sufficient difficulties are created if a given improvement in the underlying balance of payments requires a relatively severe deterioration in the terms of trade and if, in addition, the initial downward-sloping section of the J-curve is stretched out for a considerable period of time.

VIII. EXPORT CAPACITY

My own view is that elasticity pessimism is often taken much too far, especially among businessmen and politicians. The British export problem has been largely a capacity one, in the long-term sense that production facilities, design and sales organisation have not been of a kind that can be easily or quickly switched to the export market, whatever exchange rate or home demand policies are followed. Therefore short-run price or profitability elasticities are low.

[1] 'Income and Price Elasticity in World Trade', *Review of Economics and Statistics* (May 1969).

The tentative diagnosis I am suggesting should be sharply differentiated from the more usual 'too little investment' complaint. If the trouble were simply an overall shortage of productive capacity, this would be just another way of diagnosing excessive demand. For capacity can only be short in relation to the demands made upon it. My point is that the composition of productive capacity was excessively biased towards home market requirements.

The problem is to secure more investment, in human as well as physical resources, designed to cater for world, rather than British, markets. There is no reason to think that British businessmen are impervious to profitability considerations. The reason for their reluctance to adjust their long-term plans is their extreme suspicion that any profitability or price advantage in overseas markets, obtained for example by the 1967 devaluation, will soon be eroded, and that export markets are an 'unreliable' basis for expansion. Sustained experience to the contrary could remove this suspicion.

If the above account is valid, the conditions for improving Britain's competitive performance are not difficult to state. They are a pattern of exchange rates and relative cost movements that preserve at least the devaluation advantage of 1967, and preferably improve a little upon it; and a demand management policy, which is not drastically deflationary, but is designed to make 'room' for a payments surplus, with a little margin to spare. If the British Governments are to stick to a policy of this kind, and avoid panic action, two further conditions are required: a growth of world trade not too far below the average of the past decade and sufficient international financing, or favourable capital movements, to tide over any short-term difficulties. The above conditions are sufficient and no additional investment-boosting programmes are required.

IX. UNITED STATES POLICY

The enumeration of the conditions required for an export breakthrough brings one immediately to the impact of American policy. The traditional British concern has been with protectionist Congressional lobbies, the workings of the 'Buy American' Act, the American Selling Price, and so on. A more recent fear is that the United States money squeeze may lead, directly via the bidding for Euro-dollar deposits, to a higher level of interest rates in both the United Kingdom and the Continent than domestic considerations would warrant. But both these worries are less fundamental than the course of North American imports over, say, the period 1969-71.

North America accounted for nearly a fifth of total United Kingdom exports in the 1960s. A sufficiently serious setback here, which would of course have a multiplier effect on other markets, could swamp any gradual improvements in the United Kingdom's own competitive position. Whether a check to North American imports were brought about by protection or financial policy would be a secondary consideration over the relevant period. What matters would be the total movement of imports.

TABLE 4.3

AREA DISTRIBUTION OF UNITED KINGDOM EXPORTS

	Monthly rates, 1966 (£m.)	Average annual per cent rate of increase, 1957–67
Sterling Area	146	+1½
E.E.C.	100	+9
EFTA	71	+8½
United States	73	+8
Canada	22	(+½)
Latin America	19	0
Other Western Europe	18	(+13)
Soviet bloc	19	(+12)
Rest of world	47	+3½
	515	+5

Source: *Board of Trade Journal*, 21 Feb 1969.

A quick elimination of the basic United States deficit through an increase in exports would also be harmful to Britain's balance of payments. British exports would suffer from a displacement effect in third markets, instead of through the check to United States markets. (Whether an improvement brought about through the capital account could also be deleterious to the United Kingdom would depend on the exact nature of the improvement.)

Thus of all the courses which the United States might follow, a quick correction of its deficit would be the most harmful to Britain. The issue of S.D.R.s ought to be a mitigating influence. On suitable accounting conventions the world as a whole would have a net surplus; and the United Kingdom would be able to improve its own balance without any net deterioration in the rest of the world. But there are many uncertainties about the way in which a new and unfamiliar asset will in fact be treated; there will be a 'leakage' of S.D.R.s to the surplus countries, and the improvements in the national balances of payments will, if shown at all, appear in the capital or monetary account, which countries regard as more volatile and less secure than the trade balance. The trade-off for the United Kingdom between a $1 billion reduction in the annual United

States deficit and a $1 billion annual creation of S.D.R.s will be much less than 1 for 1, at least in the early days.

X. THE DOLLAR AND GOLD

The United States move most difficult to evaluate would be the much-discussed gold embargo. Its great advantage for the United Kingdom would be the removal of the pressure on the Americans to remove their deficit by deflation or trade restrictions. If other countries decided to revalue, or let their currencies float up, rather than hold dollars, then indeed the United States deficit would decline, but there would be an offset from Britain's point of view in the appreciation of the surplus currencies relative to sterling (assuming that the pound did not appreciate against the dollar!). There would, of course, be a risk of protectionist moves during the chain reaction of events following an official gold embargo; our best chance of avoiding them lies in contingency planning before the event.

A great deal is sometimes made of the agonising choice Britain would have to make in such circumstances between 'going with the dollar' or 'going with Europe'. Most such discussion is marred by a failure to distinguish between the choice of parity and choice of assets for reserve-holding. 'Going with Europe' would in any case be initially impossible on the parity front, as Continental parities will move in different directions unless there has been a major realignment beforehand. If after such a realignment the dollar floated against a European currency bloc, it would be an act of astonishing folly to tie sterling to either bloc. If such a folly has to be committed, there would be an overwhelming case for the pound being tied to the dollar on the grounds that both the United States and Britain have been experiencing a long-term deterioration in their international trading position. Such a choice would be inconsistent with membership of a tightly-knit E.E.C., and this may, indeed, be one further reason for making careful stipulations about British membership.

A big increase in the official gold price would not avoid these difficulties if there were long-term changes in the relative international competitiveness of the United States and the E.E.C. But it would have some advantages. The annual increment of new reserves, following such a change, would probably be larger and almost certainly regarded with fewer reservations by creditor countries than S.D.R.s in the early years. A waiver would be required from the I.M.F. to prevent a large increase in Britain's repayment burden (which would not be obtainable on the share provided by the G.A.B.). But the small size of the British official gold reserve, and the absence of private gold hoardings, would make the change much less inflationary for the United Kingdom than for other countries; and this country would be in a good position to benefit from the increase in the value of world trade. Thus for once the ratio of real growth to inflationary expansion would compare favourably with competitors.

British self-interest is not, of course, a sufficient reason for a gold price increase. Yet, as Professor Harry Johnson has pointed out, such an increase might well come about in any case as the end-product of the chain of events following a United States gold embargo. It could also happen after a series of devaluations which left the dollar high and dry in relation to other countries. There is therefore a great deal to be said for making the change in one move and avoiding the disruption of the long-drawn-out method; but I have no doubt that this suggestion will be treated as a mention of sex would have been treated in Victorian times, or of British devaluation before 1967.

XI. THE FUTURE OF BRITISH POLICY

Whatever one's views on these topics, it is on balance improbable that either salvation or damnation will come to the British economy from some brave, bold American act; and it would be better to conclude by returning to an earlier topic and asking how British Governments are likely to behave if elasticity pessimism comes to govern their behaviour. At the time of writing, the British balance of payments has enjoyed a turn for the better. But it would be irresponsible in the extreme to assume, on the basis of the 1969 figures to date, that previous payments difficulties will not recur. It would be irrational to hold down import demand purely by deflating real output and employment. The right policy in such circumstances might at first sight seem to be to limit imports directly. But would not the resulting inefficiency and distortions be lessened if quotas were sold at market-clearing price to importers, who would be allowed to trade them freely in the second-hand market? Leaving aside the gains from monopsonistic discrimination, the same result could be achieved simply by a floating rate combined with a variable import surcharge (or export tax) so that balance were achieved at a lower volume and more favourable terms of trade.

Unfortunately such a solution is unlikely to be either proposed or accepted internationally. The most likely source of import saving is in fact an increase in agricultural protectionism, whether Britain is inside or outside the E.E.C. Imports of temperate foodstuffs are running at about one-third of total supplies. This proportion could be reduced by fairly moderate increases in farm prices. Such a policy has been inhibited up to now by the added burden on the Exchequer of higher deficiency payments and by agreements on access with Commonwealth countries. A change to duties or levies would not, of course, reduce real costs, but such is the power of the tax illusion that it would make it politically easier to increase the effective rate of protection. Moreover, an expansion of domestic agricultural production would reduce both the real and the balance of payments costs of E.E.C. entry, although the ultimate effect of the E.E.C. agricultural policy on the British balance of payments would still probably be heavily adverse.

One can also envisage traditional liberal trading policies being eroded by 'voluntary' international import-control schemes for particular commodities on the lines of the textile or steel agreements, a 'tough-minded' use of anti-dumping legislation, and an abrasive 'Buy British' aspect of our foreign policy. On all these matters, I am discussing possible trends of British policy, not giving my own remedies, which lie in the realm of flexible exchange rates in particular, and the market mechanism in general.

TABLE 4.4

THE STRUCTURE OF BRITISH IMPORTS

	Monthly rate, 1968 (£m.)	Average annual per cent rate of growth, 1957–67
Food, beverages and tobacco	159	+2
Fuels	75	+5
Basic materials	101	−1
Chemicals	35	+11
Other semi-manufactures	142	+7
Finished manufactures	126	+16
Miscellaneous	10	
Total excl. United States aircraft, etc.	646	+4
Total incl. United States aircraft, etc.	658	+5

Source: *Board of Trade Journal*, 21 Feb 1969.

If I had to give a prognosis, it would be that as a result of parity changes and internal financial policies the underlying British balance of payments will, by one means or another, have improved sufficiently by the 1970s to allow output to grow in line with capacity and finance some net repayments of official debt. The balance of payments constraint will be much less and the British economy will enjoy better growth rates in the 1970s than in the mid-1960s; and the consumer will be less hard pressed by official policy. On the other hand the 'balance of payments constraint' will not have been removed altogether. Internal policy will still be governed by short-term balance of payments needs, and the economy will be run at a lower pressure of demand than before 1966, but partly as a result there will be less 'stop-go'. All kinds of industrial intervention, or semi-protectionist policies which would be palpable nonsense on their own, will continue to be justified by payments fears. Such fears will inhibit British foreign policy and rule out a great many initiatives at home and abroad. There could also be a shift at the margin from restraints on capital outflow to direct import restraints in periods of difficulty, on the grounds that the latter do less harm to future foreign exchange earning power.

This is not the most thrilling prospect imaginable; nor is it the most catastrophic. A guess of this kind is not worth while unless the twin temptations of wishful thinking and gloom-mongering are shunned with equal vigour.

5 International Economic Policies of a Nordic Group

Nils Lundgren
INSTITUTE FOR INTERNATIONAL ECONOMIC STUDIES,
STOCKHOLM, SWEDEN

I. INTRODUCTION

EFTA is always thought of as a very heterogeneous organisation consisting of countries who have mainly one thing in common. They were not prepared in the middle of the 1950s to sign the Rome Treaty. Even this common attitude was explained by very different underlying factors. It is usual to point to wide differences among them in level of development, geographical situation, economic structure, size of economy and population, security policy, etc. Accordingly, it seems reasonable to assume that the basis for common EFTA policies will normally be weak or non-existent. Also, it seems to follow that they could not easily be treated together in a discussion of commercial and economic policies, which is the object of this paper.

While there is some truth in this conception of EFTA, the dispersion should not be exaggerated. The notion of extreme diversity is to a large extent based on the observation of the great differences between Portugal and the other EFTA countries. Portugal is an odd bird in EFTA, however, and it is not reasonable to let it represent the extreme of an imagined spectrum. Britain, the four Nordic countries and the two Alpine countries, Austria and Switzerland, are all high-income, industrialised welfare states, situated in the same part of the world and with very similar cultural and social characteristics.

Still, it is clear that inside a European context they differ considerably due to geographical situation and economic structure in particular. As we are here interested in economic and commercial policies which are to a large extent conditioned by the European environment, we cannot press them into a common form for the analysis. It is argued here, however, that it is possible to distinguish three major actors in EFTA, namely the United Kingdom; Switzerland; and the Nordic group consisting of Denmark, Finland, Norway and Sweden. These three forces in fact dominate EFTA while Austria and Portugal tend to be both too weak and have too special problems.[1] As Britain's policies are dealt with in a separate paper,

---
[1] This structure is reflected in the EFTA Secretariat, which is headed by a British Secretary-General assisted by two deputies, who are of Swedish and Swiss nationality. The Swede may be considered the key Nordic official in the unofficial system of national quotas resorted to in most international organisations.

we may here restrict our interest to the Nordic countries and Switzerland without losing too many important elements of the EFTA contribution to the international network of interacting and conflicting economic policies.

I have chosen to let the process of elimination go one step further, however, and to exclude Switzerland also. The reason for this is not an underestimation of Switzerland's importance in international economic relations. But Swiss policies are for this very reason fairly well known and have not undergone much change in recent times. It seems that Switzerland continues to be so successful in economic respects that her worries are mainly caused by anticipations of or uncertainties about the future. Switzerland continues to run economic and commercial policies based on the cornerstones of neutrality, federalism, agricultural protection and industrial liberalism. Switzerland remains a proponent of international free trade in industrial goods, reluctant to enter into any sort of organisation that could erode national sovereignty even marginally.

This general attitude is partly explained by the fact that Switzerland derives her national identity not from ethnic and linguistic homogeneity but from her constitution and foreign policy orientation. A development towards accepting a European economic union with prospects of political federation is therefore much less likely in Switzerland than in other countries, where people can picture their nation as a member of such a federation. The Swiss generally expect their national identity to disintegrate in such a situation. This vision and the experience of success in the past probably ensure that familiar Swiss attitudes to international economic problems will not change.[1]

It is, however, not only on the basis of such a principle of exclusion that the discussion will be restricted to the Nordic countries. There are also two other reasons why the Nordic area may deserve more attention than it has normally been awarded in discussions of international economic problems. Firstly, it is quite clear that their policies and aspirations are not very well known abroad. Even if there are limits to the amount of information people in Europe and North America can absorb and memorise about four small and peripheral countries, there seems to be a case for presenting some of the important aspects of their policies, as they now exist. Secondly, there are strong indications that these four countries may shortly succeed in achieving a much closer unity in their international economic and commercial policies. If this were to happen, it would be very relevant to the general problem of this Conference, as it would really introduce a new actor on the stage – an actor who could have considerable influence on certain international economic and political

[1] See *The European Free Trade Association and the Crisis of European Integration*, by a Study Group of the Geneva Graduate Institute of International Studies (London, 1969) pp. 145–62.

issues for reasons to be discussed later on. This possibility and the policy alternatives open to Britain are probably the most interesting features of the EFTA area in the context to be studied by this Conference.

II. THE POSSIBILITIES OF COMMON NORDIC POLICIES ON INTERNATIONAL ECONOMIC PROBLEMS

The Nordic countries enjoy a basic homogeneity in ethnic, linguistic and political respects, which makes it permissible to speak of a Nordic way of life. For this reason they also share a common outlook on most international problems, whether economic or political, and they have a degree of grass-root integration in economic, legal and social matters that is unparalleled by any other set of sovereign nations. They have not just free trade in goods (except agricultural products), a common labour market and far-reaching industrial integration. It may be of equal importance that they have identical patent laws, increasingly similar commercial legislation, social security extended to all Nordic citizens, common tariff rules, transferable university degrees and other things in common.

Nordic co-operation on both internal and external policies has gone so far that there are civil servants in government departments who are in almost daily contact with their opposite numbers in the other Nordic countries. In international organisations the representative of one country often speaks on behalf of all four. In the Kennedy Round they actually negotiated as one delegation and at UNCTAD II their co-operation was so conspicuous that the delegate from India referred to 'the Nordic delegation' in his final speech. When Denmark in 1965 took an initiative on South African racial discrimination in the U.N. General Assembly without consulting the other Nordic countries, this caused a strong reaction there, and led to criticism in the Nordic Council. This shows how far co-operation has gone even in general foreign policy.[1]

This advanced degree of integration and co-operation implies that the Nordic countries have already created something very close to a Nordic economic union.[2] It is a situation that seems both to require and make possible the creation of common Nordic economic institutions. With such institutions they would become a bloc with considerable international influence. For they apparently would not have more internal differences of opinion and interest than most national states of the same size, and would therefore be able to act with as much decision and consequence.

[1] See Nils Andrén, *Nordic Integration, Co-operation and Conflict* (1967).
[2] This has apparently not been realised by the leading integration expert Ernst B. Haas. See his 'The Uniting of Europe and the Uniting of Latin America', *Journal of Common Market Studies*, v 4 (June 1967) 320.

(1) *Nordic and European Co-operation as Alternatives*

The reason why the Nordic countries have not institutionalised their economic co-operation during the 1960s is that they have had different policies on the European Economic Community question. Denmark and Norway have both asked for membership in the wake of the United Kingdom, while Sweden has restricted herself to asking for negotiations on how economic relations between herself and the E.E.C. could be arranged. Finland has not made any formal approach at all.

This situation has introduced a schizophrenic element in Danish and Norwegian trade policies, as these two countries have had reasons to fear that more formal Nordic commitments could tie their fate to that of Sweden and Finland and so, in the event, ruin their possibilities of joining the Common Market. At the same time, the prospects of having the Nordic market broken up again were equally dismal. Until de Gaulle's veto on British membership in 1967 Denmark and Norway tried to avoid a more institutional framework in Nordic co-operation for this reason, but favoured a pragmatic extension of Nordic integration in the hope that these two policy objectives were not mutually exclusive. Sweden and Finland, on the other hand, have had reasons to want such Nordic ties in order to improve their possibilities of reaching a satisfactory agreement with the E.E.C., if Britain, Denmark and Norway were to achieve E.E.C. membership.

As the differences on the E.E.C. questions have been the obstacle to common economic institutions, it is important to have a clear conception of the causes of these differences.

The reasons for differing Nordic E.E.C. policies may be classified into geopolitical conditions, economic structure and ideoligical orientation, which schematically may be said to manifest themselves respectively in security policy, trade policy and general foreign policy. There is fairly general agreement among experts and politicians in Europe and North America today that the Nordic countries could not have adopted the same security policies in the late 1940s unless they had established a Nordic defence union. The Cold War frontier was drawn through the Nordic area by outside forces and there were no political possibilities of having all Nordic countries on the same side of it. A Scandinavian defence union or the present split solution were the only alternatives.

When Britain applied for membership of the European Economic Community in 1961 and both Western European and American forces tried to make it a second pillar of the Western alliance, the possibilities of Nordic unity on Western European economic co-operation were swept away. For such unity would then have required at least some Nordic countries to change their security policies and this was excluded by over-ruling considerations of stability in the Nordic area. It is a safe assumption that no Nordic country will undertake an independent revision of its present security policy. A change can only be expected in connection with a general reform of the security system of Europe. This would probably require super-power agreement on the German question and a general political reorientation on a global scale, or possibly it could happen as a result of a slow disintegration of the two military blocs.

It follows from this that the stronger the federalist or Atlantic Alliance character of the E.E.C. is, the more security policy considerations create a conflict between E.E.C. policies and Nordic policies in Denmark and Norway. For in this situation these countries must foresee difficulties in joining the E.E.C., if they create strong ties to the two other Nordic countries who cannot then consider E.E.C. membership. If either the likelihood of gaining E.E.C. membership in the foreseeable future diminishes or the E.E.C. develops into an organisation for economic co-operation with no political connection with the Western alliance or a federal Europe, Danish and Norwegian objections to institutional Nordic co-operation also diminish. Both these factors have been at work lately.

It is also clear that different economic structures have come to reinforce the Common Market policies selected by the Nordic countries mainly on the basis of their security policies. In the short and medium term the effects of the Community were expected to come mainly through tariff discrimination and the common agricultural policy. Denmark had at least three good reasons to be allowed in before the agricultural policy was agreed upon. Firstly, Denmark wanted to influence the general construction of that policy. Secondly, it was obvious that it would be very difficult to admit new members after the policy had been implemented. Thirdly, Danish farmers who were very worried about their exports to Germany and eager to obtain high E.E.C. prices, were a politically very important group in the early 1960s because the Social Democrats were running a minority government. All this made Denmark very active and impatient to reach an agreement with the Community.

The Common Market tariffs on industrial goods are very moderate by both historical and international standards. In fact, they caused concern mainly in a few sectors of semi-manufactures and processed foods. This hit Norway much more than the other three countries, as Norway had very important export interests in metals and frozen fish. In particular, the Norwegian aluminium industry was competitive enough to sell across the E.E.C. tariff, but feared that aluminium capacity on the Continent would be expanded in response to the favourable discrimination awarded by the customs union.

Sweden had a more diversified export structure dominated by raw materials that were duty-free and engineering products that were neither very sensitive to tariffs nor subject to high tariffs. Finland had her exports concentrated to paper and the important competitors were outside the

Common Market. The main threat to Finland was that E.E.C. paper industries would expand their capacity on imported pulp, but this would have caused concern in all paper-producing countries. Finland did not stand alone on that issue.

The combined effects of different security objectives and different economic structures would seem to afford enough explanation for why the Nordic countries have not stood united on the E.E.C. issue. It has often been assumed, however, that a difference in ideological orientation is also important. Denmark and Norway would be more Atlantic and European-minded, while Sweden and Finland would be more isolationist and anti-integration. There are hardly any government statements to support this idea, however, and it seems likely that the difference in tone and vocabulary that may have been noticeable in the public debate as between the countries was rather the effect of fifteen years' experience of different security policy. Also, given the social and political similarities, one would not expect ideological differences to have a high explanatory value.

We shall accordingly assume here that the Nordic countries have adopted different E.E.C. policies, because of basic differences in security policy and economic structure, and that this has been the obstacle to the development of common Nordic economic institutions.

(2) *The E.E.C. today from a Northern Viewpoint*

During the 1960s there have been such changes in the political and economic character of the E.E.C. and in the economic structures of the Nordic countries that the basis for their E.E.C. policies and accordingly their attitude to closer Nordic economic integration is now different. The federal and Western alliance character of the E.E.C. has by now been all but effaced. In fact, Soviet military challenge has been replaced by American economic challenge as a leading argument for Western European co-operation, and the serious blows to supranational ambitions seem to have reduced the Common Market to a potentially very efficient instrument for industrial policy in the widest sense of the term. This has increased the possibilities for Finland and Sweden to reach satisfactory agreement with the E.E.C. It is significant that Sweden informed E.E.C. capitals early in 1969 that she is interested in membership.

At the same time the doubts about Britain's possibilities of achieving E.E.C. membership in the foreseeable future have increased. Denmark and Norway have no intention to try to get in without British, or at least Swedish company. Denmark must have the 55 million British consumers with her to have a chance of reaching an agreement with the Six on agricultural problems. The four Nordic countries have therefore been put much more in the same position vis-à-vis the Community. Moreover Denmark and Norway are not altogether attractive new members to the Six because of their large export surpluses of agricultural products and fish, which would increase the already formidable problems of establishing Community co-operation in these fields.

Sweden on the other hand can probably enter with very little friction, as it adopted an E.E.C. type of agricultural policy many years ago and has no need for exceptions other than those required to safeguard the credibility of its security policy. Her technically advanced industries are considered a welcome contribution to Western European attempts to meet the American technological challenge.[1] Finland, finally, in fact derives a certain strength from the weakness of her position. Her delicate position as a neighbour of the Soviet Union is now generally understood and there is hardly any risk that she would not be allowed to establish relations to an enlarged Community that took into account her security interests. There are no countries in Western Europe who would want to isolate Finland either economically or politically.

To these developments must also be added the fact that the E.E.C. agricultural policy has already been implemented. Danish farmers are no longer eager to get in early to participate in its construction. Paradoxically, Danish farmers may also have lost political influence, because the Agrarian Party is now member of a non-Socialist coalition government with a parliamentary majority behind it.

Finally, the economic structure of Denmark has changed considerably since E.E.C. was formed in the late 1950s. Agriculture is no longer a dominating sector in the Danish economy. Its share of export value was down to 38 per cent[2] in 1968 and less than 15 per cent of the working population was employed in agriculture. The loss of importance is, of course, partly a result of the adverse effects of E.E.C. agricultural policies on Danish agricultural exports to Germany. In fact, Denmark may be the only country to have had an efficient economic structure furthered by the E.E.C. agricultural policy. For even efficient Danish agriculture employs resources that could profitably be transferred to industry. Danish exports of manufactures have soared in the 1960s.

(3) A Nordic Bloc at Last

In this situation Danish and Norwegian fears of Nordic ties that could limit their freedom of action in E.E.C. policy have been reduced very considerably. The change may also have been furthered by the fact that new non-socialist coalition governments have replaced the Social Democrats in both countries in recent years. The Social Democrats have adopted very pro-Nordic attitudes in opposition and the two new Prime Ministers both come from parties that have been very hesitant about E.E.C. membership.

[1] We do not argue that this attitude is economically valid. The important thing is that it exists and affects policies.
[2] Of this a considerable share is value added in food-processing industry.

Early in 1968 the new Liberal Danish Prime Minister proposed that the possibilities of extending and institutionalising Nordic economic co-operation should be investigated. The proposals were adopted by the Nordic Council and passed on to the four governments concerned. A Committee of Nordic civil servants worked out a report that was presented on 3 January 1969.[1] The report is now being worked over and is to be presented in a more detailed form on 15 July 1969. A public debate will then start and a final decision may be taken during next year after the Norwegian parliamentary elections in September this year, and, perhaps, after the Finnish elections in March 1970.

The report proposes a customs union for industrial products, close co-operation on economic, commercial and industrial policy, some liberalisation of intra-Nordic capital movements, certain concessions to Denmark on agriculture and four common financial institutions: a general fund, an investment bank, an agricultural fund and a fishery fund. Further steps on establishment rights and industrial legislation are to be investigated.

As the civil servants concerned have been in continuous contact with their respective governments, their report is in fact to a large extent the result of political negotiations and compromise. It proved impossible to reach agreement before the deadline set by the Prime Ministers on the subjects of the customs union, on contributions to the financial institutions and on the question of new common institutions for the whole network of economic co-operation. On the latter question the Danes supported a system similar to that of the E.E.C. while the other three have expressed more sympathy for an EFTA type of organisation.

The attitude is on the whole very positive in all Nordic countries to these proposals for what is in fact something very close to Nordic economic union and is usually called Nordek. The trade unions and the Social Democratic parties in all four countries have decided favourably and they wield a very heavy influence in Nordic politics.[2] In Sweden there is really unqualified approval in all camps with only minor fears among farmers of too great concessions to Danish agricultural interests. In Finland the Communists are sceptical but this is no serious threat unless the political climate in Europe deteriorates significantly.

In Denmark industry is opposed to a Nordic customs union because it would increase the cost of certain imported inputs. Danish industry is strongly geared to finished goods, produced from raw and semi-processed materials that are imported duty-free. Danish effective protection to

[1] Nordisk utredningsserie 1969:1, *Utvidgat Nordiskt ekonomiskt samarbete. Preliminär rapport från Nordiska ämbetsmannakommittén* (Stockholm, 1969).
[2] See Declaration by the Trade Union Congresses in Denmark, Finland, Norway and Sweden of 14 November 1968 and Declaration by representatives of Social Democratic parties and Trade Union Congresses of 8–9 February 1969.

manufacturing industry is therefore considerably higher than nominal tariffs suggest and a Nordic customs union would erode part of it. Even more important is the fact that this industry exports a large share of its production duty-free to other EFTA countries, especially Sweden and Norway, whose domestic industries pay duties on such inputs. It is obvious that Danish industry does not want to lose that competitive advantage. It seems unlikely, however, that the Danish Government could turn down its own proposals, the more so as it has unanimous support from the parliamentary opposition.

Norway is the only country where there has been really vociferous opposition to the Nordek plans. Here it seems that security policy considerations and fear of Swedish big business in combination are the main cause of conservative and industrial resistance. However, it is explicitly stated in the Nordic Prime Ministers' declaration in Copenhagen in April 1968 that the co-operation should not include security policy, and Swedish big business is not very large by international standards. As Norway has already decided for E.E.C. membership, she would seem to have accepted already the risk of foreign takeover by really big German and British firms. The Norwegian opposition is, however, based on the belief that economic integration leads to political integration by necessity and that only Swedish industry has an interest in penetrating the Norwegian economy to a dangerous degree.

The idea that economic integration leads to political integration was held by the founding fathers of the E.E.C. as well. It seems to be supported neither by *a priori* analysis nor by the E.E.C. experience, but its existence remains an important political fact.

Even taking into account these disagreements, it is generally considered very unlikely that the Nordek plan can fail completely. The customs union may be watered down, but all four countries are now so committed that they could hardly let the whole thing come to nothing. Unless general political developments in Europe take a very dramatic turn, it seems safe to assume that a Nordic near-economic union with very closely co-ordinated economic and commercial policies will appear on the international scene in the near future. The only such dramatic event that can be foreseen today is the chance that President Pompidou may agree to take up negotiations about British entry into the Common Market. The implications of such a development will be analysed at a later point.

III. INTERNATIONAL ECONOMIC POLICIES OF A NORDIC BLOC

A discussion of the international policies that the Nordic countries may follow in the future and back up by the increased strength of common institutions does not have to be founded on guesswork only. There are both common ambitions and experience of extensive co-operation in the past to base the analysis on.

At the most general level it seems that the basis for the international economic policies of the Nordic countries can be expressed in the following terms. They are all small industrialised countries with high income levels made possible by far-reaching participation in the international division of labour. They are therefore whole-heartedly in favour of policies designed to facilitate international exchange. There are no protectionist groups with influence except in agriculture. At the same time their smallness and consequent weakness in the international power game makes them very eager to establish international institutions that can help to create an international society ruled by law rather than by military and economic power. This attitude is witnessed by their ardent support of the United Nations and their very active role in most global organisations and conferences.

Their general interest in international co-operation obviously does not ensure indiscriminate Nordic support for regional integration projects. A regional project cannot establish rules for the behaviour of others than its members. It may offer a desirable framework for relations with other members, but the small country's relations with the rest of the world will still be governed by military and economic strength. The group will presumably have more of that, but a small country will have to judge whether it will be used to further its interests. Similarly, it will have to decide whether the grouping will systematically adopt internal policies to which the political majority of the small country may object.

It has already been explained how such considerations have made it impossible before for Finland and Sweden to consider E.E.C. membership. For similar reasons all four Nordic countries have shown little enthusiasm for Western European political federation. They regard the economic co-operation as an end in itself and they all agree today that such co-operation could preferably be based on the Rome Treaty. The political decisions by the Nordic Prime Ministers on extended Nordic co-operation stated clearly that such co-operation should be designed so as to facilitate the four countries' future participation in or association to an enlarged European market. It also stated that the Nordic co-operation was to be compatible with their general ambitions to extend their trading links with third countries, liberalise world trade and safeguard the interests of underdeveloped countries.[1]

It is probable that these declarations were more than just phrases, as the Nordic countries have already managed to co-operate closely along those guidelines in the Kennedy Round, at UNCTAD II and in EFTA.

[1] Meeting of Nordic Prime Ministers in Copenhagen, 22–23 April 1968.

(1) Western European Economic Integration

The first and possibly most important area where the United States and Canada may be affected by the common Nordic policies is Western European integration. The United States has decided in the past that it is willing to pay the price of discrimination against its exports for the political benefits it expects from a united Western Europe. As pointed out above, the Nordic countries are interested mainly in the economic aspects of Western European integration and would generally prefer to avoid most or all of the results the Americans hope for.

There are, in principle, four ways out of the present deadlock in Western European integration. There could be a change in French attitudes to British membership. There could be piecemeal integration of EFTA and E.E.C. countries through commercial arrangements and co-operation in fields not covered by the Rome Treaty. There could be established a large multilateral free-trade area comprising most or all industrialised market economies and maybe other countries as well. There could finally be extended co-operation inside the existing organisations, EFTA and E.E.C.

The first possibility has attracted some revived interest since de Gaulle's abdication, as Pompidou is generally expected to allow negotiations on this issue. However, from the Nordic point of view there are two snags here. Firstly, it seems obvious that the British economy could not cope with the difficulties of adopting an E.E.C. type of agricultural policy and join the customs union without a very long period of transition. Britain does not merely have to maintain its present external balance. She must improve it considerably over the coming years. This implies that British membership must be many years ahead and the Nordic countries want to do something in the meantime.

Secondly, both the international monetary situation and the Community agricultural system make negotiations with Britain extremely complicated. The British pound, the French franc and the German mark have to be set in new relations to each other. This issue cannot be settled without American co-operation and presumably that of the Group of Ten, and it has to be done before the agricultural policy is settled. It will be very difficult to satisfy the French and German farmers and the British consumers and wage-earners simultaneously. For this reason and because both France and Britain want to keep down the number of small countries who could reduce French and British influence on Community affairs, the Nordic countries would most probably be excluded from the negotiations to begin with.

This would leave the Nordic countries to wait for a very long time, and their interests would be hurt by the final Franco-British agreements taken over their heads. Britain would probably have to sell the Danish farmers, as one of her strongest cards in these negotiations would be her 55 million

NA E 2

consumers, who could rescue the E.E.C. agricultural policy, and thereby the farmers, the Government and the balance of payments of France. The magnitudes involved are indicated by the following figures:

TABLE 5.1
UNITED KINGDOM IMPORTS
IN 1966
($U.S. m.)

From	Meat	Dairy products
Denmark	314	116
E.E.C.	65	44
Ireland	81	37
New Zealand	200	194
Australia	92	72
World	1048	546

Source: O.E.C.D. Series C Commodity Trade: Imports, Jan–Dec 1966.

The present shares of the E.E.C. in the world's largest food import market are very small and it is likely that Britain would have to play that card. Denmark would then take most of the beating and Nordic support of Danish agricultural interests could be important. The other three Nordic countries have very good reasons to hope that Danish agricultural exports are not squeezed out from Britain and the Continent, as this is bound to have repercussions on their own protected agriculture. Also, Nordic cohesion in the Kennedy Round was partly due to Danish willingness to allow agricultural problems to stay in the background and it would be difficult not to return this moral debt.

The British preference for dealing with the Six within the framework of the W.E.U. is a sign that Britain no longer has many interests in common with the Nordic countries on this issue. It shows both that Britain wants to have free hands in dealing with the Six, i.e. no obligations to Nordic or other EFTA partners, and that Britain is more interested in the foreign policy gains than in the economic gains of membership. Even though the latter attitude is logical in view of British economic difficulties, it means that Britain is not hunting the right animal from the Nordic point of view. The conclusion is likely to be drawn in the Nordic countries that they will have to deal with the E.E.C. question on their own with joint forces.

This is not tantamount to predicting a joint Nordic application for membership in the near future. This policy has been proposed from time to time by Danish top politicians in the past, but there are too many obstacles in the way right now. Nordic cohesion must be consolidated and the international monetary problems and the E.E.C. agricultural policy, which are partly connected, must be settled at least temporarily. There is also the EFTA commitment, which means more to the Nordic countries than to Britain. If the present deadlock should remain a few years from now, however, such a Nordic initiative might be possible and maybe even probable.

The potential conflict between the Nordic countries and the United Kingdom could materialise earlier in a different way. The mounting economic difficulties with British membership and French resistance have already lead to a proliferation of proposals for temporary or partial commercial arrangements between the E.E.C. and other Western European countries. These may now be said to be consolidated into the Harmel plan supported mainly by Benelux and Italy and the Franco-German proposals presented at the end of 1968.

There is an important distinction to make between intra-Western European arrangements according to whether they refer to fields covered by the Rome Treaty or not. In the latter case there are fewer objections by defenders of the Rome Treaty and by the United States government. There is already some progress registered in these fields. The Community has invited other Western European countries to a European patent conference and there may be proposals about Western European technological and scientific co-operation based on the report from the Aigrain group. The Harmel plan also meets these requirements as it is geared to defence and political matters. But for the same reason it seems to be doomed by French objections from the beginning. Neither does it offer what the Nordic countries want according to officially proclaimed policies: a wider European market solution.

The Franco-German proposals on the other hand are of an economic character and contain Western European preferences on manufactures plus concessions on agricultural products. These particular proposals may now be a dead horse, but they represent a principle that lives, the principle of increasing the degree of Western European economic integration step by step through negotiations between EFTA and E.E.C. countries. Britain, the United States and Canada all have their reasons to object to these proposals. Both Britain and the United States want the political gains of an E.E.C. with Britain as a member. There are no economic gains to either in the short run, as Britain lacks competitiveness and the United States would suffer a discriminatory treatment in Western Europe. So would Canada. The United States has protested officially in Brussels against the proposals, supporting itself on the GATT agreement. This is the traditional American line against all preferential tariff systems.

It is true that the United States has modified this attitude considerably, starting by sacrificing it to a political gain in the case of the E.E.C. It broke the rule itself by entering the agreement on free trade in automotive products with Canada. Finally, it has now given up its resistance against preferential tariffs on imports of manufactures from underdeveloped countries. It seems likely, however, that commercial arrangements between E.E.C. and EFTA countries would endanger American economic interests in such a direct way that these attitudes cannot be taken as precedents. The Nordic countries, on the other hand, do not have the same reasons to turn down the idea. They would probably appreciate the pragmatic character of this approach which would not force them to sign far-reaching treaties and they would then be free to go on with Nordic integration which would be a way of strengthening their bargaining position.

On the other hand it is difficult to reconcile this kind of policy with the GATT agreement, and the Nordic countries are very reluctant to weaken GATT. As was pointed out above, GATT is precisely one of these global organisations that lays down certain rules for behaviour in international trade. This will probably cause the Nordic countries to be very careful in taking a stand on intra-Western European preferences.

The question of commercial arrangements has a tactical aspect, however, which could give the Nordic countries a possibility of influencing the development of the European market question. For if they were to approach the Six on this issue of commercial arrangements, Britain and the United States would have to react. And it seems probable that the United States would then try the possibility of a large free-trade area such as NAFTA. There have already been signs of this kind of thinking. The Roth report delivered to President Johnson in 1968 contained the idea of a large free-trade area with American membership, and Mr Lawrence McQuade, who had a high post in the Johnson Administration, specifically referred to the possibility that the United States could react in this way if commercial arrangements between E.E.C. and EFTA countries were to threaten.[1] Seeing that the interest in a large free-trade area, which would comply with GATT, has increased in Britain even in parliamentary and government circles and that President Nixon's trade policy may be more liberal than expected, the chances of such scheme are probably greater than is generally realised. The Nordic countries would favour such an idea for many reasons. It would increase the extension of free trade and separate trade policy from general foreign policy again. It would stop the present tendency towards making trade liberalisation a Continental affair, which creates uneasiness in the Nordic countries with their traditional Anglo-Saxon orientation.

The Nordic countries also have reasons to regard a large free-trade area comprising North America, EFTA and E.E.C. as a step that would lead to world free trade in industrial products. For this organisation would presumably be joined by Japan, Australia and others, so that virtually all developed market economies would be members. As these have in fact just agreed to granting preferences to less developed countries on manu-

[1] See Hugh Corbet, 'Une Nouvelle Stratégie des Échanges Commerciaux', *Le Monde Diplomatique* (Juin 1969).

factures, it seems that their industrial tariffs would be directed against the state trading countries only. Trade with these countries is not really regulated by tariffs, however, and so it appears that a large free-trade area would logically end up abolishing itself in favour of indiscriminatory free trade.[1]

There is also the snag that the Six might not join such a free-trade area to begin with. France is worried about her balance of payments situation and has a strong protectionist lobby. In addition it seems that the Six face a very difficult period as regards agricultural policy. To the Nordic countries it would be a fairly simple choice, however, as a troubled Community with a protectionist France obviously would not let the Nordic countries in as members. A large free-trade area comprising EFTA, North America, Japan and Oceania would be the alternative to the *status quo*. Again Nordic co-operation would then be furthered and a Nordic economic union would most likely be the end-result. The Nordic countries must be expected to support a free-trade area also if it were to exclude the Six.

The fourth principal alternative open to the Nordic countries in European integration is further extension of EFTA co-operation. Their general feeling is that EFTA has been very successful in achieving what it set out to do, even though the Danes think that further progress on agriculture should be possible. They have all been positive in using the EFTA machinery for various new purposes, including contacts with the E.E.C.

Here again Britain is of a different opinion, as she wants to deal with the Six alone and does not want to use EFTA in a way that would indicate that she does not expect to become a member of the E.E.C. in the near future. There are, for this reason, very limited possibilities of doing anything in EFTA in addition to perfecting the present form of co-operation through work on rules of competition and the like.[2] From the Nordic point of view EFTA has achieved two very important goals, however. It has brought about intra-Nordic free trade in industrial goods and it has proved that the free-trade area construction works, even when consisting of countries with very different tariff systems and size and structure of economies. As suggested above, both achievements may have significance in a wider international context.

[1] This point was also made by the former Director-General of GATT in an address to the Canadian Club of Toronto in October 1967. See Press Release GATT/1006, 19 Oct 1967 (mimeographed).
[2] See Bengt Rabaeus, 'Current Work in the European Free Trade Association', and Charles Bruggman, 'Expansion Paths for the European Free Trade Association', papers prepared for a conference on 'The Stockholm Convention: A Successful Free Trade Area Experiment', sponsored by the Graduate School of Contemporary European Studies, University of Reading, and the Trade Policy Research Centre, London, at Sonning-on-Thames, Berkshire, England, 19–20 April 1969 (to be published).

(2) *Other Fields of International Economic Problems*

It is striking that the conflicts and interactions of interest of this Conference tend to disappear when the discussion of Nordic international economic policies is shifted from the Common Market question to other fields. There the Nordic countries have a unique record of close co-operation and they have generally been in agreement with the United States on important policy issues. It would, however, be much too big an undertaking for a conference paper to explore all the various aspects of all such international policy-making. There have been certain differences noticeable between the Nordic countries and the United States on aid to underdeveloped countries and on trade with state-trading countries. There has been much agreement on international monetary problems. It seems reasonable to restrict the discussion to the work of two international organisations where important commercial policies are being shaped at present, GATT and UNCTAD.

GATT plays a particularly important role, as it is the alternative to the regional liberalisation attempts that have occupied the centre of interest in the Nordic countries in recent years. GATT owes both its structure and its work methods to the peculiarities of the American constitution.[1] The United States and the Nordic countries both prefer the non-discriminatory approach with no formal surrender of national sovereignty. The Kennedy Round was more successful than expected and the Nordic countries managed to establish themselves as a trading unit that could negotiate as a fifth power with the United States, Britain, E.E.C. and Japan.

There are certain obstacles to further progress in GATT, however, which have to be taken into account. The ordinary tariff cutting is not as vital since the Kennedy Round, as the remaining tariffs on industrial goods are now, with a few exceptions, very low. In fact it may be that the developed countries now fear a new round of tariff cutting, because it would reduce their protection against imports of labour-intensive consumer goods from the underdeveloped countries. The Cotton Textile Agreement is a sign that the industrialised countries may not be prepared to go further in liberalising that kind of trade. The traditional strength of the major trading nations in GATT has always been an obstacle in these fields and was, in fact, the reason for creating UNCTAD.[2]

It has also been argued that the major obstacles to world free trade are now the existence of tariff disparities, non-tariff barriers and agricultural protection.[3] The European Community has and the Nordic countries will have a fairly even level of effective tariff protection, while the United

---

[1] See Karin Kock, *International Trade Policy and the GATT 1947–1967* (Stockholm 1969) chap i–iii.   [2] Ibid., p. 276.

[3] Gerard and Victoria Curzon, 'After the Kennedy Round What Trade Policies Now?', *The Atlantic Trade Study* (London, 1968) p. 14.

States in particular has very high protection for certain products and low for others. It has been assumed especially in France, that the method of linear cuts would therefore lower the general level of protection more in the former areas than in the United States. From this could follow E.E.C. resistance against a new Kennedy Round.[1] It seems unlikely that the Nordic countries would take this attitude, however, as there have been no signs of such thinking in official circles. It does not seem probable that this would be an issue between them and the United States.

Liberalisation of agricultural trade offers a very complicated picture. It is reasonable to assume that the United States and Canada will make further industrial trade liberalisation dependent on progress on the agricultural side. During his recent visit to Europe the new American Minister of Trade, Mr Stans, stressed the importance of getting support from the American farmers, who are traditionally for free trade, against mounting protectionism in industry.

It is difficult to see, however, how the E.E.C. could negotiate in GATT about changes in its agricultural policy which is so delicately balanced and which has endangered the existence of the Community several times. It is possible that there could be progress on selected products such as wheat. The Nordic countries might get a very severe test of their unity here as Denmark would have important interests to safeguard, while the other three probably would prefer to leave temperate zone products out.

The Nordic policy would obviously depend on what kind of agricultural co-operation the four countries would have established when GATT negotiations started. As no such negotiations can be expected until 1972, when the Kennedy Round cuts will be fully implemented, and probably much later, we can only speculate. If there have been no disturbances to Nordic co-operation, one could possibly venture the optimistic guess that Norway and Finland will have managed to rationalise their agricultural sectors considerably inside a Nordic framework. This would strengthen Nordic cohesion, but there might still be little enthusiasm for liberalised world trade. Regional agricultural co-operation might produce the same result in the Nordic area as in E.E.C.

Possibly Nordic countries would be able to meet American demands on cereals and compromise on meat, while retaining high protection for dairy products. This would not suit Denmark, on the other hand, and her agricultural interests were sacrificed in the Kennedy Round. It is clear, however, that there will be no obvious community of interest between the Nordic countries and North America on this issue which may dominate trade liberalisation work in the 1970s.

[1] The theoretical and empirical foundation of this view is by no means unquestionable; see R. N. Cooper, 'Tariff Dispersion and Trade Negotiations', *Journal of Political Economy* LXXII 6 (Dec 1964).

Non-tariff barriers have received considerable interest in recent years and are being investigated in GATT at present. There were also hints from Mr Stans that President Nixon may propose a GATT conference on non-tariff barriers for 1971. Such a Nixon Round would certainly get unqualified support from the Nordic countries, who have very few such barriers of importance and above all have a clear interest in reducing the differences between their small home markets and their large export markets. The United States itself probably has some of the most important non-tariff barriers, and such a conference would probably have a front line between the Nordic countries, Benelux and Germany on the one hand and the United States, Britain and France on the other.

Finally, Mr Eric Wyndham White[1] has suggested a sectoral approach, taking up certain industries for tariff negotiations again. In particular, it seems possible to achieve something in modern science-based industries. This would probably strengthen the result of the Kennedy Round in liberalising trade between developed market economies without reducing their protection against manufactures from underdeveloped countries.[2] This would leave such tariffs to be dealt with by UNCTAD, where many developed countries have already accepted the idea of preferences for the underdeveloped countries on such goods. This situation seems rather paradoxical and the Nordic countries must be expected to be rather sceptical. The sectoral approach was in vogue in the late 1940s, when it produced E.C.S.C., and it has ever since been considered uninteresting.[3]

Seeing that the Nordic countries have a principal preference for liberalising international exchange inside the GATT framework and have just been through negotiations that had very favourable results both in terms of lower international tariffs and of strengthened Nordic bargaining position, they will tend to favour new GATT attempts. It is difficult to imagine a Nordic initiative, however, for several reasons. Their common appearance is not consolidated and the complexities of Nordic and Western European economic integration will absorb their interest for several years to come. Even more important is the fact that the United States deals with GATT in such a curious way. The President needs a Trade Expansion Act from Congress and much of the GATT initiative therefore rests with the American President by necessity.

In UNCTAD, finally, there is now established such close Nordic co-operation that the four delegations to UNCTAD II in New Delhi had almost identical instructions. It was clear from the beginning in 1962 that the prospects for Nordic unity in UNCTAD were very good, and in New Delhi it was already a rule that they made common declarations. Reporting to capitals was divided out between the delegations to save effort. At

---

[1] Eric Wyndham White, op. cit.   [2] Kock, op. cit., p. 279.
[3] John W. Evans, *U.S. Trade Policy: New Legislation for the Next Round* (Council on Foreign Relations, New York, 1967).

UNCTAD I they had not yet a common line on general preferences for underdeveloped countries, which became a strategic issue. Denmark accepted this approach, while Norway and Sweden then agreed with the United States on the stand that such measures could not bring benefits that motivated a deviation from the GATT principle of most-favoured-nation treatment.[1]

On most other questions the new situation arose that the Nordic bloc voted against the United States and with the underdeveloped countries and the Soviet Union. This seemed at the time to introduce a new situation in their international economic policy-making, but during UNCTAD II the few roll-calls taken put the Nordic group on the same side as the United States. Both had then decided to support general preferences.

It seems that so far the Nordic countries do not have any policies on development and aid that lead to difficult relations with the United States. They have, on the whole, shown more willingness to accept the demands of the underdeveloped countries than other O.E.C.D. members, except the Netherlands and Canada. It is doubtful whether this indicates a tendency to disagree with the United States or whether it is a result of their being small. They may not expect to have their way, which is a chance the United States and other big countries have to take into account.

While the UNCTAD experience is too short to allow any conclusions of that kind, it is sufficient to prove that the Nordic block is determined to do its best to channel questions of trade and development through a global United Nations organisation and avoid excessive bilaterism. Here it presumably has more in common with the United States than with some of the bigger Western European countries.

IV. CONCLUSIONS

There are always uncertainties to handle in international economic relations, but it has been argued above that the uncertainties are greater than usual in the fields that concern the Nordic countries the most. The main reason for this situation is the reappraisal of the strategic question of Western European integration which has exerted a profound influence on most international economic relations in the last decade.

The conventional model of the situation can be presented crudely as follows. France is trying to keep the Community to herself to further her national ambitions, while Britain wants to get in to get a new leading role and improve her economic performance. The other Five want Britain in to balance France, while the other EFTA countries queue up behind Britain for more down-to-earth economic reasons. The United States

---

[1] Kerstin Wiklund, 'Norden: UNCTAD', in *Norden på Världsarenan*, ed. Åke Landqvist (Stockholm, 1968).

wants Britain in for the political gain of a United Western Europe, which is why the Soviet Union is opposed to the idea.

This model puts France in opposition to all other Western European countries and the United States and it follows that when French resistance is broken, for instance through a change of government, then a movement starts which ends up with a Community enlarged with Britain, Denmark, Norway, Ireland and maybe Sweden and with other EFTA countries associated in various ways.

We suggest that French resistance will not be broken in the near future and that the real obstacle in any case is the British economic weakness and the technical and economic difficulties of solving the agricultural and monetary problems. British ambitions are to reach agreement with the Six alone to get a token co-operation in foreign policy to make up for the loss of prestige suffered in the past from the vetoes on her applications. Real economic integration would probably have to wait. Finally, the experience of the past suggests that economic integration does not easily lead to political unity and we assume that the Community, enlarged or not, will remain an economic organisation, while political co-operation, if any, will take other forms.

From the Nordic point of view the conclusions would then be that Nordic economic integration is no longer a hindrance to participation in Western European economic integration of the kind that will be possible. As Britain has deliberately abdicated its leadership of the Nordic countries, they will moreover need increased Nordic co-operation as a substitute. Their success in the Kennedy Round has strengthened this view and the importance of the Nordic area to E.E.C. exports creates confidence in their possibilities of standing on their own feet in dealing with the Six. In 1966 the Six exported $U.S. 3·6 billion of goods to the Nordic group compared to $U.S. 4·1 billion to the United States, $U.S. 2·5 billion to the United Kingdom and $U.S. 0·4 billion to Japan.

Nordic economic integration is moreover parallel to that of the E.E.C. in many respects. The instructions from the Nordic Prime Ministers to the Civil servants working out the Nordek proposals state clearly that Nordic co-operation should be shaped so as to facilitate their future participation in Western European economic integration. The common tariff system proposed has been adjusted to that of the E.E.C. to a very large extent. The Nordic countries will therefore be in a successively better position to approach the Six, while the opposite may be true of Britain. This widening gap between Nordic and British interests could get a final impetus, if Britain either has to resort to quantitative import restrictions or enters alone in some kind of symbolic political co-operation with the Six, leaving economic co-operation for long fruitless negotiations.

The United States on the other hand is no substitute leader, as she has primarily political and strategic interests in supporting Western European integration. If the United States has its way, Nordic unity is endangered. The recent change in Denmark and Norway towards a positive attitude to common Nordic economic institutions and dramatically extended co-operation shows that they do not expect that the United States will have its way in the near future. However, the situation will arise that the United States and the Nordic group will have different ambitions and the latter will have more political strength than before to safeguard its interests.

On the other hand, the frustrations that both the United States and the Nordic countries encounter on Western European integration will tend to lead them to GATT initiatives. The United States favours this organisation because it is created specifically to meet American long-term trade policies and particular constitutional problems. The Nordic countries have the same interest in a non-discriminatory, global approach and are confident that their unity will allow them a role of some importance in the future.

While the Nordic countries thus seem to be in for a period during which their relations with the Anglo-Saxon great powers will be less close on trade policy than they have been traditionally, it is possible tht they will find themselves increasingly in agreement with Canada. This *rapprochement* has already been evident at UNCTAD II and it seems that the general trend in Canadian politics is towards more active international commercial policies.[1] It may be that the Canadian desire to reduce its dependence on exchange with the United States by increasing contacts with European and Pacific countries will bring Canada and the Nordic group on the same line in the future. There are also similarities in economic structure and similar attitudes on foreign investment and the multi-national firm that may cause them to enter into closer co-operation.

[1] See, for instance, H. Edward English, 'Transatlantic Economic Community: Canadian Perspectives', *Canada in the Atlantic Economy 2* (Toronto, 1968).

Discussion of the Papers by Mr Brittan and Mr Lundgren

Mr Shonfield introduced the paper by Mr Brittan saying that it raised a number of questions and Mr Brittan chased a number of his favourite ideas. He only chased them for a short distance, and had explained that he felt strictly bound by the space limit imposed on paper writers. This eccentricity should be explained to the more self-indulgent members of the Round Table. However, because of this conciseness some issues needed expanding.

In the early part of the paper, where Mr Brittan looked at some strands in British economic policy, he considered the way in which demand management had dominated British thinking. What did Mr Brittan mean by this? If there was a balance of payments deficit, what other method could one use? Or, if Mr Brittan meant not that he was opposed to demand management in principle, but to its particular shape in the United Kingdom, then he should clarify this. It was certainly true that Britain had used discriminatory fiscal measures rather than monetary policy, hitting such products as motor-cars and consumer durables very hard. Would (and will) monetary measures have been more effective?

In his discussion of trade philosophy on p. 90, Mr Brittan suggested that there were some changes in stable features of it. For example, at the bottom of p. 91, he talked of back-door protectionism; Mr Shonfield doubted whether Britain really was especially involved in this. The cases he gave – for example, the state reorganisation of the computer industry – were so commonplace that if this were regarded as back-door protection, then every country in the world was engaged in it. It merely made Britain more like other countries – not an exceptional protectionist.

Mr Brittan then went on to the question of how basic was Britain's balance of payments weakness. This was a fundamental issue which had already come up in discussion of the E.E.C., and would come up again in the discussion of EFTA. There seemed to be two issues. The first was that sterling was a reserve currency and therefore exposed to short-run movements of funds. The second was that export and import earnings moved in the wrong ways. Mr Brittan suggested that both elements were at the heart of our troubles and that they were of about the same order of magnitude.

Looking to the future, on p. 96 we came to the nub of the problem in a paragraph about export capacity. Mr Brittan said that 'the British export problem is largely a capacity one in the long-term sense that production facilities, design and sales organisation are not of a kind that can be easily or quickly switched . . . the problem is to secure more investment, in human as well as physical resources, designed to cater for world rather than British, markets'. If the British response to devaluation had been disappointing and weak so far, it was a result not of too little devaluation but reflected the fact that we had not been uncompetitive before. What had happened was that for various reasons we had not responded to market opportunities. Mr Brittan went on to look at the conditions required for improving Britain's trade performance. But at this point the essential condition for improvement, viz. the increase in the productive capacity of British industry, seemed to get lost.

Later, Mr Brittan proceeded, especially on p. 99, to ask how the United Kingdom should behave if there were a general currency realignment – which he appeared to think was likely to happen fairly soon. He asked on p. 99 whether if the United States moved to a freely-floating exchange rate, the United Kingdom should follow or remain with Europe. Mr Brittan thought it was necessary to move with the United States. He said 'If such a folly has to be committed, there would be an overwhelming case for the pound being tied to the dollar on the grounds that both the United States and Britain have been experiencing a long-term deterioration in their international trading position. Such a choice would be inconsistent with membership of a tightly-knit E.E.C., and this may, indeed, be one further reason for thinking about such membership.'

Mr Brittan had earlier given other reasons for doubting whether Britain should join the E.E.C. This was another. Yet if the dollar were to float, we could surely assume that other countries would allow their currencies to float as well. He saw no prospect that, all at once, the E.E.C. would introduce a common floating currency. Messrs Brittan and Lamfalussy had put the problem of doing so in an earlier session. He did not see this as a real dilemma; the individual E.E.C. countries would let their economies go in different directions.

The paper gave an interesting prediction of what would result from a second-best series of alternatives. It looked for a modest, insufficient improvement in the British balance of payments in the 1970s. It saw more protectionism – especially in agriculture. The British economy would be chronically weak.

Finally, since Mr Brittan had correctly identified the distinguishing feature of Britain's balance of payments weakness – the inadequate productive capacity – he wanted to raise a question about investment. How could a country like Britain raise the investment ratio (by which he meant 'investment' at large and not just in manufacturing) so that output responded more rapidly to market opportunities? The country needed a more rapid rate of growth in order to become more responsive; this was simply the other side of the medal. Britain had been the first country to have an industrial revolution; it now needed a special boost of investment characteristic of an underdeveloped country. How could this be achieved while equilibrium was maintained in the balance of payments? This was not just a British problem; the rest of the world would need to be involved in its solution.

Professor Lundberg said that the paper by Mr Lundgren contained common features with that of Mr Brittan. It was closely knit in its views on many political and attitudinal problems. He would therefore pick out some questions which were closely related to those in Mr Brittan's paper.

First, he wondered whether it was interesting for this meeting to look at the problem of a group of such small countries. He thought it was, because the four Nordic countries (Norway, Denmark, Sweden and Finland) together had large stakes in foreign trade. The E.E.C. exports to these countries were equal to their exports to the United States and greater than their exports to the United Kingdom. These were small countries, dependent on foreign trade and the way in which the world was organised.

Mr Lundgren thought that EFTA had succeeded as a free-trade area. EFTA was interesting, in that it was a free-trade area with no external tariff, which worked well. This had meant free trade for industrial products within the Nordic group. It was an example of lasting economic co-operation. Perhaps EFTA had now done its job and there was no future in developing EFTA any further.

One reason was the outlook and interests of the United Kingdom. The United Kingdom was not very interested in EFTA. Nice phrases came from United Kingdom politicians, but the Danes especially saw Britain as an unreliable partner in dealings with the E.E.C. Danish farmers especially resented agricultural competition with the United Kingdom and the dealings of the United Kingdom with the E.E.C. would be very much concerned with this. It was feared that the United Kingdom would sell out Danish farmers.

It was, however, necessary to keep EFTA in existence, not least for the co-operation of the Nordic countries. There were common institutional arrangements, and the common labour market which were there to stay. The problem of a Nordic union was perhaps close to being decided. The uncertainty depended on the relationship between the United Kingdom and the E.E.C. The four Nordic countries had different attitudes to the E.E.C. An old problem was how far the E.E.C. would move towards becoming a political arrangement. Denmark and Norway belonged to NATO and therefore had few of the inhibitions that Sweden and Finland had. But these problems had been reduced, partly because the difficulties which the United Kingdom had experienced in entering into negotiations with the E.E.C. had left the time to consolidate the Nordic Union.

Mr Lundgren referred to the difficulties of the Nordic countries – despite their homogeneity as a group in outlook on the world, in language, institutions, and their interest in the international division of labour. Danish agriculture would always lead to problems because the other three were more or less self-sufficient agriculturally. There were some fears, in Denmark, Norway and Finland, about the industrial competition of Sweden. In some ways, Sweden was too large – though she was also too small. Her national income was three times that of Norway. Norway was afraid that Sweden would absorb Norwegian plants in Swedish corporations. Though he thought all these problems would be overcome, they were very real ones.

On the attitude of Nordic countries to the rest of the world, Professor Lundberg thought that the creation of a Nordic union was not an obstacle to closer Western European economic co-operation. On the positive side, the weight of the Nordic countries would be greater when they were united. Perhaps they were biased, because they thought that countries were *unbiased* with respect to great-power complexes. Mr Lundgren pointed out that the Nordic countries could have common interests with Canada, not least because the problems of the O.E.C.D. were, as had been seen yesterday, of 'unknown' difficulty.

The Scandinavians liked a pragmatic approach. They would favour the step-by-step creation of a bigger free-trade area in the West by small movements. This conflicted with the GATT attitude – America and the Nordic countries shared the same attitude in seeing global solutions as possible.

Professor Lundberg said he wanted to stress what both papers said. In the future, GATT must deal efficiently with non-tariff obstacles to trade – with these back-door protectionist devices. Tariffs were now in most cases not the main obstacle to international trade. The real obstacle was back-door protectionism. These problems would be so much harder to deal with because they were not straightforward protection of trade, but an integral part of national economic policies. Older problems like full employment and growth had actively helped to reduce tariffs. Now, in most countries, national ambitions to development were changing – especially in Scandinavia. They were of a regional, structural nature. Sweden did not rely on the price mechanism for regional full employment and for structural development. Instead it relied heavily on public expenditure – for example in developing electronics, atomic energy, and public health. There was a move away from the general full employment approach, as indeed there was in the United Kingdom with the SET and the REP – to selective policies for further particular kinds of national and regional development. Capital movements also were being channelled with nationalistic aims. Non-tariff barriers would be important issues for future GATT conferences.

Mr Brittan said that so far as the paper by Mr Lundgren was concerned, he had been fascinated most by the description of the Nordic union's approach to economic integration. This was different both from the minimalist EFTA approach and from the emphasis of the E.E.C. on institutional elements and harmonisation policy at government level. The Nordics looked to the gradual approximation of behaviour and the assimilation of markets, with institutional arrangements simply reflecting what had already happened. When we came later to the problem of a wider E.E.C., we might learn a good deal from the Nordic model.

One could well see why EFTA felt that the United Kingdom blew hot and cold. He did not think that the United Kingdom's attitude was much better or worse than anyone else's in this respect. Perhaps this showed the difficulties that international trade organisations ran into if they were top-heavy. The United Kingdom carried too much weight in EFTA – and perhaps we should learn from this that a NAFTA organisation which excluded the E.E.C. would be much too dominated by the United States.

Turning to Mr Shonfield's remarks, Mr Brittan said that on the question of whether the pound would move more with the dollar than with the E.E.C. currencies, he had emphasised the tightly-knit structure aimed at by the existing E.E.C. The exchange-rate issue would be no obstacle to an E.E.C. which was working like a Nordic union. But there *was* the ambition of some in the Common Market Commission who were seeking a tightly-knit community based on fixed exchange rates.

There was then the question of what he had meant when he said that too big a load had been put on demand management in the United Kingdom. It was true that some people did think that the wrong instruments had been used. This was not what he was concerned with – he thought that the wrong choice of demand weapons was of marginal importance. What was needed was a *mix* of weapons going beyond the traditional ones of demand management. For example, there were exchange rates (his own preference), or the use of the GATT powers for emergency import controls. In part, the answer might be to finance, either by government intervention or by interest-rate policy, overseas investment by borrowing in world capital markets.

Mr Brittan drew attention to the revisions in the balance of payments arithmetic in the table on p. 93. One extraordinary feature of the last few years was that there had been under-recorded exports, recently, approaching £150 million per year. The under-recording had started in 1964 and had grown since. It was not right to say that the effect was simply to transfer the same amount from one negative item to others. If one looked at the table on p. 93, one saw that if the current account deficit was lower, then the effect would be mainly on items (4)–(6), which were short-term outflows of one kind and another, or perhaps even on parts of item (3). Had we had a truer picture of the current account position of the British balance of payments at the time, he thought short- and long-term capital outflows from the United Kingdom would have been smaller.

As for whether this paper showed an exaggerated gloom, he was sure that devaluation had worked more slowly than most people had hoped – but at least it was now having its effects. Recent figures for sterling balances and for British reserves suggested that in the second quarter of 1969 there had been a substantial basic surplus of £100 million. This was the first, due to more than freak long-term capital movements, since the winter of 1966–7. Economists would hardly need warning that they should not wave the flag too hard over this – with stagnant home demand in the United Kingdom at present. But at least it was a sign of movement in the right direction. Mr Shonfield saw the United Kingdom as a weak country, a liability to the international community. It was perhaps true that this was so by some absolute, ideal standard. However, he did himself expect the British balance of payments and rate of growth to be better in the 1970s than in recent years. But only when the Government could run its domestic policies without any distortion because of the balance of payments could we say that the 'balance of payments constraint' had been lifted. He did not see it being lifted in the 1970s.

On back-door protection, he did think that Mr Shonfield underrated this and Mr Lundgren had emphasised its dangers. Individual examples had been mentioned. Perhaps these did only take the United Kingdom up to the international norm; but we were in the early stages now. These measures came in with the Labour Government, but if anything the Opposition was even more taken up with this approach. Back-door protection was a small shadow over the situation at present, but it was not a British problem alone. It was a problem because defensible measures for structural change soon became back-door protectionism. If these proliferated all over the world, then there really would have to be a new, harder kind of GATT negotiation.

Professor Robinson said he was fascinated by the papers and by the introductions. He was as puzzled as Professor Lundberg as to which British activities in recent years really were parts of long-run policies, and which were spasmodic responses to short-run difficulties. What the world wanted was to know, not what the British wanted to do, but what they were doing.

Professor Robinson said he would like to look at another stated objective of British policy, that of trying to make the United Kingdom economy viable in the modern world. This was almost Britain's biggest problem. Big adjustments were necessary because of the disappearance of British assets in two world wars: they were also a result of the final disappearance of imperial advantage round the world. It was hard to say which of these problems were a result of failures to export because of competitiveness, and which were longer-term problems resulting from failures in selling and design. The British need was to contract the obsolete industries of the nineteenth century. Agriculture had already declined about as far as was possible. Coal, textiles, early iron and steel, railways and shipbuilding would have to decline as well. To a theoretical macro-economist, it was easy to say that this should be done overnight. When one turned to the applied level, it was a matter of judgement how fast one could contract large amounts of resources and transfer them to expanding industries. For example, one could look at the coal industry. If one tried to reduce this fast, did one produce unemployed coal miners or transferable resources?

Yet the main need was to expand modern industries. He had been fascinated by the paper by Professor Albert because so many European problems were also British problems. The question was how to expand the 'spearhead' industries. Britain's problems, like those of Europe, were that the British market was too small for many spearhead products. We needed a bigger market for computers, aircraft, etc. If one looked at the advantages of joining the E.E.C. in this sense they were real indeed. Joining EFTA and the E.E.C. together would provide a market for these industries in a more real sense than either could do separately. He thought that they had not sufficiently faced a good many of these difficulties in the discussions of previous sessions. He thought that the problems were very similar to those met with in East Africa, in recent attempts to establish a customs area between Uganda, Kenya and Tanzania. All the countries were too small to operate separately, yet together they could provide a market. The question was to which country each production unit would go. If all went to Kenya because it was bigger, then there would be problems for Uganda and Tanzania. The same issues were met in Europe. If all the spearhead industries went to West Germany, or to one other European country, there would be difficulties. Could one get a rational distribution or rational collaboration in distributing these industries? We had tried a little in aircraft. Britain and France were making the Concorde, and attempts had been made to make a European airbus. At the moment, the difficulties were more obvious than the successes. If Europe was going to operate as a series of separate nations then it was clear that there would be problems about where development should take place. This was a huge problem which the Conference had not yet tackled. The total European market was big enough for these industries, but would political and social influences prevent them being distributed satisfactorily?

Perhaps Mr Brittan was too good at preaching the pure doctrine of free trade. If one wanted these spearhead industries, one needed somehow to help them forward. It would not shock him if some back-door protection took place in relation to these spearhead industries. But we needed a more rational approach in handling these infant industries. This was where the conflicts with the United States began, and the difficulties of solving the problems were at a maximum. Just as developing countries had to take on more of the industries which Europe had developed in the nineteenth century, like textiles, so some industries that were now the backbone of the American economy would have to move into the middle range of countries, while the United States moved to the next generation of spearhead industries. He could see that the United Kingdom had thrown big problems on to the countries which had supplied the British market in the past, but he thought it was inevitable that such changes should go on all the time. Britain and Europe were quite different now from what they had been in 1913. This change was necessary. We had to accept that structural change took place all the time and not blame it on other people.

Professor Ashton said that one of the objectives missing from Mr Brittan's list concerned backward-areas policy in the United Kingdom. This reflected the question of income distribution. Regional policy now had a considerable impact on economic policy in the United Kingdom, and there had been large expenditures in the region in recent years. This government expenditure was the method by which something had been done in the 1960s. A recent paper by Mr McCrone showed regional public expenditure up to five times in the 1960s. Evidence could be seen of the need for this in his own area around Newcastle with traditional industries in a run-down state, and a large population with relatively low productivity. Equally, if one looked at social tension in Ulster recently, much of the underlying conflict arose because the distribution of industry policy had not been as successful as we would have liked. It did not always work well, and it always took time, as Professor Robinson had explained.

Professor van Meerhaeghe recalled that Mr Shonfield had drawn attention to what Mr Brittan said on p. 96 of his paper, about the need to secure more investment, in human as well as physical resources, designed to cater for world rather than British markets. Professor van Meerhaeghe was surprised there was no mention made of the need to increase productivity in order to cater for *both* markets. This applied also to the second paragraph. Professor van Meerhaeghe did not think he was alone in talking of overmanning in the British economy. An American industrialist, quoted in one of Professor Kindleberger's books, had stigmatised Britain as 'a half-time country, getting half pay for half work under half-hearted management'. Professor Harrod, in his review of Caves's book in *Economica*, stated: 'The British will not work any harder than they want to, just to bale the authorities out of their balance-of-payments muddles.' Of course, this was a matter for Britain, but Professor van Meerhaeghe did think that some mention of the possibility of raising productivity was necessary in the paper.

Mr Lamfalussy wondered whether Mr Brittan would develop his views on demand management. Why did he not say that there were mistakes in the mix of weapons used? Perhaps he would expand on this view, in the light of the fact that the I.M.F. had commented on the failure of the British to use monetary policy.

Second, on the British balance of payments, he wondered what surplus was necessary to repay short-term official debts, and if a surplus of this size was feasible? He was thinking of this, not so much from the point of view of the United Kingdom, because he did not think the balance would be achieved, but from an international point of view. What about the question of funding, if the balance would not be achieved?

Mr Lamfalussy said that Mr Brittan had swept under the carpet the basic question of industrial development. It could be argued that the United Kingdom had to replace declining by expanding industries, increased productivity, etc. We were back to the same basic problem. One way of doing this would be to increase the savings ratio. Could this be handled by economic policy?

M. Ferras said he wanted to return to what Mr Shonfield *did not* say. Mr Brittan's paper had missed the fact that the United Kingdom economy had to improve its performance within a world monetary system that provided a straitjacket for it. It needed a large balance of payments surplus, and this depended on the world monetary system. He did not see how the United Kingdom economy could reach the needed surplus, because the rest of the world would simply make it difficult. Mr Brittan might be right that the consequences of the present monetary system would be to lead to big changes in the United Kingdom, including a fluctuating exchange rate which was what Mr Brittan wanted.

Professor Izzo said that Table 4.4 suggested that British imports of manufactures were growing fast. It was known that they were constituted (i) by commodities, such as raw materials and to some extent food, required to contribute to the industrial process and whose growth was a function of that of industrial production; and (ii) by commodities which could be supplied either by domestic or foreign firms. If, as seemed true, the rate of growth of exports *minus* that of the second group of imports was less than the rate of growth of national income, the implication was that the competitiveness of the British economy was decreasing. Did Mr Brittan agree with Professor Harrod that a good deal of the problem arose from the way in which the level of demand was controlled (i.e. the so-called stop–go policy) which led to a small increase in industrial capacity? Was there a case for some change in the structure of taxation? For example, perhaps, one could substitute a value-added tax for the Selective Employment Tax.

M. Houssiaux said he was surprised by the contrast in Mr Brittan's paper between the argument about back-door protection on p. 91 and his conclusion on p. 101 where he described it as 'palpable nonsense justified by balance of payments fears'. This was an oversimplification, if measures to improve efficiency had been guided solely by balance of payments consideration. Without these, one would return to the problem of the development of particular industries which were relatively independent of the balance of payments. Surely the balance of payments problem had itself held back assistance to some British industries.

Professor James noted that Mr Brittan said that, since 1967, devaluation had not helped the British economy very much. He would simply say that in the present-day world no country could choose the amount of its devaluation independently. If it went too far, there would be competitive devaluation. Nor, indeed, could a country choose the amount of its revaluation. He was not surprised that the British devaluation had had few results. He wondered whether the world was now in a position where devaluation would always be inadequate.

Professor Wallich said he wanted to look first at the problem of the sum of surpluses. It was clear that individual countries which were being talked about all wanted surpluses – the United Kingdom, the United States, Germany and France. The picture which emerged was one of inconsistency of current account objectives, with no desire in surplus countries to finance other people's deficits. He wondered who had benefited recently from the big fall in the United States surplus from $8 billion to zero in four years. It was surprising how little the United Kingdom had benefited. Perhaps the reason was that surpluses and deficits were very structural. He did not think this was true of the United States, where the deficit was much more a result of minor inflationary movements. In the United Kingdom, there were more structural problems. Travelling around countries that were supplied by the United Kingdom he met the repeated observation that it was delivery dates, rather than the quality of goods, which held back British exports. He found it hard to see what one could do about this.

On the spearhead industries, he said a lot more would be heard of them during the Conference, but he wanted to point out that margins for improvement existed in other industries as well. Underdeveloped countries always wanted more industrialisation, but they then found that doubling the size of the industrial sector did not do much to increase employment. The real pay-off was still in agriculture. There would also be a pay-off in a number of countries from the installation of oxygen steel processes and this would do more than the establishment of a small electronics industry to benefit the economy.

Mr Brittan talked of a potential American gold embargo. He seemed to see a cosmic closing of the gold window, and floating E.E.C. exchange rates. Professor Wallich himself saw nothing as cosmic as this. Everything was a question of degree. He thought that European countries might feel constrained in taking American gold, but there was little likelihood of a floating European exchange rate. What was likely was gradual evolution, in as yet unpredictable directions.

Professor Hicks went on from what Professor Robinson had said to emphasise that a lot of the British troubles went back to a loss of position on current and capital account because of changes, partly due to the two wars. This was where one should start analysing the problem. He was impressed how far one could tell the whole story without taking any account of money at all. Working in terms of constant prices and ignoring money prices, one got the whole of the answers.

Effectively, the British economy had had to go through the drastic changes in structure which Professor Robinson had mentioned. The British people had refused to recognise this, and had tried to go on in the old ways. They had refused to accept the slow rate of growth which was inevitable while the exogeneous changes took effect. The balance of payments troubles in the 1960s came simply from this.

The three years when the balance of payments was really bad were 1964, 1967 and 1968. The position in 1964 was that the current deficit was matched by an increase in stocks. This had happened because of deliberate action by the British Government, which had tried to step up the rate of growth – but because we were still working in the 'old' way the policy had failed.

The deficits were essentially much more serious in the more recent years. They were caused by an excess of real consumption on both public and private account. Professor Hicks did not see how one could get out of the current difficulties without a high rate of investment, and room must be found for this. At present, a little room was finally beginning to be found.

Professor Tolpekin asked about the British position in world markets. The paper implied that Britain's export performance was relatively poor. What were the main reasons? Was it the low competitiveness of British goods? Or was there some hesitancy on the part of British exporters, who were not pushing their goods hard enough?

When Mr Brittan listed Britain's external economic policy aims on p. 87, the fifth aim spoke of the British anxiety to increase the liberalisation of trade. Yet at the same time Mr Brittan's paper spoke of back-door protection. What were the prospects for liberalisation in these circumstances?

Mr Maddison wanted to make a point on Table 4.2 of Mr Brittan's paper. It seemed very odd that a country so much in debt to international organisations could get its balance of payments figures so far wrong for five years. If this could happen by accident, perhaps other things were wrong as well. One only had to look at British tourists abroad to see that many of them were not content with the £50 travel allowance. Perhaps money which the Board of Trade statisticians thought was being spent on imports was being spent on tourism. British tax morality seemed to have moved closer to French and Italian standards and the statisticians must not have allowed fully for the increased amount of income concealed, or for the new kinds of tertiary-sector activity on which it was spent. For this reason, the measurement of income levels and of growth rates might also be wrong. It could well be that both the income level and the rate of growth were somewhat higher than imagined.

Mr Brittan replied to the discussion. He said he now realised that it was never wrong to say something in favour of virtue – hence he should have mentioned the need to increase British productivity and other pieties. He had not mentioned investment specifically because he was dealing with demand management generally. There were two sides to investment. There was the supply of savings; there was the demand from industrialists. This could be given a fancy name, or described as Keynes had done as a matter of 'animal spirits'. The position in the United Kingdom was weak on both sides. The margin of resources was not available; and when there might have been a margin available, 'animal spirits' did not exist, because the economy had been knocked on the head. On the demand side, the basic weakness was that industrialists hesitated to invest because they did not take an optimistic view of the future. They did this on the principle of 'once bitten, twice shy'. Whenever they took the predictions of British Governments seriously, industrialists found that emergency measures reduced the gains from investment. Whether this was wholly rational, he was not sure; would, say, German entrepreneurs have looked farther ahead?

On the demand side, the most important thing was to reduce the balance of payments constraint on economic growth. It was important that industrialists should not feel that investment was a mug's game. The emphasis in section VIII of his paper had therefore been on the need to increase Britain's competitive advantage in overseas markets. This was the one thing that would get the investment demand we needed. On the supply of savings it was impossible and perhaps undesirable to reduce the percentage of national income going to consumption very suddenly. One could not go from 15 per cent to, say, 25 per cent overnight. A rational economist and an unsophisticated elector would both resist this, and rightly so.

However, over a period of years, one could increase consumption rather less than national income. This would gradually increase the margin available for investment. If one looked at the growth of private consumption in Britain between 1964 and 1969, one would find a growth rather less than the output potential. In some years private consumption had been held back, while even in the others consumers had suffered all the psychological frustrations of restriction, yet those responsible for managing the economy had not been able to keep private consumption down.

The margin had been used in several ways. Part of the increase in income had gone to public consumption and investment. This phase was over. The trend of public expenditure was now in line with the growth of productive potential. Political pressures in the United Kingdom were likely to keep it around that level. Another part of the potential gain had gone in increasing the margin of unused resources. For structural reasons, when one wanted to switch resources to exports one could do this only if the rate of employment and activity were for a time reduced.

There were many calls on British potential now, as in the past. If one had a growth of the productive potential of 3–4 per cent, consumption could increase at 2–2½ per cent and this would leave a gradually increasing margin for investment.

Mr Brittan did not think that Britain had suffered from what was a simple capacity constraint. There was not enough capacity of particular kinds. If Britain devalued and deflated, as in 1967–9, in order to reduce home demand, increase exports and promote import substitution, particular kinds of capacity for exporting were not there. In the last six months, for example, from a broad macro-economic point of view, the economy in general was operating too far below capacity. Yet there were bottlenecks. In the engineering industry for example, orders had increased phenomenally. They had gone from an index of 100 ten years ago to 250. This was well above the capacity to deliver. The capacity mix was therefore more important than the absolute quantity of capacity.

Mr Brittan said it was clearly possible to extend the list of objectives on p. 87. He had tried to keep it short by looking only at external elements in policy. It was true that regional policy did affect overseas affairs, but he had tried to limit his list in the spirit of the title of the paper.

Mr Lamfalussy had asked some specific questions about the balance of payments and demand management. He did not himself think that the mix was right. What he said earlier might have given a wrong impression. For example, he thought it was wrong in 1968 to have been contracting demand through fiscal policy while, quite accidentally, expanding it through monetary policy. What he had tried to say was that this was not the only, or indeed the main, mistake. The British economy had been in fundamental disequilibrium throughout the 1960s. Apart from the need to cut domestic consumption, there was also the need to shift resources to exports and to import substitution. To have relied on demand management after 1967 (with no devaluation) would have meant a ridiculous and unnecessary increase in unemployment.

On the feasible balance of payments surplus, *The Economist* newspaper was said to have argued for a surplus of £300 million for ten years. Whether this was possible in the present situation he did not know. One should not treat Britain's central bank debts as repayable in three or six months. There were presentational advantages in keeping the impression of short-term debt, but in the end even governments would have to recognise the truth. One difficult problem was that any kind of international borrowing to further an increase in British internal investment was now pre-empted by the need to finance past payments deficits.

Mr Brittan did not take the view that the free market worked perfectly and did not suggest that there should be no help from the government in making structural changes. The difficulty was that back-door protectionist schemes were confused in their purposes. What began as an arrangement for a particular industry turned into a pretext to interfere with the export–import balance in various ways rather than altering the exchange rate. This was a perversion of the whole objective of industrial policy.

To Professor Tolpekin, Mr Brittan said that if one looked at international prices, there had been a long-term deterioration in the British position up to devaluation. However, even in given conditions of price competitiveness, there was some tendency for the British share of world trade to fall. As for the future, he thought that liberal trade policies would continue to be a major British aim, but as in the United States there would be pressures in other directions too.

Mme Marchal continued the discussion of the paper by Mr Lundgren. He had referred to the hesitations of Switzerland in joining regional blocs. This was true. Many Swiss had doubts about the purpose of setting up a market on a European scale. The other objection was that the Swiss were attached to their national sovereignty, and feared that they might lose their national identity. There were some Swiss who did not think this, however. Some claimed that one could join both regional and world groupings. Professor Rieben, especially, thought that Switzerland lived in a state of 'osmosis' with the E.E.C. and that part of her exports to developing countries would vanish if these countries did not earn the funds created by their own exports to the E.E.C.

On the political objections, one had to remember the Swiss were federalists and it seemed strange to argue that the principle that was the reason for the establishment of the Swiss nation could, if applied on a continental scale, be self-destructive.

Mr Lundgren had said that France was pursuing ends that were selfish and Gaullist. Mme Marchal thought this was unfair to General de Gaulle. First, because of France's veto which had kept Britain out of the Common Market, Denmark and Norway had been spared the difficulty of deciding whether to follow Britain in her attempt to join or to remain members of the Nordic Union.

Second, because of France's success in leading Europe towards a common agricultural policy, the Danes had been faced with a challenge which they had overcome by industrialisation. This was a benefit to Denmark. Mme Marchal thought that until now Denmark had been the only country to gain from the E.E.C.'s common agricultural policy.

Professor Kindleberger saw some ambivalance in the paper. There was love of the Market and of GATT; there was also fear of the Market in some circumstances. We were now told by our students that hypocrisy was the worst sin of the elderly. Was there not the same ambivalance (he would say that rather than hypocrisy) in the paper? Again, the Swedes seemed to fear Denmark and Norway, while both feared Sweden. To Professor Robinson, Professor Kindleberger said that Sweden had succeeded in bringing in modern industry without protectionism. This showed what could be done in a free market situation, despite what Professor Robinson had said about back-door protectionism.

Professor Rasmussen recalled that, again talking about back-door protectionism, Mr Lundgren said it was hard to eliminate. Some of the measures concerned explained the large increase in the importance of the public sector. Some had alternatives. Sweden had shown that there were other ways to reduce friction in an economy with depressed areas. The dilemma was whether to move industry into these areas, or labour out. Sweden had done very well through an active labour policy, as a substitute to this back-door protectionism. In part, the educational system was a substitute as well.

Mr Shonfield said he would like to take up the argument over the future of the E.E.C. and Britain's relations to this. In the paper, Britain was endowed with Machiavellian motives and a remarkable geriatric weakness. He was pleased to think that his country was vital in something – if only in vice.

The point was summed up on p. 122. It was argued that the Nordic countries were in a better position to approach the Six than the United Kingdom. It was also argued that the real problem was the weakness of the British economy.

How fundamental was this, and how much of an obstacle was it? If one took Mr Brittan's view that there was room for increasing the investment ratio, then the balance of payments would improve in the 1970s. However, he did not wholly accept Mr Brittan's optimism and wondered whether this was why Mr Lundgren thought that British economic weakness would dominate its relationships with Europe in the next decade. Even if Britain was relatively weak, she was not likely to have a slower rate of growth than in the past. The rate of growth in recent years had still been greater than in the early 1900s. It was not a question of exporting less. We were simply in an extraordinarily vital period for the capitalist world. In such a period, the relative position of the United Kingdom showed up unfavourably.

He did not say there were no other problems. However, if one talked of British economic weakness as a special factor, one ought to be clear what this weakness was. It was the failure to adjust the savings ratio to new realities. Mr Brittan argued that the adjustment was beginning. If it continued, and if the international community would give Britain longer credits, as indeed they were beginning to do, why should the E.E.C. be so against this allegedly decrepit and Machiavellian partner.

Professor Lebedev said that the U.S.S.R. had special economic relations with Finland. He wondered what Mr Lundgren thought the policy of the Nordic union would be if integration proceeded. Would economic relations between the Nordic countries and Russia develop along what he might call 'Finnish lines'? Or would Finland be moved farther away from the U.S.S.R.?

Professor Scott wondered whether the question was not how far state intervention would increase, but whether the liberalisation of trade was deceptive in the modern world because it was matched by back-door protectionism. Examples had been given during the session of the kind of regional policy which was being pursued and he thought this was likely to increase costs of production in the long run. As time went by, these devices would turn out to be not concealed but explicit protectionism. They would weaken the competitive position of the countries in question, and make trade patterns compulsory and rigid.

As for the Nordic union, some of its characteristics were those of a free-trade area. Others suggested political unification, and even increasing the mobility of labour and capital. He would like to refer to the latter. On pp. 110, 111 and 123, Mr Lundgren talked about the circulation of capital. In fact, Norway and Sweden invested in *Canada* and therefore capital went from Scandinavia for direct investment in Canada in industries that the capital exporters understood. Objections might arise in Scandinavia, in that external investment was popular with investors, who might resist the idea that their capital should be kept within Scandinavia.

Professor Scott said that Professor Lundberg had used the phrase 'the tail wagging the dog' and had spoken of international agricultural markets. He wanted to augment this. Perhaps the correct analogy was with small black markets for otherwise price-controlled commodities. Professor Lundberg referred to national schemes for social savings, and pointed to the difficulty of these entering the international capital market. Was the international capital market becoming smaller as a percentage of total European investment than before? Maybe this was a better example of 'back-door protectionism' than instances mentioned earlier. An illustration of this was the small amount of labour migration across the Atlantic. If the capital market was working as well as it had a hundred years ago, there would surely also be more labour migration. Labour stayed at home because capital did.

Professor Houssiaux commented on a remark on p. 119 of Mr Lundgren's paper about the so-called 'uninteresting character' of a sectoral approach to trade liberalisation. He recalled the Kennedy Round which was sometimes said to be a 'bunch of sectoral agreements', the Dillon Round and some tendencies to enlarge the scope of the two Cotton Agreements. He also recalled that, in many respects, the Kennedy Round had focused on industry-by-industry discussions. In some sectors, like steel, metals, chemicals and paper and pulp, it now seemed responsible to extend the 'sectoral approach' to trade liberalisation.

Professor Yamamato thought there were big problems for small countries. He wondered whether the Nordic countries would be in a better position if they were either to unite or to join the E.E.C. But there were difficulties for the United Kingdom in choosing. At any rate in the near future, namely the 1970s, four or five big countries or groups would continue to hold the leadership in international politics as well as in world economic affairs. Many smaller countries, whether developed or underdeveloped, should unite to defend their economic interests. This was one of the grounds for encouraging them, and especially smaller, developing countries to form a regional 'Economic Development Community'.

Mr Lundgren replied that, in general, the small fry of EFTA were backbenchers when it came to making commercial policy and being such a heterogeneous lot, they could not easily be treated together. What he had done was to exclude all possible developments among them except the Nordic economic union, as this seemed to be the only element of interest to the Round Table. However, such a union did not exist as yet, so he had to cover a lot of ground in looking at possibilities. Looking at the possible policies of a Nordic union he had to introduce a number of assumptions about what other countries would do. These had to be treated as assumptions. He obviously could not be sure what would happen in, for example, the United Kingdom, France and Switzerland. If his assumptions were proved wrong, that would be very unfortunate for his paper. All he could do, then, was to follow up the effect of any changes in assumptions on his results.

He agreed in general with what Mme Marchal had said, including what she had said about General de Gaulle, and he was prepared to reinforce what she had said about the effects on Danish agriculture of Denmark being outside the E.E.C. The rapid industrialisation of Denmark was not, of course, simply a result of this; but it had been given extra impetus by it.

Professor Kindleberger had accused him of ambivalence in his views on the benefits of free trade, when talking about the fear of Danish agriculture and Swedish big business. What he was saying was only that there were such fears present as political facts, not that he shared them himself. However, looking at what the agricultural position was like, one had to take into account social and regional factors, as well as economic ones. Change would have to be slow, and special agricultural policies were needed. The Norwegian reaction to the advent of Swedish firms was rather like the reaction of the E.E.C. to American firms moving into Europe.

He wondered whether Sweden had proved that there was no need for much institutional machinery to further economic interaction and the international division of labour. He was not an expert. He thought Sweden had proved very efficient in some industrial products, like ball-bearings. Similarly, the fact that there had been a big Dutch electronic industry before the founding of the E.E.C. showed that technologically-advanced industries could develop in small countries. It could be, however, that those countries which were already in a particular line of activity automatically had a lead, but that the establishment of such industries in the future would require more institutional integration.

He agreed with Professor Rasmussen that we needed to know how back-door protection could be avoided.

Replying to Mr Shonfield, Mr Lundgren said he did not intend that what he had said in his paper about Britain should be read as a safe prediction. However, he realised he had to defend what he had assumed about Britain. His remark about being Machiavellian was not intended as a reproach, but only as a description of the situation. This was true of most countries, and he was certainly not displaying anglophobia. He simply thought that Britain had little reason to consider the interests of other EFTA countries. As to whether Britain's economy was a sick one, the question was how bad the sickness was. He thought that his opinions were based on widely-held views expressed in newspapers, books, journals and indeed in the discussions of the Round Table. He thought it was agreed by most people that the problems would not be solved in five years, and Mr Brittan said in his paper for the Conference that there was a risk that Britain would impose quotas on imports. He thought that his assumptions could be generally accepted as reasonable ones, even if they finally turned out to be wrong.

To Professor Lebedev, Mr Lundgren said that Finland was an example of a country with a deliberate geographic position which had drawn the necessary conclusions for its security policy. That policy obviously implied something more than an official undertaking not to side with Germany in case of war. Finland probably also considered its international economic policy in the light of its general foreign policy ambitions. However, he did not like the teleological outlook implied in the question about what the effect of a Nordic economic union would be on trade with Eastern Europe. What happened would be the result of policy decisions concerning that trade. It would not be the results of the decision to create a Nordic economic union. His guess was that the share of trade with Eastern Europe would increase in all four countries in the future, not because of any change in policy but as a continuation of the present trend.

So far as direct investment across Nordic frontiers was concerned, there was already virtual freedom in the sense that permits were extended very liberally. Portfolio investment was restricted by legislation, and future plans were still vague. At present, it seemed likely that capital exports from Sweden to Norway and Finland would be encouraged. The proposed investment bank would help, but this was not so much a question of liberalisation as of governmental cooperation. However, the Nordic union would probably lead to extensive liberalisation of capital movements within a fairly short period of time.

Professor Houssiaux had rightly said that he had been too sweeping about the possibilities of using a sectoral approach. This was largely because he drew the line between sectoral and general differently. If one called the Kennedy Round an example of the sectoral approach, then he agreed there was room for it. On the other hand, if by sectoral approach was meant the getting together and talking, say, about electronics alone, then he stood by what he had said. It was too difficult to trade-off the advantages.

Finally, Mr Lundgren emphasised that if followed from his assumptions and analysis that the Nordic economic union would be a unit of the same size in relation to Europe as Canada was in relation to the United States. The Nordic group and Canada would to a large extent be interested in the same special problems, like finding outlets for agricultural goods, paper and pulp; formulating policies on multinational corporations, etc. This supported the conclusion that there was likely to be some kind of alignment between Canadian and Nordic ambitions. It would alter the situation quite significantly.

6 Portuguese Economic Development in the Presence of the Post-War Foreign Policies of the United States[1]

A. M. Pinto Barbosa
TECHNICAL UNIVERSITY OF LISBON

I. INTRODUCTION

The subject of this paper is the study of the repercussions of the foreign policies of the United States on Portuguese economic development during the post-war period.[2]

To provide a necessary background, some account will first be given of the evolution of the Portuguese economy during the period, emphasising those aspects that seem most significant and seeking always to integrate the various details into an overall perspective of the economic and social evolution of the country. Thus the whole paper attempts to interpret the phenomena observed, and deliberately avoids any merely descriptive record. Attention is concentrated on the relations between Portugal and the rest of the world. These issues in turn will, moreover, be examined only in so far as they concern the United States and the ways in which the more important foreign economic policies of the United States have had repercussions on Portugal.

The paper ends with certain conclusions, in which an attempt is made to bring together the central issues and to suggest certain problems for further investigation.

II. THE GENERAL TRENDS OF PORTUGUESE DEVELOPMENT IN THE POST-WAR PERIOD

The broad lines of evolution of the Portuguese economy in the post-war period can be summarised as follows:

[1] For the purposes of this book Professor Pinto Barbosa's paper is printed here, where it logically belongs. Owing to a misunderstanding regarding its intended content, it was much less appropriately discussed by the Conference in association with the papers by Robert Mundell and Gabriel Ferras (Chapters 11 and 12 below). The brief and rather inadequate discussion of it took place at the end of the session devoted to those papers. Readers are referred to comments by Erik Lundberg in the discussion of Chapters 16 and 17 below. (Eds.)

[2] I am very grateful to Messrs A. Labisa, E. Rodrigues Lopes and L. Arouca, of the Technical University of Lisbon, and to Messrs J. Andrade Soares and R. Martins dos Santos, of the Economic Research Department of the Institute of Economic Sciences, for their collaboration in the preparation of this paper.

(a) An average rate of growth of the national product by about 5 per cent.
(b) A slow modification of the sectoral pattern of employment, which has, however, probably accelerated in the last few years:
  (i) for most of the period, the proportion of the working population in the primary sector, particularly agriculture, remained high; only very recently has a significant decline of that proportion been seen;
  (ii) although progressively increasing, the rate of growth of the proportion of the population working in the secondary sector reflects, throughout the period, the difficulties of industrialisation experienced by the Portuguese economy;
  (iii) the proportion of the population working in the tertiary sector (mainly trade and public administration and defence) in the first stages declined both in total and as a percentage of total employment, but more recently has again been increasing; the proportion so employed seemed too high in relation to the general level of economic development of the country, particularly in comparison with that engaged in secondary activities.
(c) A more favourable trend in the distribution of gross domestic product by sectors of origin, reflecting significant differences in the sectoral levels of productivity:
  (i) a high, but decreasing, proportion of the domestic product originating in the primary sector: of particular importance is the product generated in agriculture, which, because of its large weight in the total product and of the heavy dependence of crops on climatic conditions, is still a principal factor in determining the trend of the economy;
  (ii) a growing share of the secondary sector in the domestic product; the whole of manufacturing industry, in the context of an industrialisation policy directed to import substitution, has played an important part as a dynamic factor in the Portuguese economy since the mid-1950s; during the 1960s a slackening of the stimulus of manufactures to economic activity in general, as a result of a number of less favourable short-term factors which may have been associated with certain features or deficiencies of a structural nature;
  (iii) constancy throughout the period of a comparatively high proportion of activity in the tertiary sector, particularly in respect of commercial activities and (mainly in the later years) of public administration and defence, and thus reflecting not so much the high share of the tertiary sector familiar in advanced industrial economies as a deficient structure in the sector; the excessive weight of commercial activities is

particularly to be noted, which derives principally from historical factors.

(d) Stability of internal financial conditions and in the balance of payments:
  (i) after a comparatively short period of strong inflation, resulting from post-war reconstruction and return to normal working conditions, there followed, through most of the 1950s and the early 1960s, a period of monetary stability which, in certain respects, represented a well-defined phase of Portuguese development; thereafter, as a result of factors which previously had either been absent or less potent, inflationary strains, though moderate, were generated; among the factors responsible the following seem to have been the most relevant:
  a process typical of imported inflation;
  a large increase in the average level of wages, particularly of the agricultural wages, associated with the growth of emigration;
  a relative shortage of domestic supplies (both in total and in variety of products) in face of strong pressures of demand and associated with considerable rises and changes in the consumption standards, especially in the more developed areas of the country;
  a heavy increase of public expenditures;
  (ii) a policy of equilibrium and stability of public finance;
  (iii) an accumulation of balance of payments surpluses;
  (iv) a certain rigidity and, in some respects, a comparative conservatism of the credit system, especially in relation to the needs of financing economic development.

(e) Strong dependence of the economy on the outside world:
  (i) through recourse to imports to meet basic needs of foodstuffs, raw materials and capital goods;
  (ii) through dependence on the stimulus to domestic activity represented by exports;
  (iii) through the decisive part played by certain current invisible exports, especially private transfers and more recently tourism, in the favourable balance of payments.

III. THE SIGNIFICANCE OF THESE FEATURES FOR PORTUGUESE DEVELOPMENT

It would be of little relevance to analyse the factors described above in comparison with similar events in other countries, for none of the possible alternatives can be set against the background of the general long-term development of the Portuguese economy.

The significance of each of the five items mentioned above is not equally important (nor even similar). In practice, whereas the first major feature represents, as will be realised, a mere quantitative measurement of the total rate of development, the second and third features correspond roughly to the standards common to development in all countries which have not yet attained the most advanced stages. Entirely different is the situation in respect of the remaining features mentioned, since monetary and financial stability and balance of payments equilibrium represent, as a rule, a constant feature of Portuguese economic policy throughout the post-war period, in sharp contrast not only to other countries of comparable economic development, but also, one may say, to the generality of all countries.

On the other hand, the interrelationship of the Portuguese economy with other economies and the extent of and changes in its dependence on the outside world possessed particular features which make any simple generalisation impossible. Only the last two issues will, therefore, be considered at some length. Thus, after a general consideration of Portuguese economic development, a working hypothesis will be sought to explain these characteristics of monetary and financial stability and balance of payment equilibrium in the form of a political and financial mechanism of reaction to somewhat difficult financial problems. Such a mechanism is of a somewhat unusual character and its origins, features and applications can only be interpreted in the historical, economic and political context of the Portuguese society where it operated. Thereafter, the broad features of the dependence of the Portuguese economy on the outside world will be briefly set out. Finally, special attention will be devoted to the relations with the United States.

IV. THE PROCESSES OF CHANGE

The development of the Portuguese social economy, in the two senses of the change of economic structures and of the evolution of the sociological context of those structures, does not represent an independent process: the forces which led to the changes that were taking place did not originate in internal conditions. On the contrary, they derived from efforts to adapt to stimuli or shocks, of a more or less directly economic nature, originating outside and impinging on more or less stable equilibrium conditions attained by the Portuguese social economy. The initial process of introduction of modern industry was late in comparison with that of the main Western European countries and, above all, it assumed a remarkably peripheral character, leaving untouched many clearly pre-industrial areas which, in surviving, remained as factors contributing rigidity in the economic development.

An important feature in all these processes has been a relative maladjustment between the rate of change in economic structure and that of the parallel political change. Thus, the intermixture of political concepts originating or in practice abroad and internal political concepts (of a more clearly traditional character) was facilitated, especially in the late nineteenth and early twentieth century, by the weakness and state of dismemberment of the then existing political structures.

A doubly critical situation would thus have been created: on the one hand, a more or less superficial political change not accompanied by any corresponding change in economic structures; on the other hand, as mentioned above, such a political change, in some cases of a revolutionary character, as did not reflect any actual change originating in Portuguese society, but merely an intermixture, more or less adequate to that society, of certain lines of political thought originating in wholly different sociological contexts.

Certain stresses were thus created which, in the course of time, might have two basic types of solution:

(a) One solution would be the possible reaction of the whole society to the stimulus formed by the strain of maladjustment between the different elements of its structures, taking the form of an acceleration of the process of modernisation of the various socio-economic structures, and thus establishing a consistent pattern of development of the whole society through a comparatively self-consistent set of structural changes.

(b) The other solution would involve the whole dynamic potential of such an interstructural strain of the Portuguese society becoming predominantly absorbed through a process of political transformation resulting from the shock of conflicting ideological currents, and leading to subordination to it of the practical aspects of the implied socio-economic transformation.

Actual events showed that, of these two basic alternatives, the one that predominated was the latter, thus maintaining for some decades, particularly in the early twentieth century, a sharp conflict between the economic structures and the general trends of the major political centres, especially Lisbon and Oporto.

An important process of political evolution thus appeared in Portugal, the main consequence of which was the outburst involving the destruction of the traditional society.[1]

[1] In the present study, when the expression 'traditional society' is used, what is meant is the actual Portuguese society of the period that preceded the appearance of Liberalism in Portugal – to be more precise, the society of the eighteenth century and of the early decades of the nineteenth century.

That period will correspond to a well-defined situation of existence of that 'traditional society'; many of its elements, mainly in terms of socio-economic structure and in the most backward areas, will persist for many decades. The text refers, particularly, to the

With the turn of the century (more strictly in the first two decades of the twentieth century) the dominance achieved in Portugal by the purely political aspects of the total problems became more accentuated, reducing to a secondary position the more practical problems of a social and economic nature.

If to this politicalisation we add an intense political instability and the continued aggravation of the chronic problem of public finance, severe monetary instability, an excessive external indebtedness and the consequent weakness of external credit, it is easy to understand the abnormal importance attached to the question of the equilibrium of the State budget.

Two fundamental problems have thus emerged, which affect the whole Portuguese social and economic organisation:

(a) On the one hand, concern to escape from the phase of political instability and unrest that characterised the period down to the end of the first quarter of the twentieth century, involving a very strong effort to achieve internal political stability; this naturally implies a certain caution regarding changes, both economic and social, in which the economic development is given effect, even though in practice some of the basic conditions have been laid down.

(b) On the other hand, the need (partly as a result of political considerations implied in the general ideas of the preceding paragraph) to overcome the difficulties resulting from financial disequilibrium led to an intense effort directed to achieve financial reconstruction and at the same time to accelerate growth – but a growth acceleration in the general context of a primarily stabilising control.

It is the combination of these two lines of reasoning that has led to the policy which includes in the Portuguese plans for economic development the special feature, just mentioned, of emphasis on monetary and financial stability. This feature, it would appear, has led to two different kinds of consequences: on the one hand, it may have led to a deliberate slowing down of certain development policies which might have accelerated the transformation of the Portuguese social economy and to its subordination to the safeguarding of certain equilibria regarded as fundamental – mainly those of an economic and social nature; on the other hand, it may have assured the effective creation of basic conditions favourable to a more rapid acceleration of economic development with a minimum of financial and balance of payments problems.

---

period of destruction of the traditional society which, as previously said, can be considered to have started in the middle of the nineteenth century.

Having regard to the adjustments always needed between a theoretical and general concept and the observation of a particular and concrete reality, it seems that the concept of "traditional society', in the sense used in the text, is a close approximation to Hagen's 'rural society'.

V. PORTUGAL AS AN ECONOMY DEPENDENT ON THE OUTSIDE WORLD

The second important feature in the development of the Portuguese economy that deserves special attention is that of its relation with the outside world. This problem can be considered, within the line of analysis we have adopted, from two fundamental viewpoints: on the one hand, that of the existence in Portugal of features common to the generality of the countries in an analogous economic state; on the other hand, an attempt to identify special circumstances in the Portuguese case.

The most important of all common features and, simultaneously, that of the most general character is split into a double perspective:

(1) Within the framework of the traditional society and economy, there grew up, although with some changes in its detailed product composition and in the direction of its trade flows (with which we are not concerned for the moment), a trade consisting of the export of agricultural staple goods, closely linked to the international maritime routes, with its counterpart in import of other agricultural products (mainly cereals) and of manufactures and luxury goods; in relation to these trade flows (both imports and exports) it is to be admitted that they did not affect substantially the internal working of the economy.[1] This general feature concerning the participation of the Portuguese economy in international trade[2] was to persist down to the middle of the nineteenth century;

(2) Within the framework of the transition of Portugal towards an economy in the early stages of industrialisation and all the complex structural changes that accompanied it, the repercussions of its international trade on the working of the internal economy began to be of significance; they have subsequently been strongly accentuated and the Portuguese economy has acquired a dependence on the outside world in the respects mentioned in section II above through the consequent effects on total supply and demand.

An examination, even superficial, of the various aspects of the relations between the Portuguese economy and the outside world immediately emphasises, as the most significant, the two following:

[1] The most significant effects that could be detected may presumably be reduced to the repercussions caused by the changes of the economic structure of the countries importing the Portuguese products, which in turn had repercussions on the Portuguese balance of payments, but not, as is emphasised in the text, on the deeper reality of the country's economic life, quite apart from their small scale.

[2] Taking into consideration the above-mentioned changes in the trade flows (especially those resulting from the successive political rearrangements associated with the evolution of European countries) and in the products traded, as well as the changes resulting from the successive stages of the trade between Metropolitan Portugal and her overseas territories.

(a) The process of Portuguese expansion throughout the world, the effects of which have always been reflected in the general development of Metropolitan Portugal; and

(b) the dominant role played by England in the linking of the whole of the Portuguese economy (Metropolitan Portugal and overseas territories) to the international economy.

As to the first of these points, although it refers to an element wholly integrated into the Portuguese history of the past five centuries,[1] this analysis of the implications in terms of post-war issues will be conducted in relation only to Metropolitan Portugal – leaving thus aside any analysis of the reciprocal relations established between the various territories, but emphasising the important role played by the Portuguese overseas territories not only on the development of Portugal's external relations, but also, in a particularly significant sense, on the whole of the Portuguese status in the world.

The predominance of England in the external relations of the Portuguese economy has deep roots of an historical and political nature, although some more strictly economic motivation is also to be found, closely linked to the main power lines of the international life of both States.

As a result of a complex set of causes, the changes in this trade were to have repercussions, especially on the development of the Portuguese economy. The expansion of the trade reached its maximum in the course of the nineteenth century, and especially its second half; this was precisely the period during which the first stage of transition occurred of the Portuguese traditional society towards a liberalism-inspired society, within which the first steps in industrialisation and economic modernisation were taken.

The influence of Britain cannot be measured in terms of the British share (large as it was) in imports and exports of goods. To that all the rest that seems fundamental must be added, especially the capital inflow, both in the form of loans (often linked to the precarious financial position of the State) and as direct investments, and, above all, the presence in Portugal of a wealthy and privileged British colony engaged in certain important economic activities.

More recent trends have shown a decline of the British share in Portugal's foreign trade, especially in the last decades. This is after all no more than the counterpart of the wider phenomenon of the improvement

[1] In relation to this aspect it is to be noted (although the point does not form a part of the present analysis) that the special relations between the economies of Portugal and Brazil during the colonial period and the extraordinarily important part played by the latter country in the whole of the external situation of the Portuguese economy, especially as concerns international payments down to the early decades of the twentieth century, form a subject deserving special attention.

that has progressively taken place in the geographical diversification of Portuguese external trade, although the United Kingdom still retains an important place in the complex of Portugal's foreign relations.

The Portuguese economy began, although on a small scale, as has been previously mentioned, its industrialisation process during the nineteenth century. In the period following the Second World War, after securing its internal stability in the ways and circumstances described above, Portugal appears to have achieved the possibility of developing towards effective self-sustained growth; it shows, in this respect, some of the features characteristic of an economy under development; on the other hand, certain conditions and limitations resulting from its relative retardment as compared with the other industrialised economies still persist.

Considering in this broad context the problem of Portuguese external relations, it seems reasonable to speak of a twofold trend, the understanding of which is especially relevant for a long-term perspective of such relations: on the one hand, there is some improvement in the geographic distribution of Portugal's relations, which has shown itself mainly through opportunity to offset the loss of some traditional connections which, in addition to involving a degree of dependence, increased the economy's vulnerability and affected its development; on the other hand, there still persists a very strong tendency to exercise an attraction on the world-dominant economy.

It is this line of reasoning that seems to explain the development of the mutual relations between Portugal, on the one hand, and England and the United States on the other. There can thus be found that conflict of tendencies which, in the last analysis, is nothing more than the repercussions on a small economy of the changes that have occurred during the first half of the twentieth century in the structure of world economic power.

Such a change representing the basic phenomenon of the entire rearrangement of the modern international economy had (and will continue to have) its effects in every country. In Portugal, it has forced the readjustment of her relations from an economy to which she is traditionally linked (and in relation to which strong links still remain) to another towards which she is attracted (the United States).

It must, however, be realised that a general survey of the Portuguese situation, as seen in the perspective of the growth of the post-war international economic organisations, must take account also of the repercussions on Portugal of the various European economic co-operation and integration movements. Here once again is to be found, as a fundamental feature of her policy, the need to adjust herself to a change originating outside, since her economy is of relatively small current 'size' (though with strong potentialities in the international scene) when confronted with much more complex, advanced and stronger economies and groupings of economies. As the study of this aspect of Portuguese participation in international economic life does not fall within the scope of the present paper, only this mention is made of a very important issue.

VI. THE EFFECTS ON THE PORTUGUESE ECONOMY OF THE POST-WAR FOREIGN POLICIES OF THE UNITED STATES

If one attempts to classify the economic foreign policies of any country, regarded in terms of their relation to the major forces affecting that country's internal economy, under the two broad heads of structural measures and conjunctural measures, one may perhaps say that, measured by their repercussions on post-war Portuguese economy, the most significant United States policy measures under the first head have been:

the disposal of agricultural surpluses;

the protection of the American economy, either directly (through customs duties and quantitative restrictions) or under several other more subtle forms, summarised under the general title of 'administrative protectionism';

diplomacy, exercised on an economico-political base, directed to liberalisation of the economic relations among other countries;

a continuing aid and assistance policy in a variety of fields and under a multiplicity of shapes, among which Marshall Aid had a special importance and implications.

On the basis of the last of these there has been a progressively increasing supremacy of the United States in the whole world economy. Although this fact does not reflect any one particular economic policy measure but is the result, perhaps inevitable, of the growth of the American economy in comparison with that of other economies, it is on this fact that essentially depend many of the more positive measures included under separate heads.

Under the head of conjunctural measures, those that are of special interest for their repercussions on the Portuguese economy are those consequent on the current position of the United States balance of payments, and especially those affecting the capital transactions, the remittance of profits and tourism.

The Balance of Payments as a Reflex of the Reciprocal Relations of Both Economies

For the analysis of the influence of economic policy measures adopted by a dominant economy on the development process of another relatively weaker economy, it is obvious that a record of the different transactions through bilateral balances of payments measured on an annual basis may be no more than a shadow, at most approximate, of the deeper realities we need to study.

The effects of domination, or of dependence (which amounts to the same thing), between economies are much less associated with trade transactions than with certain current invisible items and especially with certain capital transactions; and even these features as a whole will perhaps be less significant than certain more specific kinds of direct penetration, involving control of certain key positions. We thus refer to the balance of payments pattern, only to support the general line of argument that is being advanced, and with the varying importance clearly in mind of different kinds of items that are recorded; our attention is centred throughout not on the balance of payments in itself but on the more profound realities it partially but incompletely reflects.

In respect of goods transactions, the relevant features for the problem under examination are essentially two:

(a) The relatively low United States share in the total of Portuguese foreign trade, which is primarily with European countries.

(b) Two well-marked and clear-cut cases of direct and immediate influence of certain types of United States foreign economic policy on the development of the Portuguese economy, one connected with Portuguese imports, the other with exports. These two most important cases are:

(i) in consequence of permanent insufficiency and substantial conjunctional fluctuations in certain agricultural products, especially wheat, Portugal regularly makes large imports of American wheat; as the result of American policy for the disposal of agricultural surpluses, not only the continuity but also the terms on which this essential import for the Portuguese economy will be provided depend on the formulation of this policy;

(ii) a more serious matter is the grave obstacles imposed against the export of various Portuguese products, especially manufactures, by the United States protectionist measures. It is not necessary, in this paper, to multiply the examples;[1] it is important to emphasise here the obvious relation of dependence between a less developed economy, needing to secure access for its products to the largest world market, and the dominant economy, anxious to protect the equilibrium of its internal production structure, an aim that it successfully achieves by adopting more or less obvious protectionist measures.

We must, however, emphasise the damaging features of such

[1] We might mention, among others, the cases of textiles, canned fish and machine-tools.

policies when seen from the point of view of their repercussions on the Portuguese economy, in that they invalidate much of the export promotion policy, which is indispensable to the acceleration of Portuguese development; this is in effect an actual example of the general obstacles imposed in highly industrialised economies on the entrance of manufactured products coming from less developed economies when these might compete, in some cases with advantage, with internal products.

If one turns to the items recorded as current invisibles, tourism has a special importance to our problem together with private transfers and income from capital investments.

Although, as regards tourism, it is obviously unreal to speak of dependence, the problem becomes more meaningful when one considers the vulnerability of an economy that has a surplus under this heading of invisibles (which is the case with Portugal) when the other country concerned adopts economic policy measures (even if they may be regarded as being of a conjunctional character) which restrict either the exit of tourists or the amounts of their expenses abroad. Such a policy always has serious repercussions on the expected receipts from tourism of the country with a favourable balance, even when those receipts are considered in aggregate. But, as may be appreciated, the fall of receipts has particular significance if the decline of the expected tourist inflow affects the receipts of the principal international payments currency; moreover, in terms of the management of the internal economical policies of the country concerned, it will have even more serious effects if tourism has been regarded as a leading sector in the development programme, as has been the case of the Third Portuguese Development Plan, now in operation.

As is well known, Portugal is a country with a large emigration which, for a variety of reasons, has greatly increased during the past decade. In addition to the normal effect of emigration on the private transfers component of the balance of payments which in the case of Portugal is very considerable, the important role played by this large emigration as a catalyst in the overall long-term development of Portugal cannot in these days be denied. This is a matter of great importance, but its centre of gravity is obviously not in the connections of Portugal with the United States but with various Western European countries, especially France and Germany. For that reason it will not be examined in detail in this paper.

Of a greater interest to our immediate concerns is the analysis of the main features, not of human migration but of that other phenomenon that may be called 'enterprise migration'. In this sense, more than in any other, the figures in the balance of payments fail to provide a complete picture of what is actually happening; as the figures need no comment, we may more usefully try to explain and interpret our more direct knowledge of the actual course of events.

The presence of American companies in Portugal, either directly or in the form of participation on favourable terms in Portuguese enterprises, has been increasing in recent years. This, besides reflecting the interest of United States capital in the potentialities of the Portuguese economy (chiefly in areas outside Europe) and the favourable conditions offered either in the shape of political, social and financial stability or of liberal legislation in respect of external capital,[1] may also be regarded as the spread to Portugal, with a certain time lag, of the more universal phenomenon of American firms seeking a position in the various European economies. We come thus to the nub of the whole question of the dominant economy attitude of the United States, in relation to the Old World. Statistical measurement, theoretical analysis, scientific study, political application, detached impartial and realistic description as well as passionate and unreasoning reaction over this basic problem of post-war international economic life – none of this is new, and of course it will long continue and may ultimately reach some conclusion. For the moment we can only stress the repercussions on the economic development of Portugal.

Following precedent, it is probably of advantage to separate two basic types of effects associated with the presence of such enterprises within the Portuguese economy:

(a) On the one hand, and this may be the more important feature, they are a dynamic element encouraging the introduction of 'innovations' in Portuguese economic life, contributing to an extent we regard as significant to a modernisation in self-defence of structures and mentalities which has increased in recent years.

(b) At the same time, the presence of such enterprises, and especially the great disproportion of their competitive power to that of their local competitors (when there are any), creates in practice and to an increasing extent a real position of economic dependence of Portugal[2] in relation to the United States; this affects the general prospects of achieving an optimal use of resources on an international scale and

---

[1] Foreign capital, the authorisation of which is always granted, provided it is meant for undertakings considered of interest for the economic development, is under a regulation that does not restrict either the repatriation of the investment settlement amount and its accruals, or the transfer of its income. That regulation is applicable, with no discriminations as for its origin, to every country participant or associated with Portugal in O.E.C.D., I.M.F. and EFTA.

[2] Moreover, to judge from many other countries, this is probably true of the majority of market economies; in the centrally-planned economies what seems to be a similar effect is in reality only the counterpart, in terms of another super-power, of the general phenomenon of a world-wide rearrangement and rationalisation of resource-use.

has inevitable consequences on the international distribution of factor remuneration (mainly of capital and entrepreneurship) and on the distribution of decision-making power between the various world economico-political centres.

The two main types of effects distinguished above when examining the actual existing situation are of importance not entirely for themselves alone, but more fundamentally for the potential consequences that they may possess in an already foreseeable future; these very briefly and summarily would appear to be as follows:

(a) The impact resulting from the more and more vigorous presence of great United States enterprises within the Portuguese economic structures, reinforcing the conditions already mentioned that are favourable to the acceleration of the development process, may represent a very important stimulus (once again of an exogenous character) and enable the Portuguese economy to reach a final and decisive phase of structural transformation such as will, at last, permit a self-sustained growth of per capita incomes.[1]

(b) This economic development may, however, if one assumes a trend that recent events make it possible to foresee, not be accompanied by a corresponding increase in the decision-making power of the country so far as concerns its participation in international economic activities and even in limiting but not in probable cases in the actual management of its own domestic businesses where the decision regarding growth forms part of a broader policy with its origins outside Portugal; this danger is implicit in any very intense concentration of economic decision-making power in a single great dominant economy.

The changes of behaviour and outlook resulting from the presence of foreign enterprises (particularly North American enterprises) in the Portuguese economy, which has shown itself principally in the past few years, was preceded by a similar phenomenon, though at that time with its repercussions mainly on the administration: we refer to the participation of Portugal in the Marshall Plan. What has been the implication of Marshall Aid on the development of the Portuguese economy?

In comparison with most countries that accepted similar United States aid, Portugal presented some divergent characteristics that in themselves at once affected the basic principles on which the assistance was provided. The peculiar position of Portugal in that period of European life arose

[1] As an addendum to this paragraph, though outside the strict field of economics with which this paper is concerned, it is relevant to draw attention to the spread (by osmosis and imitation) of behaviours and values introduced with the industrial enterprises into the areas in which they are located.

from a whole variety of circumstances, among which the following may be emphasised:

(a) Portugal had not been directly involved in the Second World War.
(b) As an immediate consequence of this, the Portuguese economy had not been destroyed in any physical sense through military operations, though during the whole period of the war, restrictions and difficulties had inevitably occurred, especially from shortages of consumer goods, and from severe restrictions on imports of capital goods, for which Portugal was almost entirely dependent on industrialised countries, and especially on certain European countries involved in the war.
(c) The state of the Portuguese balance of payments, though reflecting in the early post-war years the result of the hectic expansion of consumption after the restrictions of the previous years, was not in any way comparable to the grave difficulties of most of the European countries, principally because of the run of years in which credit balances had been accumulated through exports of strategic raw materials and of certain consumer goods made possible by the neutral position of Portugal.
(d) Finally, as a consequence of various factors, perhaps not exclusively of an economic character, Portugal had decided not to make use initially of the United States assistance programme for Europe, asking for United States aid in the context of the Marshall Plan only at the beginning of 1949.

This summary of short-term considerations is intended to set in a more correct perspective the issues of Marshall Aid in relation to the basic conditions of the Portuguese economy; whereas in most Western European countries (chiefly the most economically developed) that programme was actually related to a reconstruction (though on conditional terms) of their economies, in the sense that it would permit the resumption, in their essential features, of certain pre-war trends, in Portugal the same form of American aid did not mean a reconstruction, but a stimulus to the intensification of a possibly too slow rate of economic development.

The background forces that had hindered, for reasons involving the economic, political and social life of the country, the economic development of Portugal have already been outlined. Now, with political, financial and exchange stability secured – the exclusive preoccupation of the period from 1926 to the middle of the 1940s – the first move was made in the direction of a controlled process of economic development; but, be it stressed again, an economic development considered in the framework of a predominantly stabilising control.

It is in this context that the participation of Portugal in Marshall Aid seems to gain its full meaning, far beyond the financial contribution in which that aid consisted, if regarded only from the much too narrow point of view of financial statistics.

It was thought necessary to make an economic development effort in which the State would be deliberately and explicitly interested; such development was thought to be possible without seriously affecting those respects in which it had been possible to overcome more or less completely certain chronic instabilities from which Portugal had long suffered. But (looking back at these problems today) it was utopian to aim at the formulation and execution of a development policy depending on a public administration that lacked the outlook, methods and, especially, the suitably trained staff for such a task – a problem aggravated by the fact that, in reality, these deficiencies were associated with the most pertinent characteristics of the whole Portuguese social economy and especially with an industrial organisation which lacked economic dynamism. And all this had been reinforced by the stabilising effort that had characterised the recent past.

It can be seen, therefore, that Portugal in the late 1940s and early 1950s was in a phase we may regard as one of disequilibrium until it achieved far-reaching changes in the structures inherited from the traditional society: the desire for economic development was evident and it could be built on a foundation of relative social and financial stability; but human and technical resources were inadequate to achieve the first phases of the actual execution of the speeding up of the change of economico-social structures.

It is, therefore, in the fields of knowledge, of the application and improvement of methods and techniques through contact with experts of other countries or in international organisations (that is to say the O.E.E.C.) and in the subsequent training of qualified and specialised home staff, that we must expect to discover the real value of the participation of Portugal in the international schemes for post-war economic reorganisation, and especially as a beneficiary from the Marshall Plan. So that it might participate, it was in fact necessary to re-examine and to systematise many features of the Portuguese economy; it was necessary to justify actual investment projects in terms of economic rationality; in short, it was necessary to learn and to apply a whole complex of techniques, typical of the economic life of industrialised societies, in everyday use in the United States but hitherto practically unknown or unused in Portugal.

And in addition to the need, then demonstrated, for sharing the methods of work of the organisations concerned with international cooperation, there came a widespread penetration of that experience, both in certain government departments (especially those nearest to these international contacts) and at the same time the spreading of the theoretical concepts through the universities which, modernising their courses, set out to ensure the training of high-grade technical staff capable of absorbing, assimilating, adapting and developing this stimulus to modernisation.

But throughout the 1950s these developments, favourable to the modernisation of the economic and social life of the country, were confined to certain government and university departments; their extension to the basic economic organisations of the country was necessary, and especially to the industrial enterprises, on which economic edvelopment in a market system is inevitably based. It is obvious that for this step in the general process of modernisation, the Marshall Plan had no direct relevance; but we have already drawn attention to the fact that the international 'migration' of industrial enterprises has played and will continue to play a part in this international transmission of the ideas and techniques of modern industry, and that the contacts and associations with foreign industrial enterprises has immensely increased in Portugal during the past decade; at the same time, private industry, competing with public administration on relatively favourable terms, has been able to recruit the more highly qualified staff which the universities have been training; all this has contributed to a modernisation of work methods, and in some cases also of forms of employment, which, though insufficient alone, have been in our view one of the fundamental conditions for the Portuguese economy to absorb the outside stimuli to which it has been exposed and thus to approach the critical level of per capita income that will at some stage make possible a continuing spiral of self-sustained growth.

In the long and complex process of the creation of the actual environment in which economic and social life may undergo, the repercussions of United States economic policy upon the Portuguese economy cannot be considered under the single and isolated respect of the inescapable domination effect. In fact, as we have just seen, the relation with the United States has also contributed – and more significantly – to the introduction of new techniques and activities and to the spread of a progressive outlook. And these are, after all, the factors which render possible the changes that embody the very essence of economic development.

VII. SOME GENERAL CONCLUSIONS

The basic elements out of which this paper has been constructed are three:

(a) The concept of interrelation and mutual dependence between different economies and groups of economies, resulting from their coexistence in a world that is becoming smaller and smaller, more and more densely populated, more and more complex in consequence of the improvement of means of communication.

(b) An attempt to apply to the special circumstances and specific peculiarities of the development of the Portuguese economy a much

more general concept of the process of economic development which envisages that, after the breakdown of an equilibrium peculiar to an agriculture-based traditional society, a long process of discontinuous development begins, involving progressive modernisation and perhaps culminating in the creation of an industrial economy.
(c) The unique position of the United States as a dominant economy on a world scale.

The position of the Portuguese economy, viewed in the perspective of the coincidence of these three basic elements, may perhaps be summarised thus: Portugal is a European economy, not only of a small size but also less developed for a variety of historical reasons which have restricted its development. The analysis of the behaviour of the Portuguese economy has meaning only when account is taken of the fact that, from the time when the decisive changes in the leading European countries occurred and they began to evolve towards industrial capitalism (at the end of the eighteenth century and in the first half of the nineteenth), Portugal made it its policy of political, economic and social change merely to respond and adapt its internal adjustment mechanism (often inadequately) to external stimuli; this has subsequently resulted in consequential disequilibrium, some of which appear to have been satisfactorily overcome only during the present century.

The reorganisation of Portugal's international economic relations after the Second World War had to insert itself into a complex system of large blocs, without being able, however, to derive from foreign trade the whole gains from larger size and more economic use of resources, partly because of Portugal's relative vulnerability, partly because Portugal's chief preoccupation lay in internal development; nonetheless, mere participation in the new patterns of international economic organisation had very favourable effects on the progress of development.

In these circumstances the participation of Portugal in the general development of the world economy appears – as in most countries – to have practically deprived Portugal of any effective initiative, and to be rather characterised by a state of dependence, more or less complete according to the fields of action considered when confronted by the large industrial organisations of today, and in a very particular sense in regard to the United States.

A final point: taking into account the particular circumstances of each case – a necessity for any fair appraisal of a concrete situation – it seems that the basic lines of analysis here adopted for the interpretation of the broad trends of Portuguese economic development might be equally applied to the study of other economies in similar conditions. We would particularly like to investigate the history of all the economies which, like

Portugal, failed to achieve endogenously and proportionately to the forces that required adjustment to new conditions, the changes that might have led to industrialisation and a new equilibrium of the whole social economy, but merely adjusted rather slowly and with considerable difficulty their own pattern of internal development. In practice, in spite of countless differences in each individual case, all such countries have as a common feature in their historical development the absence of the well-defined changes that characterised certain phases of the history of the more advanced economies. All else is the consequence once again, as we have seen in the case of the Portuguese economy, of the processes of repercussion and adjustment arising from relationships with the more developed economies.

While insisting once again on the specific features of each particular case, we believe that this is a line of investigation which, quite apart from its scientific interest, may be able, for countries in an intermediate stage of development, to help to make their economic development policies more effective and thus contribute to the more fundamental objective of making it less difficult for mankind to achieve the material conditions that will provide human dignity for all men.

Discussion of the Paper by Professor Pinto Barbosa

Professor Wallich said he found that the paper by Professor Pinto Barbosa bore on the hypothesis that a country's system of preferences depended on its historical experiences. Portugal's experience was one of monetary, political and economic instability. Recently, Portugal had succeeded in the sense of having a high degree of monetary and political stability, though perhaps at the expense of the rate of growth. Recently, perhaps Portugal's policies had been too conservative because it was too bent on stable development and stable money. Germany's preferences came from analogous historical experience. Perhaps what happened in Germany explained the present conditions in the world rather more than what happened in Portugal. Again, one had an experience of inflation and of violent dictatorship, which coloured what many Germans thought about stability and inflation.

Germany and Portugal both had strong preferences for stable prices. Britain and America, whose experience had not been that of inflation or of political instability, but of unemployment in the 1930s, wanted full employment more than price stability. With Germany and Portugal it was the other way round. These preferences were enhanced by recent analysis – for example, the Phillips curve. Portugal had relatively slow growth and stable prices. This choice seemed to have been made permanently.

Professor Amzalak said that Professor Pinto Barbosa, one of the most brilliant Portuguese economists, had a long historical introduction to the present position of Portugal. He then studied the attitude of Portugal towards North American economic policy after 1945. Finally, he looked at the balance of payments and its effect on both economies. In general, Professor Amzalak had read this paper with great pleasure and had few comments. He would just say that it was very difficult to develop and explain all this within the limits of length imposed on Professor Pinto Barbosa. As a Portuguese, he had seen what had been done; but his foreign colleagues might think the paper was too concise.

Professor Nunes said he agreed with Professor Wallich. Professor Pinto Barbosa said that Britain had a big influence on the Portuguese economy. This had now been replaced by the United States. But America's influence was different. Britain had had an almost total influence on the Portuguese balance of payments, as its biggest supplier and customer. It had also had a dominating influence on the capital balance. While the United Kingdom was still Portugal's first customer, there were few relations between Portugal and Europe. However, Germany was important. Now, from a commercial point of view, it was not just the United States which was important but the United Kingdom and Germany as well. America had a big influence on capital flows. One effect was on public administration; the other was through direct investment in modern technology. This was the difference between the influences of America and the United Kingdom.

Professor Pinto Barbosa said his paper had looked at interdependence among a group of countries. It was complex because it looked at a large number of communities. Portugal had moved from agriculture to modernisation and to growth. One could find this in the extent of industrialisation.

The United States had a unique position in the world not to be compared with that of Portugal as a small, developing economy. Portuguese development had certainly not the same effects as compared with what had happened during the industrial revolution. The effects of severe disequilibrium, during a long period, had been hard to remove. Since 1945, the Portuguese economy had become a member of a large bloc, taking gains from greater rationality in her use of resources. Development policies had been used. The development of international co-operation had helped the process of internal development. The development of the world economy had also helped, by bringing about a more interdependent system, particularly with the United States.

Professor Pinto Barbosa agreed with the conclusions of Professors Wallich and Nunes. He particularly emphasised the link between the rate of growth and both internal and external financial stability.

Part 2

Conflicts of Interest in Trade, Capital Flows and Monetary Policy

Part 2

Conflicts of Interest in Trade, Capital Flows and Monetary Policy

7 North Atlantic Trade and Payments

Angus Maddison
O.E.C.D., PARIS

I. THE REDUCTION OF TRADE BARRIERS

Since the end of the war the North Atlantic countries have made continuous progress in reducing trade barriers both on a world-wide basis and in ways which have promoted sub-regional integration. The early post-war morass of quantitative trade restrictions in Europe was removed by means of the O.E.E.C.'s liberalisation code between 1948 and 1953. Dollar imports into Europe were liberalised in the mid 1950s. The E.E.C. and EFTA arrangements have removed tariffs within the areas they cover, and the external tariffs of these two groups and of North America have been lowered by Dillon and Kennedy Rounds of negotiations in GATT. Automobile trade between the United States and Canada has been put on a free-trade basis by special bilateral arrangement.

This liberalisation in commercial policy has had no counterpart in the rest of the world which has steadily increased its degree of protection. From evidence collected by E.C.L.A. for Latin America it would seem that Latin American tariffs are now about ten times as high as those in North America and Western Europe. Asian countries have also raised tariffs and protection has been strengthened in Australia.

As a result, the concentration of European countries' exports on Europe has greatly increased, particularly since 1958 when the Common market was created. This is clear from Table 7.1.

TABLE 7.1

DEGREE OF TRADE INTERDEPENDENCE 1938–66
IN THE NORTH ATLANTIC AREA
(percentage of total exports)

Common Market Exports to:

	E.E.C.	U.K.	Other Western Europe	U.S.A.	Canada	North Atlantic Total
1938	27·5	10·7	19·6	4·7	0·6	63·1
1950	33·2	9·0	16·5	5·5	0·6	64·8
1958	32·1	5·7	20·1	7·1	1·0	66·0
1966	44·1	4·8	20·3	7·8	1·0	78·0

TABLE 7.1—contd.

U.K. Exports to:

	E.E.C.	U.K.	Other Western Europe	U.S.A.	Canada	North Atlantic Total
1938	12·8		16·3	9·5	4·8	43·4
1950	11·2		18·8	5·3	5·9	41·2
1958	13·8		16·4	9·3	5·8	45·3
1966	18·9		22·3	12·4	4·2	57·8

U.S.A. Exports to:

1938	15·2	16·8	6·9		15·0	53·9
1950	15·6	5·0	7·8		19·2	47·6
1958	16·0	5·0	9·3		19·5	49·8
1966	18·2	5·8	8·5		21·8	54·3

Canadian Exports to:

1938	6·4	40·5	2·9	32·9		82·7
1950	3·8	15·0	2·6	65·5		86·9
1958	8·6	15·8	2·9	59·4		86·7
1966	6·3	11·0	2·7	60·6		80·6

Source: *Yearbook of International Trade Statistics* (U.N., New York).

The relative importance of mutual trade between Canada and the United States increased considerably during the war and in the past two or three years there has been a further increase, particularly for Canada, because of the automobile agreement. However, the European market is much less important now for Canada and the United States than it was

TABLE 7.2

GROWTH IN THE VOLUME OF EXPORTS, 1880–1967
(annual average compound rate)

	1880–1913	1913–50	1950–67	1958–67
Belgium–Luxembourg	3·6	0·2	8·2	9·8
France	2·6	1·1	6·8	8·7
Germany	4·4[a]	−2·4	12·7	9·9
Italy	3·2[b]	1·4	12·6	15·6
Netherlands	5·0	1·2	9·1	8·7
United Kingdom	2·2	0·2	2·3	3·3
Canada	4·6	3·3	6·0	7·6
United States	3·2	2·3	5·0	5·2
World	3·3[a]	1·3	6·7[c]	6·7[d]

[a] 1881–1913. [b] 1872–1913. [c] 1950–66. [d] 1958–66.

Source: A. Maddison, 'Growth and Fluctuation in the World Economy, 1870–1960', *Banca Nazionale del Lavoro Quarterly Review* (June 1962) and *Monthly Bulletin of Statistics* (U.N., New York, Feb 1969).

TABLE 7.3
RATIO OF MERCHANDISE EXPORTS F.O.B. TO G.N.P.
AT CURRENT MARKET PRICES

	1913	1938	1950	1967
Belgium–Luxembourg		26·5	22·1	34·8
France		6·9	10·4	9·8
Germany	17·0	5·4	8·6	18·0
Italy	11·3	6·3	8·6	13·0
Netherlands		17·4	28·3	32·1
United Kingdom	19·8	8·2	16·3	12·5
Canada		15·7	17·5	18·4
United States	6·1	3·6	3·5	4·0

Source: A. Maddison, *Economic Growth in the West* (Allen & Unwin, 1964), *Monthly Bulletin of Statistics* (U.N., New York, Feb 1969) and *Gross National Product: Growth Rates and Trend Data*, RC-W-138 (A.I.D., Washington, Apr 1969).

in 1938, almost entirely because of the decline in the importance of the United Kingdom market.

As a result of the liberalisation of trade and the faster growth of the economies, the volume of exports of all countries in the area has risen faster since 1950 than ever before. But the rise is much less impressive for the United Kingdom and United States than it has been for most European countries.

The closer integration of the North Atlantic area has therefore largely been a bipolar phenomenon as far as trade is concerned. Since 1958 the benefits have been largely confined to Europe.

II. THE CONTRIBUTION OF FREER TRADE TO ECONOMIC GROWTH

In view of the political effort it takes to reduce trade barriers, it is surprising to find how little serious evidence there is of the contribution of freer trade to economic growth. The special E.C.E. study on growth factors in Europe in the 1950s never even mentioned gains from trade. The most serious attempt to measure the gains is that of Denison.[1] For 1950–62, he estimates that reductions in trade barriers made the following contributions to growth (in terms of percentage points per annum):

Belgium	0·16
Denmark	0·09
France	0·07
Germany	0·10
Italy	0·16
Netherlands	0·16
Norway	0·15
United Kingdom	0·02
United States	0·00

[1] E. F. Denison, *Why Growth Rates Differ* (Brookings Institution, Washington, 1967).

Other writers have had an even less favourable view of the gains from trade. Verdoorn's 1954 study showed likely gains from an all-European customs union to be no more than one-twentieth of one per cent of G.N.P. (not annually, but in total). Verdoorn takes into account the trade-diverting as well as trade-creating effects, but if we take Verdoorn's gross trade-creating effect, it amounts to a once-for-all gain of only one-seventh of one per cent of G.N.P. Scitovsky[1] endorsed the general conclusions of Verdoorn's study with regard to increased specialisation, but stressed that the gains from increased competition would be more substantial.

In contrast to this view, we have the Wonnacotts'[2] study on United States–Canadian integration which suggests that most of the productivity difference between the two countries is due to tariff protection and the inefficiency of smaller Canadian domestic markets. Their expectation of the potential gains from integration for Canada is about 300 times as great as Verdoorn estimated for Europe. However, the Wonnacotts tend to treat tariff barriers as a catch-all residual in explaining productivity differences, and their case seems a little weak.

Denison's analysis is inadequate on several counts, but his approach to the problem is probably the most useful starting point. He assumes that cost differentials are two-thirds as high as trade barriers i.e. that domestic production behind a 15 per cent tariff wall would, on average, involve 10 per cent higher costs than free trade. The gain from trade is two-thirds of the tariff reduction multiplied by the increase in the trade ratios.

These are several respects in which the analysis could be improved. In the first place, Denison uses Raymond Bertrand's estimates of nominal tariff levels, whereas it would be better to use Balassa's more refined estimates of 'effective' tariffs, which measure the net incidence of protection on value added, and therefore give a more accurate picture of possible cost differentials. As final goods have much higher levels of protection than raw materials, the 'effective' rate of protection is generally higher than the nominal rate and the use of effective rather than nominal rates would probably raise Denison's estimates by about three-quarters. In addition, it would be useful to make some estimate of the effect of removing quantitative restrictions.

Denison's comparisons are global ones, and it would be helpful to disaggregate them, and look at a few major sectors of manufacturing. The trade ratios have probably grown fastest in sectors where barriers have fallen most. It is also likely that these will be the sectors where domestic prices will have fallen most or risen least. I suspect therefore that disaggregation would increase the estimated gains from trade.

---

[1] T. Scitovsky, *Economic Theory and Western European Integration* (Stanford U.P., 1958).

[2] R. J. and P. Wonnacott, *Free Trade between the U.S. and Canada* (Harvard U.P., 1967).

Dension makes an allowance for economies of scale, but does not relate it to changes in international trade. The estimates of gains from scale are fairly arbitrary, but part of them should be imputed to increased trade.

Finally, Denison makes no allowance for the impact of trade on competition though he does admit that it must have had some effect. It is difficult to analyse the change in competition and its effects in any precise quantitative way. Scitovsky managed to collect quite a lot of illuminating case material, and it should be possible to do something of the same kind again. There are one or two industries like toys, shoes or cars in which the impact of 'potential' trade in reducing domestic prices and forcing increases in productivity has been substantial. And in these cases consumers in national markets have also a much wider range of choice now than in the 1950s.

All of these considerations force one to conclude that Denison understates the positive contribution of more liberal commercial policy to economic growth. However, he makes no allowance for the costs of trade diversion, i.e. the effects which discriminatory tariff reductions have had in diverting trade from non-members of the tariff-cutting group. Other people who have looked at this point in relation to manufactures do not consider that it has been significant,[1] but it has obviously been important for agriculture and has hurt the United States and Canada in particular.

In overall terms, the contribution of increased trade liberalisation to the post-war acceleration in income growth has probably been rather modest, and less important than the rise in the rate of investment, the pursuit of Keynesian full employment policies and international co-operation in trade and payments. However, it has not been negligible, and the political co-operation involved in achieving more liberal policies has also helped strengthen co-operation over payments difficulties.

III. THE SCOPE FOR FURTHER LIBERALISATION

In the past, liberalisation of trade has progressed in successive regional phases which have generally sparked off positive reactions elsewhere. Thus EFTA would not have existed without E.E.C., and nor would the Kennedy Round. At the moment there does not seem to be scope for further progress within the present regional arrangements, or any likelihood of another large-scale GATT round. The United Kingdom has been twice rebuffed in its efforts to seek entry into the Common Market, and even if it were invited to enter, it would seem hardly worth while to join an

---

[1] See B. Balassa, 'Trade Creation and Trade Diversion in the European Common Market', *Economic Journal* (Mar 1967).

arrangement which has such restrictive agricultural policies, now that industrial tariffs have been reduced by the Kennedy Round.

TABLE 7.4
EFFECTIVE INCIDENCE OF PROTECTION
AFTER KENNEDY ROUND IMPLEMENTATION

	U.S.A.	U.K.	Common Market
Nominal tariff, all commodities	6·8	9·1	6·6
Effective tariff, all commodities	11·6	16·0	11·1

Source: B. Balassa 'The Effects of the Kennedy Round on the Exports of Processed Goods from Developing Areas' (UNCTAD, New Delhi, Feb 1968).

As tariff levels are now relatively low and the main commercial policy barrier to better resource allocation is the agricultural policy of the Common Market, it might well be that the most useful next step would be the creation of a free-trade area in industrial goods between Canada and the United States. This would strengthen the power of these two countries in bargaining for a relaxation of the restrictive agricultural policy of the Common Market and would probably lead to another round of GATT negotiations which would bring all the countries a step nearer to free trade. Another GATT round would also be an effective way of helping developing countries which seem unlikely to get the tariff preferences they are demanding in the UNCTAD.

Further liberalisation of trade between developed countries would un-

TABLE 7.5
RATE OF GROWTH OF G.N.P.
IN CONSTANT PRICES, 1950–68
(annual average compound growth rates)

	1950–68	1950–60	1960–8
Belgium	3·6	2·9	4·5
Canada	4·5	4·0	5·2
France	4·9	4·5	5·3
Germany (West)	6·3	7·9	4·3
Italy	5·5	5·7	5·3
Netherlands	4·7	4·7	4·7
Sweden	3·9	3·5	4·4
Switzerland	4·4	4·5	4·4
United Kingdom	2·8	2·6	3·1
United States	3·9	3·2	4·7
Unweighted average	4·5	4·4	4·6
Japan	10·0	9·6	10·4

Source: *Gross National Product: Growth Rates and Trend Data* (A.I.D., Washington, Apr 1969), and A. Maddison, *Economic Growth in Japan and the U.S.S.R.* (Allen & Unwin, 1969).

doubtedly contribute to their growth by improving resource allocation and increasing competition. It would also provide consumers with a wider range of choice which is probably of almost equal importance. But the overall impact of such liberalisation on income is likely to remain rather modest, and possibly lower than the gains achieved in the past decade. The real justification for constantly trying to push forward is that there are strong protectionist forces with political influence and without some positive momentum there is always a real danger of sliding backwards particularly now that payments difficulties are so extreme.

IV. PAYMENTS DISEQUILIBRIUM AS AN OBSTACLE TO PROGRESS

In fact, the persistent and severe payments disequilibrium within the North Atlantic area is probably a more serious obstacle to the realisation of the full growth potential of the area than the remaining barriers to free trade. The main reason why these problems have persisted so long has been the reluctance of countries to tackle them directly by exchange-rate adjustments. This was partly because of the special difficulty of the United Kingdom and United States as reserve currency centres, but there has been a perverse and sanctimonious view about the propriety of exchange-rate changes and revaluation of gold in these two countries just as there has been in France and Germany.

The payments disequilibrium has not yet had very serious repercussions on economic growth within the area, except in the United Kingdom. In the decade since convertibility was generally established in 1958 there has been substantial improvement in the intimacy and frequency of central bank consultation, and a huge network of central bank credit has been created to bail out countries in difficulties. In spite of the universal cry for more international liquidity, there has in fact probably been overgenerous supply. If the United Kingdom had had access to less credit it might have had an earlier and better-organised devaluation.

As a consequence of the attempts to patch over fundamental payments disequilibria there has also been a new burst of restrictionist measures which are quite incompatible with longer-run liberal goals. Nearly all foreign aid is now tied. The United States has substantial controls over capital exports. The United Kingdom and France have very tight exchange control over all transactions by residents. Germany and France have a system of subsidies and taxes on trade and the United Kingdom has advance deposits on imports. There is an increasing tendency to use rebates of indirect taxes as a means of boosting exports. There is a two-tier market in gold.

Unless exchange rates are adjusted satisfactorily, it seems likely that these neo-mercantilist restrictions will grow and have a harmful effect on resource allocation. The harmful effect may not be large, but the restrictions on personal freedom, particularly on freedom to take holidays abroad, is a more substantial loss in relatively affluent societies. There is also some danger in a system that always operates near to crisis, that relations between countries will deteriorate and that self-destructive measures like those of the 1930s will ensue. Fortunately this seems less likely now than it did two years ago.

One reason why payments problems so frequently reach crisis point is the creation of an international market in Euro-dollars in the 1960s. This market is now so large that it has reduced the independence of national monetary authorities, particularly their power to isolate their interest structures from those abroad. The growth of this market has sometimes been a considerable nuisance from the viewpoint of managing a system with fixed exchange rates which are under challenge, but it has also forced institutional improvements in the banking mechanism and helped pro-provoke closer co-operation between countries on economic policy, so its overall effect may well have been helpful to economic growth.

Finally we should say something about the increased international flow of longer-term private capital.

United States private direct investment in Europe in the past decade has been almost as big as the Marshall Aid programme. Its major impact has been technological, managerial and institutional. United States companies have concentrated heavily on new products created by massive research and development expenditures. American management has pioneered the creation of new multinational companies. United States management consultants have arrived in force and are now even reorganising the British Treasury. The large-scale capital and credit needs of United States companies have greatly expanded international capital markets, and United States banks have brought new ideas and winds of competition. This type of integration between North America and Europe may well have contributed as much to accelerate European growth as has the reduction in trade barriers. Again as in the case of trade integration, impact has probably been greatest in Belgium and the Netherlands.

Europe did not need this investment for balance of payments reasons. In fact, the investment flow has helped put a strain on the United States reserve position, and the American Government now requires United States firms operating in Europe to finance their investments by foreign borrowing.

There are some reasons for thinking that the big flow of long-term capital of the past decade may not continue on the same scale. The initial stimulus to invest came from the creation of the Common Market and EFTA which effectively presented United States manufacturers with the choice between losing export markets or investing abroad. The Dillon and Kennedy Rounds of tariff reduction have now softened this incentive somewhat. Secondly, there was probably an exhaustible backlog in 'normal' capital flows (e.g. by comparison with Canada) because of the war and the inconvertibility of European currencies until 1958. Thirdly, United States payments difficulties may curtail the flow. Fourthly, many politicians in Europe consider that heavy reliance on United States investment for new technology will lead them to 'industrial helotry', or they fear that multinational corporations will limit their political power. So far, only the French have taken significant action to restrict United States investment and this was later rescinded, but the pressure for changes in policy is likely to grow stronger as time passes, particularly if a good deal of the investment has to be financed by local borrowing.

V. CONCLUSION

The post-war economic relationship between North America and Europe is much more intimate and articulate than ever before. There has been no serious transmission of deflationary influences as in pre-war years, and cooperation between governments and central banks in O.E.C.D. and the B.I.S. is so close that a serious breakdown in the present system of trade and payments is very unlikely. The liberalisation of commercial policy has made a modest contribution to European growth but has probably brought little net benefit to the United States except non-measurable increases in consumer satisfaction. The post-Kennedy Round commercial barriers are not a very serious obstacle to efficient resource allocation except in agriculture. The most pressing problem is that of chronic payments disequilibrium. It may well be that the disequilibrium can be ended within the framework of the existing exchange-rate system, but even if this system changes, the change will probably be a modest switch to the crawling-peg system.

Discussion of the Paper by Mr Maddison

Professor Rasmussen introduced the paper. He noted that the papers at the Round Table ranged, in terms of length, from 9 to 125 pages – the shortest, Mr Maddison's paper, even having 3 of its 9 pages made up of tables. In the lottery organised by the Programme Chairman, Professor Robinson, it appeared on the surface that he had gained. More profound judgement, however, might show that he was in a difficult position because of the range of problems by Mr Maddison. The paper was an iceberg – the overwhelming part of the substance being below the water. Consider the table of contents one might construct out of Mr Maddison's paper:

(1) 'Trends in International Trade in the Post-war Period in Historical Perspective' – pp. 163–5;
(2) 'Measures of the Gain from Trade' – pp. 165–7 a conference in its own – and worth organising);
(3) 'Present Trends in Policy' – pp. 167–70;
(4) 'Capital Flows' – p. 170;
(5) 'Conclusion' – p. 171.

In section I it was briefly shown that growth and liberalisation of trade in the post-war period had brought about an increase in the volume of exports in Western Europe and the United States which was – historically considered – of a record size. The United Kingdom as well as the United States, however, had lagged behind. He did want to use time commenting on this section, which summarised the facts.

In section II, Mr Maddison touched exciting questions. He did not want to repeat all the well-known, more or less classical, arguments on the gain from trade. All knew the textbook presentation of the issue. This theory was an important background to whatever we said of the gain. One problem was that the theory as such did not lend itself easily to empirical work, assuming as it did knowledge about unknown social welfare functions and production possibility curves. This was a grave difficulty. Another problem was the assumptions of pure trade theory. Two countries were capable of producing two commodities by using two factors, *identical* between countries, with production functions *the same* in the two countries. Further, we usually assumed constant return to scale and – this was important – optimisation.

He was not going to argue that this very abstract theory was of no use. On the contrary, it was an extremely useful beginning to our attempt to explain what happened. However, the theory would have to be applied to a world consisting of many countries (of unequal size), where many commodities were produced by a multitude of factors and where production was going on at many different levels in the sense that production functions were different in the n countries. He need not go into detail on these matters, but the theory also assumed that we were always living at the happy point – it was not even a region – of *profit maximisation*. In other words, to apply the theory we must adjust and modify it. Such modifications might be extremely important as a supplement to our attempt to explain what happened by way of an abstract theory. He wanted to cite two examples familiar to him.

In the 1880s, transport costs declined significantly because of technological innovation; so did the price of grain. In turn, Danish agriculture adjusted to the new situation and turned to producing butter, bacon and eggs from cheap imported grains. It had been argued that this was only an adjustment to the changing terms of trade facing Danish agriculture. However, recent research suggested that the shift was just as much the result of the steady fall in absolute income forcing the sector to adjust. It might have been optimal to alter the production-mix before it happened. However, the sector optimised because it was forced to do so.

The second, and perhaps more illuminating case, was that of the textile industry in Denmark which was facing catastrophe in the 1950s. Trade was liberalised and chances of survival seemed very small. Within a decade, employment fell to one-third. Production increased, however, particularly because exports flourished. Why? This could, or might, have happened without liberalisation; perhaps more easily because the profit made on the home market might have helped the export drive. The brutal facts, however, were such that the industry was forced to 'do something about it' in order to survive. It optimised, and it was likely that this would not have happened in the absence of pressure.

It was therefore proper to be reminded that optimising was not a once-for-all process. In a world of changing tastes and technologies, continuous adjustment was called for. And this was precisely one of the virtues of foreign trade – that it enforced this process.

Many similar cases might be quoted. However, and this was his whole point: How did one measure the gain from trade in such cases? His conclusion was that he felt we had been off the mark in attempting to quantify the gains from liberalising trade, as shown in the table on p. 165 of the paper. So, he had grave doubts on Mr Maddison's conclusion.

Trying to optimise one of our most scarce resources, time, he would not give detailed comments on the remaining sections. In section III of this paper, he was simply curious about the aside on p. 168 that the most useful next step would be the creation of a free-trade area in industrial goods between Canada and the United States. Was this really so important from a European viewpoint?

He agreed with Mr Maddison when, on p. 169, he argued that without a liberal pressure there is always the danger of sliding backwards. He even thought Mr Maddison was slightly over-optimistic when, in the third paragraph of p. 169, he argued that there has been an over-generous world supply of capital. In May 1969, Denmark lost one-third of her foreign exchange reserves in five days. She survived, *inter alia*, because of the central bank consultations and the huge network of central bank credit referred to in the paper. But to call it generosity would perhaps be to exaggerate.

Mr Maddison on several occasions referred to the misallocation of resources implied by the agricultural policies of almost every country. It was tempting to raise that issue, but as there would be a session on agriculture later, we should not go into detail. In passing, he would just venture the guess that the growth rates indicated on p. 168, Table 7.5 might, *inter alia* be very much affected by the agricultural policies pursued. He had in mind the well-known hypothesis that a manpower reserve in agriculture ready to move into manufacturing and the service industries was one of the favourable conditions for economic growth.

(He was oversimplifying.) Agricultural policy might do its best to slow down this process.

Professor Rasmussen said he would end on one small point. Without reopening the discussion on the British case, he could not but feel slightly puzzled over the fact that on two or three occasions Mr Maddison stated that United Kingdom tariffs were low. Yet Mr Brittan, in his paper, said that 'the United Kingdom market remains fairly highly protected by international standards'. Table 7.4, on p. 168 of Mr Maddison's paper, tended to support Mr Brittan.

Mr Lamfalussy wanted to make two observations on p. 170 of the paper. On the impact of the Euro-dollar market, Mr Maddison said that this was a reason for crises. He thought this was right, but would like to observe that the real problem was the external convertibility of the Euro-dollar. This allowed the Euro-dollar market to be the vehicle for speculation against a number of currencies. For example, after the recent French devaluation, the Belgian central bank had lost 15 per cent of its reserves in two weeks, more than half of this because Belgian francs were being sold by non-residents. It was very hard to stop the transfer of reserves from national currencies to non-residents' accounts. Only complete exchange control would do this.

On the suggestion made by Mr Maddison that the supply of international liquidity was over-generous, Mr Lamfalussy said that if one looked at all the major changes in the West (including those mentioned in Mr Maddison's own paper), it was hard to say that there was an excess of international liquidity. Apart from international liquidity, domestic liquidity had become an increasingly important factor, because it was so easy to switch from one currency to another. Consequently, one must look at that too. Lastly, small countries like Holland and Belgium were troubled by the activities of international business.

The share of international firms in world activity had risen quickly. Their treasurers had large amounts of money under their control and could use it to speed up leads and lags. In addition, they could cause long-run flows out of one country's currency, through the way they fixed transfer prices for supplying partly-finished goods from one part of the firm to another. Such prices were almost always arbitrary, in some sense, and even strict exchange control could do little to halt the process. It therefore reached a point where there was too little international liquidity and where governments could not separate foreign exchange policy from internal policy. For example, Belgium was having to deflate unnecessarily harshly because of the recent speculation.

Professor Marchal agreed with Mr Maddison that the Euro-dollar market had both good and bad effects on economic development. But the increase in liquidity was more closely related to the development of the Euro-dollar than Mr Maddison seemed to suggest. Did he mean that current institutions and techniques were unfavourable to the creation of Euro-dollars? Or did he mean that they were unfavourable to the creation of liquidity, apart from Euro-dollars?

Again, Mr Maddison said that the effects of the Euro-dollar market had been too narrow from the point of view of economic policy. Did he mean the effect on general economic policies? Mr Maddison concluded that the overall effect of having the Euro-dollar was good, but Professor Marchal wondered if he could justify this.

Professor Lundberg went back to the point made by Professor Rasmussen, who took up the question of the gains from trade. How far had rising trade between Europe and the United States helped growth? He had hoped that Mr Maddison would have enlarged on the Denison research. Denison had used crude methods to get his results. He had combined Cobb–Douglas production functions with small triangles of welfare gains. Professor Lundberg thought these were dangerous techniques. Alfred Marshall had described trade as the engine of growth, and Professor Lundberg thought we should need to disaggregate a lot to see what had happened to the growth of particular countries. Sweden, like other countries, had found that flexibility in the allocation of resources and economic structures as well as the adaptability in growth which trade allowed were things which could only be obtained through trade. Salter's book, *Productivity and Technical Change*, showed that most of the increase in British productivity over a period of twenty-five years came from shifts of resources. These not only took place between agriculture and industry, but between industrial sectors and within the firms. Trade was concerned with shifting resources from less to more efficient uses, and the Cobb–Douglas function overlooked that. If one took a two-factor market, or a triangle, to look for the gains of trade, one missed the point. One often found that trade was growing twice as rapidly as the economy in general, and was most effective in shifting resources. Yet its effects could never be accurately measured. There was also the problem of incentives – the compulsion of competition. One's organisation had to live or die as a corporation or a firm. It was dangerous to assume, as economic theory so often did, that the firm was in equilibrium. International trade forced the firm into search processes in order to succeed in competition. The Maddison approach understated the effects of international trade, because it looked only at the triangles of welfare gains.

Professor Rasmussen wondered how Professor Lundberg was so sure that the gains could not be measured. *Professor Lundberg* replied that he had only said that it was difficult to measure them using triangles. They could clearly be measured in other ways.

Professor Patinkin said that Mr Maddison was using absolute and not relative numbers. In Belgium the contribution of trade to growth was given as 0·6 per cent. Was this small or large? We did not know the rate of growth of Belgium. However, the table at the end of the paper said it was 2·9 per cent. It was therefore of more significance than the 0·6 per cent, by itself, would suggest. However, even this was not sufficient. If one took electronics, one found there were significant technological improvements within a short time period. Even in the United States, however, developments in electronics would represent only a small proportion of growth in any year. So, one needed a new deflator, for example the relative importance of trade to the G.N.P. One could not use gross figures, but perhaps one could look at net added value going into exports as a percentage of the G.N.P. Then Denison's figures would be more significant.

Mr Maddison said he had tried to put the impact of particular influences on economic growth into perspective. The most reasonable starting point in evaluating the influence of trade on growth was Denison's recent model. He was unhappy with the contribution of Verdoorn, backed by Scitovsky, which seemed to mean that the development of the E.E.C. and the reduction of tariff barriers, etc., had had no effect on growth at all. At the opposite extreme was the work of the Wonnacotts. Denison's was the only really empirical approach. He might have omitted some aspects of trade's contribution to growth and it might be reasonable to double Denison's figures. But this would mean that trade had contributed only 0·2 percentage points a year to growth. Professor Rasmussen wanted a more sophisticated analysis, but did not say how this should be done.

Professor Kindleberger said that Denison had suggested that the biggest contribution of trade was into shifting labour from low-productivity to high-productivity activities. Even if the total size of foreign trade did not change, one had another measure of the gains from trade through the reallocation of resources. He wanted to side with Professor Lundberg (despite the latter's attacks on Denison). Professor Kindleberger wanted to return to what Professor Rasmussen and Mr Lamfalussy had said about the Euro-dollar and liquidity. Both took a dim view of the present supply of international liquidity to individual countries and Mr Lamfalussy was against convertibility.

Mr Lamfalussy denied that he was against convertibility. It was simply that, once one had it, one needed more international liquidity than before.

Professor Kindleberger said that Mr Lamfalussy wanted small countries to pursue an independent policy in a large capital market, because if there was convertibility one had leads and lags. One could argue that exchange control over capital movements was desirable; but was it feasible?

Professor Kindleberger had been disturbed by Mr Brittan's remarks, likening a discussion of the gold price to discussion of sex in the Victorian era. Now Mr Maddison was talking about perverse and sanctimonious views on this issue. He did not want to argue that doubling or trebling the price of gold was a populist argument. He simply wanted to object to the colourful language used by Messrs Brittan and Maddison.

Mr Lundgren noted that part of the disagreement with the paper was over the quantitative importance of the gains from trade. However, the paper did not discuss the gains from trade, but the gains from further trade liberalisation. The former were clearly large, and if technical change accounted for an important part of economic growth and required larger markets than national ones, then it could be said that the gains from trade were increasing. This was true in the sense that the cost of a return to autarky would then be increasing over time. The latter, the gains from trade liberalisation, were an altogether different matter, and it seemed very likely that the quoted findings from the literature were very near the truth. Obviously, if there were important, unrealised gains from trade at any point of time, these would, under a reasonably efficient pricing system, give rise to large competitive advantages which would make it possible to overcome the prevailing trade barriers easily.

On p. 166 of his paper, Mr Maddison said that if one performed Denison's calculations, using effective rather than nominal rates of protection, one would get higher figures for the gains from trade liberalisation. This was not correct. The result would be the same as before, expressed in terms of G.N.P. This could easily be checked with the use of a little algebra. Mr Maddison's main argument was accordingly stronger than his own presentation indicated.

Professor Cooper wanted to qualify Mr Maddison's contention that there was little net gain to the United States from trade liberalisation except that consumers benefited from wider choice. The process of trade liberalisation had warded off strong protectionist moves. In the absence of United States initiatives for further trade liberalisation, protectionist pressures would have prevailed in the Congress, and the United States might have found itself with the very high levels of protection that had prevailed in the 1930s. Taking into account this political dynamic, the relevant welfare comparison was not between the gains from trade before and after liberalisation, but between the gains from trade after liberalisation and those that would have occurred at much a higher level of protection than the one prevailing before liberalisation.

Mr Maddison had suggested that there was a reluctance in the United States to tackle the payments deficit. It was in this connection that he spoke of perverse and sanctimonious views on the price of gold. But in what sense would an increase in the price of gold represent a solution to the balance of payments problem? A change in exchange rates might be expected to offer a solution, but a change in the price of gold was not the same as a change in the dollar price of other currencies; other countries must refrain from changing the price of gold in terms of *their* currencies, a prospect that was doubtful in the event of a change in the dollar price of gold. Was Mr Maddison using casual language, or did he have some other hypothesis in mind?

Mr Maddison said an increase in the price of gold would make it easier for other countries to change exchange rates. *Professor Patinkin* wondered whether it would not simply raise the price of gold. *Mr Maddison* said that all currencies would not need to move to the same extent, and in any case there would be a gain in liquidity. *Professor Kindleberger* noted that Mr Maddison thought there was enough liquidity already.

Professor Wallich said that while he shared the view that the benefits from trade were understated, he thought perhaps one should look elsewhere than to the gain to the G.N.P. Maybe it was a question of what kind of country one was dealing with. Did small countries gain more than big ones? Did undiversified countries gain more than highly diversified ones? Table 7.4 seemed to bear out this view a little, in the sense that the United States had no gain to the growth rate from trade. This would not be surprising with its low ratio of trade to G.N.P.

Some time ago, he had run regressions of the rate of growth in various variables for forty countries over ten years, eliminating the effects of population growth and changes in income per head. He had focused on the ratio of investment to national income and that of exports to national income as two explanatory variables, among others. The latter showed itself to have significantly negative coefficients, with more open economies experiencing lower rates of growth. The investment ratio came out with a strong positive coefficient. It seemed that trade had a negative effect on growth. He felt he was now in danger of being lynched for telling a group of economists that trade had a negative effect on growth.

Professor Sohmen said he was sympathetic intuitively to the idea that the Denison figures were much too low. He had nothing much to offer in their place, but thought that much more work was needed in this area. The reason for the lowness of the figures might be, apart from the fact already stressed by Professor Kindleberger, that they did not take trade in intermediate products into account. Theoretical work, by MacKenzie, Enke, and others, had shown that trade in intermediate products could improve production possibilities a great deal. Future empirical work ought to pay more attention to this factor.

Professor Hicks said he had been looking at Table 7.4 in Mr Maddison's paper, together with the figures on the rate of growth in Table 7.5. It was unfortunate that the figures were for different periods. However, if one took, for example, the Netherlands, one found that it was a country which came out well in the Denison calculation, but that growth had been steady over two decades. He would like to see how the two tables fitted together.

Professor Rasmussen said he had not argued that Mr Maddison should have made more measurements himself; he just wanted Mr Maddison to show a more critical attitude to the figures he had quoted.

Somehow, Professor Rasmussen was getting the feeling from the Round Table that economics was harder than we had imagined! Surely it was an error always to assume that we could treat questions as though the elements in them were additive.

Professor Mundell said that trade arose because of differences between countries. With increasing factor mobility, countries would become less different and the potential gains from trade therefore less. Big countries gained less from international trade than small ones, so that as countries got bigger the potential for diversification was greater and the gains from trade less.

As world population and capital stock increased, he thought that the gains from international trade in existing goods would diminish, and large countries like the United States would be beyond the point where they needed to rely on increasing trade to obtain growth. There would, of course, be problems where particular resources were not available in any one country. There might, for example, be problems for small countries in these circumstances if substitution of other factors were not possible. But for large countries the gains from trade would decline, except for trade in new goods. Thus, future trade would become increasingly based on capital movements.

Professor Lundberg had spoken of the underestimation of the gains from trade by the welfare triangle method, and Professor Sohmen had said this was perhaps not the whole story because there would be changes in production functions arising out of trade in intermediate products. Perhaps the protectionism we could now see arising was caused by the smallness of gains from trade which depended on the absolute size of countries when the transfer of knowledge was difficult.

He would disagree wholly with Mr Maddison on the monetary system. In the future world, he thought that more fluid flows of capital would take place than in the past. The world would become more like the American federal system on a world or continental scale. There would not be changes in exchange rates but movements of funds. There might be a period of chaos before countries discovered that the gains from exchange-rate alterations were disappearing and the easy flow of information could demolish confidence in existing exchange rates. This was important because if residents in a country got used to the idea that its exchange rate might change, they would keep their accounts in dominant currencies. However, he expected fewer exchange-rate changes in the long run because the maintenance of confidence would be necessary to protect existing currencies. However, the more exchange-rate changes there were in the short run, the longer it would be before this happened.

Mr Ferras did not think that Professor Mundell was right. If he were, there would have to be a change in the whole approach to the political arrangements. Countries would not accept monetary policy being set by other countries.

He agreed on the perverseness of discussions on changing the price of gold. Certainly, it was true that the American authorities, trying to stop pressure on the dollar, had forced Britain to stick to her own parity for too long before 1967.

To Mr Lamfalussy, Mr Ferras said that, with aid, the best basic question was whether the receiver was following the right or wrong policy. In the United Kingdom, a lot of short-run assistance before 1967 had helped the authorities to stick to the wrong parity for too long.

Mr Brittan said that undoubtedly there had been American pressure to keep the parity of sterling unchanged, but while it was right to blame the United States for this, the pressure was quite welcome to the Government of the time. American pressure had helped those in the Bank of England and elsewhere who wanted the Government to stick to its policy of defending the parity.

Replying to Professor Kindleberger, *Mr Lamfalussy* said he did not pretend that countries had to be independent from the international capital market. He was simply saying that a central bank today could not wait for a long time to know why it was losing reserves. It needed sufficient reserves to allow it to find the reason before taking drastic steps. Owned reserves were simply not big enough.

Mr Grogan pointed out that Mr Maddison, on p. 163 of his paper, had said 'Asian countries have also raised tariffs and protection has been strengthened in Australia'. In 1962 Australia removed the tight import licensing which it had imposed in 1952. Since then, imports had increased more or less in line with economic growth. There had been a dramatic decline in the percentage of Australia's exports to and imports from Britain. A recent study at Newcastle upon Tyne indicated closer correlations if the decline in Australian imports from Britain were related to decline in exports to Britain in the preceding year than if the comparison were reversed. This might suggest that Britain was the primary sinner, rather than Australia, with respect to protection.

Mr Maddison said that participants at the Round Table were naturally rather sensitive to the suggestion that trade did not play a very important role in explaining growth. But, as Sir John Hicks had said, how could one explain Japanese growth if one thought that trade liberalisation was so important for growth. The Japanese trade ratio was still less than before the war but it had the fastest-growing economy. Obviously, freer trade had contributed to faster growth in post-war Europe, but one could not claim the whole of the post-war acceleration in growth for trade. Such factors as the increase in investment, full employment and co-operation between countries were more important.

Though he would criticise present liquidity arrangements, they were much better than before the Second World War. Severe deflation had not been a consequence of balance of payments disequilibrium. The United Kingdom seemed to be the only country with a growth rate significantly below her potential, and even here, lack of liquidity was not the sole cause.

Mr Maddison noted that Professor Mundell thought that payments would be equilibrated in future through capital movements and changes in the rate of interest, not through changes in exchange rates. He was not ready to accept this. The system would have to rely to some extent on exchange-rate changes. Apart from anything else, governmental attempts to check tax evasion must ultimately limit the extent of capital movements.

8 Economic Relations between European Socialist Countries and Capitalist Countries of Europe and North America

K. Plotnikov
U.S.S.R. ACADEMY OF SCIENCES

I. INTRODUCTION

Today the question how to achieve better relations between 'East' and 'West' and between European and North American countries is of concern to all. There is reason to think that the system which the European socialist countries have evolved to develop trade between themselves – the Council for Mutual Economic Assistance (C.M.E.A.) – might usefully serve as a model for the countries of the West and might be extended to relations between socialist and capitalist countries.

In this paper an attempt is therefore made firstly to outline the economic ties between the socialist countries of Europe and the prospects of their further development. An attempt is made secondly to analyse the economic relations between the European socialist countries and the capitalist countries of Europe and the United States.

II. ECONOMIC RELATIONS BETWEEN THE EUROPEAN SOCIALIST COUNTRIES

The council for Mutual Economic Assistance (C.M.E.A.), created twenty years ago by Bulgaria, Hungary, the D.D.R., Poland, Rumania, the U.S.S.R. and Czechoslovakia, has as its main aim 'to promote through co-ordination of efforts of the C.M.E.A. countries the planned development of their economies and the speeding-up of their economic and technical progress, the rise in the level of the industrialisation of countries with less developed industries, the consistent growth of labour productivity and the well-being of the peoples of the C.M.E.A. countries'. During these twenty years all the activities of the C.M.E.A. countries have been directed to the attainment of these goals. The experience accumulated has demonstrated that co-operation between the C.M.E.A. countries has served as an important stimulus to rapid growth of their economies. In the past decade the combined national income of the C.M.E.A. countries has increased by 93 per cent, while in the same period that of the developed capitalist countries has increased by 63 per cent. The C.M.E.A. countries, with only 10 per cent of the world's population, now account for about one-third of the world's industrial production: in 1968 the C.M.E.A. countries produced 855 billion kWh of electricity, 1,129 million tons of coal, 324 million tons of oil, 142 millions tons of steel, 323 thousand metal-cutting machine-tools, 503,000 tractors and over 16 million tons of fertilisers. These figures well illustrate the achievements of the C.M.E.A. countries in the sphere of industrialisation.

The economic co-operation and international division of labour within the framework of C.M.E.A. is designed to enable every member country to develop a pattern of industries which best suits the conditions in that country. The main form of co-operation between the C.M.E.A. countries is the co-ordination of national economic plans. This gives member countries the opportunity to plan in advance their economic exchanges. It helps to solve economic problems of common interest, such as expansion of fuel, power and raw materials production, specialisation and co-operation in production, more rapid scientific and technical progress, desirable changes in the structure of production and location of industries. The co-ordination of national economic plans for the period 1966-70 was worked out in 1966 and the inter-C.M.E.A. economic exchanges were based on it. This co-ordination opened up great possibilities for international specialisation and co-operation in production. The agreed specialisation arrangements cover more than 4,000 types of machinery and equipment and 2,200 chemical products. At the same time a great deal is being done in the sphere of standardisation.

The experience of co-operation within C.M.E.A. shows that for some socialist countries integration is becoming a vital necessity. The scientific and technological revolution makes it necessary to concentrate and specialise production, to expand scientific and technological research and to modernise industries. This cannot be achieved if each national economy is developed separately. The socialist systems of ownership of the means of production, of international division of labour, and of specialisation and co-operation in production all influence the process of integration of production within C.M.E.A. The establishment of international associations of enterprises in the socialist countries has contributed to the process of integration. Optimum scale is possible only when industrial enterprises are guaranteed large (in some cases larger than national) markets for their products. Within C.M.E.A. integration is proceeding rapidly in such key branches as fuel production, electricity generation, metallurgy, the chemical and machine-building industries. The planned growth of the European socialist countries depends greatly on fuel supply and the rationalisation of fuel and energy use; in some countries there are fuel and energy deficiencies. For this reason saving of fuel and the building of big and efficient thermal power stations is of the utmost importance. So also is the utilisation of water resources for electricity generation and other purposes. A general plan for the integrated utilisation of the water resources of the Danube in the common interests of all C.M.E.A. members and all purposes – electricity production, river transport, agriculture – has been worked out. Rumania and Yugoslavia are jointly building the Iron Gate hydro-power station. Similarly, the C.M.E.A. countries are planning jointly to build a number of atomic power stations with a combined capacity of 8–9 million kW and designed to produce 55–60 billion kWh of electricity annually. Important steps have also been taken towards unifying the power grids of the C.M.E.A. countries. In 1962 a Central Control Administration of the Power Grids of the C.M.E.A. countries was set up; since then electricity exchanges between the U.S.S.R. and other C.M.E.A. countries increased more than tenfold.

In 1964 the International Organisation for Co-operation in Metallurgy ('Intermetal') was established by Bulgaria, Hungary, the D.D.R., Poland, the U.S.S.R. and Czechoslovakia. Within 'Intermetal', the volume of rolled steel products, pipes and other items exchanged grows annually and measures to improve the utilisation of capacity in rolling mills, bloomings, and other processes have been introduced. In future, developments will be based not only on co-operation in metallurgy as such but also in mining iron ore, production of coking coal, and the building of blast furnaces and steel-making capacity.

Integration in machine-building has also contributed to raising the technical efficiency of the enterprises concerned. The formation of an organisation for co-operation in the ball-bearing industry has resulted in rapid expansion of the production of ball-bearings. There are, again, great prospects for integration in the chemical industry.

Integration extends into the sphere of trade. Within the framework of the socialist system the world socialist market, which functions in conformity with its own laws, different from those of the capitalist market, has come into being; it covers two-thirds of the trade turnover of socialist countries. In the world socialist market the volumes, structures and prices are determined on a planned basis and trade policy is guided by principles of mutual benefit and mutual aid.

Currency and financial relations within C.M.E.A. are so conducted as to strengthen economic co-operation and encourage further integration. The establishment of the International Bank for Economic Co-operation (I.B.E.C.) has improved currency relations between the C.M.E.A. countries and broadened trade and other economic links between them; the present credit system adequately meets the needs of the socialist countries for credits; the total of credits extended during the past five years amounts to 8·8 billion transferable roubles. A large part of the operations of the I.B.E.C. is carried out in gold and convertible currencies; the I.B.E.C. has established broad links with the banks of C.M.E.A. countries as well as with important banks in third countries.

TABLE 8.1

COMPARISON OF TRADE BETWEEN C.M.E.A. COUNTRIES AND SELECTED OTHER COUNTRIES WITH THAT BETWEEN C.M.E.A. COUNTRIES AND THE UNITED STATES, 1962

(Trade with United States = 100)

	U.S.A.	Britain	West Germany	France	Italy	Austria	Finland	India
U.S.S.R.	100	741·5	726·2	536·5	517·5	252·0	889·8	442·0
D.D.R.	100	1054·5	8136·3	502·2	491·0	813·6	584·0	931·8
Czechoslovakia	100	596·0	7542·0	269·9	356·8	371·8	132·0	373·2
Poland	100	184·0	121·0	42·3	57·4	51·6	37·0	32·3
Hungary	100	1428·2	2346·2	967·1	1228·2	1618·0	205·1	700·0
Rumania	100	1973·3	3946·6	1456·6	2323·3	986·6	133·3	403·3
Bulgaria	100	1988·8	5100·0	2433·3	330·0	3111·0	144·5	222·2

III. ECONOMIC RELATIONS OF EUROPEAN SOCIALIST COUNTRIES WITH EUROPEAN CAPITALIST COUNTRIES AND THE UNITED STATES

Before trying to describe the general trends in the economic relations between the countries of the socialist and capitalist systems, it is desirable to consider the actual state of these relations. The volume of foreign trade is the best indicator of this. An analysis of the foreign trade of the U.S.S.R. and other socialist countries shows that the trade between them and the capitalist countries increases progressively. During the period 1950–62 the Soviet Union's trade with the capitalist countries of Europe grew 5·3 times, that of Czechoslovakia 1·2 times, the D.D.R.'s 3·4 times, Bulgaria's 8 times, Hungary's 2·3 times, Poland's 1·7 times, Rumania's 8·9 times. In 1966 the developed capitalist countries' share in the trade of the C.M.E.A. countries amounted to 23 per cent.

The main items in C.M.E.A. imports from the developed capitalist countries are machines and equipment (1·5 billion roubles in 1966) and agricultural raw materials (1·5 billion roubles in 1966). The main items of C.M.E.A. exports to these countries are fuel and metals (1·4 billion roubles in 1966) and agricultural and mineral raw materials (0·8 billion roubles in 1966). The structure of C.M.E.A.'s countries' trade with capitalist countries, and especially with developed countries, is undergoing significant changes. In the C.M.E.A. countries' exports the share of machinery, equipment and other industrial goods is constantly growing.

A comparison of the trade between C.M.E.A. countries and certain capitalist countries with that between C.M.E.A. countries and the United States is of interest. The figures in Table 8.1 cover the year 1962; the figure 100 is taken to represent the trade turnover between a given C.M.E.A. country and the United States.

The table shows how damaging to Soviet–American trade and to trade between the United States and other socialist countries were the discriminatory measures against trade with socialist countries then in force in the United States; the United States, taking into account the volume and the structure of its production and trade, has great opportunities where trade with the Soviet Union and other socialist countries is concerned and might have been expected to have far the largest volume of transactions with the world socialist system.

The table reflects the situation as it was several years ago. But so far as Soviet–American trade is concerned it has unfortunately remained practically static to this day. In this respect recent official returns of Soviet foreign trade are instructive (See Table 8.2). It is significant that the statisticians of the Soviet Foreign Trade Ministry did not find it necessary to include the United States separately in the table.

TABLE 8.2

THE SHARE OF CERTAIN COUNTRIES AND GROUPS OF COUNTRIES IN THE FOREIGN TRADE TURNOVER OF THE U.S.S.R.

(percentages of total trade)

	1965	1966	1967	1968
Total	100	100	100	100
All socialist countries	68·8	66·5	67·8	67·4
C.M.E.A. countries	58·0	56·0	57·1	57·5
All capitalist countries	31·2	33·5	32·2	32·6
Developed capitalist countries	19·2	21·1	20·6	21·3
Austria	0·7	0·7	0·8	0·7
Belgium	0·5	0·6	0·7	0·8
Britain	2·7	3·0	2·8	3·2
Italy	1·5	1·5	2·1	2·2
Canada	1·6	2·2	0·9	0·7
Holland	0·6	0·7	1·0	0·8
West Germany	1·7	1·9	1·9	2·2
Finland	2·8	2·8	2·8	2·5
France	1·4	1·7	1·8	2·2
Sweden	0·7	0·7	0·7	0·9
Japan	2·2	2·8	2·9	2·9

The table that follows gives an idea of how small is the trade turnover between the U.S.S.R. and the United States in relation to the total volume of Soviet foreign trade and to Soviet trade with some capitalist countries.

TABLE 8.3

TRADE TURNOVER BETWEEN THE SOVIET UNION AND CERTAIN CAPITALIST COUNTRIES

(million roubles)

	1966	1967	1968
World	15,078·6	16,370·1	18,039·9
Finland	426·7	461·3	458·9
France	261·4	299·6	388·4
Britain	449·0	450·5	575·7
Canada	324·8	147·0	131·2
United States	99·0	91·7	69·5

There is no necessity to repeat that the present state and scale of the economic relations between the Soviet Union and other socialist countries on the one hand and the capitalist countries, including the United States, on the other hand stems to a great degree from the economic policies of the capitalist countries; the socialist countries do not apply any restrictions to economic relations between East and West. These restrictions on trade with the socialist countries are in the long run equally disadvantageous to all who practise them. It is self-evident that the more goods socialist countries sell to capitalist countries the more they can buy from them.

The process of socialist economic integration continues; the policies of all C.M.E.A. countries aim at its furtherance. It is necessary to take into account socialist economic integration as well as the integration processes between Western Europe and North America, if one seeks properly to evaluate the future prospects in the field of international economic relations. Socialist integration does not exclude the possibility of expansion of relations between C.M.E.A. countries and third countries. On the contrary, the policies of the socialist countries are based on the assumption that co-operation between the socialist and the capitalist countries will make headway, once it is realised that such co-operation is a practical necessity.

The Soviet economic plan for 1966-70 provides for further increase of Soviet trade with those developed capitalist countries which in turn show readiness to develop their trade with the Soviet Union. Long-term trade and credit arrangements between the Soviet Union or other socialist countries and such capitalist countries will help to make possible a mutually beneficial expansion of economic relations.

Discussion of the Paper by Professor Plotnikov

Professor Khachaturov said there were two parts to the paper. The first looked at co-operation in Eastern Europe; the second at co-operation between Eastern and Western Europe and the United States. Professor Plotnikov explained that in relations between socialist countries the C.M.E.A. played a decisive part.

Professor Plotnikov's data showed the share of Eastern European trade in the world economy. The development of socialist countries was linked to co-operation between them. This made possible the development, in each country of the industrial complexes best suited to its own resources and position. In the first part of the paper, Professor Plotnikov mentioned the co-ordination of national Plans; an Eastern European Common Market for certain goods; co-operation in research and development; and plans for further integration. The main form of co-operation between C.M.E.A. countries was in the co-ordination of national Plans. This allowed members to provide mutual economic exchanges and to solve common problems – for example, problems such as fuel supply, raw materials, scientific and technical policy were all considered. Agreement for specialisation between countries covered 4,000 kinds of machines and 2,000 kinds of chemical products. They allowed the production capacity of enterprises to increase and reduced costs. They allowed mass production; for they needed bigger markets than national ones. Thus, there were new organisations for co-operation in metallurgy, chemicals, etc. Scientific and technical co-operation was an important goal. Already this covered hundreds of research topics. Economic co-operation, and the enlargement of the market covered by C.M.E.A., was helped by an international bank. Its total lending over five years had amounted to 9 billion transferable roubles. Professor Plotnikov found all this interesting in the light of possible co-operation with the West.

This was what he looked at in the second part of the paper. On the foreign trade of the U.S.S.R., Professor Plotnikov showed that her main partners were the United Kingdom, West Germany, France, Italy, India and Finland. Another major sphere for co-operation was in science and technology. For example, there was already co-operation with France over colour television. Under the Franco-Soviet treaty, research into scientific problems was being carried out.

There were, of course, insignificant trade links between the United States and the U.S.S.R. Professor Wallich had wondered how many Russian goods were of interest to the United States, and had advocated payments in gold. Professor Khachaturov did not agree with this. The Soviet Union had a big national economy, and a developing industry; it also had a large internal market. This was why foreign trade plays a comparatively small part in national income of the U.S.S.R. However, the U.S.S.R. did want trade, especially with the United States. This trade might be profitable to both partners, and the paper suggested possible developments. The Soviet Union was anxious to import, for example, scientific instruments and some consumer goods. The first need was for the United States to remove the embargo on some kinds of trade with socialist countries. This had been introduced in the United States a long time previously, and many goods were banned. Professor Khachaturov ended by saying that trade would also help peaceful coexistence.

188   *Conflicts of Interest in Trade, Capital Flows and Monetary Policy*

Professor van Meerhaeghe referred to the passage in the paper arguing that co-operation through C.M.E.A. helped growth. What calculations had been made to show how fast the Eastern European countries would have grown without it? This kind of calculation was made for the E.E.C.; was it made for the Eastern bloc? For example, Yugoslavia was not a member. Had Yugoslavia grown differently?

Professor van Meerhaeghe wondered whether one could say what were the disadvantages of the C.M.E.A. All international organisations had their disadvantages and he wondered what those of the C.M.E.A. were, especially in establishing the criteria which helped to determine the industries 'which best suit the conditions in each of the C.M.E.A. countries'.

Mr Maddison said that, on p. 185 of his paper, Professor Plotnikov showed a faster rate of growth of trade between socialist countries than between socialist and capitalist countries. Yet there were big differences within the socialist world. The Soviet Union, Rumania and Bulgaria seemed to have increased their trade in recent years, while this was not true of Czechoslovakia and Poland. Did this represent differences in policy about trade within the Eastern bloc?

Professor Yamamoto noted that Professor Plotnikov said that the Soviet Union was anxious to broaden further its trade with industrialised countries. As a developed country in Asia, Japan was also anxious to trade with the Eastern countries and indeed with mainland China. Trade with China was a big problem for political reasons, but there seemed to be possibilities of trade with the Soviet Union. The American share in Japanese trade was more than 20 per cent and there would be bad effects if economic difficulties arose in the United States. In trying to diversify its trade, Japan would be happy to increase its trade with the Soviet Union.

Professor Lundberg was surprised that everything seemed to go so well in the East, compared with the West. Those who had written papers for the Round Table were enjoying the difficult problems of the West. Was it really true that there were none in the East?

On p. 182 Professor Plotnikov said that trade between socialist countries developed according to its own laws. These appeared to be different from those in the capitalist world. Trade grew rapidly despite the fact that socialist countries had no international pool of convertible currency. So much trade took place on the clearing basis. Was this the law of trade in the East?

At the bottom of p. 185, Professor Plotnikov said that most trade problems arose in East-West trade. Professor Lundberg agreed that there was the embargo on trade with the United States, but Sweden would like more trade with the Soviet Union. However, there were always payments difficulties, and lack of contact with the ultimate consumer. Was this a deficiency of socialist trade? What was there really in the policy of the West which caused trade to be so small between East and West?

Professor Campbell said he would like to protest light-heartedly at the exclusion of Canada from the main trading partners of the U.S.S.R. In fact, it was the third biggest. So far as wheat was concerned, many people did not realise that the U.S.S.R. produced as much wheat as America, Canada, Australia and the Argentine added together. In a year of bad harvests, a 20 per cent reduction in the wheat harvest in the U.S.S.R. equalled the normal output of Argentina and Australia. There were obviously difficulties in the world wheat market as a result. He wondered whether Professor Plotnikov could give any information about the likely developments in wheat production in the U.S.S.R. What were the prospects for imports into Siberia, even if there was a surplus in the West?

Professor Izzo wondered if Professor Plotnikov could say what was the percentage of trade to G.N.P. in the U.S.S.R. *Professor Plotnikov* replied that the figure was 2 per cent.

Dr de Mello said that, in his introduction, Professor Khachaturov had said how hard it was to increase East–West trade because of embargoes. Was there the same problem the other way round? Could such obstacles be removed?

Professor Wallich said that on p. 182 of his paper, Professor Plotnikov said 'the volume, structure and prices in the world socialist market are determined on a planned basis'. His understanding of trade between private firms and government organisations was not great, and he wondered if one could see how flexible the Eastern countries' plans were. When the plan was formulated, one clearly needed to aim at some balance between products coming from foreign and domestic sources. What was the basis for this? Was price important? After formulation of the national plan, suppose that the price of a product altered on the world market. What room was there for substituting this change into the plan?

Professor Wallich wondered at what level in the administrative machine such decisions were taken. For example, the Soviet Union did not import steel. If there were a fall in the price of steel, and if the plan allowed this, at what level in the administration would the decision to import steel be taken? Would it be in an office in Moscow or would the decision be taken by a plant manager?

Professor Sohmen said we were told that trade between the Soviet countries and the West was based on world market prices. Was this also done in intra-bloc trade? If world prices were used, he could see many reasons why these would not be ideal. For example, factor endowments were not the same in Eastern countries as in the West. Other equilibrium prices must therefore hold. In addition, Western prices were often distorted by monopoly power or government intervention. For example, home prices for agricultural foods in most countries were higher than export prices. If these prices were used for socialist trade, it was hard to see how proper results could be obtained.

Professor Plotnikov replied to the discussion. To the question on the prospects for economic relations between the Soviet Union and Western capitalist countries, he replied that the future of economic relations between the Soviet Union and Western capitalist countries depended mostly on the policy of the latter. Unfortunately, the capitalist countries had some powerful forces that were against the expansion of trade with the U.S.S.R. and other socialist countries, and they pursued a policy of discrimination. However, in business circles and among the statesmen of Western countries, there appeared to be more and more supporters of economic co-operation between the West and the East. Here, the economic, scientific and technical achievements of the Soviet Union and other socialist countries played a considerable role, as well as recent recessions both in Western Europe and the United States.

These changes had led to the expansion of trade between the U.S.S.R. and Western countries and had led to new forms of scientific and technical co-operation. For example, there had been close Soviet–French relations in recent years. The U.S.S.R. maintained trade and scientific relations with the United

Kingdom, Italy (which supplied equipment for a number of automobile plants in the U.S.S.R.), Japan, Finland, Norway, Iran and many other countries.

However, the development of trade with most Western countries, particularly with members of the O.E.C.D., had been slowed down by various discriminatory measures on their part. They maintained quantitative restrictions on imports of a number of goods from the Soviet Union and other socialist countries. These goods were being discriminated against by customs duties and taxes. In NATO, up to now, there had been an embargo on exports of many goods to the socialist countries. Because of this, trade relations between the U.S.S.R. and the United States were at a rather low level.

Such tariff barriers prevented the development of international trade and the strengthening of good-neighbour relations. But those who hoped to slow down the economic growth of the Soviet Union by using trade discrimination were misleading themselves. At present, the economic power of the Soviet Union and the other socialist countries was so great that they could develop successfully by using their own resources and through mutual assistance.

As for whether a shortage of convertible currency in the Soviet Union and other socialist countries prevented the development of foreign trade, Professor Plotnikov said that, at present, currency relations between the socialist countries were based on the collective currency note of the C.M.E.A. countries – the convertible rouble. This currency note had a stable gold content and there were fixed exchange rates between the convertible rouble and the currency of each socialist country. This currency note kept prices stable and provided the basis for foreign trade between the socialist countries. The establishment of an International Bank for Economic Co-operation in 1964, with the aim of facilitating payments, granting credits and easing currency restrictions, was of great importance.

The socialist countries still faced the problem of moving to a collective, convertible currency. But the necessary conditions had first to be established. If this problem were solved in a proper way, a convertible currency would help to expand and strengthen economic relations both between socialist countries and throughout the world market.

As for the possibility of the U.S.S.R. expanding trade relations with the United States, Sweden and other countries, Professor Plotnikov explained that the Soviet Union was interested in the development of mutual economic co-operation with other countries. This was shown by the fact that the U.S.S.R.'s foreign trade turnover had increased more than tenfold; it now held seventh place among trading countries, as against sixteenth in 1938. The trade turnover of the U.S.S.R. with the developed capitalist countries had grown considerably. For example, between 1950 and 1962 the Soviet trade turnover with Western European countries had grown 5·3 times.

Unfortunately, the situation was different with Soviet–American trade. The United States, because of the size and structure of its national production and foreign trade, had an important potential for trade with the Soviet Union; but under the influence of the 'cold war' policies, and by deliberately refusing mutual economic benefit, the United States had allowed Soviet–American trade to fall almost to zero. Trade with a small country like Finland, which kept good relations with the U.S.S.R., was nine times greater than trade between the U.S.S.R. and the United States.

The Soviet Union had a great trading potential, possessing rich natural resources and a large international market for industrial and agricultural produce. The U.S.S.R. was therefore interested in developing trade with all the countries of the world on a mutually beneficial basis.

Professor Campbell had asked if the Soviet Union would continue to buy wheat from Canada. Professor Plotnikov reported that the Soviet Government was carrying out a major programme for the technical re-equipment of collective farms and state farms and further land reclamation. It was increasing the use of chemicals and was reorganising agriculture, as well as training more specialists.

By 1968, the gross value of agricultural output increased twofold by comparison with 1940. Because of this growth in agricultural output, the U.S.S.R. did not need to buy wheat abroad.

Professor Plotnikov said that in socialist countries trade was carried out on the basis of world prices, but with some amendments. This was because prices in the world market were influenced by various marketing factors. So far as the foreign trade of socialist countries was concerned, it should be mentioned that they still carried on trade at world prices, as they could not yet be abandoned. Collaborative research was being carried out in the socialist countries to establish world socialist prices.

Finally, on possible changes in the national economic plan, Professor Plotnikov said that changes could be made after the national plan had been adopted by the government. But these changes were always under the control of the government. In an emergency, the government decided on amendments to the plan.

9 Towards an International Capital Market ?

Richard N. Cooper
YALE UNIVERSITY

I. INTRODUCTORY

This paper discusses the growth and development of the international capital market during the past decade, considers whether it can be said that a genuine international capital market now exists, and discusses the advantages and disadvantages of one integrated capital market transcending national economies. 'Capital markets' involve the mobilisation of savings by those who want or are willing to accept financial claims, for investment (or consumption) by others who are willing to accept financial liabilities or share their equity. Capital markets are usually distinguished from 'money markets' by the maturity of the claims that are traded there, the capital market referring to transactions in claims with maturities in excess (definitionally) of one year, and usually in excess of five years, although any clear distinction between the two must be arbitrary, for these markets may be, and typically are, closely related. Medium-term bank lending, for example, involves maturities in excess of one year but ordinarily does not give rise to marketable securities.

Several geographically distinct capital markets can be said to be integrated – that is, effectively one market – to the extent that a significant number of savers do not distinguish among claims on the basis of the geographical location of the borrower. In the international context, this means that a significant number of savers do not distinguish among borrowers on the basis of nationality. This failure to distinguish must include, of course, both the willingness to accept claims on foreigners and the ability to do so, the letter implying an absence of balance of payments and other restrictions against foreign investment.

The extent to which there can be said to be an Atlantic capital market, encompassing Canada, the United States, and many or most of the countries of Western Europe, can be approached empirically from two angles. We can ask about the absolute and relative volume of long-term financial transactions crossing national boundaries and about the nationality and other characteristics of the borrowers and lenders. Or we can apply the economically more meaningful test of the extent to which bond yields and share prices have been brought into harmony. One market implies one price for identical goods or claims, and similar prices for similar goods or claims. A genuine Atlantic capital market would therefore imply similar interest rates or yields for financial claims of similar risk and liquidity. The next two sections of this paper offer some sketchy evidence on both of these approaches. Following this evidence, I will draw some implications for economic policy of the tendency towards one market, and offer an assessment of the advantages and disadvantages at the present time of a unified capital market spanning national boundaries.

II. THE SIZE AND GROWTH OF INTERNATIONAL CAPITAL MOVEMENTS

The rapid growth in foreign bond flotations during the decade of the 1960s has been a source of universal astonishment. From barely more than $200 million in 1958 (close to $400 million if the United Kingdom is included), foreign bond issues in Europe grew to over $4·7 billion in 1968, a compound growth rate of nearly 30 per cent a year. The growth is far less dramatic, but still dramatic, if the United States market is included: total foreign bond issues on both sides of the Atlantic rose from $1·5 billion in 1958 to $6·3 billion in 1968[1], a fourfold increase (Table 9.1). A

TABLE 9.1

FOREIGN BOND ISSUES,[a] 1958–68
($ million)

| | Foreign issues on domestic markets | | International | |
	United States	European[b]	issues[b]	Total
1958	1138	302	82	1522
1959	802	337	31	1170
1960	636	393	29	1058
1961	558	559	79	1196
1962	1185	430	–	1615
1963	1414	426	119	1958
1964	1191	263	838	2293
1965	1532	264[c]	1192	2989
1966	1317	550[c]	1155	3021
1967	1619[d]	404[c]	2002	4025
1968	1576[d]	1185[c]	3517	6278

[a] Including private placements and convertible bonds.
[b] Foreign bonds issued in Germany after imposition of the 25 per cent coupon tax on German bonds in March 1964 are treated as international issues, since they are exempt from the tax.
[c] Including the Canadian market.   [d] Excludes portion purchased by foreigners.
Sources: 1958–66: O.E.C.D., *Capital Markets Study*, vol. III, *Functioning of Capital Markets* (Paris, O.E.C.D., 1968) p. 717; 1967–8: Department of Commerce, *Survey of Current Business*, and Morgan Guaranty Trust Company, *World Financial Markets*.

---

[1] It might be noted in passing that recent levels compare favourably in absolute magnitude to the average annual $2·0 billion in foreign bonds issued in Europe and the United States during 1924–8, the alleged heyday of the international capital market.

distinction may be drawn between foreign bonds issued in national markets, denominated in the national currency of the market in which it is floated, and 'international' bond issues, which are denominated in a currency (usually United States dollars but also German marks, two or more currencies, and units of account) different from that of the country (or countries) in which it is floated.[1] International issues grew from negligible amounts in the early 1960s to $3·5 billion in 1968.

The overwhelming bulk of the long-term foreign borrowing in the United States is by Canadians, although Japan, Israel, the World Bank, and (before the imposition of the interest equalisation tax in 1963) several European countries have also been important borrowers. United States corporations and their subsidiaries have been the single most important group of borrowers in European markets, accounting for nearly half of all new issues (many of them convertible bonds) in 1968. Non-American corporations accounted for nearly a quarter of the borrowing, and governmental bodies and international institutions for the remainder. Characterising the lenders is more difficult, since it is not known who ultimately purchases these bonds. In the United States, insurance companies and pension funds provide a steady source of demand for new bond issues. In the European market, individuals and family trusts are relatively more important (leading to correspondingly higher selling costs for the 'retail' market). It has been estimated for the mid-1960s that about half the purchases of foreign bonds issued in Europe were by banks and trusts in Switzerland, acting on behalf of customers from all over the world; another 20 per cent of the funds came from other continental European countries.[2]

Over three-quarters of the international bond issues, narrowly defined, were denominated in United States dollars, and therefore over two-thirds of total foreign bond issues outside the United States were so denominated. Like a language, a currency is useful in proportion to the number of people who use it. By using a common currency, the market is widened and the potential liquidity of financial claims is increased – potential since this liquidity depends on the development of secondary markets where securities are bought and sold after issue and before maturity, and secondary markets in Europe have developed more slowly than the new issues market. During 1968 and 1969 use of the German mark became more prominent, as the German monetary authorities deliberately maintained low interest rates and took other steps to encourage the export of

---

[1] Foreign bonds denominated in German marks are considered 'international' bonds after March 1964, even when floated on the German market, since they were exempt from the coupon tax levied on interests payments to foreign holders of German bonds and hence had lower yields than German bonds floated on the domestic market.

[2] David Williams, 'Foreign Currency Issues in European Security Markets', *I.M.F. Staff Papers* (May 1967) p. 61.

capital, making DM.-denominated bonds less costly to borrowers than dollar-denominated ones.[1]

Foreign and international bond issues have grown rapidly relative to the total activity on the various national capital markets, as well as in absolute volume. Comparable measures are difficult to obtain, but on the basis of total net new bond issues on the eight major European capital markets plus the United States, as computed by the O.E.C.D., the share of foreign and international bond issues rose from 5 per cent in 1960 to 11 per cent in 1965 and to an estimated 14 per cent in 1968.[2]

Equity shares comprise another part of the capital market. Here one must turn to the secondary market for relevant information, since it is far more important, relative to new issues, than is the case for bonds. Until 1967 and 1968, net movements of funds between countries on account of purchases of stocks (excluding direct investment, aimed at management control) was rather small. Americans added very little to their holdings of foreign stocks during the 1960s, while the British engaged in large-scale net liquidation of their foreign share holdings. Net foreign purchases of American stocks rose sharply after the mid-1960s, however, from $200 million in 1963 to nearly $2·3 billion in 1968, with purchases from Europe and Canada accounting for the bulk of them. Mutual funds spread rapidly in the late 1960s, especially in Germany and Italy, and many of these specialised in the purchase of foreign – mainly American – stocks.

From the viewpoint of the integration of capital markets, however, it is *gross* rather than net transactions that count. These have been substantial, even when net transactions were small. In 1968, for instance, foreigners bought $13·1 billion in American stocks, and sold $10·8 billion, over six times the levels of 1960; American purchases of foreign stocks (except for dealers, generally subject to the interest equalisation tax of 15 per cent) amounted to $1·6 billion in 1968, while sales came to $1·2 billion, both over double the levels of 1960. These sums are of course small relative to the total gross value of stock sales ($125 billion on the New York Stock Exchange alone in 1968). But here, as elsewhere in economics, it is the marginal buyer that counts. The question, therefore, is whether international transactions in stocks and bonds were sufficiently large at the margin to influence or even to govern prices in the various national markets.

Before turning to an examination of the evidence on that point, two other important dimensions of international capital movements should be mentioned, for while they are not strictly part of 'capital markets' as defined here, both short-term capital movements and direct investments

---

[1] Expectations of a future revaluation of the mark also helped lower coupon rates on DM.-denominated bonds.

[2] O.E.C.D., *Capital Markets Study*, op. cit., *Statistical Annex*, pp. 122–3, and the sources there cited.

provide potential indirect linkages between capital markets to the extent that there is some substitutability between short- and long-term financial claims, on the one hand, and between long-term financial claims and real assets on the other. Capital markets could be fully integrated in the economically meaningful sense of price equalisation for claims of similar quality even with no movement of long-term portfolio capital between countries, for instance, provided that money and capital markets were tightly linked within each country and that national money markets were closely linked internationally.

National money markets are linked these days primarily through Eurodollars, a market in short-term dollar claims located in London and other European financial centres. Where national exchange regulations permit the outward movement of short-term funds, those with such funds to invest will compare their earning opportunities at home with those in Eurodollar deposits, and will shift funds accordingly. Even where regulations limit the outward movement of funds, credit-worthy borrowers will draw funds from the Euro-dollar market when rates there are more attractive than in their home markets. In this way national money markets tend to be tied together.

The Euro-dollar market has grown to substantial proportions. At an estimated $25 billion of total liabilities by the end of 1968, excluding interbank deposits, the Euro-dollar market was roughly equivalent in size to the total money supply in Italy, Japan, or the United Kingdom, and was substantially exceeded only by the money supplies in France and the United States. It has shown surprising responsiveness, moreover, to new demands placed on it. Switches of borrowers or lenders between the Euro-dollar market and domestic markets can therefore exert a powerful influence on domestic monetary conditions, and for many countries could in principle largely undercut monetary policy as an instrument of economic stabilisation. This extreme has not yet been reached, in part because a switch between dollars and local currencies requires either that the switching party take on an exchange risk or that he insure against it, e.g. by selling forward the currency he has purchased. The presence of exchange risk serves to insulate national money markets from one another even when all the technical facilities for one integrated market are present.

Direct investment abroad can also provide a link between capital markets. Recent work on the motivation for direct investment has rightly emphasised the exploitation of quasi-monopoly powers arising from patents or other unique technological or managerial advantages. Many direct investors borrow in local markets, both to establish credit lines and to hedge against exchange risks, and this practice suggests that direct investment is not primarily in response to national differences in long-term bond yields. Nevertheless, direct investment does usually involve the transfer of funds from one country to another, and since the early 1960s such transfers have taken place on a substantial scale.

United States takeovers of European firms bid up the price of existing assets, and takeovers for cash shift funds from the United States capital market to the capital or money markets of Europe. Investments in new plant and equipment are more ambiguous in their effects, since any flow of funds from the parent company is accompanied by an increased demand for funds that may more than offset it, depending on the extent of local borrowing and the size of multiplier effects. But many international corporations, with access to two or more national capital markets, are influenced in their source of funds by relative costs, and hence tend to bring borrowing conditions in national markets into closer harmony. Direct investment also plays a role in bringing national money markets together, as corporations with temporarily idle funds place them where the yield–risk combination is most attractive, or fill short-term cash needs by borrowing in the money market where costs are lowest. Indeed, international corporations have been among the major participants both in the Euro-dollar market and in the Euro-bond market.

In passing, it is of interest that both the Euro-dollar market and the international bond market were encouraged by the imposition of national controls that inhibited the most advantageously situated national market from serving an international role. In 1957 the British commercial banks were circumscribed in their ability to lend sterling outside the United Kingdom, but were left free to carry on in other currencies, so began to accept deposits and lend in dollars. In 1963 the interest equalisation tax effectively closed the New York bond market to a large class of foreign borrowers and thereby generated a demand for issues in Europe, a demand that was greatly augmented two years later by the voluntary limitations placed on United States financing of direct investment abroad.

III. INTEREST RATES AND ASSET PRICES

The flow of funds across national boundaries unquestionably increased sharply during the 1960s, both absolutely and relative to internal financial transactions. Identifiable international money and capital markets appeared. But were these developments sufficient to integrate the national financial markets in the sense of bringing together prices of similar financial assets? A unified market requires a single price for the same commodity prevailing everywhere at each point in time. When this condition is not met, markets are to that extent fragmented.

It is difficult to test empirically the extent to which we have achieved integrated money and capital markets among the major industrial countries, since assets in different countries continue to be different in one important respect; they are denominated in different currencies. The possibility of changes in exchange rates among the currencies introduces an element of risk which, from the viewpoint of a resident of any particular country, is not present when all assets are denominated in a single currency. The assets also differ in other, less important respects. A comparison of interest rates on high-quality short-term assets and on long-term government bonds none the less reveals a marked tendency towards convergence following the move to currency convertibility by the major European countries in late 1958. Table 9.2 shows that the dispersion around the

TABLE 9.2

INTERNATIONAL CONVERGENCE OF INTEREST RATES,[a] 1958–68

	Short-term[b]			Government bonds[c]		
	Mean	Standard deviation	Coefficient of variation[d]	Mean	Standard deviation	Coefficient of variation[d]
1958	2·86	1·22	0·43	4·48	0·94	0·21
1960	3·37	1·21	0·36	4·66	0·93	0·20
1962	2·96	0·95	0·32	4·80	0·89	0·19
1964	3·66	0·74	0·20	5·36	0·93	0·17
1966	4·80	0·83	0·17	5·89	1·13	0·19
1968	4·74	1·75	0·37	5·97	0·81	0·14

[a] Average rate for June of indicated year.
[b] Unweighted mean and standard deviation of three-month Treasury bill or call-money rates for Belgium, Canada, France, Germany (West), Netherlands, Switzerland, United Kingdom, and United States.
[c] With maturity in excess of twelve years, for countries listed in preceding footnote plus Italy and Sweden.
[d] Standard deviation divided by mean.
Source: Underlying data from *International Financial Statistics*.

mean of short-term interest rates for eight countries declined substantially after 1958. The decline in dispersion was less marked for long-term bond rates, but except for 1966 the dispersion declined steadily relative to the mean bond yield, suggesting some convergence in the long-term capital market as well. The sharp increase in bond-rate dispersion in 1966 is attributable solely to a 2 percentage point increase in German bond rates, to 8·4 per cent, in a period in which the German state and local authorities were borrowing at an exceptionally heavy rate and the Bundesbank tightened credit to dampen total spending. The increase in absolute and relative dispersion of short-term rates in 1968 is attributable to a combination of high rates in Britain and France, reflecting doubts about the exchange rates of their respective currencies, combined with an exceptionally low rate in Germany designed both to stimulate capital

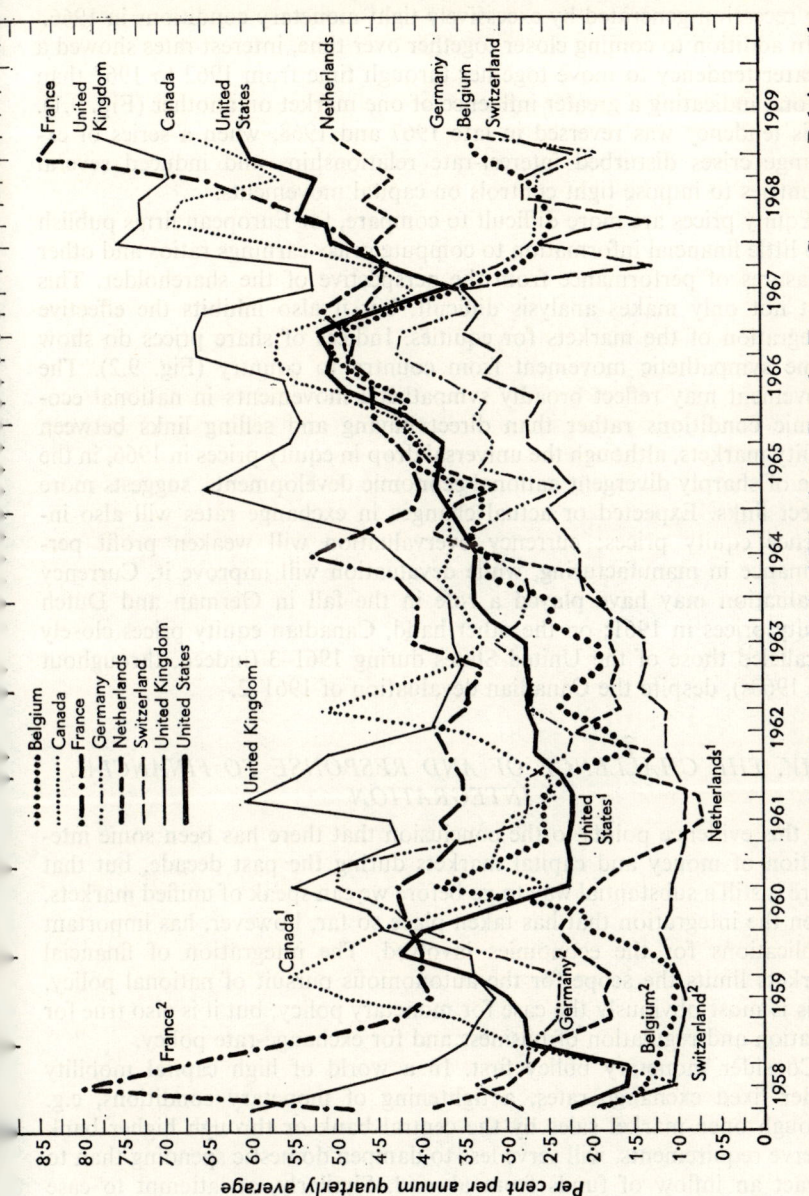

FIG. 9.1 Short-term rates for the United States, the United Kingdom, Canada, France, Germany, Belgium, the Netherlands and Switzerland, 1958-69.
[1] Average tender rate for three-month Treasury bills.   [2] Average of daily or weekly call-money rates.
Source: I.M.F., *International Financial Statistics*.

outflow and to promote domestic capital spending in the aftermath of the recession generated by excessively tight monetary conditions in 1966.

In addition to coming closer together over time, interest rates showed a greater tendency to move together through time from 1962 to 1967 than before, indicating a greater influence of one market on another (Fig. 9.1). This tendency was reversed in late 1967 and 1968, when a series of exchange crises disturbed interest-rate relationships and induced several countries to impose tight controls on capital movements.

Equity prices are more difficult to compare, for European firms publish too little financial information to compute price–earnings ratios and other measures of performance from the perspective of the shareholder. This fact not only makes analysis difficult, but it also inhibits the effective integration of the markets for equities. Indices of share prices do show some sympathetic movement from country to country (Fig. 9.2). The movement may reflect broadly sympathetic movements in national economic conditions rather than direct buying and selling links between equity markets, although the universal drop in equity prices in 1966, in the face of sharply divergent national economic developments, suggests more direct links. Expected or actual changes in exchange rates will also influence equity prices; currency overvaluation will weaken profit performance in manufacturing, while devaluation will improve it. Currency revaluation may have played a role in the fall in German and Dutch equity prices in 1961; on the other hand, Canadian equity prices closely paralleled those of the United States during 1961–3 (indeed, throughout the 1960s), despite the Canadian devaluation of 1961–2.

IV. THE CHALLENGE OF AND RESPONSE TO FINANCIAL INTEGRATION

All this evidence points to the conclusion that there has been some integration of money and capital markets during the past decade, but that there is still a substantial way to go before we can speak of unified markets. Even the integration that has taken place so far, however, has important implications for the economies involved. The integration of financial markets limits the scope for the autonomous pursuit of national policy. This is most obviously the case for monetary policy, but it is also true for taxation and regulation of business and for exchange-rate policy.

Consider monetary policy first. In a world of high capital mobility under fixed exchange rates, a tightening of monetary conditions, e.g. through open-market sales by the central bank or through higher bank reserve requirements, will serve less to dampen domestic spending than to attract an inflow of funds from abroad. Similarly, an attempt to ease domestic monetary conditions to stimulate spending will instead simply stimulate an outflow of funds. Financial integration thus poses a profound

Cooper – Towards an International Capital Market? 201

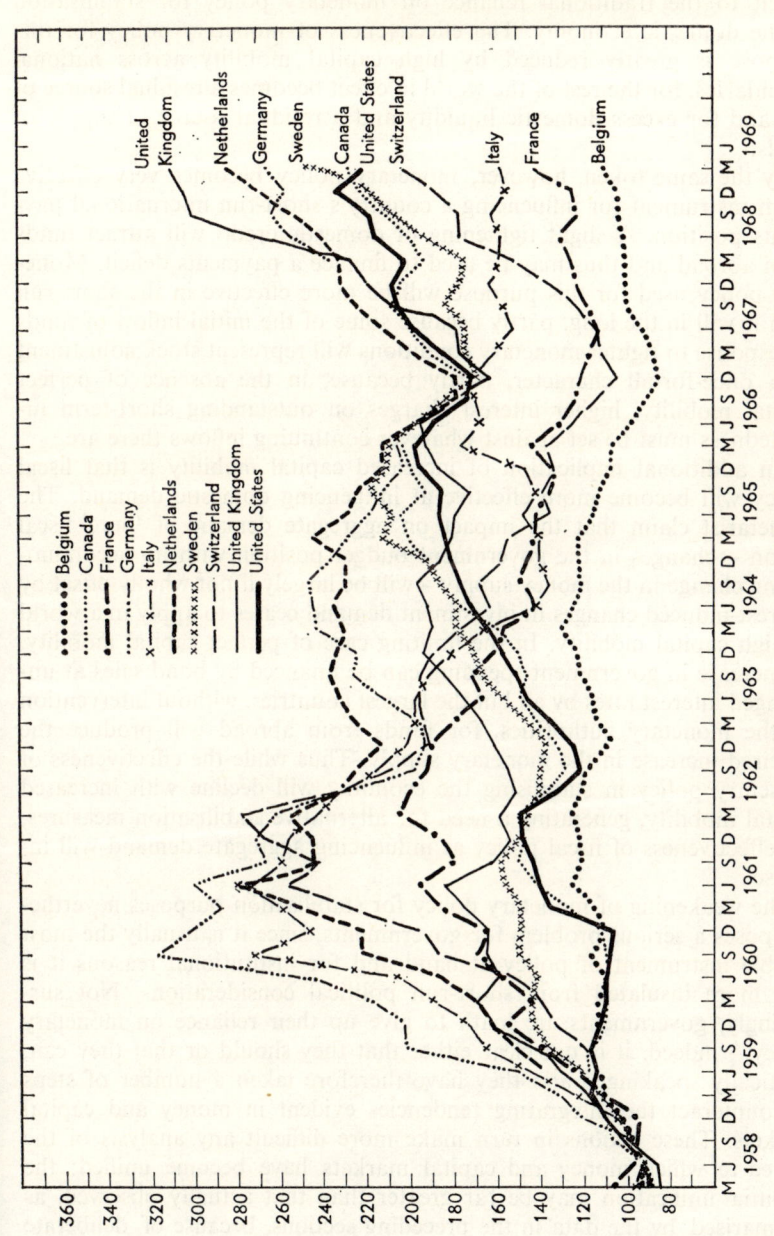

FIG. 9.2 Index of industrial share prices, quarterly, March 1958 – March 196 (1958 = 100).

NA H

threat to the traditional reliance on monetary policy for stabilisation of the domestic economy. The effectiveness of monetary policy for this purpose is greatly reduced by high capital mobility across national boundaries, for the rest of the world in effect becomes a residual source of demand for excess domestic liquidity and a residual source of supply of funds.

By the same token, however, monetary policy becomes very effective as an instrument for influencing a country's short-run international payments position. A slight tightening of domestic credit will attract funds from abroad and thus may be used to finance a payments deficit. Monetary policy used for this purpose will be more effective in the short run than it will in the long, partly because some of the initial inflow of funds in response to tighter monetary conditions will represent stock adjustment of a once-for-all character, partly because, in the absence of perfect capital mobility, higher interest charges on outstanding short-term indebtedness must be set against whatever continuing inflows there are.

An additional implication of increased capital mobility is that fiscal policy will become more effective at influencing domestic demand. The monetarist claim that the impact on aggregate demand of 'pure' fiscal action – changes in the government budget position with no accommodating change in the money supply – will be largely if not wholly offset by interest-induced changes in investment demand ceases to apply in a world of high capital mobility. In the limiting case of perfect capital mobility, an increase in government spending can be financed by bond sales at unchanged interest rates by all but the largest countries. without intervention by the monetary authorities, for funds from abroad will produce the required increase in the monetary supply. Thus while the effectiveness of monetary policy in stabilising the economy will decline with increased capital mobility, generating a need for alternative stabilisation measures, the effectiveness of fiscal policy at influencing aggregate demand will increase.

The weakening of monetary policy for stabilisation purposes nevertheless poses a serious problem for governments, since it is usually the most flexible instrument of policy at hand and for institutional reasons it is also more insulated from short-run political considerations. Not surprisingly, governments are loath to give up their reliance on monetary policy – indeed, it is not clear either that they should or that they can, politically speaking – and they have therefore taken a number of steps to counteract the integrating tendencies evident in money and capital markets. These actions in turn make more difficult any analysis of the degree to which money and capital markets have become unified: the potential unification may be far greater than that actually observed, as summarised by the data in the preceding sections, because of deliberate countervailing steps to reduce the integrating pressures in the interests of preserving some degree of national autonomy in the exercise of monetary policy.

Government response to the greater interdependence between national capital markets has been widespread. These responses have often been taken under the guise of balance of payments' policies, but that is merely the other side of the coin. Special measures to restrain capital outflows serve to protect the balance of payments in periods in which for domestic reasons the monetary authorities desire to maintain a greater degree of monetary ease than prevails abroad. That these measures are not governed principally by balance of payments considerations is indicated by the fact that countries in payments surplus have also taken steps to insulate their economies from high international capital mobility, even though balance of payments pressures were not so acute as for countries in deficit.

The devices used are well known. Virtually all countries restrict foreign access to their domestic capital markets, usually on the grounds that unlimited access by foreigners could create undue disruption of imperfectly developed national capital markets. Britain and the United States, however, restrict access on balance of payments grounds, in the case of the United States through an 'interest equalisation tax' on United States purchases of European and certain other issues, which is to say that the authorities in those countries would not like to be obliged to maintain interest rates at the levels required to limit foreign borrowing. Both countries also limit purchases by their residents of outstanding foreign securities. The interest equalisation tax applies in the United States, and Britain in effect imposes a tax by requiring British residents wanting to invest abroad to buy foreign currency at a premium but to sell a portion of receipts from liquidation of foreign assets to the authorities at the official exchange rate. These and other countries also limit the amount of short-term investment that can be undertaken abroad.

High capital mobility can be as frustrating to countries wanting to tighten domestic monetary conditions as to those wanting to ease them. At various times France, Germany, the Netherlands, and Switzerland have all prohibited interest payments on deposits by foreigners, to inhibit an inflow of short-term funds. Special reserve requirements have been imposed on foreigners' deposits with the same aim. Since 1964 Germany has imposed special withholding taxes on interest paid to foreign holders of domestic bonds, a kind of negative interest equalisation tax. (Foreign bonds floated in Germany are exempt from this tax, so they command lower nominal yields and therefore draw funds largely from outside Germany.) Both Germany and Italy, and to a lesser extent the Netherlands and Switzerland, have encouraged their banks to channel short-term funds abroad through directives or attractive forward swap arrangements, thereby regaining some control over domestic monetary conditions. But this technique will work only so long as domestic non-bank borrowers do not have direct access to foreign sources of funds, a condition that has eroded over time.

International transactions in equities do not escape the national restraints. The taxes imposed by Britain and the United States apply to equities as well as to bonds. Several countries limit purchases of foreign equities by their residents to those quoted on the national stock exchange, which in turn are restricted. In the late 1960s the growth of mutual funds in Europe provided a closer link between equity markets, especially in Germany and Italy, for they permitted residents to purchase balanced and diversified packages of foreign securities of which they had little direct knowledge. In 1969, however, the Italian Government limited sharply the activities of these mutual funds, despite the fact that Italy was running a large payments surplus at the time, because they were drawing equity away from prospective domestic issuers at a time when the Italian authorities wanted to stimulate domestic investment.

In sum, national authorities do not yet seem ready to accept the limitations imposed on their own freedom to influence domestic financial conditions by an integrated capital market spanning national boundaries.

High international mobility of capital also imposes limits on national autonomy in matters of taxation and business regulation, although these limitations are both less obvious and far less evident than is true for monetary policy. There is little question, however, that one of the principal attractions of foreign bonds to investors is that income on them can be more easily concealed from the domestic tax authorities. Foreign bond issues registered on the London market, unlike domestic issues, are not subject to British withholding tax (where tax treaties eliminate British withholding on domestic issues, they also provide for exchange of information between taxing authorities); but they are not generally subject to withholding tax by the United States or by any other country either. High international capital mobility under these circumstances will erode the ability of international authorities to tax interest income except in those countries where the tradition of voluntary tax compliance is strong, for prospective bond-holders can readily invest in international bonds to escape taxation.

High capital mobility also weakens national regulation of securities markets and corporate financial activity. In early 1969 a Swiss company subverted a Swiss requirement that existing stockholders be given preference on new stock issues, for example, by establishing a financial subsidiary in the Netherlands Antilles to raise desired funds through a convertible bond issue. This kind of escape from regulation through migration was a familiar phenomenon in the United States around the turn of the century, where business regulation by the constitutent states was gradually eroded as the railroad and the telegraph transformed local markets into a national one. Those states most aggressive in the competition for business location set a tone for lax business regulation, and as a result regulatory responsibilities were gradually taken over by the Federal Government.

Pressures for supranational action in the field of business regulation and taxation have not yet reached an advanced stage, but the beginnings of such pressure can be seen both in the desire for increased inter-governmental consultation on such matters and in the attempts, largely so far by the United States, to tax 'foreign' income and to extend its national regulations beyond national boundaries. The Revenue Act of 1962 levied United States taxes on the income of United States-owned corporations operating from tax-haven countries; and the Kennedy Administration had asked for a much broader extension of the United States tax than that finally passed by Congress. Similarly, in 1965 the Securities and Exchange Commission instructed a number of foreign (mostly Canadian) companies to submit information reports because their securities were being traded in the over-the-counter market in the United States. The foreign companies regarded this as an unwarranted intrusion into their business affairs, and they were supported by their governments; but the S.E.C. was merely carrying out its Congressional mandate to protect American investors from possible exploitation by unscrupulous corporate management. The problem of national jurisdiction arose because securities markets transcend national boundaries.

A third area in which high international mobility of capital has important implications is exchange-rate policy. A technically well-developed international money market, among other things, facilitates the movement of funds into or out of different currencies in anticipation of exchange rate changes, so the volume of currency speculation is greatly enlarged during periods of uncertainty about exchange parities. The presence of exchange risk might be expected to inhibit the development of an international capital market.[1] When foreign loans are involved, either the borrower or the lender (or both) runs an exchange risk. If the borrower's home currency is devalued, the burden of a foreign-currency debt will be increased in terms of his own currency. (Whether the real burden on the borrower is increased by devaluation depends on a host of other factors as well, such as whether devaluation raises the profitability of his local investment.) Nevertheless, financial integration may proceed rapidly when exchange risk is perceived to be low. The subsequent emergence of exchange-rate uncertainty will induce many lenders to insure against parity

[1] Canadians floated fixed-interest bonds in New York (in United States dollars) on a large scale during the 1950s, when the Canadian dollar was on a floating rate. But expectations (and Canadian monetary policy) kept the Canadian dollar close to parity with the United States dollar. Moreover, Canadian borrowing in New York increased sharply in the 1960s, after Canada switched to a fixed exchange rate. How much of the dramatic increase in foreign borrowing was due to factors other than the change in exchange-rate regime is difficult to say.

changes either by borrowing or by selling forward. As the volume of outstanding international indebtedness increases, the volume of hedging activity in periods of uncertainty will also increase, resulting in corresponding pressure on national reserves. These large and sudden movements of funds in turn may force reserve-short countries into unnecessary parity changes, or, on the contrary, delay needed changes because of the reduction in national wealth (in the form of loss of reserves) implied by a change in exchange rate when there is a large but temporary short (for devaluation) or long (for revaluation) foreign position in the currency.

V. THE ADVANTAGES AND DISADVANTAGES OF AN INTERNATIONAL CAPITAL MARKET

Turning now from the analytical and empirical to the normative side, we may ask whether such financial integration as has taken place is a good thing or a bad thing. Or to cast the question into policy terms, are the defensive reactions by governments desirable or undesirable? These questions cannot be answered sensibly without a point of comparison. What are the alternatives? On the standard competitive model, a reduction of artificial barriers to capital movements, whether by reducing ignorance or by removing policy restrictions, will lead to a more efficient use of the world's scarce resources and hence would generally be regarded as desirable. The economic theorist's presumption in favour of free markets is applicable to capital as well as to goods and services. Under competitive conditions, capital will seek higher rates of return, moving from regions of relative abundance to regions of relative scarcity. Total output will rise. In addition, free movement of funds permits individuals and institutions to diversify their risks, and this too is desirable to the extent that individuals deem high risks to be undesirable. Thus there is a diversification as well as an efficiency argument for international capital mobility.

An assessment of the desirability of international capital mobility becomes more complicated when competitive conditions are not fulfilled, for example because of the presence of import tariffs or income taxes. International capital movements may either mitigate or aggravate the efficiency losses arising from the tariffs, depending on whether the tariffs raise the return to capital more in capital-poor countries than in capital-rich ones. Similarly, different national tax rates may either foster or inhibit the efficient allocation of capital among countries. Tax treaties strive for tax neutrality in the location of capital. But lower tax rates combined with tax deferral or other tax-avoidance devices presumably contribute to better allocation when they draw American capital to Belgium than when they draw French or Italian capital to Switzerland, perhaps to be re-lent to the United States.

Arguments based on allocative efficiency assume that economies have adjusted fully to prevailing conditions. In particular, they assume that balance of payments equilibrium is assured, so that real capital movements correspond to non-compensatory private and official movements of funds across boundaries, and they also assume that the various domestic economies respond quickly and properly to changes in the pattern and level of demand. Neither condition is met in practice. The failure of balance of payments adjustment to take place promptly and appropriately, in the short or even medium run, may lead to no more than opposing movements of private and official capital. In this case the increased mobility of capital implies a need for additional international liquidity. But it may instead lead to the imposition of restrictions on other transactions, introducing resource misallocations or aggravating those already present; or it may lead to unwanted unemployment or inflation, the former entailing obvious resource costs and the latter involving costs of a more subtle sort. Although international capital movements are not ordinarily the source of unwanted deflation or inflation, they may inhibit the prompt correction of excessive deflationary or inflationary tendencies by constraining the use of monetary policy. Fiscal policy can in principle fill the breach left by monetary policy for stabilising the domestic economy, though not without occasional help from changes in exchange rates if balance of payments equilibrium is also be to maintained. But if for political or other reasons fiscal policy is not in fact readily available for this role, the costs of international capital mobility are correspondingly higher. The United States during the period 1960–4 perhaps offers the clearest, and certainly the most costly, case in which high capital mobility inhibited the use of monetary policy to stimulate a sluggish economy in a period in which fiscal policy could not be brought rapidly into play.

Finally, the increased international mobility of capital will affect the distribution of income. Real capital movements will raise the marginal product of labour in capital-importing countries and will lower the marginal product of labour (relative to what it would otherwise have been, except where the foreign investment has come entirely from increased savings) in capital-exporting countries. Under competitive conditions, labour will be made relatively better off in the former countries, capital better off in the latter. Even imperfect adjustment of real to financial capital flows will produce these effects, although to a lesser degree. In principle, of course, we can separate efficiency from equity, allow flows to take place on principles of efficiency, and correct for equity through the tax system. In practice, we have found great difficulty in incentive-free taxes, so a clear separation between the two considerations is not possible. Furthermore, redistributional taxation cannot be laid with impunity on internationally mobile factors, for they can escape taxation through migration or through evasion permitted by high mobility. Redistributive taxation relies on fragmented factor markets to be effective.

A second distributional effect of high capital mobility arises during the transition to a fully integrated capital market. Only the best known (and generally largest) firms and banks can borrow in the major international markets, and by shopping around such firms can lower the total cost of their borrowed funds – not least because of the lower international bond rates occasioned by tax evasion. Thus the growing international capital market may foster the concentration of industry. (A countervailing tendency, at least during the transitional phase to full integration, is the invasion of national markets by new foreign competitors.)

How does one weigh these conflicting considerations in assessing the pros and cons of an evolution towards an Atlantic capital market? I conclude that such an evolution is desirable, provided we can co-ordinate monetary policies effectively among countries and obtain more active fiscal policies within countries, and provided we can assure that real capital movements correspond closely to net financial flows. An international capital market is no substitute for changes in exchange-rate parities, and in fact its presence greatly aggravates the currency speculation that can take place in anticipation of changes in parities. It thus suggests the need for smaller and more continuous changes in exchange rates, which in turn may reduce somewhat the high mobility of capital. If balance of payments equilibrium is not assured through co-ordinated monetary policies and provision made for more frequent changes in exchange rates, however, high capital mobility will exert pressures for trade controls and/or unwanted domestic inflation or deflation. Under these circumstances high international mobility of capital may well leave us with a third- or fourth-best world, and governments may be wise in the meantime to restrict international flows in the interests of attaining at least a second-best one.

10 European Capital Markets and Financial Intermediation by the United States

Alexandre Lamfalussy

BANQUE DE BRUXELLES AND UNIVERSITY OF LOUVAIN

I. INTRODUCTION

The balance of payments of the United States has undergone dramatic changes in 1968, and preliminary figures for the first quarter of 1969 suggest that so far these changes have not been reversed. Since early 1968, the surplus on merchandise trade – a traditional feature of the United States external accounts for more years than I can remember – has vanished; at the same time, the similarly traditional deficit on private capital account has turned into a surplus. Thus the United States has ceased to acquire long-term private assets; in fact, there has been a *decline* in the net long-term private claims of the United States economy over the rest of the world. This can also be put in a different way. In 1968, the surplus on current account has diminished to the point – $2 billion – where it hardly any longer covers grants and donations by the United States Government and private United States residents. Hence the conclusion that, for the first time since many years, there has been no increase in the net worth of the total sum of international assets held by the United States, long- *and* short-term.

Eighteen months is, of course, a very short period and it would be foolhardy to regard these changes, on the basis of the available evidence, as a reversal of trends. A recession is quite likely both to produce a trade surplus and to put an end (for a while at least) to European portfolio investments in United States common stocks; indeed, there is some fragmentary evidence that security purchases by Europeans have slowed down substantially since May–June this year.

I do not propose to re-examine *all* the problems connected with this new pattern of the United States balance of payments. I suggest, however, that even if this new pattern of external accounts turned out to be rather short-lived, its mere emergence casts serious doubts on the theory put forward in 1965–6 by Desprès, Kindleberger and Salant and therefore warrants a re-discussion of this theory.[1] In a book published a year ago – hence written at a time when the 'familiar' pattern of the United States

---

[1] *The Economist*, Feb 1966, by Desprès, Kindleberger and Salant, and 'Capital Markets and the Balance of Payments of a Financial Center', by Salant, in *Maintaining and Restoring Balance in International Payments* (Princeton, 1966).

balance of payments was still very much actual – I suggested a reinterpretation of the D.K.S. thesis.[1] In short, I argued there that while there was no reason to believe that the United States is performing the function of a financial intermediary for the benefit of an excessively liquid Europe, it could be said, on the other hand, that American industry is playing the role of entrepreneurship through its direct investments in Europe financed to a large extent in Europe itself. I based this argument on an analysis of European capital markets and their comparison with these same markets in the United States rather than on a study of international capital flows. The balance of payments figures for the years 1964–7 seemed to justify the D.K.S. thesis rather than mine – although the figures on international assets and liabilities at the end of 1964 had been open to alternative interpretations.[2] Now that the balance of payments data themselves have turned more in favour of my argument, I would like to seize this welcome and unexpected opportunity to reopen the debate and to restate my thesis.

II. FINANCIAL INTERMEDIATION BY THE UNITED STATES

There seems to be a double origin to the theory that the United States is (or has been) performing the function of a financial intermediary for Europe.

First, business experience and direct observation of financial markets prior to the establishment of the interest equalisation tax in July 1963 suggested quite spontaneously such an interpretation. Many European governments, public bodies and companies had been issuing bonds in the New York market, while a high proportion of these issues were bought by the Europeans themselves. To this extent, the function of the New York market was that of an entrepôt. It was argued that New York had been playing this role because of the poor organisation of European capital markets: the skill and know-how of the New York investment banks, the large institutional support for new issues, the size and 'breadth' of the secondary markets made it possible to float issues of a size which was beyond the reach of individual European capital markets, London being an obvious exception in this respect.

The second and economically more significant argument stems from the observation of the United States balance of payments figures, especially for the period 1959–66. During this period, the United States accumulated through a rising flow of direct investments substantial long-term assets in Europe, while at the same time the overall deficit of the United States balance of payments, coupled with European surpluses,

[1] *Les Marchés financiers en Europe* (Presses Universitaires de France, 1968) pp. 171–7.
[2] Robert Triffin, 'The Balance of Payments and the Foreign Investment position of the U.S.', *Essays in International Finance* (Princeton, Nov 1966).

resulted in an accumulation of short-term claims by the E.E.C. countries over the United States. Borrowing short and lending long is, of course, what most financial intermediaries actually do; hence it was possible to say, almost by definition, that the United States was playing the role of a financial intermediary for the benefit of Europe. In the light of this, the United States balance of payments deficit acquired the much less disturbing nature of a 'deficit' proper to a financial centre, i.e. to any financial intermediary. D.K.S. regarded this as a justification for the United States deficit and warned us that its disappearance would be apt to create a number of financing problems first of all in Europe itself. Europe would therefore discourage the proper functioning of its own financial markets, if it were to push the United States authorities towards checking the outflow of private United States capital.

To explain how the European countries got themselves into this situation, the D.K.S. school of thought assumes that the preference for liquidity is higher in the European countries than in the United States. In doing so, they adopt a view which has been – and still is – widely held in Europe. It has been pointed out many times since the end of the war that per capita currency circulation is much higher in countries like Belgium, Switzerland, France, Italy – even Germany and the Netherlands – than in the United States or the United Kingdom, and this has been regarded as a sign (although obviously not a proof) of a higher liquidity preference. Both the E.E.C. and the O.E.C.D. reports on capital markets reaffirm this belief and quote more extensive statistics than simply the partial figures of currency holdings. Finally, it had been accepted (until the recent rise in long-term interest rates in the United States and the United Kingdom) as a matter of evidence that the higher level of long-term interest rates in Continental Europe could be explained, partly at least, by higher liquidity preference.

The tenants of the D.K.S. thesis add a novel element to this diagnosis by assuming that European financial intermediation is deficient in so far as it is unable (or unwilling) to transform these liquid assets into long-term claims on final borrowers. The result of this is that the gap between interest rates on highly liquid financial assets and those carried by long-term claims is higher in Europe than in the United States. This may be the result of government regulations or sheer lack of competition, but the final conclusion is that the social cost of financial intermediation is much higher in Europe than in the United States. While (to the best of my knowledge) no systematic studies have so far been made to compare interest differentials in various countries and therefore to test this theory, many examples have been quoted to enhance its plausibility. The strongest example of the kind is the comparison of the rates on New York C.D.s with those on high-grade corporate bonds.

This, then, is the summary of the theory which I propose to criticise. As all summaries of this kind, it may be incomplete or biased and probably does less than justice to an ingenious theory which embraces in a brilliant synthesis almost all interesting features of international finance and money over the last twenty years.

III. PROBLEMS OF METHODOLOGY

Let us first review a few problems of methodology which are raised either in the field of statistical testing or in the formulation of the assumptions underlying the theory. There is little hope for confirming or invalidating this theory or indeed any other theory in this area (including the one I am going to put forward) so long as we are unable to solve these problems.

(1) The first of these problems is to find out what interest rates really are. Because of taxation and a number of other related facts, this is far from being an easy exercise and this is probably why there are no fully comparable statistics on rate differentials.

Let me quote you a few examples. European households keep a very high proportion of their semi-liquid assets in form of savings deposits. The degree of liquidity of these savings deposits varies considerably from one country to another: not only in terms of administrative regulations but even more so in fact. Measuring actual velocities of circulation (in those few happy cases where such statistics are available) is of no use: what really matters is whether the individual holder of a savings booklet believes that he will be able to withdraw from his deposit whatever amount he would like to and at first notice. Practice in this matter varies not only from country to country but also from one financial institution to another. In addition to this, the tax advantages attached to these deposits are general, ingenious and complicated to the extreme. In some cases no income taxes are due at all so long as the income does not exceed x francs (as in the case in Belgium); on the other hand, this tax exemption is valid for all individual savings booklets held by physical persons, while income tax is calculated on a household basis. A family of seven, for instance, can earn a tax-free interest income of $7x$, while the rate of taxation as well as the total amount of income tax to be paid is derived from the total income of the household. You must bear in mind, moreover, that this is a simplified example. In some more complicated cases, savings deposits generate special rights to borrow from the banks, either for instalment finance or for house building. The result is that the current 3·5 per cent on savings deposits can, in some cases, be as high as 6 or 7 per cent in terms of pre-tax interest income. In others, it will only be 4 per cent or even less. I have not been able to invent so far a meaningful statistical technique capable of yielding some reliable, general conclusion in this field; and to assess what this means, one has to remember that acquisition of savings deposits of this subsidised kind may well represent in a number of European countries (Germany, Belgium, Italy to say the least) anything between 20 to 40 per cent of the annual acquisition of gross financial assets by households.

If one tries to by-pass these difficulties by jumping directly to the measurement of the cost of financial intermediation, one is likely to encounter even more formidable problems. The most obvious is that neither the balance sheet nor the profit and loss account of the financial intermediaries are published in a way which would permit the linking of a meaningful income to a meaningful asset. The example of English bank returns is too well known to be dwelt upon. But even in a country like Belgium where the yearly returns by banks are standardised and fairly detailed, I have been unable so far to compare the costs and returns of various categories of liabilities and assets for the three large banks of the country, of which one is my own. Returns on long-term government bonds vary from one bank to another by more than 2 per cent! This quite clearly cannot be true. And even if we were ready to give up measuring the yields on categories of assets, the comparison of the overall yield gap would be only marginally more significant, for banks earn more and more income from fees, underwriting and selling commissions which have nothing to do with their borrowing and lending activity.

(2) The second problem is related to the measurement of the *social* cost of financial intermediation, as opposed to the cost of individual financial transactions or of a group of transactions performed by one category of intermediaries. This is a major problem and there are reasons to believe that by overlooking it, one has come to doubtful conclusions as regards the comparison of *social* costs between the United States and Europe.

This is due to the fact that financial transactions flow from final lenders to final borrowers in quite different ways according to countries. Let us quote just one major example. Governments, public bodies and companies finance themselves in many Continental countries by issuing bonds. These bonds are placed to a very large extent with households, through the retail-sales organisation of nation-wide branch banks. To this extent, there is no financial intermediation involved: funds flow directly from the household sector to the non-financial final borrower. Now both in the United States and in the United Kingdom bonds are placed predominantly with institutional investors: in the case of the United States, with life insurance companies and with the pension funds of public bodies; there are practically no direct sales to households. Given these differences between Continental Europe on the one hand, and the United States and the United Kingdom on the other, one can *not* derive conclusions as to the *social* cost of financial intermediation by simply comparing the actual costs related to the underwriting and selling of bonds. These latter are undoubtedly higher in Europe than in the United States or the United

Kingdom but they are the *only* costs involved in chanelling the savings of households towards the final non-financial borrower, while this is by no means the case in the 'Anglo-Saxon' countries. Both in the United States and in the United Kingdom, we ought to add the cost involved in acquiring a life insurance policy and so on. On the other hand, if one compared the underwriting and selling profits made by banks in the process of selling bonds to other financial intermediaries, one would come to the conclusion that these commissions are practically the *same* in all major developed countries.

It can therefore be argued that the higher (apparent) cost of financial intermediation in Europe can in many cases be explained by the simple fact that this cost covers the entire flow of funds from households to final non-financial borrowers. One could even quote examples the other way round, especially in the field of mutual funds. Here we have a good comparison, since mutual-fund shares are bought in most countries directly by households; yet it is a well-known fact that the sales costs in the United States are substantially higher than those in Europe.

(3) The third problem is not a statistical but a theoretical one. It is often said that the yield gap between short- and long-term financial assets or, more generally, between financial assets held by final lenders and liabilities incurred by final borrowers is a good measure of the efficiency of financial intermediation. Stated in this way, without qualification, this proposition is apt to be misleading.

The mistake is most obvious in international comparison: it does not follow from this proposition that if the yield gap in country A is narrower than in country B, then we are entitled to draw the conclusion that financial intermediation is more efficient in A than in B. The *actual* yield gap is significant only in comparison with what the yield gap would be in the absence of financial intermediation; hence the international comparison of yield gaps would be meaningful (for the purpose of comparing the efficiency of intermediation) only if these actual gaps stood in the same relation to each other as the potential ones. It may well happen that in country B, final lenders have strong and very sticky preferences as regards the structure of their portfolio; and if these preferences do not coincide with those, also strong and sticky, of the final borrowers regarding their debt structure, the yield gap could become very wide indeed if there was no intermediation at all. In this instance, finanical intermediation in B might, in fact, be very efficient by reducing the potential gap to a much narrower actual one, yet this latter could still be wider than the yield differential observed in A.

Since we are unable to re-create a situation without financial intermediaries, we will never be able to measure in a fully satisfactory way the efficiency of financial intermediation. I think, however, that we could improve upon the simple comparison of actual yield differentials by comparing the output (value added) of *all* financial intermediaries in a given country during a given period with the total sum of financing deficits and surpluses by sector (as these are given in Table 10.1). Such a measure, of course, raises a number of questions: to what extent should we disaggregate sectors? Should one not take into account *gross* rather than *net* financing flows? On the other hand, this measure answers at least some of our problems by taking into account the *complete* range of intermediation from final lenders to final borrowers and by assuming (implicitly) that the burden of intermediation increases with the size of financing deficits and surpluses.

This problem is of great importance in the comparison of United States and Continental European financial markets. As will be shown in the following pages, we have good reasons to believe that, for a number of reasons, the tasks of financial intermediation are much heavier and in a sense more 'difficult' in Europe than in either the United Kingdom or the United States. Given these difficulties, one should by no means discard the possibility of reversing the assumption underlying the D.K.S. theory by arguing that financial intermediation, at least in the area of bond issues and long-term loans, is more efficient in Europe than in the United States.

IV. FINANCING SURPLUSES AND DEFICITS BY SECTOR

The first major difference between the United States (and the United Kingdom) on the one hand, and Continental Europe on the other, lies in *the size and structure* of financing deficits and surpluses by sector. This can be seen at once from Table 10.1. First, it is obvious that (relative to any meaningful statistical aggregate) the size of net financing flows from surplus to deficit sectors is much bigger in all three Continental countries mentioned in the table than either in the United States or in the United Kingdom. It is striking to see that, even in *absolute* figures, the financing needs of corporations were bigger in France or in Germany than in the United States, while they were as much as one-sixth of the United States figure in Belgium. It is worth mentioning that while this relation might have changed to some extent since 1964, the basic proportions have remained the same. Second, it is equally obvious that the pattern of deficits and surpluses varies considerably from country to country and that there is a particularly sharp contrast between Germany and France on the one hand, and the United States and the United Kingdom on the other. In both large Continental countries, the net flow of financing is quite simple – it goes from the households to the corporations – while the flows are more diversified in the two 'Anglo-Saxon' countries: in the United States, a (relatively) much smaller financing surplus of the household sector faces a government deficit and a 'relatively' very small financing deficit in the corporate sector; in the United Kingdom, an equally small household surplus finances exclusively the government and the *public* corporations.

TABLE 10.1

FINANCING SURPLUSES AND DEFICITS BY SECTOR IN 1964
($ billion)

	Households	Corporations Private[a]	Public	Government	Residual[b]
United States	+14·6	−3·6		−5·7	−5·3
United Kingdom	+1·9	+0·3	−1·5	−1·0	+0·3
France	+3·6	−4·3	−1·5	+0·2	+2·0
Germany	+2·8	−3·9		+1·1	−0·1
Belgium	+1·0	−0·6		−0·4	0·0

Note: 'Financing surplus' is defined as an excess of savings over investment; 'financing deficit' as an excess of investment over savings.

[a] 'Private' corporations include in Germany, Belgium and the United States *all* corporations.

[b] The residual item comprises the international sector, financial intermediaries as well as errors and omissions.

Source: *Les Marchés financiers en Europe* (Presses Universitaires de France, 1968) p. 55.

One can do a lot of research in order to refine these conclusions. It can be shown, for instance, that the bigger financing deficit of the corporate sector on the Continent is due to a large extent to faster capital accumulation (if this is measured in terms of investment as a percentage of the gross domestic product) and probably only to a lesser extent to smaller profit margins. It can also be shown that the differences in the financing surpluses of the households can in no way be explained away by the undoubtedly higher propensity of United States households to become indebted, but must be connected with the higher propensity to save on the European Continent. But none of this research can alter the two conclusions given above.

I suggest that these provide us prima facie with two presumptions. First, that the sheer quantitative task of financial intermediation is much heavier in Europe than in the United States: to channel net flows of this size from one sector to another is likely to require a more complex process of intermediation in Europe than in the United States or in the United Kingdom – unless, of course, there is a remarkable coincidence between the portfolio preferences of the households and the ideal debt structure of the deficit sectors. The second presumption is that the more limited choice open to Europeans is also likely to increase the burden of intermediation: French and German households will have to finance corporations and only corporations, while United States households can choose between acquiring claims either on the corporate sector or on the government.

V. FINANCING NEEDS OF CORPORATIONS

These presumptions become quite strong when one goes in some detail into the financing needs of the corporate sector. The O.E.C.D. study of capital markets provides us with a number of revealing figures in this respect.[1] The most important ones relate to the respective size of equity financing: it appears from the O.E.C.D. statistics that for the period 1959-65 as a whole, net equity financing amounted to about only 2 per cent of the total external finance of United States corporations, while the proportion came to 25 and 27 per cent in Germany and France.

A priori, there are two possible explanations for this striking difference. The one is that the cost of issuing new equity in Europe made this type of finance more attractive for corporations than other sources of funds. This would imply relatively high equity prices, hence a strong final demand for equities or some sort of fiscal (or administrative) advantages in favour of equity issues. This explanation can be safely discarded, for yearly statistics make it abundantly clear that net equity issues both in Germany and in France continued quite strong even in periods of declining stock prices. Thus in Germany, net equity issues had reached 3·3 billion D-marks in 1961 when stock prices stood at their post-war maximum; in 1965, after a decline of about 25 per cent in stock prices, net equity issues grew to 4 billion. In France, the decline on the Paris stock exchange was even stronger; yet for these two years, the respective figures for equity issues were 3·5 and 4·7 billion francs. It could also be shown that this increase in stock financing could in no way be justified by the fact that meanwhile the cost of bond financing has also risen.

The other, valid, explanation lies in the fact that their weak financial structure has compelled - and still compels - European corporations to issue a substantial amount of new equity. I do not think that we need detailed statistics to prove that in terms of *all* financial ratios European corporations are under-capitalised, while the position of both the United States corporations and of British companies is very strong indeed.[2]

The weak financial structure of European corporations has been a powerful stimulus for equity financing for at least two reasons: first, because management has recognised that under-capitalisation is a continuous threat to independence; second, because bondholders and other institutional lenders made future loans conditional on capital issues.

As a result, new equity have been substantially higher in Continental Europe than in the United States. Table 10.2 shows conclusively that the new issue market in common stocks has been much stronger in Europe than in the United States: for the years 1960-5, the four E.E.C. countries

---
[1] *Études sur les marchés de capitaux* (O.E.C.D., Paris, 1967).
[2] See, however, ibid., Annexe statistique, pp. 73-7.

given in the table issued about two and a half times more new equities than the United States.

TABLE 10.2

NEW EQUITY ISSUES

	Yearly averages, 1960–5 ($ million)	Fixed capital formation of corporations	As per cent of Stock exchange capitalisation	Total issues of securities
United States	1,030	1·5	0·3	7
Germany	660	5·0	3·0	20
France	790	8·5	3·6	41
Italy	810	9·3	9·3	29
Belgium	170	8·5	3·8	20

Source: *Études sur les marchés de capitaux* (O.E.C.D., Paris, 1967) Annexe statistique.

A very similar picture emerges when one examines the other sources of long-term finance for the corporate sector. This, of course, is not astonishing: the net financing needs of corporations being so substantially larger in Europe, one would expect much heavier long-term borrowing in Europe than in the United States. This turns out to be true. One single set of figures will show it. While, in 1964, German corporations issued long- and medium-term debt for the equivalent of about $3·4 billion and the French corporations (public and private) for $5 billion, the same figure amounted for the United States corporations to $4·9 billion. The proportions for the period 1960–5 as a whole are not basically dissimilar from these.

VI. PORTFOLIO PREFERENCES OF HOUSEHOLDS AND FINANCIAL INTERMEDIATION

The main question raised by the foregoing argument is this: how are these heavy equity issues, as well as the issue of all kinds of long-term debt, channelled towards the portfolios of European households? I have tried to answer this question in my book and there is little point in repeating the statistics which are used there to reach my conclusions. Since the purpose of this paper is to discuss the interrelations between the North American and European capital markets and not European financial intermediation proper, I will simply sum up here the main line of my argument.

(1) As regards the common stocks issued in Europe, they are brought to a very large extent *directly* by households, on a retail basis. This is in striking contrast with United States and British practice, where households have been *dis*-investing in direct stockholdings and where the net

equity issues have been taken up by insurance companies, corporate pension trusts and (to a lesser extent) by mutual funds. All these three categories of intermediaries exist in Continental Europe but they play only a relatively small role in the new issues market.

(2) The same is true for *bonds*, both those issued by corporations and those sold by various government agencies. European bond issues have been placed quite predominantly with households. Again, this is in contrast with both the United States and the British practice where institutional investors take a very high proportion (and, in some case, all) of the bonds.

(3) As a result, direct security purchases form a substantial proportion of the acquisition of financial assets by European households. According to my statistical guesses and estimates, the percentage may have been around 20 to 25 in France, Germany and Italy and as high as 33 in Belgium, for the period 1960-5, while there were during the same years security *dis*-investments in the United Kingdom and a nearly balanced situation in the United States. On the other hand, European households direct only a relatively small proportion of their financial investments towards those institutional investors (insurance companies and pension trusts) which in the United States and the United Kingdom are the main purchasers of securities. It is to be noted, however, that the *total* of direct security purchases *plus* investments with institutional investors form approximately the same proportion of the gross acquisition of financial assets by households in Europe as in the United States or the United Kingdom, the only exception being France where this proportion is lower. Or, to put it the other way round, the accumulation of money balances (currency plus bank deposits) plus the constitution of savings deposits form also the same proportion in all countries considered, the only exception being France where this proportion is higher.

(4) This is not to say, however that financial intermediation is so much less important in Europe than in the United States or the United Kingdom; for a high proportion of bonds taken up by households are in fact issued by financial intermediaries, usually of the nationalised or semi-nationalised type. Most of these institutions finance themselves by issuing bonds and use their resources to grant long- or medium-term loans to corporations. These specialised lending institutions play a very powerful role in financial markets in France, Italy, Belgium, even in Germany. They practically do not exist in the United States and are much weaker in the United Kingdom.

(5) Both these specialised intermediaries and the commercial banking system lend long- and medium-term funds to corporations, in proportions unknown both in the United States and in the United Kingdom. Ten-year loans have become a common feature in Continental banking; they are not, to the best of my knowledge, in England or in the United

States. The banks are deriving their resources from a wide range of deposits, of which savings deposits form an increasing proportion. Hence it can be said that in Europe, the dominant type of financial intermediary – specialised in long- and medium-term *loans* – is the group of commercial banks and that of the specialised lending institutions, just as the dominant type of intermediary in the United Kingdom and the United States for long-term finance (both in the equity and the bond markets) is the insurance companies and the pension trust funds.

(6) The European commercial banking system plays, however, an additional role in financial intermediation, which again is quite alien to commercial banking practice in the United Kingdom or the United States. This is the system of direct retail sales of all kinds of securities to households. European commercial underwrite security issues or are part of selling groups; they sell these securities to their retail customers through their nation-wide branch network. This is not intermediation in the proper sense of the word; it is distribution but on a very wide scale. I have no doubt in my mind that the primary issue market of all kinds of securities could not be as powerful as it is today in Europe without this system of distribution. But this also explains the well-known weakness of the *secondary* markets: retail sales of securities to households being final sales, there is little scope for the development of secondary markets. But it must be clearly understood that the weakness of the secondary market is not equivalent to a weakness in the primary market. Indeed, the opposite is true.

VII. UNITED STATES FINANCIAL INTERMEDIATION IN EUROPE?

The main propositions put forward in the previous section throw a fairly different light on European financial markets from the one implied by the D.K.S. theory. The figures quoted above show that European *primary* markets are very vigorous, since they have been able to accommodate substantially larger equity and debt issues than the United States market. There is no clear evidence for a high liquidity preference among European households, since what really seems to happen is that European households buy securities directly, instead of buying them indirectly through the insurance companies or the pension trust funds. This, to my mind, cannot be regarded as a sign of a higher liquidity preference. Finally, financial intermediation is powerful in Europe but in a very different way from the United States or the United Kingdom pattern: it is based on a different group of intermediaries; it channels funds more easily towards long-term lending than towards equity investment; it also plays a simultaneous role in the *distribution* of securities. These were the main reasons for my scepticism about the validity of the D.K.S. reasoning.

Now let us turn back to international financial statistics. Table 10.3 demonstrates two basic facts.

First, the international investment *position* of the United States – i.e. the pattern of assets and liabilities at a given date – does not justify the D.K.S. argument. This is obvious for the figures at the end of 1964: at that time, the United States as in a net debtor position towards Europe (– $5·4 billion), with long-term private and official assets and liabilities being roughly in balance, while there was a net *short*-term debt towards Europe. This can hardly be described as the position of that of a financial intermediary.

TABLE 10.3

THE INTERNATIONAL INVESTMENT POSITION OF THE UNITED STATES TOWARDS WESTERN EUROPE
($ billion)

	1964	1967
1. Long-term private assets and liabilities		
United States claims	+17·5	+22·6
(of which direct investment)	(+12·1)	(+17·9)
United States liabilities	–17·7	–20·2
(of which European portfolio investment in United States securities)	(–10·2)	(–10·5)
Net United States private long-term claims (+) or liabilities (–)	–0·2	+2·4
2. Short-term private assets and liabilities		
United States claims	+2·1	+2·7
United States liabilities	–7·1	–10·8
Net United States private short-term claims (+) or liabilities (–)	–5·0	–8·1
3. Net United States Government claims (+) or liabilities (–)	–0·2	+0·2
Total net United States investment position towards Western Europe	–5·4	–5·5

Source: *Survey of Current Business.*

Second, the *changes* in these balance-sheet data show, however, that in terms of *flows* the United States *did* act as an intermediary between 1964 and 1967. During these three years, the United States private sector acquired net long-term claims of the order of $2·6 billion over Europe, while Europe acquired additional net short-term claims over the United States for about $3·1 billion. With some compensatory changes in long-term government finance, the net *overall* position of the United States remained the same.

In the absence of any other confirmation of the D.K.S. thesis, I regard these flows as far too small to warrant any definite conclusion.

These doubts have now been confirmed by the spectacular changes which occurred in 1968 in the United States balance of payments. Unfortunately, the data on international assets and liabilities at the end of 1968 have not yet been published. Nevertheless, the balance of payments figures clearly indicate that the United States private sector did *not* increase its net long-term claims on Europe; it is even quite likely that there was a decrease in these claims. We know that net capital exports by United States corporations declined from their $3 billion level in 1966 and 1967 to a mere $400 million in 1968, as a result of the massive Eurobond issues by United States corporations last year which nearly offset direct investment abroad. We also know that a great proportion of these issues was sold in Europe. Finally, we know that the purchase of outstanding United States securities – mostly common stocks – by Europeans increased by about $1·5 billion in 1968, thanks to the remarkable sales organisation of the United States offshore funds and the none the less remarkable *in*ability of Europeans to time properly their portfolio investments in the United States. With these figures in mind, it is not unreasonable to believe that 1968 and the early months of 1969 may well have reversed the flows registered in 1965–7.

If this is so, the international financial statistics of the United States – both the stocks and the flows – confirm the view that the United States does not play the role of a financial intermediary for the benefit of an overliquid Europe unable to turn its liquid assets into long-term investments. The fact that European households probably bought United States securities for at least $3 billion in one single years shows, on the contrary, that there is not much wrong with Europe in this respect. The problem seems to lie elsewhere: in the area of industrial direct investment. Here the role of the United States is unquestionable: it is that of an industrial entrepreneur, carrying out investments project and financing himself locally by issuing equity and bonds and borrowing short-, medium- and long-term funds from local institutions.

Discussion of the Papers by Professor Cooper and Mr Lamfalussy

Professor Hicks said that these were two very serious, important and far from easy papers. He would deal with Professor Cooper's, which fell into three parts. The first looked at the growth of the international capital market, centring on the figures in Table 9.4. This first part did deal to some extent with the problem of the Euro-dollar and of equities, but the most precise information was for the market for bonds.

Looking at the table, and at what Professor Cooper said, two issues seemed to arise. First, there was, in a way, the straightforward, traditional development of international lending by purchases of securities across frontiers. Second, there was the new development of the purchase of securities denominated in currencies other than those of the countries where they were issued. The first was not new. It was something that the free enterprise system naturally bred. It had begun to do so about 1900; had done so again in the 1920s; and was doing so once more in the 1950s and 1960s. In a way, this was part of a development going much further back. Another part was the reaction to a particular kind of restriction imposed by national governments to stop the first kind of movement getting out of hand. However, this division was not precise. In Table 9.1, one saw an extraordinary jump in the second column for 1968 – a reaction to particular constraints. This seemed to correspond with the movement in the third column. He would therefore like to ask if the movement, over the last three or four years, in the total of long-run lending was important or just a flash in the pan.

In the third section of this paper, Professor Cooper raised a general issue. Professor Hicks did not feel so much in agreement here as on the rest of the paper, and wanted to go into this. Early in section III, Professor Cooper said that the real test of the unification of the capital market was how far the rate of interest was the same in all markets. Was this true? The condition for a perfect market was that the price of the same thing should be the same everywhere. Were bonds in different currencies the same or not? Some participants would say yes; others would say no. He thought one could have conditions where one had different currencies, with fluctuating relationships between each of them and free movement of funds between them. The rate of interest then adjusted to general market expectations about these movements and rates of interest were not equal everywhere. It was true that this would not be an equilibrium situation, but, at the same time, it was possible for the increasing theoretical perfection of the market to proceed in a way that was important, even though exchange rates could and did move a good deal.

On section IV, where he was more in agreement with Professor Cooper, Professor Hicks said that the issue was fundamental, and not an easy one. He was very much on the same side as Cooper because he thought that the free enterprise system, without government interference, led to a single market which was bigger than any government. For thirty-five years he had held the view that such a system would be inherently unstable. Often there was opposition between general monetary stability and optimisation in real terms. One therefore needed a second-best alternative. There was no international institution that could really control international money. We had to do this through national stabilisation policies. How could it be done without moving farther away from the real optimum conditions than was necessary?

Finally, Professor Hicks said that he was puzzled by a remark on p. 202. There, Professor Cooper said that 'an additional implication of increased capital mobility is that fiscal policy would become more effective at influencing domestic demand'. Relatively, he would agree; but if Professor Cooper meant absolutely, he wondered what was meant. If he did mean absolutely, what was the argument?

Professor James introduced the discussion on the paper by Mr Lamfalussy. He said he could not hope to deal with the whole of this paper, but would look at key points. We had now reached the real problem facing the Round Table, the relationship between the United States and the rest of the world – especially Western Europe. This paper was concerned with monetary policies and relationships between the United States and Western Europe. At the moment, the view of Desprès, Kindleberger and Salant was generally accepted. He was therefore glad that Professor Kindleberger was here. He thought that Mr Lamfalussy basically accepted the D.K.S. thesis, and that he had simply completed, or reinterpreted it.

Mr Lamfalussy looked at the D.K.S. thesis in the light of a new situation. Since 1968, the flow of funds from the United States to Europe had been much smaller.

The D.K.S. thesis was that the United States played the role of a financial intermediary. In principle, this was useful both for America and for Western Europe. It was useful for the United States, in the sense that it was normal for the American balance of payments to be out of equilibrium. It was useful for Europe, because if the United States were only a financial intermediary, then Europe would not suffer. It would be possible for the United States to borrow short-term in Western Europe, while leaving long-term investment decisions to be made in Western Europe.

Mr Lamfalussy had tried to complete, to reinterpret. He approved the D.K.S. view with two kinds of argument – methodological and factual.

On methodology, the D.K.S. thesis depended on the rate of interest. Mr Lamfalussy said he was not sure what this was; it varied between the short and the long run. Apparent rates of interest also included a large number of impure elements – so it was hard to compare American and European interest rates. One also had to calculate the cost of financial intermediation, and again this was hard to work out. Nor was it easy to discover what was the efficiency of financial intermediaries.

There were also observations of fact. For Mr Lamfalussy, the need for finance on the market was no doubt greater in Europe than in the United States. European firms had a smaller financial margin. Again, the organisation of the market in Western Europe included several institutions which were nationalised or quasi-nationalised. There was also the question of the roles which banks played in linking individual investors and firms wanting finance.

On institutions, Mr Lamfalussy concluded, on p. 220, that the European market was vigorous and that there was no excessive preference for liquidity in Europe.

Again, on fact, Mr Lamfalussy said that statistics for purchases of European securities in the United States and for American purchases of European securities did not support the D.K.S. thesis. In 1964–7 there was no excess of American borrowing in Europe, but a slight balance in favour of Europe. For the period since 1968, the position was not yet clear. If one took account of Euro-bonds, America lent part of its funds to Europe and American firms financed subsidiaries in Europe by borrowing Euro-dollars. Did this mean that one had to abandon the D.K.S. thesis? The answer was no, but Mr Lamfalussy had altered the thesis. He said that the American role was not one of a financial intermediary in Europe; it was the role of an entrepreneur – in the Schumpeterian sense. American firms created innovation in Western Europe, but they did this in part with European capital. This was the essential thing in the paper. Professor James said he did not want to contradict any of this because Professor Kindleberger could defend himself. But he was very much attracted by the Lamfalussy thesis.

On one detail, if we did not recognise the role of the United States as a beneficient financial intermediary, and replaced it with that of an entrepreneur, this would mean that centres deciding on investment in Western Europe would be partly in the United States, This was not very reassuring for a Europe which feared being dominated, if not colonised, by the United States.

Professor van Meerhaeghe asked Mr Lamfalussy whether there were no figures for 1965 and 1966, similar to those he gave for 1964.

He returned to the passage on p. 202 of Professor Cooper's paper, mentioned by Professor Hicks, which implied that increased capital mobility would make fiscal policy more effective in influencing domestic demand. This might be true, but everything would depend on how easily the government could obtain funds; most governments were short of money.

Professor Wallich said he mainly wanted to consider the Cooper paper – especially its findings about interest. He was particularly concerned with the problem of calculating progressively narrowing interest-rate differentials in the kind of situation we had been in for the last year. Professor Hicks had doubted whether one really could look at interest-rate differentials without making some adjustments. He would suggest possible ones.

When one spoke of short-term rates, it was important to remember the cost of cover. This might or might not widen differentials, but it was there. For long-term bonds, it was not very relevant. Then there was the impact of inflation. As Professor Cooper said, there were big time-lags before people became accustomed to a rate of inflation. United States experience suggested that it probably took twenty years or so, though the lag was perhaps now less.

Professor Wallich wondered how far fiscal policy was strengthened when capital mobility increased. He thought Professor Cooper meant that complete mobility of capital eased fiscal policy by providing an infinitely elastic money supply. If the government were to run a deficit, there was no problem about financing in the United States or the United Kingdom. However, some governments would have difficulties in financing deficits. In the United States the rate of interest could rise only if the Federal Reserve System did not allow the money supply to increase appropriately. If, owing to international capital flows, the government had lost control of the money supply, the rate of interest would not rise with a tough fiscal policy. One ought also to look at institutional arrangements. Much of what had been said depended on how the money supply increased when the balance of payments was in deficit. The United States was a country where an inflow did not increase the supply of money. Both official and private foreign holders simply transferred funds to United States citizens. The money supply was therefore constant. All that happened was that if United States banks' borrowings of Euro-dollars increased, and if the Federal Reserve System did not offset this, the money supply rose marginally.

M. Ferras thought that Professor Cooper overemphasised the dangers from international capital movements. These did bring dangers for national monetary policy, but countries used various devices to keep some independence in their own affairs. Switzerland was an example. She had had some independence despite being a country which attracted a good deal of capital.

On the pros and cons, Professor Cooper said in his paper that underdeveloped countries often received too little capital. However, even in industrial countries one often ended up with extraordinary situations over capital flows. The United States, the richest country in the world, was importing it; Italy, which was most in need of capital, was exporting it. This was a very awkward situation and M. Ferras thought measures were needed to redress it.

Professor Sohmen noted that Professor Cooper had pointed out that in an integrated capital market one would always have the same rate of interest for the same type of debt. Considering that most people thought that the fixing of exchange rates fostered integration of capital markets, he wondered whether, when Canada had a floating exchange rate in the 1950s, there had been a noticeable de-integration between the Canadian and United States capital market. Conversely, had there been a narrowing of interest differentials after 1962, with fixed exchange rates? He did not think that, in fact, the differences were very great. With fixed exchange rates, Switzerland had been able to keep a considerably lower rate of interest than, for example, Germany. There was usually a difference of about 2 per cent. So, the degree of capital-market integration, even with fixed exchange rates, was not much in evidence.

If one took the case of floating exchange rates, with different rates of inflation, some currencies would tend to fall in value continuously relatively to others. With competition and good foresight, forward exchange rates would tend to be where the spot rate was expected to be at the later point of time. Therefore, a country with a high rate of inflation could need a rate of interest that much higher. There would then be agreement not only between the rate of inflation and the rate of interest, but also between both of these and forward discounts. In this way, real rates of interest would be equilibrated. With different rates of inflation and fixed exchange rates, on the other hand, real rates of interest would necessarily differ.

Those who argued that a system of fixed exchange rates and an integrated capital market would lead to uniform interest rates tended to overlook the fact that this held only for nominal interest rates at best. There was an element of money illusion. As economists, we were accustomed to think that what mattered was relative rather than absolute prices. Relative prices on the capital markets were the real rate of interest.

Mr Lamfalussy discussed Professor Cooper's paper. He wanted to join M. Ferras in arguing that making bond issues, and financing, could raise serious political problems. Because many Euro-bonds were sold to South American holders, they actually financed United States investment in Europe. This seemed to be the opposite of an optimally distributed capital flow. The main thing was that if there were enough international liquidity, then, with better co-ordination of economic and monetary policies, the world could accommodate capital flows. The alternative was that they might lead to controls or to the import or export of inflation. In fact, we were already reverting to controls. Over the last seven or eight months, there had been a sharp fall in the number of issues in the Euro-bond market. This was due in part to supply factors. Few D-mark issues had been made because of the fear of revaluation. There were also accidental factors like the fall of prices on Wall Street, which reduced issues of convertibles. The rise in American interest rates had made people unwilling to buy. There were also a number of political moves in European countries, not least the step Italy had taken to prevent Italian banks underwriting or selling Euro-bonds. Italy had been a big buyer of short bonds. France had also been out of the market since exchange control, and the same situation was arising in Belgium.

Why had this happened? Professor Cooper said that balance of payments difficulties were the main reason. But there were two others. First, there were simple S.E.C.-type considerations. This was a free market, and while the standard of information in the prospectuses was good, the procedure was often so telescoped that many investors did not yet know what the prospectus said at the time when they had to decide whether or not to underwrite an issue. This practice should be criticised. Second, there were tax considerations, which could not be overemphasised. The main characteristic of the Euro-bond was that there was no withholding tax and that these were bearer bonds. Tax evasion was easy and most governments could not prevent it. Euro-bond issues took a large percentage of current national savings.

To conclude, he would expect government measures of all kinds, and was not optimistic about the large-scale development of the Euro-bond market.

Professor Kindleberger said he was reminded of the remark of the butler in Oscar Wilde's *The Importance of being Earnest:* 'Skip the chapter on the Indian rupee, because it is so exciting.' He had found this discussion exciting and was having difficulty in organising his many views. He could not speak for Desprès and Salant, and they would reply in full in due course. However, this might take a long time; Dr Salant was a deliberate man.

On Professor Cooper's paper, he was sorry that Professor Hicks was against the argument that it was better to have international regulations in these matters than to rely on national markets. He would see fiscal problems tackled by international negotiations; he would try to tackle the kind of problem Mr Lamfalussy had raised by an international S.E.C. However, he thought that the international capital market was a useful device for shifting capital from advanced countries to underdeveloped areas. If this system had worked for a hundred years under the British, he thought one might be patient for a little, while the system was under different management. For example, Mexico showed the benefits of such a system. Mexico did not want foreign aid; but it wanted to borrow on the New York and Euro-dollar markets. Mexico had proved her credit-worthiness and was now able to obtain funds in this way. This seemed to him a paradigm of what was desirable.

He could not say whether the international capital market would be unified by the year 2000, or the year 2070; he simply did not know. He was just talking about trends. Professor Cooper had said that regulation of the market would work only about 50 per cent of the time, but that this was good enough. This simply was not true. He wanted large and small borrowers to be able to use the international capital market. He did not want rich people to be able to avoid regulations while poor people had to obey them.

On the problem of international financial intermediation, he thought it was interesting that Professor George Holm had recently given twelve reasons why the D.K.S. thesis was wrong. His own wife always said that if one did not want to go to dinner, one reason was better than twelve. Twelve reasons sounded like scratching around for a good one. He was impressed that Mr Lamfalussy had scratched around to find new grounds for a second attack; this delighted him. He wanted to make two points. First, the current fact of financial disintermediation did not prove that financial intermediation could not have occurred in the past. He would agree that things had gone wrong in the last year or so, but this was not a powerful argument bearing on the interpretation of an earlier period. He would stress the need to prevent past arrangements unravelling, but this did occur. Second, many attacked the thesis in unacceptable ways. Mr Lamfalussy talked of quantities without prices. If one looked at M1, M2, or even M3, and yet not at the rate of interest, this was unacceptable. To say, as Mr Lamfalussy did in his paper, that the European equity market was as good as the American one without looking at price earnings ratios, the size of issues, or the thinness of markets, was not fair. I.B.M. had not been able to raise a loan of adequate size in Switzerland; it had to do so in the United States. D.K.S., and especially K, agreed that it was wrong to limit intermediation to short- and long-term debt. The United States lent long and borrowed short; that was intermediation. But gross lending and borrowing within each category constituted intermediation too. The numbers relevant to the short and long run separately did not give the essence of the idea. Professor Triffin criticised the thesis in an unfair way. He had taken figures for 1964. Professor Kindleberger had always felt that the use of first differences was the last refuge of a scoundrel; but in this case it was only by first differences that intermediation was revealed, because many long-term assets held in the United States were of long standing. When Triffin said that the United States long-term investments in Europe were not greater than European loans to the United States, he dealt with outstanding amounts, not recent changes. For 1964–7 financial intermediation was a fact of life.

Professor Kindleberger thought that, in an earlier discussion, M. Albert had been unduly harsh on Professor James in rejecting out of hand his use of domination as a description of United States–European relations. Domination might not be a completely accurate description of the position, but these relationships exhibited a number of asymmetries, similar to the domination effect, and it was well to take note of them. For example, in financial questions, the United States served as a financial centre, and Europe as a borrower. This asymmetry made it inappropriate to apply the same kind of balance of payments accounting to the two areas. The United States was a bank; Europe a firm. If a firm incurred net demand liabilities, it could be said to be in deficit; this was not necessarily true of a bank. When a firm borrowed from a bank, it was not necessarily in surplus, nor the bank in deficit. On this showing, Professor Kindleberger was not disposed to regard the increase in United States short-term liabilities to Europe and the world in the period from 1950 to 1966 as indicating United States deficits. United States net assets rose in this period. Lending long and borrowing short provided liquidity to the rest of the world. The United States earned a net return for giving up liquidity; and European economies paid for their gain in liquidity.

Professor Mundell said one should distinguish between the location of the international capital market, where intermediation was important, and the types of assets trade. In Professor Cooper's paper he found a view he had held for a long time – that major differences between rates of interest around the North Atlantic were due to the different prospects of the currencies in which assets were expressed. If one asked how perfect international capital markets were, the main thing to look at was differences in rates of interest; but since assets were different, to make a relevant comparison one needed to translate everything into the same currency. Therefore, at least all short-run assets should be translated into the same currency equivalents.

In the previous year, Professor Earl Hamilton had talked to him about rates of interest in the eighteenth century, quoting figures for various capital markets in the 1720s. In that decade, differences in rates of interest between Geneva, Amsterdam, London, Paris and Frankfurt varied by less than 0·5 per cent. This was true not just in any one year, but for seasonal changes as well. There was a very high degree of perfection of the market in the 1720s. The reason why there was not such perfection now was that we were now comparing different things. In the 1720s, all rates of interest were gold rates of interest; everything was calculated in the same asset.

The table on p. 198 of Professor Cooper's paper showed what had happened recently. There were big differentials in interest rates when expectations of changes in exchange rates developed.

As a general philosophy, he thought that if one asked how perfect the international movement of funds was, the answer was that it was like movement of goods. With barriers to anything, one had differences in price. Taking single assets, and allowing for exchange rates, one had perfect capital movements.

This was quite separate from the intermediation issue. Here he was on the side of some version of the D.K.S. thesis. One traded where the economies of scale from the centralisation of information were greatest – that was to say, mainly in New York – apart from the impact of American balance of payments measures.

Professor Cooper said that Professor Mundell had clarified an important point that had not been clear in his paper. When he said that one market meant one price, the condition 'one market' in this context implied fixed exchange rates and the absence of expectations that exchange rates would change. Over the past ten years, large deviations in interest rates among major countries had generally been associated with expected changes in exchange rates. Thus, Britain had exceptionally high interest rates in 1961 and during the period 1964–7. He therefore agreed with Professor Sohmen that in the long run divergent rates of inflation would give rise to payments disequilibrium and would require alterations in exchange rates. As the disequilibrium was building, there would be a divergence between real and nominal rates of interest and the capital market would not allocate resources efficiently. To the extent that divergences in rates of inflation were expected to result in future changes in exchange rates, however, they would be reflected in forward exchange rate. This would correct those distorting effects.

In response to Messrs Lamfalussy and Ferras, Professor Cooper said that some national independence in the pursuit of monetary policy had been preserved because countries resisted the integrating pressures of the international capital market by imposing barriers to the international flow of funds. The Swiss, for example, had on occasion taken severe measures to resist the inflow of liquid funds. At the same time, they limited foreign access to the Swiss capital market. They had also objected strongly to a bond issue in London denominated in Swiss francs, because such issues would substantially reduce their influence on the flow of funds through the Swiss capital market. By thus inhibiting full integration, Switzerland was able to maintain lower long-term interest rates than prevailed elsewhere.

Professor Cooper replied to Professor Sohmen's question about the integration of the American and Canadian capital markets in the 1950s, when Canada had a flexible exchange rate, as compared with what happened in the 1960s, when Canada moved to a fixed rate. Comparison between the two regimes was difficult, because the Canadian authorities had behaved very much as though they had a fixed exchange rate, even during the period in which the Canadian dollar was free to move. Developments in the Canadian economy paralleled those in the United States, rather than being insulated as might have happened under flexible rates. In particular, Canadian monetary policy during most of the period kept Canadian interest rates in line with those in the United States. So, financial integration was greater than might have been expected under a regime of flexible rates. It was interesting, however, that after the Canadaian rate was pegged in 1962 the flow of debt capital from the United States increased very sharply; but this development could not be linked unambiguously to the change in the exchange-rate regime.

In explaining his remarks about the effectiveness of fiscal policy, Professor Cooper said that he had introduced what was probably a parochial American concern. 'Fiscal policy' here meant pure fiscal policy, namely, changes in government expenditure (or taxation) without accompanying action to change the money supply. The 'monetarist' school of thought argued that pure fiscal policy could have little or no influence in stabilising a national economy, since any increase in government expenditure financed by the sale of bonds would simply raise the rate of interest and thereby induce an offsetting decline in private investment and consumption. With a world capital market, however, monetary expansion automatically accompanied fiscal expansion (under fixed exchange rates) because of inflows of capital. When the State of California floated a loan to finance additional expenditure, it drew funds from the rest of the country. Similarly, with close integration of national capital markets, increased government sales of securities would put upward pressure on local interest rates and would thereby draw funds from outside the country. The United States represented a possible exception to this process, however. It was so large that expansionary fiscal policy without accommodating monetary policy would tighten monetary conditions throughout the world.

Mr Shonfield recalled that Professor Kindleberger had argued that the United States ought to be treated differently because it was not a firm but a bank. In fact, the United States was a bank and also a firm. In most countries, there were elaborate regulations to stop banks being firms at the same time. If the United States wanted to be both a bank and a firm, then it must be subject to international control in its aspects as a firm. Would Professor Kindleberger elaborate on this question?

As he understood it, Mr Lamfalussy did not deny that the United States fulfilled the function of a financial intermediary. However, Mr Lamfalussy said that the essential function, the one Europe needed, was that of entrepreneurship. He demonstrated this by asking us to imagine that the United States ceased to perform the financial function. What would happen? There would be no serious disadvantage. Europe had a reasonably efficient capital market for financing what Europe did today. However, if one took away America's entrepreneurial function, this would be a serious loss to Europe. Therefore, as Professor James said, this was not a contradiction of the D.K.S. thesis; it simply said that one function was more essential than the other.

Mr Lamfalussy replied that if one redefined the action of a financial intermediary to mean either a swop or direct investment, he would have to agree with Professor Kindleberger. There had clearly been an enormous amount of such activity. However, he himself called direct investment entrepreneurship. If one extended definitions like this, there was no point in going on discussing.

On quoting quantities without prices, Mr Lamfalussy said he would go back to what he had said in his book. He agreed that prices were important; so were price–earnings ratios. In his book, he worked these out for the European stock exchanges. He did decide that something was wrong with the European stock markets, but the poorness of secondary markets did not prove the poorness of primary markets. It was undesirable; however, one should not reverse the argument.

Despite the fact that primary equity issues were important, this was not enough. One could not say that stock markets were all organised. He did say that the task was so big that poor performance of prices in secondary markets was understandable. Also, the institutional set-up made possible long-term lending and debt financing, so making it easy for American firms to borrow. They were ideal borrowers for financial institutions with long-run funds to lend, and this bias consequently helped American firms to move to Europe.

To Mr Shonfield, and implicitly to Professor Kindleberger, Mr Lamfalussy said that the reason why clear discussion of these issues was needed was that there were political implications. Professor Kindleberger's first statement was that intermediation was in the interests of the American balance of payments context. Professor Kindleberger did not want to destroy European markets, but to keep the United States balance of payments deficit. When one got to such political issues, one had to be careful.

Mr Lamfalussy said he did not say that the D.K.S. thesis was wrong because yield curves were the opposite of what they should be. He said that he did not know. One could say that he had been unscientific; one could also say the opposite. If one had poor information, there was danger in deriving political proposals from it.

Second, he accepted that the fact that there had been disintermediation since 1967 did not prove that there had been no intermediation before. What he said was that because disintermediation took place so rapidly, and in such big amounts, two things suggested themselves. First, stability of performance was not great; second, the size of financial intermediaries was not big enough to warrant a policy thesis of this kind. Could one base a major defence of the American balance of payments position on such small movements so easily reversed?

To Professor van Meerhaeghe, Mr Lamfalussy said he had tried to study the questions discussed in his paper before he found the O.E.C.D. figures. If one took these for the 1961–5 period, the results were not significantly different. He also thought that later figures would make the same case. There was some increase in American lending, but there was an increase in lending in Europe too.

Professor Eastman said that Stephen Potter had taught that a person should always answer to any proposition; but not in the South. Here one should say: not in the North. The close ties between the American and Canadian capital markets explained the stability of the relationship between their rates of interest. In the early 1950s, when Canada was borrowing little, the differential between rates on long-term Canadian and American bonds was about 0·5 per cent; since then it had usually been about 1 per cent. In the late 1950s, by dint of the most desperate efforts which consisted of increasing the riskiness of Canadian bonds, the Canadian central bank managed to raise the differential to about 1·5 per cent. At that time, new issues by Canadian borrowers payable in United States dollars followed United States rather than Canadian interest rates. These experiences showed great, though not perfect, elasticity of supply of foreign capital to Canadian borrowers. Perhaps this justified the assumption, for analytical purposes, that the elasticity of supply of capital was infinite.

Mr Merigó said he would go back to what Mr Shonfield had said about the United States behaving as a banker. The American presentation of its balance of payments on a liquidity basis was unfair to the United States. One could have a liquidity deficit as a firm, financed by foreign claims on American banks. The United States could lend long and borrow short; then it was behaving like a private banker, if the short borrowing was from foreign individuals or private firms.

The problem came when the United States borrowed from central banks. In that case, America was really acting as a central bank *and* as a private firm. It borrowed short from foreign central banks, as a central bank did; but it invested directly abroad. Perhaps this was pushing intermediation too far, and foreign central banks should therefore be cautious.

It was interesting that in years when central banks thought perhaps that they were holding too many dollars and moved into gold, the United States had had to apply 'voluntary' controls, not on investment but on the way it was financed. Finally, the United States borrowed long and invested directly. For European countries, it was right to look at the domination aspects of this. One day they might not want to accept this system of allowing the United States to finance its direct investment by borrowing in European markets at higher rates than in the controlled United States market.

Professor Lundberg said a major issue was raised in Professor Cooper's paper. He wanted to look at the background to the capital market in individual countries. The savings market in a country like Sweden was very compartmentalised. Looking at it from a Swedish Socialist point of view, one would not fully accept the results of a more perfect capital market. This would simply send funds to already developed parts of the country, and make the system work worse in some respects. One had to help agriculture and the weak regions. Perhaps the working of international capital markets would appear even worse than we thought if we judged it by looking at the distribution of resources between rich and poor countries. In Sweden, funds coming from the international market made up a small percentage of its whole capital market activity. It regarded the Euro-dollar market as a disturbance. This was a natural reaction, where countries did not accept perfect capital markets. How would such countries react internationally?

On income distribution, the question was whether the working of the international capital market would reduce the gap in income per head between, say, the United States and Portugal. He did not know. But this was the kind of problem that was always raised in discussions with devoted Swedish planners. He thought some parts of the market would work better than others, and that there was a danger that the international capital market would become like the international agricultural market. There one had enormous disturbances and had to make compromises. One might correct social problems caused by capital markets by fiscal policy; perhaps we should create some sort of social-saving funds internationally, to correct unwanted changes in income distribution.

Professor Sohmen said he would underline what Mr Merigó had said about the need to distinguish private from official capital movements. In the last ten years, central banks in Europe had accumulated United States funds at low yields. Americans had been investing privately at high rates of return in Europe. In effect, one therefore had European taxpayers subsidising American investors in Europe.

On a different point, it was hard to be sure what were the preferences of European 'countries'. In 1966-7, President Blessing of the German Bundesbank used to say that Germany was losing reserves at a dangerous pace, in face of the enormous pile of foreign exchange the country was holding. He therefore felt it necessary to keep interest rates high. Some European officials, indeed, seemed to have an inordinate love of foreign exchange reserves. Private citizens had no reason to be happy about this, but it was difficult for them to reveal their preferences effectively.

Part of private transactions was probably not following the dictates of rational resource allocation either. For example, American mutual funds took large amounts of money from Europe to invest in American shares. The main reason was that they had very hard-hitting salesmen. By contrast, European bankers were used to pushing much less hard. There was therefore an asymmetry in capital flows.

Professor Wallich wanted to emphasize the difference between the actual institutions and the assumptions we made about them. The demand for assets was altered by institutional pressures. He agreed that mutual funds were sold very hard. There were also credit arrangements. It was hard to say what liquidity would be in Europe without these institutions. The real thing was therefore the selling effort. He would suggest that the Federal Reserve System needed to use a horde of mutual-fund salesmen to correct the balance of payments – and not the discount rate.

About firms and intermediaries, there seemed to be an ambiguity. Mr Shonfield said that a firm was a merchant or investment bank. To put it another way, was the firm a profit-maximising entity? The United States capital market was not a profit-maximising entity; the United States was (hopefully) a welfare-maximising entity. The aim was to maximise the welfare of United States citizens, by incidentally increasing the welfare of the rest of the world. This seemed to him a worth-while distinction.

Professor Scott said that Professor Lundberg had used the phrase 'the tail wagging the dog' and had spoken of international agricultural markets. He wanted to augment this. Perhaps the correct analogy was with black markets for otherwise controlled commodities. Professor Lundberg referred to national schemes for social savings, and pointed to the difficulty of allowing these to enter the international capital market. Was the international capital market becoming smaller as a percentage of European activity than before? Maybe this was a better example of backdoor protectionism than instances mentioned earlier.

As for the small amount of labour migration across the Atlantic, if the capital market was working as well as it had a hundred years ago, there would surely be more labour migration relative to movements of capital.

Professor Kindleberger said that Mr Shonfield's view implied that the United States should be treated as if it were a firm, when it was in fact a bank. A firm normally had a quick-asset ratio of $2\frac{1}{2}$ or 3 to 1, and viewed an increase in demand liabilities as a deficit. The liquidity definition of equilibrium in the balance of payments of the United States treated that country as if it were a firm: increases in liabilities were treated as a deficit; and increases in quick assets were regarded as not available to meet withdrawals. What was needed rather was a definition of disequilibrium appropriate to a bank which looked at its liabilities very differently from a firm.

He did not know if the United States should have its balance of payments behaviour regulated. Perhaps there was a case to be made for GATT-type regulation of attempts to improve the balance; for example, extending the presumption against restrictions from trade items to service items such as tourist expenditures. But he did not accept the view that the United States had had significant deficits on the average for twenty years – prior to 1966–8. In 1964, for example, the United States had a current account surplus of $8 billion. What did Mr Shonfield mean when he talked about regulating the firm? Professor Kindleberger had himself advocated the internationalisation of monetary policy – with countries like Switzerland and Sweden opting out if they wished. He could not accept complaints about the United States payments deficit when it was behaving like a prudent bank.

In separating private and official holdings, Mr Merigó was in the company of Bernstein, Johnson, etc. He did not make this distinction himself for several reasons. First, it was hard to tell which were official and which were private assets – especially when central banks conducted market operations in dollars. Second, financial intermediation often joined two markets at different levels of completion. The borrowers might acquire dollars; the savers might hold local currencies which required the central bank to hold dollars. If the intermediation process were short-circuited in this way, the central bank had a choice whether to complete it by holding dollars or not. For example, it could lower the rate of interest to complete the transfer process, or it could reduce the degree of monopoly in the capital market. But, unless a country cut itself off like Sweden, to complain that it held dollars was to miss the point. European countries and Americans were mainly interested in short-term movements; what was wrong if financial intermediaries brought them together? The United States was said to be buying plants with European money. If European countries lowered the rate of interest and increased domestic liquidity, local firms would be able to pay a higher price for the plants than American firms.

On entrepreneurship, he would like to put the issues in a formula:

$$C = \frac{I}{r}.$$

That was to say, the capital value of the firm depended on I, the income flow, divided by r, the rate of profit. Either American firms had a higher C because they could earn a higher I; or because they accepted a lower r. Mr Lamfalussy and Professor James thought that it was because they accepted a lower r; Mr Merigó and Professor Sohmen thought there was a higher I. He thought it was hard to resolve these two views.

President de Gaulle had suggested that America could pay more for French firms because America had cheaper money. He thought this might have been true on occasion, but the best way of reducing the rate of interest and rate of profit was to move towards a perfect international capital market. He had been impressed when General Electric bought Machines Bull, which had already been hawked around Europe. European firms had too little liquidity to buy it. Only the big, liquid American corporations could do so. Was this a matter of liquidity preference, or was it because the hope of a higher rate of return made the American firm able to buy Machines Bull?

Mr Brittan said he would like to ask Professor Cooper a question about second-best solutions, though he was sure Professor Kindleberger would disapprove even of the question.

At the end of his paper, Professor Cooper said 'If balance of payments equilibrium is not assured through co-ordinated monetary policies and provision for more frequent changes in exchange rates, however, high capital mobility will exert pressures for trade controls and/or unwanted domestic inflation or deflation.' This was a familiar issue in the United Kingdom and, in the chapter in the Brookings volume on Britain, Professor Cooper had shown that, to obtain an improved balance of payments, it was possible to use either control over capital outflow, or controls on trade, or changes in exchange rates, or cuts in government spending overseas. Assume that the last two were ruled out in a particular situation. How, from a welfare point of view, should one then choose between trade controls and controls over overseas investment? The latter were always immediately attractive, but in the long run it would reduce overseas earnings. This would not happen if one cut down on the trade side. He thought probably the theoretical answer was that one should do a bit of both.

In reply to Professor Scott, *Professor Cooper* agreed that there was less labour mobility today than in the past, particularly in the latter half of the nineteenth century, and that labour mobility then also involved substantial mobility of capital. But the roles of labour and capital mobility had both changed. As Ragnar Nurkse pointed out, over a decade ago, labour and capital movements tended to be complementary in the nineteenth century, both aiming to take advantage of unexploited natural resources. More recently, capital and labour had tended to become substitutes. Regional policies within countries typically encouraged capital to move to workers. Foreign assistance could be viewed as an attempt, by moving capital, to raise incomes where heavy concentrations of people were, thereby reducing the pressures for outward migration. More concretely, the United States recently reduced the seasonal inflow of labour from Mexico; it took only one season for American capital to move to Mexico to use the agricultural labour there and export the produce to the United States.

Mr Brittan had raised a difficult question. It was far easier to assess the effects of balance of payments measures on financial flows than it was to assess their effects on social welfare. There was no universally valid answer. On some occasions, capital movements offset other distortions in the world economy, such as tariffs; controlling them would involve substantial costs in terms of efficiency. On other occasions, capital movements reinforced the efficiency costs of other distortions in the world economy, such as certain differences in national taxation; controlling them would actually contribute to allocative efficiency.

Professor Cooper answered Professor Lundberg's question by saying that he did not think that insulation between national economies would be possible in the long run – over a period of several decades. Governments might resist, but most pressures, both technological and sociological, were towards greater interdependence among nations.

In the concluding remarks of his paper, Professor Cooper said he had been concerned with the pace and the method by which we should move to this long-run position. When he said that capital controls were second-best, he meant that pressures on national monetary and income distribution policies seemed to be too great for countries to absorb at the present time. Some orderly restraint on capital movements might be needed to reduce the pressures for greater integration into a world economy; otherwise we might experience a nationalistic backlash that would engender extensive and disorderly restrictions on all kinds of international transactions.

Mr Lamfalussy returned to the question of entrepreneurship. There were three points:

First, there was an explanation based on European financial markets. American firms did have advantages in borrowing in Europe, because of their good financial structures. This was important, even when one compared them with large, reputable European firms.

Second, on the higher potential rate of profit of American firms, perhaps one could explain this by talking of the 'management' gap. However, one feature was that this might be related to size. Perhaps bigger firms could attract genuinely gifted managers. Maybe the time factor was important too. United States firms could wait. Their profit performance in Europe tended to be low at the beginning. It took four, five, or even six years before they began to make profits. This was again linked to size.

Third, perhaps the United States was wrong to invest in Europe at all. If one looked at profit rates in recent years, one found that these were falling and that detailed figures on individual firms showed a very wide spread. Whether the United States was right to invest in Europe or not he did not know; he simply left open the possibility of a global miscalculation.

11 Monetary Relations between Europe and America

Robert A. Mundell
UNIVERSITY OF CHICAGO

I. INTRODUCTION

The monetary history of the past century can be conveniently divided into three periods: the sterling-dominated gold standard prior to the First World War, the dollar-dominated gold standard following the Second World War, and the transition period in between (1914 to 1945). The transition period saw the attempt to restore sterling in 1925, the separation of sterling from gold in 1931, and the rise of the dollar to international status after devaluation in 1934. The post-war system has been dominated by the United States. The monetary order established at Bretton Woods in 1944 created a code of conduct for the adjustable peg system in addition to a multilateral credit facility, but it was the interaction of national power rather than the International Monetary Fund that dominated the form into which the post-war system evolved.

My subject is European and American monetary relations. I have had to decide between an historical review and a theoretical analysis. Both are needed, but I have chosen a theoretical approach. There is a great need, I believe, for a shift of emphasis in the theoretical models used to analyse the mechanics of the international monetary system and to interpret the United States balance of payments deficit.

Economic policy is made in the context of totality of international relations. The international monetary system is only one of the constituent parts of the international system. The monetary system, however, is not a static system because the institutions occupying central roles in it evolve over time. Economic theory can elucidate the mechanics of the system in a given institutional setting, but when the institutional setting changes (as from 1914 to 1945), our technical models have to take into account new modes of conduct. Thus traditional gold standard theory is not applicable to the modern dollar-dominated gold standard any more than Keynesian depression economics is applicable to the inflationary environment of the world economy in recent years. Of course a grand parent theory that encompassed all conceivable subsystems could be constructed, and then all short-run theories would emerge as special cases. But to build such a general theory is not necessarily the most economical way to proceed. Most theories that are simple enough to be useful are partial theories conditioned by the institutional 'constants' at the time. But the risk of the use of partial theories is their misuse in transition periods. During periods of great transitions it is necessary to be alert to the signals that structural parameters are changing. This need is especially relevant today because our own times have involved great transitions.

Two illustrations relevant to my paper may bear this out. Consider the much quoted Cunliffe Report on the operation of the gold standard. This influential document built a fairy-tale image of the nineteenth-century system that was distinctly inferior to accounts of earlier economists like Thornton, Ricardo, Lord Overstone and Bagehot; it was an overly *simpliste* analysis suitable, if at all, to the world of David Hume, and not to the complicated financial system that had grown up by 1914. Yet the Cunliffe Report exerted a profound effect on thinking in Britain and America about the gold standard in the post-war period.

A second example is the applicability of Keynesian theory to the modern world economy. *The General Theory* was written in the pessimistic milieu of mass unemployment, deflationary expectations, economic autarky, population stagnation, economic controls and a general trend towards international disharmony. No wonder Keynes adopted inelastic expectations, a closed economy, a constant stock of productive equipment, an elastic supply of labour and no technological change, as his simplifying assumptions. But what economist today would regard these assumptions as relevant characteristics of the modern world?

The three decades, from 1940 to 1970, have been characterised by inflation, rapid growth, the population explosion and fantastic technological leaps. Ours is the atomic age, the electronic age, the age of the explosion of modern science and space travel. The assumptions Keynes selected to symbolise the attitudes of the 1930s are almost the opposite of those relevant today.

I am not saying that the Keynesian model is 'wrong' or useless. Rather its premises are no longer applicable. More work would be necessary to make his model applicable to the world economy today than to start on a fresh track. The assumptions of inelastic expectations, zero growth and technical change, elastic supplies of labour and a closed economy do not fit any country in the world today. Now if we had a grand general theory to cover all cases we could simply modify the assumptions. But since we lack such a general theory, one can argue, as I do, that the Keynesian model should be put on the shelf until his world of pessimism and gloom returns (hopefully never).

The first part of this paper develops a system that I believe better captures many relevant features of monetary relations in the modern world economy than does the traditional Keynesian model. It focuses attention on the special position of the United States monetary system and the role of the United States deficit as the supply line feeding reserves (often unwanted) to the rest of the world. This monetary pipeline sets the tune of world inflation as long as individual nations adhere to the fixed exchange-rate systems.

The monetary mechanisms of the system, however, represent only one aspect of the problem. In lieu of a general long-run theory there is no escape from historical analysis. The system has to be put also in the perspective of its historical setting in order to form judgements about its evolution and to find a framework for judging the adequacy of current suggestions for reform of it.

The major conclusion of my theoretical analysis is that the post-war period can best be interpreted as a period of disguised equilibrium misinterpreted as disequilibrium. The main conclusion of my practical analysis is that the alternatives now facing the Atalntic nations reduce to three competing ideas: (1) European acquiescence to American monetary leadership; (2) an international solution based on world monetary management; and (3) creation of a monetary bloc in Europe competitive to the dollar.

II. THE MONETARY MECHANICS OF THE INTERNATIONAL SYSTEM

(1) *Credit Expansion and the International Distribution of Money*

Important revisions in economic thinking are needed to understand the connections between growth, interest rates and the balance of payments as they are determined in the modern gold standard. The theories of world monetary equilibrium of Hume, Ricardo and Mill establish the nature of international general equilibrium for a static world economy, but need drastic adjustment to make them suitable for a growing world economy experiencing secular changes in the price level. An acceleration of monetary growth, for example, will initially lower interest rates, but in so far as the acceleration of monetary expansion leads to price increases that are anticipated, interest rates will eventually rise, altering the ratio of money to income and creating ambiguity with respect to the interpretation of the effect of monetary changes on the balance of payments. It is vital in all theories to specify the time period during which particular markets are allowed to adjust to equilibrium. Thus distinctions can be made between theories based on hypothetical time periods during which (*a*) balances of payments are equilibrated, (*b*) capital stocks are relocated between countries, and (*c*) growth ceases. Over the very long run it is necessary to allow for the rise and decline of different national currencies as international power relationships change.

In order to interpret the interaction between some of these variables, and the instruments of international monetary policy, it will be useful to construct a monetary model[1] of the world economy, divided into two regions: America, and the rest of the world or 'Europe'.

In Figs. 11.1(a) and 11.1(b), interest rates are plotted on the ordinate and real money supplies on the abscissa. $L_A L_A$ and $L_E L_E$ depict the liquidity preference schedules – the loci of interest rates and money supplies that indicate the willingness of each community to hold real money balances. These schedules can be symbolised by the equations $i = \phi(M_E)$ and $i = \psi(M_A)$ on the assumption that interest rates, after adjusting for exchange risk, are the same in each country.

In addition to the liquidity preference schedules we need equations specifying equilibrium in the world capital market. I assume that each country has a given labour force rooted to its respective region, but that the capital stock, which is fixed in the short run for the world as a whole, is mobile between countries. The marginal efficiency of capital (M.E.C.) is assumed to be an increasing function of real money balances and a decreasing function of the capital stock located in each region. Consider, for example, the curve $K_A K_A$ in Fig. 11.1(a). This schedule indicates that the marginal efficiency of capital (the real rate of interest) rises with the level of real money balances for a certain quantity (K_A) of the world capital stock located in America. If the amount K_A of capital is in America, then $K - K_A$ of capital is located in Europe, where K is the world capital stock,

---

[1] The model developed below departs from the Keynes–Hicks model in the treatment of expectations, stocks and flows, and money as an argument in the production function. The Keynes–Hicks model assumes constant expected future prices, whereas mine assumes, not just that expected future prices rise with spot prices, but that current rates of change of spot prices are extrapolated into the future. A second difference is that income in Keynes's system is determined by the equality of current flows of saving and investment, whereas it is implicit in my system that the price level is determined in the commodity (stock) market and flows of saving and investment determine the rate of growth.

My system bears some superficial similarities to the Metzler–Patinkin model in so far as it places the level of real balances at the centre of the analysis, but their models more closely approximate the Keynes–Hicks model in the exogenous treatment of expectations and the interpretation of stocks and flows. In certain respects, therefore, my model integrates Fisher's system with the Metzler–Patinkin system, siding with the former with respect to the role of expectations; in part it follows up the line pioneered by Chicago economists (especially Cagan, Friedman and Bailey), and Maurice Allais, while it departs from all three groups in its treatment of money in the production function; in the latter respect it is closer to some of the work of Tobin, Sidrauski and Stein in growth theory. International developments of related models have been made by Komiya, McKinnon and Arthur Laffer; the latter has found that a somewhat different version of the model achieves successful empirical results.

My own work on the subject was begun in 1963 when I engaged in work on inflation at the I.M.F., and some of it is contained in articles in the *Journal of Political Economy* (June 1963, Feb 1965, Apr 1965) and the *American Economic Review* (May 1969); *International Economics*, chap. 9; 'The International Distribution of Money in Growing Economies' (forthcoming in a book of readings); and other miscellaneous papers forthcoming in a book on monetary theory.

and this fixes the location of the corresponding capital equilibrium schedule, $K_E K_E$, in Europe.

The implied distribution of the capital stock (K_A in America and $K - K_A$ in Europe) is not an equilibrium quantity because the intersection of $K_A K_A$ and $L_A L_A$ would result in a lower M.E.C. in America than would the corresponding intersection of $L_E L_E$ with $K_E K_E$ in Europe. Part of the capital stock would accordingly move from America to Europe until the M.E.C.s are equated. A migration of capital shifts $K_A K_A$ upward and to the left and $K_E K_E$ downward and to the right. In the final equilibrium the two schedules $K'_A K'_A$ and $K'_E K'_E$ establish the interest rate $BC = DF$, and the level of real money balances, $O_A B$ in America, and $O_E D$ in Europe.

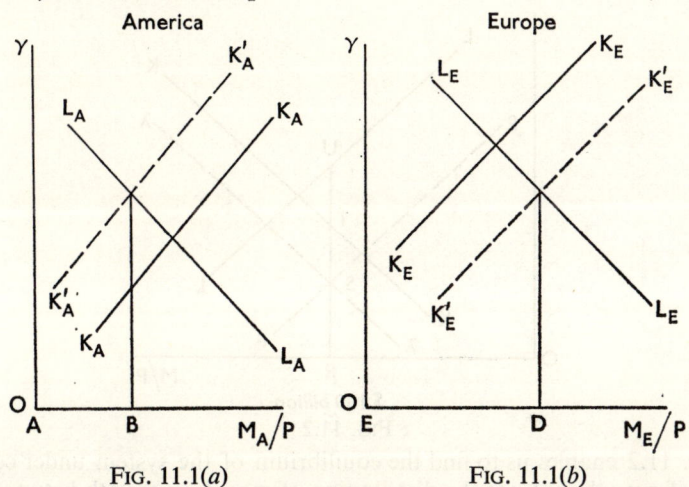

Fig. 11.1(a) Fig. 11.1(b)

In order to find the equilibrium of the system when the world economy is growing and credit expansion in each of the regions is allowed for, it will be convenient first to continue the two graphs. Adding $L_A L_A$ and $L_E L_E$ horizontally gives us (Fig. 11.2) the global liquidity preference schedule, LL; and adding money supplies for corresponding capital schedules gives us the global capital requirements schedule, KK. Let us assume, for simplicity, that the income elasticity of the demand for money is unity. Then subtract the rate of growth of the world economy from KK to get $\lambda\lambda$; this equals the real rate of increase in the demand for money. Now by an analogous procedure we can subtract the rate of growth in the supply of money from LL to get $\rho\rho$. The equilibrium of the system is determined at the point where the growth of the nominal supply of money is equal to the growth of the nominal demand for money. Taking into account the fact that the nominal demand for money is composed of two parts – a real increase and an increase needed to compensate for a depreciation of nominal balances due to inflation – it is readily established that the equilibrium of the system will be established at the intersection of the two schedules $\lambda\lambda$ and $\rho\rho$, since the rate of growth in the nominal demand for money will be the vertical difference between $\lambda\lambda$ and LL. Illustrative values for the variables at equilibrium of the G-10 economy in 1968 would be

M/P = OR = \$400 billion (money balances)
i = RU = 7 per cent (interest rates)
r = TR = 4 per cent (real interest rate)
π = TU = 3 per cent (rate of inflation)
ρ = US = 6 per cent (rate of monetary expansion)
λ = TS = 3 per cent (rate of growth)

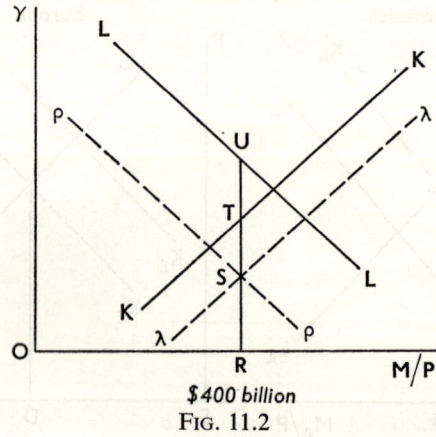

Fig. 11.2

Fig. 11.2 enables us to find the equilibrium of the system under conditions of growth, but not the distribution of monetary growth between the two regions. Our major concern is the division of the money supply between the two regions and the balance of payments of the United States and Europe. To specify these variables the world economy must be broken into its component parts, as in Figs 11.3(a) and 11.3(b). From the apparatus of Fig. 11.2 we got the equilibrium interest rate and the position of the $K_A K_A$ and $K_E K_E$ schedules. The balance of payments of the two regions is then determined by the fact that any excess supply of money produced by one region must in equilibrium be equal to the excess demand for money produced in the other region. Since the rate of inflation is common to both regions, the balance of payments will be established at the point where the excess of the 'equilibrium' rate of monetary expansion over the sum of the rate of growth and the rate of inflation in one region, weighted by the money supply of that region, plus the corresponding excess in the outer region, is zero. The shaded areas in the left- and right-hand graphs represent the United States balance of payments deficit and the European balance of payments surplus. A representative value for this area is about $4 billion or 2 per cent of the United States money supply.

Now consider the effects of an increase in credit creation in one of the regions, say the United States. In Fig. 11.3(a) this involves a downward movement in the curve $\delta_A\delta_A$ and a rearrangement of capital stocks between the countries. After an initial adjustment (during which interest rates will fall), the expected rate of inflation in the world will increase, lowering the real quantity of money demanded in both regions and raising the world price level. But after this adjustment process has been com-

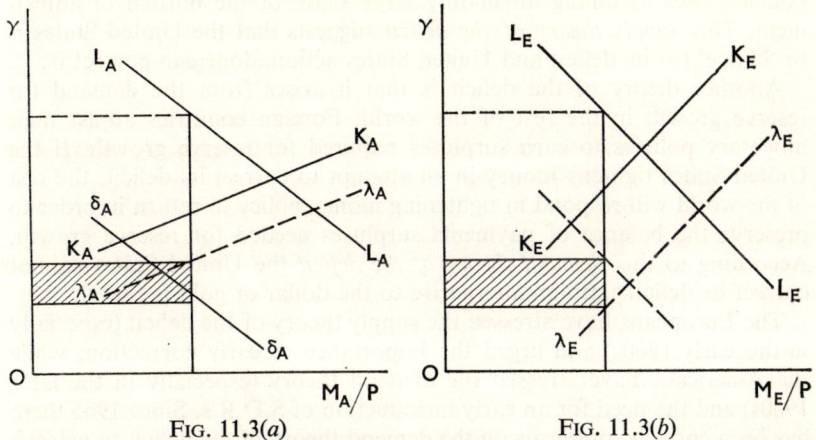

FIG. 11.3(a)   FIG. 11.3(b)

pleted there will be an increased flow demand for money in both countries to compensate for the depreciation of real money balances. In the absence of any change in the rate of credit expansion in Europe, the United States balance of payments deficit will increase. An increase in credit expansion in the United States will therefore result in an increased monetary expansion in the United States that is less than the increased credit expansion; and there will be an increase in the rate of *monetary* expansion in Europe (arising from the balance of payments surplus) even though there is no change in the European rate of *credit* expansion.

We can see, therefore, that an increase in United States monetary expansion can lead to an increase in the United States balance of payments deficit. But consider now an increase in the growth rate in Europe which leads to an increase in the demand for money in Europe; this amounts to a downward shift in the schedule $\lambda_E \lambda_E$. In the absence of additional credit creation in Europe, monetary tightness will induce a balance of payments surplus and an increase in the rate of monetary expansion and deflationary) pressure in the world economy, again leading to an increased balance of payments deficit in the United States.

(2) Demand and Supply Theories of the Deficit

We have now seen how both an increase in the rate of credit expansion in the United States and an increase in the rate of change of the demand for money in Europe can worsen the United States balance of payments. These two possibilities are closely related to two theories of the United States deficit.[1] One view of the deficit is that it arises from excess money creation in the United States, which forces European central banks to accumulate dollars they must either hoard (giving a zero or low-interest loan to the United States) or get rid of by more expansive monetary policies, thus assuming an unduly large share of the burden of adjustment. This *supply theory of the deficit* suggests that the United States is to 'blame' for its deficit and United States action alone can correct it.

Another theory of the deficit is that it arises from the demand for reserve growth in the rest of the world. Foreign countries adjust their monetary policies to earn surpluses required for reserve growth. If the United States tightens money in an attempt to correct its deficit, the rest of the world will respond in tightening money policy in return in order to preserve the balance of payments surpluses needed for reserve growth. According to this *demand theory of the deficit* the United States cannot correct its deficit until an alternative to the dollar or gold is found.

The Europeans have stressed the supply theory of the deficit (especially in the early 1960s) and urged the importance of early correction, while the Americans have stressed the demand theory (especially in the later 1960s) and the need for an early introduction of S.D.R.s. Since 1965 there has been enough consensus on the demand theory of the deficit to achieve agreement on the S.D.R.s, but not enough to reach agreement on the size of the allocation desirable over the first few years.

Our foregoing analysis shows, however, that it is unnecessary to resort to one-sided theories of the deficit or even to the concepts of disequilibrium they imply. The existence of the deficit is compatible with equilibrium between demand and supply over the past two decades, not only in the tautological sense in which demand and supply are always in equilibrium but in the operational sense of equilibrium.

Consider again increased (desired) hoarding in Europe. In the absence of a corresponding acceleration of credit in Europe, this will bring deflationary pressure in the world as a whole and a European surplus. However, the deflationary pressure may induce the United States monetary authorities to *accelerate* credit to maintain monetary growth in the United States, or to *decelerate* it to prevent a worsening of the balance of payments. Similarly an increase in United States credit expansion that

---

[1] Robert Aliber, in a paper given at the International Economics Workshop at the University of Chicago, has made the distinction between supply-determined and demand-determined deficits.

worsens the United States deficit may induce additional or slower credit expansion in Europe as the authorities act, respectively, either to reduce their surpluses, or to slow the pace of inflation. The first European reaction would be equilibrating with respect to the balance of payments, but it would aggravate world inflation; whereas the second reaction would have the opposite effect. In none of these cases can it be said that the United States deficit is either demand-determined or supply-determined.

A central issue in the conduct of monetary relations between the two regions, therefore, is the type of reaction of one monetary authority to a change in policy in the other region.

To investigate these interactions, let us consider as two independent variables the rates of expansion of credit in the United States and Europe, δ_a and δ_e, plotted on the axes of Fig. 11.4. The equilibrium relation between these variables and the rate of world inflation is

$$\pi = (\delta_a - \lambda_a)\sigma_a + (\delta_e - \lambda_e)(1 - \sigma_a)$$

where σ_a is the share of dollars in the world money stock. Price stability ($\pi = 0$) requires that changes in δ_a are offset by changes in δ_e. The line $\pi \pi$ depicts the values of δ_a and δ_e at which price stability can be maintained.

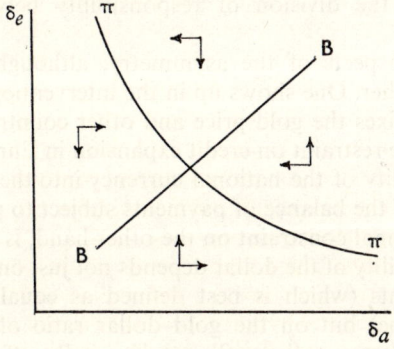

FIG. 11.4

The second consideration is the United States balance of payments deficit. From Figs 11.3(a) and 11.3(b) it is readily seen that the deficit (B) is equal to $[\delta_a - (\lambda_a + \pi)]m_a = B = [(\lambda_e + \pi] - \delta_e]m_e$. There are variations in δ_a and δ_e that will preserve a given value of B; the zero balance of payments line is BB and it has a positive slope. A simultaneous increase in both δ_a and δ_e will raise the rate of inflation and both regions will have to participate in the credit expansion producing it if a zero balance of payments is to be maintained.

Now consider a policy matrix (Fig. 11.5) based on the targets of balance of payments equilibrium and price stability.

Both countries could co-operate to achieve the same target, following policies A and C (adjusting towards the *BB* line) or policies B and D (adjusting towards the $\pi\pi$ line). Or a division of functions based on A and D or B and C could be adopted. Slightly more complex possibilities with alternatives in function could be adopted, with, for example, the surplus region assuming responsibility for adjustment when $\pi > 0$, and the deficit country when $\pi < 0$.

In fact, however, there is an asymmetry built into the system by virtue of the post-war position of the dollar as the settlement currency. The

Target \ Instrument	Balance of payments	Price stability
δ_a	A	B
δ_e	C	D

FIG. 11.5

United States currency bloc encompasses a transactions area covering half the world and its currency is an ultimate reserve. This fact imparts an asymmetry to the division of responsibility between Europe and America.

There are two aspects of the asymmetry, although they are closely related to one another. One shows up in the intervention system by which the United States fixes the gold price and other countries fix their dollar rates. Formally, the restraint on credit expansion in Europe is the requirement of convertibility of the national currency into the dollar, which implies equilibrium in the balance of payments subject to possible variations in reserves. The formal constraint on the other hand, is convertibility into gold. But convertibility of the dollar depends not just on the United States balance of payments (which is best defined as equal to the collective surpluses of Europe) but on the gold–dollar ratio of reserves abroad. However, United States policy will not be vitally affected by the convertibility requirement, since any serious conflict between internal balance and convertibility will be decided in favour of internal balance.

This leads up to the second aspect of the asymmetry which stems from size. The United States constraint is not convertibility but the rate of inflation. In theory, therefore, the United States economy adapts to achieve a given rate of inflation and, in view of the size of the United States transactions area, this should correspond to rates of inflation throughout the world.

The pairing of instruments and targets is therefore suggested by the policy arrangement as represented by B and C in the policy table: United States credit expansion is matched with the world requirement of price stability, and European credit expansion is matched to the requirement of balance of payments equilibrium, as the arrows in Fig. 11.4 indicate.

III. MONETARY CONTROL

We now turn to the actual behaviour of rates of monetary and credit expansion in the United States and the rest of the world. If both European and American monetary authorities followed balance of payments equilibrium policies, money expansion rates should move in opposite directions in Europe and America. Such has not been the case over the past few years. The prevailing trend of money expansion rates has been sympathetic. Since 1964 at least the core of the world economy has been behaving like a single monetary area. Let us consider the cycles of monetary expansion rates in the United States and nine other industrial countries (G-9).[1]

(1) Cycles of Monetary Expansion

From the first quarter of 1965 to the first quarter of 1966, the average rate of G-10 monetary expansion was 8 per cent, compared to 6½ per cent for the same period a year earlier. (This is a weighted average of the G-9 rate of almost 11 per cent and the United States rate of 5·4 per cent.) In the second and third quarters of 1966 the expansion rate was cut to 3·3 per cent and 2·9 per cent respectively, the period of the crunch. This was divided between a reduction in the G-9 rate to 7·5 per cent and 5·3 per cent; and a reduction in the United States rate to −0·7 per cent and 0·5 per cent. Both the United States and G-9 were implicated in the restriction and interest rose abruptly.

The reversal came in the fourth quarter of 1966 when the G-10 rate was stepped up to 5·9 per cent and followed by further acceleration to 9·0 per cent and 10·0 per cent in the succeeding two quarters. Again, both G-9 and the United States were implicated in the acceleration, with G-9 rates of 8·2, 12·1 and 9·9, and corresponding United States rates of 3·6, 6·0 and 10·2. This brings us up to the second half of 1967 when a new period of monetary restriction was introduced with an average rate for the two quarters of 3 per cent. But this time the restriction was extemely sharp in Europe compared to the United States, respective figures for G-9 and the United States being 1·4 and 4·8.[2]

G-10 monetary expansion was again stepped up in the first three

[1] I am grateful to Miss Elaine Goldstein for organising the data on which the analysis of the present section is based.

[2] The G-9 figures were, however, especially influenced by the United Kingdom devaluation; since we are using dollar values of money supply, the United Kingdom devaluation cuts G-9 money by Britain's weight in the index multiplied by the devaluation of 0·14. The results, therefore, exaggerate the degree of monetary restrictiveness during the last quarter of 1967, which in terms of local currency was mainly concentrated in France.

quarters of 1968, rising to 4·8, 10·4 and 9·4. Corresponding figures in G-9 were 5·0, 13·7 and 10·3, and in the United States 4·3, 6·1 and 2·1. A reversal was again introduced at the beginning of 1969 (comparable figures are not available to me at the present time and place of writing).

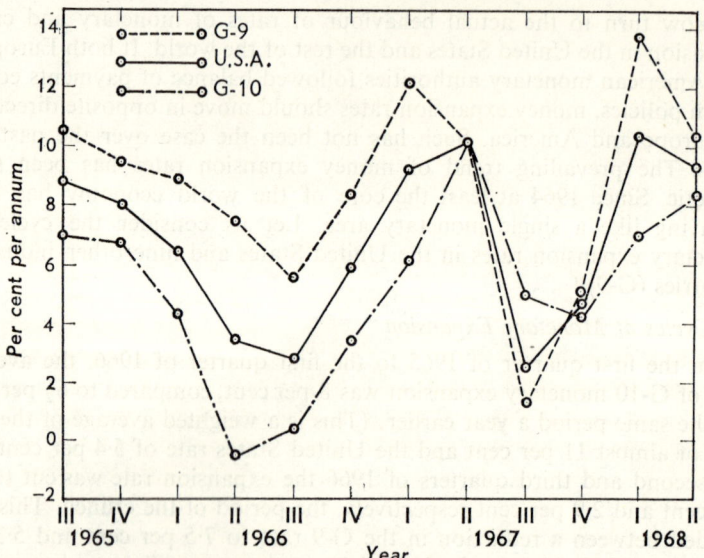

FIG. 11.6 Annual rates of monetary expansion of G-9, the United States and G-10, 1965-8.

Fig. 11.6 illustrates the high degree of sympathy of the rates from G-9 and the United States and illustrates the extent to which the world as a whole follows similar monetary cycles. It is, I believe, ample evidence that it is useful to regard the G-10 monetary areas as a single unit and not as two or more independent areas each following monetary cycles dominated by the balance of payments. The evidence is at least consistent with the theory that the United States money supply is to a large degree autonomous while the rest of the world follows balance of payments equilibrium policies.

This does not imply tacit acceptance of a division of responsibility along the B-C arrangement of the policy table.

A United States monetary policy that is independent of the balance of payments does not imply one that is directed at United States or even world stability. In Fig. 11.4 the European rates of credit expansion may adjust to the BB line while the United States rates of expansion may move in stabilising or destabilising directions from the standpoint of a given rate of inflation in the world economy. Indeed, since 1965 United States monetary policy has been erratic partly because of miscalculation and partly because of the Vietnam war. This brings us to the question of control of the global money supply.

(2) *Control of the Global Money Supply*
The world money stock can be defined as

$$M = \Sigma P^i M_i$$

where M_i is country i's money supply (currency and demand deposits) and P_i is the exchange rate (the dollar price of currency i). The I.M.F., strangely enough, does not compute this total,[1] but a fair approximation to it can be got by using the figures we have already developed for the United States and the G-9 group (Japan, Germany, France, the United Kingdom, Italy, Canada, the Netherlands, Belgium and Switzerland). In 1968 the total[2] was $400 billion of which dollars accounted for half. A rough figure for the total non-communist world would be $500 billion.

The concept of a global money supply would not be a very interesting one if each country's monetary policy were independent of one another, as they would be under a regime of flexible exchange rates. Under such a system each country could establish its own rate of inflation and nominal interest rates in each nation would reflect the expected internal and external depreciation of the unit of account. But flexible exchange rates have only rarely been resorted to by the major nations, and, except for Canada (1950–62), only as a temporary expedient. The major countries commit their monetary policies to the fixed exchange parities subject only to the fluctuations permitted by the exchange margins and variations in foreign exchange reserves. Those countries that have got out of step with the mainstream of the world economy – Britain and Germany are outstanding examples – have sooner or later had to reverse monetary policies or change their exchange rate. Whatever gains are believed to have been achieved by the sporadic exchange-rate adjustments that have actually taken place (the gains have never been measured even by economists who advocate exchange flexibility), it is doubtful whether they have been significant enough to offset the harm produced by their chaotic effect on exchange markets.[3]

[1] Devaluation of one of the currencies in a global money supply figure can be handled statistically the same as a partial bank failure is handled in national money totals.

[2] In calculating this magnitude it is of some significance to avoid double counting due to the holding of foreign exchange reserves. When European central banks hold deposits in New York banks, this magnitude is counted as part of the United States money supply as it is measured by the Federal Reserve System. These deposits, however, are assets of the European banks and they have corresponding liabilities in pounds, francs, etc. The correct global figure, therefore, can include these dollars in the United States component or in the European component of the world money supply, but not in both.

[3] It is hard to believe that the 5 per cent upvaluation of the German D-mark and Dutch guilder in 1961 justified the increased uncertainty spread over European markets

The degree of monetary integration indicated in Fig. 11.6 has been obscured by the substantial disparities between interest rates that have developed in different centres in the past two years. But these disparities have almost entirely been reflections of the waves of international currency speculation that have rocked the system in the events leading up to and following the devaluation of the pound sterling in November 1967 and the franc–mark crises of 1968 and 1969. Given the high international mobility of capital that has developed over the past decade, interest-rate differentials (after adjustment is made for taxes and transactions costs) can be almost entirely accounted for by the expected gain or loss from exchange control or rate changes. It is exchange risk and the price changes devaluation induces that explain the high interest rates on sterling loans, the low interest rates on D-marks securities and the exorbitant rates on French franc bills in 1968. The low Swiss franc rates, on the other hand, which at first appear as an exception (because the Swiss authorities, by eschewing exchange-rate variation as an instrument of adjustment, have preserved confidence in the Swiss franc), are due to the comparative absence of risk of exchange control. International interest-rate differences can thus be accounted for now almost entirely by Irving Fisher's theory of appreciation and interest extended to the different currencies of the international economy.

Some idea of the disruptive effect of speculation and its impact on interest in recent years can be got from the 'tension index'[1] which since 1967 has reached crisis proportions. Yet the actual exchange-rate changes that have occurred have been too insignificant to have produced a market effect on equilibrium. It is hard to resist the weight of empirical evidence that suggests it would be better to take the exchange-rate issue out of current politics and abandon it as an instrument of international adjustment.

We return, therefore, to the question of the global stock of money and its rate of increase. The significance of this variable is clearly brought out by a consideration of the relations between annual rates of monetary expansion and annual rates of G.N.P. growth. The correspondence of these two rates of change for the G-10 countries over the twelve-year period 1955–67 is clearly brought out in Fig. 11.7.

Two points may now be noted. The first is that the correlation between rates of growth of income and money does not imply independence of monetary policy as an autonomous instrument for determining the level of income. In a single open economy the money supply is an endogenous variable and there is no point to saying that it is determined by, or that it

---

in the following spring or the shock effects that weakened sterling that summer. It would have been simpler to increase the supply of D-marks and guilders by 5 per cent.

[1] Computed by H. Stokes at the University of Chicago, based on a weighted average of interest arbitrage differentials and forward exchange premia.

Mundell – Monetary Relations between Europe and America   251

determines, prices or income. If a country attempted to expand credit beyond normal hoarding demand, the change in the money supply would fall short of the increase in credit by the reserve losses that would automatically follow; on the other hand, of course, an exogenously determined increase in exports would permit (indeed, cause) an increase in the money supply. The causation is not unidirectional.

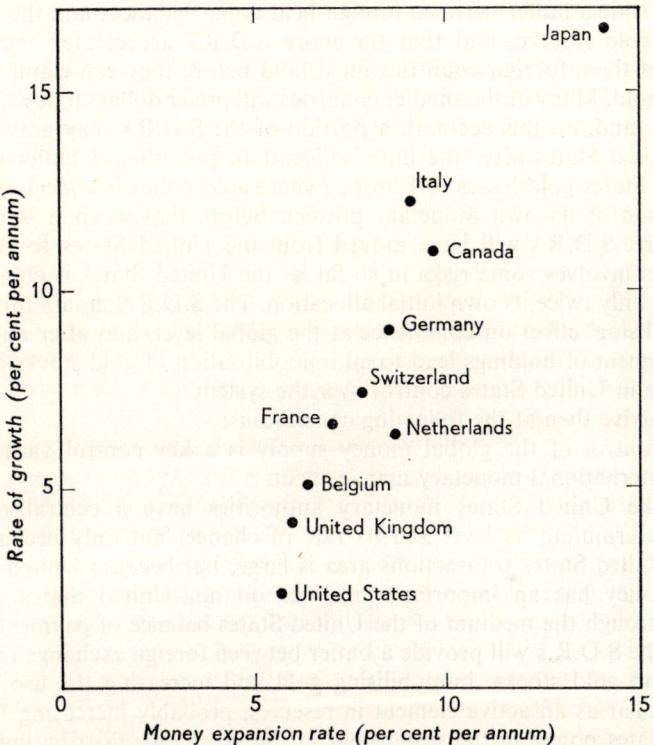

FIG. 11.7 Annual rates of increase of G.N.P. and money supply, 1955–67 (G–10 countries).

The second point is that the stock of money for the world as a whole is in a sense autonomous. While a single country cannot accelerate credit expansion without losing reserves, all countries can do so simultaneously, in so far as they are prepared to accept the consequent decrease in the ratio of external reserves to inside money. This means that control of the world money supply, or its reserve base, is an instrument of world monetary management.

Although in a formal sense gold is the only 'outside money' (money which is no one's liability) in the present system, dollars rather than gold represent the bottom of the world credit pyramid as long as other countries protect the system by not converting dollars into gold. An increase in dollars alters the ratio between gold and dollars in the system and portfolios have to be adjusted accordingly.

The introduction of S.D.R.s complicates the credit base of the system. Currencies are convertible into S.D.R.s but S.D.R.s are not convertible into gold although they have a gold guarantee. This means that S.D.R.s will provide a buffer between foreign-held dollar balances and the United States gold reserve, and that the more S.D.R.s are created the larger stock of them foreign countries must hold before they can claim United States gold. Many of the smaller countries will prefer dollars to low-interest S.D.R.s and, on this account, a portion of the S.D.R.s may gravitate to the United States after the initial allocation, providing a buffer against United States gold losses to Europe (where gold policy is conceived of as a weapon of its own monetary power). Before that weapon is played, therefore, S.D.R.s will have moved from the United States to Europe, and this involves some risks in so far as the United States is committed to hold only twice its own initial allocation. The S.D.R.s should thus have a 'stabilising' effect on confidence at the global level, and after an initial arrangement of holdings lead to an immobilisation of gold stocks and an increase in United States control over the system.

We arrive then at the following conclusions:

(1) Control of the global money supply is a key control variable of international monetary management.

(2) The United States monetary authorities have a central role in determining its level and its rate of change, not only because the United States transactions area is large, but because United States policy has an important influence on non-United States money through the medium of the United States balance of payments.

(3) The S.D.R.s will provide a buffer between foreign exchange reserves and gold stocks, immobilising gold and increasing the use of the dollar as an active element in reserves, probably increasing United States power in the system but at the same time distributing more equitably the seigniorage gains from reserve creations in so far as the United States holds a substantial share of the S.D.R.s.

IV. CONCLUDING OBSERVATIONS

Because of its great size, internal balance in the United States is a precondition for global balance as well as a 'vital interest' of the supereconomy. The asymmetrical position of the United States economy and the international attributes of the dollar as a world currency suggest that United States monetary policy be conditioned by the state of activity in the centre of gravity of the world economy (which incorporates the United States), while credit policy in the rest of the world be governed by balance of payments constraints (including the need for reserve growth). The quasi-liturgical function of preserving the official gold price is achieved in the first instance by the United States, but rests ultimately on discretion on the part of the big central banks in the management of information and uncertainty, by variations in their gold–dollar portfolios, and by proper timing of the introduction, acceptance and use of gold or dollar substitutes like the S.D.R.s.[1]

This scheme of instrument–target relationship is consistent, but its implementation rests more on general acceptance, suasion and co-operation than on coercion. Since 1965 each of the major countries can be accused of policies inimical to the general interest. Britain has run a chronic deficit and will probably continue to run one as long as she has access to credit at interest rates well below market rates. Germany has run a chronic surplus because of a high and perhaps increasing saving rate, the scarcity of alternative foreign assets in which official savings can be held, and the poor management of uncertainty with regard to the exchange rate. Japan has adhered to protectionism and exchange control in the face of ample resources for engineering convertibility of the yen. France has temporarily initiated what can best be described as a currency cold war against the dollar and the pound, publicly advising in 1967 a medicine (devaluation) for the pound that she refused to take herself in 1968. And the United States has pursued inflationary policies as an instrument of wartime finance, self-righteously expecting applause for military policies which her NATO partners did not share in making and which they either opposed or sympathised with, if at all, only half-heartedly. In the face of these political tensions (even conflicts) it is not surprising that the international system has failed to generate faith in its stability. There is a lack of effective coercive instruments for enforcing discipline in the system, beyond the voluntary methods of co-operation, and the system has accordingly become an overly permissive one approaching international monetary anarchy.

The permissiveness of the system has extended even to the creation of international money. The mushrooming of swap agreements over the past two years has injected a variable and potentially destabilising element into the system introducing a scrounge-for-yourself method of creating international money substitutes that frustrates chances for rational monetary

[1] The S.D.R.s are close substitutes for gold in so far as their gold weight guarantee (which can be waived by 85 per cent vote in the I.M.P.) is believed; but close substitutes for the dollar in so far as they yield interest. In view of the currently high interest rates on liquid dollar assets and the relatively low belief in United States interest in raising the price of gold, the S.D.R.s are now closer substitutes for gold than dollars and will have the effect of making dollars convertible into S.D.R.s rather than gold, thus decreasing the interest in reducing dollar holdings. This is perhaps one reason why Japan, Germany and Italy have been less anxious than the United States for a large initial allocation.

management of the world economy. Perhaps the only reason the system has not broken down is that the United States economy has managed, subject to the qualification of excessive inflation, to remain stable. Because the world economy has become dependent on the stability of the United States economy and the use of the dollar, and because national stability is a vital interest of the United States government, all hopes for disciplining the United States by ordinary methods have to be reconsidered. Any change in the system leading to an overpricing of gold increases the inflationary potential in the world economy. Gold can become overpriced when demand is reduced or its price increased. The dollar exchange standard itself has high inflationary capabilities. Once – or if – speculation over a higher official dollar price of gold subsides, a new possibility arises as central banks take advantage of the higher interest rates on liquid dollar assets. In the absence of a co-ordinated gold portfolio policy on the part of Europe, this would increase the options of the United States and create a new inflationary potential. A greater danger (perhaps now remote) is that the United States might raise the price of gold, again setting the stage for renewed inflation. No better is a system of flexible exchange rates, which, initially, would throw countries more formally on to a dollar standard. The I.M.F. rules on exchange margins would in all likelihood be waived in Germany, France, Britain or Japan if one or all of these countries wanted to adopt flexible rates. The long-run barrier to a system of flexible exchange rates is not the legal trappings of the Bretton Woods monetary order but the understandable fear that the national currencies could not compete in the long run against the dollar, even in the domain of domestic transactions.

The only feasible alternatives to a United States-dominated international monetary system, are an international solution based on world monetary management, a world reserve currency and supranational influence over United States monetary policy. One barrier to the adoption of this solution is that it involves an apparently gratuitous concession of monetary power by the United States.

The alternative is a monetary coalition among the European countries beginning with a reserve pool and ending with a European currency. The economic gain from a reserve pool would be huge; for the Six and Britain alone the gains from the reserve saving stemming from the internationalisation of formerly external transactions would be billions of dollars.[1] But the long-run success of a deeper European monetary coalition depends on

[1] Suppose half the trade of European countries is intra-European. Then half the dollar reserves held by the pool can be replaced by intra-European credit while the otiose dollar reserves can be replaced by earning assets. Thus the capital gain from the reserve pool would amount to $15 billion if current desired reserves are $30 billion; if $15 billion are invested in United States earning assets, there would result a current seigniorage gain of $1·5 billion per annum assuming an interest return of 10 per cent.

its inclusiveness. The principles of monetary integration suggest that monetary union in a polyopolistic world differs from that of a world containing a super financial power; and that a *sine qua non* for the success of a monetary coalition is that it approach the financial size of the United States. The E.E.C. alone is probably too small a monetary area to make effective competition for the dollar, and the inclusion of the United Kingdom along with the rump of the sterling area may be necessary to give the coalition the chance of success that only confidence in the viability of its reserve asset can provide.[1]

To conclude, then, the course of European–American monetary relations over the next decade will depend on whether any monetary leadership exists in Europe capable of building an alternative to a dollar-dominated world. The 'American challenge' in the field of finance has hardly begun; and the dollar has by no means approached its zenith as a world currency, so time is on the side of the dollar system. Because of the competitive monetary aspirations of England, France and Germany, the national jealousies blocking monetary collusion of any type, the widespread failure to recognise the inexorable expansion of the domain of the dollar as but one aspect of the financial dimension of the American challenge, only the emergence of vigorous financial leadership in Europe would defeat the more likely prospect that the European countries will bow to the comparative benevolence of United States leadership rather than striking out on their own.

[1] Given the incipient weakness of a declining reserve currency domain, the disadvantages of Britain's weak reserve position conceal the long-run potential advantage of the greater size British inclusion would ensure, but it may involve a complicated arrangement of mutual concessions such as the acceptance of a loss for Britain in the field of agriculture, in exchange for a gain in the field of finance. Because time is short, the switch from the dollar to the pound as the intervention currency would be one means of setting the system into operation quickly.

12 The Problems of International Monetary Arrangements

Gabriel Ferras

GENERAL MANAGER,
BANK FOR INTERNATIONAL SETTLEMENTS, BASLE

I. INTRODUCTION

In order to keep the present paper within reasonable bounds, it is proposed to treat this subject in the context of the general economic relationship between North America and Western Europe. Even thus restricted, it covers problems which actually require deeper analysis. It is, however, principally intended to provide food for thought by describing the working of the international monetary system as it is now, some quarter of a century after the Bretton Woods Conference. I shall therefore commence by outlining the fundamental characteristics of the system established at Bretton Woods and continue with a review of the different aspects of its recent development, as regards both the factors determining world liquidity and the composition of reserves. This somewhat didactic distinction is made for ease of exposition. The final comments – even if they do not show how international payments may evolve in the future – will at least emphasise certain underlying factors that should affect their developments.

II. FUNDAMENTAL CHARACTERISTICS OF THE BRETTON WOODS SYSTEM

The two essential characteristics of the system established at Bretton Woods are the free transferability of currencies at fixed rates of exchange, and their convertibility into gold at a fixed official price, for the benefit of central banks. Fixed exchange rates are maintained through the intervention of central banks in their foreign exchange markets by selling or buying dollars against their own currency so as to ensure that exchange rates do not deviate more than 1 per cent either side of the parities declared to the International Monetary Fund. The parities themselves are defined either in terms of a weight of gold or in terms of a dollar with a fixed gold content. They can be modified only with the agreement of the Fund and only in order to correct a fundamental disequilibrium. The parity of the dollar itself is of necessity based on a fixed weight of gold; the American monetary authorities are not obliged to intervene in their market, since they have undertaken freely to buy and sell gold, for the settlement of international transactions, at a price related to the parity of the dollar. A uniform change of parities, i.e. in effect a change in the price of gold for all currencies, can be decided upon by the Fund with a majority of 85 per cent of the total voting rights.[1]

In order to ensure that the above principles are observed, monetary authorities have at their disposal owned reserves (gold and foreign exchange), drawing rights in the I.M.F. and numerous credit facilities.

Gold and foreign exchange represent the essential elements of central bank reserves. As at 31 March 1969, the gold holdings of member countries of the International Monetary Fund and Switzerland totalled $38,956 million, the gold stock of the United States amounting to $10,836 million and that of the European members of the Group of Ten, plus Switzerland, to $18,858 million. The proportion of gold in official reserves varies widely from country to country; at the end of March, for example, it ranged from 69 per cent for the United States to 30 per cent for Sweden. The foreign exchange assets of central banks are not so large; at the end of March 1969 they were of the order of $29 billion for all the members of the Fund, of which $3·6 billion was held by the United States and $6·3 billion by the European members of the Group of Ten plus Switzerland. These assets can, of course, together with the foreign exchange assets of the national banking systems, be influenced to a certain extent by central banks. The monetary authorities can, as a general rule, vary the amounts of foreign exchange held in the official reserves in order to influence the level of these reserves or the domestic liquidity of the banking system.

I.M.F. drawing rights have developed considerably since Bretton Woods; on 31 March 1969, total drawings outstanding were $5,820 million and the total of quotas exceeded $21 billion.

Parallel with the I.M.F. drawing rights, certain central banks and the Bank for International Settlements have established – in some cases following special arrangements in periods of crisis, in others in a more institutionalised and permanent form – short-term credit facilities amounting to considerable sums. To quote an example, the facilities arranged between the Federal Reserve Bank of New York on the one hand, and the Bank of Canada, the central banks of the Group of Ten, the National Bank of Switzerland and the Bank for International Settlements, on the other hand, amount to $10,050 million.

The basic principle of the monetary arrangements set up at Bretton Woods, with the high degree of priority attached to fixed exchange rates, is inseparable from two other fundamental aims of economic policy: liberalisation of trade and, with certain exceptions, freedom of capital movements. The free exchange of goods is an aim that has been increasingly pursued since the war. It has been one of the major objectives of the

[1] Articles of Agreement. Article IV, section 7, is in the process of being amended.

international organisations that were subsequently founded (I.M.F., GATT and O.E.C.D.), and the success achieved in the dismantling of different types of protection – import restrictions, discriminatory measures and even tariff barriers – has been considerable. Progress towards the removal of controls on capital movements, however, has been more erratic. The very philosophy behind the I.M.F. in fact indicated a distrust of these movements, and monetary authorities – even while preaching the merits of freedom – have willingly resigned themselves to maintaining certain types of restrictions or to setting up controls each time a dangerous reserve crisis arose. In spite of these obstacles, movements of funds unconnected with commercial transactions have assumed a volume which was quite unforeseen at the time when the present international monetary system was established.

The monetary system set up at Bretton Woods has on the whole been successful. Expansion of world trade has continued at an ever-increasing pace. In terms of the monetary value of imports, the total trade of I.M.F. members has almost doubled in the period from 1961 to 1968 alone. The development of international commercial transactions has thus contributed greatly to economic growth and to the maintenance of a high level of employment, in accordance with the aims of the authors of the Bretton Woods Charter. As regards the countries of North America and Western Europe, the pace of expansion has been even greater. In spite of the various restrictions to which they are subjected, capital movements have become larger than ever, so much so that serious problems have arisen. Admittedly, since the end of the war, exchange rates have had to be revised several times, even those of major currencies, which is quite understandable in the light of all the underlying modifications of structure, incomes, prices and productivity which have taken place in the individual economies over a quarter of a century; however, stability does not mean rigidity and changes of parity have been made, under the aegis of the I.M.F., in conditions of co-operation unknown before the war. The international monetary system which arose out of Bretton Woods has therefore had one essential merit: it has on the whole enabled the Bretton Woods objectives to be achieved.

To say that the system has worked well does not mean that it has not suffered some setbacks. On the contrary, weaknesses have appeared, increasingly numerous and frequent in recent years. The serious crises of 1967, 1968 and 1969 have brought to light a certain number of faults, not inherent in the system itself, which have demonstrated that under the effect of various rigidities a critical stage is finally being reached.

III. RECENT DEVELOPMENTS IN THE DETERMINATION OF WORLD LIQUIDITY

If one confines oneself to the present decade, it must be stated that world liquidity has in recent years originated principally in the balance of payments deficits of the industrialised countries, and especially those countries whose currencies are used as exchange reserves. Sometimes these deficits have given rise to a straightforward increase in foreign exchange assets; at other times they have been financed by credit operations between central banks or through the intermediary of the I.M.F. This has resulted in an increase of reserves for central banks in the form of either short-term credits among themselves or credit positions in the Fund. It has been estimated that from 1964 to March 1969 reserve increases arising out of special financial operations have amounted to $11·5 billion. The growth in reserves resulting from multilateral or bilateral credits has – simultaneously with the exchange crises that have, with increasing frequency, shaken the international monetary system – come about under the pressure of events. The real trend in reserves is not easily discernible, since the indebtedness which forms the counterpart of these credits is disregarded in published statistics. There has thus been an accumulation of short-term debts, the repayment of which can only be envisaged as a long-term affair; these credits cannot always be said to have served the best interests of the recipient countries, since less generosity might have led to earlier corrective measures. Finally, although the system has shown great flexibility, its mechanism has been the antithesis of the systematic reserve creation at which numerous reformers are aiming, notably through the introduction of Special Drawing Rights.

The deliberate creation of reserves first of all raises a number of problems concerning the assessment of the volume of existing liquidity. Because it covers all usable means of international payments, including banking assets and both official and private credit facilities, the concept of world liquidity is vague, ill defined and frequently confused with the much more specific and definite concept of monetary reserves. Before concluding, therefore, that there is a shortage of world liquidity, it is necessary to realise that the volume of liquidity is not fixed, but varies according to circumstances. In this respect, the existence of the so-called Euro-dollar market is of particular importance. According to estimates made by the Bank for International Settlements, the volume of Euro-dollars, i.e. the short-term United States dollar liabilities of commercial banks in the Group of Ten countries, excluding the United States – other than liabilities to the United States – has risen from $7·7 billion at end-September 1963 to $30 billion in June 1969.

The Euro-dollar market, in which funds are volatile, can greatly affect the level of official reserves. Some of the recent movements recorded in this market have been especially noteworthy in this respect; thus, as at the end of May 1969, the American banks had borrowed $9·8 billion from their European branches in order to augment their internal liquidity; this has had the indirect effect of reducing European reserves and of improving the United States net reserve position. Thus, too – conversely – it is estimated that during the two weeks at the end of April and the beginning of May, at the time of the speculative crisis over the Deutschmark, the reserves of the Bundesbank increased by $4 billion, of which some $2 billion came from other central banks and nearly $1 billion from the Euro-dollar market. These movements are large enough to cast doubt on the value of the statistical concepts used to arrive at an estimate of the optimum volume of liquidity.

A further difficulty concerns the criteria to be applied in judging the advisability of creating reserves and the amounts to be so created.

Although it is generally agreed that world liquidity should, broadly, vary in accordance with world economic growth, the expansion of production and the development of trade, no precise ratio can be set. The advisability of an increase in reserves can therefore only be judged on the basis of the various aspects of economic policy which indicate that the individual countries' struggle to preserve their reserves has become the major preoccupation of the monetary authorities at the expense of more fundamental considerations such as the development of full employment or the maintenance of free trade. Furthermore, it should be noticed that certain aspects of restrictive policy – for example, rising interest rates or the control of capital movements – are not necessarily connected with the preservation of reserves. The objective of price stability and internal equilibrium also plays its part. Although the current restrictions on capital outflows in the United States form part of the arsenal to defend the reserves, the raising of interest rates, increasingly followed in Europe, represents one of the chief means employed to arrest domestic inflation. In other words, the existence of restrictive measures would only be proof of a shortage of liquidity if in other respects economic policy could be considered adequate. Otherwise, it could only be a sign of misguided policies, for example of too great a rigidity in the exchange rate, or of inadequacies in the process of domestic adjustment to balance of payments disequilibria.

One of the weaknesses of the monetary system which has recently come to light is the increasing rigidity of exchange rates. The I.M.F. Statutes provide, on the one hand, for a procedure to avoid competitive devaluations and, on the other hand, for methods of financing designed to allow countries to meet possible balance of payments difficulties. The initiative for exchange-rate adjustments lies with member countries. The aim of the authors of the Statutes was not to establish rigid exchange rates, but on the contrary to construct a system of parities which could be altered under the control of the Fund members in the event of fundamental disequilibria. In this respect, the international monetary system has not, over recent years, functioned satisfactorily. There has been strong resistance, mainly of a political nature, to exchange-rate adjustments. Devaluations have carried the stigma of defeat, which has made them more difficult. This lack of flexibility has been reinforced by the general desire not to weaken the position of the dollar, since a change in the parity of the dollar implies a change in the gold price of $35 an ounce. To these causes of rigidity on the part of the deficit countries can be added, in the case of persistent surplus countries, an opposition to exchange-rate revaluation often based on political considerations but also motivated by a reluctance to be compelled, in the last analysis, to take action because of others' mistakes.

Numerous ideas have been advanced for making the exchange-rate mechanism more flexible, thus giving countries greater latitude in the conduct of their affairs. These range from suggestions for parity adjustments at regular and frequent intervals (known as the 'crawling peg' system) to the adoption of freely fluctuating exchange rates. The major defects of a non-fixed rate system are that it destroys one of the restraints on inflationary pressures, provokes an atmosphere of uncertainty detrimental to the development of international trade and, probably, leads in the end to the introduction of controls. The I.M.F. system, flexibly applied, retains great advantages.

IV. RECENT DEVELOPMENTS IN THE COMPOSITION OF RESERVES

Parallel to these problems relating to the total of world liquidity are those concerning the composition of reserves. Each of the three components of reserves (gold, foreign exchange and other items) has, in effect, individual characteristics which in a sense limit their use. Their juxtaposition thus raises what can be called the problem of their order of precedence.

(1) *Gold as a Component of reserves*

Gold remains the fundamental element in monetary reserves, of which it still forms about 52·5 per cent. There is no question here of listing its merits and its demerits as a reserve asset, except to mention that it is the only non-fiduciary one, i.e. the only type of reserve asset which does not give rise to a coresponding liability elsewhere in the system. In other words, when new monetary gold enters the system there is an increase in total reserves, both gross and net, while an expansion in the other existing components of reserves does not add to the net total of reserves, since the surplus country's gain is offset by the increase in liabilities of the deficit country. The recent addition of gold to monetary reserves has been small, following a period during which the gold stock actually fell. Between 1 April 1967 and 31 March 1968, Western countries' gold reserves diminished by $2·6 billion owing to central bank intervention in the free market. Over the following twelve months the flow of gold into reserves recovered to the extent of $1,130 million, but gold acquired by the South African Reserve Bank accounted for $625 million of this. On the whole, central banks participating in the Washington declaration of 17 March 1968 have refrained from acquiring gold arising out of new production, considering that 'as the existing stock of monetary gold is sufficient in view of the prospective establishment of the facility for Special Drawing Rights, they no longer feel it necessary to buy gold from the market'. The International Monetary Fund itself has so far not taken up an offer of sale at $35 an ounce made by the South African authorities on the basis of Article V of the Statutes. As the United States opposed this purchase, on legal grounds which are at least open to question, there has been a quasi-stability of the official gold stock since the Washington declaration. Even so, in the longer term, it is doubtful whether the normal private demand for gold – for industrial use and for holdings as a form of saving – can be satisfied at the price of $35 an ounce. This means that, under existing conditions, there would be no chance for any newly-mined gold to flow into official reserves. The risk of official gold reserves diminishing is not great, for, in spite of the difference between the official rate and the prices prevailing on the free markets, it is doubtful whether central banks would engage in arbitrage operations by which they would purchase gold from the United States Treasury for resale to the market. However, the existence of a sizeable difference between the official price and the free market price (nearly 25 per cent on 30 April 1969) can only strengthen central banks' propensity to hold gold. This means that in the event of reserve losses they would only use gold as a last resort, either divesting themselves first of other assets or having recourse to the numerous credit facilities available; while, in the case of reserve gains, they would endeavour to acquire gold first – at the expense of the monetary gold stock of the American Treasury and the I.M.F. From 1 April 1968 to 30 April 1969, in spite of French sales of $750 million – sales which the French authorities made rather liberally, thus showing that their preference for gold and their defence of the gold standard were not irreversible – the United States gold stock rose by only $235 million. Thus gold has become a static asset in two senses: first, as regards the world total, and secondly, as regards the use to which it is put; and this in spite of oft-repeated assurances that gold is the essential base of the monetary system. Such a situation is hardly founded on perfect logic.

Two diametrically opposed suggestions for reform currently advocated at least have the merit of consistency. The first is a rise in the price of gold. The second is the demonetisation of gold.

The possibility of a rise in the price of gold was provided for in the Statutes of the I.M.F.; it could even be said to form an essential cog in the monetary system established at Bretton Woods, for the equilibrium of that system depends on the production of gold and its inclusion in reserves.[1] Various arguments have been put forward against a uniform change of parities. Some of them are political. Others are economic in nature and concern, for example, the wish to see the expansion of world reserves result from agreed decisions rather than to rely on new supplies of gold. At a time when countries remain deeply attached to their sovereignty in the monetary field, there is a large element of paradox in the attitude of many economists who, on the one hand, advocate an expansion of reserves and, on the other hand, accept that the part of reserves which they themselves still regard at least for the moment as 'the major and dominant element'[2] should remain static.

The demonetisation of gold, too, is not without its advocates. It is difficult to see how this would serve the interests of the world economy while, as mentioned above, gold still forms 52·5 per cent of world reserves. The tenacity shown by the United States Administration in defending the United States gold stock shows that, in the country where it has most often been advanced, the demonetisation thesis has not taken hold in official circles. After all, the demonetisation of gold cannot be considered in isolation without taking into account the nature of the system which would be called upon to replace current monetary arrangements. In this regard, three solutions are, broadly speaking, conceivable: the establishment of a supranational central bank with power to inject reserves into the system as and when needed; the adoption of exchange rates more or less free from official intervention, so that reserves would become much less necessary; and the reliance of many countries on a dollar standard, with their parities fixed in relation to the dollar and their reserves held in dollars. The first solution is perhaps that of the future, but it disregards current political circumstances. The adoption of free exchange rates has already been mentioned above. Without doubt it is the creation of a dollar standard which some people consider to be the likely way in which the reserve currency system will develop, with perhaps other currency blocs besides the dollar bloc.

(2) *Foreign Exchange as a Component of Reserves*

Exchange reserves consist essentially of dollars, pounds sterling and, to a certain extent, French francs and Deutschmarks. The dollar has long been

---

[1] Milton Gilbert, 'The Gold–Dollar System: Conditions of Equilibrium and the Price of Gold', *Essays in International Finance*, no. 70 (Princeton University, Oct 1968).

[2] Final Report of the Colloquium on *The Future of the International Monetary System*, John F. Kennedy Institute, Tilburg, 16–19 Apr 1969.

the most important currency and now accounts for about 60 per cent of the total world exchange reserves of $31 billion.

The smooth working of a monetary system which includes the accumulation of exchange reserves can only be ensured if certain conditions are fulfilled. It presupposes that those countries whose currencies are used as exchange reserves follow policies designed to maintain the confidence of foreign holders as regards both the par value and convertibility of the currency. It also implies the maintenance of a convincing ratio between the reserve currency country's gold or gold-convertible assets and its short-term foreign liabilities. If, therefore, the smooth working of the system requires at the same time an increase in world reserves, such an addition in the form of foreign exchange alone carries within itself the seeds of conflict, since the supply of reserves by way of the deficits of key currency countries can only be allowed up to a certain point. In all these respects, the present system has for several years shown increasing signs of weakness.

In the United Kingdom, the authorities have succeeded, little by little, in establishing a monetary and budgetary policy which, there is reason to hope, will lead to the appearance of a surplus in the balance of payments. They have not been able to avoid the devaluation of the pound and the burden of short- and medium-term external debt has become substantial. The sterling balances of non-sterling area countries have been reduced to a minimum. Those of the sterling area countries are the subject of special bilateral arrangements in accordance with the Basle Agreement of 9 September 1968. Under the terms of this agreement twelve central banks and the B.I.S. granted to the Bank of England a credit facility of $2 billion to enable it to meet possible reserve losses caused by the conversion of pounds. The sterling area countries, for whose benefit the agreement was largely drawn up, undertook to maintain for a period of at least three years an agreed proportion of sterling in their reserves; these assets themselves enjoy an exchange guarantee expressed in dollars. The Basle Agreement has certainly played a very important part, since the sterling area balances had, by the end of March 1969, more or less recovered to the initial level on which the agreement was based. It represents a tentative practical attempt at stabilisation – and at this stage a successful one – as a compromise between the consolidation and the dismantling of the sterling area.

More difficult to appraise is the current status of the dollar as a reserve currency. The gold convertibility of the dollar remains the cornerstone of the monetary system. After increasing by $5,800 million since the beginning of 1960, the official external dollar liabilities reached $15,950 million on 31 March 1969; having been reduced by $8,670 million over the same period, the gold stock fell to $10,840 million. The American monetary authorities have reached the point where any further decrease in their gold stock is viewed with alarm, and where any transaction which shows up for the partner countries of the United States as a conversion of official assets into longer-term claims or into private assets, for example through the Euro-dollar market, is welcomed. For their part, the central banks of these countries are showing such restraint as regards their possible acquisition of gold from the United States Treasury that Professor Friedman in a recent speech felt able to say that, following the Washington meeting of March 1968, the availability of gold at $35 an ounce for transactions between monetary authorities was in the nature of a fiction. Incidentally, his appraisal of the present situation was resented in some European countries.

In considering future prospects, what conclusions can be drawn from the present position? Is the flow of reserves provided by the dollar and the American balance of payments deficits now in the process of drying up? Or is it true that, as Professor Friedman says, the partner countries of the United States, especially the countries of Europe, are more or less consciously on their way – if they have not already reached it – towards a dollar standard which they could only avoid by letting their exchange rates fluctuate? This latter forecast is certainly in accordance with the underlying tendencies of the monetary system. All the same, various factors still allow doubts to be cast on the validity of Professor Friedman's statement: the development of the American balance of payments; the role to be played by the new forms of reserves, in particular the Special Drawing Rights; and the attitude of the partner countries of the United States. Most particularly, some countries of Europe could stop using the dollar as their international currency, peg their currency to gold, and let the dollar rate float. From the technical standpoint alone, it would be difficult for central banks to hold as reserves foreign assets the value of which would fluctuate in terms of their own currencies. The division of Europe into several groups; the lack of cohesion among the countries of the European Community, where co-ordination of thought and action in the monetary field should be close; and a certain amount of inertia in regard to the development of the international monetary system do not, however, afford any perceptible indication of European unity. Three regional groupings exist side by side and to a certain extent overlap, without any of them having overmuch strength.

The widest of these groupings is that covered by the European Monetary Agreement. By the end of 1958 the economic and financial situation of the European countries belonging to the O.E.C.D. had strengthened so much that most of their currencies were declared fully convertible for non-residents. As a result of this move the E.P.U. was terminated. It was, however, decided to continue co-operation in a new form, that of the European Monetary Agreement (E.M.A.). This agreement has two principal features: (a) the *Multilateral System of Settlements*, which provided for the continuation of limited interim finance facilities, together with an exchange guarantee for central banks' holdings of each other's currency; and (*b*) the *European Fund* which, with an original capital of $600 million, was intended to take over some of the credit functions of the E.P.U. The financing activity of the E.M.A. has been rather limited in size and directed mostly to the advantage of the less developed of its members.

The Convention of 1960 setting up the European Free Trade Area does not provide for special arrangements in the monetary sphere.

More important have been the efforts of the European Economic Community. Common institutions have been established. The Monetary Committee, created under Article 105 of the Treaty of Rome to promote the co-ordination of monetary policies of member countries, and the Committee of Central Bank Governors, set up in May 1964 with a view to holding discussions on the general principles of monetary policy, are of a consultative nature. The Council of the Community and the Commission, on the other hand, wield their own powers of decision. Thus, the Council has decided that member governments should consult with each other in advance on any change in the parity of the currency of one or more of its members. Likewise, consultations should be held on any important position adopted by participating countries in the field of international monetary relations. In principle, individual decisions should only be taken once these discussions have been held unless special circumstances, such as the time factor, prevent it. It should be noted that the common agricultural policy does not imply that it is impossible to change parities among members of the Community, but such changes would entail certain difficulties, owing to the fact that common prices have been fixed (in units of account equal to the United States dollar) for almost all of the main agricultural products.

In fact, the Community's achievements in the monetary sphere remain to this day very modest. In particular, there exists no unity of view among member countries of the Community on fundamental aspects of the monetary system (the role of gold, the merits of reserve components destined possibly to supplement gold, the conditions for the creation of Special Drawing Rights). To recommend now the establishment of a European currency is utopian; it is not even certain that the member countries of the Community could concur in collective decisions aimed at harmonising the composition of their reserves. Would they be capable of adopting a common attitude should the gold convertibility of the dollar one day be suspended? The desire to maintain communal bonds forged in other fields (trade, agricultural policy, etc.) could undoubtedly lead them towards a unification of views. However, in view of the various alternatives – the tying of all currencies to the dollar, the acceptance of fluctuating rates between the dollar and the European currencies, the setting up of a gold bloc in Europe – the sources of friction could still be numerous. Even though, *a priori*, the prospect of a dollar standard holds no attraction for the European countries, the variety of their individual preoccupations and objectives leads one to the conclusion that in a dialogue between the United States and Europe the latter might not give all the weight that real cohesion would lend it.

(3) *Other Reserve Components*

There are various reserve components other than gold and foreign exchange, although they are relatively less important. Into this category fall the various forms of bilateral credits which have replaced exchange assets, for example Roosa bonds and claims on the I.M.F. which give rise to automatic drawing rights. For the countries of the Group of Ten and Switzerland, the former amounted at the end of March 1969 to above $2·9 billion and the latter to $4·8 billion.

A much more important role has been assigned to the Special Drawing Rights to be issued by the I.M.F., which are intended not to replace but to supplement gold. As at 31 May 1969, fifty-four countries out of the Fund membership had ratified the agreement providing for the creation of these drawing rights, and it is likely that by early next year the first tranche will have been issued. According to recent estimates, it could amount to a considerable sum, of the order of $4 billion for the first of the five years for which the activation of S.D.R.s is to be decided. If we assume – and, admittedly, this is pure conjecture – that the issues in the following four years are of the same size as the first, the total of S.D.R.s issued would reach by the end of the period $20 billion, or 51 per cent of the present monetary gold stock.

In fact, there are a number of considerations which could, or should, restrain the issue of S.D.R.s. The first concerns the general uncertainty about the present degree of liquidity in the world economy in view of the doubtful value of the criteria used. The second relates to the possible effects which a universal increase in liquidity would have on the determination of I.M.F. members to correct a deterioration in their balance of payments. This determination should stem from the need to maintain internal and external equilibrium, and should not be strongly influenced by the allocation of drawing rights. However, recent experience, which suggests that the willingness to correct deficit positions has been weakened rather than strengthened by foreign credits, is not very encouraging. That the present system of reserve creation through the financing of deficits may continue is also a risk which cannot be ignored. The continued acceptability of drawing rights as reserve instruments will depend on whether, in fact, the drawings are repaid without undue delay so that the issue of drawing rights is not looked upon either as a simple device for helping countries to finance their deficits or as a method of substituting one debt for another. The third factor to be considered is the nature of the drawing rights themselves. Without attempting to describe their legal status, although this would be a very interesting exercise, one can say broadly that, once they have been generally allocated, their use will constitute the incurring of a fixed gold value debt and their accumulation the acceptance of a fixed gold value claim. Their use and acceptance will therefore depend, over and above the contractual obligations, on a number of opinions concerning the quality of these reciprocal credits and debts, the risks or advantages arising out of the gold guarantee, and above all the comparative merits of other reserve assets. There is reason to assume that, for a time at least, some central banks will maintain their preference for gold. It is in order to avoid the risks inherent in this preference that certain economists advocate that from now on rules should be adopted under which central banks should harmonise their reserve policies.[1]

V. CONCLUSIONS

It is relatively easy to analyse the recent development of the monetary system, even though the existence of rules of conduct that have been more or less explicitly tacked on to or substituted for the Bretton Woods obligations has understandably led to some confusion of thought. What is much more difficult is to draw fundamental conclusions on the basis of this development and to try to take stock, even if one makes no attempt to forecast how international arrangements are likely to develop in the future. This may happen in four ways, not all of which are mutually exclusive: an adjustment in the present system by a change in the price of gold, evolution towards the dollar standard, adoption of floating rates or the development of a managed system involving reserve creation and harmonisation. However, several observations are called for.

The first is that numerous rigidities or strains which have appeared in the system are not due to the system as such, but to the way in which it has been used. The drawbacks arising from the rigidity of exchange rates, for example, would be less great if the Statutes of the Fund and, in particular, the provisions of Article IV concerning changes in parities were observed in the flexible way their authors intended.

The second consideration is that certain aspects of the recent development of the system constitute radical changes, or carry within them the seeds of such changes. The system created at Bretton Woods has certainly not been abandoned, but one must be aware of the extent of the changes it has undergone and of their probable consequences. For example, to make the maintenance of the price of gold in dollar terms one of the dogmas of the system is to necessitate more frequent upward exchange-

---

[1] Edward M. Bernstein, 'The Future of International Reserve Assets', paper prepared for the colloquium on *The Future of the International Monetary System*, held at the John F. Kennedy Institute, Tilburg, 16–19 Apr 1969.

rate adjustments in future; the result will be to lower the price of gold in terms of currencies other than the dollar, increase the demand for non-monetary gold and thereby widen the gap between the free and the official price of gold. This can only make the operation of the two-tier system more difficult and hasten the time when the United States may have to face up to the question whether to abandon the gold convertibility of the dollar or to raise the price of gold. To take another example of a change in the system that may have momentous consequences, the decision to create fiduciary reserve instruments is likely to lead not only to the harmonisation among countries of different types of reserve assets, but also to a strengthening of the powers of initiative and coercion vested in organisations such as the Fund, even in the field of exchange rates.

Such prospects would not in themselves be a matter for concern if they were accompanied by substantial headway along the road of political co-operation and co-ordination. Spectacular progress has, it is true, been achieved since the war and there is no lack of machinery for financial co-operation and assistance. But so long as there are at times real conflicts of interest between countries and, in some cases, fundamental political issues involved, obstacles will often stand between the recommendations made by consultative bodies and political action. There is no small risk, therefore, that monetary arrangements might one day seize up because their implications went far beyond what the authorities would be prepared to accept. For example, can the member countries of the International Monetary Fund be expected to harmonise their reserves when the six members of the Common Market have, despite their close links, apparently never broached the question of harmonising theirs? The real obstacle to the establishment of more 'concerted' systems than the one that emerged from Bretton Woods is that close enough integration is not desired and is anyway very difficult to visualise. It is necessary, therefore, to make sure that the monetary machinery which has proved its usefulness is not dismantled with undue haste, and that great care is taken in introducing innovations into the system.

Moderation would also be required to assure the success of such innovations, as there is reason to fear that they will not make the maintenance of internal and external equilibrium any easier. And here I must repeat – commonplace though it may be – that good results cannot be expected from any international payments system if the participating countries, and especially those with the largest economies, do not subject themselves to the necessary discipline to keep their balances of payments in reasonable equilibrium. This is self-evident with a system of fixed exchange rates. It would be no less true with a flexible rate system. Even the establishment of a dollar standard would not protect the United States from dollar crises unless it was managed in a way that would remain acceptable to other countries.

Discussion of the Papers by M. Ferras and Professor Mundell

Mr Brittan said this should be an interesting session following the discussion of the papers by Professor Cooper and Mr Lamfalussy, though there would now be more emphasis on short-run issues. It was the difficulties of the American balance of payments which had to be discussed this afternoon.

The American authorities were not sure if they were dealing with a balance of payments constraint of the kind we knew only too well in the United Kingdom. Perhaps it would be better if the United States *either* decided it had no balance of payments problem (*à la* Mundell), *or* went to the other extreme and adjusted in a fundamental sense. If the United States tried the second policy, and the rest of the world would not let it, then it would know that the first alternative was the right working assumption.

M. Ferras posed, clearly, the problems of the future of the world monetary system – to which Mundell had suggested some tentative answers. It seemed important that M. Ferras believed that the world's payments arrangements were in a critical phase. In section III of his paper, he dealt with the development of world liquidity. In discussing the shortage of reserves, some might think they knew an elephant even if they could not define it. It was true that the position was eased by reserve creation, credits and changes in the distribution of reserves resulting from United States Euro-dollar borrowings. He agreed with M. Ferras when the latter said there was too much generosity in granting conditional liquidity to various countries – including the United Kingdom. This had simply removed the incentive to take corrective measures earlier. But Mr Brittan was sceptical when M. Ferras said that the Bretton Woods agreement required exchange-rate changes as a normal response. The trouble was that exchange rates had become political symbols. The present system of pegged rates, with occasional jumps, was based on an inbuilt deception. This was not just a pious statement. The whole system depended on Ministers of Finance being believed, when they said that the exchange rate would not move. They must believe this *themselves*. Often, also, the penalty for devaluation was their departure.

There was a serious point here. Once one got a knowing and cynical attitude to all denials of devaluation or revaluation, then once there was the slightest possibility of a rate being out of line, torrents of funds would move across the exchange. A swap system could hardly hope to cope. So, in the end, one would have to choose between fixed rates with alterations only in emergencies, or more gradual and continuous adjustment.

In section IV, tactfully entitled 'Recent Developments in the Composition of Reserves', M. Ferras covered some very controversial questions. There was a statistical summary of developments affecting official gold reserves which, by implication, criticised the two-tier gold system and America's policy of sticking to the existing gold price.

He would like to make two observations on p. 269. There, M. Ferras said that in an inflationary world the real price of gold tended to fall over time. Apart from other considerations, there would be only a limited amount of time before the ordinary commercial forces of supply and demand for gold, as a commodity, took the price above $35 an ounce.

On p. 267, M. Ferras implied that the successful working of S.D.R.s required some harmonisations of the composition of reserve assets between countries. Once such harmonisation had been achieved, there would not be too much difficulty in increasing the supply of S.D.R.s year by year, or alternatively of raising the price of gold to official holders. On balance, it was probably more likely that the S.D.R. system would be used.

The important thing about S.D.R.s was how these would enter into balances of payments. We had seen that countries had incompatible balance of payments targets. If S.D.R.s came to be seen as worthwhile assets for countries to hold, one might get more modest balance of payments targets. One might even get a little more modesty in current account aims.

At the end of his paper, M. Ferras formulated the options open to us. These were (1), a change in the official price of gold; (2), a shift to a dollar standard; (3), flexible or fluctuating exchange rates; (4) man-made reserve creation. Mr Brittan said he would stress that M. Ferras said that not all of these were mutually exclusive. Probably only (1) and (2) were.

Professor Mundell had three options – two of them the same as two of M. Ferras's. These were a dollar standard and man-made currency creation. Professor Mundell did not include a change in the price of gold or floating exchange rates. However, he did have as his own third option the creation of a European monetary bloc. It was interesting, and perhaps saddening, that M. Ferras, who was in daily touch with European finance, thought this kind of option was not open.

In considering Professor Mundell's paper, one had to do so on two levels. First, it was an important theoretical contribution to the subject, which would be studied for a long time. Second, it contained policy suggestions which were not directly dependent on his model. Mr Brittan could accept the analytical tools more easily than the policy suggestions.

The Keynesian model of the kind used by the United Kingdom Treasury or the O.E.C.D. did focus directly on real magnitudes in the economy: demand at constant prices, the percentage of production capacity in use and the percentage of unemployment. It was right to say that Keynes's methods could be unwisely used, in particular through a failure to allow for the effects of price expectations. Existing Keynesian models were excessively short-run. There was too little attempt to see what happened if one projected recent price inflation forward. Mr Brittan's problem with the 'neo-quantity' models that were now coming into fashion was that they dealt with unemployment indirectly. It was now seen as a function of the rate of change of prices and of its acceleration or deceleration. The merit of the Mundell paper was that it went more deeply into this – especially the effects of wage contracts and of expectations.

For international questions, the heart of the model lay in Fig. 11.4. In Fig. 11.4, on the X-axis, one had the rate of United States credit expansion. Corresponding to any United States rate of increase, there was a rate of European credit expansion which produced an American balance of payments deficit of a specified size. If the European monetary authorities were willingly to adjust to American monetary policy, there would always be a rate of credit expansion which would reduce the American balance of payments deficit to what was tolerable. There was also a whole family of curves showing the rate of change of world prices following any rate of credit expansion in the United States or Europe. As one went north-east in the diagram, one had a higher rate of inflation, and the $\pi\pi$ line showed price stability.

This system worked if there were consistent aims on the two sides of the Atlantic. One possibility was that the American monetary authorities would be responsible for price stability. The Europeans would then be responsible for adjusting their rate of credit expansion to obtain whatever United States balance of payments result they regarded as tolerable. This, and other more complicated compromises, were discussed by Professor Mundell. All of them needed underlying harmony of aim between America and Europe.

The matter could also be put in terms of supply and demand theories of the American deficit. Supply theories said that America created the deficit. The demand theory said that Europe needed the deficit to add to its reserves. The system was in harmony only if the deficit in the United States' balance of payments gave the increase in official dollar holdings in Europe desired by central banks and other authorities, and no more.

Mr Brittan said that his interpretation was that the system could be in disharmony for two reasons: first, the United States could create a bigger deficit than Europe wanted, and Europe might be unwilling to respond by increasing its internal rate of inflation. This was the D-mark problem at the moment. A problem could also arise (as M. Ferras showed) if Europe did not want to accumulate reserves in dollars. This then raised the whole issue of what the future international reserve medium should be.

A more fundamental objection to using domestic credit expansion as the equilibriating device was implicit in the remarks by Professor Wallich earlier, on the attitude of the United States to reducing its deficit quickly. This could involve a disproportionate rise in American unemployment – with fears of increasing Negro and teenage unemployment.

On pp. 267–8, Professor Mundell gave a useful computation of the world money supply. Mr Brittan thought there was enough exchange-rate stability for this total to be of interest.

Fig. 11.6 in Professor Mundell's paper showed the similarities between monetary behaviour in different countries. Europeans woud say that the extent to which their policy had been parallel to that of the Federal Reserve System was regrettable. It was implicit in the Mundell paper that the system worked badly. For various reasons, United States monetary policy had not led towards price stability in the United States or in the world. Europe was reluctant to alter its own policies to fit in with the rate of American and world inflation.

Discussing the options ahead, Professor Mundell said that any subordination of American monetary policy to a world authority would require concessions of sovereignty by the United States. What would American get in return?

Mr Brittan wanted to take issue briefly with Professor Mundell's scattered remarks on exchange-rate changes in general. On p. 267, Mundell thought that the damage had been greater than the gains in the last ten years. Would he distinguish two propositions? Let us grant that in the United Kingdom demand expansion in the 1960s was above the rate compatible with exchange-rate stability, and that increased demand had led to inflation rather than real growth. In that case, the United Kingdom should at the very beginning have adopted policies to maintain the exchange rate. The case for this was arguable. However, one should *not* go on to the second proposition – that in 1967 Britain could have avoided devaluation through deflation of the money supply. This could only have been done at a severe cost in unemployment or trade restrictions.

Later, Professor Mundell said that the basic argument against flexibility was that in the long run the American dollar would drive out all other currencies. We should not lose all that much sleep because in the year 2000 the American dollar might have the position in the Western world that the mark now had in Europe. American 'domination' was likely anyway in the view of many speakers – whether exchange rates were fixed or flexible. But this was not a very relevant problem to a government which had a fixed exchange rate and which was concerned about potential conflicts between its economic objectives. Certainly, it did not provide a strong enough argument for moving either to severe restrictions on trade and capital movement – or to restrictions which would cause a severe fall in employment and output here and now.

M. Lamfalussy was disappointed by the way M. Ferras had treated the creation of reserves in recent years and looked especially at the relative quantities of gold and foreign exchange. M. Lamfalussy thought he had seen a calculation by Professor Triffin that in the last ten years the gold exchange standard could not function well. All increases in foreign exchange reserves were a result of negotiation. If one took account of increases in reserves due to drawing rights, then in the last ten years neither gold nor dollars had helped to increase liquidity. Did M. Ferras agree with this? He did not want to contradict the text of the paper, but what did M. Ferras mean?

The second problem was that in the post-war system we had preferred trade liberalisation to liberalisation of capital investments. It was true that capital liberalisation had been a bit slow, but he wondered how, given the interpenetration of Western economies, the movement of capital goods could be separated.

His doubt was essentially on the place of big countries and on the role of intra-firm trade in international trade. There were many possibilities for disguising movements of capital within the firm as current movements. This was not a statistical question, but essentially one of definition. The problem could be put differently, but it was a growing one.

If one looked at events, one found two things. First, one found that a country which had tried to institute capital controls had soon been led to interfere with commodity trade. Second, there was a more macro-economic point. If one looked at the evolution of capital balances, another extraordinary phenomenon appeared. For example, France had had very rigorous exchange control for a year. There was no fall in the loss to reserves. Britain, too, had imposed rigorous controls, but the trade balance was still bad. America had stopped capital exports, but was in difficulties on current account. Germany had tried to do all it could to increase capital exports but the current surplus rose in line with the increased capital outflows. All this was very bothering. Perhaps the rules of the macro-economic game caused it to happen.

Professor Phelps said the principal message in Professor Mundell's paper was that if American monetary and fiscal policy led to faster inflation than the rest of the world wanted, then the rest of the world would either have growing balance of payments surpluses, or too much inflation. This might lead to a wish in Europe to form a coalition against the dollar.

The theoretical contribution in Professor Mundell's paper was more novel and important. Some simplifying assumptions were employed: a perfect world capital market leading to one rate of interest; fixed exchange rates; the same rate of inflation in all countries; a tendency towards full employment equilibrium; and the same equilibrium rate of unemployment at every inflation rate. The paper showed how the world inflation rate was determined and the world real rate of interest too.

There were, however, some peculiarities. First, there was no international means of payment; neither gold nor really the dollar acted in this capacity. There was no tendency for the United States to have a balance of payments deficit because dollars were used. Nor was it clear how the money supply in the two areas grew. Perhaps it grew through a budget deficit of the Treasury and a passive monetary policy; or perhaps there was an active monetary policy and a passive budget deficit. This made for difficulties, because either policy step affected the KK schedule in Figs. 11.1 and 11.2. Correspondingly, Professor Mundell had left out of the account how variations in the fiscal and monetary mix could alter the current account surplus in the country. The rest of the world was supposed to be under a single intelligence and perhaps it would have been more natural to treat it more atomistically.

Professor Phelps said he had some thoughts on a model of a pure dollar standard. He would argue from it that the dollar standard left open the opportunity for every foreign government to choose the quantity of international liquidity and the rate of growth of national wealth that it wanted. If it were willing to engage in managed and gradual currency appreciation or depreciation, it could also have the rate of inflation that it preferred. The costs of having these things were about as low as or lower than in any monetary system. His message, then, was how to stop worrying and love the dollar. He assumed a world capital market and a world commodity market which kept interest rates and price differentials within bounds. Countries other than the United States were small, with no monopoly power. America controlled its own and the world price level via its monetary and tax policies.

Under this dollar standard, foreign governments would run balance of payments surpluses in order to acquire the real quantities of dollars they wanted for international liquidity in order to protect themselves against unforeseen balance of payment swings. America's monetary policy would control its own price level and thus that of the rest of the world. Indirectly, this would determine the nominal amount of dollars that central banks wanted to hold. If the world price level rose 10 per cent, the world demand for dollars would rise 10 per cent too.

In a growing world economy, even if the price level were constant, there would be a continuing overall American balance of payments deficit because of the corresponding growth in the demand of the world's central banks for real dollar reserves. But there was nothing perfidious about this American deficit. Foreign central banks would get interest on their dollar reserves. There would be some loss to foreigners as compared with an own-currency standard, to the extent that the artificial addition to demand for assets in the United States would improve the terms on which the United States could borrow abroad. (In truly perfect capital markets this could not occur.)

What would happen if the United States chose to inflate? This decision need not increase the burden on foreign economies. In real terms, he saw no implied increase in American indebtedness.

The rest of the world, as individual countries, could have whatever current account surpluses they wanted, through fiscal measures, while the size of their dollar holdings would be the object of their monetary policy. More rapid accumulation of wealth owned domestically and abroad through an increased current account surplus could be engineered by tax increases. However, the reconciliations of wishes around the world for current account surpluses puzzled Professor Phelps. If one country increased taxes to raise the current account surplus, others would raise their taxes too, and where would the process stop? Eventually the real rate of interest would fall until countries were reconciled to aggregate balance. But what of the short run?

The final point was on the rate of inflation. Professor Phelps said he had argued that countries could have the real rate of growth they wanted. But with fixed exchange rates, countries might not like the American rate of inflation. If they wanted to contract out of it, they must appreciate. That would not normally be so costly.

Professor Phelps added that one should not confuse managed parities with wild exchange-rate fluctuations. He also contended that the United States would not go back to a zero rate of inflation, because the social costs would be too high.

M. Ferras replied to M. Lamfalussy on the recent behaviour of reserves. In his paper, he was not so much thinking of the American deficit as of others, especially the British deficit. First, reserve creation could be in a form that involved double counting. The global reserves would increase, but the increased indebtedness of central banks would be hidden. Second, these operations arose in times of crisis. Therefore credit given was too generous. Third, such reserve creation was often fortuitous.

On current versus capital account, he thought Mr Lamfalussy and he agreed. It was just a fact that in the hierarchy of policies, liberalisation of commercial trade was usually seen as more important than liberalising capital movements. Restrictions on capital movements were often the first measures taken to safeguard the balance of payments. Was this national? Our order of priorities might be wrong. He would put trade first. He accepted the distinction as seeming logical, but thought that it was less logical in fact. It was hard to distinguish current from capital movements, and conventions differed between countries. But he thought that for adequate liquidity one needed capital movements without restriction.

Mr Brittan had said that the Bretton Woods agreement provided for a good deal of rigidity in exchange rates. This was true, but did not Mr Brittan agree that in the last four years there had been more rigidity than the framers of the agreement had expected? Maybe this was for political reasons, and also arose from the feeling that the depreciation of important currencies – especially the pound – was a threat to others – especially the dollar. This was why there had been so much aid to the United Kingdom in order to keep the old parity.

M. Ferras said he had not yet dealt with the problem of the gold prices. If the dollar price of gold were fixed, then the pressure on currencies was greater. For example, with a surplus currency, there was great pressure for revaluation. This was even more difficult and more undesired than devaluation. In the end one could not avoid devaluation; but the difficulty with appreciation was that countries thought that they were being forced to pay for other countries' mistakes. This made revaluation hard from a political point of view.

M. Ferras was sceptical of floating rates of exchange. M. Schweitzer used to say that rates did not float, they sank. He thought a system of fixed exchange rates was best if we were to avoid inflation. If rates floated, the fight against inflation was abandoned and this was bad. Similarly, he could not see any country really allowing a rate to float freely. There would always be intervention – but when? So many things were involved that it was very hard to manage a currency. He therefore thought it was best to keep to the Bretton Woods rules. There should be changes in exchange rates, but under I.M.F. control.

On Mundell's third option, he agreed on the way the system might evolve. There were three options. First, an American-dominated system; second, managed currencies supervised by a supranational central bank; third, some form of currency bloc in Europe. He had not dealt with option three because he did not think the prospects for it were bright. Co-operation on monetary policy was weak within the E.E.C., and one could not leave out the United Kingdom and at least part of the sterling area.

Professor Mundell said he would be selective in replying to the discussion. On the 'benevolence' of American leadership he had nothing to add except to note that it was easier for a Canadian than an American to say it. He added that when he talked of Europe he had no intention of excluding Japan.

There were two ways of approaching his paper. First, it looked at the world economy as it was – with all economic, political and social issues. Second, it built a model and tried to see how good the conclusions looked, from the standpoint of interpreting that world.

In the real world, political, economic and social issues were all lumped in, so that the conclusions of the paper did not all flow from the model. The model looked only at economic aspects.

On the mechanism, Professor Phelps had given an alternative model. But the significance of his own model lay in the perspective it gave on the world – not in the detail. The perspective of Keynesian models had been tolerably satisfactory in the 1930s – they were better than those they replaced. But the Keynesian model simply did not explain things very well. Applying Keynes's model directly was very misleading – except when it was handled by the most astute theorist. For example, the best application of it had been by Keynes himself in his *New Statesman* article when he had explained how to cure the slump. Keynes was fully aware of his assumption of inelastic expectations. But, in rigidly Keynesian models, expectations were held constant. The model was therefore unrealistic as it was used by the ordinary economist. Geniuses did not need models.

For example, an increase in the money supply would reduce the rate of interest, but only if expectations did not change. Similarly, what would one expect if prices increased? Would expectations not change? Going back to J. S. Mill's analysis of the effect of a change in the money supply on the rate of interest we should recall that Mill had said that the rate of interest would rise or fall depending on how the change was brought about. If the increase in the money supply were brought about by a budget deficit, the rate of interest would rise; if by an extension of credit, it would fall in the short run. In the longer run, if expectations were for an increase in prices, this would lead to a rise in the rate of interest. Keynes would have reached these conclusions by suitable shifts in his investment schedule, but in practice we became imprisoned by the model. Professor Mundell thought it was more useful now to give up Keynesian stereotypes, and to build on expectations in a world where inflation was accepted. He was now emphasising different things, with more relevant policy implications. It was a 'Keynesian' theory, but with adaptive expectations built into it endogenously.

On the question of the operation of the international system, the traditional notion of gold moving to bring about equilibrium, was found to be a rather romantic notion. This was especially true for economists like Arthur Bloomfield who had studied the working of the gold standard in the nineteenth century. In fact, things were not like this at all. When the United Kingdom had tightened its monetary policy in the nineteenth century, all countries did. There was no 'separate rate of inflation or deflation' in different countries.

Since 1945, we had moved to a system that relied on exchange controls – and then, when convertibility came, increasing mobility of capital. The qualification was that exchange rates could alter, so that expectations of change developed strongly and rates did alter. Up to the middle 1960s, there had been a tendency towards the equalisation of rates of interest between countries. Since then, with inflation in the United States and secular problems in the United Kingdom, there had been a fall in confidence in current exchange rates and a widening gap between different national rates of interest. Now, the rate of interest was not a good indication of the relative sympathy between monetary policies in different parts of the world. The indicator he had used was the rate of monetary expansion, and his graph showed very similar movements in the past four years between countries. The situation was very similar to what Bloomfield, Triffin and others had shown for the late nineteenth century.

Professor Cooper wanted to draw attention to one implication of Professor Mundell's suggestion that today expectations regarding price changes were elastic, in contrast with Keynes's assumption of inelastic expectations. If all factors of production – businessmen and landowners as well as workers – had elastic expectations with regard to prices, and if they all took steps to maintain their expected real income by raising money wages and rents correspondingly, then currency devaluation would have a deflationary impact on the economy of the devaluing country. Devaluation under these circumstances would not improve the trade balance through relative price effects – the lower value of the currency having been offset by higher factor prices. The higher level of domestic prices would increase the demand for money which, with supply unchanged, would reduce the demand for goods and services. The result would be much the same as if the nominal supply of money had been reduced in the first place, without devaluation.

What public expectations are was an empirical question, and the answer would undoubtedly vary from time to time and place to place. But expectations did have a time dimension; we did not make much of the price changes of yesterday, or even last week or last month, but only over some longer period of time. In addition there was a period of adjustment between the time at which it was collectively decided that observed price increases would last and the time at which this expectation could be translated into higher money incomes.

During both of these periods, typically, productivity was growing. Thus, by the time money incomes had caught up with price increases, real incomes might have been restored and might still be lower than they would have been in the absence of the price increases. The net effect on behaviour was likely to be somewhat closer to Keynes's assumption, and the relative price effects of devaluation might generally be expected to work.

Professor Izzo said that the interaction between the current balance of payments and the balance of international capital movements, to which Mr Lamfalussy was referring, could be explained as follows. If part of the saving supplied by the private sector of a country neglected domestic investment, it followed that the level of domestic monetary demand was reduced by the amount of saving going abroad, unless the latter was offset by domestic forces (e.g. negative saving by the government). Under these circumstances, part of domestic production, of an amount equal in value to that of saving flowing abroad, was made available for exports. If the economy were competitive, they would be exported, thus leading to an excess of current exports over imports of commodities. Therefore, one might say that capital exports produced the trade surplus and that the latter was financed by these same capital exports.

Professor Rasmussen said he wanted to make what was not really a technical point. Professor Mundell was in effect arguing that the rate of growth of monetary expansion was equal to the rate of growth of prices plus the rate of growth of output. If monetary expansion were exogenous, then there would be no increase in output. Therefore, it was implied that the rate of price increase was equal to the rate of growth of monetary expenditure. This was a crude quantity theory.

If he had understood Professor Mundell's model right, he was using at another point a different rate of growth of prices and a different rate of interest. If the rate of interest was i, then real monetary balances would be determined, and the real rate of interest and the level of output also determined. He thought the system was over-determined. This was shown to be true if one counted the variables and equations. Some greasing of the system was needed. Perhaps this result depended on the assumption about velocity.

What was desired velocity? One could work with expected rates of interest or of price increase. One could deduce the behaviour of households or businesses, or say what was a desired portfolio. But who desired a velocity? What economic behaviour lay behind it?

Professor Hicks said he had long stood by the view that greater attention should be given to the effect of current events on expectations. But we knew little about these, and were therefore in danger of introducing a particular way of reacting and drawing policy conclusions.

Professor Robinson said he sympathised with what had been said about Keynes by Mr Brittan. If Professor Robinson had believed that Keynes thought the things attributed to him by Mundell, he would agree with Professor Mundell. Having worked during the war with Keynes on inflation, he knew that the true (and English) image of Keynes was very different from that of the bogyman created by Professor Hansen.

Professor Mundell replied to the debate. To Professor Cooper he said that on the first point, he had not interpreted the model correctly. The elasticity of expectations and devaluation could still affect the balance of payments through real balance effects. Devaluation was another way of changing the money supply. With a constant stock of nominal money balances, it lowered the real value of liquidity. He would agree that the time dimension of expectations was important. He had gone into this superficially in the first appendix of his paper. showing the importance for employment of wage contracts, expectations of the future and the structure of current and expected wage contracts.

Professor Mundell said he did not agree with Professor Rasmussen that his model was over-determined. The variables were the money supply, unemployment, π and λ. The equation containing velocity was definitional, and not a restriction on the system.

He had been asked whether there was any value in the concept of desired velocity. It was the reciprocal of the desired money supply per unit of output – a notion used in many works in the past. He thought the concept was a valid one.

To Professor Hicks, Professor Mundell said he was not sure what Professor Hicks meant when he said that we knew 'little' about expectations. We did have writings on the dynamics of inflation, including expectations. For example there was Irving Fisher's appendix to the *Theory of Interest*. There was also the work of Gibson and papers by Meisleman and others. We had direct evidence on the behaviour of expectations from stock markets and from the structure of interest rates. Moreover, he himself had high expectations that our knowledge would increase in the future.

Part 3

Conflicts of Interest in Agricultural and Industrial Policies

13 Mutual Repercussions of Western European and North American Agricultural Policies[1]

D. R. Campbell
UNIVERSITY OF TORONTO

I. INTRODUCTORY

Agricultural policies and developments in Western Europe and North America have mutual repercussions in three ways – from the direct effects European policies have on imports from North America, from indirect effects through trade with third countries, and from differing stances adopted in international agencies and around bargaining tables.

The United States exported agricultural products valued at $6·2 billion in 1968, of which $1·4 billion went to the E.E.C. and $0·84 billion to other Western European countries.[2] Exports to Western Europe thus represented one-third of total American agricultural exports and a considerably larger share of 'commercial' exports if P.L.480 and other concessional exports are excluded. About 10 per cent of American agricultural output is exported.

Canadian agriculture is highly dependent upon international trade, with about 25 per cent of output going into export markets. Of $1,379 million[3] of farm products exported in 1967, $192 million went to the E.E.C. and $271 million to the United Kingdom. The policies and developments of Western Europe obviously can have a significant direct effect on the agricultural sectors of Canada and the United States.

The indirect repercussions, through trade with third countries, are in some cases as important as the direct relations of North Atlantic trade. The competition of France in world wheat markets or in the Japanese barley market, or the development of E.E.C. butter and skim-milk powder surpluses of remarkable proportions all have their impact on North American agriculture.

Finally, the varying positions taken by the North Atlantic countries in the Kennedy Round, UNCTAD, and in the negotiations and observance

---

[1] The author wishes to express his appreciation to T. K. Warley, Visiting Professor at the University of Guelph, for invaluable help. Errors are, of course, the author's own responsibility.
[2] EFTA, plus Spain and Ireland.
[3] All dollar values in this paper are given in United States dollars. One unit of account in the E.E.C. equals one United States dollar.

(or otherwise) of the International Grains Arrangement have serious repercussions on European and North American agriculture.

This paper discusses in turn the policies and developments of the past decade in the E.E.C., the United Kingdom, the United States and Canada. It then turns to a consideration of policy repercussions, primarily those of Europe on North America. Finally, it considers some of the main repercussions which would occur if the United Kingdom were to enter the E.E.C. Limitations of space prevent discussion of the policies of other Western European countries, relevant though they may be.

II. OBJECTIVES OF AGRICULTURAL POLICIES

The main objectives of the agricultural policies of the E.E.C. and the United States appear to have been identical – to increase farm incomes. It is true that many fine words have been spoken about improved farm structure, low-cost production, consumer prices, balance of payments, food aid, and so forth, but the basic objective seems to have been to produce higher farm incomes than could possibly have come about through the working out of free markets. In Great Britain the main objective of government policy has been to save foreign exchange. In an important policy statement late in 1968, the Minister of Agriculture, Fisheries and Food proposed further selective expansion of output to save £160 million in food imports by 1972–3. In Canada, objectives have not been clear; certainly increasing farm incomes has been an important element particularly in the costly dairy support programme since 1966, but, possibly because of the much greater dependence of Canadian agriculture on international trade, policies have tended to be *ad hoc* and to favour quick adjustments to exogenously determined economic forces. Sweden has been the only Western country in which a major objective has been to restrict agricultural production (even to the point of being a net importer) as part of an overall programme of national economic development.

III. THE EUROPEAN ECONOMIC COMMUNITY

Agriculture is an important sector in the E.E.C., accounting for about 7 per cent of Gross Domestic Product and employing about 14 per cent of the Community labour force. Although agricultural imports have increased, the E.E.C. is now about 90 per cent self-sufficient in food production compared to an average of about 85 per cent before the Second World War. The rapid growth of agricultural output is indicated in Table 13.1.

The Community farm labour force has declined rapidly in numbers; between 1950 and 1967 the decline was about 40 per cent in the E.E.C. compared with 46 per cent in the United States and 45 per cent in Canada.

TABLE 13.1

PHYSICAL VOLUME OF AGRICULTURAL PRODUCTION, SELECTED EUROPEAN COUNTRIES, CALENDAR YEARS 1964-8
(1957-9 = 100)

	1964	1965	1966	1967	1968[b]
Belgium-Luxembourg	110	108	108	122	121
France	121	129	125	136	142
West Germany	115	108	112	123	125
Italy	108	114	116	126	120
The Netherlands	122	120	125	137	139
E.E.C.	116	117	118	129	131
Denmark	124	124	121	122	126
Sweden	117	115	105	117	115
United Kingdom	127	132	131	137	135
All EFTA	120	122	120	127	127
Western Europe	116	119	120	129	131

[a] Preliminary.

Source: *Foreign Agriculture*, 27 Jan 1969, United States Department of Agriculture, p. 6.

The decline in farm labour forces in North America seems to have been more rapid, however, in the earlier years and to have slowed in the past three years. A comparison of experience in France and Canada is revealing: between 1962 and 1968 the French farm labour force[1] as a whole declined by 21 per cent, the number of farm operators by 17 per cent, of family help by 22·5 per cent and of hired workes by 27 per cent. The corresponding reductions for Canada were: total, 15 per cent; operators, 19 per cent; family help, 5 per cent; and hired workers, 9 per cent.

In spite of huge transfers from other sectors to agriculture via national budgets and FEOGA[2] and high levels of protection, average farm incomes in the Community are only about one-half the level of non-farm incomes. The structure of the farm sector is weak; almost one-half of all farm holdings are 12 acres or less in size and the fragmentation of holdings inhibits the efficient use of modern techniques and wastes the time of operators required to move from plot to plot. Marketing institutions and arrangements have been criticised as being inadequate for a modern efficient agricultural sector.

Estimates of direct national government and Community assistance to agriculture indicate annual expenditures of about $5 billion. This is in addition to the assistance provided by the very high levels of protection shown in Table 13.4 (see p. 288 below).

It would be inappropriate here to describe in any detail the national and Community institutions and their relationships. The E.E.C. has

[1] Reported in *Agra Europe*, 19 Feb 1969.
[2] European Agricultural Guidance and Guarantee Fund.

TABLE 13.2
GOVERNMENT SUPPORT TO AGRICULTURE IN THE E.E.C.
(U.S. $million)

	1960	1967
1. *Expenditures*		
Market support	495·9	1,519·0
Structural improvements	858·3	1,897·0
Miscellaneous	370·2	423·5
Total	1,724·4	3,839·5
Social measures	378·1	1,109·6
Total	2,102·5	4,949·1
2. *Countries*		
West Germany	730·7	1,520·5
Belgium	53·9	112·8
France	693·4	2,057·5
Italy	481·5	923·2
Luxembourg	9·4	12·2
Netherlands	133·6	322·9
	2,102·5	4,949·1

Source: *Kommission der Europäischen Gemeinschaft*, COM (68)100. Quoted in *Agriculture Abroad*, Canada Department of Agriculture, Apr 1969, p. 36.

made remarkable progress in eliminating internal trade barriers and developing a common agricultural policy and institutions in spite of the considerable price and other adjustments which were entailed. Central among the institutions developed is FEOGA, which, as its name indicates, provides funds for two main purposes – guidance or structural change, and price guarantees. The latter has absorbed far more funds than the former, a fact which reflects the greater emphasis placed upon maintaining or increasing farm incomes through high prices than through structural changes at the farm level. It is, of course, true that product prices can be affected much more readily than major adjustments at the producer level. Furthermore, in the merging of six different agricultures many objections may be expected; they can be partially met by high prices. Expenditures under the Guarantee Section are of two main kinds – 'intervention' or offers-to-purchase, and 'diversion', including export subsidies and subsidies for secondary utilisation such as denaturing wheat or skim-milk powder.

The Guidance Section budget of FEOGA is expected to rise from $80 million in 1965–6 to $285 million per year during 1967–8 to 1969–70, compared with Guarantee expenditures of $240 million in 1965–6 rising to an estimated $2,750 million in 1969–70 (see Table 13.3). FEOGA Guidance expenditures have been limited to 25 per cent (in 1969 up to 45 per cent) of costs of approved projects (approved by the nation-state as well as by FEOGA) in which the beneficiaries also contribute 30 per cent of the cost. To date a high proportion of Guidance expenditures has gone to marketing projects and a low proportion to farm structural adjustments.[1]

TABLE 13.3

EXPENDITURES OF THE E.E.C. AGRICULTURAL FUND[a]
(all figures in $U.S. million)

	1965–6	1966–7	1967–8	1968–9	1969–70
Guarantee Section					
Grains	120·3	136·5	535·0	587·5	587·5
Pork	14·5	15·2	40·0	65·0	65·0
Eggs	1·2	0·7	2·0	2·5	2·5
Poultry	2·1	2·8	5·0	5·0	5·0
Rice	0·1	0·8	7·0	11·2	11·3
Dairy products	98·0	131·7	370·0	975·0	1,270·0
Beef	–	–	2·0	52·5	52·5
Fruit, vegetables	–	0·1	29·0	30·0	30·0
Olive oil, grape kernel oil	–	79·2	147·0	147·5	145·0
Oilseeds	–	–	48·0	50·0	50·0
Processed products	–	–	18·0	–	–
Sugar	4·0	3·5	110·0	310·0	310·0
Tobacco	–	–	–	–	100·0
Wine	–	–	–	–	125·0
Total, Guarantee Section	240·2	370·5	1,313·0	2,236·2	2,753·8
Guidance Section	80·0	123·5	285·0	285·0	285·0
Total Guidance and Guarantee Sections	320·2	494·0	1,598·0	2,521·2	3,038·8
Special Sections	–	–	208·2	140·3	69·2
Total Fund expenditures	320·2	494·0	1,806·2	2,661·5	3,108·0

[a] Projections through 1969–70 by German Ministry of Finance.
Source: *Foreign Agriculture*, 26 Aug 1968, U.S.D.A.

FEOGA expenditures on Guarantees through price support and surplus disposal amounted to about $36 per hectare devoted to soft wheat and $105 per hectare of sugar beets in 1967–8.[2] This direct assistance is in addition to the protection afforded by variable import levies which amounted to 85 per cent of the world market price for soft wheat and 338

[1] Of the Guidance funds actually allocated in 1967, about one-third went to farm structural improvement projects and two-thirds to marketing (excluding special and emergency assistance in that year to Italy). Proposals for the following three years indicate a similar balance.

[2] For data on costs per hectare for other products, see *Agra Europe*, 19 Mar 1969.

per cent for sugar (see Table 13.4). Financing[1] of FEOGA comes from the variable import levies and from the contributions of the member states according to agreed 'fixed key scales'. These budgetary contributions thus become a form of open-ended obligation to meet that part of FEOGA's expenditures not met by revenue from the variable import levies.

TABLE 13.4

E.E.C. PRICES AND WORLD MARKET PRICES, 1967-8

(all prices in $U.S. per 100 kg.)

	Import price	World market price	Col. (1) as % of Col. (2)
Soft wheat	10.73	5.79	185
Durum wheat	16.14	8.07	200
Hulled rice	17.96	15.34	117
Barley	9.07	5.67	160
Maize	9.01	5.63	160
White sugar	22.35	5.10	438
Beef and veal	68.00	38.82	175
Pigs	56.71	38.56	147
Poultry	72.33	55.00	131
Eggs	51.14	38.75	132
Butter	187.44	47.25	397
Olive oil	115.62	69.84	166
Oilseeds	20.19	10.11	200

Data are wholesale prices, and include direct support for production of durum wheat, olive oil and oilseeds. Col. (1) is headed Community Price and Soft Wheat is called Common Wheat in source.

Source: *Newsletter on the Common Agricultural Policy*, Directorate-General for Agriculture of the European Communities Commission, Brussels, Nov 1968.

The variable import levies represent the difference between the Threshold Price[2] (calculated back from Target Prices) and world prices. That E.E.C. farm prices are high relative to world prices is indicated in Table 13.4. For example, world barley prices at E.E.C. port of entry were $5.67 per 100 kg. ($1.24 per bushel), to which a levy of $3.40 per 100 kg. (74 cents per bushel) was applied in 1967-8 so that the import price was $9.07 per 100 kg. ($1.98 per bushel). Column (3) of Table 13.4 indicates the wide variation in the degree of support for various commodities.

[1] To 31 Dec 1968, Germany had contributed a total of $683 million and received $359 million; France contributed $576 million and drew $919 million (*European Community*, Dec 1968–Jan 1969).

[2] Threshold Price is the term used for grains. Guide Price and Sluice Price are terms used for beef and pork. All refer to the price at which imports may occur and are roughly equal to world prices plus variable import levies.

The results of the E.E.C. policies have been discouraging both within and without the Community. The Vedel Commission in its study of French agriculture to 1985 criticised market support as 'ineffective and unjust' and stated that structural reforms have 'probably merely accompanied developments which would have occurred in any case'. Sorenson and Hathaway seem to have assessed the situation accurately:

> Those who believe that a move to a Common Agricultural Policy is likely to solve, or even appreciably alleviate, the low-income problem in E.E.C. agriculture are likely to be disappointed. First, the most prosperous farms are found in northern France and the Low Countries. These are the countries where the greatest increases in farm incomes will occur under the new policies. This is especially true for the Paris Basin area where the large farms will benefit from both higher prices and the removal of the quantum tax. The lowest-income farms in Germany, Italy and western France will benefit least from the new price policy. Thus, the policies as now formulated will, if anything, increase the income disparities within E.E.C. agriculture; and, moreover, the countries with the lowest-income farms will pay the largest share of the costs of the policy.
> It should be noted that no price policy will solve the income problem of most of these low-income farms. Only structural improvement can solve the problem and it will require a continued reduction in farm numbers, which is a long and difficult process. In this sense the E.E.C. policy is not unlike that of the United States; it gives great emphasis to income transfers from non-farm to farm people, but the money that is transferred goes predominantly to those who are best off in agriculture, not to the poor.[1]

The 'Mansholt Plan', proposed in late 1968, offers a new orientation for agricultural policy to 1980. Emphasis, which up to this point has been predominantly on the support of product prices, would shift to farm structural adjustments. Incentives to move from agriculture would be increased by grants, advanced retirement pensions, vocational training and the creation of 80,000 new jobs per year in agricultural areas. The Plan proposes the creation of much larger production units, some consisting of joint ownership and operation by a number of existing producers. With improved structure would come greater output, and, to offset this at least partially, the Plan proposes that 5 million hectares out of 71 million currently in use should be retired from farming. It is hoped that the farm labour force, which will have decreased in numbers by 4·7 million to 10 million between 1960 and 1970, will fall by another 5 million by

[1] V. L. Sorenson and D. E. Hathaway, *The Grain–Livestock Economy and Trade Patterns of the European Economic Community* (Institute of International Agriculture, Michigan State University, 1968) p. 117.

1980. Average annual cost of the Plan for the 1970s would be $2·5 billion. The Plan also makes medium-term proposals to deal with the pressing surpluses of butter, skim-milk powder, and sugar.

IV. THE UNITED KINGDOM

The United Kingdom is one of the few countries in which farm incomes are about equal to average incomes in the non-farm sectors. Production has increased at a very rapid rate, spurred on and assisted by the Government. 'At this year's Annual Review, we want to see the upward trend in production maintained, so that agriculture can make its full contribution to import saving on the broad lines of the selective expansion programme. . . .'[1] Production in 1966–7 to 1968–9 was 39 per cent greater

TABLE 13.5

PRODUCTION AND IMPORTS OF AGRICULTURAL PRODUCTS, UNITED KINGDOM, SELECTED YEARS
(all figures in '000 long tons)

	1953–4		1961–2		1967–8[a]	
	Home	Imports	Home	Imports	Home	Imports
Wheat	2,664	3,853	2,573	4,609	3,836	4,023
Barley	2,521	1,255	4,974	531	9,242	180
Oats	2,821	82	1,822	42	1,361	20
Maize (corn)		1,413		3,938		3,608
Total grains[b]	8,917	6,632	9,556	9,675	14,568	8,091
Meat	1,421	1,000	2,141	1,106	2,376	960
Butter	29	288	58	407	41	467

[a] Forecast.
[b] Also includes rye, mixed grain and sorghum.

Source: *Annual Review and Determination of Guarantees, 1968*, Cmnd 3558 (H.M.S.O.).

than in 1954–5 to 1956–7. Table 13.5 gives details of the remarkable accomplishments of United Kingdom agriculture in replacing imports by domestic production. Food imports in 1960–2 accounted for 31·2 per cent of all British imports; by 1966 the percentage was 26·5.

Production increases have been stimulated by substantial government assistance: expenditures by the Exchequer on price guarantees and production grants in 1968–9 and 1969–70 are estimated at £281 million and £318 million compared with net farm incomes of £477 million and £516 million respectively. Since the technique used to support prices is primarily that of deficiency payments, consumers have had the advantage of purchases at world prices. This is in contrast with the E.E.C. in

[1] Excerpt from statement by Mr Peart, Minister of Agriculture, Fisheries and Food, in the British House of Commons during debate on the 'Annual Review and Determination of Guarantees, 1968'.

which price supports are implemented by offers-to-purchase and by high variable import levies.

The United Kingdom has brought more order to her own markets by negotiating a series of bilateral agreements by which imports to the United Kingdom are allocated to exporting nations. In the case of the Cereals Agreements of 1964, signed bilaterally by the United Kingdom and about twenty supplying nations, suppliers were to share in the growth of the United Kingdom market. Domestic production increased so much that this provision was embarrassing to the United Kingdom and the Agreements were quietly dropped in the 1967-8 negotiations which culminated in the International Grains Arrangement. Import quotas (by nation) were begun for sugar in 1951, for butter in 1962, and for bacon in 1964.

V. THE UNITED STATES

In many ways the farm policy of the United States has been similar to that of the E.E.C. in spite of the fact that the United States has an agricultural surplus and the E.E.C. a deficit and that agriculture in the United States is only about one-half as large relative to the American economy as is the case in the E.E.C. The American offer-to-purchase support programme in the 1950s led to the accumulation of large stocks which in turn led to Public Law 480 disposal, primarily in less developed countries, to import restrictions, export subsidies, and, in addition, to acreage retirement and acreage allotment programmes.

United States wheat-marketing policy took a dramatic turn in 1964 when the high offer-to-purchase price was reduced drastically and a domestic milling certificate programme introduced. The result has been a continuation of a two-price system which allows exporters to compete in world markets. Sales to less developed countries through P.L. 480 have been de-emphasised in favour of aggressive selling in commercial markets since 1966.

Table 13.6 indicates the remarkable growth of United States agricultural exports to the E.E.C., reaching a peak in 1966; 1968 exports at $1·4 billion show a continuation of a slight downtrend since 1966. United States agricultural exports to EFTA countries in 1968 were valued at $650 million, of which tobacco accounted for 30 per cent, feedgrains for 16 per cent, oilseeds and meal for 13 per cent, and wheat and flour for 9 per cent.

United States corn and soybean exports have grown dramatically and steadily for the past fifteen years, particularly to the E.E.C. The acreage devoted to soybeans expanded from 23 million in 1959 to 42 million in 1968, partially because of acreage allotment programme for other crops.

TABLE 13.6

AGRICULTURAL EXPORTS FROM THE UNITED STATES
TO E.E.C. COUNTRIES

($million)

	1958	1962	1964	1966	1967
Feedgrain	159·8	320·5	333·9	495·8	392·5
of which corn	48·1	166·5	238·9	340·3	304·3
Other grain	68·1	89·1	81·9	130·6	126·5
of which wheat	63·7	56·2	60·9	107·3	96·5
Soy beans	62·1	162·3	213·9	278·7	294·2
Soya meal	6·4	42·0	71·1	140·6	142·3
Tobacco	89·5	105·5	105·8	119·9	149·0
Cotton	197·4	106·0	189·1	65·9	71·8
Fruit	59·8	66·7	61·0	66·3	64·5
Eggs and poultry	3·6	53·5	31·7	23·6	18·5
Other products	174·9	205·1	327·5	242·8	190·8
Total	821·6	1,150·7	1,415·9	1,564·2	1,460·1

Source: *Agra Europe*, 16 Apr 1969.

VI. CANADA

Whereas both the United States and the E.E.C. have been fairly free to follow the kind of farm policy they wish – the United States because agricultural exports are only 0·7 per cent of G.N.P., and the E.E.C. because she is a net importer of food – Canada has been circumscribed by the need for large exports, especially of wheat. Canadian policy has been to avoid large government expenditures and to make Temporary Wheat Storage Payments and provide 'stop-loss' price supports for other products to overcome what were hoped would be short-run problems. This Micawber-like policy was vindicated by big wheat sales to China and the U.S.S.R. in the early 1960s but now seems to be in difficulty.[1] Total federal and provincial expenditures on agriculture, including research and extension as well as price supports, amounted to $470 million in 1966-7.[2] The only major programme which has been out of keeping with Canadian emphasis on 'ad hoc-ery' and adjustment has been an embargo on butter imports and an extensive subsidy programme to the dairy industry.

Canada's heavy dependence upon exports of high-quality milling wheat has placed her farm sector in an unenviable position given the current world surplus. About 10 million of the 30 million acres sown to wheat in

[1] Micawber, a creation of Charles Dickens, was always 'waiting for something to turn up'.
[2] S. W. Garland and S. C. Hudson, *Government Involvement in Agriculture* (Federal Task Force on Agriculture, Ottawa, 1968).

TABLE 13.7

AGRICULTURAL EXPORTS FROM CANADA, 1963 AND 1967

(all figures in millions of Canadian dollars)

	E.E.C.		U.K.		All agricultural exports
	1963	1967	1963	1967	1967
Wheat and flour	134	118	162	130	801
Barley	–	23	10	12	73
Oilseeds and products	8	28	48	41	127
Animals, meat, animal products	1	5	15	15	181
Dairy products	1	5	11	10	34
Tobacco	3	1	24	42	47
Fruits, vegetables	3	3	16	15	71
Other products	31	23	35	29	149
Total agricultural exports	181	206	321	294	1,483

Source: *Canada, Trade in Agricultural Products with the United Kingdom, the United States and All Countries, 1966 and 1967* (Canada Department of Agriculture, Ottawa, 1968).

recent years will have to be diverted to grass, oilseeds, and feedgrains. Canada, then, has a particular interest in Western European programmes which affect wheat and feedgrain production and imports.

VII. DIRECT REPERCUSSIONS OF EUROPEAN POLICIES

(1) The elasticity of supply of aggregate agricultural output in the E.E.C. is obviously decisive, given the very high level of farm prices in the Community. The conclusions of a study of the E.E.C. by Sorenson and Hathaway are particularly relevant:

> Most of our analysis suggests that the total area planted to grain is not very sensitive to price changes, at least not price changes of the magnitude that appear likely under the proposed E.E.C. policies.
>
> Grain yields in the E.E.C. appear likely to be almost exclusively a function of technology and shifts in the location of production. Improved knowledge and management is more likely to influence fertilizer use and other production practices than are changes in grain prices.[2]

The authors add a pertinent footnote at this point. 'U.S. readers are reminded that fertilizer use in the U.S. and yields of grain have climbed rapidly in recent years with stable or falling product prices.' Between 1950 and 1966–7 the tonnage of the three main fertiliser ingredients used in the E.E.C. countries apparently increased by 150 per cent; in Canada the increase was about 300 per cent.

[1] Sorenson and Hathaway, op cit., p. 73.

Sorenson and Hathaway project a continuing small downtrend in grain acreage, from 21·8 million hectares in 1955, 21·5 million in 1964 to 20·4 million in 1970 and 19·9 million in 1975. The decline in acreage has been more than offset by increased yields so that output increased from 47·8 million tons in 1955 to 61·2 million in 1964 and is projected by Sorenson and Hathaway to increase to 66·5 million in 1970 and 73 million in 1975.

It seems reasonable to conclude that the very high farm prices of the E.E.C. have encouraged greater grain production and thus had an adverse effect on North American exports. However, it appears that increases in output have come about more because of technology and structural change (shifting the supply curve) than because of high prices (moving along the supply curve).

With government support, the United Kingdom has quadrupled her barley production (Table 13.5) and become self-sufficient. Her major imports from North America are wheat, corn, oilseeds and tobacco, of which only the first can be produced in the United Kingdom.

(2) In the E.E.C., beef and milk are joint products, based primarily upon forage rather than grain, and with few of the specialised beef feed lots to be found in North America. The joint nature of beef and milk production poses a dilemma because the E.E.C. has huge surpluses of dairy products but is deficient in beef and veal and likely to remain so for some years.[1] Because imports of beef come from sources other than North America whereas most of the feedgrain imports come from North America, a Community policy to become self-sufficient in beef would have some advantage for North American grain producers.

The embarrassing E.E.C. dairy surplus has led to a proposal which would have serious repercussions on United States exports. The proposal is to tax oilmeal and vegetable oil. Such taxes would raise the price of margarine and thereby contribute to higher domestic butter consumption; they would also raise the price of oilmeal (protein supplement) and thereby both discourage heavy feeding of cattle and encourage substitution of skim-milk powder for oilmeal in feeds. Naturally the United States objects because soybeans now earn more foreign exchange for the United States than any other farm product and 35 to 40 per cent of these exports go to the E.E.C.

(3) Relative prices set by FEOGA for different grains and livestock appear to have a considerable effect on levels of production for each and consequently on imports. The high levels of support for wheat relative to those for barley and corn (Table 13.4, col. (3)) have tended to result in a Community surplus of wheat and deficit in feedgrains.[2] Thus the E.E.C.

---

[1] Sorenson and Hathaway, p. 103.

[2] See D. J. Epps, *Changes in Regional Grain and Livestock Prices under the European Economic Community Policies*, Institute of International Agriculture Research Report No. 4 (Michigan State University, 1968) pp. 73 ff.

relative prices of wheat and feedgrains have made exports more difficult for countries such as Canada which, like the E.E.C., export wheat and import corn and soybeans, and more favourable to the United States. Since 1967–8 the Threshold Prices of both barley and corn have been raised but that of wheat kept stable. This will tend to reduce the Community wheat surplus and feedgrain deficit.

The relative Threshold Prices of barley and corn in the E.E.C. produce some peculiar and probably unintended results in North America. The Threshold Prices[1] for 1967–8 were: barley, $9.00 per metric ton; corn, $88.38 per metric ton. On a total digestible nutrient basis, barley is worth only 86 per cent as much as corn; thus if corn were priced at $88.38, barley should have been priced at about $76.00 in order to be competitive. The high Threshold Price for barley in the E.E.C. has been a factor in its expansion from 11·5 per cent of E.E.C. grain acreage in 1955 to 18·3 per cent in 1964 and a predicted 23·5 per cent in 1970.[2] Of equal importance however, the over-pricing of barley has meant that most of the tremendous expansion in the E.E.C.'s imports of feedgrain has been in corn, not barley. For the United States, which can produce export surpluses of both corn and barley, this is probably not particularly important. For Canada, an importer of corn but potentially a large exporter of barley (especially if 10 million acres must be removed from wheat), this is a matter of great moment. Given the current relative Threshold Prices, Canada cannot, by lowering the price of barley, bid her way into the huge E.E.C. feedgrain market.

VIII. INDIRECT REPERCUSSIONS

The Guarantees Section of FEOGA provides for export subsidies as well as for price supports and subsidised secondary domestic utilisation (such as skim-milk powder used for livestock feed). The export subsidies must inevitably affect other exporters to third markets.

The most important E.E.C. commodities receiving export subsidies and affecting North American agriculture are wheat and barley exported by France. Wheat, in particular, has been in competition with both the United States and Canada. French exports of wheat and flour (equivalent) averaged 60 million bushels per year during 1955–9 or 4·8 per cent of world exports; in 1965–8, they averaged 156 million bushels or 7·8 per cent of world exports. France has recently sold 900,000 tons of soft wheat to China at what is reported to be 50 per cent of the lowest French intervention price. Transportation costs must be added to this subsidy.

The indirect repercussions from export subsidies emanate from both sides of the Atlantic. The United States operates a pricing system for

---

[1] *Foreign Agriculture*, 5 May 1969, U.S.D.A., p. 6. Threshold Prices for 1968–9 were: corn, $92·69; barley, $92·19.

[2] Sorenson and Hathaway, op. cit., p. 77.

wheat which allows exporters to make purchases at well below the average national price, as shown in Fig. 13.1. The net effect of subsidies by the United States, France and other countries, including Australia, is to put at a serious disadvantage producers in countries like Canada which would, in a free market, have a considerable cost and price advantage.

IX. A QUESTION OF STANCE

The total of repercussions between European and North American farm policies cannot be covered by a discussion of direct and indirect trading relationships. In UNCTAD, I.G.A. and the Kennedy Round, there

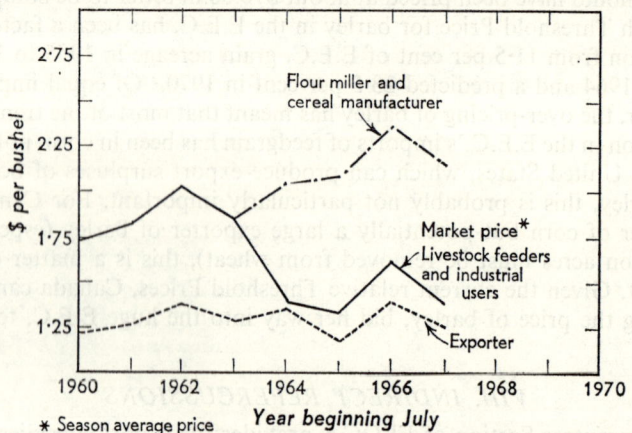

FIG. 13.1 The market price of wheat no longer tells the full story about the cost of wheat to different users. Beginning with the 1964 crop, processors of wheat for use as human food in the United States must pay a fixed amount per bushel to the U.S.D.A. The market price, beginning that crop year, is lower and continues to reflect the cost of wheat to other users. Exporters continue to pay less than other wheat users since their price represents that of the open market less the export payment. Such payments are made by the U.S.D.A. to the exporter, enabling him to compete in the lower-priced world market.

Source: *The Wheat Situation*, May 1969, U.S.D.A. Reproduced by courtesy of the United States Dept. of Agriculture.

seemed to be a series of actions and reactions across the Atlantic. In I.G.A., for example, the French proposals were widely at variance with those of the United States and I.G.A. provisions resulted from a compromise. This subject deserves considerable attention and certainly more than can be given to it in this paper. The unedifying sight of heads of state devoting their time to rather acrimonious discussions of broiler markets is evidence of the primacy of short-run considerations.

X. A LARGER COMMUNITY?

If the United Kingdom and some other EFTA countries were to be accepted into the E.E.C., it is highly likely that they would have a very few years in which to make the transition to the E.E.C.'s agricultural policy and institutions. Leaving aside the considerable adjustments necessary on the part of British farmers and complaints about higher food prices by British consumers, what would be the repercussions of an enlarged E.E.C. on North American agriculture? The current E.E.C. surpluses of dairy products and sugar could be largely absorbed in the United Kingdom without any serious effects on North America. When the higher E.E.C. feedgrain prices apply in the United Kingdom and other Western European countries, production would increase and imports fall.

Higher consumer prices in present EFTA countries as they join the E.E.C. would reduce consumption somewhat, especially of butter and meats, but would not have serious repercussions across the Atlantic. Imports of North American fruits and vegetables by the United Kingdom could be expected almost to disappear. Those small Commonwealth Preferences enjoyed by Canada in the United Kingdom market would disappear with only modest damage.

XI. CONCLUSIONS

In the E.E.C., the United Kingdom and the United States there have been transfers on a major scale from non-farm to farm sectors, primarily through various forms of price support. In the E.E.C. and the United States these transfers have come about primarily because of low farm incomes. Yet without a major structural change, higher prices cannot solve the problems of very low-income farmers but merely give increased returns to those who are large and already fairly prosperous.

In the E.E.C. the path of least resistance in merging six different agricultural economies involved setting high prices. The facts of politics probably dictate that there could have been only slight variations from this course.

The remarkable declines in farm labour forces in the North Atlantic countries have been almost as rapid as even economists might recommend. A decline of 50 per cent in a generation is almost staggering in its implications for social facilities in farming areas, for education and for adjustment in urban centres. A more rapid rate of structural change might have been detrimental not only to individuals but to nations.

Nevertheless, the peculiar circumstances of the E.E.C., only 90 per cent self-sufficient in food, and the United States, with small agricultural exports compared to G.N.P., and the United Kingdom, with a need to save foreign exchange, are not duplicated by Canada, Denmark and many other exporting nations. For these countries, necessary adjustments have been and will be hard; it is to their credit that so much adjustment has already occurred.

14 The Common Agricultural Policy of the European Economic Community and North American Exports[1]

Luc Fauvel
UNIVERSITY OF PARIS

The purpose of this paper is to recall the social imperatives and the various pressures which have shaped the agricultural policy of the European Economic Community (E.E.C.) and then to analyse the repercussions it is likely to have in the future on United States exports to the Common Market.

I. THE PURPOSES OF THE COMMON AGRICULTURAL POLICY

In 1959 there appeared to be little chance that the six signatory countries of the Treaty of Rome would ever effectively harmonise their agricultural policies. Agriculture is the last refuge of national economic idiosyncrasy. Policy unification was out of the question. In each country, national policy was made up of a somewhat incongruous medley of legislative and financial provisions, most often wrested from Parliament piecemeal, without any really comprehensive plan, in the course of the thirty years which had passed since the 1929 crisis. The representatives of each group of producers (cereal growers, producers of milk, beef, pork, fruit, vegetables, sugar beet, potatoes, oilseeds, wine, cheese, flax, and so on) had managed to get government support for their particular products, but with results and in forms which varied greatly from case to case and from country to country. In most cases they had succeeded in getting a price that was considered 'reasonable' by the producers after the domestic market had been isolated from the fluctuations of international trade. This price enabled the farmer to go on cultivating his land. It diminished his worries with respect to the recurring annual uncertainties about the size of the harvest, and made him less vulnerable to the threat which the rapid growth of production under the impact of technical progress implied for those least able to adjust to the inevitable fall in prices. In the case of many products of crucial importance for the incomes of farm families, national prices were often between 130 and 300 per cent of average world market prices.

It soon became evident, in the years between 1959 and 1962, that notwithstanding all the differences in national policies, they all served two purposes very widely accepted by public opinion and Parliaments in

[1] Translation from the French by Elizabeth Henderson.

industrial countries. One purpose, ever since 1929, had been to 'reduce the instability of prices and incomes'; the other was 'income parity', an objective accepted in Europe since about 1955. This deep unity of purpose had to some extent been masked by the wide range of techniques employed; but it provided a basis for the system of market regulations for separate products, which began to be put into effect in Brussels from 1961 on. And so, between 1962 and 1968, joint regulations binding on all the six member countries were adopted and gradually came to replace the support policies previously ruling in each separate country. It proved unnecessary to make major changes, either upward or downward, in the benefits hitherto available to any particular group of producers. The Commission was able to propose to the Council of Ministers temporary compromise solutions worked out for each product even in the most difficult situations, without serious detriment to the overall policy line. To be sure, the transition from national to common policies more than once seemed politically 'blocked', but it did in all essentials take place within the time limit of the seven- to ten-year transition period originally set.

There is thus nothing abnormal in the support enjoyed by the Community's farmers. It rests on what is euphemistically called the policy of 'organisation and stabilisation of agricultural markets', such as had been widely practised since 1929, though it had increasingly been called into question both in Europe and in North America. Actually, what causes misgivings is not so much the two objectives mentioned above, but the rigidities they cause. It is not the principle of reducing the instability of farm prices and incomes which is criticised, nor the wish to diminish the gap between the incomes of farm households and of skilled workers in the same region (which is the more precise definition of the concept of income parity). The contested point, rather, is the more and more general spread of price and sales guarantees at a time when the past twenty years' rapid technological progress in agriculture keeps threatening to upset the situation at every new stage. It has been clear for twenty years that we are moving towards agricultural production without peasant farmers. Price stabilisation at relatively high levels with a view to helping small isolated peasant farmers to survive merely means keeping part of the industrial countries' agriculture in a state of underdevelopment. Price and income guarantees are nothing but permanent oxygen-tents which prevent the disappearance of sub-marginal farms, and these government guarantees are sources of unjustifiable profits for the big, well-managed family farms.

It is, of course, true that the objective of income parity, as explicitly stated in Germany's Green Law of 1957 and later, in almost identical terms, in the French Orientation Laws of 1960 and 1962, does in the first place presuppose a structural policy. The real, long-term objective, and the hard way to achieve it, is to improve the productivity of farm enterprises and at the same time quickly to reduce their number and the size of the farm population. Both in Germany and in France, successive governments have for ten years secured the passage of a whole series of legislative and financial measures designed to achieve this. But in practice the easy way of price supports still has the upper hand. It is the result of pressures brought to bear on government by the most varied groups, pressures both of regional politics (e.g. Bavaria, Brittany) and of the majority of farmers' associations. Admittedly, there are nowadays movements favouring free-enterprise farming, and 'young farmers' movements which, in France and elsewhere, have come to realise that the policy of high prices is dangerous and obsolete. But they are in a minority. The way of least resistance is to go on helping farmers to live where they are, as best they can. Not long ago a French Minister of Agriculture made a public statement which meant just that. It needs far too much political courage to make any real attempt at reducing quickly the number of inefficient farmers by speeding up their move to other occupations, for their family background and training gives them little chance of success elsewhere.

What the Common Market has achieved, then, in its first seven years and along the lines of the first Mansholt Report (1960), is in essence to unify market policies – that is, the methods of supporting farm incomes. It was not until the end of 1968 that the second Mansholt Report at long last shifted the emphasis to structural policies. Among other things, the Commission hopes that within ten years, before 1980, measures will be adopted to 'eliminate the legislative and financial obstacles which obstruct an enlargement of the size of farms as well as greater mobility of land ownership and labour'. The intention is not merely to speed up the reduction in the number of farmers, but to withdraw certain acreages from farming altogether. (It may even pay, for instance, to plant certain species of poplars in the Netherlands; within eight years they will yield paper pulp, and within sixteen years they can be used as timber.) Another proposal aims at reducing the number of dairy cows by slaughtering premiums. The governments and producer organisations of the six member countries are now face to face with the real problem. Not all of them find this particularly pleasant, but no one denies that the common policy must move in this direction.

There has been, however, one aspect which has distinguished the Common Agricultural Policy sharply from *British policy*. The cost of agricultural support in each of the six countries was borne essentially by households, through a system of high domestic prices and isolation of the domestic market. The British system was economically, and technically, very different, in that it rested on some sort of true price system which attempted to reconcile domestic consumer prices with international prices. And it is the British taxpayer who has to foot the bill for the 'deficiency payments' which make up the farmers' income to a 'reasonable' level regarded as necessary to induce them to go on farming in Great Britain. Economists are naturally inclined to regard this system as clearer, more candid and, perhaps, more honest than the Continental system. The taxpayers (and the farmers) may get the impression that they are better informed in this way about the mounting size of the bill to pay. However that may be, the experts at Brussels were at a loss when they were asked to suggest how the British system might be reconciled with the one which, by some miracle, was in the process of unification on the Continent. No satisfactory solution was put forward in 1965, or none at any rate that did not imply abandoning what was being so laboriously built up at Brussels.

But since then the approach to agricultural problems has changed a good deal everywhere in the world. In the early days of the Common Market organisation, in the years 1960 to 1962, it was implicitly taken for granted that the Community as such would be a net importer of agricultural commodities. There might perhaps be some French exports of wheat or meat, and some Dutch exports of dairy products. But the import requirements of the Federal Republic of Germany alone would keep the E.E.C. as a whole in deficit. It soon became clear that technological progress was gaining ground very quickly in the underdeveloped parts of European agriculture. But technological progress could not be of much benefit to small farmers unable to afford the growing cost of inputs. It may lead to waste through over-equipment of small farms and prestige investments. And it yields less returns than it should, because of the unwieldy distribution channels and the inefficiency of food-processing industries in certain countries. France is a case in point. None the less, output of one product after another has been expanding beyond the limit of self-sufficiency for the Community as a whole, thanks to an income effect associated with the familiar behaviour patterns of agricultural producers. And so surpluses pile up, which can be exported only at world market prices, at prices, that is, barely 50 per cent or in some cases 30 or 20 per cent of the Community's guaranteed price. More and more often, the *'joint financial responsibility'* of the Community is called into play. In other words, contrary to what was expected in 1960, the import levies on agricultural commodities entering the Community are not sufficient to finance the export rebates, or subsidies. The Community finds itself faced with a financial problem. And the governments of those countries which happen to export least (that is, which have fewest products to export at a loss) need a good deal of prodding to go on playing the game of 'joint financial responsibility'. They declare that they do not like having to ask their taxpayers for the money needed to pay equal shares of the mounting cost of export subsidies.[1] The Council of Ministers of the Six finds itself forced

---

[1] And yet, the closer the economic union of the Six becomes, the more will surplus disposal have to remain their joint responsibility. Otherwise they will have to retreat to the EFTA solution.

to think of lowering the support prices. Of course, it is (politically) hard to talk of a price 'fall'. This is a word best left unsaid. Nevertheless, some Finance Minister in one or other exporting country can be heard nowadays telling his farmers that the money they claim in growing amounts so as to get rid of their unsaleable surpluses must now in some part be extracted from the pockets of taxpayers in other countries. This may be a very honest argument, but it does worry the farmers just a little.

Nor, for that matter, is it an argument that must always be taken very seriously. It has been said with reference to French agriculture, which owns almost half the Community's farm land, that there is no point nowadays in talking of French surpluses, or Italian or German surpluses. The sub-marginal farms are not all in one country, they are scattered all over the Community. There are some in every member country. The situation cannot be analysed in aggregate terms, country by country, but only in terms of each of the individual agricultural regions in all the six countries; that is, it must bear on several hundreds of different regional situations. Surpluses have to do with local, detailed situations, not with national statistical averages.

But no beginning has as yet been made with the *regionalisation of the Common Agricultural Policy*, though a debate on regional specialisation has been launched by J. Klatzmann, of the Agronomic Institute in Paris. Starting from farm management analyses of the Heady type, Klatzmann looked at the conditions in which different commodities are produced in each region and then tried to determine what should be produced from the point of view of the best practicable use of local resources, that is, at each region's lowest cost for each product. At the end of a laborious study, Klatzmann came to the conclusion that France produces less, and Germany far more, than it should do. This is hardly surprising.

The regions most definitely overpopulated and overexploited in the E.E.C. are Hesse, the Rhine Palatinate, Baden-Württemberg, Bavaria, Sicily, Sardinia, the Abruzzi, Apulia and Calabria. At the other end of the scale Klatzmann places northern France, the Paris region, Picardy, Upper Normandy, Belgium and the Netherlands. He makes out a case for indicative regional planning.[1] But Ministers will hardly be in a hurry to accept Mr Klatzmann's 'fantastic accounts'.[2]

Mr Klatzmann's final suggestion is that the outflow of manpower from

---

[1] The French Ministry of Agriculture, in its turn, has since 1963 been financing research on various overall planning models for agriculture, with two chief purposes: (*a*) to make individual plans mutually more consistent and to make the activities of different regions more consistent at the national level; (*b*) to provide an instrument capable of indicating the consequences of proposed policies, especially the effects of a price change for one or more products on the geographical distribution of production.

[2] The cost of transferring one farmer to industry seems to be lower, and easier to calculate, in West Germany than in France and Italy. West Germany has a greater range of established industries which can absorb rural manpower.

agriculture should be stemmed in France, just when instead every effort is being made to depopulate the countryside. The price of land is lower in France than in Germany, and should attract farmers from the other side of the Rhine. Klatzmann concludes: 'If the Common Market represents an opportunity for French farming, this does not necessarily mean that it represents an opportunity for every French farmer.'

In the meantime, there is general agreement to the effect that agricultural prices in the E.E.C. must come down. Politically, this has found expression in a formula that combines a price decline with aids for farm modernisation. This is known in France, and elsewhere, as the *three-sector theory*. Some Ministers of Agriculture are trying to persuade producer organisations that there are nowadays three categories of agriculture, each to be treated in its own way:

(1) *Competitive agriculture* is composed of profitable farm enterprises, such as, say, farms of more than 100 ha. growing a variety of grain crops in the Paris region. With intensive farming methods, these can provide a living for a family at prices not all that far removed from those guaranteed to American farmers.

(2) At the other extreme, what is called *social agriculture* is composed of farms too small even to think of modernising them, and capable of surviving only as a subsidised group. The term 'social agriculture' is meant to imply that the farm families which form part of it should be subsidised *intuitu personae* by the nation, rather than kept on the brink of bankruptcy, with their heads just above water, by a general high-price policy. This may cover farms of less than 10, 15 or 25 ha., or even 50 ha. in regions where wages are high. There can be no question of earning enough by general or livestock farming to bring up a family in decent conditions, unless prices are kept artificially high throughout the E.E.C., which would be against the interests of 180 million inhabitants. There is no way out except for the government to subsidise these families until their children have learnt some other trade, and such members of the older generation as cannot be retrained become eligible for old-age pensions.

(3) The third category, *potentially viable agriculture*, is by far the most important and the hardest to deal with. It consists of farms that could be made to pay by means of an adequate modernisation policy. These may be general farming enterprises of, say, 20, 30, 50 or up to 100 ha. In the country around Paris it is a life's work for a farm family to try to buy up enough land in the neighbourhood to increase the holding from 50 to 100 ha.

It is the multiplicity of intermediary situations between competitive and social farming which has created most headaches for governments during the last fifteen years. Young farmers in France have got into debt by drawing heavily on agricultural credit facilities. But in spite of a price policy still on the whole very favourable to the producers, they cannot always manage to break even, and then they turn on the government and blame it for having encouraged them to modernise farms which, in the event, turned out to be less easy to make pay than was originally thought. There certainly are aids towards structural modernisation, which in some cases have proved too generous; they are dangerous for the people concerned and turn them into angry men.

The main point of these comments is that the problems of lowering costs and modernising farms, and also the food-processing industries and the marketing channels, have indeed been faced in the Common Market and occasionally tackled in some earnest. It was not originally expected that there would be so many and such large surpluses; thus the Common Agricultural Policy, Model 1, has now to be revised. 'Social' prices above world market prices become intolerable when they have to be paid throughout the Community for an increasing number of products at a time when technological progress should actually bring prices down.

For some years, then, a certain convergence of agricultural policies has been in evidence. It seems to be generally agreed that prices must be brought closer to a level which will more nearly balance supply and demand.

For forty years, the industrial countries' agricultural policy has been essentially aimed, under the deceptive slogan of market organisation, at keeping farmers quiet to the extent that Parliament needs their votes. Down to 1970, the Common Agricultural Policy has been able to do nothing but carry on as in the past. But it is not immutable.

II. EFFECTS ON INTRA-COMMUNITY TRADE

The discussion will be limited to one highly characteristic case, that of *French exports*. In France, the associations of agricultural producers had accepted the idea of a common policy for a variety of reasons, not all of them equally sound and including some that are a little disturbing if one thinks of the somewhat naïve underlying reasoning:

(*a*) Prices were expected to go up – for at the outset French prices as a whole did indeed look rather lower than the average of guaranteed prices in the other five countries.

(*b*) The Six taken together were net importers, which would facilitate intra-Community exports.

(*c*) French farms are generally larger than farms in the other member countries (18 ha. on an arithmetical average).

(*d*) There is a high potential for expanding output in France, which has half the E.E.C.'s farm land.

As things have turned out, the Common Market has created more problems for French farmers than it has solved.

(1) *Wheat* was a first relative disappointment. It has been thought that there would be enough French wheat to cover the Community's deficit in bread grains. But the millers of the five other countries went on importing from Argentina, Canada and the United States the strong wheats that nowadays have to go into the flour mixtures for industrial baking. In France, baking and milling are still largely artisan industries, lagging far behind developments elsewhere. In the course of time, however, the other member countries came to realise that the quality of certain varieties of French wheat was as good as any they could get locally for breadmaking, and intra-Community trade expanded. In the end it was wheat from the other countries, especially Germany, which was offered for sale to intervention agencies – a circumstance helped by speculation against the franc in 1968–9. French barley and maize, of which production has greatly expanded, have so far had no great difficulty in finding export markets within the Community.

(2) *Sugar beet* accounts for only 3 per cent of farm incomes in France. From 1931 on, production was regulated by bilateral monopoly agreements under the supervision of public authorities. Exports (at a loss) were limited because growers themselves had to meet 70 per cent of the cost of export subsidies, under the so-called sugar plan by which public funds were available only for limited amounts of surplus (about 20 per cent of domestic consumption). Moreover, French prices were the lowest in the Community, and so the common price was bound to be higher. French beet growers did in fact see their price go up by 35 per cent in two years. They are on the whole an efficient group of farmers, and it can easily be imagined how much profit they made out of so conspicuous a price rise. The discrepancies between farmers' incomes (per ha.) according to crops and regions, such as they now appear in the national accounts, have become so large as to constitute documentary condemnation of the allegedly social agricultural policy jointly sponsored by the government and producer organisations. In the case of French sugar beet, the price elasticity of supply is so high that the E.E.C. Commission could do nothing but recommend national production quotas. French growers acquiesced. At the French price, which was already twice or three times as high as the world market price, they could have supplied the whole Community, after building a few additional factories. The Commission had to persuade them to give up the idea of free trade. They have nothing to complain of.

To the extent, therefore, that French farmers grow cereals or sugar beet, and especially if they go in for large-scale farming, they gained greatly during the early years of the Common Market. But these crops together account for only 15 per cent of the gross product. Elsewhere developments were much less favourable.

(3) *Beef and veal.* Between 1960 and 1964, it looked as though France

was going to become an exporter of beef and veal. The first few years of the Common Market proved disillusioning in this respect. The Community's prices seem to be settling at a level about 20 per cent higher than those in Great Britain and the United States. In France, as everywhere on the coast of north-west Europe, farmers generally prefer to produce milk, which, at its present guaranteed price, yields a larger gross income for the farm family and gives employment to excess labour. Milking requires labour not required in meat farming. However, meat consumption has expanded very fast in Italy and other member countries. The E.E.C. has to import about 15 per cent of its requirements. But in France modern cattle farms do not pay. The marketing system is deplorable. An Italian steer is often a French calf fattened with maize imported from across the Atlantic. Admittedly, Italian veterinary legislation permits the use of hormones forbidden in France. And, under a special clause, maize is imported into Italy at lower prices than into France, where it costs livestock farmers twice as much as in the United States. Thus French livestock farmers, and their associates in the meat industry and the meat trade, proved less efficient than those in other member countries when they had an opportunity to expand their exports. A modern livestock farm may well earn no more than 3 or 4 per cent net profits. Production cost in France roughly equals the E.E.C. guaranteed price. This presupposes programmed marketing, a far cry from peasant habits. All profit melts away if an animal is kept a fortnight or a month too long at the farm because the farmer was not prepared to sell at the price offered by the dealer or current at the cattle fair. The small farmer has no clear notion of the amount of his 'profit', but a modern livestock farm cannot survive without it.

(4) *Pig meat* is not a product that France exports. On the contrary, it has been importing more and more of it since the unification of the market. As of 1967, Belgian and Dutch pig farmers were quick to take advantage of free trade. French production costs are high enough to prevent any expansion of output at the guaranteed price, which nevertheless seems to be good enough for competing pig breeders. French pig farmers have managed for ten years to get government approval for a market organisation such that it discourages efficient industrial pig farming in France, much to the benefit, at present, of other E.E.C. countries.

(5) Exports of *broilers* from Brittany to Germany have been declining year after year since the beginning of the Common Market. For supplying the markets of London, Hamburg or the Ruhr, the agricultural areas of western and south-western France will always be handicapped by higher transport costs than those of producers located near the ports and the waterways of the Rhine delta. Distance and backwardness together make costs so high that the product could be made competitive only by the farmers accepting lower earnings than is politically feasible at this stage.

Here, too, backwardness is attributable to the producer organisations concerned. In 1968, French poultry farmers again succeeded in obtaining from the government the introduction of a para-fiscal charge on the large poultry farms, which are the only efficient ones. Nor was this the first of the measures of this kind taken, in Brittany or elsewhere, in aid of the 'small producer'.

(6) But it is in *dairy products* that the inability of French farmers to export is most blatant. Dairy products provide a quarter of the farm family's income, its 'wage', and the only income that comes in regularly month after month. Before prices were unified, France had the most expensive butter and the cheapest milk of the Six. Inefficiency is common to all levels, and much of it is due to the wide dispersal and small size of dairy farms. Average yields per cow are only three-quarters of those in the Netherlands or Denmark. Milk collection per litre costs twice as much. The same applies to milk processing. France never had dairy surpluses until 1953; prices have been guaranteed since 1957, when the government started subsidising exports. Dutch dairy farmers have had the incentive of an opposite situation for more than half a century; they could survive only by exporting to unprotected markets. Dutch co-operatives can export butter at 6 francs per kg. At that price, the income elasticity of demand for butter on the part of private households is still reasonable. But the Common Market price is about 9 francs, a price barely sufficient for French farmers. Common Market stocks of surplus butter are approaching 500,000 tons for 1970, the equivalent of five-sixths of a year's world butter exports (of which three-quarters go to Great Britain). A good part of this butter is produced efficiently with feedgrains, soya or fish meal imported from Peru. This does not often happen in France, though yields here, as elsewhere, are increasing by 80 per cent thanks to the use of more nutritious fodder than natural pastures. So French agriculture contributes in its own, rather unprofitable, way to the creation of those surpluses that are exported at 1.50 francs per kg. It costs the E.E.C. 8 francs (including storage costs) to earn 1.50 francs in that way. A proposal to introduce a charge on soybeans is designed to raise the cost of milk production in modern dairy farms and so to cut down their profits – a surreptitious way of giving a little help to the less efficient pasture farmers. By raising the price of butter from 6 to 9 francs in the Netherlands, the E.E.C. regulation strengthened people's inclination to use margarine instead of butter, and that in a country where housewives are notoriously anxious to keep down their food expenses. When the consumption of margarine goes up, distribution costs diminish. Sometimes, too, the government keeps a close watch on the big firms that make margarine.

No wonder, then, that there was little chance of French butter exports to the rest of the Community expanding. The great hope was that it would prove possible to sell more fermented soft cheeses, but this would have needed a very good sales organisation. The French co-operatives have little experience in this field. What happened instead is that France became the world's biggest exporter of skim-milk powder, which means that proteins are exported at relatively low prices to the United States and to some of the countries of Eastern Europe.

The example of France is highly instructive. If one examined the situation in other countries one would reach much the same conclusion. The Common Agricultural Policy does not work in cases where a region's farm and food economy lags far behind the general development elsewhere.[1]

III. THE FUTURE OF NORTH AMERICAN EXPORTS TO THE E.E.C.

The creation of the European Economic Community caused many misgivings among the traditional exporters of one or the other of the six countries. This was particularly so in the case of countries that used to export to West Germany, which, by virtue of the size of its industrial population, will no doubt always remain one of the two main food-importing countries in Europe, the other being Great Britain.

The E.E.C.'s neighbours naturally stood to lose most as a result of the new policy. These are the Scandinavian, East European and Mediterranean countries – including, to name but a few, Denmark, Hungary, Roumania, Greece, Turkey, Spain and Algeria. They export pigs, dairy products, grains, fruit, vegetables, oilseeds, tobacco, citrus fruit and grapes. By and large those are the same products that Western Europe produces, and exporters do not always have the comparative advantage. It is open to these countries to negotiate with E.E.C. with a view to obtaining 'associated' status, but under GATT rules it is difficult to create preferential zones.

However, the problems that generated most heat were not those facing this group of European countries, individually or collectively. Troublesome negotiations started with the *United States*. The creation of the E.E.C. had attracted large amounts of capital to Europe, to the detriment of the United States balance of payments. The Federal authorities had decided to champion a frankly expansionist trade policy, in the hope that an appreciable improvement of the United States trade balance with the Six would, in the short run, offset the heavy outflow of capital for invest-

---

[1] One reservation should be made at this point. The traditional agricultural exports of France do not need the E.E.C. They are essentially luxury products, like fine wines, cognac, champagne, Roquefort and similar cheeses. They are the fruits of centuries of agricultural civilisation. But their supply is rather inelastic. Exports are more likely to increase in value than in volume. The classical example is the contrast between cognac and whisky. The great wines, in particular, are associated with named plots of land, the qualities of which have in many cases been known and appreciated for a century or more, but the area of which cannot be increased.

ment abroad and particularly in the E.E.C. In October 1962, Congress passed the Trade Expansion Act, and this led to the general round of tariff negotiations (covering both industrial and agricultural products) which opened at Geneva in May 1964. The idea was to arrive at a multilateral reduction of tariffs and other forms of protection. These negotiations have often been spoken of as involving only two partners, the United States and the E.E.C. This is juridically inaccurate, since all the contracting parties of GATT were involved; but in practice the United States and the E.E.C. were the chief protagonists. If indeed the E.E.C. was the main beneficiary of the deterioration in the United States financial position, it was a matter of pressing concern to the latter to improve their balance of payments as quickly as possible. Those responsible for United States commercial policy declared the progressive establishment of the Common Agricultural Policy to be *an unsurmountable obstacle* not only to the expansion of agricultural trade between the United States and the E.E.C., but even to the continuance of United States 'traditional' exports. The Kennedy Round quickly took a dramatic turn. The Americans were defending their 'historical' outlets and putting forward claims for access to the market of the Six to be kept open or widened.[1] The others replied that it was absurd to negotiate about the obstacles set up at the frontiers to the entry of agricultural products so long as the exporting countries were free to give their own farmers whatever support they chose. It so happens that under the Common Agricultural Policy the level of protection for the major commodities is equivalent to the support level, thanks to the mechanism of import levies and export rebates – a system simple at least in principle. The E.E.C. was proposing to negotiate that level of protection.[2] But ultimately the E.E.C. felt that the claims of Washington had to be rejected. The negotiations ended in failure. All that came out of them was a new cereals arrangement and a food aid programme in cereals.

But this 'failure' was of no importance either for the United States or for the E.E.C., for the simple reason that the negotiations were in practice pointless. This, at any rate, was the view of those who had taken the trouble to think for a moment what course the E.E.C.'s imports must inevitably take.

The United States was bound to expand its exports to the E.E.C. for three reasons:

(1) The disappearance of quantitative restrictions (quotas, obligatory admixtures of domestic products, state trading, abusive administrative regulations). It would once again become possible to export to any particular member country thanks to *the quality of the product*, a chance

---

[1] Requests were even made that guarantees should be given as to the quantities of American agricultural products that the E.E.C. would continue to import.

[2] This would have given the civil servants of Brussels the opportunity to underline for the benefit of public opinion in the E.E.C. the level of support received by agriculture.

that had been slim ever since 1929. This would happen, for instance, in the case of the best bread grains, the best oilcakes, and the various feed-grains. Together with cotton fibre and tobacco, this group of products alone makes up 90 per cent of E.E.C. imports from the United States.

The unified system of protection by import levies must not be seen just as a set of prohibitive tariffs subject to weekly adjustments. The system has no such inexorable aspects. What the E.E.C. does guarantee its farmers is priority for the sale of Community products. The farmer can count on getting at least the intervention price (which lies between 2 and 10 per cent below the target price), whereas imported products cannot, in practice, reach the Community market at any price lower than the target price because of the import levy, which makes up the difference from the world market price. At equal quality, therefore, there never is a big gap between the price of the imported and the local product. And the buyer is always free to buy abroad if he prefers to, and need no longer make do with the E.E.C. product if he does not like its quality.

(2) The North American and the E.E.C. food economies have become *complementary* to a high degree. The E.E.C., like the rest of the world, is short of proteins, but can afford to buy them. There are surpluses of carbohydrates and fats everywhere, but proteins are in relatively short supply. Soybean cake is the main product nowadays, and the oil provides merely a bit of extra income. Butter has ceased to be the prized yield of milk, and has become its principal by-product. The fats are an inconvenience; it is the protein content of milk that is wanted. Among cereals, the protein-rich grains are preferred. In developing its output of animal products, the E.E.C. was bound to develop its fodder industry, on the basis of soybean cake and sorghum, which the E.E.C. does not produce, and of maize, of which it does not produce enough. As regards bread grains, it became clear as of 1964 that French wheat surpluses were not much better in quality than those elsewhere in the Community (what is called E.E.C. standard wheat). So there could be no question of self-sufficiency, since industrial bakeries, in Germany and elsewhere, need flour with an admixture of strong wheats such as are not grown in Western Europe. Under the impact of consumption changes in Europe, therefore, the technical complementarity between agriculture in North America and the E.E.C. has become very marked during the last twenty years or so, and should soon become even more marked with the development of new cattle-feeding techniques. This phenomenon is a fundamental one. It was in the United States, from 1940 on, that the headlong pace of technological advance in farming began. Europe depends on the United States for its hybrid maize seeds (at least for the time being), for selected breeds of broilers and laying hens which make it possible to transform compound feeds at a competitive level into eggs and poultry for meat. Europe uses United States veterinary products, adopts many of the United States

techniques of agriculture without soil and without farmers, not to speak of the techniques and patents of the United States food industries. Finally, Europe's modernisation of marketing methods and promotion of new products are based on techniques tried out in the United States and, often enough, financed by United States capital. All this must have been known in 1964.

(3) Last but not least, the E.E.C. as a group has had *a high rate of economic growth*, which has meant the prospect of a high propensity to import the foods (or their agricultural components) associated with a standard of living approaching that of the United States. It was important not to forget the essential lesson of the monetary and tariff wars of the 1930s. Whatever the outcome of the Geneva negotiations, United States exports to the Common Market were going to expand first and foremost in response to the E.E.C.'s import needs. And food consumption in the E.E.C. was going to be determined by the E.E.C.'s rate of industrial growth. Inevitably people in the Community were more and more going to adopt American food habits. The consumption of meat (broilers, barley beef, lean pork), of fruits and vegetables (fresh or canned), of fresh cheese, fruit juice and various convenience foods was going to expand very fast in Western Europe, which itself was in many cases ill prepared to meet this new demand from its own resources.

Have the facts proved this optimistic analysis correct? To answer this question we must look separately at each of the major European imports from the United States and see how they have fared.

(*a*) *Soybeans and soybean cake*, and other oils and oilseeds, have met the forecast precisely. They now account for 30 per cent of the E.E.C.'s agricultural imports from the United States, and the volume of imports is still growing. Import statistics distinguish between oilseeds and oilcake, but the same applies to both. E.E.C. imports of oilcake from the United States rose from $7 million to $167 million in the eight years between 1958 and 1966, a twenty-five-fold increase. The reason is that soybean cake is the perfect answer for the fodder industry, which prefers simple rations. Qualitatively, the only comparable product is groundnut cake, but soybean cake has the advantage of an appreciably higher content of amino-acids. At prices not far apart, soybean cake is preferable because oilcakes with the highest and most balanced protein content are the most economical in use. This applies equally to feed for poultry, pigs and dairy cows. Before the establishment of the E.E.C., oilseed imports into France were subject to a permit by a semi-public agency, which gave priority to groundnuts from Senegal and the (small) French crops of rape and sunflower seeds. Thus the United States, which has a virtual monopoly in the export of soybeans and soybean cake, had the double advantage of rapid demand expansion and of the disappearance of quantitative protection in one of the E.E.C. countries. In 1966, soybeans from the United States accounted for more than half the volume of all oilseeds purchased by the E.E.C. For the United States, which exports about 40 per cent of its output (beans and cake), the E.E.C. has become the chief foreign buyer.

(*b*) *Sorghum* is another simple example of the technical complementarity of the two food economies concerned. As poultry and cattle feed, it has a higher nutritive value than barley and wheat. The advantage is confirmed by the calorie cost of sorghum, which, in poultry and cattle feed, is lower than any other except that of maize. The Community produces no sorghum, and the United States has become its principal supplier, accounting for more than three-quarters of E.E.C. imports.

(*c*) *Maize* occupies more cultivated area in the United States than any other crop. Annual production of it is more than 100 million tons, compared with 35 million tons of wheat, 15 million of sorghum and 25 million of soybeans; the proportion of the crop exported is, respectively, 15, 16, 20 and 40 per cent. The United States is the world's biggest maize producer, and the country best able to sell very large quantities on the world market. In the E.E.C., maize is grown only in Italy and France. In France, production doubled between 1960–4 and 1968 to reach 5 million tons, or one-twentieth of United States production. It cannot in the long run expand at the same pace as demand. The same applied to Italian maize production, which is of the same order of magnitude. Over the same period, United States maize shipments to the E.E.C. increased spectacularly from 1 million tons in 1958 to 6·5 million in 1966 (out of a total of 10·3 million tons imported by the E.E.C. in the same year). The future of American maize in the E.E.C. seems assured, since maize is the cheapest energy food in livestock farming. Its excess fat content can be readily offset by the easy process of mixing it with sorghum, barley or wheat. It should be added that under a special abrogation a lower import levy is charged in Italy, where the production of 'vitelloni' and 'baby beef' has been greatly developed on the basis of calves bought from France and imported maize.

The sum of coarse grain imports and bread grain imports (one-seventh of the total) accounts for 40 per cent of E.E.C. agricultural imports from the United States. In 1966, the Community imported from non-members $4,840 million worth of products subject to Common Market regulations; the bill for fats and oils was $1,515 million, and that for grains $1,345 million.[1] The bulk of this total came from the United States. But some uncertainties nevertheless do surround the future. United States grain exports to the Community seem to have reached their ceiling, or even to have declined since 1967. Guaranteed prices (and production costs) for grains seem to be higher in the United States than in Canada and the Argentine. Italy is going to import something like 5 million tons of maize

[1] The corresponding import figures for 1960–1 were $3,300 million, $1,000 million and $900 million.

in 1969 (five times as much as Germany), but largely from the Argentine and South Africa. And here we come to a world problem – the glut of wheat since 1968.

(d) *Wheat.* Even at the time of the creation of the European Economic Community, member countries produced almost enough soft wheat to meet E.E.C. demand for human and animal consumption. In terms of volume, soft wheat accounts for roughly half the total grain production of the Six. It soon became clear that there would be surpluses to export at a loss. Wheat prices were guaranteed at fairly high levels in each of the member countries before the E.E.C. was set up. In the country that produces most wheat, France, prices went up by 7 per cent. Even though E.E.C. prices are relatively high for wheat in comparison with other grains, there seems to be no danger of any increase in wheat acreage. But yields per hectare keep growing. Since 1967, the world wheat market has been in a state of collapse, and the same applies, by reflex, to other grains, in spite of the new International Grains Arrangement of 1968. Certain import markets have disappeared. The East has had good harvests. Unit yields seem to have increased in India and Pakistan, as they have been doing in the United States for the last thirty, and in Europe for the last fifteen years.

Pending a constructive solution, wheat of poorer quality is being denatured in the E.E.C. in mounting quantities. It looks as though in ten years denatured quantities will have doubled from 1 to 2 million tons out of a total annual surplus of 7 million tons. The E.E.C. finds it even harder to export its surpluses than does the United States, because qualities are poorer and less varied. In July 1969 there were large stocks everywhere that could not be exported at the minimum price of the Wheat Convention. The United States complains of a decline of wheat sales to the E.E.C., but actually it is American coarse grain exports, which had flourished during the last ten years, which are in most danger of stagnation or decline. Animals can take a certain amount of wheat instead of sorghum, barley or maize, if only the E.E.C.'s own denatured wheat is cheap enough. The feed manufacturers use a computer, and every week they work out in the light of seasonal price changes (and biological needs) what product-mix is cheapest for the given rate of animal growth. In any event, the relative price of wheat with reference to the price of other grains will have to be lowered. For forty years wheat producers everywhere have enjoyed relatively better guaranteed prices than other grain growers, just because at the outset their vote carried more weight (especially in France and Italy).[1]

[1] Degree of self-sufficiency for cereals in the E.E.C.:

	1957–60	1964–7
Wheat	93·0	103·9
Other cereals (barley, oats, maize, rye, etc.)	77·7	72·5
Total of cereals (excluding rice)	84·5	84·9

In the case of animal products, conclusions are less straightforward. It must be remembered that it is impossible to export both the final products (pigs, chickens, beef, dairy products) and the animal feed that is an input in their production.

(*e*) *Broilers.* The Community's imports of poultry meat (95 per cent of which go to Germany) increased rapidly from $3 million to $52 million between 1958 and 1962. Then there was a sharp drop to $21 million in 1966. In 1961, Germany completely abolished its quantitative import restrictions, but at the end of 1962 the E.E.C. levy on the so-called transformation products of cereals came into effect. At that time, European poultry breeders, and more especially those in the Netherlands, were adopting American techniques of industrial production, as it was inevitable that they should do. European imports of maize, sorghum and soybeans increased, while those of chickens declined. It should be added that in the case of the 'transformation products' the import levy contains a fixed element which amounts to a duty on value added in the 'manufacture' of the broiler. This duty is high and, to this extent, the E.E.C. is protectionist. Why? When the duty was fixed, in 1962, the cost of transforming grain into broilers was still much higher in Europe than in the United States and insufficient allowance was made for the fact that this cost was coming down rapidly. The protective duty is based on the production cost of old-style broilers. Among others, French farmers seem to have favoured this high duty in order to encourage the rapid spread of the new techniques (infant industry protectionism), but it was the Dutch farmers who took advantage of it to best effect. The new techniques are, in fact, quite independent of any natural resource endowment so far as supplies to the E.E.C. markets are concerned. The most modern broiler factory is in West Berlin.

(*f*) *Other meat.* Is it to be concluded that E.E.C. imports of meat from the United States must inevitably and continuously decline? Certainly not. Taking animal products as a whole, the E.E.C.'s net import requirements keep growing. The United States on the average exports about half the E.E.C.'s extra-Community purchases, and is by far its biggest supplier of carcass meat. France has since 1963 become the chief buyer of United States meat, after the abolition of import quotas on carcass meat from the dollar area. The E.E.C. as a whole is likely to remain dependent on non-member countries for many years for the coverage of its overall requirements of beef and veal. The United States could furnish some of these imports directly[1] or could find in them a source of a further expansion of their maize and soybean exports. As regards pig meat, on the other hand, the situation seems to be developing rather more on the lines of the poultry market. Since European farmers have discovered the new tech-

---

[1] By using large-capacity cargo planes for high-priced products such as liver, tongue, brains, fillet, etc.

niques of intensive production, they tend increasingly to take care themselves of the transformation of home-produced or imported vegetable proteins into animal proteins.

(*g*) E.E.C. imports of United States *canned fruit in syrup* (pineapples, peaches, mixed fruit, etc.) have been rising steadily since 1958. Germany is the chief buyer, accounting for 70 per cent of the annual value of Community imports of canned fruit and vegetables from the United States. Germany's imports from member countries, on the other hand, consist mostly of vegetables (tomatoes, beans, peas) and tomato juice. The Benelux countries mostly import canned fruit from the United States. Import quotas for canned fruit were abolished in 1968 by all member countries except France and Germany, but the German quota is very large. Thus trade with the United States has not been disturbed. In the medium run, the United States has enough technical lead for the abolition of quotas to raise their exports. A great effort has been made in the field of plant breeding so as to select such varieties of fruits and vegetables as lend themselves to mechanised handling. The technological lag of Italy and France keeps production cost in these countries high and confers upon the sale of fruit and vegetables to canneries a residual character further aggravated by the lack of concentration in the industry. American capital is the answer, provided the local farmers accept it. It should be added that the Community produces neither pineapples nor grapefruit, and that for canning purposes the different variety of Italian oranges can hardly compete for colour and price with those of Florida. There are many reasons, therefore, to conclude that United States exports of canned fruit and fruit juice to the Community are very likely to expand.

(*h*) *Tobacco*. The Treaty of Rome provided for modifications in the French and Italian State monopolies in the manufacture and distribution of tobacco and cigarettes. It is to be expected that this will lead to an appreciable increase in the European consumption of American-type cigarettes. It will also lead to the abolition of quantitative import restrictions, and to the establishment of European branches by the great tobacco manufactures. Competition among European brands will become keener, and the income share spent on tobacco will increase. New smokers have no fixed taste. Freed of administrative restrictions, manufacturers will be induced to buy more light tobacco. Given the very varied range of tobaccos produced in America, and especially the homogeneity and quality of flue-cured, burley and Kentucky types of tobacco, the liberal nature of the E.E.C. regulation as regards sources of supply is bound to be favourable to United States exports to the Community. Indirectly, the United States balance of payments should, in addition, benefit from French tobacco purchases in Latin America. Italy, it is true, already produces enough to meet half its domestic demand. But American firms have proved heretofore how successful their sales promotion can be in continental Europe. Swiss smokers have already rallied to the American taste. The Germans are about to do so, and are turning away from the consumption of Near East tobaccos. The procedure is as follows: an American firm with a world name grants a manufacturing licence to a European firm; as soon as half that firm's output consists of American-type products, it is asked to accept equity capital from the American sponsor, which is hard to refuse lest the licence which keeps the European firm going be withdrawn.

(*j*) In the case of *cotton*, it would seem that the application of the common external tariff as the sole means of protection for European producers of textile fibres should have no appreciable effect, given the liberal nature of the preceding national regulations.

The above survey covers the problems associated with more than 90 per cent of United States agricultural exports to Europe. These exports are complementary to the E.E.C.'s agricultural production. They are indispensable for the expansion of animal husbandry (soybeans, coarse grains) or capable of competing successfully, thanks to a number of technical or commercial advantages (canned fruit, tobacco). What more is there to be hoped for?

In many cases the situation has changed very greatly since the application of the Common Agricultural Policy. It may be recalled that the six countries of the Common Market used to adjust their grain imports on the basis of domestic production, each by its own regulations. There were different systems, like the system of import certificates in Germany, or of compulsory admixtures in the Netherlands. Now, all these specific regulations have been abolished. The mechanism of import levies is very flexible; it allows any products produced outside the E.E.C., and qualitatively superior to those produced by member countries, to be imported for reasons either of a technical nature (wheat) or of an economic one (coarse grains, canned fruit and vegetables, tobacco, cotton, soybeans). In other words, it may be said that the Common Agricultural Policy establishes a very acceptable framework for international competition by making a distinction, on the one hand, between a liberal market of full competition, which is proving favourable to the United States (canned fruit, oilseeds, tobacco), and, on the other hand, a market of potential competition on the basis of quality (grains, certain animal products).

IV. THE REAL PROBLEMS

It has been shown in some detail why the United States has nothing to complain of in the development of its agricultural exports to the European Economic Community. These exports doubled between 1958–9 and 1966, while the corresponding exports of the rest of the world expanded by less than 50 per cent.[1]

The real problems lie elsewhere. They are three:

(1) The phase of accelerated technological progress, which began in the 1940s, seems to be coming to an end in the United States while it is still at its height in Europe and merely at its beginning elsewhere in the world, including the developing countries.
(2) It is hard successfully to negotiate international agreements such as have been proposed to soften the impact of the sudden emergence of new surpluses on the stability of commercial flows. Things are not made any easier by existing differences in the approach to commercial problems, especially as between the United States and the E.E.C. These differences are due in particular to the cumbersomeness and rigidity of the governmental and legislative machinery involved.
(3) Last but not least, the political intention of the advanced economies to get rid of traditional agriculture has reached actual application only in a very few countries so far.

(1) *The Phase of Accelerated Technological Progress*

The United States complains that its exports to the E.E.C. have become static since 1967, or indeed are in decline. A matter of much more concern to America, in fact, is the expansion of E.E.C. exports to non-member countries, which exports rose from $1,900 million to $2,900 million between 1958 and 1966. The E.E.C. has become a rival of the United States in certain export markets (especially for wheat), because E.E.C. yields per hectare nowadays sometimes increase by 7 per cent annually, as they did in the United States ten or fifteen years earlier.

The pace of technological progress began to speed up in the 1940s, and worked its full effect in the 1950s. However, for a long time prices remained relatively high. There were no great problems for exports: the German miracle, the Italian miracle, and then the creation of the European Economic Community. But since the years 1955–60 unit yields and, generally speaking, the productivity of agro-business have been rising fast in all the industrialised countries of the temperate zone.

In spite of a considerable decrease in the agricultural labour force, production is increasing faster than domestic consumption – by 4 per cent as against 1 per cent – hence the appearance of surpluses termed structural. To be sure, they are due to the general support of agriculture in industrial countries. This applies as much in Switzerland, Sweden and Great Britain as in the E.E.C. and the United States. But support is relatively weaker in the United States. It has been said that agricultural support in the E.E.C.

[1] E.E.C. agricultural imports (in million dollars) rose from 7,350 to 11,200; imports from the United States alone increased from 900 to about 1,900, which leaves an increase from 6,450 to 9,300 for agricultural imports from the rest of the world.

costs $14,000 million out of an annual gross national product of $400,000 million. In France, the annual cost to the nation of one of its farmers is estimated to be $2,000. In the United States, support seems to have reached its peak around 1960. This was also the time when new institutes were set up in several industrial countries for the sales promotion of new American agricultural products, such as the Poultry Institute at Frankfurt, and soybean institutes elsewhere.

Today, the E.E.C. countries are still in a phase of very rapid productivity increase. Surpluses pile up, and the system of export rebates is used in an attempt to sell them abroad. These rebates are treated by the United States Administration like export subsidies. The optimists are waiting for the moment when things will go in the E.E.C. as they have been going for seven or eight years in the United States. The problem of lowering the guaranteed prices is with us. The E.E.C. is inevitably entering a second phase in its price policy. After merely harmonising the former national prices, the E.E.C. will now have to align its own prices to those of the world market, lest it remain stuck with an underdeveloped, high-cost agriculture. Some day, prices will have to follow the downward trend of the production costs of farmers of average efficiency. The most sanguine optimists add that the Community has less cultivable land per inhabitant than the United States, and that, in time, it is bound to adopt a somewhat more 'industrial' (secondary and tertiary) economic orientation than in the past. The problem therefore is how to reconcile the conflicting interests of exporters during the next ten years or so.

(2) *Difficulties of Negotiation*

Officials whose business it is to work out solutions for this conflict complain of two things. It is difficult to come to any agreement with the United States Administration, which is often hamstrung by Congress decisions. It is also difficult to get the Community's Council of Ministers to take such constructive decisions as might, in some cases, have been obtainable from national governments. Two examples may illustrate the point.

(*a*) In 1968, the United States introduced a countervailing duty on tomato preserves from Italy and France, to offset the rebate paid by the E.E.C. on exports. But this does nothing to protect the American market. The only result is to make it easier for Spanish and Portuguese preserves to be sold in the United States. This was not the intention of the United States Administration, but it was obliged by law to take this step, since there was, after all, a rebate and it had to be treated like a subsidy. What the officials of a number of countries want is a system by which representatives of the government departments concerned get together and agree on a minimum import price for particular foreign products in any given country. This has been done for imports of Emmenthal cheese into

Switzerland. Could it not be done for tomato paste in the United States? Here again we find the same attitude of the technocrats in Brussels at the time of the Kennedy Round.

(b) The Brussels Commission complains that the Council of Ministers no longer has the courage to take any decisions. It said as much in the introduction to its Annual Report in December 1968. More bluntly, the officials say: 'You've got to slip some money into everyone's pocket before taking a decision.' What this means is that Community policy makes progress only via horse-trading at ministerial level. The Ministers don't settle problems, they make mutual concessions to each other. If one of them has to go home and admit that he has had to give way on one point, the important thing is for him to be able to announce that, in exchange, he has secured a far bigger advantage. In 1969, for instance, negotiations on the important problem of reducing dairy surpluses and expanding beef production have run into an impasse. The idea is to replace milk production by meat production. But this problem involves 40 per cent of farm incomes. The same problem arose in Switzerland in 1968. Butter surpluses per head of the population had become very large (larger than in the E.E.C.); the Federal Government managed to reduce them within a year, by the method of calling a meeting of the farmers' organisations and consumer co-operatives concerned and notifying them that in future they would themselves have to foot the bill for surplus disposal. It is hard to say whether a major advance towards political unification in the E.E.C. might soon make it possible to take such decisions. It is not easy to imagine Dutch dairy co-operatives or poultry breeders getting the Community's political authorities to levy a surplus disposal charge which might get their French competitors into difficulties, or else French wheat or sugar-beet growers getting official prices fixed at a level which might cut deeply into the often low enough net income of wheat and sugar producers in other countries.

(3) *Getting Rid of Traditional Agriculture*

Sometimes one country presents others with what appears to be the model of what they should do. What happened in Japan a century ago, after 1867, has for fifteen years been regarded as the pattern of an efficient policy for economic development. As far as agriculture is concerned, what we lack is not analyses of what should be done, but governments willing to do it. During the past ten years, all eyes have turned to Sweden, where the government was evidently more firmly determined to tackle the difficult task. It has been said that in Sweden, agricultural policy was better integrated with general economic policy than elsewhere, that Swedish co-operatives were used to better purpose, that the Swedish Government had the courage to tell the producer monopolies that it would go as far, or nearly as far, as autarky for farm products, if the farmers insisted, but not one step further. It would not call on the taxpayers to subsidise the disposal of unsaleable surpluses. This attitude has been simplified to the point of caricature by saying: 'Grow strawberries and tomatoes in the Arctic Circle if you like, but don't ask for taxes on our workers so that you can export your strawberries and tomatoes at a loss.' The curiosity and admiration of Western European 'experts' became stronger after the announcement of the 1966 'plan'. Today this is talked of as a Mansholt Plan before the event: 'Sweden is preparing the way for its entry into the Common Market.' As elsewhere, structure policy in Sweden aims at enlarging the size of farms, improving the training of farmers, diminishing their number, etc. But its great contribution is that it proves it to be politically possible for the government of an industrial country in full expansion to get its voters to accept the following points against the protests of some farmers:

(a) The degree of the country's self-sufficiency in food will deliberately be reduced within a few years from 95 to 80 per cent, so as to regain some of the benefits of the international division of labour.[1]

(b) The agricultural population will be reduced by two-thirds in fifteen years, and so brought down to 3 per cent of the working population, which will be enough to feed the country for four days out of five.

(c) The government will not bear the full cost of restructuring farms. If change is justified, it will be helped by credits, which are a better incentive than subsidies. And as regards any costly transformation of farms, the private banks will finance it if it can be proved to be profitable; there is no need of public funds.

Even now no Swedish farmer produces anything without prior agreement with the agency that sells his output and shares the risk with him. This attitude encourages the banks to give credit.

Thus the Swedish example is crucial and encouraging after the catalogue of so many 'social' constraints which farmers everywhere have invoked for forty years in order to obtain the crutches which have enabled them to limp along well behind in the national economy. It has been proved that agricultural policy can make a new start, if only public opinion has become aware that this is necessary. It is in this sense that the Mansholt Report of December 1968 is, in its turn, an act of courage.

[1] A degree of 80 per cent self-sufficiency in food was the case in Germany and France in 1939.

15 The Mutual Impact of North American and Western European Agricultural Policies

John Ashton
UNIVERSITY OF NEWCASTLE UPON TYNE

I. NATIONAL POLICIES

Since the 1930s, national policies for domestic agriculture have been such as to exert a major influence on agricultural production and trade in and between countries of North America and Western Europe. These policies have been, in a broad sense, support policies, protecting home producers from foreign competition and generally encouraging the expansion of domestic production. Although there has been considerable similarity in the domestic objectives underlying these policies, the levels of protection, the extent of coverage and the administrative devices employed have varied both from country to country and, within countries, over periods of time. In contrast with the similarity of domestic objectives the two regions have developed a wide gap in their underlying approaches, in other words in their 'philosophies', towards trade policy. This has increased the problems of harmonising national support policies and thereby reducing any adverse impact on the development of international trade.

As a starting point in the discussion, the main characteristics of policies in the countries principally concerned are discussed below. A preliminary *caveat* should, however, be entered. Although agricultural trade between North America and Western Europe represents a very substantial proportion of world trade in temperate products, its significance extends beyond these regions. The way in which the agricultural policies of North America and Western Europe impinge upon other nations, including both less developed countries and Commonwealth countries exporting temperate-zone products, is not discussed in this paper. Nevertheless the importance of this aspect needs to be emphasised.

(1) *The United States of America*

Since the Reciprocal Trade Agreements Act of 1934, the policy of successive American administrations has in principle been towards expanded and freer world trade. Implementation has, however, been hindered by protectionist pressures within the United States. These pressures have caused Congress to limit to a varying degree the President's power to negotiate in the trade field and to insist on safeguards for domestic agriculture, as well as for other sectors. Nevertheless, through bilateral and multilateral negotation over the past thirty years, culminating in the Kennedy Round, the United States has conceded substantial reductions in its tariffs especially on industrial items. These are estimated to have declined from an average of 50 per cent in 1931–5 to about 8 per cent following the Kennedy Round.[1]

For agriculture, since the 1930s, there has been a system of comprehensive price-support measures for a wide range of products. These measures have stimulated great increases in production which have encouraged innovation and continuing technological advance. The new technology itself has also greatly contributed to increases in output. In turn this situation has created some marketing problems and, on occasion, has given rise to considerable surpluses of particular commodities. Generally, such supplies in excess of the requirements for commercial outlets have been channelled to less developed and needy countries on a variety of concessionary terms.[2] The United States has endeavoured, by consultation with interested countries, to ensure that these less-than-fully commercial transactions do not disrupt the markets for its competitors selling the same products on commercial terms. The United States has also, especially in recent years, restricted domestic production where surpluses were troublesome. This has been mainly implemented by compensatory payments for exclusion of acreage from specific crops. Yield increases, resulting from better technology, have done much to offset such efforts. Besides inducing increased production, the relatively high domestic prices, resulting from the support system, have attracted imports of some products. Action has been taken to restrict such competition from imports, notably in the case of dairy products, where a waiver from GATT obligations has been maintained since the mid-1950s. This move has aroused criticism by countries such as Denmark, New Zealand and Australia.

Following the Second World War, the United States had taken the lead in advocating international co-operation aimed at expanded and freer trade. This policy and the importance of its agricultural export trade to Europe made protectionist policies in that region a matter of concern to the United States. The Common Agricultural Policy (C.A.P.) of the E.E.C. which emerged in the early 1960s reinforced the protectionist effect of existing policies of member countries. In effect, it reserved the E.E.C.

[1] Based on data in V. Galbraith, *The General Agreement on Tariffs and Trade*, chap. 44, Table 44:1, 'Foreign Agricultural Trade', ed. R. L. Tontz, and on estimated reductions effected under the Kennedy Round.

[2] 'A clear distinction between concessional sales, export dumping and food aid is a hopeless task ... concessional grants and sales constitute about a fourth of total U.S. exports since 1955'. Agricultural Economics Report No. 33, July 1967, Department of Agricultural Economics, Michigan State University.

home market for domestic producers using import levies to protect the internal price structure. Apart from any restrictive effect on imports, this policy encouraged expanded home production.

These developments led the United States and other exporting countries to press, during the Kennedy Round, for a modification of the C.A.P. and for greater harmony in national agricultural policies so as to encourage international trade on a basis of efficient use of resources. The Kennedy Round largely failed on the agricultural side. Since then, the United States has shown some signs of adopting a tougher line, involving more aggressive marketing and the enforcement on its competitors of their fair trading commitments.[1] In some cases there has been a move towards market management, as in the voluntary control by the principal suppliers of their exports of certain classes of meat to the United States market. Such arrangements are a compromise between open access on the one hand and import restrictions on the other. This development indicates the recognition given in the United States to the wider aspects of its trading policies. Currently the United States is re-examining its trade policies in the light of the Kennedy Round and agriculture is an important element in this re-examination.

(2) *Canada*

Canada's agricultural policies aim at assuring adequate farm incomes and at assuring supplies for domestic and export markets. Various programmes are used in an attempt to achieve these goals. They include deficiency payments and offer-to-purchase schemes on a number of commodities as well as the promotion of more orderly marketing by government and producer marketing boards, agricultural credit programmes and various types of grants to foster resource adjustment within the industry. Some products, notably grains and dairy products, are subject to import permits. About one-half of agricultural imports move into Canada duty-free; duties on the remainder averaged about 8 per cent in 1966. Also, some subsidies have been paid on dairy exports.

Because of the importance of the United Kingdom market, the system of special preferences between Commonwealth countries, stemming principally from the Ottawa Conference of 1932, continues to have importance for Canada. In the agricultural as well as the industrial field, trade relations with the United States are increasing in importance and the Kennedy Round strengthened this relationship. Broadly, in its approach to the conduct of international trade, Canada is greatly influenced by its degree of dependence upon the competitive export of agricultural products.

[1] H. L. Worthington, address given at a conference sponsored by North Carolina State University, 27 Jan 1969.

(3) The European Economic Community

Individual policies of the member countries of the E.E.C. are now being replaced by the Common Agricultural Policy. The individual policies had incorporated a major degree of support for agriculture, and production was expanding prior to the formation of the E.E.C. In broad terms, the aim of the C.A.P., is to establish a common market for the various products, with government intervention where necessary to support prices, and with levies on imports to prevent the undermining of the resulting price levels. Surpluses, where existent, are exported with the aid of subsidies. The costs of the system are met from the proceeds of the import levies, augmented by subventions from the member governments. In addition to the price-support system the policy has other major aims, such as the reorganisation of the highly unfavourable farm structure, the improvement of markets and provision of better credit facilities.

The degree to which individual member countries satisfy their respective requirements for various agricultural products differs between products and between countries. For the Community as a whole, however, with the major exception of beef and fats and oils, the level of self-sufficiency is high and appears to be increasng. Furthermore, the trade increases which have taken place within the E.E.C. are evidence that the policy is operating to give strong preference to suppliers within other member states.

Although some regional specialisation in production may gradually emerge, the policy does not even purport to aim at optimum allocation of world resources, notwithstanding the clause in the Treaty of Rome that provides for encouragement of world trade. The E.E.C. has in fact proposed that the rationale of its system become the basis of world-wide arrangements for agricultural trade. Domestic producers in all countries would be protected by a system of world reference prices below which exports would not be sold. Quantities which could not be absorbed commercially at these prices would be disposed of, as best as might be, to needy or underdeveloped countries. These proposals were rejected during the Kennedy Round by the United States and other exporting countries on the grounds, *inter alia*, that the level of prices suggested would not make a contribution to expanding world trade or to restoring equilibrium to markets already distorted by conflicting intervention by importing and exporting countries.

(4) The United Kingdom

Before the Second World War, there was little direct financial support for agriculture and the country depended upon imports for about half of its requirements of temperate-zone agricultural products. During the war, food prices were controlled and prices to farmers were raised to stimulate increased domestic production. In the post-war period fixed prices and guaranteed outlets were continued until the mid-1950s when the government relinquished control of food supplies with the easing of the international supply position. At this stage, a system of guaranteed farm prices was introduced which was implemented through payment of the deficiency between the open-market price and the guaranteed price of farm products.

The combination of price guarantees and technological advances had led to greatly expanded domestic production of foodstuffs. The introduction of the deficiency payments system, however, allowed imports to compete freely and to set the market price to the consumer. Food prices in the United Kingdom have remained relatively low by standards in the rest of Europe. With increasing supplies from the mid-1950s onwards, there has been a tendency for government support to be tapered off, to become more selective and to be restricted to specified quantities of production. More recently, however, recurrent balance of payments crises have reinforced requests from the producers for continued and increased support, on the grounds of need for import-saving.

Supplies of agricultural products from domestic production now account for two-thirds of total requirements of temperate-zone products, and one-half of all food requirements, i.e. including tropical products. Periodic over-supply on the United Kingdom market for a number of products has led to depressed prices with complaints both from overseas and domestic suppliers, and with the need for increased United Kingdom Treasury subsidies. For a number of commodities, notably wheat, bacon and butter, the United Kingdom has moved towards market regulation and sharing, with provision for minimum import prices or import levies to prevent United Kingdom market prices falling to unduly low levels.

The problem of small farms in the United Kingdom and the need for structural reform is less acute than in the E.E.C. The proportion of relatively large-scale farms is substantially higher than in the E.E.C. On these farms, economies of scale can be achieved, permitting substantial substitution of capital for labour and the attainment of reasonably efficient standards of production. As a result, there has been heavy investment in modern technology.

At present, there are some signs of changes in agricultural policies, which reflect the possibility of future entry of the United Kingdom into the E.E.C.

(5) *The European Free Trade Area*

In the European Free Trade Area, agriculture is exempted from the free trade provisions of the Stockholm Convention, under which EFTA was founded. Agricultural trade between EFTA members, which include the United Kingdom, is, however, regulated by a series of bilateral agreements. In practice, though, major development of agricultural trade has not proved easy because of the degree of agricultural protectionism in all member countries.

Denmark is an important exporter of agricultural products and has much to gain from liberalisation in the markets to which it exports, or, alternatively, from membership of the E.E.C. Until recently it has been an exponent of liberal trade policies, but in the early 1960s the 'chain-effect' of protectionism in other countries has led it to adopt support measures for its farmers. Sweden has recently given indications of wishing to reduce its degree of agricultural self-sufficiency as a step towards more efficient use of national resources. Switzerland, while operating high levels of agricultural protection and support, has limited agricultural resources and is the world's largest per capita importer of agricultural products. Norway, Austria and Portugal have acute problems of farm structure and modernisation. In the case of Austria, trade with Eastern Europe is important.

(6) *Other Countries*

Among the remaining European countries, Greece and Turkey are associate members of E.E.C. Ireland's agriculture is now closely linked to the United Kingdom market. Spain has been a major importer of agricultural products from the United States, notably feedgrains, soybeans, tallow and cotton.

II. TRADE PATTERNS

The broad trade flows of agricultural products between North America and Europe, and within Europe between the E.E.C., EFTA and other European countries, shown in Table 15.1, indicate the much greater importance to North America of agricultural exports to Europe than such trade in the reverse direction. Thus, in 1967, North American agricultural exports to Europe were $2,851 million, while the trade in the opposite direction was $1,089 million.

Within Europe, the E.E.C. has become of prime importance as an outlet for North American agricultural exports, especially in contrast to the comparatively static nature of the EFTA market for these products in recent years. During the period 1959–67, the former has increased by 66 per cent while the latter by only 8 per cent. In contrast, during the same period, agricultural exports from E.E.C. and EFTA countries increased by roughly the same proportion, i.e. 67 per cent and 74 per cent respectively.

The largest increases in agricultural trade were experienced between E.E.C. countries. Thus in the 1959–67 period, intra-E.E.C. trade increased by 177 per cent. The corresponding increase within EFTA was 66 per cent.

TABLE 15.1

INTRA-O.E.C.D. TRADE IN AGRICULTURAL PRODUCTS[a]
(export values – f.o.b. $million)

From \ To	North America	EFTA	E.E.C.	Other European O.E.C.D. countries[b]	Total[b] including intra-regional trade
1959					
North America	729	259	223	101	1,312
EFTA	933	536	680	244	2,393
E.E.C.	957	645	1,252	159	3,013
Other European O.E.C.D. countries[c]	76	39	24	4	143
Total[c] including intra-regional trade	2,695	1,479	2,179	508	6,861
1967					
North America	992	451	372	266	2,081
EFTA	1,008	951	1,127	650	3,736
E.E.C.	1,588	860	3,464	518	6,430
Other European O.E.C.D. countries	255	132	136	14	537
TOTAL	3,843	2,394	5,099	1,448	12,784

Increase in Value of Agricultural Trade between 1959 and 1967
(percentage increase in brackets)

North America	+263(36)	+192(74)	+149 (67)	+165	+769
EFTA	+75 (8)	+415(66)	+447 (66)	+406	+1,343
E.E.C.	+631(66)	+215(33)	+2,212(177)	+359	+3,417
Other European O.E.C.D. countries	+179	+93	+112(–)	+10	+394
Total including intra-regional trade	+1,148	+915	+2,920(–)	+940	+5,923

[a] S.I.T.C. Items 0, 1, 4, 22 and 29.
[b] For this comparison Japan is excluded from the O.E.C.D. member countries. Spain was also excluded in 1959 but included in 1967. Therefore, no percentage changes have been calculated for trade with and between 'other European O.E.C.D. countries', or for 'total trade'.
[c] In comparing trade totals for the regions, it needs to be remembered that the totals for the European groups include intra-regional as well as external trade, whereas for North America no figures for internal trade in the United States or Canada are included.

Source: 1959 figures from O.E.C.D., *Agricultural Policies in 1966*, Table 10, p. 49. 1967 figures calculated from O.E.C.D., *Commodity Trade: Exports*, series c (Jan and Dec 1968).

Although not covered explicitly in Table 15.1, some additional comments should be made. The demand for agricultural products in European countries has risen in recent years because of population growth and some increase in per capita consumption, especially in relation to certain products.[1] Supplies to meet these increases have been forthcoming both from increased domestic production and from increases in exports from supplying countries. The increase in market requirements within European countries has not, however, been shared equally between local producers and exporting countries. By and large, it is the former who have benefited most as degrees of national self-sufficiency have increased for most commodities.

In contrast to this general tendency, it appears that the United States has been able to maintain the proportion of its agricultural exports which go to the E.E.C., in spite of the total of those exports having increased. Some of the other suppliers of temperate-zone products, however, have failed to maintain the proportion of their exports going to Europe. Although it is not within the scope of this paper, this certainly applied to Oceania, as well as to Canada. Even when those other countries have, in absolute terms, maintained the level of their exports to Europe, the growth in European production has meant for them failure to obtain the share they might otherwise have gained of the expanded consumption in Europe. Furthermore, the diversion of supplies that might otherwise have gone to Europe has meant intensified pressure on markets in third countries.

III. TRADE PROJECTIONS

So much for the backcloth of recent experience. In looking to the future, the most straightforward way to proceed is to assume that current policies and underlying trends in demand, technology and suchlike will continue and to extrapolate on this basis. Much useful work has been accomplished from this standpoint.

Thus Sorenson and Hathaway have analysed policy issues in the E.E.C. with special reference to future supply–demand effects from the main agricultural products.[2] Broadly they foresee self-sufficiency in pork, poultry meat and eggs with continuing surpluses of dairy products. They think there will be some change in composition of the feedgrain output, with some shift towards barley, but no major expansion of total grain output. Beef and milk support prices will tend to prevent any major shift from forage to grain. Germany and Italy will continue to have deficits

[1] E. A. G. Robinson, 'The Desirable Level of Agriculture in the Advanced Industrial Economies' (Table V, p. 37) from chap. 2 in *Economic Problems of Agriculture in Industrial Societies*.

[2] V. L. Sorenson and Dale E. Hathaway, *The Grain–Livestock Economy and Trade Patterns of the European Economic Community with Projections to 1970 and 1975*, Research Report No. 5 (Michigan State University, 1968).

but not of those products that are in surplus elsewhere within the E.E.C., e.g. French wheat and dairy products. They give estimates, for each member country, of projected growth (to 1970 and to 1975) of output of grain and livestock products in the E.E.C. These vary from 1·5 to 2·8 per cent compound annual growth rate, and they predict that imports from third countries of red meat and grains are likely to increase. They do not see the primary policy tool of the E.E.C., i.e. price, as being very potent for control of either the level or composition of output. Also price support could aggravate rather than solve the low-income problem, by channelling assistance to the farms that need it least and by widening the gap in land values between the more productive and less productive areas. Structural adjustment, which is a *sine qua non* for such income adjustment, will be a long and difficult process.

Price policies may be rather neutral so far as rate of technological and structural change is concerned; the member countries have in fact had support policies before the E.E.C. was formed. Competition in the marketing sector is a potentially dynamic force for benefiting both farmers and consumers. Europe, because it will have to import and export (surpluses), cannot isolate itself from world markets. From the viewpoint of the United States, some European markets like poultry and eggs are likely to be lost for technological reasons irrespective of support policies.

The admission of the United Kingdom and certain other European countries may have a far greater impact on third countries than has the development of the E.E.C. policy to date. The possibilities of import substitution appear quite high with E.E.C. farmers gaining markets at the expense of third countries. Overall, however, Sorenson and Hathaway consider that so far United States response to the E.E.C. agricultural policy seems to have been more reaction than reason.

The prospects for United States agricultural exports have also been examined in detail by Q. M. West, Director of the Economic Research Service of the United States Department of Agriculture.[1] He has summarised the outlook as very bright, with an increase in agricultural exports of $1,500 million over the period 1965–70, and with further increases for particular commodities, notably feedgrains, and soybeans and products, to 1973–4 and again to 1980. Most of this will, he considers, be in the commercial market and will result largely from increased feed requirements for the expanding livestock industries in Western Europe and in Japan. His views and those of Hathaway and Sorenson quoted above appear to be in broad agreement.

[1] Q. M. West, 'Foreign Supply and Demand Projections: Outlook for U.S. Agricultural Exports', *Journal of Farm Economics*, vol. 48(2) (1966). See also 'Southern Agricultural Trade: Its Trends and Future Direction', being a paper given by the same author at the North Carolina State University, 27 Jan 1969.

There seems no reason to query the demand assumptions underlying the above forecasts. Per capita consumption in North America and in Western Europe (except the South) is already high and in the future rising incomes are likely to change the pattern of consumption rather than raise the level of per capita demand.

On the supply side, the outcome is likely to be rather more speculative and will depend upon whether the E.E.C. does in fact use price and other policy weapons to condition total supply to a greater extent than Hathaway and Sorenson apparently envisage. Moreover the development of new technology and the rate of its uptake will also play a decisive part in the future evolution of European agriculture. Even though the recent Mansholt proposals[1] for restructuring agriculture appear to have had a cool reception, it seems certain that governments within the Community will have to devote increasing attention to this problem because of the mounting cost of support. In 1969, it is estimated that the Community and member states between them will spend $5,500 million in respect of price support and structural reform policies.[2] Economic growth in other sectors will no doubt provide increasing opportunities for employment and continue to attract labour out of farming, apart from any special measures introduced to stimulate a reduction in the farm population. As larger and more economic farm units emerge, these are likely to give farmers greater flexibility in their production decisions.

IV. POLICY ADAPTATION

The remaining question concerns the extent to which policies are likely to, or should, for some economic or social reason, change. And straight away it must be acknowledged that any changes in the short run are likely to be small. Policies are becoming complex and interlocked so that, even were they desirable, revolutionary changes are becoming less and less likely. Nevertheless there are several indications that policy adaptation is being considered. At the individual national level, countries as diverse as Australia and Finland are attempting to reduce some sections of agricultural production, while Canada is currently considering a proposal

[1] *Memorandum on the Reform of Agriculture in the European Economic Community* (E.E.C., Brussels, 1968). The Memorandum contains comprehensive proposals from the Commission of the E.E.C. for a major reform of the structure of production, by increasing the size of the individual farm, reducing the number of farms and by encouraging co-operation between farmers. These alterations will call for readjustment in the marketing framework and this is envisaged in the proposals along lines of establishment of producer groups, of a European type of company and of groupings of Product Councils more or less analagous to Marketing Commissions.

[2] J. Van Lierde, 'Agricultural Adjustment in an International Setting', a paper presented at a Conference held by the Agricultural Adjustment Unit, University of Newcastle upon Tyne, July 1969.

of a public committee for major adaptations in Canadian agriculture including a reduction from 29 million to 20 million acres in the area of wheat.

Within the E.E.C., it looks very much as if the current policies will prove too expensive to sustain over the longer period, although preliminary reactions to the Mansholt Memorandum suggest that policy reform will be far from easy. Within GATT, discussions are continuing, apparently to some purpose – if slow – on trade liberalisation in agricultural products. Concurrently, and on a wider front, there is considerable preoccupation among governments and international agencies on such key issues of the world economy as development aid programmes, commodity stabilisation schemes and international liquidity problems.

An exploration of the possibility of policy adaptation is a speculative exercise which includes political considerations and even normative economies. But it may be that if economists wish to contribute to the policy debate and to influence affairs, they must sacrifice at least some part of their scientific virtue. A logical beginning is a redefined maximisation axiom, namely that a nation will only change policies to benefit (in some sense) itself – or, at the margin, will only go as far as a zero net loss in the cause of altruism. An improvement in a nation's policy can therefore arise if objectives are reformulated or if they can be better attained by alternative means. Such possibilities may arise from changing underlying economic conditions, changes in the assessment of self-interest or better administrative machinery. At the risk of being simplistic, it may be helpful to recapitulate the general reasons for agricultural support policies, commentary about which may throw light on the directions for policy improvements.

Initially intervention in agricultural matters aimed primarily at reducing instability in prices and farm incomes, an instability which arose from combination of relatively inelastic demand, unplanned variations in supply and imperfections in the market (some of the latter two elements may have been induced by the actions of foreign governments). This function of policy is difficult to evaluate, but, without making a fetish of constancy, the economic cost of wild fluctuations can be recognised. The principal method by which control of price instability on world markets has been sought has been by international commodity arrangements. The degree of success which has been attained in particular instances is debatable but, taken over the whole range of agricultural products, has not been great.

A second purpose of agricultural intervention has been to close the 'income gap' between agricultural and non-agricultural incomes, a gap which has arisen from the relatively slower rate of adaptation of the agricultural industry to changing economic and technological conditions compared with some other sectors in the economy. Table 15.2 indicates that, whatever ameliorative results may have accrued from current

TABLE 15.2
RELATIVE INCOMES IN AGRICULTURE, 1966

	(1) Total G.D.P. ÷ Total economically active population (U.S. $)	(2) G.D.P. from agriculture ÷ Economically active population in agriculture (U.S. $)	(2) as percentage of (1)
France	5,073	1,792	35
Germany	4,433	1,747	39
Austria	2,997	1,313	44
Finland	4,279	1,931	45
Norway	5,405	2,846	46
Sweden	6,504	3,304	51
Italy	3,118	1,690	54
United States	9,180	5,024	55
Ireland	2,167	1,487	57
Denmark	5,348	3,060	57
Netherlands	4,989	3,722	75
United Kingdom	4,814	3,332	79
Canada	6,949	5,477	79
Belgium	4,742	5,055	107
Australia	5,420	5,987	110

The above figures vary considerably from year to year. The table is, therefore, intended to be illustrative only.

Sources: G.D.P.: *International Financial Statistics* (I.M.F., Dec 1968). G.D.P. in Agriculture: *U.N. Statistical Year Book, 1967*. Population: *Year Book of Labour Statistics, 1967* (I.L.O.).

policies, there is generally a considerable shortfall in attaining comparable incomes. Two further significant points can be made here. In the first place many policies for supporting farm incomes have, implicitly or explicitly, inhibited the structural adjustment of the agricultural sector, which offers the only long-run solution of the income problem.[1] In other words, the short-run solution actually worsens the long-run problem. Secondly, it is possible for a country to 'export' its adjustment problem – at least to some extent – by allowing domestic production to expand, by maintaining high food prices and/or by transfer payments by government.

Thus it can be argued that, for instance within the E.E.C., there must be a balancing of interests between the costs of the present policy to the consumer and the taxpayer on the one hand, and, on the other hand, the social and political disruption, in addition to the economic hardship for

[1] Some 80 per cent of the 6 million farms (of more than 2½ acres) in the E.E.C. are below 25 acres in extent and are often fragmented. The same type of pattern applies for individual enterprises; for example, 80 per cent of milk producers have less than 10 cows. Van Lierde, 'Agriculture in an International Setting'.

rural communities, from following an alternative policy of, say, free trade and no subsidies. Such analysis is beyond the capacity of current evaluation techniques. But one might suppose that there is a rate of industrial and social transformation beyond which costs (in some total sense) mount rapidly, while on the other hand complete stagnation is neither necessary nor desirable. It is not obvious that governments have been fully aware of the interrelationship between trade policies and domestic structural policies for agriculture; even when this awareness exists, strength at the international bargaining table is not necessarily related to the ability or inability of a country to tackle its structural problems.

One can conclude, then, that future trading policies will continue to be tempered by considerations of domestic farm policy. Perhaps, however, international acceptance of protectionist policies could be linked in some way to appropriate structural policies being followed in the country concerned, the degree of allowable protection being related in some flexible fashion to the ease or difficulty of adaptation – in economic and social terms. (On this basis, one might conclude, for example, that Ireland could be more protectionist than the United Kingdom.)

Another objective of policy has been the expansion of production *per se*, as opposed to an expansion to solve the income problem. The reasons underlying such a policy can vary. On the non-economic level, there may be strategic, military or other national considerations. In some countries, the objective is to earn foreign exchange to facilitate general economic development. In the United Kingdom there is the possible import-saving contribution of agriculture to the deep-seated balance of payments disequilibrium. Finally, there is the suggestion, widespread but not always specific, that 'comparative advantage' is a somewhat mythical concept and no firm basis for trade policies. Some progress towards improved policies may arise from demonstrating, in terms sufficiently convincing to what may be a partisan decision-making system, that measures currently being implemented will not lead to the achievement of the defined goals.

In looking at the merits of any agricultural expansion, one is concerned with marginal resources, mobility of factors and the like, yet there is seldom adequate economic arithmetic brought to bear on the problem. And for this economists themselves must take some of the blame. Admittedly the analytical situation is complex, lacking neatness and precision, but some contribution can be made if one is prepared to be brash.

To conclude this discussion of expansion policies it may be worth mentioning, firstly, that since technological advance looks likely to continue, the pressure to expand output from a gradually diminishing labour force will continue. Secondly, the contemporary problem of threatened agricultural surpluses is a psychological novelty to mankind. Popular thinking encompasses more easily food scarcities as a continuing background to policy-making. These considerations may suggest that the task of persuasion towards acceptance of more rational policies could be as important as the economic analysis. Perhaps therefore the most important point to stress is the overlapping relations of two sets of problems.

First, there are the domestic policy problems where each country concerned must find the political will to tackle contentious and difficult problems of internal adjustment. The role of agriculture in the present and future economy of the country concerned has to be assessed and the appropriate measures planned and implemented so that agriculture can fill this role. Alongside this problem, there is that of the international trade problems which have largely arisen out of the domestic policies. Here it is desirable, if not essential, for nations to reach some agreement on the role of international trade in agricultural commodities. Such agreement will probably involve some compromise between the views and attitudes of the United States and of the E.E.C. respectively. Despite the spread of technology, one must believe that fundamental differences in resource endowments are likely to remain which, in turn, predicate gains to be obtained from rational use of the resources and of trade in broad conformity with comparative costs. For trade to take place on such a basis, observance of what may be called 'rules of fair trading' seems a *sine qua non*. It must be a primary purpose of international negotiators to spell out such rules and secure a workable consensus. There is a great wealth of experience and expertise that can be tapped for this task and the major international organisations and forums have an obvious contribution to make. In a less obvious but still useful way, academic economists should be able to contribute both to disentangling the complex details involved and to clarifying the public debate on the broad issues.

Secondly, in arriving at solutions the needs of the short and longer terms must be weighed and, if feasible, reconciled. For the short term, the main problem is to keep the channels working. This will involve the practical negotiations and compromises mentioned above. For the longer term, the problem is to ensure that trade takes place in a manner, and on terms, which will help rather than hinder the balancing of production and of demand and which will encourage the location of this production in conformity with rational use of world resources. Undoubtedly, national interests will continue to be imperative for each country and probably optimum, or even rational, trade patterns can only be expected as the operations of constraints imposed by national sovereignty are modified towards greater harmony in such matters as international investment and international monetary arrangements. There are lessons in this field to be learned from the progress of European economic integration.

V. CONCLUSIONS

In conclusion, in relation to the central theme of this paper, it should be stated that the mutual impact of agricultural policies in North America and Europe has been significant. On the one hand, pressure on European markets has been sustained by North American suppliers who, generally, are comparatively low-cost producers. On the other hand, European policies have been highly protectionist and possibly tending towards autarky while at the same time production tends to be much more fragmented and high-cost. The result has been that North American suppliers have not had unlimited access to markets and, with massive technological developments, have had to resort to restriction of their basic output. Thus the United States, for instance, has retired from production more than 50 million acres of farmland. At the same time, the European policies have done nothing to solve the agricultural problems in the respective countries – problems of income disparity between agriculture and the rest of the economy and problems of physical structure of agricultural resources which, basically, give rise to the income problem. As Dr Mansholt has said, 'market and price support policies alone cannot solve the fundamental difficulties of farming. . . . All policy decisions to be taken in connection with the Common Agricultural Policy should from now on be guided by the double purpose of contributing as much as possible to the establishment of equilibrium of agricultural markets and of improving the structure of agriculture.'

Over the next few years, that is, before the full implementation of the Kennedy Round by January 1972, the rate of change of agricultural and trade policies in North America and in Europe may be relatively slow, although the impact of policies in these areas on other countries producing temperate-zone products will continue to be great.

There is no sign of significant change in the underlying economic forces. Economic growth generally is likely to continue. Effective demand for food will expand, but relatively slowly. Agricultural technology will continue to advance and to spread at a rapid rate. Differences in trade 'philosophy', if not resolved, will impede a unified approach to trade problems and will prevent optimum development of trade in temperate-zone products.

How North America and Western Europe cope with the problems which these factors represent will depend upon:

(1) The degree to which individual countries adopt rational policies, especially to restructure agriculture and modify existing support policies.
(2) The degree to which reciprocal liberalisation of tariff and non-tariff barriers to trade is adopted. Restructuring agriculture will not, of itself, solve surplus problems.

(3) Measures, such as improved international commodity agreements, aimed at price stability as well as at market regulation to ensure better that supply is brought more into balance with demand.
(4) The adoption of national production and trade policies – perhaps strengthened by such means as international agreement on self-sufficiency ratios and maximum support levels – which will be in general conformity with the pattern indicated by comparative costs. Admittedly, this cannot be a static concept.
(5) Integration with commercial trade policies of national and international policies aimed at assisting the economic and development programmes of the less developed countries.

As a closing observation, may I reiterate that this paper has stressed the particular problems of farm structure and resulting low farm incomes that underlie the agricultural policies I was asked to discuss. The economic, social and political difficulties involved in adjustment of these basic causes are great and give rise in each country to continuing pressures for short-term solutions on a national basis. However, I believe that, in the longer term in agriculture as in other sectors, the efficiency with which resources are used must become a major, if not the major, criterion of policies if the problems which, for over half a century, have characterised agriculture at both national and international levels are to be solved.

Discussion of the Papers by Professors Ashton, Campbell and Fauvel

Professor Robinson introduced the discussion. He said that in a previous session we had looked at possible conflicts in international monetary policy. The programme committee had tried to identify three other sensitive areas: agriculture, industry, and migration and movement. The Round Table would begin by looking at agriculture with three very complementary papers.

He wanted to concentrate on the agricultural policy of the E.E.C. and on the paper by Professor Fauvel. He would leave the discussion to bring out the relationship of these issues to policies in North America and the United Kingdom. These were dealt with by Professors Campbell and Ashton respectively.

Professor Robinson thought it was good to start with the E.E.C. because its external image had been created by its agricultural policy rather than by its very open and liberal industrial policy. He would like to start with a question that all three papers asked. This was why one had agricultural policies at all – especially agricultural support policies. These had started all over the world in the 1930s during a deep depression. In industry, the depression created high unemployment; in agriculture, a ruinous fall in prices. Governments therefore wanted to seek methods to insulate agriculture from all of this. Now, having created the machinery, even though the original problem had disappeared, governments were using this machinery for two main purposes.

First, there was the perennial problem that agriculture faced markets with low income elasticities of demand; there was also low price elasticity of demand for agricultural goods as a whole, even though there was high cross-elasticity between individual agricultural products. There was now very rapid technological progress in agriculture. Both in the United Kingdom, and he thought in France, technological progress in agriculture was more rapid than in industry. Thus, generation by generation, more people were forced to leave agriculture. One needed to keep agricultural incomes at a level which would encourage them to move out.

Second, Europe, the United Kingdom, the United States and Canada were all concerned with the problem of rural poverty. All wanted to narrow the gap between rural and industrial incomes. This was the nub of the problem. If one had prices which brought rural incomes closer to those in industrial areas, one expanded output and created surpluses.

This was the central issue in the agricultural policy of the E.E.C. It had needed all the available diplomatic skill to get an agricultural policy at all. Some of us were now puzzled as to how far agricultural policy had been upset and modified in the wake of the French devaluation. He was not clear what had happened.

In the first stage, agricultural prices in the E.E.C. had been set high enough to narrow the gap between rural and industrial incomes. However, this remained wide, as one could see from p. 332 of Professor Ashton's paper. One had to remember, however, that if one looked at the proportion of G.N.P. coming from agriculture, this also had to support those providing fertilisers, building tractors and keeping them running, and other inputs. To divide the proportion of G.N.P. coming from agriculture by those directly engaged in it would overstate the income per head of those actually in agriculture.

Prices in the E.E.C. were high enough to increase output faster than the likely growth of demand. This meant that surpluses would arise sooner or later. In the E.E.C., elasticities of supply were highest in areas of high productivity, like northern France and the Benelux countries. These produced higher-quality products. Surpluses came from less efficient, high-cost areas. Therefore, the question was whether the present agricultural policy was the end of the story, or the beginning.

Professor Robinson said he was not shocked that those making the agricultural policy of the E.E.C. had felt obliged to find a common solution, and had therefore concentrated on solving short-run problems. However, we had to look ahead. He wondered what the long-run consequences of these short-run policies would be, as growing surpluses emerged. Here, he saw one conflict of interest. What he had said about the need to move manpower out of agriculture was not inevitably true for one, individual country; it could, if it wanted, export its problems of adjustment by reducing imports and pushing the burden on to other countries. Those not in the E.E.C. wanted to know whether the long-run policy of the E.E.C. was to export its problems of adjustment in this way. It could then plan to cover a growing proportion of its agricultural needs. Or was the point simply that this was a short-run effect of getting agreement? He wondered how the whole E.E.C. expected to increase rural incomes, and yet get incentives to contract agricultural manpower. He was left in the air at the end of Professor Fauvel's paper on this.

To look at the problem from a more realistic angle, if one tried in the short run to say how much agriculture was economic, one had to assess realistically how much of the manpower in agriculture was quickly transferable to other activities. For example, if an agricultural worker in the Dordogne could not be transferred elsewhere, the opportunity cost of keeping him where he was was zero. It might therefore be economically wise, as well as humane, to leave him in agriculture.

Professor Fauvel had suggested that current thinking in France divided agriculture into three types. First, there was efficient agriculture. Second, there were farms which were capable of modernisation. Third, there were farms which were incapable of modernisation, so that incomes were provided on a personal basis. How could one ensure that this generation of non-transferable agricultural manpower would not be replaced by a new generation of non-transferable, inefficient producers on farms that remained too small?

As he had said, he was not shocked that the E.E.C. should encourage low-cost agriculture, nor was he shocked if the incentives to expansion were unnecessarily big. However, he was worried by a policy which, in Germany, left the country with rapid industrial progress and at the same time with some of the most backward, medieval agriculture in Europe. In Hesse, the Eifel and Bavaria, agricultural prices failed to make use of industrial expansion to draw people out of agriculture. Instead, Germany acquired industrial manpower when it needed more from Greece, Sicily and other less developed countries.

On import policies, the E.E.C. seemed to aim at making itself self-sufficient in what it could produce. As Professor Fauvel said, this did not mean that American exports to the E.E.C. would contract. There were large numbers of agricultural products which the E.E.C. could not produce, or where it was at present short. Soybeans and proteins were two examples. Professor Fauvel claimed that the E.E.C. would provide a growing market for the United States and Canada, but Professor Robinson was not convinced. At the first round, there might well be growing wheat surpluses. He would be surprised if these did not soon become barley surpluses, and then displace imports of soybeans and other products. In addition, quantitative restrictions on quality products from the United States had gone. Where American products could compete through their higher quality, they could be imported even if this led to greater surpluses in the E.E.C. This was true of wheat, though he had explained why he thought it would lead to a barley surplus.

What was the justification for this general policy of self-sufficiency? The E.E.C. prices, as shown in Table 13.4 of Professor Campbell's paper, were not far from double the world price for some important products. A liberal economist had to ask himself whether it was an efficient long-run policy to support direct agricultural production rather than exchanging industrial products for low-cost North American agricultural products. He found it hard to distinguish the purely short-run policy of supporting agriculture to the minimum desirable extent, and that of getting it to contract into the pattern which in the long run would lead to a more efficient world situation. He thought that American agriculture had a high potential for low-cost, elastic supply. Was the world using this to best advantage?

Professor Robinson said he had talked about the E.E.C. rather than the United Kingdom, because Professor Ashton had covered this in his paper. In the United Kingdom, agriculture was about half-way between that in the backward areas of Germany, and the efficient agriculture of the New World of America. It was closer to the highly efficient producers of northern France and Benelux. Rapid technological progress was leading to falling real costs of production. The problem was analogous to the E.E.C. one. How could one get rural incomes nearer to industrial incomes? In the United Kingdom, G.D.P. per head in rural areas was about 80 per cent of its level in the whole economy. This was close to the ratio for Canada, and for the more efficient parts of the E.E.C., like the Netherlands, but less than the ratio in Belgium.

The United Kingdom problem was less that of rural incomes than of making bargains with agricultural producers which would give incentives, and yet not lead to excessive farm income levels. The United Kingdom was worried by the secondary effects of the high bargaining strength of the agricultural sector and the way that the 3 per cent of British resources devoted to agriculture were used. Given her bad balance of payments, agriculture was a not wholly inefficient way of reducing the balance of payments gap.

To sum up, the central danger was that of conflict of interest. All of us faced the question of how to put pressure on agriculture to modernise, reduce its use of labour and take its share in the process of adjustment. He wondered whether some countries were attempting to export their problems of adjustment rather than face them. He would, however, emphasise the difficulty which an outside observer had in d stinguishing between the short-run and long-run policies of the E.E.C. countries.

Mr Lamfalussy said that because the effects of the French devaluation were so important, he would like to ask Professor Fauvel what results it was likely to have.

Professor Fauvel said that the guaranteed agricultural prices were guaranteed in dollars. When French devaluation was first mooted in June 1968, it was said that devaluation was impossible because it would raise agricultural prices. This would give an even bigger impetus to agricultural production in France. The Brussels technocrats had a year in which to reflect on this. It seemed that the E.E.C.'s economic division at Brussels looked at agricultural policy in a very relaxed way and suggested reducing agricultural prices slowly because France was an important part of European agriculture. It was therefore suggested that, if France devalued, there might be a 2-3 per cent cut in agricultural prices. The Ministers simply did not dare to agree. All that was being done was to try to hold back French agricultural prices as far as possible.

Professor Eastman said he wanted to emphasise Professor Robinson's point that, in most countries, agricultural policy seemed to be to export one's problems. For agricultural price support did little to increase the income of the farmer; it was soon capitalised in an increased price of land. The farmer left a larger estate and there was very little effect on his current activities. Indeed, the need for large amounts of capital to buy farms became a barrier to new entry and so to rationalisation of the industry.

Professor Campbell had mentioned the costs of social capital where rural population decreased, but this could easily be overemphasised. During the depression, in the Canadian West, if, for instance, students were not present for existing schools, the schools were shut at zero marginal cost. The problems came rather if one had to build new schools where there were more children.

One had to remember that both American and E.E.C. policies had a heavy cost for underdeveloped countries. A Swedish model had tried to evaluate the effect of agricultural price supports on world prices. Although the conclusions were tentative, it seemed that the world price of sugar, for instance, had been depressed by 20-30 per cent. This increased the problems of underdeveloped countries, since so many of them had marked comparative advantages in this kind of product. We therefore had to look at the ways such policies could be renegotiated in future. He had already claimed that domestic policies were becoming negotiable, and had been challenged because the Kennedy Round had achieved little except an alteration in the grain agreement. However, it had been perhaps optimistic to hope for much from negotiations with the European countries, at a time when the internal E.E.C. arrangements were still being completed. Europe could not make major concessions to the United States at that time but, in the long run, simplification of European policies achieved by the Common European agreement might make concessions easier to grant. Professor Eastman said he had in mind the United States position, which did not take agricultural support policies out of the Kennedy Round negotiations. This was why he was optimistic.

Professor Sohmen commented on the position of German agriculture. He agreed that Germany was the main obstacle to a sensible E.E.C. agricultural policy. Without necessarily wanting to defend German policy, he would say that the main reason for it was a political dilemma. Policy-makers feared that farmers might react violently to major changes. He could see no hope for change until after the election, and not too much after it either. It was important not to forget, however, that when the European agricultural policy was launched, German farmers suffered most through reduced prices. French farmers got higher prices. So German farmers could claim that they had already made a major sacrifice and could hardly be asked for more. One further argument was that many thought that the preservation of Western European agriculture would maintain an indispensable asset if there were to be a war.

Professor Yamamoto said that although Japan's problem was different, it was a difficult one. Internally, Japan had a rice surplus and the government was pressed to maintain price supports. Externally, countries like Thailand want Japan to buy more rice.

He had been interested in three points on p. 320 of Professor Fauvel's paper. The paper suggested that the degree of Sweden's self-sufficiency in food would be deliberately reduced within a few years from 95 per cent to 80 per cent; that the agricultural population would be reduced by two-thirds in fifteen years; and that the government would not bear the full cost of restructuring farms.

These points were suggestive, and maybe in future world food supply would exceed world demand. He thought there was therefore a need for regional agreements. Regional division of labour should be encouraged not only in the E.E.C. and EFTA but in Asia too.

Professor van Meerhaeghe said that Professor Eastman had mentioned the repercussions of price-support policy on underdeveloped countries. He did not think that the E.E.C. alone was guilty in this respect. For example, Professor Eastman had mentioned the sugar problem; yet the transactions on the 'free' market (outside international agreements) represented only 45 per cent of total transactions.

Mr Shonfield returned to what Professor Robinson had said about short- versus long-run aims. He wanted to bring out another aspect. The E.E.C. had initially set up its agricultural policy on two very respectable assumptions. First, there was the welfare aim of increasing the standard of living of a large section of society, the peasants, and of sustaining their incomes when the market ceased to be favourable. Second, there was the free-trade aim – the removal of visible obstacles to trade. This had been achieved by using minimum prices as the welfare instrument and introducing them into trading procedures. They ended up, however, with the negation of competition in agriculture.

He thought that as members of the world community who were hurt by this E.E.C. folly, we might suggest that, if either objective had to go, it should be the trade and not the welfare one. The French devaluation had already begun to move matters in this direction.

There was a third, less clear, objective of the E.E.C. The Community had wanted to collectivise the subsidisation process – making it central rather than national. The aim was to increase the amount of power exercised at the centre. This political objective was also a respectable one; but it explained why there was the reluctance to see the contradiction between the two major objectives. The consequence of sacrificing the free-trade objective would be to push responsibility for subsidies back to national governments. He would propose that this should happen.

The result would be that the individual E.E.C. countries would be made to make welfare payments directly to the recipients, and the taxpayers would exert the normal pressure to limit their size. At present, foreign countries paid the big subsidies. With no common E.E.C. government, German taxpayers could not make their indignation felt in Paris. If one brought subsidies back to where they belonged, one would get some limitation on their size. In essence, in order to run an agricultural policy as ambitious as that of the E.E.C. (and this was a remarkable piece of machinery), one needed a powerful government at the centre to take charge of the bargaining process between the various interests. This did not exist, so it was better to push the bargaining back within national states.

Perhaps the best solution might be for the Commission to play some judicial role. It could do what the European Court of Justice had done when, for example, the French imposed import restrictions on Italian refrigerators. There should be a body of final instance to look at questions of global subsidisation. Each year, the E.E.C. policy-makers could work out various kinds of limitation for each stage of short-run or medium-run policy. This arrangement would make subsidies explicit. And it would simplify the problem of short-run welfare arrangements.

Professor James said he had been interested by what Mr Shonfield said. He wondered whether this solution would have the effect of giving responsibility for agricultural support back to national governments and so would be retrograde so far as integration was concerned.

He would now like to come down to earth, and ask Professor Fauvel whether it was correct to say that the French thought in terms of the three sectors mentioned on p. 303 of his paper. He seemed then to have used the criterion of size of farm more than anything else. Was not the product important as well? Professor James spent his holidays in a rich area of Charollais – between Bourges and Nevers. A curious phenomenon over the last ten years was that the price of land for cereals had risen ten times. That for cattle raising had not risen at all. He had wondered why. The answer was that the price of cereals was high enough to give a better profit than the price of meat. Agricultural technology had changed in cereal cultivation, but not in cattle raising. In cereals, much less labour was needed than ten years ago; in cattle raising there had been no fall at all. Perhaps the technological gap between the United States and France had been reduced in cereal production; no reduction at all in cattle raising.

Professor Houssiaux said that he would take a different approach from Mr Shonfield and put the development of the E.E.C. in the context of the historical development of agricultural policies. In fact, the creation of the E.E.C. agricultural policy was a specific event at a specific point in European history. On agricultural policy in general, he agreed that the aim was to keep up the income of the agricultural population. Up to the 1930s, agricultural incomes had been too low, but external protection enough to keep them up. Later on, subsidies were needed to complete external protection. In the years before the E.E.C. agricultural policy, nothing had been done and surpluses reappeared about 1956 at the time of the Rome negotiations. There was never any long-run policy for European agriculture in the E.E.C. up to the Mansholt Report. The E.E.C. did not have a long-run policy for itself or for its members, so the Common Agricultural Policy was being constructed in an ivory tower. From 1956, agricultural policy had been mainly a matter of expediency. What had been done was to try to keep up income but also to deal with some structural problems, without logical basis for doing so.

First, there was the objective of stimulating investment in agriculture. Investment incentives in agriculture had been given and everyone had been surprised at the way agriculture had responded to them – especially those who did not know how rapidly information travelled between French farmers.

The second objective was to improve the organisation of farms and to encourage a better product-mix. In the 1960s there had been proposals to form cooperatives, and financial support from the European Investment Bank. There was also a setting up of new 'agro-businesses'. Again, concentration had gone much more smoothly in agriculture than many people thought it could.

Third, there was the aim of encouraging vertical integration into the processing industry – assisted by the chicken war. There were many difficulties, not least budgetary restraints.

In the end, the Mansholt Plan had shown that the agricultural problem would find its solution outside agriculture, and that it was important to push surplus labour towards industry. This was a classic issue, but it raised all kinds of problems for public finance. There probably was disguised unemployment in French agriculture, though perhaps not much in the United Kingdom (but not in the same sectors). The need was to find some way of using this surplus labour. The cost of agriculture was not mainly in subsidies but in speeding up transfer. It was possible to move fairly fast; there was a real elasticity in what could be done.

Mr Merigó said he did not think that the agricultural policy in Europe was a 'folly'. The results were not wholly satisfactory, but America had also had subsidies of enormous size for a long time and their adverse effects had often affected the underdeveloped areas rather than the E.E.C. because of dumping. He would mention cotton.

Mr Merigó wanted to discuss the idea of pushing subsidies back on to national governments. The E.E.C. was mainly an industrial community and therefore the important moves were on industrial issues. He thought the policy of economic integration within the E.E.C. had been surprisingly successful in France, but with severe social costs. Many of the troubles in May 1968 were perhaps a result of the efforts imposed by E.E.C. membership. Had more people been moved out of agriculture into industry, the troubles would have been even bigger. The E.E.C. agricultural policy was therefore vital for France.

Finally, he wanted to point out that state budgets showed how big the cost of agricultural support was, and it was easy to see the amounts of transfers to and from the Agricultural Fund in the balance of payments figures. In the French balance of payments, $200 million to $300 million per annum were being received in European agricultural subsidies.

Mr Grogan said he was glad that Professor Ashton had reminded the Conference that countries other than those in Europe and North America were interested in agricultural issues. He thought Professor Fauvel was unrealistic in believing that present E.E.C. policies provided any assurance about future markets to countries exporting primary products. The first priority for governments within the E.E.C. was to find markets for their own agricultural production. It was necessary to be clear what was the basic cause of the international agricultural marketing problems. Undoubtedly, most countries had a structural farm problem. After 2,000 years of relatively slow change, agriculture in developed countries was faced with rapid modernisation, which led to technical and social problems. The problem in international markets, however, arose from the fact that, partly because of advancing techniques, production of a number of commodities had run ahead of relatively inelastic effective demand for them. Production was likely to be increased rather than lessened by structural reform of farms. Recent efforts, including those in GATT and UNCTAD, to solve the problem of markets had not been encouraging. The Kennedy Round discussions appeared to recognise that for some commodities the international free-market price mechanism had largely broken down; it was not the prime determinant of the allocation of resources either nationally or internationally.

If one ignored the possibility of any return to *laissez-faire*, two lines of approach appeared to be under study at present. One related to commodity agreements and the other to the 'problem areas' approach under which international co-operation would be sought in restricting support measures and subsidies and in agreeing on rules to govern trade practices. Detailed negotiations were unlikely before 1972, by which date the Kennedy Round provisions should be fully implemented. An interesting recent development in Australia had been the action taken by wheat-growers to obtain government legislation to restrict wheat production compulsorily in order to cope with the marketing and storage problems that had accompanied a surplus of wheat. This action had arisen from the responsibility of the grower-controlled Wheat Board for marketing the whole of Australia's wheat production.

Professor Cooper noted that Professor Fauvel said that American farmers had nothing to complain of over the agricultural policies of the E.E.C. because the E.E.C.'s imports of agricultural products from the rest of the world and from the United States had grown from 1958 to 1968. This observation required three qualifications. First, a peak was reached in 1966 and agricultural imports had declined thereafter; *net* imports declined even more sharply. Second, the composition of imports had changed substantially under the Common Agricultural Policy, and this confronted foreign farmers with the task of reallocating resources to meet the new pattern of demand. Third, and not least, the current level of agricultural imports into the E.E.C. had been maintained only by a process of continual bickering between nations, involving threats and counter-threats. In 1969, for example, the E.E.C. had threatened to impose special taxes on soybeans, a major export from the United States to the E.E.C., to help reduce the dairy surplus. Strong American representations were required to avoid these taxes. He was therefore less comforted than Professor Fauvel by the fact that United States agricultural exports to the E.E.C. increased after 1958.

Mr Merigó had justified the E.E.C.'s Common Agricultural Policy by arguing that the United States had pursued similar policies in the past. Professor Cooper pointed out that this policy had been instituted under very different circumstances, in the depths of a world-wide depression in the 1930s, and also that the American Government had been attempting to extricate its economy from this folly for two decades. Europe might have many things to learn from the United States, but in the area of agricultural policy it was from United States mistakes rather than from its successes that lessons should be drawn.

Professor Robinson said that he agreed with a lot of what Mr Shonfield had said, but did wonder about the precepts he was offering. Was it really better to go back on trade liberalisation in agriculture? The E.E.C. was trying to make industry and agriculture more specialised. One could not have an E.E.C. policy unless one had agricultural free trade to balance that of industry. There were two questions here. Should one have free trade in agriculture? Should one share the support of welfare policy between countries? The case seemed stronger for not sharing support than for going back on general free-trade policies.

Professor Rieben reverted to the transfer problem. On p. 284 of Professor Campbell's paper, it was said that the Community farm labour force had fallen by about 40 per cent in the period 1950 to 1967, compared with 46 per cent in the United States and 45 per cent in Canada. With his own region in mind, he wondered whether there would be an acceleration in decline for social reasons. For example, in his own canton, two-thirds of peasants' daughters married non-farmers. If this happened on a European scale, he wondered what would be the result. The problems of transfer were psychological rather than price problems. Differences occurred according to whether the movement was from the South to the North, or from Northern agriculture to industry. Labour from the rural South appeared to adapt quickly to the industrial North; but it was young manpower. In the North, the transfer was very slow. In many cases, the peasant who left the land simply became a labourer in industry. This was a traumatic experience about which there was a good deal of medical and psychological evidence. Young agricultural workers represented an elite and were not much of a problem. It therefore seemed unfortunate that so few moved from primary to secondary school and then on to university. Was it not important to concentrate on education in agricultural areas?

Professor Houssiaux thought there were two reasons why there should be decentralisation of agricultural policy in the E.E.C. along the lines suggested by Mr Shonfield. First, attacks on the Brussels bureaucracy were very fierce. The problem would be simplified if the bureaucrats were under national control. Second, the problems were not really agricultural but educational, and social. Agricultural secondary schools simply encouraged children to leave the land.

Professor Fauvel agreed with Professor Rieben on his first point, and with Professor Houssiaux on his last point. Peasants no longer wanted to stay in the villages. Girls were eager to escape from such jobs as milking cows in the fields in all weathers, as was still the lot of their mothers. Every evening the television demonstrated what seemed a much more attractive way of life. Before 1940 there had been a stable agricultural population; this was no longer the case. Like Britain and Sweden, most countries in Western Europe were now quickly losing labour from agriculture at an annual rate which depended on the growth in employment outside agriculture. Indeed, it was generally agreed that the E.E.C.'s agricultural problem had to be solved outside agriculture. It was a problem of backward areas in industrial societies. No one imagined that it would be in the interest of the E.E.C. to go on producing more and more grain or butter, to be exported at half or a quarter of internal cost. Agricultural prices were high but family incomes were low for inefficient farmers. The problem was to create new jobs in activities that would not result in the same permanent fiscal burden for the Community and keep the cost of food high.

There was no an *arrière pensée*, aiming to 'export' the problems of the agricultural policy of the Community, for the simple reason that no one was satisfied with the high cost of this policy for the taxpayer and the consumer in each country. This policy resulted in maintaining or even creating in the longer run backward areas in the member countries. The aim was progressively to reduce agricultural prices to something like the level in the U.S.A., when the efficiency of the marginal E.E.C. farmer would be nearer the efficiency of the marginal U.S. farmer. The high profits of the efficient farmers in France, northern Italy and the Netherlands would be reduced simultaneously. The high agricultural prices in the E.E.C. were not a result of the Rome Treaty. They existed before it. The 'miracle' of the last ten years consisted merely in the unification of the procedures of price support, which ten years ago differed in form from one country to another. Before the Common Market little had been done for agriculture in the long run. In France agricultural policy consisted mainly in a follow-up of the market support system of the thirties. This system was resumed and developed in the fifties. The price support for dairy products, for instance, was effective only from 1957. Although rapid technical progress lay ahead, no one in the 1950s foresaw the scale of the problem. Even early in the sixties the experts in Brussels did not foresee with any precision the amount of the surpluses. They envisaged the future E.E.C. as a net importer of food, so far as concerned the majority of its needs. Now that the surpluses had occurred, the financial problems created were sufficiently great to oblige the E.E.C. to move to a new stage in its agricultural policy. This was the meaning of the new Mansholdt Plan, published at the end of 1968.

It was now agreed that it would be necessary to reduce prices, but it was difficult to say so openly. The farmers' organisations would not accept it. The solution would probably consist in maintaining the family income of the older and less efficient peasants by personal allowances. This would not reduce the arable area in Western Europe, but would make it possible to reduce prices and bring about a change in the size and operation of farms. Professor Robinson had rightly underlined the difficulty at this point: it was to ensure that the present generation of non-transferable agricultural manpower would not be replaced by another generation of non-transferable albeit more efficient producers on farms that remained too small. As in Sweden, the aim was to reduce both production and agricultural population. No such action had been attempted in the 1930s or 1950s; it would, however, be easier when the number of agricultural voters had fallen.

Why an agricultural policy at all? We were no longer in Ricardo's time. M. Albert had said that an agricultural policy was of secondary importance; industrial and monetary policies were far more necessary. It did not follow that agriculture could be allowed to look after itself. There were underdeveloped agricultural regions in all developed countries including the U.S.A. They could not be ignored. To do so would be to say to the peasants in southern Italy, or western France, or Bavaria, that they were not regarded as members of the new Europe. They would not accept this. National unity presupposed measures to help the backward parts of a nation. The same was true for a community of nations. New developments would take place across the former national borders. In France one-fifth of the active population in agriculture was foreign. Were they to be sent home because a new Europe was created? Agricultural 'segregation' would be economically stupid. The geographical distribution of the agricultural surpluses would change. For the past fifty years, Belgian, Dutch, Italian and German farmers had become richer in the French countryside than they could have done at home. It could happen tomorrow with British farmers.

After the first ten years of the E.E.C. we had to start facing the long-term problems. It was difficult to prepare for the political unity of Western Europe if the depressed areas of rural life were to be regarded as a *maladie honteuse* to be cured at the expense of the member state alone, the peasant population being considered as a reservoir of unskilled manpower used to exert pressure on wages in the industrial areas.

Professor Campbell said that Professor Robinson had asked the big question – why should one concern oneself with agriculture? There were two reasons for this. First, there was the political reason mentioned already by Professors Sohmen and Fauvel that agricultural voters were normally over-represented in parliaments. Furthermore, in most countries, those of our generation had been born when about 30 per cent of the population was working on the land. We had a sentimental link with agriculture and city people found it quite easy to sympathise with the idea of subsidising farmers. The second reason was the fact that farm incomes were much lower than the incomes of non-farmers.

The problem arose mainly out of a remarkable technological revolution in agriculture. This occurred first in the United States and Canada, and then moved to the United Kingdom. It was now occurring in the E.E.C. countries and in socialist countries. It would no doubt come next in underdeveloped countries. In industrial countries, there was a decline in the size of the farm labour force and one could identify various stages in this. First, one had a major fall in the amount of family labour on farms. Second, one had a fall in the number of operators, though there was little fall in the amount of hired labour used as the size of farms increased. The technical revolution occurred first in the United States. Professor Cooper had said that the rest of the world should not follow American agricultural policy. It seemed peculiar that the United States, with the largest surplus of highly trained agricultural economists had followed such perverse agricultural policies. Under Public Law 480, exports of agricultural products had reached about 1 5 billion per annum. We had seen some of the effects of this on underdeveloped countries. America had taken land out of cultivation. While there was a fall in agricultural surpluses, there were also 50 million acres of retired land in America which could be brought back into use. We were clearly in for a long period of agricultural surpluses.

So far as Mr Shonfield's views on the E.E.C. were concerned, perhaps high agricultural prices were the only way in which the E.E.C. could achieve its political objective of common prices and free trade within the Community. It was following the line of least resistance. Structural changes had probably been too slow, but this was the inevitable direction in which the E.E.C. must move. Similarly, high prices did achieve the welfare objective of keeping up farm incomes. However, this was not necessarily the most efficient way of doing so. The amount transferred from taxpayers and consumers was enormous. For example, the total cost of E.E.C. agricultural support had been put at more than $14 billion per annum. In most countries, a more efficient way of achieving these social welfare objectives would be to give direct income transfers. Even half of the $14 billion would go a long way towards providing satisfactory minimum incomes by direct income payments, considering that there were 10 million people in the farm labour force of the E.E.C. and many of these 10 million were not potential income recipients at all.

Professor James had suggested that there had been more technical change in cereal production than in beef production in France. This was true. There were few 2,000–3,000 steer feedlots in Europe, though there were in the United States. One might expect them to develop in future. So far, the fact that dairy and beef prices had been linked in the E.E.C. had meant that France had a dairy surplus but a deficiency of beef production. One problem was that expanding the output of cattle to meet the beef deficit simply increased the dairy surplus, given the present joint-product nature of production.

Professor Eastman had raised the interesting question of whether increasing prices also increased costs. Higher agricultural prices usually had most effect on the most inelastic factor – often land. In the 1960s, when Canada had been selling more wheat to China and Russia, the price of prairie land had doubled. It was now falling. So farmers lived poor and died rich!

On the exodus from agriculture, economists talked very blithely about the benefits of mobility. It was important that Professor Rieben had reminded us of the social and psychological costs of moving, or indeed of staying behind when everyone else moved. Professor Campbell wondered, sometimes, when one thought that there had been a fall in the American and Canadian farm labour force of 50 per cent since 1945, how much faster the process could have gone. The social costs, in both psychological and economic terms, would have been unbearable. It was undoubtedly true that some countries had followed foolish policies. For a time since the war, displaced persons moving to Canada had been forced to spend a year in argiculture – even though highly trained for other work. Professors Fauvel and Rieben had mentioned the problem of girls leaving rural areas. In Canada, an interesting thing was that the birth-rate in Quebec, a largely agricultural province, was now the lowest in Canada. This was not for quite the reasons that Professor Rieben gave; there were many other social factors.

Professor Campbell wanted to refer to the kind of dilemma that faced a country like Canada or Denmark. Other countries followed protectionist and subsidy policies that seemed unwise. With a large proportion of agricultural exports to national income, Canada would find it expensive to engage in competitive export subsidies. The dilemma was that Canada had to match what she saw as bad policies if others engaged in this kind of activity; or she had to let her efficient, low-cost agriculture decline.

Professor Campbell wondered whether national agricultural policies could be the subject of international negotiations. The Kennedy Round suggested they could not; so did the International Grains Arrangement. However, this was the only way out of a very long-standing dilemma. As one reduced the number of farms, farm size would increase and the more efficient producers would produce still more.

Professor Ashton said that he was glad that the Round Table had brought agriculture into the discussion. So far, when it had appeared it had firmly been pushed away again. Much had been written and said about agricultural policies. In his speech of the opening of the F.A.O., Mayor La Guardia of New York had suggested that 'ticker-tape ain't spaghetti!' Although there was a lot of paper on the subject, perhaps not very much had yet been achieved.

There were many sacred cows in agriculture – both metaphorical and literal. There was more folklore and emotional reaction about agriculture than about any other sphere of economic activity. First, it was said that agriculture was a special case. The idea of self-sufficiency had haunted Europe since Bismarck. The United Kingdom, having got off this hook in 1846, now seemed to be climbing back again. One could have a whole paper on this issue alone. Politicians praised the quality of farming people (independent and sturdy) as different from city dwellers. Perhaps this mystique went back in Britain to the early responsibilities of raising local troops. A lot of nineteenth-century institution-building had been enshrined in, for example, agricultural co-operatives and land banks. Unfortunately, these products of a bygone age were now being copied indiscriminately by less developed countries, and not all of them were worth copying.

The objective of equalising farm and industrial incomes was perhaps the most misleading outcome of one of those sacred cows. It left out the question of how high an income one was going to achieve for how many people. The *quid pro quo* for higher agricultural incomes was, in fact, a more rapid decline in the agricultural population.

Professor Robinson had raised a number of very relevant questions. It was largely a matter of national trade philosophies. The United Kingdom had moved away from its nineteenth-century attitude. It was seen to be harsh and unrealistic to abandon a whole sector of the economy, and we had seen the pendulum swing to bring the United Kingdom into line with other countries. In all contexts, agriculture was production-oriented. In the E.E.C., with its protectionist context for agriculture, one forgot about markets, effective demand, etc. This became very clear in the 1963 debate on Britain's entry into Europe. For instance, the Commission suggested that an increase in the price of cereals of £5 per ton would not affect output. It was thought that output was limited by the full exploitation of technical capacity. The British had said, for tactical reasons, that a rise in price of £5 would bring 3 million acres back into production; in fact, it would probably have been substantially higher. The product-mix of British farmers was very responsive to price changes. British producers had accepted the need to move to new outlets. Deficiency payments had led to too much milk; there had therefore been a quantitative restriction – but the politicians would say no more than this. They simply said that they wanted efficient production.

In Sweden, the problem was more logically recognised. The Swedes said that high self-sufficiency had a rather high opportunity cost. So they were laying the foundations for change.

Professor Ashton found it interesting that, during the whole session, the consumer had not once been mentioned as an interested party. Yet if one proposed to pay for agricultural policies via the market, it was a very regressive way of doing so. One should perhaps say to Mr Shonfield that, in the end, it was the consumer who would have to pick up the bill. It was now suggested that the strongest lobby for stable prices in the E.E.C. was the French Ministry of Finance. The Commission had delayed restitution payments to member governments by up to two and a half to three years. Meanwhile, this was a charge on the national budget. Even though the money would be paid in three years' time, the budgetary problems caused could be disturbing.

To Professor James, on the milk/beef problem, Professor Ashton said the moral was that high prices engendered quite rapid technical progress. Prices had favoured milk producers who could thickly convert working capital into income. With beef the time-scale was longer and it was correspondingly harder, because this part of agriculture had become very neglected in a technological sense. There was little research and not much change in methods over the centuries. In milk, the situation was the reverse. The crux was therefore the beef/milk price ratio. But dairy lobbies were strong, and the danger always was that the ratio would move in the wrong direction.

Professor Robinson had asked how one distinguished long-run from short-run policies. Professor Ashton did not know what the answer was, but thought long-run policy must take us back to trade philosophy. Did we really believe in trade liberalisation? The aim must then be an economic environment in which competent people could make a living from agriculture; one certainly did not want the pre-war situation of chronic instability. Then, short-run issues became the special cases – help for upland areas, small farms, and so on.

16 American Influence on Industrial Policy in Western Europe since the Second World War

Jacques R. Houssiaux
UNIVERSITY OF PARIS

I. THE MEANING OF INDUSTRIAL POLICY

Despite the recent use of this term by economists, perhaps as an analogy with agriculture, there are many ways of defining industrial policy. 'Industrial policy' may in one sense be regarded as the combined effect on industry of a variety of macro- and micro-economic policies, including monetary, budgetary and fiscal policies, anti-trust policy, policy for government purchases and policy for wages and prices, etc. It is in this way that the United States, for example, has tackled its industrial control.[1]

Alternatively, a systematic list can be made of the objectives, the instruments and the measures adopted by or imposed on the aggregate of business interests in relation to their industrial activities. The aim will then be to establish a continuing systems analysis showing the strengths and weaknesses of industry as a whole, its principles of change, the constraints placed on it and the long- and short-term effects on industry as a whole[2] of the direct or indirect measures taken by public and private business interests. Following the United States, the French Government recently turned its attention to the identification in this sense of the major issues of industrial policy.

Finally, it is possible to regard the appearance of industrial policies as the reflection of a 'general view that is both systematic and consistent, of development problems and a mutual balance between the various industrial sectors'.[3] In this sense, while 'industrial policy has been formed progressively by adding limited measures, it is still only based to a small extent

---

[1] See *The Industrial Policies of the United States*, Report by the O.E.C.D. Industry Committee, May 1969.

[2] See para. 135 in the above-mentioned Report: 'The methods used by Government to identify the main problems that it would like to discuss with industry, and in general to pinpoint the principal issues of industrial policy, are still rather crude. What we *need* to do is to employ the systems analysis approaches that have worked so well in our military and educational planning.'

[3] See G. Colonna di Paliano, 'La politique Communautaire des Structures Industrielles', Introductory Report to the International Conference on the Industrial Policy of the European Economic Community, Milan.

on a general analysis . . . it is not a specific policy. It is rather an approach which uses economic forces to ensure the effective and smooth development of industrial activity.'[1]

If we adopt the first approach, it is unrealistic to speak of the appearance in Western Europe of industrial policies, since from 1945 onwards they have formed an integral part of the reconstruction programmes and the accelerated growth policies of almost all the Western European economies.[2]

If, on the other hand, like many observers, we hold that it is too late to introduce systematic and consistent measures into the industrial system and that it is only possible to take effective action at the two extremities, the declining sectors and the 'peak' activities, we favour two basic features of industrial policy in Europe in the last few years – an emphasis on:

(i) *international competitiveness* in national industrial activities rather than simple quantitative growth;

(ii) the *flexibility* of the national industrial system, in preference to protecting and preserving outdated activities.

Regarded in these terms, it can be reckoned that there was no real industrial policy in Western Europe before the 1966 recession. It will therefore be the more difficult to assess its content and efficacy; its content because the authorities concerned have themselves seldom attempted to clarify their industrial policies; its efficacy because there are no adequate statistical indicators to show the respective effects of industrial policies and other simultaneous measures. Thus, foreign trade statistics, a review of the actions taken to modernise the structures of firms through mergers and the establishment of new plants, statistics of productivity indicators, do not at present make it possible to measure the technical progress achieved in industry as a result of adopting given industrial policies.

II. THE NORTH AMERICAN INDUSTRIAL SYSTEM AS A MODEL FOR EUROPE

The North American industrial system has been used as a model and has played a major role in the forms and objectives of industrial policies in Western Europe in the last few years. For example:

(*a*) the composition of industrial output, which has been studied over a long period by the European countries, is attributable to the structure of American production;

(*b*) the size of the big American enterprises sets a target for the merging of European firms;

(*c*) the rate of introduction of advanced technologies into American industry is taken as an objective by European managements;

---

[1] See G. Colonna di Paliano, op. cit., p. 27.
[2] See O.E.C.D., *Gaps in Technology*, General Report (1969).

(d) European managers are trying to popularise modern managerial methods similar to those of American firms;
(e) European countries are aiming at increasing the proportion of new products in their exports, taking as a target the composition of American foreign trade.

This is not a new phenomenon. Since the 'American challenge' and the emphasis placed on the technological gap – that is to say, since the beginning of the post-war period – European governments have been trying gradually to reduce their dependence on advanced North American technology; the nuclear policies of Great Britain and France, the prestige expenditure on aeronautics or electronics have had this as their objective. What is new is that European governments are now trying to imitate the methods used in the United States to develop new technologies and spread them throughout their industries. There has been emphasis on the efficiency of the management techniques which made the Apollo programme possible, on the value for Europe of the former pupils of American business schools, on imitating the methods of creating and of managing the big mergers on the other side of the Atlantic. There has been an infatuation in administration circles for planning–programming–budgeting methods. All these and many other signs show the growing influence of the American industrial system on European thinking. Mobility, decentralisation and competition are in conflict with the older system of bureaucratic efficiency that is still characteristic of industrial organisation on the Continent.[1]

Yet any closer examination of the industrial policies that have progressively been put into effect in European countries[2] shows, on the one hand, that they differ considerably from the American conception of Federal action in relation to industry and, on the other hand, that there is danger of probable clashes with the American Administration.

In the following sections of this paper a brief description will first be given of the objectives of industrial policy in Europe. This will then be broadly compared with American policy or what takes its place. Thereafter an examination will be made of the problem of integrating national industrial policies into policies for wider regional associations, such as the European Economic Community. Finally, an attempt will be made to discover where, in the application of European industrial policies, there

[1] The failure of the European Productivity Agency after 1948 to spread American industrial ethics in Europe is well known. Nevertheless, it is undeniable that the old system of bureaucratic efficiency had outstanding success in certain European industries, particularly in Germany, especially during the post-war reconstruction period. An earlier experience also shows that in the past under the July Monarchy, the industrial organisation of the Colbertists and the Anglo-Saxon industrial revolution were both examples of successful achievement.

[2] See O.E.C.D. reports on industrial policy in the different European countries, 1967 to 1969. We would particularly like to thank Mr Roelants du Vivier for making these reports available to us.

might be clashes with American official and private decision-making bodies.

III. THE GRADUAL INTRODUCTION OF INDUSTRIAL POLICY IN WESTERN EUROPE

Industrial policy makes its appearance when individual and separate economic measures introduced to help the traditional organisations in certain sectors of industry become so numerous that the authorities realise that co-ordination is necessary. The signs of the beginnings of an industrial policy are similar in all European countries. There are programmes, research and development planning, the promotion of mergers and the rationalisation of enterprises. It is only gradually that the profile of industrial policies becomes clear, but it generally includes the following seven elements:

(1) *The reorganisation of public administration* to strengthen the points of contact between the administration and the business sector; for example, in Great Britain the setting up of a Ministry of Technology and an Economic Development Council (E.D.C.); in France, the creation of a Ministry of Industrial Development, the reorganisation of the planning commissions, the creation of an industrial development committee and co-operation with enterprises to apply a more liberal price policy (policy of programme contacts); and in Sweden, the setting up in 1968 of the Industrial Policy Council. There are also many more examples.

(2) *The introduction of measures to modify industrial structures:* this takes the form of the creation of new enterprises, the formation of business groups, the setting up of giant enterprises of 'international dimensions', the improvement of the profitability conditions for national enterprises, etc. Examples of actions of this kind are those taken under the auspices of the Industrial Reorganisation Corporation (I.R.C.) in Great Britain, technical planning in France (iron and steel, larger computers, electronic components, machine-tools, armaments, etc.).

(3) *A more systematic organisation of the reconversion of declining economic sectors*, such as the reconversion of the Ruhr, closure of mines and the concentration of coal yards in Germany, the successful reconversion of the naval dockyards in France, direct financial aids for reorganising certain industries in Great Britain.

(4) *The promotion of technologically advanced industries.* This policy of action on the *sectoral structures* has been encouraged in Great Britain by the I.R.C. and the E.D.C. and the various economic Ministries. The enterprises in these sectors have benefited from financial assistance for investment in France, Germany, Great Britain and Sweden either directly or through the various measures taken to assist scientific and technical research.

(5) *An infrastructure policy* based on a new conception of the role of

common-service equipment in the growth of industrial productivity. These measures in the fields of vocational and higher education, basic research, transport infrastructure and urban organisation have been reoriented in various European countries since 1960. For instance, in Great Britain the 1964 Act on vocational training led to the setting up of a series of sectoral bodies for vocational training; it was the same in France after December 1966. Germany followed later in the same direction. This movement towards collective services linked to industrial policy recalls the substitution of equipment programmes in France after 1840.[1] In those days 'the sudden irruption of the railways led to the problem of superimposing one level of equipment on another'[2] both of which could not be financed at the same time. It was to be for the Saint-Simonian school to provide the financial institutions so that the essential part of their industrial policy could be put into effect.[3]

In Sweden, Germany and later in France industrial development funds were instituted and private financing sought for the collective equipment needed to fulfil the increasingly heavier collective equipment programmes.

(6) *Action to reorganise the main sectors of the services needed for the development of the industrial activities*, as, for example, the commercial and banking sectors. In France and Great Britain the banking system has had to be considerably modified in order to develop new industrial services. Banks have merged and national banks have recovered their active role in industrial development, in the case of the Crédit Mobilier in about the year 1865 and the Crédit Lyonnais at the end of the century. There is talk in some countries of setting up Industrial Development Banks. It would seem that a fairy had suddenly transformed the timid and somnolent banking circles. The state has obviously played an appreciable role in reviving the banking sector in France. Perhaps it has needed it more than other sectors. The use of credit schemes is still the key to industrial policy in European countries as, for instance, in Sweden, where the required collective services have been financed by large investment institutions such as the National Superannuation Fund.

(7) *Measures for changing the industrial values of a nation*. The authorities are trying to encourage the acceptance by the public of concepts of efficiency, mobility and competition. The Report of the French Industrial Development Committee, published in July 1969, devotes an entire part of its government action programme to describing the new industrial ideas which should be disseminated through the various levels of society. Similarly, efficiency measures are more widespread in various European countries because of official or semi-official institutions such as the R.K.W.

---

[1] See L. Girard, *La politique des Travaux Publics sous le Second Empire* (Paris, 1952).
[2] Ibid., p. 4.
[3] See J. B. Vergeot, *Le crédit comme stimulant et Régulateur de l'Industrie* (Paris, 1918).

in Germany and the British Institute of Management (B.I.M.) in Great Britain.

The establishment in France of the Centre National d'Information sur la Productivité des Entreprises (National Information Centre on Business Productivity) and the Fondation Nationale pour la Gestion des Entreprises (National Foundation for Business Management) is a result of the same line of thought.

Action on *sectoral structures*, measures for the adaptation of enterprises, strengthening of the infrastructures and industrial environment are some of the principal industrial policy guidelines which European countries are gradually introducing. There is nothing very new about these concepts or even about the measures recommended. But the wide range of action undertaken in certain countries is surprising. For instance, the trend towards concentration in Great Britain, the reconversion policies in Germany and France, the reorganisation of the critical sectors in Great Britain and France, all these actions are becoming more consistent, permanent and efficient.

There are still, however, marked differences from the American concept of industrial policy. In Europe, industrial policy is still very much guided by tradition. Governments continue to correct the effects of the rigid structures of the past. To a certain extent, they are trying to remedy the deficiencies of the private sector in introducing modern industry. They have welcomed it and have then discovered the difficulty for European private enterprises in introducing certain advanced technologies. In the States, it appears that there is less need to fear a *lack of development opportunities* in industry or the *lack of means* to tackle them. Industrial policy simply becomes an arrangement for joint action with the private sector. Let us briefly recall the organisation of this policy since its main points are well known and will be found in detail in the O.E.C.D. Reports.[1]

IV. THE CONSISTENCY OF AMERICAN INDUSTRIAL POLICY

The state's contribution to the development of industrial activities in the United States in the form of industrial policy has been limited to the following lines of action:

(1) *The setting up of an effective system of co-operation with the business community.* Traditionally, the different administrative departments have rather close links with the various sectors of industrial opinion. However, since 1967, with the introduction of the prices policy, restriction of direct foreign investments and the campaign against 'hard-core' unemployment, periodic discussions have taken place between senior officials of the Federal Administration and business executives. These 'government-

---

[1] See O.E.C.D., *The Industrial Policies of the United States*, Report by Industry Committee, May 1969.

industry' dialogues do not take the place of the administration's traditional contacts with the organisations representing industry. But they enable certain specific action programmes to be prepared more efficiently and ensure the dissemination of the 'guidelines' in the industrial community.

(2) *The application of the guiding principles laid down for business practices.* These rules mainly concern anti-trust policy, patents, direct foreign investment, measures to protect the consumer, measures to protect shareholders, and the elimination of industrial nuisance and are not in principle concerned with the particular situation in one sector or one enterprise. They are constraints affecting the whole business community; the market is regarded as an efficient regulator of industrial activity so long as the guiding principles are observed.

(3) *Limited measures to promote the adaptation of enterprises.* These policies mainly affect employment and investment and the small business sector. These are anti-cyclical policies rather than policies for developing businesses.

(4) *Action in the field of infrastructure and industrial environment.* This is the major field for government action. The main items are the Federal credits for scientific research, town development, transport infrastructure and educational programmes.

The combined measures grouped under the title 'industrial policy' present undoubted consistency and force, but it would be an exaggeration to suggest that this is a result of studied and systematic formulation. American industrial policy is, moreover, a product of the economic history of the United States and is at the same state of progress as its industrial system. Certain aspects of the industrial policy are indeed of recent origin, as, for example, the dialogues which have given to the relationship between the Federal Government and major-industry a wider role in defining and applying economic micro-policies – the 'guidelines'. In addition, these dialogues have been used for other purposes, for discussions on the formulation of macro-policies (credit, budget and taxation), for consultations on the conditions for applying the guiding principles (patents, mergers, nuisance) and exchanges of view on the possible improvement of public institutions.

As regards measures in the field of infrastructure and industrial environment, their rapid development since 1962 has been encouraged by the high growth of the economy after the recession in 1961 and by the present economic and budgetary doctrine of the 'New Economics'.

The measures for promoting the modernisation of businesses and business managements have been extended remarkably since 1931. Some of the major institutions responsible for seeing that the guiding principles laid down by the economic regulations are respected date from that period.

Finally, the American Government and Congress have not hesitated to add a conceptual or institutional measure to the stock of industrial policy instruments when it has become necessary to eliminate a bottleneck, to help the producers to understand industrial development, or to give a fresh start to technical progress. A recent example may be given. The new Ministerial Committee for Price Stability has been considering how to improve the upkeep of domestic appliances with the result that under the Fair Packaging and Labelling Act of 1967 mandatory and voluntary standards are being developed.

This brief examination of European and American industrial policies shows that similar instruments are used in many of the measures adopted on both sides of the Atlantic. And they are adopted with the same objective: to make industrial progress faster and smoother. The differences are none the less considerable, particularly in the general approach of those responsible for industrial policy. On this side of the Atlantic priority is given to measures for the adaptation of businesses and industries; on the other to guidelines and leadership. Is this a simple result of the historical difference in industrial development or a preference for a particular system? One can only judge for oneself.

V. THE INTEGRATION OF EUROPEAN INDUSTRIAL POLICIES

The organisation of regional groups in Europe, and particularly the setting up of the European Economic Community, came at the very moment that individual member states of these groups were systematising the different lines of industrial action within their own national industrial policies. The creation of regional groups should result in a progressive transfer to joint institutions of some of the functions formerly carried out by the national states, or at the least a co-ordination of strategies and national policies.

Again taking the example of the Common Market, an industrial policy for the Community gradually appeared, dividing various instruments for action permitted by the Treaty between the institutions of the Community, the Commission and the Council.

The content of the Community's industrial policy closely resembles the guidelines described for the United States, only differing on a few minor points. The Treaty of Rome gave the institutions of the Community wide powers to control business practices. The regulation on combines and monopolies is one of the first of the guiding principles specifically for the Community (Articles 85 and 86). Since 1960, the Commission has been trying to bring in another regulation on brevets.

In our opinion, the implementation of the guiding principles is probably the most important item in the Community's industrial policy at the present stage of the trend in thinking in Europe and of European integration. The Treaty has also provided the Community institutions with various instruments to promote the modification of businesses and industrial structures in Europe. But in this field *the direct means of action* of Brussels authorities must be distinguished from their work on *co-ordination, harmonisation and incentive* for the benefit of the member countries. Thus, as regards aid, government purchases, standardisation, technical obstacles to trade within the Community, alignment of legislations, *direct action* is limited to financial aid by the European Investment Bank. For the rest, the Community bodies, especially through the Committee for Medium-Term Policy and its specialised Working Parties, can help the states to modify their strategies, can induce them not to practice policies unfavourable to their partners (beggar-my-neighbour policies), to avoid outbidding between member countries, to have regular discussions on policy steering and the major industrial projects of the states, and to prepare special projects of joint activities by several member countries. Efforts have already been made in this direction: in iron and steel, textiles, shipyards and oil. They have not always given very satisfactory results. Thus, it is probable that, when the Treaties are merged, provisions will be laid down for the joint use of the existing instruments, which is a field in which the Treaty of Rome gives little scope for effective action.

A procedure for effective co-operation with the industrial community also seems to be necessary, even more so than in the United States. In fact, the development of industry in its national traditional locations has increased the differences within the Community as a whole; the abolition of customs barriers widens the gaps, making dangerous a policy limited to guidance and *laisser-faire*. A passive policy of that kind would not be accepted either in industrial circles or by the populations of the member states.

Co-operation on employment, the migration of workers, business mergers beyond the frontiers of individual countries, the practical application of freedom to decide location, social charges and taxation, and similar matters are made more difficult by the absence of close community of interest within European industrial circles. This was seen, in particular, during the industrial 'hearings' which the Community organised for each sector at the time of the Kennedy Round. Each crisis in the Community has divided the industrial Community and disrupted European industrial associations to such an extent that it sometimes seemed as though the enterprises repudiated their national associations.

The stage when the work on industrial policy can be divided between the Community bodies and national administrations is far from having been reached. In the future several arrangements are possible:

1st approach: Industrial policies remain the responsibility of national states. The Community bodies show what the effects of these policies will be on the member countries and discuss with the states the objectives, instruments and measures taken to apply these policies.

2nd approach: The states establish with the Commission the main guidelines of the Community's industrial policy. They decide in the Council the choice of instruments and make a periodic report on the measures taken to apply the agreed programme.

3rd approach: The states give the Commission the task of advising businesses on techniques, markets, and locations. The Community bodies are also responsible for improving the industrial environment of the European enterprises by creating favourable legal and fiscal conditions. The aids and subsidies for adapting sectoral structures are decided directly by the states but are governed by rules laid down by the Community bodies.

4th approach: The states leave the Community with the task of organising and financing the common infrastructure programme (scientific research, town development, transport infrastructure, educational institutions and specialised research). The Community bodies are also made responsible for files such as foreign investment in Europe, the organisation of European financing instruments, the constitution of a few public enterprises on European lines, the economic development of regional areas covering several national territories, etc.

5th approach: The states make the Community bodies responsible for the macro-economic policies (a European system of reserves, setting up of an inter-regional equalising fund, co-ordination of taxation systems, etc.).

The efforts of the various European countries rapidly to adapt their national industries to competitive conditions will probably limit the concessions that states will make to administration by the Community to the following lines of action:

(i) The Community studies the development of European industries, points out the disparities, indicates the reconversions needed and in some cases even organises, for limited periods and in well-defined sectors, a Community system of aid.

(ii) The Community informs the businesses of the development of modern industrial techniques. It helps them with their rationalisation and training programmes either directly or through bodies similar to the Industrial Training Boards in Great Britain. It develops the vocational training programmes for the workers in the Community.

(iii) The Community undertakes, as a part of the medium-term policy, studies on joint technological action by the member countries which can be decided by them.

(iv) The Community applies the provisions of Article 92 on aid and continues to improve the overall guiding principles for businesses, in particular on patents and anti-trust.

It is thus probable that the regional groupings in Europe will benefit to a large extent from the conception of overall industrial policy formulated by the member countries. But, except in fields where innovation is needed or where the historical experience of member countries is inadequate – as for example on the subject of anti-trust – it is doubtful whether the national states will agree to relax appreciably their control over the instruments of industrial policy.

The regional body will never be more than a centre for co-ordinating national policies and a study centre for the benefit of administrations and businesses. Industrial policy will only go beyond the simple stage of inter-state co-ordination when the regional or Community body has control over global economic policy, that is to say over the economic institutions of a federal unit and, in particular, over monetary and budgetary instruments.

It is unlikely, then, that Community policy will become a mere sum of present national industrial policies retaining the existing characteristics of the economic interventions in the various states. In fact, the experience of the United States tends to show that expectations of the probable consequences of an inevitable broadening of European markets may be exaggerated.[1]

In these circumstances, the effect of future development of European integration may not be expected to be a transfer to the Community administration of the instruments which the Federal Government of the United States at present possesses for control of businesses and sectors of industry. There can be no certainty, as with the Common Agricultural Policy, that industrial affairs in Europe will be subjected to a heavy and ineffective bureaucracy.

VI. THE AREAS OF CONFLICT BETWEEN EUROPE AND THE UNITED STATES AND THE INTERNATIONAL CO-ORDINATION OF THE INDUSTRIAL POLICIES OF DEVELOPED COUNTRIES

Europeans have reason to be concerned about the actions of American decision-makers when they have repercussions on objectives of industrial policy on the Continent. It is easy to make a list of these matters of complaint:

(a) exploitation of the European financial market by American financial institutions;

---

[1] See O.E.C.D., *Industrial Policies of the United States*, May 1969, paras. 10 ff.: 'The United States economy undoubtedly benefits from the large size of its internal markets, but probably not to the extent that many people may believe.... We are also experiencing a fractionalisation of markets as a result of the affluence and the diversity of goods offered.... The ability of the manufacturer to deal with the market as though it were a uniform entity disappears....'

(b) the development of direct investment in Europe and the taking over of a growing number of European companies by American big business;

(c) attraction of European investment to the United States and the American authorities' appeal to European businesses to enter American markets;

(d) attraction of highly qualified manpower and the brain drain to America;

(e) American protectionist trade policy and the existence of large barriers to the entry of European products (in particular non-tariff barriers);

(f) American aid to industry for scientific research, distorting competition with European enterprises;

(g) government purchase with the same effects;

(h) the economic power of the big American companies which enables them to exercise certain discriminating practices in the European market.

Clearly the majority of these complaints against American industry and the Administration are based on a misunderstanding of the way in which industry functions in the United States. But even so, and quite apart from the effects of the international monetary situation, Europe finds itself placed in an ambiguous situation as regards American industry which may encourage it to intensify its own measures of protection.

First, Europe, which is trying to increase the use or advanced technologies in its own enterprises, may find itself forced to discriminate against American subsidiaries. This discrimination may take various forms: a stricter application of anti-trust rules to non-Community businesses, in particular the rules relating to monopolies; the drawing up of a special statute for European firms, a tightening up of the right to establish firms and of access to the financial market by non-European enterprises; control over the acquisition of joint ventures and over take-overs by non-European enterprises. Such a policy will never be made public, but none the less it will be put into effect more and more often. Moreover, the European authorities will attempt to insist that European components in the international corporations shall be independent of the decision-making and control centres in the United States. Thus, the phase of establishing multinational companies of American origin in Europe is likely to be followed by a phase of intensive Europeanisation of these companies.[1]

This policy designed to protect the European industry was difficult to imagine when the European states were still able to outbid one another to

---

[1] Which will start with the voluntary return to 'polycentralism', to use Mr Perlmutter's expression, *Columbia Journal of World Business* (Jan 1969).

attract American businesses to their countries. It now seems that in various European countries, including Great Britain,[1] there is similar action and a common attitude which may restrict United States direct investment in Europe during the coming years, despite any relaxing of restrictive measures by the American Government.

It would seem to many responsible Europeans that Europe has filled the technological gap sufficiently to be much less afraid of the effect on its advanced industries of a slowing down of direct American investment. On the contrary, Europe has reason to fear the hold that multinational companies may have on European industry, with its possible reactions on the whole system of work, on the international division of labour, on international trade, and on relative autonomy of economic policy, if the two continents should make bilateral negotiations on industry easy between Europe and America.

Despite our beliefs and our desires, despite the development of freedom in international trade during the last few years, the world can still be divided.

Today, it appears clearly that Europe will not be a second market for the decision-makers of the North American industrial system. It is by different methods that the association of the two continents at industrial level should be achieved.

[1] As implied by the attitude of Mr Wilson's government to direct American investment since January 1969.

17 United States Foreign Investment and the Technological Gap

John H. Dunning
UNIVERSITIES OF READING AND WESTERN ONTARIO

I. THEORETICAL EXPLANATIONS OF THE GAP

Much has been written, in recent years, about the technological gap between Europe and the United States, and its significance in influencing the rate and structure of economic growth of the two regions.[1] The extent and character of the gap have been variously evaluated,[2] but one index of technological *usage* now commanding increasing attention is the export competitiveness of Europe and the United States in technologically advanced products. Several studies have shown that there is a strong positive correlation between the level and share of world trade of particular manufactured products accounted for by the United States and their research and development content.[3] But it has also been observed that such an advantage may more reflect the Americans' comparative ability to innovate new products than their efficiency in manufacturing these products once innovated;[4] and that where this is the case, over time, unless there are continuing dynamic scale economies in the innovating country, or a complete blockage in the transmission of knowledge,[5] production will gradually spread to countries where production and marketing conditions are the most favourable.

The sequence and form of the diffusion of knowledge between countries,

[1] The latest and most comprehensive analysis is contained in the O.E.C.D. study, *Gaps in Technology: An Analytical Report* (Paris, 1969) and the related industry case studies.

[2] See, for example, C. Layton, *European Advanced Technology* (Allen & Unwin, 1969).

[3] D. Keesing, 'The Impact of Research and Development on United States Trade', *Journal of Political Economy*, LXXV (Feb 1967) 38–45; W. Gruber, D. Mehta and R. Vernon, 'The Research and Development Factor in International Trade and Investment of United States Industries, *Journal of Political Economy*, LXXV (Feb 1967) 20–37; W. Gruber and R. Vernon, 'The Research and Development Factor in a World Trade Matrix', paper presented at Conference of Technology and Competition in International Trade, sponsored by Universities–National Bureau Committee for Economic Research, New York, Dec 1968.

[4] G. C. Hufbauer, *Synthetic Materials and the Theory of International Trade* (Harvard University Press, 1966).

[5] M. V. Posner, 'International Trade and Technical Change', *Oxford Economic Papers*, XIII (Oct 1961) 323–44; K. J. Arrow, 'The Economic Implications of Learning by Doing', *Review of Economic Studies*, XXIX (June 1962) 155–73.

and its impact on the level and pattern of international trade, has been examined in the literature mainly from two approaches,[1] known respectively as the *product cycle* and *technological gap* theories. As they have so far been tested,[2] the United States has been cast in the role of the innovating country, and the impact of the introduction of a variety of new products, e.g. synthetic materials, electronic goods, consumer durables, etc., traced out. Although differing in emphasis, the two models may be formulated in similar sequential terms. These, very briefly, and expressed in terms of *product* innovation, are as follows:

(1) the innovating country is initially the sole producer and exporter of the new product;
(2) foreign producers begin either to displace, or reduce the rate of increase of exports from the innovating country;
(3) foreign goods become competitive with the innovating country's exports in third markets, thereby further reducing their volume or share in world trade;
(4) foreign goods compete with those domestically produced in the innovating country.

There is nothing mechanistic about this cycle of events or its timing; it does not necessarily follow that foreign production will always become competitive in third markets or that the innovating country will finally import large quantities of the goods it first exported. Much will depend on comparative world trade and production advantages, and the extent to which these are interfered with by trade barriers of one kind or another.

The theories offer alternative explanations of the initial monopoly position of the innovating country and the process by which production and trade are internationalised. The product cycle theory assumes the initial barrier to production by importing countries is the inadequacy of their domestic markets: it is essentially a *demand*-oriented theory. The technological gap theory suggests that local production is not undertaken principally because the relevant knowhow is not available or is too

[1] For a summary of these and other modern trade theories, see G. Hufbauer, 'Theories of International Trade and Technological Progress', paper presented at Conference on Technology and Competition in International Trade, sponsored by Universities – National Bureau Committee for Economic Research, New York, Dec 1968.

[2] R. Vernon, 'International Investment and International Trade in the Product Cycle', *Quarterly Journal of Economics*, LXXX (May 1966) 190–207; S. Hirsch, *Location of Industry and International Competitiveness* (Oxford, 1967); L. T. Wells, 'Test of a Product Cycle Model of International Trade: U.S. Exports of consumer Durables', *Quarterly Journal of Economics*, LXXXIII (Feb 1969) 152–62; B. N. Wilkinson, *Canada's International Trade: Analysis of Recent Trends and Products* (Private Planning Association of Canada, Montreal, 1968); R. B. Stobaugh, Jr, 'The Product Cycle, U.S. Exports and International Investment', unpublished Ph.D. dissertation (Harvard University, 1968); G. K. Douglass, 'Product Variation and International Trade in Motion Pictures', unpublished Ph.D. thesis (Massachusetts Institute of Technology, 1963).

expensive to acquire: it is basically a *supply*-oriented model. In practice these theories complement each other in so far as both set forth necessary conditions for the internationalisation of production and trade.

Both the extent to which and the speed at which production is diffused from the innovating country will depend on a variety of factors influencing comparative cost and demand conditions. Obviously, the more alike economic conditions in the non-innovating countries are to those in the innovating country, and the easier technology can be transmitted, the more likely production will be internationalised, particularly if restrictions are placed on the exports of the innovating country.

Both the product cycle and technological gap theories of trade are essentially micro-oriented. Neither theory, for example, explicitly predicts future levels and composition of exports of the *innovating* country, though both seem implicitly to assume that, even if its exports (or share of exports) of one generation of product discoveries eventually decline, these will be replaced either by product discoveries of a new generation or, where foreign production is in the hands of subsidiaries of the innovating country, by an increase of its invisible exports. Moreover, except where technological advance takes the form of completely new products, these models are difficult to test at a *macro*-level, as the existing classification of commodity statistics – even at a four-digit level – make little allowance for the age or type of product.[1] Neither does the technological gap theory shed much light on trends in the balance of technological power between advanced industrial nations.

One important aspect of both the product cycle and technological gap theories concerns the speed and manner in which the *use* of technology is internationalised. In this paper, we shall first outline the main changes which have occurred in the level and composition of exports of technological goods from Europe and the United States between 1955 and 1965. More particularly, we shall attempt to assess whether there has been an improvement in Europe's competitive performance vis-à-vis the United States, and how far this reflects a narrowing of the transatlantic gap in the use of technology. Second, we shall examine the extent to which the changes revealed have been due to Europe's increased *production* of technology[2] and how far to an increase in technological borrowing from the United States in the form of licensing agreements or direct investment by United States companies in Europe.

We start our analysis with a brief historical excursion into the impact made by the transfer of knowledge from the United Kingdom to the United States on the structure of Anglo-American trade and production in the nineteenth century. This *inter alia* illustrates the relevance of the

---

[1] Obviously, as the commodity statistics are classified in more detail, the possibility of making effective tests is improved.
[2] Vis-à-vis the United States.

two trade theories under discussion where the innovating country is a (relatively) low-wage economy and the non-innovating country is a (relatively) high-wage economy.

II. THE TRANSFERENCE OF CAPITAL AND KNOWLEDGE

For most of the nineteenth century, technology was transferred from Europe to the United States by the migration of skilled labour and entrepreneurs on the one hand, and the exports of machinery and paper knowledge (e.g. blueprints, designs, formulae) on the other. There were comparatively few licensing agreements between European and United States firms, and, until the latter part of the period, there was no European direct investment in the United States. In the main, though similar in their timing, the transference of capital and knowledge were independent of each other.[1] We outline the main features of each, before and after the Civil War.

(1) *Down to 1860*

Prior to the Civil War, most foreign capital – which was almost entirely United Kingdom supplied – was directed to state and municipal governments, and used, in the North, to build an infrastructure of transport and communication facilities, upon which the American 'take off' rested,[2] and in the South to help finance the production and marketing of cotton for sale to United Kingdom factories.[3] By current standards, the amounts invested were small. Between 1830 and 1839, the net international indebtedness of the United States increased by $222 million and, at this latter date, the cumulative foreign capital stake stood at $297 million.[4] After a short recession, capital imports resumed, and by 1860 the net indebtedness has risen to $379 million.[5] Most foreign investment in the 1850s went into railroad expansion.

The technological contribution of European capital was primarily indirect. It was to help accelerate and sustain structural changes in American capital formation then emerging. Technologically, the discovery

---

[1] R. Nurkse, 'International Investment Today in the Light of Nineteenth-Century Experience', *Economic Journal*, LXIV (Dec 1954).
[2] W. W. Rostow, *The Stages of Economic Growth* (Cambridge, 1961).
[3] For a comprehensive account of United Kingdom investment in the United States in the nineteenth century, see T. C. Coram, 'The Role of British Capital Development of the United States, 1600–1914', M.Sc. (Soc. Science) thesis (University of Southampton, 1967).
[4] D. C. North, 'The U.S. Balance of Payments, 1790–1860', in *Trends in the American Economy in the Nineteenth Century*, Studies in Income and Wealth, No. 24 (National Bureau of Economic Research, New York, 1960). At this latter date it was reckoned that at least one-half of the total state debts were in foreign hands.
[5] Ibid., p. 581.

of the cotton gin, the opening up of the Erie Canal and the coming of the railroad were the main dynamic forces: each of these was indigenously generated. Little foreign capital was invested in manufacturing industry, partly because of the risks involved and partly because United Kingdom investors felt that this would reduce export opportunities of domestic industry. But indirectly, United Kingdom investment released local capital for manufacturing outlets – particularly in the metals and textile industries.

Europe's main technological contribution to the development of United States industry came mostly by other means. There are several examples of British firms transferring their activities or setting up branch units to overcome tariffs,[1] notably in the linen and woollen industry. As part of the new Republic's attempt to promote secondary industry, American agents visited the United Kingdom with tempting offers to attract skilled workers in the iron, textiles, glass and other industries. Following the migration of Samuel Slater, the founder of the modern cotton-spinning industry in the United States, hundreds of cotton workers migrated across the Atlantic. The first woollen factory with power machinery was started by two Englishmen.[2] In spite of British legislation, designed to restrict the outflow of knowledge, machinery, drawings and patterns were smuggled out of the country. In the metal industries, the immigrants were fairly senior technicians or superintendents of plants; they sought to sell their ideas and know-how to United States capitalists and frequently became entrepreneurs in their own right. The canning and brewing industry also owed much to United Kingdom migrants; most of the technical improvements in the carpet industry originated from Scotland; Dundee capitalists and mill superintendents set up the jute industry in Paterson. The pottery and cutlery industries were largely found by English journeymen – complete with tools and equipment; the silk industry was in the hands of German, French and English interests. Sometimes these immigrants brought with them substantial sums of money, but more often than not the amounts involved were very small.[3]

In summary, up to 1860, while United Kingdom *money* capital helped to finance the social infrastructure which advanced the United States 'take-off', United Kingdom *human* capital helped create and sustain the basis of secondary industry on which the future wealth of the United States was built. Immigration accounted for 31 per cent of the increase in population in the 1850s, and the contribution of manufacturing as a proportion of national output was still quite small. Less than 20 per cent of the population was engaged in manufacturing, mining and constructional activities in 1860 and more than three-quarters of American imports took the form of manufactured goods.[4]

[1] Coram, op. cit., p. 134.   [2] Ibid., p. 139.   [3] Ibid., p. 232.
[4] R. A. Gallman, 'Commodity output, 1839–1899', in *Trends in the American Economy in the Nineteenth Century*.

What of the impact of this migration of knowledge and capital on the structure of Anglo-American production and trade? While, in its early stages, the American industrial machine tended to converge with that of the United Kingdom, it soon diverged due to the different factor-price structure and technological needs of the two economies. At the same time, United States producers were quick to improve and adapt technologies imported from England; even before the Civil War, the principle of interchangeability of parts had been widely adopted, and a series of new innovations, e.g. the typewriter and the sewing machine, marketed. Often new British inventions were exploited in the United States with greater success than at home. Not only was the United States, unhampered by the constraints of industrial traditionalism, able to learn from the United Kingdom's mistakes; from the start, labour – particularly skilled labour – was at a premium, and there was considerable pressure to introduce capital-intensive methods. But because of domestic market limitations, American producers were unable to compete with United Kingdom producers for export markets; indeed, for the most part they had to be protected by a high tariff wall against United Kingdom imports. Nevertheless, up to 1860 and beyond, the United States was a substantial net importer in the products in which foreign expertise and capital, directly or indirectly, played an important role. Trade both followed and stimulated the movement of capital and labour.[1] The *proportion* of imports from Europe declined as she became more self-sufficient, but in most cases the absolute volume continued to increase quite rapidly. By 1860 about two-fifths of all Britain's manufactured exports were sold to the United States, who dispatched 70 per cent of her exports (mainly cotton and tobacco) to the United Kingdom.[2]

In spite of Britain's efforts to restrain the export of knowledge, the period up to 1860 was one in which its international mobility was high and the imitation lag small. Quickly the imported technology was adapted to suit the needs of the importing country. If a technological gap existed between Europe and the United States at the beginning of the nineteenth century, it was closed by the middle of the century. Already by that time the United States was more mechanised than the United Kingdom, and her output per head was at least as high. The idea that the initial product innovator maintains its lead is not borne out in this instance, though it is true the most marked progress occurred in those American industries in which the United Kingdom was at a comparative disadvantage.

(2) *After the Civil War*

Between 1860 and 1914, foreign investment in the United States expanded

---

[1] J. Potter, 'Atlantic Economy, 1815–60: The U.S.A. and The Industrial Revolution in Britain', in *Studies in the Industrial Revolution*, ed. L. Presnell (Athlone Press, 1960).
[2] H. C. Allen, *The Anglo-American Relationship since* 1783 (Allen & Unwin, 1959).

from $400 million to about $7,000 million: at the same time gross national product rose from $5 billion to $35 billion.[1] Although for short periods, notably between 1869 and 1873 and 1887 and 1891, investment accounted for more than 10 per cent of domestic capital formation, for most of the period it was less than 5 per cent – and in the latter years, viz. 1890–1914, around 2 per cent. Most capital exports continued to be directed to railway and public securities. In 1913, for example, of the total United Kingdom portfolio investment of $3,667 million, $2,997 million or 82 per cent was invested in United States railroads.[2] Apart from breweries and distilleries there was very little money invested in American manufacturing industry. Paish has estimated United Kingdom *direct* investments in the United States at this time to be around $700 million;[3] Cleona Lewis puts the figure of all foreign direct investment at 14 per cent of all investments.[4]

The fifty years before the First World War saw a diversification of European corporate activities in the United States and rather more interest was directed to the equity stock of United States companies. More than $40 million was invested in the cattle industry between 1875 and 1890,[5] and about the same amount of money in Western mining industry between 1870 and the turn of the century.[6] In neither case was much technological transference involved; in neither case were the investments very successful. However, the economic development of certain areas was stimulated, notably in Texas and the Far West. Foreign investors also bought large tracts of American land and supported land mortgage companies.

In secondary industry, syndicates were incorporated in England with the specific purpose of buying a controlling interest in promising United States companies. These were quite extensive,[7] although the amount of capital involved was only large in three industries – brewing and distilling, flour and milling and iron and steel. Again, however, these ventures were rarely profitable, and only in the brewing industry was there any direct managerial or technical participation.[8]

One motive for direct investment during these years was the United

[1] J. H. Dunning, *Studies in International Investment* (Allen & Unwin, 1969); D. C. North, 'International Capital Movements in Historical Perspective', in *U.S. Private and Government Investment Abroad*, ed. R. Mikesell (University of Oregon Press, Eugene, 1962).

[2] G. Paish, *Transactions of the Manchester Statistical Society*, Feb 1914 (session 1913–14). [3] Ibid.,

[4] *America's stake in International Investments* (Brookings Institution, New York, 1938).

[5] W. Turrentine Jackson, 'British Interests in the Range Cattle Industry', in *When Grass Was King*, ed. M. Prink (University of Colorado Press, 1956).

[6] C. Spence, *British Investments and the American Mining Frontier* (Cornell University Press, 1958).

[7] Coram, op. cit., pp. 330 ff. [8] Ibid., pp. 332 ff.

States tariff which had been progressively raised after 1860. This induced a number of United Kingdom firms in the cotton and tinplate industry. Before the Civil War three-quarters of the trade of J. and P. Coates had been with the United States. The tariff forced the company to manufacture, and together with another United Kingdom subsidiary – American Thread – it supplied four-fifths of the cotton thread produced in the United States at the outbreak of war. Up to 1890, the United States bought 70 per cent of the tinplate produced in South Wales. Then an *ad valorem* tariff of 90 per cent was imposed, as the result of which some sixty Welsh mills were closed down.[1] In an effort to recapture the market, there was a steady migration of capital, technology and labour across the Atlantic. A similar salvage operation had occurred earlier in the silk industry: some 16,000 people migrated from Macclesfield between 1870 and 1893. Several United Kingdom companies moved the whole or part of their plants to the United States; sometimes they crated their machinery and moved lock, stock and barrel with their employees.[2] These fared rather better than the tinplate manufacturers and developed in the high-class fields of velvet and satins.

The prospects of market growth prompted other United Kingdom enterprises to set up branch plants in the United States. One outstanding example in an industry in which modern technology played an important role was the United States investment of Courtaulds in man-made fibres. This soon grew to be the most important company in its field in the United States. But most British subsidiaries operated in fairly traditional sectors, and though they transmitted expertise, they did not carve out an important market for themselves. They were mostly in the labour-intensive industries or in very specialised lines of activity.

Some firms or trades migrated completely due to depressed conditions in the United Kingdom. As a result of mechanisation, employment in United Kingdom lace and lace-curtain industries fell by one-half between 1851 and 1891.[3] Encouraged by trade union support there was also a substantial exodus of cutlery workers in the depressed 1880s.[4] In other cases the enterprising spirit was well in evidence. In 1885 a Nottingham manufacturer established the British hosiery company in Rhode Island with 120 British operatives which was intended 'to pioneer British manufacture in coming to America to sell directly to the trade'.[5] Sometimes American companies went out of their way to attract United Kingdom firms: there is at least one case of an American firm buying out a United

[1] R. T. Berthoff, *British Immigrants in Industrial America, 1790–1900* (Harvard University Press, 1953).
[2] F. R. Mason, *The American Silk Industries and the Tariff* (London, 1920).
[3] J. Clapham, *An Economic History of Modern Britain*, vol. II (Cambridge University Press, 1932) p. 513.
[4] S. Pollard, *A History of Labour in Sheffield* (Liverpool University Press, 1959).
[5] Coram, op. cit., p. 357.

Kingdom cutlery firm and persuading 150 of its employees to emigrate en bloc to work for the parent company.[1]

While it is easy to catalogue examples such as these, it is more difficult to evaluate the overall significance of the flow of United Kingdom capital and expertise on United States industrial development. Perhaps the best sources are still migration data. Paul Strassman has documented the origin of British-born textile workers who died between 1880 and 1915. Of the 224 names obtained from obituaries of trade journals, 8 manufacturers came to the United States to set up plants for United Kingdom companies, 26 started mills on their own account, 33 began in the United States as superintendents or overseers and 59 came to America as operatives and 29 as children.[2] R. T. Berthoff has estimated that in 1890 there were still 15,000 British workers in the United States iron and steel industry and that one-tenth of all the machinists were United Kingdom immigrants.[3] At the same time one-seventh of workers in the pottery industry were United Kingdom born: in the glass industry 6 per cent, in the glove industry 7 per cent, in the stone industry 28 per cent. In the cotton industry 20 per cent of the foreign-born operatives were of British stock, and in the woollen industry 33 per cent.[4]

From these and other data, it is fairly clear that the United Kingdom technological contribution to United States industrial development after 1860 largely originated from industries in which the United Kingdom had a comparative advantage. But it also appears that this knowledge was quickly assimilated, improved upon, and adapted to United States conditions, and that the United Kingdom control over it was lost. To this extent, there does seem a significant difference between what is happening today with the United States as the leading innovator. There are two main reasons for this. First, the technology transferred in the nineteenth century was largely very simple, easily learned and imitated, and needed only a small skilled labour force to service it. Even today, the industries in which European firms are represented in the United States are among the least research-intensive. Once the initial knowledge barriers had been overcome, the catching-up process was very quick indeed. What is more, there was comparatively little product or process development in these industries in the United Kingdom after the mid-nineteenth century. The innovating firms did not consolidate their early advantages in the way the product cycle infers.

Second, the reservoir of United Kingdom (and other European) knowledge was transferred from an economy in which labour was relatively

---

[1] C. Erickson, *American Industry and the European Immigrant, 1860–85* (Harvard University Press, 1957) p. 42.
[2] Quoted in Coram, op. cit., p. 358L.
[3] Berthoff, *British Immigrants in Industrial America*, p. 67.
[4] Ibid., pp. 38, 76, 77, 81.

plentiful to one in which it was scarce, and, reflecting this, to an economy geared to mechanisation and standardisation. That this sort of economic structure was a forerunner to others in the twentieth century was not apparent at the time. There appeared to be greater impetus to exploit innovations: both the rewards and the competitive pressures were more pronounced than the United Kingdom. From early times, the United States was forced to invest in process technology.[1] The fact that these processes did not infiltrate back to the United Kingdom was partly because there were few connections between United States and United Kingdom firms and partly because there did not seem the impetus for United Kingdom industry to adopt them.

We conclude, then. The European technological impact on United States development was largely ephemeral in character. Such a technological gap as existed was quickly closed, initially by the migration of skilled manpower and the export of 'paper knowledge', and later from indigenous sources. Since, however, the major contribution of Europe was in labour-intensive activities, United States production costs were generally higher than European costs, and up to 1914 the United Kingdom and Germany continued to enjoy the lion's share of most world markets.[2]

In terms of the product cycle thesis, since most European capital flows in the nineteenth century took the form of portfolio investment, the impact on the production and exports of the investing countries was indirect. Where direct investment occurred, this was prompted largely for defensive reasons and was within traditional United Kingdom industries. The United Kingdom, however, remained the main supplier of United States imports throughout the nineteenth century. In some cases, as we have seen, domestic production replaced the United Kingdom exports: in others the growth of United States incomes encouraged the United Kingdom to supply certain special consumer and capital goods which otherwise would not have been produced.

III. THE IMPACT OF UNITED STATES DIRECT INVESTMENT IN EUROPE SINCE 1955

We now turn to the main, and statistically more rewarding, part of our analysis. It is to assess the impact of United States direct investment in Europe since 1955 on both United States and European growth and trading patterns – again in the light of the hypothesis of two cyclical models of international trade referred to earlier. We take as our starting point two reasonably well-established and related propositions. The first, well

---

[1] S. Kuznets, *The Meaning and Measurement of Economic Growth*, ed. B. Supple (Random House, New York, 1963).

[2] D. Aldcroft (ed.), *The Development of British Industry and Foreign Competition, 1875-1914* (Allen & Unwin, 1968).

documented by the O.E.C.D. and several United States economists,[1] concerns the relationship between the composition and competitiveness of United States trade in manufactured products and their research and development content. The second is the technological gap existing between the United States and Europe – a stock concept – as revealed *inter alia* by the 5:1 technological balance of payments in favour of the United States, and its considerably greater volume of research and development expenditure. These have been enlarged upon elsewhere and will not be repeated here.[2]

The link between these two propositions – a link which is partly a reflection of the extent of the technological gap, but also one of the main vehicles by which it may be reduced – is the *flow* of knowledge between the United States and Europe. This may take various forms, but today – unlike the nineteenth century – the greater part of a country's technological superiority lies in its control of *proprietary* knowledge[3] – which is transmitted across national boundaries mainly through the operations of multinational companies and licensing agreements. Because of the almost complete absence of any information about the industrial or geographical composition of the latter, we shall concentrate our attention in this paper on the impact of United States direct investment on (*a*) the competitiveness and (*b*) the composition of European trade in technological products and how this, in turn, has impinged upon United States trade.

First an important point of clarification. As we have pointed out elsewhere,[4] the term technological 'gap' popularly refers to the gap between the *production* of technology of two (or more) countries. But whether it pays a country to produce or import technology depends on the structure of its resources. For it is not the production but the use of the technology which is one of the key components of economic development. One can point to a number of classic examples where it is obviously best for a country to import all or most of its technology embodied in finished products. Or, it may be appropriate for an economy to import its technology, but be a major producer of products embodying that technology. Only, perhaps, in a comparatively few cases will it pay a country to be a producer – net exporter of technology or knowledge *per se*.

But technology, as well as being an end-product in its own right, is also an agent of growth, and a means of changing the comparative trading and

[1] See references in footnotes 1 and 3 on p. 364.
[2] O.E.C.D., Gaps in technology.
[3] J. B. Quinn, 'Scientific and Technical Strategy at the National and Major Enterprise Level', paper prepared for UNESCO Office of Economic Analysis Symposium on *The Role of Science and Technology in Economic Development*, Paris, Dec 1968.
[4] J. H. Dunning, 'Technology, U.S. Direct Investment and European Economic Growth, paper given to C. K. Kindlegerger's Seminar on the International Corporation at the Sloane School of Management, Boston, Apr 1969 (to be published).

production advantages of particular countries. It by no means follows that the country which innovates new products will be the best suited to manufacture those products. On the other hand, countries which have the advantage in this respect cannot exploit their position without the necessary knowledge of *how* to do this – and it is the transference of such knowledge the multinational corporation facilitates. In such cases, international investment often becomes the prerequisite of international trade.

As a frame of reference for our discussion, let us classify countries according to whether they are mainly:

(1) net exporters of technology and of technology-embodied products;
(2) net exporters of technology-embodied products, but net importers of technology;
(3) net importers of both technology and technology-embodied products.

Countries in the first category may be distinguished by their substantial allocation of resources to higher education and research and development, by their high ratio of (*a*) receipts of royalties and fees from foreign firms, relative to those paid to foreign firms, and (*b*) export of research-intensive products to all manufactured products. Countries in the second category include those with a considerable domestic production of technology-embodied products but which are net importers of technology. Countries in the third category, which include all of the less developed economies, normally engage in little indigenous research, and only a very small proportion of their population would expect to have a university education; these countries would import most of their technologically advanced products.

In Table 17.1 we set out the state of technological development of a number of European countries and the United States for the latest year about which data are available. The definitions of the terms used are given in the notes to the table. Such a classification is, of course, descriptive rather than analytical and tells us nothing about whether countries are allocating their resources efficiently. A time series of the data in Table 17.1 would take us a little further in this respect, but unfortunately only the United Kingdom and the United States publish regular information on research or development expenditure, and even these are not directly comparable either with each other, or at different points of time. However, the gist of Table 17.1 is, perhaps, clear enough. The United States is the only country of those listed which can be classified as a net exporter of technology. The European statistics portray a rather mixed picture, but the United Kingdom, West Germany, Sweden and France would appear to be the most technologically advanced and Italy the least advanced. The table also shows, however, that those Europeans countries which are the leading producers of indigenous technology also import the most technology from the United States.

TABLE 17.1
INDICATORS OF TECHNOLOGICAL MATURITY

	(a) Production of indigenous technology					(b) Dependence on foreign technology			
	(1) Numbers in university education (as % of population),[a] 1966	(2) R. & D. expenditure ($ per head of population) 1963 or 1964	(3) % of R. & D. in science-based industries, 1963 or 1964	(4) Export of research-intensive products, 1965 (% of all manu-factured exports	(5) ($ per head of population)	(6) Receipts of royalties and fees from foreigners ($ per head of population), 1963 or 1964	(7) Payments of royalties and fees to foreigners ($ per head of population), 1963 or 1964	(8) % of patents taken out by foreigners, 1958–61	(9) Import of research-intensive products,[b] 1965 ($ per head of population)	(10) U.S. direct investment,[c] 1965 ($ per head of population)
United States	43·0	109·7	46·4	76·5	68·0	n.a.	n.a.	n.a.	8·6	26·7[a]
Europe										
(i) E.E.C. countries										
Belgium	10·0	14·7	40·9	37·6	88·2	0·8	n.a.	85·1	22·6	49·8
France	16·0	27·1	33·7	53·9	81·6	1·0	2·5	59·4	13·8	27·7
West Germany	7·5	24·6	39·7	72·1	181·2	0·8	2·6	32·4	13·2	36·8

United Kingdom	4·8	39·9	41·3	67·2	130·9	1·4	2·0	47·0	23·1	80·6
Sweden	11·0	33·5	33·6	54·3	169·7	0·9	n.a.	68·8	33·4	31·0
Norway	n.a.	11·4	16·8	31·2	71·1	n.a.	n.a.	80·0	26·7	31·4
Denmark	n.a.	n.a.	n.a.	54·6	117·5	0·8	n.a.	79·3	20·0	35·6

n.a. = not available.

[a] In the 15–24 age group.
[b] Groups 1 and 2 products imported from the United States (from EFTA and E.E.C. in the case of the United States)
[c] In manufacturing and petroleum.
[d] Foreign direct investment in United States manufacturing and petroleum.

Sources:
Column
(1) D. N. Chorafas, *The Knowledge Revolution* (Allen & Unwin, 1968) Table VI, p. 89.
(2) O.E.C.D., *The Overall Level and Structure of R. and D. Effort in O.E.C.D. Member Countries* (Paris, 1967).
(3) O.E.C.D., *Gaps in Technology*, General Report (1968) Table 1, p. 14.
(4) United Nations, *Commodity Trade Statistics*, Jan–Dec 1965.
(5) (4) above and O.E.C.D., *Main Economic Indicators*, Apr 1967.
(6) O.E.C.D., *Observer*, Apr 1968.
(7) As (6) above.
(8) *Journal of the Patent Office Society* (Washington), Feb 1964.
(9) As (5) above.
(10) U.S. Department of Commerce, *Survey of Current Business*, Sep 1966, and (5) above.

TABLE 17.2
UNITED STATES AND EUROPEAN SHARES OF TOTAL UNITED STATES AND EUROPEAN EXPORTS OF SELECTED PRODUCTS, 1955–65

	United States			EFTA			E.E.C.			Europe		
	1955 %	1960 %	1965 %	1955 %	1960 %	1965 %	1955 %	1960 %	1965 %	1955 %	1960 %	1965 %
Group 1												
Aircraft	84·3	77·4	60·6	13·2	11·5	13·4	2·5	11·1	26·0	15·7	22·6	39·4
Instruments	24·1	29·8	33·6	24·5	24·3	24·0	50·4	45·9	42·4	75·9	70·2	66·4
Agricultural machinery	46·8	44·4	41·0	28·5	35·1	29·6	24·7	20·4	29·4	53·2	55·5	59·0
Office machinery	37·5	33·4	36·0	27·0	24·1	18·8	35·5	42·3	45·2	62·5	66·4	64·0
Electrical machinery	32·1	29·4	25·2	30·2	26·3	24·3	37·7	45·3	50·4	67·9	71·6	74·8
Chemicals												
Drugs	38·2	31·3	21·1	33·9	32·9	35·7	27·9	35·8	43·2	61·8	68·7	78·9
Other chemicals	28·6	28·8	26·0	27·2	24·4	22·8	44·2	46·7	51·2	71·4	71·2	74·0
All Group 1	37·1	36·0	30·6	27·0	24·9	23·8	35·9	39·1	45·7	62·9	64·0	69·6
Group 2												
Motor vehicles	43·3	24·7	24·5	25·7	26·5	23·2	31·0	48·8	52·3	56·7	75·3	75·5
Other non-electrical machinery	37·2	30·5	29·2	31·8	30·5	27·7	30·9	39·2	43·1	62·8	69·7	70·8
Rubber products	31·4	26·9	20·5	28·3	28·7	26·3	37·6	41·5	53·2	65·8	70·2	79·5

Primary metals	18·5	26·7	19·6	33·9	31·7	31·9	47·7	41·6	48·5	81·5	73·3	80·4
Non-ferrous metals	20·5	12·6	10·3	21·0	21·3	22·0	58·4	66·1	67·6	79·5	87·4	89·4
Ferrous metals	20·6	16·1	15·6	32·0	27·2	24·0	47·4	56·7	60·4	79·4	83·9	84·3
Stone, clay and glass	34·6	30·6	28·1	27·0	27·9	26·6	38·4	41·5	45·3	65·4	69·4	71·9
Printing and publishing	42·8	51·0	39·6	47·7	33·3	33·4	9·5	15·6	27·0	57·2	49·0	60·4
Tobacco	35·1	35·8	26·6	25·0	23·9	27·2	39·9	40·3	46·1	64·9	64·2	73·4
Food products	1·8	1·1	0·9	44·1	43·6	33·0	54·2	55·3	66·1	98·2	98·9	99·1
Drink	14·0	12·9	10·6	33·2	28·3	26·1	52·8	58·8	63·4	86·0	87·1	89·4
Textiles and clothing	20·2	14·4	12·8	39·3	38·1	31·1	40·5	47·5	56·1	79·8	85·6	87·2
Lumber and wood products	26·4	24·3	23·3	50·1	48·6	45·6	23·4	27·1	31·1	73·6	75·7	76·7
Paper and allied products	20·2	18·1	15·4	31·0	28·5	28·1	48·8	53·4	28·4	79·8	80·9	56·5
All Group 3												
All products	30·5	26·3	23·7	28·8	27·2	25·7	40·6	46·5	50·6	69·5	73·7	76·3

Source: United Nations, *Commodity Trade Statistics*, 1955, 1960 and 1965.

Notes:
Group 1 products include those in which R. & D. expenditure as a percentage of sales in 1962 was 4 per cent or more *or* where scientists and engineers employed in R. & D. were 2 per cent or more of total employment.
Group 2 products include those in which the corresponding percentages were 2 per cent but under 4 per cent and 1 per cent but under 2 per cent.
Group 3 products include those in which the corresponding percentages were under 2 per cent and under 1 per cent.
Figures were taken from Table 1 of W. Gruber, D. Mehta and R. Vernon, 'The R. and D. Factor in International Trade and International Investment of United States Industries', *Journal of Political Economy*, LXXV (Feb. 1967) 23.

TABLE 17.3

INCREASE IN EXPORTS OF SELECTED PRODUCTS: UNITED STATES AND EUROPE, 1955–65

	United States			EFTA			E.E.C.			Europe		
	1955–60 (1955 =100)	1960–5 (1960 =100)	1955–65 (1955 =100)	1955–60 (1955 =100)	1960–5 (1960 =100)	1955–65 (1955 =100)	1955–60 (1955 =100)	1960–5 (1960 =100)	1955–65 (1955 =100)	1955–60 (1955 =100)	1960–5 (1960 =100)	1955–65 (1955 =100)
Group 1												
Aircraft	169·2	88·7	150·2	160·3	132·3	212·1	820·2	264·5	2169·4	264·9	197·4	522·92
Instruments	218·2	228·0	497·4	174·6	199·3	348·0	156·7	186·9	292·8	162·5	191·1	310·66
Agricultural machinery	433·1	119·5	517·4	560·3	108·9	610·0	377·4	185·9	701·7	475·5	137·2	652·51
Office machinery	192·7	226·6	436·6	193·0	164·1	316·8	259·5	222·6	577·3	230·7	201·5	464·83
Electrical machinery	138·5	155·2	215·0	136·1	162·0	220·5	188·2	194·7	366·5	165·0	182·7	301·57
Chemicals												
Drugs	119·3	94·2	112·4	141·4	151·6	214·3	186·5	169·0	315·1	161·8	160·6	259·81
Other chemicals	165·4	145·2	240·3	147·5	150·2	221·5	173·4	176·1	305·4	163·5	167·3	273·58
All Group 1	169·7	134·8	228·7	161·0	150·9	242·9	190·2	185·5	352·9	177·7	172·0	305·71
Group 2												
Motor vehicles	91·9	158·9	146·0	166·0	139·6	231·8	253·6	171·6	435·2	213·9	160·3	342·94
Non-electrical machinery	121·6	158·8	193·2	142·7	149·9	213·9	190·4	174·2	331·9	166·3	163·6	272·09
Rubber products	121·8	105·3	128·2	146·7	123·2	180·7	155·8	168·5	262·6	152·0	150·3	282·416

Primary metals												
Non-ferrous	248·1	108·3	268·8	160·8	148·4	238·6	149·5	172·4	257·8	154·1	162·1	249·8
Ferrous	98·3	94·9	93·3	161·5	120·7	194·9	180·6	119·0	214·9	175·6	119·4	209·6
Stone, clay and glass	102·1	138·9	141·8	110·6	126·9	140·3	155·8	153·0	238·4	137·6	144·6	198·9
Printing and publishing	149·6	160·8	240·7	175·2	166·9	292·3	183·6	190·1	351·0	180·1	181·4	326·7
Tobacco	155·7	126·1	196·3	91·5	162·7	148·9	211·9	279·8	592·8	115·9	199·5	231·2
Food and drink	137·0	98·0	134·2	135·3	154·8	209·4	140·8	188·7	265·7	138·6	175·2	246·7
Textiles and clothing	109·2	118·6	129·5	101·6	132·6	134·7	128·0	160·9	206·0	120·8	147·5	178·2
Lumber and wood products	117·3	132·1	154·9	159·9	120·7	193·0	193·7	174·8	338·5	177·1	137·8	243·9
Paper	129·2	152·6	197·2	136·5	148·7	203·0	162·2	181·2	295·0	144·7	160·6	232·4
All Group 3	126·2	118·5	149·5	123·0	144·5	177·8	153·9	134·9	207·7	144·5	142·1	205·3
All products	130·6	135·6	177·1	147·4	142·7	210·4	173·1	164·4	284·5	160·7	156·3	251·2

Source: United Nations, *Commodity Trade Statistics*, 1955, 1960 and 1965.

IV. THE CHANGING STRUCTURES OF UNITED STATES AND EUROPEAN EXPORTS

We now look at the changing structure and competitiveness of United States and European manufacturing exports between 1955 and 1965. Table 17.2 classifies the export of a selection of manufactured products,[1] ranked approximately in order of their knowledge content.[2] Group 1 consists of *high* research-intensive products, Group 2 *medium* research-intensive products and Group 3 *low* research-intensive products.

This table shows that, with the exception of instruments and non-ferrous metals, Europe's share of the combined European and United States exports of all products increased between 1955 and 1965. In general, this increase was fairly evenly spread over the two sub-periods, but was rather more pronounced for the *high* research-intensive products in the latter years. Over the ten years, Europe's share of Group 1 and 2 products rose nearly three times more than her share of Group 3 products. A rank correlation between the change in Europe's export share and particular products between 1955 and 1965 and their research-intensity[3] works out at only +0·22. That it is not higher suggests that the United States has largely retained her comparative advantage in the export of certain research-intensive products.

Table 17.3, which presents the comparative increases in exports since 1955, confirms these impressions. It shows that, on average, European exports rose by 151·2 per cent between 1955 and 1965, compared with an increase in United States exports of 77·1 per cent. In the *high* and *medium* research-intensive products, the increase was substantially greater both for Europe and the United States, but *relatively* the most pronounced for the E.E.C. countries.

Taken together, these tables show:

(1) The improvement in Europe's trading position vis à vis the United States was most marked in *medium* research-intensive products in the period 1955–60 and in the *high* research-intensive products in the 1960–5 period. In these latter years, Europe increased her exports of *high* research-intensive products 27·6 per cent faster than the United States compared with 4·7 per cent faster in the earlier period.

(2) The major part of this improvement was concentrated in E.E.C. countries, which suggests a strong technological 'catching up' process was at work, with the time-lag being positively correlated with the degree

---

[1] See Appendix 1 for further details. These products accounted for over 90 per cent of American and European manufacturing exports in 1964.

[2] See notes to Table 17.2.

[3] Measured as the proportion of research and development expenditure to net sales in 1960. See Appendix 1, Table 1.

of product sophistication. The EFTA countries, noticeably the United Kingdom, decreased their share of all groups of products throughout the period – though their actual rate of increase in exports was, in general, more favourable than that of the United States.

(3) In terms of export shares, it remains true that the United States still has the greatest comparative advantage in research-intensive products – but this is tending to decline as these products become more standardised, and the process by which knowledge is internationally diffused accelerated.[1] Taking the United States share of all exports as 100, then, in 1955, that of high research-intensive products was 121·6 and that of medium research-intensive products 127·2. The corresponding figures for 1960 were 136·9 and 110·6 and for 1965 129·1 and 111·1.

(4) In terms of individual products, the greatest improvement in Europe's export performance since 1955 has occurred in three directions:

(i) those products which, in general, have a high income elasticity of demand or ownership[2] and/or which benefit from the economies of large-scale production. Notable among these are motor vehicles, domestic electrical products, printing and sophisticated clothing and furniture. These last two items are essentially unstandardised products and are examples of areas in which Europe has led the United States in product innovation in recent years.[3] Both contain a high skilled labour content but require comparatively inexpensive plant and equipment. Their knowledge content consists of creative design rather than technological expertise.[4]

(ii) Those products which were either not produced or only produced on a very small scale in at least some European countries in 1955. Aircraft, petroleum and tobacco fall into this category.

(iii) Those products which are essentially those of the technologically advanced industries and which, in the main, were first commercially exploited in the United States. All products classified in Group 1 except other chemicals are of this kind.

So far, our analysis has taken no account of imports. It may be argued,

---

[1] This would then suggest that part of the United States advantage has rested on the international immobility of knowledge. The patent system still ensures this, in part, but the greatest force making for mobility has been the multinational company.

[2] The concept of income elasticity of ownership is explored in L. T. Wells, 'Test of a Product Cycle Model of International Trade: U.S. Exports of Consumer Durables', *Quarterly Journal of Economics*, LXXXIII (Feb 1969).

[3] It should be noted that in the period 1952–3 the greatest increase in United States exports of consumer durables was in the luxury class of products, i.e. those which people are willing to do without until they are comparatively wealthy. See L. T. Wells, 'A Product Life Cycle for International Trade', *Journal of Marketing*, XXXII (July 1968).

[4] Dunning, 'Technology, U.S. Direct Investment and European Economic Growth.'

TABLE 17.4
GROWTH OF NET EXPORTS[a] OF SELECTED MANUFACTURED PRODUCTS OF THE UNITED STATES AND EUROPE, 1955-65
(1955 = 100)

	United States	EFTA	E.E.C.	Europe
Group 1				
Aircraft	143·6	289·9	..[b]	2,965·5
Instruments	535·9	390·7	292·8	321·1
Office machinery	423·5	229·0	581·5	428·2
Agricultural machinery	524·2	600·1	687·8	640·1
Electrical machinery	229·1	197·4	353·6	283·1
Chemicals				
Drugs	105·9	216·6	337·6	268·8
Other chemicals	237·2	210·8	288·3	260·4
All Group 1	225·9	231·0	348·3	298·0
Group 2				
Other non-electrical machinery	177·0	200·6	355·3	283·8
Motor vehicles	115·3	247·0	458·8	364·2
Rubber products	116·9	172·6	278·3	252·1
Petroleum products	70·8	365·2	201·3	229·0
All Group 2	139·7	221·6	347·6	297·5
Group 3				
Fabricated metals	200·7	176·6	249·1	218·5
Primary metals				
Non-ferrous	211·3	234·6	277·2	258·4
Ferrous	37·2	242·5	220·5	225·8
Stone, clay and glass	181·6	137·0	246·2	196·8
Printing and publishing	208·9	279·4	351·9	323·0
Food and drink	133·6	218·7	278·0	254·8
Tobacco	190·2	137·4	823·2	221·6
Textiles and clothing	77·7	132·7	204·6	176·5
Lumber and wood products	146·2	187·3	334·3	263·7
Paper	176·7	197·7	272·6	221·1
All Group 3	135·6	179·8	235·3	214·1
All products	166·6	204·5	289·2	256·2

[a] Exports of United States minus imports from E.E.C. and EFTA countries; exports of Europe minus imports from the United States.
[b] Negative in 1955.
Source: United Nations, *Commodity Trade Statistics*, 1955 and 1965.

however, that if two countries are increasing their exports of a particular research-intensive product at the same rate, but that one is increasing its imports (of this same product) at twice the rate of the other, then the former is technologically less progressive. To take some account of import substitution as a possible index of technological self-sufficiency, we recalculated the data contained in Table 17.3 by deducting, from the exports of manufactured products of European countries, the imports of those

TABLE 17.5
DISTRIBUTION OF EXPORTS BETWEEN INDIVIDUAL EUROPEAN COUNTRIES AND THE UNITED STATES BY BROAD INDUSTRIAL GROUPS, 1955–65

	% of all countries' exports in Group						Total		Increase in exports, 1955–65, in Group (1955 = 100)			
	1		2		3				1	2	3	Total
	1955	1965	1955	1965	1955	1965	1955	1965				
E.E.C. countries												
Belgium	3·6	3·8	2·1	4·1	11·1	11·8	6·3	6·8	289·1	460·1	209·4	248·5
France	7·2	9·2	7·0	8·0	14·3	12·9	10·1	10·1	352·5	266·2	177·6	228·8
Germany	17·6	20·3	16·9	25·2	11·6	16·0	14·7	20·4	326·0	349·7	268·9	315·9
Italy	2·7	5·7	4·4	7·8	6·3	8·9	4·8	7·6	576·0	414·0	275·7	359·9
Netherlands	5·1	6·8	3·4	3·5	5·5	6·8	4·7	5·7	370·6	240·2	242·5	276·4
EFTA countries												
United Kingdom	18·2	14·0	21·4	16·7	19·3	13·6	19·7	14·8	212·4	182·9	138·5	171·4
Austria	0·7	1·0	0·6	0·9	2·5	2·7	1·4	1·5	367·5	325·6	209·1	246·1
Denmark	0·8	1·3	0·9	1·1	1·2	1·8	1·0	1·4	412·5	308·4	295·2	323·8
Norway	0·8	0·8	0·1	0·4	1·7	2·2	0·9	1·1	277·9	1,002·2	253·5	280·9
Sweden	1·9	2·4	1·8	3·2	3·3	4·2	2·5	3·3	356·2	407·3	246·0	306·2
Switzerland	4·4	4·2	2·5	2·6	2·1	2·3	2·8	2·9	264·9	244·6	212·5	242·2
Portugal	0·2	0·2	0·2	0·1	1·1	1·3	0·6	0·6	331·7	196·4	231·4	237·1
United States	37·1	30·6	38·8	26·3	20·1	15·4	30·5	23·7	228·7	158·4	149·5	177·2
Total	100·0	100·0	100·0	100·0	100·0	100·0	100·0	100·0	277·0	233·7	196·0	228·1

Source: United Nations, *Commodity Trade Statistics*, 1955 and 1960.

TABLE 17.6
PERCENTAGE DISTRIBUTION OF EUROPEAN AND UNITED STATES EXPORTS BY PRINCIPAL PRODUCT GROUPS

Groups	1955				1965			
	1	2	3	Total	1	2	3	Total
EFTA countries								
United Kingdom	23·7	31·9	44·4	100·0	27·7	32·9	39·4	100·0
Austria	23·1	35·8	41·2	100·0	27·9	39·3	32·7	100·0
Denmark	12·4	14·4	73·2	100·0	18·6	19·2	62·2	100·0
Norway	21·1	29·1	49·8	100·0	26·9	27·7	45·4	100·0
Sweden	21·1	2·9	86·0	100·0	20·8	10·4	68·8	100·0
Switzerland	18·9	24·3	56·8	100·0	22·0	32·3	45·7	100·0
Portugal	38·7	29·4	31·9	100·0	42·4	29·7	27·9	100·0
	8·2	7·4	84·4	100·0	11·5	6·1	82·4	100·0
E.E.C. countries								
Belgium	21·9	27·5	50·6	100·0	27·0	32·6	50·0	100·0
France	14·3	11·1	74·6	100·0	16·9	20·7	62·4	100·0
Germany	17·6	23·0	59·4	100·0	27·2	26·7	46·2	100·0
Italy	29·0	38·7	33·2	100·0	30·1	42·0	27·9	100·0
Netherlands	14·1	30·3	55·5	100·0	22·8	35·1	42·2	100·0
	26·8	23·9	49·3	100·0	36·2	20·9	42·9	100·0
United States	30·2	42·0	27·8	100·0	39·0	37·5	23·5	100·0
All countries	24·8	33·1	42·1	100·0	29·9	33·8	36·1	100·0

Source: United Nations, *Commodity Trade Statistics*, 1955 and 1965.

same products from the United States; and similarly from the exports of the United States we deducted the imports from EFTA and E.E.C. countries. Table 17.4 presents the results of the increase in exports between 1955 and 1965. These, in general, support the conclusions of the previous two tables. Indeed the changes in net exports correspond very closely indeed with those of gross exports.[1]

We next turn to examine data for individual countries in Western Europe. Table 17.5 sets out the proportion of total European and United States exports supplied by individual countries in 1955 and 1965 and the increase of these exports between these years. In the *high* and *medium* research-intensive groups, only the United Kingdom suffered a fall in its export share, while Austria, Denmark, Sweden and Italy each recorded above-average performances. All European countries, apart from the United Kingdom, expanded their exports of each group of products faster than the United States, but the largest relative gains were in the research-intensive products. This conclusion also holds good for trends in net exports as well.

One result of the trends so far described has been that the structure of European exports has tended to converge with that of the United States. This is revealed in Table 17.6 and confirmed by a more detailed industrial classification.[2] In all countries, except Norway, exports of *high* research-intensive products have increased faster than average, while in all countries the share of the *low* research-intensive products has fallen. A rough idea of the extent to which there has been a convergence of European and United States export patterns is obtained by calculating the difference in the mean deviation of each country's share of each group of exports from that of the United States (ignoring minus signs). In 1955, the mean deviation for the E.E.C. worked out at 15·1 per cent and in 1965 it was 10·3 per cent. The corresponding figures for EFTA countries were 11·1 per cent and 9·5 per cent.

Table 17.6 also shows that the countries which were technologically the most divergent in their patterns of trade from the United States in 1955 are those which have tended to reduce their mean deviation the most since that date. Moreover, referring back to Table 17.2, it can also be seen that, with the exception of instruments, the percentage reduction in the difference between the European and United States share of exports of particular products is most pronounced in Groups 1 and 2, which lends additional support to both the 'catching up' thesis and the argument that, providing she can acquire the necessary knowledge, Europe can compete very favourably in the *production* of research-intensive goods with the United States. The question now arises: how has Europe acquired this

[1] The rank correlation coefficient between European net and gross exports worked out at +0·933 and United States net and gross exports at +0·931.
[2] Not presented here but available, by request, from the author.

TABLE 17.7

DISTRIBUTION OF UNITED STATES CAPITAL STAKE, NEW INVESTMENT AND EXPORTS IN EUROPE, 1954–5 TO 1964–5

	U.S. capital stake and new investment in manufacturing and petroleum			Exports and increase in exports of Group 1 and 2 products		
	1954 %	1964 %	1954–64 %	1955 %	1965 %	1955–65 %
E.E.C. countries						
Belgium	4·5	3·8	3·6	4·4	5·5	6·1
France	13·5	12·3	12·0	11·5	11·9	12·2
Germany	11·0	19·6	22·0	27·5	31·9	34·3
Italy	4·8	7·6	8·4	5·9	9·5	11·3
Netherlands	5·3	4·7	4·6	6·7	7·1	7·3
	39·1	48·0	50·6	56·0	65·9	71·2
EFTA countries						
United Kingdom	48·0	40·5	38·2	32·3	21·9	15·9
Denmark	1·6	1·5	1·5	1·4	1·6	1·8
Norway	1·0	1·0	1·7	0·6	0·8	0·9
Sweden	3·5	2·1	1·7	3·0	3·9	4·4
Switzerland	1·1	2·1	2·4	5·3	4·6	4·3
Other[a]	5·7	5·0	4·6	1·4	1·4	1·4
	60·9	52·0	49·4	46·0	34·1	28·8
Europe	100·0	100·0	100·0	100·0	100·0	100·0

[a] Including non-EFTA countries in Europe.

Source: U.S. Department of Commerce, *Survey of Current Business*, Aug 1955 and Sept 1965; United Nations, *Commodity Trade Statistics*, 1955 and 1965.

knowledge in recent years? In particular, to what extent has it been borrowed from the United States through the operation of United States-financed firms in Europe?

V. THE EFFECTS OF UNITED STATES TECHNOLOGY ON EUROPEAN EXPORT PERFORMANCE

Data on United States direct investment in Europe since 1955 are available for individual countries, classified by broad sectors of economic activity, but a detailed industrial breakdown has only been published for the E.E.C. and the rest of Europe for selected years since 1957. Nevertheless, even this very limited information does allow us to make a tentative assessment of the impact of this vehicle of technological transplants on the growth of European exports of research-intensive products. In the following paragraphs, we examine the relationship between United States investment and European exports first on a country basis and secondly on an industrial basis.

Even a most cursory glance at the geographical distribution of the United States direct capital stake in petroleum and manufacturing between various European countries reveals that this is very closely associated with the proportion of the total exports in Group 1 and 2 products accounted for by those countries. In 1954–5, the rank correlation between the data in columns 1 and 4 of Table 17.7 worked out at + 0·926 and in 1964–5 to + 0·985. On the other hand, there appeared to be little relationship between the cumulative United States investment in 1954 and *changes* in export performance between 1955 and 1965, nor between this latter variable and the proportion of domestic capital formation accounted for by United States subsidiaries (see Table 17.8). This is not really surprising, as many of the products in Groups 1 and 2 have only been exported in quantity from Europe since 1950, whereas the average 'vintage' of United States capital invested in Europe, and particularly in the United Kingdom, is a good deal older. However, when one introduces an additional variable reflecting the growth of United States capital, the picture becomes much clearer. Taken together, Tables 17.7 and 17.8 show that the share of exports of European countries of research-intensive products in 1965 is strongly associated with (i) the distribution of the United States capital stake in 1954, (ii) the rate of new United States investment since 1954, and (iii) the share of plant and equipment expenditure by United States firms to total domestic capital formation in 1957–64.[1]

We are not suggesting, of course, that United States investment has

---

[1] We do not have any data on plant and equipment expenditure of United States firms before 1957.

TABLE 17.8

EUROPEAN EXPORTS, INDUSTRIAL PRODUCTION AND UNITED STATES INVESTMENT, 1955–65 AND 1957–64

	1955–65 increase in exports (1955 = 100)			Increase in industrial production (1955 = 100)	1957–64 increase in U.S. capital stake in manufacturing (1957 = 100)		1957–65 U.S. investment as % of domestic fixed capital formation[a]
	All products	Group 1	Groups 1 and 2		Total of industry	Including petroleum	
EFTA countries							
United Kingdom	174·6	212·4	199·6	131·8	230·3	233·8	7·84
Austria	246·1	367·5	345·0	166·2	n.a.	n.a.	n.a.
Denmark	323·8	412·5	352·2	n.a.	395·2	423·5	3·12
Norway	280·8	277·9	366·1	166·7	252·9	288·2	2·25
Sweden	306·2	356·2	384·9	181·0	238·5	249·4	2·60
Switzerland	242·2	264·9	256·2	202·2[b]	2,708·6	450·0	1·86
E.E.C. countries							
Belgium	245·5	289·1	362·1	150·0	236·9	217·2	4·83
France	228·9	352·5	303·4	173·0	315·9	300·2	2·44
Germany	314·3	326·0	339·4	185·9	358·3	327·0	3·68
Italy	357·7	576·0	465·5	215·3	337·3	337·4	2·84
Netherlands	274·6	370·6	309·1	183·6	310·4	317·2	4·37
Europe	251·2	305·7	281·5				

[a] Plant and equipment expenditure of United States firms as a proportion of gross domestic fixed asset formation in machinery and equipment.
[b] Calculated on basis of 1959–65 data.

Source: O.E.C.D, *Main Economic Indicators: Historical Statistics, 1955–64*, and Apr 1967; *National Accounts Statistics, 1955–64*.

been the only or even the main factor influencing a European competitiveness in supplying research-intensive products. Neither Germany's impressive export position in 1965, nor the United Kingdom's poor performance between 1955 and 1965, can be explained in these terms. Price, delivery dates, types of markets served, structure of exports and product innovation arising from an increase in indigenous research are, or may be, equally important variables.[1] But at least the data contained in Tables 17.7 and 17.8 do nothing to refute the hypothesis that the transfer of technology from the United States to Europe by subsidiaries of American firms has helped to improve the relative export position of the recipient countries.

United States investment has, in general, moved to countries which have recorded the fastest rate of growth of real output in recent years.[2] Inasmuch as such investment has also been concentrated in the research-intensive industries of these economies, it is not unreasonable to postulate that it has contributed to this rate of growth as well as being affected by it. Certainly American participation has grown the most in those countries where productivity improvements associated with advances in knowledge and economies of scale have been the greatest.[3] Unfortunately, no industrial breakdown of United States investment *within* particular European countries has been published since 1957, so that it is not possible to estimate the extent to which differences in the technological *structure* of United States investment – as opposed to its volume – are related to growth.

A hint that such an association does exist is given by the data contained in Table 17.9, which relates increases in the manufacturing sales of United States affiliates to increases in research-intensive exports in the E.E.C., United Kingdom and the rest of Europe.[4] In the E.E.C., where the expansion in Group 1 and 2 products has been the highest, the sales of United States firms have risen above average in all industries, but most of all in the research-intensive industries. In the United Kingdom, by contrast, the sales of United States affiliates have increased less than elsewhere in Europe, while the export performance of technologically advanced products has been the least impressive.

Table 17.8 sets out details of the increases in exports in various European countries between 1955 and 1965 and the increase in the United States

---

[1] Again, in the absence of any time-series data on research and development of individual European countries (apart from the United Kingdom), it has not been possible to test the significance of this latter variable.

[2] V. N. Bandera and J. T. White, 'U.S. Direct Investments and Domestic Markets in Europe', *Economia Internationale*, Aug 1968.

[3] Dunning, 'Technology, U.S. Direct Investment in Europe and European Economic Growth', and E. Denison, *Why Growth Rates Differ* (Brookings Institution, Washington, 1967).

[4] *Survey of Current Business*, Nov 1966; *U.S. Business Investment in Foreign Countries* (U.S. Department of Commerce, 1960).

TABLE 17.9

MANUFACTURING SALES OF UNITED STATES AFFILIATES IN EUROPE, 1957–65, AND EXPORT PERFORMANCE OF ALL EUROPEAN FIRMS, 1955–65

	E.E.C.			United Kingdom				Other Europe			
	Sales of U.S. firms		Index of growth 1957–65 (1965 =100)	Exports of all firms: Index of growth 1955–65 (1955 =100)	Sales of U.S. firms		Index of growth 1957–65 (1957 =100)	Exports of all firms: Index of growth 1955–65 (1955 =100)	Sales of U.S. firms		Index of growth 1957–65 (1957 =100)	Exports of all firms: Index of growth 1955–65 (1955 =100)
	1957 ($m.)	1965 ($m.)			1957 ($m.)	1965 ($m.)			1957 ($m.)	1965 ($m.)		
Groups 1 and 2												
Chemicals and allied products	275	1,302	473·5	306·4	517	1,241	240·0	188·6	31	200	645·2	271·7
Rubber products	77	232	301·3	262·6	139	219	157·6	129·1	46	86	187·0	489·2
Machinery	502	1,960	390·4	368·1	480	1,121	233·5	202·3	27	65	240·7	300·6
Electrical machinery	299	1,172	392·0	366·5	270	706	261·5	172·5	109	224	205·5	356·3
Transportation equipment	764	2,864	374·9	435·1[a]	789	1,798	227·9	212·5[a]	147	398	270·7	482·5[a]
All Groups 1 and 2	1,917	7,530	392·8	363·3	2,195	5,085	231·7	197·8	360	973	311·1	314·4
Group 3												
Food products	225	670	297·8	204·5	491	730	148·7	160·0	19	100	526·3	213·8
Paper and allied products	13	62	476·9	295·0	21	102	485·7	165·8	–	2	–	214·0
Primary and fabricated metals	145	600	413·8	228·6	230	546	237·4	165·6	61	170	278·7	254·9
Other products	225	1,020	453·3	228·6	366	1,047	286·0	165·6	48	124	258·3	254·9
All Group 3	608	2,352	386·8	207·7	1,108	2,425	218·9	138·5	128	396	309·4	242·3
All products	2,524	9,882	391·4	284·5	3,303	7,510	227·4	171·4	485	1,369	301·1	274·3

[a] Motor vehicles only.

Source: U.S. Department of Commerce, *Survey of Current Business*, Nov 1966; United Nations, *Commodity Trade Statistics*, 1955 and 1965.

capital stake between 1954 and 1964. (We have assumed a one-year time-lag.) Apart from Switzerland, the association is a fairly close one – although that between United States investment in manufacturing and petroleum and European exports of the more technologically advanced products is no better than that between all United States investment and all exports.

It is difficult to read very much into these data: this is because they make no allowance for the different composition of United States investment between countries nor its contribution to domestic capital formation. Moreover, the increase in the exports of some EFTA countries since 1955 has sometimes reflected the establishment of completely new industries. Both Sweden and Norway's performance in Group 2 products, for example, was strongly influenced by a very rapid growth of output of vehicles and petroleum refining, while few European countries exported substantial quantities of aircraft in 1955. But one thing which does emerge from a study of the export trends of particular countries is that the Scandinavian economies have increased their share of research-intensive exports without relying heavily on United States investment.[2]

This does not mean, however, that they have been less reliant on imported know-how. In 1957–61, the percentage of licensing agreements taken out by foreign applicants averaged 80 per cent for Norway, 79·3 per cent for Denmark and 68·8 per cent for Sweden, compared with 52·6 per cent for all Western European countries.[1] Then, too, the proportion of total foreign capital invested in these countries by United States firms is considerably lower than in other parts of Europe. In the period 1962–5, it accounted for only 30 per cent of inward direct investment in Sweden and 40 per cent in Denmark. The corresponding proportion for E.E.C. countries for 1963–5 was about 55 per cent.[3]

We now turn to see how far the export performance of particular industries in Europe has been affected by technological importation. Here again, the paucity of official data forces us to deal in only very broad product categories, but it is possible to combine these into the tripartite classification already adopted. There is also available a large amount of scattered evidence on the participation of United States firms in various European countries.[4]

Table 17.10 compares the increase in United States direct investment in Europe with that of European exports in nine industrial sectors. At

[1] *Journal of the Patent Office Society* (Washington), Feb 1964.
[2] *EFTA foreign investment* (EFTA, 1968).
[3] 'International Direct Investment by Private Enterprises in Western Europe and North America', *Economic Bulletin for Europe*, XIX 1 (Nov 1967) 52.
[4] See especially ibid.; J. Behrman, *Some Patterns in the Rise of the Multinational Enterprise*, Research Paper No. 18 (University of North Carolina Press, Mar 1969); Booz-Allen and Hamilton, *New Foreign Business Activities of the U.S. Firms* (New York, 1967).

NA O

TABLE 7.10
UNITED STATES INVESTMENT, 1957–64, AND EUROPEAN EXPORTS, 1955–65

	(1) Increase in U.S. capital stake 1957–64 (1957 = 100)	(2) Increase in U.S. capital stake 1960–4 (1960 = 100)	(3) Increase in European exports 1955–65 (1955 = 100)	(4) Increase in European exports 1960–5 (1960 = 100)	(5) Increase in European/Increase in U.S. exports × 100 1955–65	(6) Increase in European/Increase in U.S. exports × 100 1960–5	(7) Increase in European sales 1957–64
Groups 1 and 2							
Chemicals	336·4	199·8	271·6	166·3	127·2	121·1	189·8
Rubber products	284·7	186·7	232·4	160·6	178·1	142·7	155·3
Non-electrical machinery	243·0	151·7	300·3	162·5	135·0	103·7	143·1
Electrical machinery	236·4	175·7	301·5	182·7	140·2	111·7	164·9
Transportation equipment	375·3	166·0	342·9	160·3	241·4	131·8	165·1
Petroleum products	247·1	177·0	187·1	135·1	262·2	146·8	n.a.
All Groups 1 and 2	279·1	172·9	267·4	166·0	147·2	117·1	165·8
Group 3							
Food products	261·1	173·7	199·9	149·0	149·4	153·8	132·0
Paper and allied products	242·9	161·9	232·4	160·6	117·8	105·2	152·2
Metals	305·6	167·9	218·8	133·6	149·7	119·6	131·4
All Group 3[a]	279·8	174·6	205·3	142·1	137·3	119·9	133·6
All products	279·2	173·2	251·2	156·3	141·8	115·3	149·42

[a] Including products not specified.
Source: U.S. Department of Commerce, *Survey of Current Business*, Aug 1961; United Nations, *Commodity Trade Statistics*.

first glance, there appears little association here between the two sets of figures. United States investment has expanded least in the electrical machinery industry, which has the second-largest export growth. Metal products rank third in United States investment but seventh in export growth.

Part of the increase in European exports, of course, reflects the operation of world economic forces rather than any improvement in Europe's competitive position. Columns 5 and 6 of Table 17.10 make some allowance for this by expressing the increase in European exports as a proportion of the increase in American exports. This materially improves the rankings of the two series, but the coefficient of correlation at +0·67 (+0·73, 1960–5) is still only moderately suggestive. Export competition is, of course, only a proxy for technological competitiveness. Another is import substitution. But the relationship is not much improved by substituting net exports for gross exports, nor by making a similar adjustment for United States exports.

Again the product classification is too broad for any firm conclusions to be drawn about the technological impact of United States investment: American participation in the European metal industry, for example, is concentrated in a very narrow range of products. Moreover, our calculations take no account of the changes in the share of exports to total European sales – which may themselves have been affected by the presence of United States firms – nor of the contribution of such firms to these sales. For example, between 1957 and 1965 the proportion of output of electrical machinery exported by all firms in Europe rose from 16·9 per cent to 22·9 per cent and that of non-electrical machinery from 23·0 per cent to 32·7 per cent. The final column of Table 17.10 presents Messrs Haufbauer and Adler's estimates of increases in the total sales of European firms between 1957 and 1965.[1] These, in general, correlate rather better than do exports with the growth in United States investment – but electrical machinery still fits rather awkwardly, even after adjustment is made for its exceptionally favourable capital–sales ratio.[2] One suspects that the extension of licensing agreements and an increase in indigenous research in Europe may have been proportionately more pronounced in this sector than in others.[3]

[1] *Overseas Manufacturing Investment and the Balance of Payments*, Tax Policy Research Study, No. 1 (U.S. Treasury Department, 1968).
[2] For an analysis of United States investment in E.E.C. manufacturing industry which comes to similar conclusions, see L. B. Krause, *European Economic Integration and the United States* (Brookings Institution, Washington, 1968) pp. 125 ff.
[3] G. Freeman and Young, *The Research and Development Effort of Western Europe, North America and the Soviet Union* (O.E.C.D., 1965).

TABLE 17.11
CONTRIBUTION OF UNITED STATES AFFILIATES IN EUROPE TO EUROPEAN SALES AND EXPORTS OF SELECTED MANUFACTURED PRODUCTS, 1957-64

		All firms in Europe		U.S. affiliates			(7) Exports from U.S. to all areas ($m.)	(8) (7)/(2) %	(9) (4)/(7) %
		(1) Total sales ($m.)	(2) Exports ($m.)	(3) Total sales ($m.)	(4) Exports ($m.)	(5) (3)/(1) %	(6) (4)/(2) %			

		(1)	(2)	(3)	(4)	(5)	(6)	(7)	(8)	(9)
Groups 1 and 2 Chemicals	1957	19,132	2,931	822	134	4·3	4·6	1,376	46·9	9·7
	1962	29,765	4,408	1,760	365	5·9	8·3	1,771	40·2	20·6
	1964	36,312	5,737	2,273	553	6·3	9·6	2,345	40·9	23·6
Rubber products	1957	2,713	257	262	36	9·7	14·0	300	116·7	12·0
	1962	3,641	570	460	75	12·6	13·2	332	58·2	22·5
	1964	4,214	731	517	116	12·3	15·7	362	49·5	32·1
Non-electrical machinery	1957	20,429	4,706	1,009	213	4·9	4·5	3,160	67·1	6·7
	1962	28,062	8,084	2,090	510	7·4	6·3	3,927	48·5	13·0
	1964	29,242	9,571	2,735	795	9·4	8·3	4,704	49·1	16·9
Electrical machinery	1957	11,480	1,947	678	100	5·9	5·1	810	41·6	12·3
	1962	16,234	3,321	1,320	210	8·2	6·3	916	27·6	22·9
	1964	18,926	4,245	1,968	332	10·4	7·8	1,284	30·2	25·9
Transportation	1957	22,206	2,793	1,700	616	7·7	22·1	1,566	56·1	39·3

Group	Year									
	1964	125,350	26,165	12,193	3,018	9·6	11·5	10,428	39·9	28·9
Group 3										
Food products	1957	34,919	2,291	734	34	2·1	1·5	444	19·4	7·7
	1962	42,757	3,204	1,185	55	2·8	1·7		15·4	21·3
	1964	46,104	3,683	1,308	121	2·8	3·3	567		
Paper and allied products	1957	7,222	1,496	34	5	0·5	0·3	324	21·7	1·5
	1962	9,488	1,824	80	10	0·8	0·5	457	25·1	2·2
	1964	10,994	2,425	148	10	1·3	0·4	596	24·6	1·7
Metals	1957	33,303	5,014	435	111	1·3	1·9	1,423	28·5	7·8
	1962	40,498	5,862	715	105	1·8	1·8		20·6	14·9
	1964	43,749	6,819	1,115	209	2·6	3·1	1,405		
All Group 3	1957	75,444	8,801	1,203	150	1·6	1·7	2,191	24·8	6·8
	1962	92,743	10,890	1,980	170	2·1	1·6	2,568	19·9	13·2
	1964	100,847	12,927	2,571	340	2·6	2·6			13·3
All products	1957	151,404	21,435	5,674	1,249	3·7	5·8	9,403	43·8	25·8
	1962	202,858	31,830	10,890	2,175	5·4	6·8		33·2	
	1964	226,197	39,092	14,764	3,358	6·5	8·6	12,996		

Source: G. Hufbauer and F. M. Adler, *Overseas Manufacturing Investment and the Balance of Payments* (U.S. Treasury Department, Washington, 1968); *Survey of Current Business*, Nov 1966; *U.S. Business Investments in Foreign Countries* (U.S. Department of Commerce, 1960).

VI. THE CONTRIBUTION OF UNITED STATES INVESTMENT TO EUROPEAN TECHNICAL PROGRESS

The previous paragraphs have shown:

(1) that those countries which, in 1954, attracted the largest share of United States capital also exported the highest proportion of research-intensive products in that year;

(2) that between 1954 and 1964, those countries which most improved their competitive position in the export of research-intensive products, relative to the United States, also attracted the greatest expansion in foreign (and in particular United States) investment and/or had the largest proportion of patents taken out by foreign (and in particular by United States) firms;

(3) that between 1957 and 1964, the increase in United States investment was, in general, concentrated in those industries which recorded the most impressive increase in exports. There were, however, one or two exceptions: the electrical equipment industry achieved a marked increase in exports but without a corresponding expansion in United States investment, while the chemical industry did not record the export gains which might have been expected.

To what extent can one assess the contribution of United States investment to European technological exports? First, Table 17.11 sets out the share of United States affiliates of both European sales and exports of a number of products, classified, again very broadly, according to their research intensity. This table reveals not only that the American share of both the sales and exports of technologically advanced products is considerably higher than that of other products, but that it has risen quite rapidly since 1957. Again, however, classification is insufficiently detailed to measure the extent of the United States participation in the highly research-intensive industries. In several sectors – electronic computers, pharmaceuticals, office and agricultural machinery, etc. – American firms account for the greater part of the output in many European countries;[1] only in the aircraft industry in their representation quite small.[2]

Another interesting feature revealed by Table 17.11 is the proportion of output exported by the United States and all firms in Europe. In some industries, notably motor vehicles and chemicals, the contribution of United States firms is considerably larger or increasing with the passing of time. In others, e.g. electrical machinery and paper products, it is smaller,

---

[1] For further details, see Behrman, op. cit.; J. H. Dunning, *The Role of American Investment in the British Economy*, P.E.P. broadsheet, No. 507 (Feb 1969); C. Layton, *Transatlantic Investments* (Atlantic Institute, 1968).

[2] Table 1 in the Appendix ranks our estimate of the share of the total output of various products accounted for by United States firms.

or increasing less rapidly than that of all European firms. The final column in Table 17.11 clearly shows that the sales and exports of the European subsidiaries of United States firms are growing much faster than United States exports of the same products. This suggests that such subsidiaries are supplying an increasing proportion of the total world sales of United States corporations[1] – and, to the extent that the technology embodied in these products is essentially United States-owned, and the profits earned on them accrue to American shareholders, the European exports of these companies, in part at least, can be thought of as an extension of United States exports.

In Table 17.12 we have extracted the exports of United States affiliates in Europe for 1957 and 1964 and in columns 4 and 8 credited these to the United States.

The result of this exercise is to reduce the extent of the improvement of European research-intensive exports between 1957 and 1964 and widen the 'indigenous' technological gap. In some cases, e.g. chemicals and electrical machinery, United States subsidiaries have accounted for at least one-half of the increased share of European exports over the period. For Group 1 and 2 products as a whole the share of European exports has risen by 7·8 per cent (63·7 to 71·5 per cent), of which United States firms were responsible for 2·7 per cent or 34·6 per cent. Moreover, not only is the contribution of United States firms accelerating over time; it would be shown to be even more marked if a narrower industrial classification were adopted.

An alternative measure of the transmission of technology made possible by United States investment is to estimate the research and development content of the products manufactured. This might be done, very roughly, by multiplying the sales of United States affiliates in particular industries by the percentages of research and development expenditure to sales in these same industries in the United States. While this measure has its deficiencies – it by no means follows that all or even a large part of the United States research and development will be relevant to the activities of European affiliates – it does give some guide of the extent to which Europe imports its research and development in this way. Again one cannot get very far in this exercise with the statistics currently available,[2] but using the data in Table 17.9 and United States research and development statistics, the total value of technological borrowing from the United States worked out at $674 million in 1965. This was approximately 11·3 per cent[3] of all European expenditure of indigenous research at that

---

[1] This is confirmed by the data on United States and European plant and equipment expenditure by United States firms presented in Table 2 of Appendix 1.
[2] Though these are being gradually improved. See O.E.C.D., *The Overall Level and Structure of Research and Development Effort in O.E.C.D. Member Countries* (Paris 1967) vol. 2.   [3] 18·5 per cent of that undertaken by private industry.

TABLE 17.12

EUROPEAN AND UNITED STATES EXPORTS OF SELECTED MANUFACTURED PRODUCTS AND THE CONTRIBUTION OF UNITED STATES AFFILIATES IN EUROPE, 1957–64
(percentages of all European and United States exports)

	1957				1964			
	(1) Other firms in Europe	(2) U.S. affiliates in Europe	(3) U.S.	(4) (3)+(2)	(5) Other firms in Europe	(6) U.S. affiliates in Europe	(7) U.S.	(8) (7)+(6)
Groups 1 and 2								
Chemicals	64.9	3.1	32.0	35.1	63.8	6.9	29.3	36.2
Rubber products	40.6	6.5	53.9	59.4	56.3	10.6	33.1	43.7
Non-electrical machinery	57.1	2.7	40.2	42.9	61.4	5.6	33.0	38.6
Electrical machinery	67.0	3.6	29.4	33.0	70.8	6.0	23.2	29.2
Transport equipment	50.0	14.1	35.9	50.0	61.1	16.0	22.8	38.8
All Groups 1 and 2	58.2	5.5	36.3	41.8	63.3	8.2	28.5	36.7
Group 3								
Food products	82.5	1.2	16.2	17.5	83.9	2.8	13.3	16.1
Paper and allied products	78.0	0.3	21.7	22.0	80.0	0.3	19.7	20.0
Metals	76.2	1.7	22.1	23.8	80.5	2.5	17.0	19.5
All Group 3	78.7	1.4	19.9	22.3	81.2	2.2	16.6	18.8
All products	65.4	4.1	30.5	34.6	68.5	6.5	25.0	31.5

Sources: G. Hufbauer and F. M. Adler, *Overseas Manufacturing Investment and the Balance of Payments* (U.S. Treasury Department, Washington, 1968); *Survey of Current Business*, Nov 1966; *U.S. Business Investments in Foreign Countries* (U.S. Department of Commerce, 1960) and Table 17.11.

time.[1] The corresponding figures for the United Kingdom were $90 million and 11·6 per cent[2] respectively.

VII. CONCLUSIONS ON THE EFFECTS OF UNITED STATES INVESTMENT IN EUROPE

The previous two sections have sought to summarise the contribution of United States firms to the growth of European technological exports. They have not, however, attempted to measure the *effects* of United States investment in any systematic way. This is indeed an area for fruitful research, but one about which there are currently few facts and figures.[3] We would, however, just make four points in conclusion.[4]

First, it is true that in some European industries, if less investment had been undertaken by United States firms, a similar amount of investment would have been undertaken by domestic or other foreign firms and a certain quantity of exports generated by them.[5] On the other hand, if the Kindleberger–Hymer hypothesis is correct and United States firms go overseas to exploit a technological advantage which the recipient countries do not possess,[6] then, in the absence of other forms of technological borrowing, much of United States investment in the research-intensive industries would represent a net addition to capital stock. Even assuming that European countries were successful in their efforts to maintain full employment, there is still the structural impact of United States investment on exports. Some idea of this is given by calculating the difference between the proportion of sales exported by United States firms and what this would have been had the distribution and proportion of exports been that of European firms in general. In 1964 this worked out at 5·8 per cent (22·7 – 16·9 per cent).

Second, no account was taken in section VI of the technological spill-over or multiplier effects of United States investment – especially as they impinge upon the performance of competitor firms. In some industries, the presence of United States firms has undoubtedly stimulated technological advances which have spread to other firms – though how far this is due to increased competition or better management in the United States

[1] Including that of United States subsidiaries in Europe.
[2] 19·5 per cent of that undertaken by private industry.
[3] But see A. Safarian, *The Performance of Foreign Firms in Canada* (Canada Economic Committee, 1969); Dunning, *The Role of American Investment in the British Economy*.
[4] These are enlarged upon in two other of my papers, viz. 'Technology, U.S. Direct Investment and European Economic Growth', op. cit., and 'U.S. Investment: The Effects of U.S. Direct Investment on British Technology' (with M. Steuer), in J. H. Dunning, *Studies in Foreign Investment* (Allen & Unwin, 1969).
[5] For an analysis of the implication of this assumption from the viewpoint of the investing country, see W. B. Reddaway, *Effects of U.K. Direct Investment Overseas* (Cambridge University Press, 1967, 1968).
[6] C. Kindleberger, *American Business Abroad* (Yale University Press, 1969).

firms is a debatable point. However, we know of no attempt to quantify the technological multiplier of United States investment. Yet it could well be as important as the immediate technological effects.[1]

Third, we have not discussed the possible technological (or other) *costs* of United States investment in Europe. Nor have we examined ways and means of maximising the net benefits and minimising the net costs of inward investment from the viewpoint of the investing countries. We have assumed that both were outside this paper; in any case, they have been discussed elsewhere.[2]

Fourth, as our research for this paper progressed we were disappointed to find that we would not obtain the kind of data we required to evaluate the contribution of United States direct investment to Europe's technological development in recent years, relative to other forms of technological borrowing and indigenous research and development. We have suggested that, in 1965, the research and development expenditure embodied in products supplied by United States firms in the leading European countries averaged about 11 per cent of domestic research and development expenditure; including royalties and fees paid to United States firms, this proportion rises to nearer 15 per cent. But we have little knowledge whether this is increasing over time. We suspect it is. Almost certainly, United States investment in the technologically advanced industries in Europe is growing considerably faster than domestic research and development. One country about which there is some published data is the United Kingdom. Here, between 1955–6 and 1966–7, total research and development expenditure increased from £300 million to £883 million or 294·3 per cent and that in private industry from £185 million to £56 million or 303·2 per cent. Over this same period United States investment in manufacturing and petroleum industry increased by 420·0 per cent. As this investment was fairly strongly concentrated in the research-intensive industries (67·7 per cent of the sales of United States subsidiaries in Britain were of Groups 1 and 2 products), it seems reasonable to suppose the United States contribution to Britain's total stock of technological expertise has increased over this period.[3]

We conclude. There seems little doubt that Europe has improved her

---

[1] Quinn, op. cit., p. 9 ff.

[2] See also H. Johnson, 'Efficiency and Welfare Effects of the International Corporation', paper given to C. Kindleberger's Seminar on the International Corporation at the Sloane School of Management, Boston, May 1969.

[3] One aspect of the technological gap not touched upon in this paper is the migration of skilled manpower from Europe to the United States. Between 1961 and 1966, some 72,000 Europeans classified as "professional, technical and kindred workers' entered the United States as immigrants. Assuming one-half of these people had been employed in European research and development at an average cost of $10,000 a year, this would have allowed the total research budget of Europe in 1965–6 to be increased by about 12 per cent.

technological and scientific capabilities relative to the United States in the last decade or so – except, perhaps, in certain very high-income and advanced research-intensive products.[1] Equally, it would appear that the transference of knowledge – particularly enterprise-specific knowledge – from the United States to Europe by way of American direct investment in research-intensive industries has contributed in no small measure to the reduction in the technological *usage* gap. These facts tend to support both the product cycle and technological gap theories of trade, and emphasise the significance of the multinational corporation as influencing both the character and the timing of the sequence. However, before we can say much more on the subject, we need a far more detailed country-by-country breakdown of the product composition both of United States corporate activities in Europe (and other forms of technological transfers) and of indigenous research and development expenditure.

[1] L. Wells, 'A Product Cycle of International Trade', op. cit.

STATISTICAL APPENDIX

TABLE 1

DISTRIBUTION OF PRODUCTS BY EUROPEAN
RESEARCH INTENSITY AND EXPORT GROWTH

	R. & D. expenditure, 1960	Net export growth, 1955–65	U.S. participation ranking
Group 1			
Aircraft	22·5	2,965·5	15
Office machinery	19·5	423·8	1
Instruments	11·8	321·5	7
Electrical machinery	10·9	283·1	8
Agricultural machinery	6·4	371·9	3
Drugs	4·4	268·8	2
Other chemicals	4·1	260·4	10
Group 2			
Motor vehicles	3·3	364·2	4
Other machinery	2·5	281·9	9
Rubber products	2·1	252·1	5
Petroleum products	1·1	229·0	6
Group 3			
Fabricated metals	1·5	218·5	11
Primary non-ferrous metals	1·1	258·4	12
Paper and allied products	0·7	221·1	14
Lumber and wood products	0·6	263·7	16
Textiles and clothing	0·6	176·5	17
Primary ferrous metals	0·6	225·8	18
Food and kindred products	0·3	199·9	13

Source: (1) *R. & D. expenditure* – D. Keesing, 'The Impact of Research and Development on United States Trade', *Journal of Political Economy*, LXXV (Feb 1967) Table 2.

National Science Foundation data figures on office machinery and agricultural machinery estimated separately from (1963a, Table A.18) on R. & D. expenditure as a proportion of *net* output.

(2) *Net export growth* – Table 17.4 in text.

(3) *U.S. participation ranking* – Author's estimate of proportion of output of European products supplied by United States-financed firms.

TABLE 2
DOMESTIC AND EUROPEAN PLANT AND EQUIPMENT EXPENDITURES BY UNITED STATES FIRMS IN SELECTED INDUSTRIES, 1960 AND 1965

	1960					1965			
	Total ($m.)	Domestic ($m.)		European ($m.)		% of European to domestic	Total ($m.)	Domestic ($m.)		European ($m.)		% of European to domestic
		($m.)		($m.)				($m.)		($m.)		

	Total ($m.)	Domestic ($m.)		European ($m.)		% European to domestic	Total ($m.)	Domestic ($m.)		European ($m.)		% European to domestic
Groups 1 and 2												
Chemicals	1,837	1,600	21·0	86	15·7	5·4	3,452	2,590	20·8	321	19·0	12·4
Rubber products	298	230	3·0	26	4·7	11·3	514	340	2·7	73	4·3	21·5
Non-electrical machinery	1,232	1,100	14·4	96	17·5	8·7	2,837	2,210	17·8	446	26·4	20·2
Electrical machinery	784	680	8·9	39	7·1	5·7	1,082	850	6·8	124	7·4	14·6
Transportation equipment	1,646	1,310	17·2	202	36·8	15·4	3,433	2,560	20·6	458	27·1	17·9
All Groups 1 and 2	5,797	4,920	64·8	449	81·7	9·1	11,318	8,550	68·7	1,422	84·3	16·6
Group 3												
Food products	1,017	920	12·1	35	6·4	3·8	1,426	1,240	10·0	83	4·9	6·7
Paper and allied products	828	750	9·9	5	1·0	0·6	1,371	1,120	9·0	25	1·5	2·2
Metals	1,143	1,010	13·2	60	10·9	5·9	1,887	1,527	12·3	157	9·3	10·2
All Group 3	2,988	2,680	35·2	100	18·3	3·7	4,684	3,887	31·3	265	15·7	6·8
All products	8,785	7,600	100·0	549	100·0	7·2	16,002	12,437	100·0	1,687	100·0	13·6

General source: Derived from data in *Survey of Current Business*, Aug 1961 and Sep 1966.

Sources of Trade Data

Export–import data were taken from the United Nations Statistical Papers *Commodity Trade Statistics*, Jan to Dec 1955, 1960 and 1965. The following S.I.T.C. categories were used:

Industry	S.I.T.C. (for each year except where otherwise stated)
Food and kindred products	013, 032, 046, 047, 048, 053, 055, 062, 073, 091, 099, plus beverages 111 and 112
Tobacco products	122
Petroleum products	332 (313 in 1955)
Chemicals and allied products	5
Drugs	541
Chemicals minus drugs	5, minus 541
Rubber products n.e.c.	62 (621, 629 in 1955 and 1960)
Lumber and wood products, furniture	63, 821 (631–3 and 821 in 1955 and 1960)
Paper and allied products	641, 642
Textiles and clothing	65 (651–7 in 1955 and 1960), 84 (841 and 842 in 1955 and 1960)
Stone, clay, and glass	661, 662, 663, 664, 665, 666
Ferrous metals	67 (681 in 1955, 670–9 in 1960)
Non-ferrous metals	68 (682, 683, 684, 686, 687 and 689 in 1955, 681–7 in 1960)
Fabricated metal products	69 (699 in 1955, 691–9 in 1960)
Machinery, except electrical	71
Agricultural machinery	712
Office machinery	714
Other machinery, except electrical	71 minus 712, 714
Electrical machinery	72
Motor vehicles	732
Aircraft	734
Instruments and related products	891
Printing and publishing	892

Discussion of the Papers by Professors Houssiaux and Dunning

Professor Izzo opened the discussion. He said that Professor Houssiaux had tried to outline the main characteristics of industrial policy in Europe and compare them with those in the United States; he then considered the integration of the industrial policies of the European countries; finally, he examined the possibility of conflicts on industrial policy between Europe and America and argued for the co-ordination of industrial policy in Europe and the United States.

On Professor Houssiaux's European industrial policy, whose main characteristics described on pp. 354–6 of his paper, Professor Izzo said that European governments were making use of direct controls (e.g. consumer rationing, controls over investment, price controls) as well as fiscal and monetary policy.

On American policy, which Professor Houssiaux described on pp. 356–8, it was suggested that the United States authorities put more stress than did the European governments on the use of fiscal and monetary policy, while selective credit controls were a more common practice in Europe than in America. He wondered why Professor Houssiaux thought the influence of monetary and fiscal policy on industrial activity cause only through expenditure on infrastructure. There was no mention of its influence on aggregate demand or its composition. For example, in America, industrial production had grown faster in 1962–8 than in 1950–62; this might be taken to indicate some weakness in performance over the 1950–62 period, probably due to the low level of demand caused by fiscal and monetary policy.

On E.E.C. policy, Professor Houssiaux emphasised the need for co-operation. He said that 'the development of industry in its national traditional locations has increased the difference within the Community as a whole; the abolition of customs barriers widens the gaps, making dangerous a policy of leadership and *laisser-faire*'. One might add that present industrial policies in Europe were imposing some non-tariff barriers on trade. However, the past record of the E.E.C. showed that its authorities were particularly concerned with eliminating all kinds of back-door protectionism; a case in point was agriculture. Therefore, one might argue that the E.E.C. countries could have to agree to a common industrial policy which could perhaps be worked out by negotiating the total amount of support to be accorded to each industrial sector in each country.

On the relationship between the American and European industrial policy, Professor Houssiaux said on p. 362: 'Europe, which is trying to increase the use of advanced technologies ... will have to discriminate against American subsidiaries.' This implied that the establishment of American corporations in Europe impaired the adoption of advanced technologies there. What evidence was there for this?

Professor Izzo said he agreed with Professor Houssiaux that 'Europe will have to devote a growing proportion of its resources to the development of basic industrial infrastructures'. The same was true in the United States and one therefore wondered why America should be expected to become an important source of funds for financing European expenditure.

At another point, Professor Houssiaux suggested that 'possible clashes between the United States and Europe in industry as far as direct investment and the functioning of the financial market is concerned, made it particularly necessary for the frequent discussions of the politics of the two continents'. Later, Professor Houssiaux mentioned the opportunity for bilateral negotiations between Europe and the United States. This might be true, but if a group of countries wanted to negotiate with an outsider on industrial investment and the financial market, there would be need for some centralised control. Professor Houssiaux could not advocate bilateral negotiations and still say there was no need for the E.E.C. to acquire some control over national monetary and fiscal policies. While perhaps direct American investment in Europe should be restricted, it had almost certainly played an important role in narrowing the technological gap in the past. Professor Dunning dealt with this issue. He had tried to see whether there was an improvement in American competitive performance relative to Europe. He examined the extent to which changes were due to greater 'production' of technology in Europe and how much to licensing agreements and direct investments. He looked at the performance of American and European exports in the period 1955–65. Apart from the United Kingdom, Europe had improved its position, i.e. there had been an increase in the European share of combined United States–Europe exports. The improvement was most marked in medium research-intensive products in 1955–60 and in highly research-intensive products in 1960–5.

More particularly, Professor Dunning argued that the greatest improvement in European export performance had been in goods with high income elasticities and/or, goods with big economies of scale, though he gave no data about income elasticity or economies of scale. Two other types of commodities where European performance had been good were: commodities which were not produced at all, or had been produced on a small scale in 1955; and products which were essentially from technologically-advanced industries.

Table 17.5 implied that there had been a better performance in Italy, Denmark, the Netherlands, Austria and Sweden. These were the countries which in Table 17.1 were shown as less technologically-advanced (except for Sweden). He added that on the basis of his own calculations for 1953–68 he had worked out that the growth trend of Japanese exports was 2·2 times that of the rest of the world. The ratios for other countries were: Italy 2·1; Germany 1·5; France 1·1; United States 0·7; and United Kingdom 0·4.

If one turned to the influence of American direct investment on European performance, one could perhaps not put too much reliance on the data provided. For instance, Tables 17.7 and 17.8 showed that for the European countries considered, the share of exports of highly research-intensive products in 1965 was closely associated with the distribution of American capital in 1954 and the rate of American investment since 1954. However, the same data seemed to imply that, for the same countries, the share of exports of highly research-intensive products in 1955 was equally closely associated with the distribution of American capital in 1954 and the rate of American investment since 1954. He did not think that the data contradicted the suggestion that direct investment had helped a great deal; but there was no very strong proof. The data in Tables 17.9 and 17.12 suggested that the propensity of America to invest abroad was higher in research-intensive industries than elsewhere. Perhaps one should compare American exports with the sales of American firms in Europe. The latter could be import substitutes. Finally, he could not refrain from observing that the data had some weaknesses, e.g. the conversion from S.I.T.C. to S.I.C. could only be approximate.

Professor van Meerhaeghe said that on p. 352 of his paper, Professor Houssiaux argued that it was legitimate to ask whether there had been industrial policies in Western Europe before 1966. Why did he take 1966? Professor van Meerhaeghe contended that there was no real industrial policy in Europe either before or after that date. Then, on p. 355, Professor Houssiaux said that there were some important measures in 1960. Was this not a contradiction?

In a section beginning on p. 354, Professor Houssiaux discussed the progressive development of industrial policies in Western Europe. Professor van Meerhaeghe wondered whether what happened really was this. He knew there were discussions of plans, programmes, etc., but one could have these and other activities intended to impress public opinion. However, he would argue that the important things were done by the private sector.

On p. 356, Professor Houssiaux talked of the logic of American industrial policy. This again implied that American industrial policy was an example for Europe. In fact, the American industrial system was no more advanced or progressive than that in Europe. Professor Houssiaux tried to give the essence of industrial policies on p. 357, but it was not at all clear what the difference was. Also on p. 358, Professor Houssiaux said that a Community industrial policy was gradually emerging. What followed was not proof of this. On the contrary, on p. 359 he said that these policies had not always given satisfactory results. M. Albert in his own paper had said that there was no common E.E.C. industrial policy.

Finally, on the role of American firms in Europe, one sensed contradictions in policy. One attracted American firms to Europe, and then said that one did not want them after all. The suggestion now was that we should discriminate against them. Professor Houssiaux wanted the severe application of antitrust laws against non-European firms. This implied that there was no competition policy within the E.E.C. itself. It was true, as he had said in the discussion of M. Albert's paper, that competition policy was much more fully worked out in its juridical aspects than in its effects on market performance. However, he did not think it was useless. He also noted that while the E.E.C. had talked for years about a policy to merge European firms, the present situation had prevented Agfa in Germany and Gevaert in Belgium from merging.

To Professor Dunning, Professor Meerhaeghe said many thought that there was not so much a technological as a managerial gap. About some statistics on Table 17.1, he would like to say that these were O.E.C.D. figures. He was not very convinced by them. The manager of a major European firm had said that when O.E.C.D. asked for information he gave some figures, but not all that he might have given. To base conclusions on these statistics was therefore a bit dangerous. Professor Dunning said there were no sectoral statistics of United States investment in various countries, but in fact there were statistics for Belgium and the Netherlands.

Mr Shonfield said that Professor Meerhaeghe had thrown doubt on the O.E.C.D. figures in Table 17.1. What was it that troubled him most?

Professor Meerhaeghe said it was columns 2 and 3. *Mr Shonfield* said this was because these figures were obtained from individual firms.

Professor Lundberg said that, at one point in his paper, Professor Houssiaux spoke of means of changing the industrial ethos: efficiency, mobility and competition. He would like to broaden the issue. When one discussed industrial policies, one was really referring to leading firms; when one looked at production per unit of labour in America and Europe, one used average or aggregate figures. He would like to refer to sectoral studies done in Sweden. How did new technology spread to the firms in a whole sector? In Sweden, one found big differences in efficiency between old and new plants in the same industry. There was always something of a technological museum. He would like to take this up from a Portuguese point of view. In his paper, Professor Pinto Barbosa had referred to the equilibrium and disequilibrium of the economic structure. One might learn something by comparing Swedish and Portuguese problems in these respects. Was he right that industrial policy had the broad implications as pictured in Fig. 17.1?

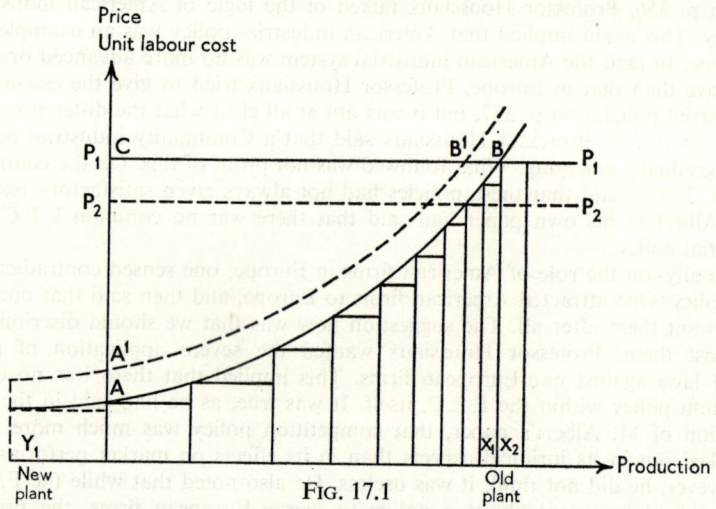

Fig. 17.1

Fig. 17.1 showed that, as had been found in Swedish research in the wood and paper industries, one could arrange the plants in a given industry in terms of their value added per unit of labour input. Declining labour productivity and rising labour costs were shown as one moved from left to right in this diagram; the bars were broader nearer the origin because plants were bigger. One had added value at a given price of product.

In the pulp industry in Sweden, for instance, value added per unit of labour in the most efficient plants was four times as high (at the left-hand end of the diagram) as in the least efficient (at the right-hand margin). There was more capital and more modern techniques at the left-hand end. The shaded area above the cost lines then gave a measure of total gross profit in the industry. The least efficient firms covered their direct costs well enough to keep going, but earned no gross profits.

We could now introduce the Schumpeterian concept of creative destruction. When one added new plants on the left, and value added was reduced to the amount shown by the dotted line, or there were higher wage costs, what happened? There was an increase of productivity at both ends. Competition would force the disappearance of the least efficient plants and shift resources from right to left in the diagram. In the paper, pulp and sawmilling industry, this reallocation of labour within the industry had accounted for about 60 per cent of the total increase in productivity during a period of about ten years.

A dominating part of these export industries had to sell at *given* prices, because it was so small compared with the world market. This kind of perfect competition implied that the industry could not compensate itself by raising wage rates; in fact, prices were about constant over the ten-year period. Productivity had to rise a good deal just because higher wages costs had squeezed out inefficient plants, and resources moved to those plants that could pay the higher wages. The aim of industrial policy must be to create the necessary mobility of resources to move as much output as one could to the more modern plants, and to force inefficient plant out of business by competition – or make them rationalise.

In Sweden, a large part of the story of rising productivity could be told by looking at industries in this way. It suggested that one could transform the economy rapidly by structural change if the 'tails' of inefficient plants were too long.

In Portugal, with a good deal of American, British and Swedish investment in new plant in various branches of industry, and with some good plants of her own, the country had new technology and yet probably very long 'tails' of inefficient and small firms. Average productivity was therefore low, and could be raised rapidly as the gaps between the best and worst plants were probably very large. It was not enough to obtain new investment; it was necessary to see that competition worked efficiently. His interpretation of Portugal's situation was that the profits of the best firms were very high, as on the left of Fig. 17.1. These firms liked to 'compete' with the 'tail'. Low wages in inefficient plants meant fairly low wages also in efficient plants, and therefore high profits and large savings for new development. Was this analysis of structural disequilibrium realistic? One needed enough efficient plants and no very long 'tails'. He thought that in full employment one should not underrate the role of creative destruction. The welfare aspect of the 'tail' was that one needed to move people from inefficient plants and branches to more efficient ones in order to transform industries. But there was an optimal rate of transformation. There were different degrees of perfection within the capital market. Mobility of labour and access to capital were obviously important. In the Swedish paper industry, capital was mobile enough. However, even if there were no change at the left-hand end, a large part of the explanation of rising productivity would be a shift of labour from right to left – a shift of employment from less to more efficient firms.

Professor Nunes said he thought that Professor Lundberg's interpretation was generally correct. There had been transfers of labour in Portugal over the last five years. New firms had higher productivity. However, certain conditions, like perfect transferability of capital, did not exist. Firms remained far to the right (in Professor Lundberg's diagram) with productivity standards that were low.

Professor Kindleberger shared Professor van Meerhaeghe's astonishment at discovering that industrial policy had started in 1966. The E.C.S.C. was industrial policy; so were the Monet plans. He knew that we were now in a period of of 'deplanification'; but all of this was industrial policy. The Agfa–Gevaert case had been mentioned, but the Citroën–Fiat merger was also industrial policy. M. Servan-Schreiber had said that in three years the French had followed five policies on foreign investment. There were strong arguments for excluding foreign investment, which were essentially the same as for tariffs.

First, Sweden and Japan had important arguments. He was impressed by the fact that Sweden wanted independence and therefore allowed in foreign firms selectively. The economics of nationalism showed that nationalism was a public good. It had its demand and its cost sides, and in equilibrium one could buy as much nationalism as one wanted.

Second, there was the infant-industry argument. Portuguese, Belgian and Italian experience showed that American firms helped the locals to learn by doing. This helped to spread techniques. The malaise of the Walloon area of Belgium had been overcome by expansion in the Flemish area. Professor Dunning had not established the case beyond peradventure, but it was hard to say there were no infant-industry effects in Europe. There was then the second-best argument. This was a powerful one. For example, it was said that the balance of payments was important; or that employment was more important than growth. One must therefore keep the Lundberg 'tail'. This was simply a variant of the infant-industry argument.

Third, there was the monopoly argument. If I.B.M. had bought Machines Bull, or now bought I.C.T., that would be a disaster. Resisting monopoly was a legitimate thing. But one might achieve the same results by reducing protection. The French, for example, had wanted to join the E.C.S.C. once they saw that big French steel arms could compete in it. They therefore let the E.C.S.C. kill off a merger with small French steel firms, because they could then blame what happened on European rather than French activity. Alternatively, one could, of course, do what had happened in June 1968 – raise minimum wages by 35 per cent. This was proving disastrous for small, labour-intensive firms. It also had serious social implications.

One could see the desirability of keeping down industrial protectionism. However, one should look ahead. A speaker at a seminar in M.I.T. had suggested that the European automobile industry would fairly soon consist of four companies. Of course, the key question was which. How far could existing firms hope to survive? The speaker had said that Fiat would do well; that Citroën could not; that Chrysler could not; and that General Motors would not wish in the long run to continue production at a lower profit than it earned at present. The expectation was that B.L.M.C. would remain, mainly because of its bus and truck production; that Volkswagen and Daimler would unite completely and survive; that Fiat Lancia would remain. Strictly, he should have said that there would be four and a half firms, because Volvo was expected to remain. There would thus be no wholly French firm. What should industrial policy do here? Should it deal with the political, or the market, issue? He doubted whether the politicians would do any better than in the past. It needed *one* policy, and nothing had shown that more clearly than monetary affairs. He would be interested to know why Professor Houssiaux thought it would be easier for the E.E.C. to have an industrial than a monetary policy.

Professor van Meerhaeghe suggested that a major argument in favour of discrimination against American firms was that the United States spent much more on research and development than did European countries.

Professor Hague said he would like to look at some details in Professor Houssiaux's paper. On p. 354, Professor Houssiaux rightly said that Britain had set up a Ministry of Technology, and a number of Economic Development Councils. He could perhaps explain that the main body in this field was the National Economic Development Council; under this, and rather deliberately following the French, we had set up the equivalent of the French modernisation commissions. These were known as E.D.C.s, or 'Little Neddies', and related to particular industries. Although Britain had followed the French in setting up the E.D.C.s, these had worked rather differently. The French modernisation commissions worked in the early stages of drawing up the plan. They took the overall plan and produced sectoral plans. Since Britain had already worked out what was called a national plan in 1965, before most of the E.D.C.s had been set up, a job had had to be found for them. There had been a good deal of difficulty over this, and most of the E.D.C.s were now devoting most of their attention to problems like increasing exports and import substitution, and improving marketing.

On p. 355, Professor Houssiaux spoke of the reorganisation of the British banking system to provide new industrial services. It would have been very nice if this had actually happened. Although a number of British banks had merged, this seemed to him to have been mainly merger for merger's sake. The main contribution of the banks to economic advance recently had been to close on Saturday mornings!

On p. 353, Professor Houssiaux, spoke of the 'infatuation' in administrative circles for the 'planning–programming–budgeting technique'. While he agreed that there was this infatuation even in the United Kingdom, he thought it important to understand why it happened. High-level thinking and teaching on such issues, as one had in business schools, was concerned with enabling managers to analyse and solve problems in a sophisticated way. Consultants tried to do much the same job by putting a set of principles into a package, and selling the package as a kind of gimmick, given what was effectively the trade name of the particular consultant. One problem was that managers then tended to see the most recent gimmick as an answer to all their problems. They were not, as one hoped business school students were, able to see the thinking lying behind the techniques. The ideas behind planning, programming and budgeting were desirable; the problem was that they were tied up into this sort of package. However, given the managers and civil servants we had, perhaps nothing better could be done.

Professor Kindleberger had spoken about the problems of international co-operation on merger policy. Professor Hague said he had recently been asked by a government-department whether English Calico should be allowed to merge with Courtaulds, and why the price mechanism was not working here as economists thought it would. The obvious answer was that the Government was not letting it!

Turning to Professor Dunning's paper, Professor Hague said he thought it arguable that Professor Dunning could equally well have been asked to write a paper dealing with the managerial gap. If the result of American investment in Europe was that entrepreneurs, in the Schumpeterian sense, moved in, one would expect them to be operating where income elasticity of demand was high. It would turn out that many of these high-elasticity industries were also high-technology industries. To return to Lancashire textiles, one found that in an industry like this the British Government was much more anxious to stop American firms moving in than where, for example, a small electronics firm wished to enter the United Kingdom. He thought that, quite apart from the fact that entrepreneurs would be attracted to rapidly expanding industries, with high income elasticity of demand, there was also a political interest in keeping foreign firms out of declining industries.

The question was, therefore, whether we were concerned with closing a technological or a managerial gap between Europe and the United States. Mr Lamfalussy had earlier raised the possibility of 'buying good management' abroad if one did not have it in one's own firm and had suggested that only big firms could afford to do this. While agreeing that big firms were probably more likely than small firms to buy foreign managers, Professor Hague thought that a major reason for this was that if a small firm bought better management, the existing top management would have to go. In a family firm, or a small cohesive social group of managers, this was unacceptable. Only the large firm could afford the disruption of bringing much better management in.

Mr Brittan said that examples like that of English Calico led him to the general feeling that one should be increasingly sceptical about what passed as 'positive political invention'. It was very important to make some crucial distinction. Few would argue against industrial policy where it was simply supplementing the work of the market economy. For example, in Professor Lundberg's diagram, one might approve of measures to accelerate the elimination of the long 'tail', since this often took place in a market economy at less than the optimum welfare rate. Confused with this welfare objective, however, there was a quite illegitimate consideration – especially in the United Kingdom and perhaps France. Basically, this was back-door protection, interfering with exports and imports. In theory, one could argue that it was legitimate to try in this way to turn the *terms of trade* in a country's favour. But country after country found no substitute for general monetary methods of adjusting the balance of payments. Countries which had tried to avoid them were, in the end, driven back to them.

The proliferation of such back-door subsidisation underlined the role of organisations like GATT. We had already reached the conclusion in the Conference that GATT would need in future to look at non-tariff protection and at the protectionist aspects of industrial and agricultural policies.

One main objection to the balance of payments aspect of industrial policy was that it brought industrial policy itself into disrepute and made people doubtful about what *was* legitimate in it. If the price mechanism was used as the main balance of payments instrument, then industrial policy could be concerned with improving the working of the market, prodding sluggish entrepreneurs, and so on. When a country was in both internal and external disequilibrium, it was almost impossible to say whether its problems arose from an overvalued exchange rate, or from excessive home demand, or from industrial weakness. It was then very difficult indeed to say which industries were operating in wrong or inefficient ways, and needed government intervention.

Mr Brittan suggested that the E.D.C.s had been a relative disappointment because they had looked at import substitution and ways of increasing exports. He thought the industry-by-industry approach was not a second-best but a fifth-best or sixth-best approach as compared with general financial measures for improving the competitive position of the British economy. Because Britain's exchange rate had been over-valued for so long, it was not possible for the 'Little Neddies' to see where their special attention was really needed. He was therefore rather suspicious of the high-level committees mentioned by Professor Houssiaux. While we did not want to go back to an imaginary nineteenth-century world, there were different kinds of industrial policy to be distinguished. One ought to separate the legitimate use of genuine industrial policy and the back-door intervention by governments which were not making enough use of macro-economic measures.

Professor Sohmen also expressed surprise that Professor Houssiaux had not mentioned one outstanding example of 'industrial policy', namely, French planning. Many economists had felt, about ten years ago, that this was the most promising road to progress. Now that there was a good deal of disillusionment about it, economists should do much more in the way of *ex post* evaluation. How far had French planning succeeded? Countries such as Portugal could obviously learn a lot from this kind of experiment.

Professor Campbell wondered if Professor Houssiaux would elaborate on what he had said about anti-monopoly legislation. He had the impression that this was quite different on the two sides of the Atlantic, and was especially interested in what was said on p. 362, when Professor Houssiaux talked of discrimination against European firms. Could one apply anti-trust policy strictly against non-European firms? On p. 362, Professor Houssiaux also talked of the intensive Europeanisation of non-European firms. What did he mean by this?

Professor Khachaturov said that the important question about the technological gap was whether it was growing or diminishing. If it was growing, how could it be narrowed? There was no direct way of measuring it. However, in some cases one could be much more accurate. It was evident, for example, that the technological gap had been reduced in the Soviet Union during the period after the October Revolution. The U.S.S.R. was now ahead of many other countries. The technological gap between Japan and most developed countries had also been diminished since 1945 with Japanese development of electronics, shipbuilding, automobile industry, etc.

It was often said that American investment in Europe, by bringing new techniques, reduced the technological gap. This was true to some extent, but would it liquidate that gap altogether? In his view, complete equalisation of technology was possible only if European countries could catch up with the United States in research and development and in education. America spent more than 3 per cent of its national income on research and development, more than $25 billion per year and several times more than Western European countries taken together; expenditure in the United States on education was about 8 per cent of the national income. He did not see that one country could hope to catch up by borrowing American technology. Some would say that the U.S.S.R. and Japan had borrowed it first, but this happened long ago, in the first stages of their industrialisation; now the U.S.S.R. was itself spending more than 3 per cent of its national income on research and development. If Western European industrial countries found it hard to finance such activities, maybe it was possible to organise international co-operation. The socialist countries had experience of this; for example, they had the nuclear physics institute near Moscow; Franco-Soviet scientific co-operation could also be mentioned. What were needed were more scientific institutions in Western Europe, and higher incomes for Western European scientists.

Professor Eastman replied to Professor van Meerhaeghe, who had argued that American direct investment in Europe should be held back because the American Government subsidised research and gave American firms an advantage not possessed by others. He thought that the positive analysis was correct. A good deal of foreign ownership was based on knowledge. A study of his own had shown some major examples of foreign ownership in Canada resulting from economies of scale in knowledge. Professor van Meerhaeghe was right on the facts. However, Professor Eastman did not believe that this justified impeding European countries from obtaining free knowledge from the United States Government. One was led back to the proposition of Professor Viner about the appropriate measurement of gains from trade for an individual country. What one should do was to compare actual foreign prices, however determined, with domestic real costs (today we would speak of shadow prices). Applying this logic to foreign investment, it was not relevant that American firms had a competitive advantage because of help given by the United States Government in research and development rather than some other reason. If foreign firms lowered costs of production in a country by bringing superior technology, they should be welcome, whatever the source of the superiority.

His own view was that if one could obtain something for nothing, one should not refuse it, though others might argue that there was something 'unfair' about this. If one went back to Professor Lundberg's diagram, foreign firms would make big profits and some would have an advantage over local firms. Certainly there was a legitimate reason for concern here, but it was hard to identify the national loss, and usually impossible to have the technology without the foreign firms. If one reduced tariff barriers and reduced prices to raise efficiency, this also would cut off the 'tail' of small domestic firms. It was his own view that somehow local firms must acquire knowledge, and there was advantage in spreading information among local firms by allowing foreign firms to enter. He would agree with Professor Khachaturov that one ought to finance as much research and development as was necessary within one's own country; but one should surely add this to, rather than substitute it for, international knowledge when the latter was free in this way.

Professor Robinson said that in the discussion we had been asking three things at once. First, what was the value for European development of American technology? Second, what was the value to European development of American management? Third, what was the value to European development of American ownership? He thought it was necessary to keep these issues more separate than had been done so far. As good Europeans, he thought all of us would accept that we badly needed the first two. Most of us would be prepared to have more American management expertise in Europe. Europe would benefit from American ideas about manning scales. In the United Kingdom, for example, we had very extravagant ideas, and an American manager coming in was usually able to economise on labour a good deal. One also got benefits from American consultants. Having American eyes looking at European industry enabled us to see where it was inefficient. However, the nub of the problem was American ownership. Here, he thought the first part of Professor Dunning's paper fascinating. This showed that in the nineteenth century the rapid transfer of European technology to the United States took place without European ownership, especially in railways.

We ought to go to face this issue. He knew that many French economists were worried by the problems of domination. Professor Kindleberger had talked about what might happen to the automobile industry in Europe and there would be a good deal of fear in Europe if this pattern actually developed. For example, in the United Kingdom, one big firm – British Leyland – held 40 per cent of the market. Rather more than that was in the hands of three American groups: Vauxhall (General Motors), Ford, and Rootes (Chrysler). Between them these American firms did almost 50 per cent of the business. Could one really see them as competing plants? Was one right to see the American group as having common responses to changes in the world situation?

Nor was the responses always favourable to the country where the subsidiary happened to be. The response took account of the effect of changes in conditions in individual countries on the total welfare of the whole concern. The international corporation was more willing to shift production from its plant in one country to a plant in another country. The response was fundamentally different from that where a corporation was wholly based in the country where it was situated. The welfare of the plant was then much more closely related to the welfare of the country. He thought there were some grounds here for worry – and that Professor Kindleberger was not facing up to them. It was not a problem of monopoly, but of a highly oligopolistic response to situations as they developed over a very wide area. There were no quick or easy answers, but we had not faced these problems so far.

Professor Šik said it was true that all countries wanted to reduce the technological gap, but how a country did it depended on its own economic system, the aims of managers and planners, and how far there was more or less competition. He would use the socialist countries as an example. In their conditions, they needed rapid technological development. But in the existing conditions of economic development, the main aim of planners and managers was to have the broadest and quickest growth of industrial production. For this reason there existed, among other things, a general protective system. However, in a country like Czechoslovakia, for almost two decades this had protected the most hopelessly backward production. The aim was to increase output, but in most firms and industries this happened at the expense of technical development. Most plants could obtain the greatest quantity of production only with more or less conservative methods and by avoiding innovation. Even the most backward and ineffective plants were kept going to secure the greatest volume of production.

The great advantage of socialist economies was said to be that they gave every worker the right to work. It was understood that the state had a duty to keep all plants in operation, without respect to their efficiency.

The issue therefore began in the plant. To keep up output, the socialist economies were often moving in the opposite direction to that in Professor Lundberg's diagram. The profits from the best plants were given to the worst in order to keep the latter in operation. So, one had a high level of industrial production but at the cost of necessary structural development. For example, the development of agriculture, transport, infrastructure and the service industries was being held back in socialist countries. The high level of output was also at the cost of real technological development because one needed a large amount of less and less effective investment simply to build up new plants, without renewing the existing ones. It would be better to close some of the old and less efficient plants, which could not be reconstructed, and to use the workers and resources in other more progressive and effective units. It was true that there would be some social problems, but the cost of permitting the present situation to continue was that it held back technological progress and kept up costs. This was not to the advantage either of socialism or of the workers. We needed to see how other methods of planning and managing, together with real competition in a socialist economy could work. Impressive technical development in some branches preferred by the state (mostly for military reasons) could not negate the fact that the administrative planning system braked the real technical and qualitative development.

Professor Houssiaux said that when he had been asked to write on industrial policy, he was not sure that he was capable of it. As a liberal economist, he was not at all sure what was hidden under the carpet! The result was that he seemed to have taken over the role of villain in the discussion.

He would first like to try and define industrial policy. He had tried to give several definitions in his paper. The O.E.C.D. had looked intensively at these issues. The first notion was that industrial policy was one way of looking at the implications of general economic policy for particular industries. He had not looked at monetary and fiscal policy; he had also ignored the infrastructure for this reason. Some elements in American policy did give a form of aid to industry – for example, research and development. The second definition was that industrial policy was a weapon used by administrators to help industries. They might do this, for example, if the private sector was not responsive to market signals. Before the coming of industrial policy, governments simply gave subsidies to declining industries and incentives to spearhead ones, but without any rational organisation.

Professor Houssiaux accepted that Swedish industrial policy was not on these lines. Nor, indeed, was German policy. But there were two broad groups of countries in Europe. In the North, Sweden and Germany put less emphasis on aid to various industries and more on trying to eliminate inefficiency. In the South, other countries interfered more directly with the market forms. But he still thought the differences were ones of degree rather than nature.

He had said that industrial policy began in 1966 because there was then a recession in Europe. Recession made it more obviously necessary to interfere in spearhead industries and showed how necessary it was to co-ordinate policy. In one sector, one could have some parts of the administration trying to eliminate small firms while others, through a small business administration, were trying to encourage them.

So far as American industrial policy was concerned it was largely a question of nuances. He thought it was true that there were more incentives in the United States and more direct action in Europe. Europe was also more willing to act upon particular sectors and firms. For example, there were the activities of the E.D.C.s and of the I.R.C. in Great Britain. But Professor Houssiaux thought there was an industrial policy as such in the United States, even under a Republican Administration.

As for differences between various E.E.C. countries, he thought that the Europeans believed, above all, in the importance of a large market. He thought himself that markets were always more segmented and that the argument of the big market was not the key to the situation. If it were, individual countries would not have grown as they had without that market. For example, Sweden and the Netherlands had grown efficiently despite their small size. It was quite impossible to generalise. He still felt that the E.E.C. had copied the United States rather than any other country and maybe, was wrong to do so.

As for anti-trust policy, the E.E.C. had no means of acting directly on competition in individual countries. It therefore used anti-trust weapons and tried to set up the rules of the game. In its competition policy, the Commission had started to look at individual sectors and industries. Within each industry, it tried to eliminate unprofitable activities.

Professor Houssiaux thought there was a kind of opposition of nature between the industrial policy of the E.E.C. and the action of individual countries. This was why there sometimes seemed to be no E.E.C. policy at all. Professor Kindleberger was right that there was no more the indication of a coming industrial policy in Europe than of a coming monetary policy: and for the same reasons. He saw no reason why there should be any sudden change, because in this situation the generals always seemed to be behind rather than in front of the troops.

As for American–European relations, participants had spoken of the managerial gap. He did not believe that there was one. Ideas were transferred quickly, and the gimmicks that Professor Hague had mentioned were soon learnt by everyone. Large numbers of people went to hear about the latest techniques. What had not changed was the structure of authority. In France, there was a very old-fashioned business system. One did not find the mobile system of the United States. The French system had its merits, however, but it did continue to keep old-fashioned methods – as indeed seemed to happen in socialist countries. He thought the performance of the German economy owed more to a very efficient bureaucracy than to the working of competition. There was no managerial gap in Germany. She had accepted new techniques gladly, but her industrial system had not changed much. He did not think that the size of the world market, or of the European market, was any longer fundamental.

On French planning, he was not ready to judge. The evolution seemed rather similar to the one followed in the United Kingdom. National planning was at the moment out of fashion.

On the European policy for competition, the aim was to avoid private barriers replacing tariff barriers. The policy was also seen as the ground for the integration of the economy, broadening the market. The reason why European policy was less severe on cartels than American was that monopoly practices were less understood as against 'public interest'. However, there had been some change. He did not think one could speak seriously of monopolistic 'domination' in Europe, though there certainly were oligopolistic markets where competition was limited. An anti-trust policy was therefore needed. As for increasing the efficiency of firms, competition could probably do very little for long.

On the Europeanisation of multinational firms, Professor Houssiaux thought that such firms, multinational *and* European, were needed. The systems in Europe and the United States were very different, and it was often necessary for European firms to be more European first, and less international. He thought we were moving towards a 'polycentric' system.

Professor Dunning said that in his paper, especially on p. 374, he tried to distinguish between the different interpretations of the technological gap. So far the discussion had focussed on the *production* of technology in Europe, but he thought we should think less in these terms rather and more of the implications of differences in the *use* of technology between Europe and America.

Most of the writings on the technological gap assumed that the best way for Europe to increase her rates of growth was to become more technologically independent – or at any rate increase indigenous research and development a good deal. In his paper, he had tried to look at how Europe's use of (world) technology could be improved. Should Europe produce more technology; import more technology; or import products which embodied technology?

He had concentrated on the first two. One way of importing technology was to encourage direct investment. It was true that most American investment in Europe was in the research-intensive sectors. He thought that such figures as there were suggested that American firms had made a substantial contribution to the rate of growth of technologically advanced products in Europe. Assuming this was the only way to borrow technology the question was: how did one minimise the costs and maximise the benefits of doing this? He thought that part of the reaction against American investment in Europe was that Europe was not properly organised to take advantage of it. Christopher Layton, in his book *European Advanced Technology*, had quoted a European research director as saying that all that America needed to do was to erect fifty-one sets of customs barriers, laws, tax systems, etc., and the technological gap would be gone within a year. There was some truth in this. The industrial machine of Europe was not geared to maximise the benefits from American investment; indeed it was inhibited from doing so. The Watkins report on Canadian economic policy emphasised the need for receiving countries to encourage the diffusion of the benefits of investment around the economy and to create effective countervailing power. This could best be achieved through an appropriate policy for increasing the competitiveness of the system. Much of the criticism of American investment centred around the issue of the *distribution* of benefits.

Moving to wider contexts, Professor Dunning said that the multinational corporation now seemed to be the main vehicle for diffusing technological expertise and managerial ability. Canada had become dominated by American subsidiaries; Europe could still choose whether American investment there would take a similar route. How far was it possible to get the benefits from American investment in other ways, e.g. by licensing agreements and joint ventures? It was important to notice that Japan and Russia managed quite well without much foreign investment, and there was much to learn from them – especially post-war Japan.

Professor Dunning thought we should get the multinational corporations in the right perspective. *Fortune* data showed that European-based corporations were now growing faster than American ones. In the last few years too, overseas investment by European-based corporations had been expanding more rapidly than that of American ones.

Professor Robinson tried to emphasise the problem of ownership, but it was important to remember that not all multinational corporations were based in America. The National Industrial Conference Board had estimated that in fifteen or twenty years about 30 per cent of all manufacturing output outside the United States would be in the hands of multinational corporations. One therefore had to see these in broader perspective, though Professor Robinson was right to raise the points he had about whether there were alternatives to direct investment as vehicles for spreading technology.

Professor Rasmussen said he was reminded of the fact that there had been a Danish study in the 1950s by Hoffmeyer which had tried to provide information on the technological gap by tracing it back to the turn of the century. The conclusion was that from about 1900 America had had a competitive advantage in research-intensive products. Hoffmeyer had used time series like those of Professor Dunning. The difficulty of all such analyses was that one had to use very broad categories and this made it difficult to draw water-tight conclusions. The O.E.C.D. had produced a study on the basis of cross-section analysis which was not wholly convincing either. They had started from the hypothesis that there was a technological gap. However, while this was true for some sectors, it was less certain for others. While Europe was not behind in fundamental research, it was probably behind in the application of that research. America often took fundamental research from Europe and turned it into improved technology.

Mr Shonfield said that Professor Hague had asked whether one could distinguish between the transmission of technology and of management in the context of Professor Dunning's paper. Professor Hague had suggested that high-income-elasticity products would very often be the same as high-technology products. One way to approach the problem was to try to find some products with high income elasticities but with no great technological content. One could then ask whether America had a significant influence in them. He could, in fact, think of some – for example, hotel management. This was an old industry in Europe, but where the American role was important. In order to proceed further with this kind of analysis, it would be necessary to disaggregate the figures.

Finally, Mr Shonfield referred to the problem of textiles. In Professor Dunning's paper these came under Group 3. But synthetic textiles were clearly in Group 1. So if one had found, say, that the United States had had a major investment in synthetics, this would have shown up as an influence on 'textiles' which was not a high-technology activity. We clearly needed much more disaggregation of statistics if we were not to draw the wrong conclusions.

Part 4

Conflicts of Interest in Migration Policies

18 Transatlantic and North American International Migration[1]

Anthony Scott
UNIVERSITY OF BRITISH COLUMBIA, CANADA

I. INTRODUCTION

The aim of this survey is to provide background for discussion of the North Atlantic flows of goods and services between Europe and North America by indicating the magnitude and timing of population and labour-force movements. The point of view will be almost entirely that of North America, that is of a region of immigration. This is just as well, for, seen as the continuation of the great European waves of nineteenth-century migration to the countries of new settlement, the movements of the past two decades have been disappointly unworthy of notice. They have had little impact on the United Kingdom, Ireland, Germany or Scandinavia, countries which until 1890 were continuously adjusting to the outflows of young artisans and peasants. Among north European countries, probably only Holland and England took post-war overseas emigration seriously, as a force which, if properly guided, could work to the advantage of both emigrants and those remaining behind. But just as northern European migrants were, in the decades before 1914, over-shadowed by new flows from southern and eastern Europe, so the British, Germans and Scandinavians have again been overhauled by flows from Italy and other countries along the Mediterranean and east of Germany and France. Moreover, the countries of northern and western Europe, far from concerning themselves with their role in the peopling of America, are bemused and concerned about their capacity to employ and absorb the circuits of migration across their borders from Europe and North Africa.

Immigration affects population growth three ways: by direct addition to existing population; by affecting the brith rates of the augmented population; and by affecting the re-migration rates of the augmented population.

The combined effects of these three forces is shown in Table 18.1, which, dealing with North America as a whole, naturally reflects chiefly the growth of the United States population, ten times that of Canada.

---

[1] In writing this paper, I have had the co-operation of Professors A. Farley and J. Vanderkamp; Mr T. J. Samuel; and the research assistance of Masako Darrough and Tony Burger.

NA P

TABLE 18.1
IMMIGRATION AND POPULATION GROWTH,
NORTH AMERICA, 1850–1960

	Population			Ratio of immigration	
Decade-ending census date	U.S.A.	Canada	Total	to population (per cent)	to population increase (per cent)
	(millions of people)				
1850–1	23·2	2·4	25·6	..	..
1860–1	31·4	3·2	34·7	7·8	30·1
1870–1	39·8	3·7	43·5	4·9	24·0
1880–1	50·2	4·3	54·5	5·0	24·8
1890–1	62·9	4·8	67·8	7·4	37·9
1900–1	76·0	5·4	81·4	4·3	25·8
1910–11	92·0	7·2	99·2	9·6	53·4
1920–1	105·7	8·8	114·5	5·2	39·0
1930–1	122·8	10·4	133·2	3·1	22·6
1940–1	131·7	11·5	143·2	3·0	4·3
1950–1	150·7	14·0	164·7	0·7	5·6
1960–1	177·5	18·2	195·7	1·9	11·8
1965–6	191·9	20·1	212·0	1·0	13·0

Note: Immigration has been corrected for Canadian–United States migration.
Sources: *The Statistical History of the United States*; *Historical Statistics of Canada*.

TABLE 18.2A
IMMIGRATION TO CANADA BY AGE AND SEX

Year	% male adults of all immigrants	% children of all immigrants
1912–19	56·3	17·9
1920–9	51·3	20·1
1930–9	32·2	32·0
1940–9	34·5	24·1
1945–9	35·2	23·8
1950–4	43·0	25·3
1955–9	40·6	26·8
1960–4	34·5	26·2
1965–8	36·2[a]	29·3[b]

[a] Excludes immigrants aged 18 and 19 years 1967, 1968.
[b] Includes immigrants aged 18 and 19 years 1967, 1968.
N.B. Prior to 1925, children were 0–13 years. After 1925, children were 0–17 years.

Sources: *Historical Statistics of Canada*; *Canada Year Book*; *Quarterly Immigration Bulletin*.

TABLE 18.2B
IMMIGRANTS TO UNITED STATES BY AGE AND SEX

Year	% males of all immigrants	% male adults of all immigrants	% of children
	(1)	(2)	(3)
1850–9	57·1		20·9
1860–9	60·3[a]		18·5
1870–9	61·0		20·9
1880–9	61·2		21·3
1890–9	61·5		14·9
1900–9	69·6		12·1
1910–19	65·1		13·4
1920–9	56·1		17·7
1930–9	44·7		17·0
1940–9	38·8		14·1
1945–9	37·0		14·1
1950–5	46·5		21·9
1955–9	46·2	34·4	23·2
1960–4	45·3	32·9	23·3
1965–7	43·4		26·4

[a] Excluding 1868.
Notes: 1850–98 children are all those under 15.
1899–1917 children are all those under 14.
1918–67 children are all those under 16.
If the sex distribution of children were even, then the following relationship would hold:
$$(1) = (2) + \tfrac{1}{2} \times (3).$$
Sources: *Statistical History of the United States*; *Statistical Abstract of U.S.*; *Annual Report for 1964*, Immigration and Naturalization Service, U.S. Department of Justice.

The rate of net immigration per thousand to the United States between 1850 and the First World War was at least one-quarter of the total population increase per thousand. It rose to above 40 per cent in 1880 and above 50 per cent in the 1900s, then fell off heavily in the 1920s, was negative in the 1930s and has been below 5 per cent since the Second World War.

Until the twentieth century, Canadian net immigration was negative, draining off part of the natural increase to the United States until the three explosive decades from 1901 to 1931. In the pre-First World War decade it provided about 40 per cent of the population increase (compared to 50 per cent in the United States). This percentage contribution remained appreciable but gradually slackened until the Second World War. Since 1951, however, net migration has again become an important source of growth, rising to 35 per cent of total Canadian increase in years of high immigration. We shall return to this subject later. But it is obvious that while the quantitative importance of migration to the United States must now be simply a reflection of its importance to the nations that are a source of immigrants, Canada (like Australia and Israel) still must take net immigration seriously as a main contribution to its development.

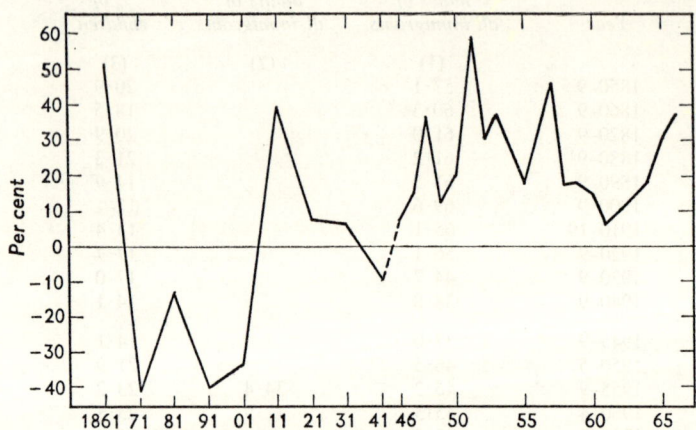

FIG. 18.1   Canada: migration as percentage of population growth, 1851–1966.
Sources: *Historical Statistics of Canada*; *Statistical History of the United States*.

The second effect of immigration on population growth is its averaging effect on the birth rate per thousand people. If the rate of natural increase is higher among immigrants than among natives, and if both rates remain fixed, total population will grow at a rate that is a weighted average of the two. In the recent past, European immigration has tended to increase North American birth rates both because the fraction of immigrants in child-bearing ages and the customary size of completed families was higher than among the North-American-born. (On the other hand, the combination of the availability of birth-control methods, economic incentives to earn funds to assist the arrival of parents and relatives, and the possible selection of female immigrants with high labour-force participation rates may offset the supposed high fertility of immigrants.) In any case, both crude birth rates and female net reproduction rates have failed to fall as far or as fast in Australia, Israel and Canada as in the United States, Western Europe or Japan; immigrant countries' rates were all above emigrant countries' in the period since 1945.

Population forecasts are also fairly sensitive to the fertility of immigrants: a recent Canadian study estimated that even with age-specific fertility rates equal to those of natives, a million immigrants spread over the next decade would increase the end-of-decade population by 1·2 million.

The third effect of immigration, 'replacement', or 'displacement', works through the impact of new immigrants on natives and immigrants of earlier years. The usual assumption of North American demographers is that a native family's rate of natural increase and its mobility are unaffected by the number of immigrants. But two important exceptions have been suggested. One concerns fertility: the greater the immigration, the greater the decline in reproduction by the natives. Consequently, the immigrants simply 'replace' native-born children. That this phenomenon (described first by General F. A. Walker in the 1890s) existed is no longer widely accepted, though it is possible to argue that immigration accelerated general urbanisation, which appeared to reduce fertility.

The other effect, 'displacement', concerns emigration. This is that the absorptive capacity of a country being fixed, or growing only slowly, the consequence of immigration is simply to 'displace' natives who, in the case of Canada, migrated to the United States. 'Displacement' was said by Professor Hurd in the 1940s to exist because Canada's century of immigration had simply balanced its century of emigration. But continuous net immigration since then has 'disproved' this theory also.

(A variant of this pair of hypotheses was that Europeans used Canada as a 'back-door' for entry to the United States. There is some support for this view in the sense that it contradicts the 'displacement' theory; more immigrants do seem to make for the United States back door than displace Canadians. But the 'back-door' hypothesis cannot be literally valid, for the United States quota restrictions on entry applied against would-be immigrants according to their birth, not their last residence.)

Of course, displacement is simply emigration that is more or less simultaneous with the immigration of which it is believed to be a consequence. Other emigration, of the immigrants themselves, is lagged behind the arrival for distinct periods. First, there are the seasonal workers (called *golodrinos* – swallows – by Kindleberger and 'transilient' short-term immigrants by Richmond), who do not attempt to put down roots, but soon return to their own country, or move on to another. Second, there are the returnees who, to fulfil (or abandon) their original emigration plan, return 'home'. Third, there are the former migrants who move permanently to a third country. It is difficult to distinguish these three types of migrants among the aggregative data on offsetting flows. But in the century following 1820, perhaps 30 per cent of all United States immigrants eventually returned home; the percentage returning rose every decade until in the 1900s the outflow equalled half the inflow; and in the Great Depression, the outflow from the United States to all countries and from North America to Europe made both Canada and the United States countries of emigration. For Canada, whose immigrants may either return home or continue to the United States, it is estimated by Richmond that since 1946 about 60 per cent of Americans, 70 per cent of Britons, and 80 per cent of other origins have stayed in Canada; about half the re-migrating Britons appear to have returned home and the other half moved to the United States.

But because most countries do not count either their emigrants, or their own nationals returning home, the available data are very unhelpful. All that needs to be said is that many immigrants do not stay in Canada, or North America, for long.

II. TRENDS TO NORTH AMERICA

The purpose of this section is to examine the trends in migration to North America, by continent and country of origin and by such personal characteristics of the migrants as age, sex and profession. In general it will be seen that while the flow of European migrants to North America has neither waxed nor waned since the Second World War, it has

(*a*) declined as a percentage of immigration from all continents;
(*b*) shifted its origin somewhat from northern to southern Europe;
(*c*) shown little trend with respect to age or sex;
(*d*) moved steadily towards increased skill and professionalism.

Is Europe remaining the principal source of North American immigrants? Taking the post-war period only, it can be seen (in Figs 18.2(*a*), (*b*) and (*c*)) that the flow from the 'rest of the world' is becoming larger, both absolutely and relative to the European flow. One irrelevant com-

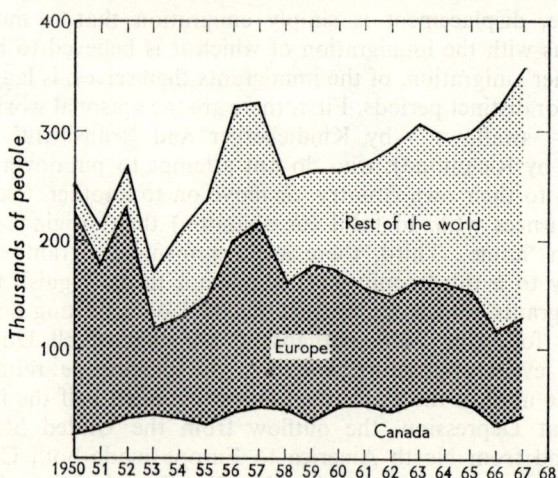

FIG. 18.2(*a*) Immigration to the United States by last permanent residence. Source: *Statistical Abstract of the United States.*

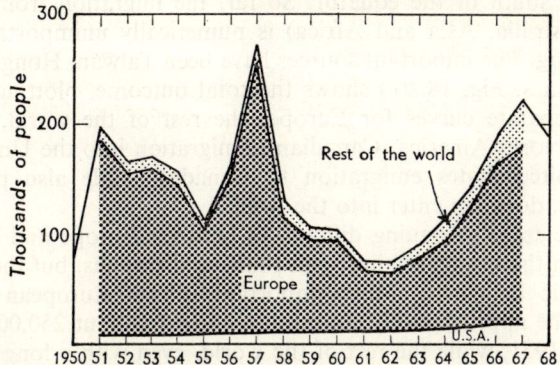

FIG. 18.2(b) Immigration to Canada by last permanent residences
Source: *Bank of Canada Statistical Summary*, March 1969, p. 224.

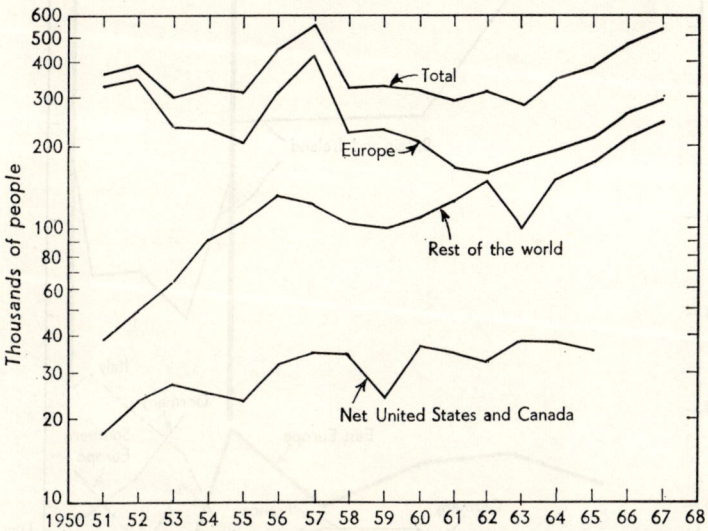

FIG. 18.2(c) Immigration to North America by last permanent residence.
Sources: *Statistical Abstract of the United States*; *Bank of Canada Statistical Summary*

ponent of the increase in arrivals is the augmented reciprocal migration between Canada and the United States. The rest of the world's increase consists mainly of Mexicans, Cubans and others from the western hemisphere moving to the United States. Most arrivals have been from the Caribbean and Central America, while comparatively few have been from the nations south of the equator. So far, the migration from the third source (Australia, Asia and Africa) is numerically unimportant though steadily rising. The important sources have been Taiwan, Hong Kong and the Philippines. Fig. 18.2(c) shows the total outcome, plotting against a log scale separate curves for Europe, the rest of the world, and total arrivals to North America. Canadian immigration into the United States (net of United States emigration to Canada), while also plotted for comparison, does not enter into the total.

There are some intriguing differences between Europe and the rest of the world in the timing of short-run peaks and troughs, but these are not all economic in source. More important is that European migration appears to be approximately constant, tending to about 250,000 per year gross since 1951, while the rest of the world, even with a long plateau to cross between 1956 and 1964, has displayed an increase of six-hundred-

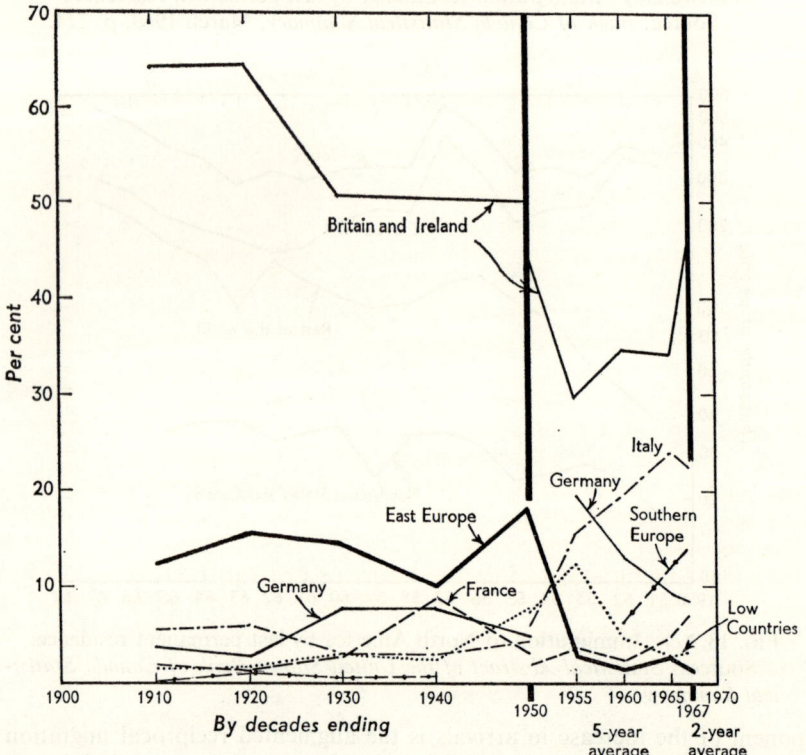

FIG. 18.3(a)   European immigrants to Canada by ethnic origins and country of last permanent residence.

Sources: *Historical Statistics of Canada*; *Canada Year Book*; *Quarterly Immigration Bulletin*.

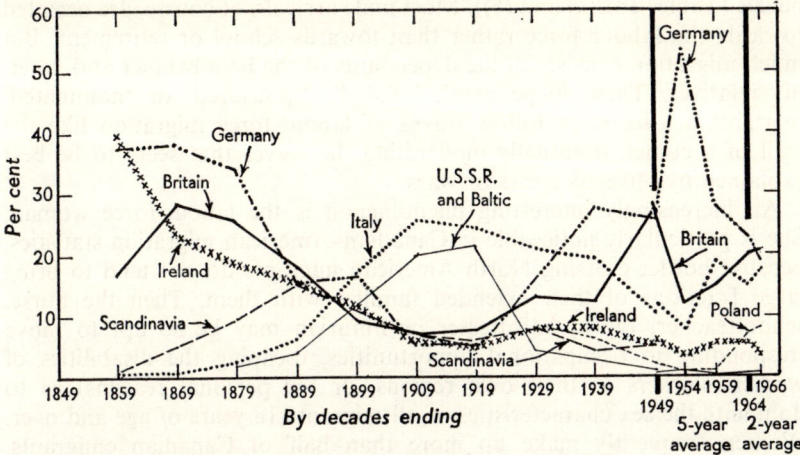

FIG. 18.3(b) Immigration to the United States by European country of last permanent residence.
Source: *Historical Statistics of the United States.*

fold. It is not clear that Europe will long remain the principal source of immigration to North America.

It is difficult to summarise the European 'national origins' information (Figs 18.3(a) and (b)). It is clear that Canada has had a high and continuing dependence on United Kingdom or British immigrants, with the numbers from German-, French- or Italian-speaking regions fluctuating from decade to decade.

The United States, between 1930 and 1965, experienced the failure of its quota system to duplicate the composition of the country by origin in 1910. Northern and western Europe was assigned about two-thirds of the total quota, but between 1930 and 1965 consigned only one-third of the migrants. Southern and eastern Europe got a quarter of the quotas but sent one-third of the migrants. Forty per cent of the immigrants came from the Americas and other regions, whose share in the 1910 national stock was less than 10 per cent. The statistics show that Great Britain, or the United Kingdom, has sent the greatest number of American immigrants, with Germany (and, in some decades, Austria–Hungary), Italy, Ireland, Greece and Russia rising and falling from decade to decade.

It is difficult to avoid the conclusion that such fluctuating proportions and differing levels represent the differences in national intensities of desire to leave, and hence give some strength to the theory that migration is best explained by changes in 'push' rather than in 'pull'. But it should be noticed that some fluctuations simply represent wartime or political closing of emigration.

The age and sex distribution of North American migrants is an intriguing puzzle (Tables 18.2(a) and (b)). Most male arrivals, of course, are oriented towards the labour force rather than towards school or retirement. But much migration consists of the dependants of the breadwinner and, later, his relatives. These 'dependent', 'related', 'sponsored' or 'nominated' migrants are likely to follow waves of labour-force migration like the trail of a comet, eventually moderating the waves that seem to be best explained by business cycles or wars.

An increasingly interesting phenomenon is the labour-force woman. She is particularly noticeable in Canadian–American migration statistics, because border-crossing North American migrants do not tend to bring large fractions of their extended families with them. Then the nurse, schoolteacher, typist, hairdresser or librarian may be so apt to move (responding to occupational opportunities, escaping the disabilities of women workers in their own regions, or for personal reasons) as to dominate the sex characteristics of all migrants 18 years of age and over. Women frequently make up more than half of Canadian emigrants, whereas immigrants to Canada from Europe are chiefly male. It may be, however, that the falling age of marriage in both Europe and North America will increase the number of dependants moving with even the youngest adult male workers. Furthermore, the generous arrangements for dependants and relatives may enable immigrants, in these affluent days, to bring their retired parents. Finally, we should not forget the large flows of students, not all of whom are immediately shown in the immigration data.

In any case, demographers have concluded that the age-and-sex distributions of international immigrants are now unlikely to make a noticeable imprint on the population pyramids of the receiving countries; relatively, the inflows are too small. This impact, of course, may be different from that of *internal* migration.

A more pronounced trend in the North American immigration time series has been the increased proportion of technical, managerial and professional manpower. This is the statistical manifestation of the 'brain drain', seen here in Fig. 18.4. While the chart fails to display the joint distribution of both skill and country of occupation, it does suggest that at the same time as the percentage of immigration from traditional sources has been falling, the demand for immigrants simply as unskilled labour (the traditional role of immigrants from Asia, Italy and parts of eastern Europe) is also declining.

The 'professionals' time series fluctuates very unsatisfactorily: definitions change, and for decades at a time there has been no incentive to get intended occupations reported correctly. Furthermore, the series reveals abrupt discontinuities which reflect, usually, a pronounced fall or rise in the denominator, the total number of immigrants, rather than in the flow

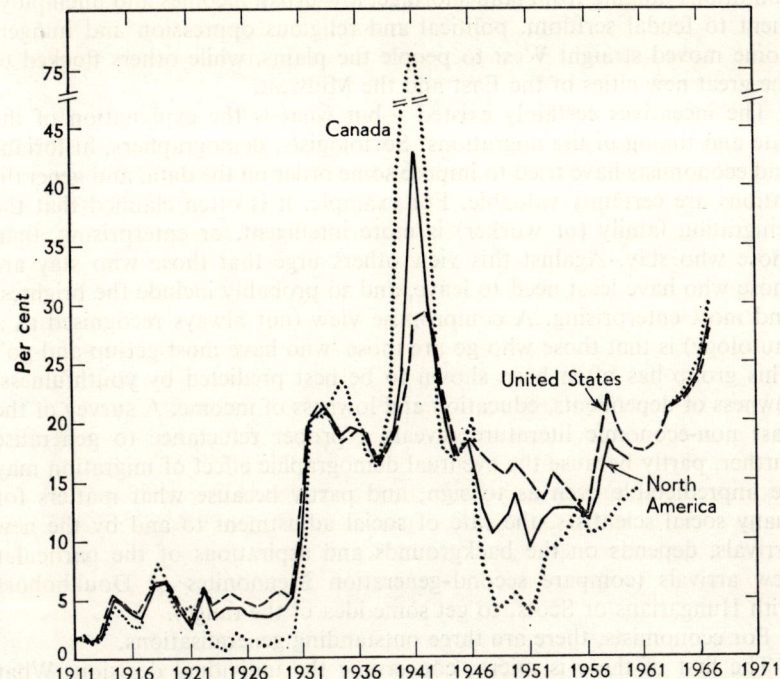

FIG. 18.4 North America: Professional immigrants as percentage of total labour-force immigrants.
Sources: *Historical Statistics of Canada*; *Statistical History of the United States*.

of professional immigration. This reflects the generalisation that the placing of immigrant professionals in North America proceeds steadily; it expands with supply, as when refugees wish to leave Europe; but its cyclical amplitude is slight.

Nevertheless, the long-run expansion of professional immigration is plain. At the height of the great inflow, near the turn of the century, professional persons amounted to less than 5 per cent of immigrants destined to the labour force. Immigration has continued to expand, and is not cyclically depressed today; nevertheless, professionals now are approaching *30 per cent* of immigrant manpower.

III. PULL AND PUSH

Historians seem unanimous that the hordes of nineteenth-century migrants had little to lose and much to gain. Depending on their origins, they left conditions ranging from land shortage, low urban incomes and unemployment to feudal serfdom, political and religious oppression and hunger. Some moved straight West to people the plains, while others flocked to the great new cities of the East and the Midwest.

The incentives certainly existed – but what is the explanation of the rate and timing of the migrations? Sociologists, demographers, historians and economists have tried to impose some order on the data, and generalisations are certainly valuable. For example, it is often claimed that the emigrating family (or worker) is more intelligent, or enterprising, than those who stay. Against this view others urge that those who stay are those who have least need to leave, and so probably include the brightest and most enterprising. A compromise view (not always recognised as a tautology) is that those who go are those 'who have most get-up-and-go'. This group has often been shown to be best predicted by youthfulness, fewness of dependents, education and lowness of income. A survey of the vast non-economic literature reveals a proper reluctance to generalise further, partly because the eventual demographic effect of migration may be unpredictable even as to sign, and partly because what matters for many social scientists, the rate of social adjustment to and by the new arrivals, depends on the backgrounds and aspirations of the particular new arrivals (compare second-generation Mennonites or Doukhobors with Hungarians or Scots, to get some idea of the range).

For economists, there are three outstanding generalisations.

The first of these is micro, concerning the individual decision. What leads a man to migrate? Various cross-section studies have been based on the hypothesis that a man moves wherever and whenever his wealth (the present value of his future real and psychic income stream) increases, after making allowance for removal costs. That this truistic hypothesis does not seem to lead to good predictions may be due to

(*a*) incorrect personal perception or discounting of future incomes, because of either misinformation or uncertainty;
(*b*) unknown weights attached to psychic (intangible) income items;
(*c*) unknown real or psychic costs.

Sociologists and demographers urge that (*b*) and (*c*) are most important, referring to surveys and questionnaires in which migrants or returnees have usually minimised financial differences as a motive for migration, and stressed opportunities, standards of living, and attitudes of the people.

This brings us to the second generalisation. It seeks to explain the *timing* of aggregate migration time series. Often referred to as a 'pull' model, it states that as conditions in the home country build up a 'propensity to emigrate, the volume, direction, and timing of the movement are largely set by the business cycle in the receiving country' (Peterson,

p. 287). In this generalisation, the 'propensity to migrate' evidently consists of the continued existence of some income differential (as a precondition, or dummy variable) and also upon the level of aspiration, the desire to profit from the differential (which may be represented by the passage of time or by the cumulation of previous emigration). For example, a recent study of Canadian growth found that changes in postwar immigration from overseas (all occupations and dependants) could not be explained by income differences or tax changes, but were sensitive to employment (actually, the lagged ratio of actual to potential demand).

Thirdly, a generalisation due to Kuznets and Brinley Thomas is that in the nineteenth century a unified North Atlantic economy experienced long swings in proletarian mass migration, population-sensitive investment, and overseas portfolio capital export. European capital was loaned alternately to domestic and overseas borrowers. When North American immigration induced capital formation, emigration 'pushed' from depressed Europe encouraged capital exports. And when European population growth was greatest, domestic lending and capital formation flourished and capital exports to depressed North America languished. Thomas also has suggested that the propensity to emigrate, the 'push', was in some way related to a cycle of births that caused a periodic swelling of the emigration age groups. But he now argues that, following the two world wars, this pattern was first blurred and then reversed so that capital exports and emigration move in *opposite* directions across the North Atlantic (and indeed between the United States and the less developed countries).

A more modest 'push' model, also based on Canada since the Second World War, is simply that emigration to the United States rises when, after a three-year lag, employment in Canada falls. The authors suggest that the family head moves first, bringing his dependants later, so that total emigration's complete response to low aggregate demand is considerably delayed. ([Wilson & Lithwick, pp. 77–8.] Although this is a short-term model, it does seem to invalidate J. Dales's long-term emigration-and-trade model, in which Canadians move to the United States as the relative income differential widens, even though Canada has increasing excess demand for labour. [Dales, pp. 34, 38.])

The chief importance of the pull-or-push debate is in its significance for policy. If migrants chiefly respond to a push, then European countries can influence migration by varying their rate of extra push and North American receiving countries need only open or close the gates. Contrariwise, if migrants respond chiefly to a pull, European countries can only allow or prohibit exits, while American countries can vary the strength of their pull.

The 'extra pushes' can be of two types. One is direct, such as the encouragement by Britain to Commonwealth countries between the wars, and that from Holland around 1950. The other, more roundabout, exists when some policy of the home country squeezes emigrants out. For example, income-distribution policies, by holding down particular wages or salaries, may, like excessive schooling, produce an excess supply of certain occupations or skills. Dales has suggested that a general tariff like a general income tax, can reduce the incomes of labour relative to those of capital and in the process produce an emigration of those whose incomes are reduced, to be eventually replaced by those who have not known high incomes. And both centuries have plentiful evidence of emigration pushed by personal persecution, or the confiscation of wealth.

Assisted emigration is no longer common, and roundabout pushing of emigrants is less common in Europe than formerly (though the low incomes and status of some European professionals, and the fleeing of Hungarians, Czechs and Algerians in the last twenty years, remind us that these emigration incentives still work). Hence the push from Europe tends to be more or less steady, with immigration regulated less by European than by North American admission policies.

If on the other hand migration responds to 'extra pulls', the effectiveness of European policy is confined chiefly to varying the legal difficulty of emigration. In fact, in Western Europe, these difficulties scarcely exist, although France and Spain have not been keen about emigration. North American policy, again, can be either direct, as in the assisted immigration available from some regions or for some professional occupations, or roundabout, as when public spending creates or supports an excess demand for these professions, or when tax rates (or exemptions) or other means of redistribution inspire immigration. In fact, assisted immigration certainly has been offered at various times, but cannot be nearly as important as the deliberate creation of employment for space and defence scientists and supporting professions, or as the (less deliberate) sustaining of full employment. Hence, once again, it must be North American rather than European policy which may explain both the level and the fluctuations in most transatlantic migration.

This conclusion provides the occasion to outline North American immigration restrictions. Before the First World War, American immigration was almost unrestricted, though heavily self-selected by age, health, knowledge (contacts) and adaptability. But in the 1920s, under nationalistic pressure, rigorous restriction was placed on the quantity, source and type of immigrants. The outstanding principles were that Canadians, Mexicans and South Americans were admitted freely, but that from the rest of the world, the national composition of the entrants should be in the proportions of the 1910 foreign-born population. Consequently, Great Britain at 65,000, Germany at 26,000, Eire at 18,000 and Scandinavia at 7,000 absorbed nearly three-quarters of the 150,000 total quota permitted by the 1950s. The restrictions are thought to have excluded many persons, not only Asiatics but also southern and eastern Europeans, during the 1920s, but their effectiveness during the 'no-pull' period of the 1930s is open to dispute, especially because the quotas were under-utilised in the late 1940s, and one-quarter of the Europeans admitted came under special non-quota legislation for displaced persons and refugees. All this changed in 1965. In 1969 each nation of the 'eastern hemisphere' has a United States immigration quota of 20,000 per year (exclusive of close relatives of United States citizens) up to 170,000 per year, with another 120,000 annually for the entire western hemisphere. Parallel to this United States system of national quotas are two hemispheric systems of 'preferences' which prevent the full utilisation of certain countries' quotas unless there are the right proportions of people who are educated, skilled or related to United States citizens. Unfilled preferences within national quotas are then made available to emigrants from other countries within the same hemisphere.

In Canada, before 1962, British Commonwealth, American and French subjects, and close relatives of previous arrivals, were fairly freely admissible, but other Europeans were admissible only 'in the light of social and economic conditions prevailing in Canada', while few Asians were admissible at all. The policy was drastically changed in 1962, and the revision was carried a step further in 1967-8. Apart from relatives, admission is now free to unrelated nationals of any country if they can amass 50 'units' or points out of 100, based on their education, skill, age, literacy, employability and some rather controversial immigration officers' assessments of 'adaptability and motivation'.

Both new systems promise to be less discriminatory against groups not heavily represented in North America; to be more flexible, less insistent on certain indispensable characteristics; but to reinforce the prevailing strong discrimination against unskilled, uneducated workers, unrelated to North American residents. The United States system has barely begun full operation, and is preoccupied chiefly with handling Cubans. The new Canadian system is being tested chiefly by its 'assessments' of American draft-dodgers and deserters.

There is some indication that the two systems will gradually *tend* to move the composition of migration away from its prevailing dominance by Canadian-American flows. This is because both systems give generous permission to citizens or new arrivals to sponsor or nominate relatives, or give 'preferences' to relatives. It is believed that Asians and southern Europeans with strong economic incentives to migrate will make very full use of this admissibility of relatives, while Canadians and Americans (and perhaps northern Europeans generally) will not. Thus the new laws give an official blessing to models of migration favoured by sociologists: migration is a function of the cumulative number that have already migrated.

IV. TRENDS WITHIN NORTH AMERICA

Two inconsistent generalisations about migratory behaviour have long been current. On the one hand it has been said that domestic mobility of populations and labour forces has been in declining proportion to distance. One man in five changes his home every five years, but only one man in twenty moves as far as the next state or province, etc. Thus even the European refugee may settle in the next country, and the typical American certainly moves a few miles west or south every decade. On the other hand, we are accustomed to thinking of streams of 'overseas migrants' from Europe leap-frogging neighbouring regions en route to distant destinations. In this generalisation the typical European does not move across the English Channel nor up from the Mediterranean; if he moves at all he crosses the ocean or the equator.

The increase in world mobility is probably working to reconcile these two generalisations. In spite of an increase in the number of international boundaries and sets of immigration barriers, Europeans are increasingly moving along the shorter routes between European countries while North Americans are lengthening the removal within their own continent which they calmly undertake in one trip.

First of these tendencies is the movement of whole families towards the city, even if such urbanisation takes them to different regions or even different countries. The following table demonstrates the decline in the rural fraction of the population in the past century.

TABLE 18.3
PERCENTAGE OF NATIONAL POPULATION IN RURAL AREAS

	United States	Canada
1850–70	85	85
1900	60	65
1950	36	37
1960	..	31

It is not profitable to carry these series closer to the present because of the blurring pattern as increasing suburbanisation of metropolitan populations encroaches on declining 'rural' areas. Suffice it to say that by 1965 the North American *farm* population, which in 1850 must have been almost co-extensive with the rural population, and so about 85 per cent, is now less than 9 per cent of the two countries' total population.

Of course, urbanisation is not simply a matter of farm people moving into the nearest town, though that *does* happen in the United States Midwest and in Quebec. More important, it is a matter of rural people perceiving an opportunity to better themselves in a particular city of rapid growth and expending employment opportunities. Hence southern Negro people move into Chicago, south-western rural workers move into

Los Angeles, and upper Midwest farmers move 1,500 miles to the west coast. The rural–urban and inter-regional movements coincide. (History records that such movements can swing very wide indeed: the urbanisation of many rural southern Italians was accomplished by a sojourn in United States cities followed by return migration to the cities of northern Italy.)

Hence domestic inter-regional migration is often precisely the means by which the labour force shifts from low-productivity to high-productivity employment; such shifts can still increase per capita G.N.P. as much as 0·5 per cent per year, in Canada.

The second tendency is inter-regional movement itself. United States census data show how extensive is this mobility among members of the male labour force.

TABLE 18.4

MOBILITY BETWEEN 1955
AND 1960, MALE CIVILIAN
LABOUR FORCE OF THE
UNITED STATES, 14 YEARS
AND OVER

(per cent of labour force)

Same house	40
Different house, same county	28
Different county, same state	13
Different state, contiguous	6
Different state, non-contiguous	11
Different country	2
Total	100

Source: Ladinsky, *Demography*, IV 1 (1967) 308.

If the data had been chosen to deal with the total population, rather than the male labour force, the five-year mobility would have been less striking. But a 1965 sample census showed about 6 per cent *annually* of the entire population moving to another county, and about half of these to another state.

How can we summarise the geographic sources and destinations of such moves? A state-to-state matrix gives too much detail, for there are 48 states and 10 provinces, each pair having a pair of flows between them. A better compromise is the attached map (Fig. 18.5), showing the United States divided into four regions and Canada into five. The figures shown are typical of the post-war period. The United States Western region has gained population from all the other regions, though even here the million in-migrants met 600,000 out-migrants leaving. The movements between the pairs of other large regions were more or less balanced, showing tremendous flows from the Midwest to the South,

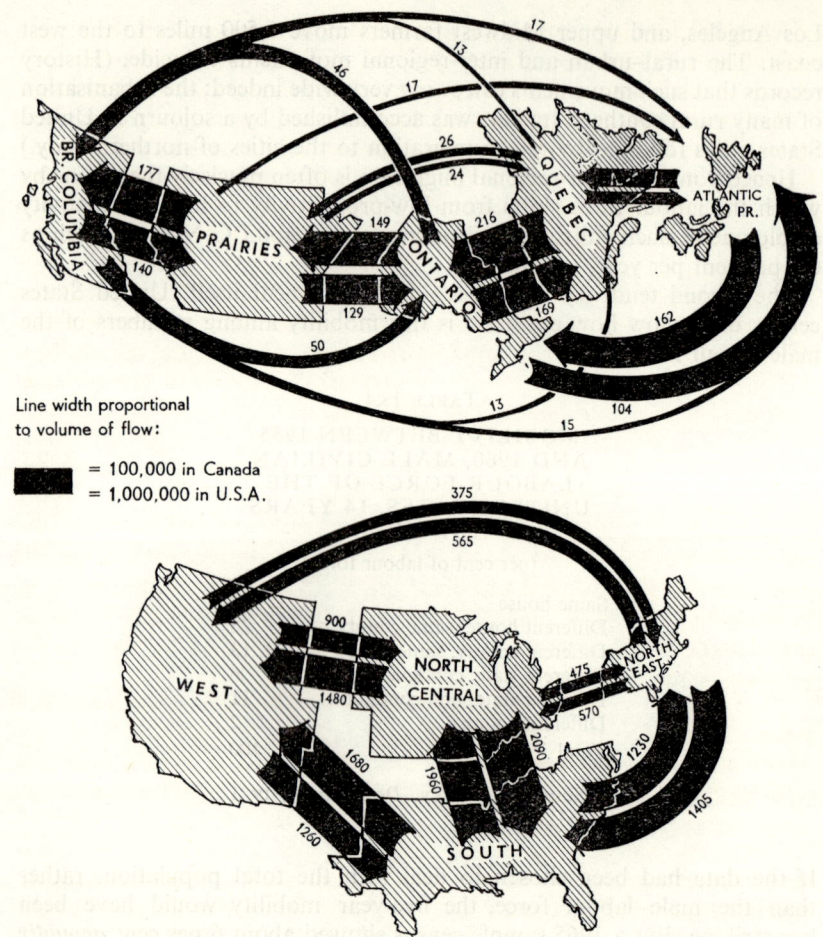

FIG. 18.5 Internal migration, Canada 1956–61, United States 1955–60: total five-year flows in thousands.
Sources: T. R. Weir, 'The People', chap. 6 in John Warkentin (ed.), *Canada, A Geographical Interpretation* (Methuen, Toronto, 1968) Fig. 6.14; United States Bureau of the Census, *Current Population Reports*, P–23, No. 16, Mar 1966, p. 23.

and the reverse. A previously large stream from the South to New York and New England is now diminishing.

The Canadian map also indicates the striking near-equality of the opposing flows within each pair of regions. The Canadian map has the advantage that most of the inter-regional boundaries run through unpopulated areas, so that inter-regional flows are less likely to be merely reflecting short-distance, inter-county moves within metropolitan regions on the Ohio, or within the Philadelphia–Baltimore part of the east-coast megalopolis. The Atlantic provinces, the prairies and Quebec are here shown to have been losing population to Ontario and British Columbia.

Both these sets of within-nation flows are very large, even after some allowance is made for the short distances that are concealed by the arbitrary division of inter-state migrants into inter-regional or intra-regional migrants. Perhaps we can best attain perspective by concentrating on the West, separated by mountain and plain from population centres in adjoining regions. The one million annual long-distance movers into the Western states (and British Columbia) from other parts of their respective countries are at least *twenty times* more numerous than the largest yearly recorded United States immigration of Canadians since the war. Here is striking endorsement of the trade-theory assumption that inter-regional mobility far exceeds international migration.

V. IMMIGRATION AND CAPITAL FLOWS

The preceding sections suggest that North America's post-war immigration from Europe is now less than from elsewhere; that it is becoming dominated by the educated and the highly skilled; and that although large in absolute terms, it is too small to have much effect on North American population growth. The purpose of this section is to sketch some of the political economy of North American immigration.

First, general population growth. Many or few, immigrants and their extended families do add to population. It is indeed odd that neo-Malthusians concerned with the menace of pollution, and with conservation for future food and materials supplies, have not been more active in opposing immigration. (Although a Canadian banker has just surprised the press by making a speech in England deprecating further economic development and immigration.) Given the mobility of North Americans within their continent, and the likelihood that they will in the next decades spread themselves out evenly enough to fill the vacant areas of coast, mountain, forest and desert, it is perhaps surprising that governments permit immigration policy at all.

The United States, obviously, admits immigrants because (*a*) it does not wish to close itself completely to the friends and relatives of its own citizens; (*b*) it does not wish to offend the regions other than northern Europe against whom it has discriminated for nearly fifty years; and (*c*) it wishes to gain the services of the skilled and educated immigrant. Motive (*a*), for example, evidently accounts for the continuous arrival of many unskilled Italians, Mexicans and Canadians. Motive (*b*) may account for the admission of almost 60,000 epople from Asia last year, of whom at least 25,000 were not the Chinese and Filipinos to whom the United States has some continuing obligation. And motive (*c*) has resulted in almost one-third of American labour-force immigrants being professional, technical, managerial, craftsmen or foremen; this proportion has been rising steadily.

Canada's motives are not dissimilar. In addition to these, she wishes also to augment her total population, (*d*) 'to develop her resources', which may suggest belief in further economies of scale, and (*e*) to provide a sufficiently large population to guarantee political independence, a motive she shares with Australia and Israel. These extra motives have dictated her higher immigration rate.

But the ideal immigration, or population, policy cannot be concerned solely with the ratio of man to land. The ideal density of humans must be a function of the amount of capital per person which may be brought in from abroad. And the very process of investment can be as important as the ultimate stock of capital per worker.

In the nineteenth century, the countries of origin sent both humans and capital to the New World. Simon Kuznets and Brinley Thomas, as already noted, have detected alternating long swings of social-capital growth coincident with population growth, by natural increase in Europe, and by immigration in America. The social capital was financed by European, saving and portfolio investment. When European population growth and social investment slowed, stagnation, unemployment, emigration and capital exports followed, and America boomed. These alternating long swings, based on population growth, have been recommended by Keynesians as a preventative of 'secular stagnation'. Although it is, obviously, difficult for economic policy to do much about the rate of natural increase, it is possible to regulate immigration. Mabel Timlin, in *Does Canada Need More People?*, some years ago actually recommended an immigration boom as a substitute for an expanded, unstable, export trade; and Hansen and the other stagnationists seemed to have implied a similar recommendation. The exhilaration, adaptability, enterprise and opportunity that typify the rapid peopling and developing of empty land is an unforgettable national experience – and an unrepeatable one.

Most population growth, by immigration or natural increase, will lack this experience of increasing returns. People and empty land, without capital and enterprise, can produce a Siberia, with steadily diminishing returns. This was prevented in nineteenth-century America by capital imports, equipping each new man with an outfit that would pay for itself and raise his income.

What is the situation today? Capital now flows *away from* the United States. Consequently, the equipping of immigrants must be financed by resources that would otherwise raise domestic labour productivity, be loaned abroad, or be transformed into current consumption. United States data show that while the aggregate capital–output ratio is slowly falling (La Tourette, 1968–9), indicating some rise in the average productivity of capital (or a defect in measurement methodology), capital per man, with some adjustment for price level, is rising. Obviously, therefore, a simple marginal productivity-of-labour curve, with all other inputs constant, does not indicate what is going on. It is indeed possible that the immigrants not only absorb capital, but also both induce more domestic saving and capital formation, and are the route by which new technology is introduced. Hence, as immigration slides the labour force along its marginal productivity curve, the immigrants may also be shifting the curve upwards.

There are two sides to the immigration-and-capital question. On the one hand, capital leads to growth. On the other hand, immigrants bring and create capital.

First, what would have happened if saving and capital inflows had been maintained, but immigration had not taken place? To suggest an answer, we may consult the well-known studies of the contribution of capital to growth. A recent work by D. Walters brings national Denison-type calculations together, and introduces Canada to them. They make it possible to get some idea of the cost of immigration, in terms of income growth in Canada during 1950 to 1962.

Over the whole period, G.N.P. grew at 3·8 per cent per year, or 1·8 per cent per person. Now it is not absurd to ask what would have happened if, in a typical year, labour-force growth had not been swollen by immigration, but had been one-third less. Then G.N.P. would have grown more slowly by the fall in the increase of labour times the relative share of labour, or 0·5, giving a G.N.P. growth rate of 3·3 per cent per year. But G.N.P. per person would actually grow more quickly: 3·3 per cent less 1·3 gives a growth rate of 2·0 per cent per year. If capital and other inputs were being contributed at the same rate per year (and if all the Denison–Cobb–Douglas assumptions had applied), per capita income would have been increased 0·2 per cent per year more because of the absence of immigration!

Taking Canadian G.N.P. per capita as $2,000, the gain in annual growth

TABLE 18.5

CALCULATED INCREASES OF GROSS PRODUCT AND LABOUR FORCE WITH AND WITHOUT IMMIGRATION, CANADA, 1950-62

(annual percentage growth rates)

	With immigration (actual)	Without immigration
G.N.P.	3·8	3·3
Labour force and Population	2·0	1·3
G.N.P. per person	1·8	2·0

Sources: Walters, Tables 20, 100 and 102.

of income would have been something like $4.00 per person or $8.00 per worker. In any case, it is about one-tenth the annual increase in per-person income.

How realistic is the assumption that, in the absence of immigration, the growth rate of real capital and of other inputs would have been maintained? (*a*) Immigrants bring or generate some of the capital; if they hadn't come, they wouldn't invest in Canadian capital formation. (*b*) Capital imports are largely direct investment and provincial borrowing. The latter are very population-sensitive, and the former are used, partly, to equip producers selling in expanding domestic markets. Hence capital imports would have declined somewhat. (*c*) But a very large part of domestic saving and capital imports are invested directly, or destined for improving facilities for the existing market (without growth) and for exports. These are more or less independent of immigration, assuming that new enterprises can make do with existing Canadian skills and enterprise. (*d*) Education depended mostly on domestic teachers, except at the university level. In universities, the end of immigration might reduce the growth of faculties by as much as one-half, in the short run. But as elementary, high and vocational schools would be unaffected, so would most of the growth of the educational content of the labour force. In brief, a one-third fall in labour-force growth would not cause most of the other contributions to G.N.P. per person growth to fall by the same percentage; per capita income would probably still rise.

Second, immigrants bring and create their own capital. It is difficult to know how much capital formation is generated by immigrants, or whether this amount differs significantly from that of natives. Female participation rates are higher and other dependents per breadwinner are fewer; therefore, per thousand immigrants, the rate of saving per year will presumably be higher than for a thousand native-born. But it is fairly clear that immigrants do not bring much physical capital (or its financial equivalent), though I do not know of any studies of this question; on the contrary, they are best known for their remittances to their last permanent residence, which is an offset to capital formation.

What some of us have studied is the human capital, or schooling brought by immigrants. The data on earlier pages have shown that, in the immediate post-war years, the United States brought a higher percentage of professionals than Canada. This was presumably the result of Canada's search for unskilled labour for mines, farms and logging, simultaneous with a selection of skilled and professional workers from advanced countries. But both countries, in fairly automatically admitting the relatives of citizens or residents, while also searching for skilled and professional workers, received the same result: in spite of near-equality in the median years of education of immigrants and native-born, the proportions of immigrants both with almost no education and with university education or more exceeded the proportions among the native-born. Hence, because the cash and opportunity costs of primary-school leavers are less than 5 per cent of those of university graduates, the immigrants brought much more human capital than either their mere numbers or their median schooling would suggest to the unwary observer. (The proportion of unskilled or little-schooled immigrants to the United States is less than to Canada, primarily because United States policy immediately after the war was relatively more favourable to professional or educated applicants. But this paragraph's main points also apply to the United States.)

Ideas of the relative importance of immigrant human capital can easily be obtained. For Canada, for example, one approach is to say that as immigrants have already spent 6 per cent more time in school, on average, than the native-born, then the annual 0·6 per cent contribution of immigration to the size of the labour force must also have added to the stock of human capital measured in educational years 0·04 percentage points more than if the average immigrant had only the schooling possessed by native-born workers.

A second and preferable approach to the Canadian data would, following the procedures of Scott & Grubel (1969), value schooling so as to give greater weight to the cost and foregone earnings of university than of primary years. The *value* of the average post-war immigrant's education (Table 18.6) was in 1967 18 per cent higher than the average native-born worker's. This extra schooling raised the average stock of education of all labour-force members by about 3 per cent, a number more than twice the increase if years of schooling alone had been used for the estimate of the importance of the extra educational endowment of post-war immigrants.

TABLE 18.6

IMMIGRANTS AND NATIVES AGED 14 YEARS AND OVER,
AND HUMAN AND PHYSICAL CAPITAL, CANADA, 1967
(1964–6 prices)

	Number (millions)	Embodied human capital Per person ($)	Total ($ billions)
(a) Post-war immigrants	1·6	7,800	13
(b) Native-born population	12·1	6,600	80
(c) Total population	13·7	6,800	93
(d) Industrial net physical stock	–	–	200
(e) (d) per native-born	–	16,500	–
(f) Total capital stock ((c) and (d))	–	–	293
(g) (f) per native born	–	24,000	–

Sources: Population and education: Davis & Gupta. Education values: Scott & Grubel, 1969. Physical capital stock: La Tourette, 1969, extrapolated.

Table 18.6 also shows that the post-war immigrants brought an average of $7,800 each or $13 billion to Canada. Is this a significant figure? It is equal to about 14 per cent of the 1967 native-born human capital stock in the labour-force ages, about 13 per cent of the total 1967 human capital stock, about 6 per cent of the physical capital stock, and so about 4 per cent of the combined total of human and physical capital stock. Although these are impressive figures, a more important conclusion would run as follows: although post-war immigrants have added disproportionately to the stock of human capital, the fact that they bring human capital but not physical capital indicates that they have tended to reduce the stock of all types of capital per member of the labour force. In terms of the theoretical analysis of the impact of immigration by H. G. Johnson (1967) and others, this means that post-war immigration has reduced the welfare of the natives of the country of destination. (This point also applies to the United States. Although it is true that immigrants to the United States bring a greater endowment of education per immigrant than immigrants to Canada, it is also true that the physical capital stock per member of the labour force in the United States is much greater than in Canada.)

But this conclusion is unimportant for the recent economic history of North America, and particularly of the United States, because the magnitude of immigration relative to the total population has been small. This should be remembered when the estimates of the total 'gain' to the United States or to Canada from the immigration of scientists, engineers or professionals are being used. Some of the estimates (for example those by Grubel and myself) are large in absolute terms, and are even more impressive when seen in their own partial context. For example, more than half the human capital embodied in all academic economists in Canada was acquired in graduate training in the United States or overseas. That is, it was acquired by temporary or permanent migration. But relative to the North American totals, such figures are not large: the percentage saving in education bills (for the continent as a whole) from recruiting foreign professionals rather than training them at home is so small (about one-third of 1 per cent) as to be within the margin of error of such aggregative statistics and the ratios among them.

This is not to say that the arrival of outstanding foreigners has not, in particular cases, been of critical importance for certain activities, industries or institutions. But just as it is obvious that immigration to North America is not, in these days of the 'global village', the chief means of transmitting European technology to North American industry, nor of bringing together the comparative advantages of the two continents, so it is also obvious that migration of Europeans to North America has an almost imperceptible effect on the United States economy. Even in the fields of science, foreign-born scientists of all ages are rarely more than 10 per cent of all United States scientists, and more than half of these have received the majority of their years of schooling in the United States. The 'brain gain', from the United States point of view, is of undergraduates and bachelors (Grubel, 1968). The Ph.D.s and Royal Society members migrating are an important portion of the teams and groups which they leave, but they are simply imperceptible in the country which they join. They are less unimportant in Canada, but most of the immigrant scientists and professionals are Americans or Europeans, largely overseas natives but trained in the United States.

VI. CONCLUSIONS

To conclude, I can do no better than to paraphrase much of Brinley Thomas's excellent summary of his own encyclopedia article. International migration from Europe no longer plays the role in economic growth it did in the nineteenth century. Legislative restrictions, changes in determinants of migration, and the population upsurges in various regions have all tended to reduce the importance and the scale of movement. Countries that once welcomed many immigrants are finding that the flood of entry into the labour force from their own swollen lower age groups makes immigration on the old scale unnecessary.

Intercontinental migrations have lost much of their significance and have been replaced by intracontinental movements; but the international circulation of skilled manpower has gained in relative importance.

It is not surprising therefore that the future research that Thomas recommends and that appears from this paper to be necessary are scarcely topics of great concern for relations between Europe, Canada and the United States. The adjustment of immigrants to their new environments, their mental health, their rates of increase in their new environment, and the effects of the brain drain on countries of emigration are either subjects for sociology, or for economists chiefly interested in Europe or in the less developed countries. (While Canada is indeed a country that is gaining and losing large gross flows of professionals, mostly in exchange with the United States, these flows are part of her perennial problem of adjustment to her enormous neighbour.)

BIBLIOGRAPHY

Adams, W. (ed.) (1968) *The Brain Drain*, New York: Macmillan.
Blume, S. (1968) ' "Brain Drain", a Look at the Literature', *Universities Quarterly*, pp. 281–9.
Borts, G. H., and Stein, J. L. (1964) *Economic Growth in a Free Market*, New York: Columbia University Press.
Carrothers, W. A. (1929) *Emigration from the British Isles*, London: Cass (reprinted 1965).

Corbett, D. C. (1957) *Canada's Immigration Policy*, Toronto: University of Toronto Press.
Dales, J. H. (1966) *The Protective Tariff in Canada's Development*, Toronto: University of Toronto Press.
Davis, N. H. W., and Gupta, M. L. (1968) *Labour Force Characteristics of Post-War Immigrants and Native-Born Canadians, 1956–67*, Special Labour Force Studies, No. 6, Ottawa: Dominion Bureau of Statistics.
Fein, Rashi (1965–6) 'Education Patterns in Southern Migration', *Southern Economic Journal*, XXXII 106–24.
Gilkey, G. R. (1967) 'The United States and Italy: Migration and Repatriation', reprinted in F. D. Scott (ed.), *World Migration in Modern Times*, Englewood Cliffs, N.J.: Prentice-Hall, 1968, pp. 44–51.
Grubel, H. G., and Scott, Anthony (1966) 'Immigration of Scientists and Engineers to the United States', *Journal of Political Economy*, LXXIV 368–78.
—— and —— (1966) 'The International Flow of Human Capital', *American Economic Review*, LVI 268–74.
—— (1968) 'Characteristics of Foreign Born and Educated Scientists in the United States, 1966', Philadelphia: the author (mimeo).
Isaac, J. (1947) *Economics of Migration*, London: Kegan Paul.
Johnson, Harry G. (1967) 'Some Economic Aspects of Brain Drain', *Pakistan Development Review*, VII 379–411.
Kindleberger, Charles (1965) 'Emigration and Economic Growth', *Banca Nazionale del Lavoro Quarterly*, XVIII 235–54.
Kuznets, Simon, and Rubin, Ernest (1954) *Immigration and the Foreign Born*, Occasional Paper 56, New York: National Bureau of Economic Research.
Ladinsky, Jack (1967) 'Sources of Geographic Mobility among Professional Workers: A Multivariate Analysis', *Demography*, IV 293–309.
La Tourette, John E. (1969) 'Trends in the Capital–Output Ratio: United States and Canada 1926–65', *Canadian Journal of Economics*, XI 1, 35–64.
Michalopoulos, C. (1968) 'Labour Migration and Optimum Population', *Kyklos*, XXII 2, 130–43.
Mishan, E. J., and Needleman, L. (1968) 'Immigration: Some Long-Term Economic Consequences', *Economia Internazionale*, XXXI, pt A, no. 2, 281–301; pt B, no. 3, 515–26.
Pankhurst, K. V. (1966) 'Migration between Canada and the United States', *Annals of the American Academy of Political and Social Sciences*, CCCLXVII 53–62.
Parai, Louis (1965) *Immigration and Emigration of Professional and Skilled Manpower* ..., Economic Council of Canada, Study No. 1, Ottawa: Queen's Printer.
Petersen, Wm. (1968) 'Migration – Social Aspects', *Encyclopaedia of the Social Sciences*, X, New York: Macmillan, pp. 286–91.
Richmond, A. H. (1967) *Post-War Immigrants in Canada*, Toronto: University of Toronto Press.
Rubin, Ernest (1966) 'Demography of Immigration to the United States', *Annals of the American Academy of Political and Social Sciences*, CCCLXVII 15–22.
Scott, Anthony (1968) 'The Human Capital Approach to International Migration', in *Proceedings Conference on Research in Income and Wealth*, New York: National Bureau of Economic Research (forthcoming).
—— and Grubel, H. G. (1969) 'Flux and Reflux: The International Migrations of Canadian Economists', *Candian Journal of Economics*, forthcoming.
Sjaastad, L. (1962) 'Costs and Returns of Human Migration', *Journal of Political Economy*, LXX 80–98.
Spengler, J. J. (1956) 'Some Economic Aspects of Immigration into the United States', reprinted in Spengler, J. J., and Duncan, D. D., *Demographic Analysis*, Glencoe, Ill.: Free Press, 1963, pp. 277–96.

Thomas, Brinley (1954) *Migration and Economic Growth* . . ., N.I.E.S.R., Study No. 12, Cambridge: University Press.
—— (ed.) (1958) *Economics of International Migration*, London: Macmillan.
Thomas, Dorothy S. (1941) *Social and Economic Aspects of Swedish Population Movements*, New York: Macmillan.
Timlin, Mabel F. (1951) *Does Canada Need People?*, Toronto: Oxford University Press.
Urquhart, M. C., and Buckley, K. A. (1965) *Historical Statistics of Canada*, Toronto: Macmillan.
United States Department of Commerce, Bureau of the Census (1966) *Americans at Mid-Decade*, Current Population Reports Series P-23, Washington: Government Printing Office.
Walters, Dorothy (1968) *Canadian Income Levels and Growth: An International Perspective*, Economic Council of Canada, Study No. 23, Ottawa: Queen's Printer.
Wilkinson, B. W. (1965) *Studies in the Economics of Education*, Canada, Dept of Labour, Economics Research Branch, Occasional Paper No. 4, Ottawa: Queen's Printer.
Wilson, T. A., and Lithwick, N. H. (1968) *The Sources of Economic Growth, An Empirical Analysis of the Canadian Experience*, Studies of the Royal Commission on Taxation, No. 24, Ottawa: Queen's Printer.

19 Intra-European Migration of Labour and Migration of High-level Manpower from Europe to North America[1]

H. Rieben
CENTRE DE RECHERCHE EUROPÉENNE, LAUSANNE

I. INTRODUCTION

Intra-European migration and immigration from Europe to North America both stem essentially from differences in the levels of economic development of the countries involved. Emigration of industrial workers from Europe to North America has remained at moderate levels: it is the movement of highly qualified manpower that has been the more significant phenomenon in this connection. In contrast, the pattern of migration between the countries of the Mediterranean littoral and industrial northern Europe has been characterised by very large-scale movements of manual workers. And, in fact, intra-European migration has largely consisted of rural agricultural workers moving to the factories and construction sites of industrialised northern Europe, where they have been rapidly transformed into an industrial labour force. The steps towards European integration taken through the E.E.C. and EFTA have accelerated and enlarged these migratory movements.

To what extent, it may be asked, is this type of migration actually leading to a *rapprochement* or integration of the regions, countries and continents between which it takes place, and whose widely different levels of development it reflects? Economic history abounds with examples which show that it is difficult, if not frankly impossible, to solve the problems of a country's backward regions, or of backward nations that are bound within a single tariff zone to more prosperous nations, by relying solely upon the operation of market mechanisms.

Let us take Italy as an example. Before the unification of the country, industrial growth in the southern provinces, protected by their tariff barriers, was only marginally inferior to the rest of Italy. Unification, however, simultaneously exposed the South to competition from northern Italy and from abroad – the latter being encouraged by the relatively favourable attitude towards free trade adopted by the regime of 1860–80. The consequence was a rapid decline of the South's industries and the emergence of an ever-widening gap between the rates of development of the two parts of the country that has only recently begun to narrow.

Another interesting and important example is that of the Hapsburg

[1] Translated from the French by Robert Price.

Empire. In the eighteenth century, under Maria Theresa, a considerable amount of industrialisation took place. Subsequently, the rate of industrial development in Austria slackened, while in neighbouring Prussia it increased. Lacking entrepreneurial resources and an experienced industrial labour force, Austria was unable to associate with the Zollverein, and when she did experiment with lowering her tariff barriers she found herself forced to fall back upon her agricultural strength. Having thus missed the opportunities which an association with the more dynamic states of the Zollverein would have brought, the Empire began the slow process of economic decline which eventually culminated, after the First World War, in the disintegration of the achievements of a thousand years of Hapsburgs.

Similarly, the example of Russia is significant and important. After the efforts to industrialise the country under Peter the Great and Catherine II, there came a period of convalescence in the wake of the Napoleonic Wars. In 1819, however, spurred on by a vigorous population growth, Russia attempted to re-establish trade links with the West by lowering her tariff barriers. But entrepreneurial know-how and industrial manpower were thin on the ground; consequently the result of trade liberalisation was to flood Russia with the manufactured goods of the more advanced countries and to push her back to 'cottage' industry and to agriculture under heavy protection.

These two unsuccessful attempts to catch up with the more advanced industrial nations left Europe in a state of profound imbalance.

These historical examples would seem to provide some support for the conclusions of a commission of economic experts who, as the first steps towards European integration were being taken, wrote that 'the abolition of tariff barriers between poor and rich nations is likely to lead to greater specialisation of production within Europe only in the highly undesirable form of casting the South increasingly in the role of an exporter of agricultural products and an importer of manufactured goods. The implication of this is that the gap between the levels of economic development in the high and low income regions will continue to grow – hardly a desired effect of successful economic integration.'[1]

What, then, can be said about the subsequent evolution of intra-European migration? In general terms, it would seem that the linking of industrialised northern Europe with the countries of the Mediterranean has had the effect of turning these latter into a vast reservoir of manpower for the industrial nations. Italy was the first to experience the phenomenon, and subsequently it spread to Greece, Spain and Portugal: still more recently, Yugoslavia and Turkey have also been affected. Since the main impact was felt initially by the regions of south-west Europe, before going

[1] Commission Économique pour l'O.N.U., *Étude sur la situation économique de l'Europe depuis la guerre* (Geneva, 1953) pp. 255–9.

on to Yugoslavia and Turkey, it will be useful to identify the special characteristics common to these regions.

It should, first of all, be noted that it is an area whose natural resources have been heavily exploited for nearly two thousand years: consequently the agricultural land, forests and mineral deposits that have been worked since the time of the Greeks and the Romans are at least partially exhausted. It is also generally agreed that deforestation has aggravated erosion and thereby severely handicapped agricultural development. In addition, from the very earliest times onwards, the extractive industries and secondary sectors attached to them have moved away from Italy to France and Spain, attracted there by higher-quality minerals and the available labour resources of these countries.

Then, although Portugal, Spain, Genoa and Venice led the way in opening up the principal sea routes, they did not manage to exploit this immense achievement by linking the ports to an industrial hinterland. Had they done so there would have been a powerful motive force working for the economic development of the Mediterranean area. Thus, it was left to those powers that were capable of creating these industrial hinterlands to realise the full benefits of the opening of the trade routes. When, in 1703, Lord Methuen linked Portugal, the pioneer of inter-continental navigation, with the country that was about to become the cradle of the first industrial revolution, Britain, he helped to confirm for many years to come the industrial vocation of northern Europe and the agricultural fate of the South.

The long-term results of these historical events are to be seen in the demographic and economic changes that occurred in these regions during the first half of the present century. Thus we observe that the male agricultural labour force of southern Europe grew by 7 per cent between 1900 and 1950, while the area cultivated per worker fell by nearly 6 per cent. In the same period, the agricultural population of central Europe fell by 25 per cent, while the area under cultivation increased by 27 per cent.[1] To these basic statistics should also be added the effects of such other factors as the slow growth of world demand for the types of products exported by southern Europe and the unfavourable trend of prices.

As demographic saturation became an accomplished fact in the South, in the North the industrial reconstruction gathered pace, helped on by the Marshall Plan on the one hand and by the first steps towards integration on the other. It was a colossal task, absorbing all available manpower, and the industrial concentration thus created so outstripped the growth of the labour force that Western Europe was only able to avoid a manpower crisis thanks to the influx of more than 10 million refugees

---

[1] Folke Dovring, *Land and Labour in Europe, 1900–1950* (M. Nijhoff, The Hague) 1965; Kristian Antonsen, 'Zones sous-développées', in *Besoins et moyens de l'Europe*, ed. J. Frederic Dewhurst (Berger-Levrault, Paris, 1962) 556.

from the East and the massive supplementation of the labour force by the surplus workers from the rural South.

Italy, led by Alcide de Gasperi, linked herself from the very first moment to the moves towards European unification that were being made by the countries of the Rhine. De Gasperi thereby not only re-created the old 'spinal cord' of Europe which ran down the Rhine and continued over the St Gotthard Pass into northern Italy but he also pulled southern Italy (and, in its train, the whole Mediterranean area) into the mainstream of European industrial expansion. For the unemployed and under employed workers of the Mediterranean littoral, this policy created new opportunities: instead of having either to resign themselves to poverty at home or go overseas in search of prosperity, they were now able to go north to the factories and construction sites of industrial Europe. And many millions of people from the South took advantage of this new opportunity.

We shall now examine the phenomenon of post-war intra-European migration in more detail, (*a*) from the standpoint of the countries from which emigration has mainly taken place, and (*b*) from the standpoint of the host countries.

II. ITALY

Up to 1950, the majority of emigrants from Italy went overseas. From 1951 on, the majority have gone to other European countries, and by 1957 more than twice as many were going to European countries as were going overseas. By 1968, the rate was almost three to one. In Europe, the principal host countries up to 1954 were France and Switzerland; in 1960, Germany overtook France, and by 1968 Switzerland and Germany accounted between them for 87 per cent of the total intra-European Italian emigration. More striking still is the fact that Switzerland alone absorbed almost half of all the Italians who emigrated to a European country in this period.

The Italian population grew by 4·7 million between 1955 and 1968 to a total of 52·9 million. In contrast, the total working population declined by 952,000, from 20,520,000 to 19,568,000. Unemployment fell from 836,000 in 1960 to 694,000 in 1968.

TABLE 19.1

SECTORAL DISTRIBUTION OF THE
ITALIAN WORKING POPULATION

Sector	1951	(%)	1966	(%)	1968	(%)
Agriculture	8,640,000	42·2	4,660,000	24·2	4,247,000	22·3
Industry	5,803,000	32·1	7,621,200	39·8	7,890,000	41·3
Tertiary	5,249,000	25·7	6,875,600	36·0	6,932,000	36·4

Source: Istituto Centrale di Statistica (ISTAT), Rome.

Two important phenomena are revealed by these figures:

(1) The agricultural labour force has been drastically cut, falling by some 4,393,000 in the seventeen-year period. To this we should add the reduction in the number of marginal workers in the agricultural sector of 2,117,000 (2,947,000 in 1951 and 850,000 in 1968).
(2) Contrasting with the declining agricultural labour force (−4,393,000) is the expansion of employment in the manufacturing and service sectors (+3,743,000).

The industrialisation which occurred in the period immediately following the unification of Italy was confined to a few prosperous centres and took place under considerable tariff protection. In these circumstances, northern industry destroyed the industry of the South and pushed that region into an agricultural role. Tariff protection was positively harmful to the development of the rural southern provinces: with the operation of market forces unable to stimulate their growth, a policy of assistance was introduced which tended to keep the surplus population on the land in a state of chronic underemployment. What is more, it was a policy which had to rely on emigration overseas as a safety valve. The limited size of the protected domestic market was a formidable obstacle to any policy of ambitious industrial growth. Thus, the combination of agricultural support and tariff protection hindered growth and change both in the countrysides and in the few industrial areas.

The policy of introversion and protectionism was succeeded after the Second World War by an entirely different approach to the conduct of the economy. The aim was to create an economic structure based upon the transformation of primary products and the export of increasingly sophisticated manufactured goods; and it was to be achieved within the framework of an 'open-frontier' policy. The North was to be pushed to as high a degree of industrial specialisation as possible by linking it to the dynamic industrial areas grouped around the Rhine; this was to be underpinned by an ultra-modern iron and steel industry built on coastal sites and operated within the context of the European Coal and Steel Community; finally, the structure of agriculture in the Mezzogiorno was to be reformed and industry brought to help in the development of the South by incentives to set up factories in the areas where there was surplus labour. From the standpoint of this policy, emigration became another phenomenon closely allied to the 'logic' of backwardness, and thus destined to disappear with the increasing prosperity of the country.

An immense effort has been made since the end of the Second World War to turn Italy into a modern industrial power and to bring the Mezzogiorno fully into the scope of this economic transformation. The South provided 1,092,000 people between 1951 and 1968 to support the industrial effort of northern Italy. Over this period, the population distribution between the two halves of the country has changed as follows:

TABLE 19.2

POPULATION DISTRIBUTION BETWEEN REGIONS OF ITALY

	1951	1958	1961	1968
Centre–North	29,810,113	31,372,019	32,350,000	32,022,000
South	17,685,424	18,988,646	18,090,000	19,940,000

Source: ISTAT, Rome.

TABLE 19.3

DISTRIBUTION OF THE WORKING POPULATION BETWEEN REGIONS OF ITALY
(as a percentage of the total population)

	1961	1968
Centre–North	45·5	39·9
South	37·1	31·4

Source: ISTAT, Rome.

Alongside this transfer of labour from South to North, government efforts to encourage investment in the South have been intensified. Thus, from 1951 to 1968, investment projects sponsored or encouraged by the Cassa per il Mezzogiorno amounted to nearly 7,000 billion lire (48 billion Swiss francs) of which 3,743 billion went to industry.

In the light of these considerations, what can be said about the significance and the possible future course of Italian manual worker emigration to northern Europe? It should first of all be borne in mind that these emigrants mostly remain firmly attached to their homeland. Eloquent proof of this is provided by the sacrifices which they make to be able to send money back to their families. At Ford's in Cologne, Giovanni Russo found that 50 per cent of the Italian workers were sending 60 per cent of their pay back to Italy; 15 per cent were sending back 80 per cent and the remaining 30–35 per cent sent back 'only' 20–40 per cent.[1]

The total amount repatriated by Italian emigrants in the period 1961–8 was $5·9 million.

Table 19.4 below indicates the general trend of emigration during the 1960s.

It can be seen from these figures that the principal source of Italian emigration remains the South; but on the whole the phenomenon is in decline. It seems to have been stablished within the ceiling of 300,000,

[1] Giovanni Russo, *Quinze millions d'Italiens déracinés* (Les Éditions Ouvrières, Paris, 1966) p. 130.

fixed for the period 1965–70. In the 1970s Italy aims to reduce net emigration to zero.

TABLE 19.4
TRENDS OF MIGRATION, 1960–7

	Emigration		Net migration		Between South Italy and non-European countries
Year	Italy, total	South Italy only	Italy, total	South Italy only	
1960	383,908	252,948	−191,673	−147,045	−37,538
1961	387,126	269,644	−176,927	−142,842	−22,743
1962	365,611	268,034	−136,523	−117,247	−26,064
1963	277,611	208,128	−56,461	−53,861	−24,845
1964	258,482	181,210	−68,314	−51,850	−22,418
1965	282,643	185,992	−86,267	−63,970	−32,443
1966	296,494	194,565	−90,008	−68,706	−55,075
1967	229,264	149,469	−59,936	−50,909	−43,149

Source: *Problemi di lavoro italiano all'estero* (Rome, 1969).

Some 71·4 per cent of the emigrants are aged between 15 and 49. An analysis of their origins shows that 47 per cent describe themselves as 'non-active', 17 per cent come from agriculture, 30 per cent from industry and 1·5 per cent from the service trades. 2·5 per cent of the emigrants are highly qualified.

TABLE 19.5
DISTRIBUTION OF ITALIAN MIGRANTS BETWEEN HOST COUNTRIES

Year	Belgium	France	Federal Republic of Germany	Switzerland	Europe, total	Other continents
1949	5,311	52,345	–	29,726	94,959	159,510
1950	4,226	18,083	24	27,144	54,927	145,379
1951	33,308	35,099	431	66,040	149,206	143,851
1952	22,441	53,810	270	61,593	144,098	133,437
1953	8,832	36,687	242	57,236	112,069	112,602
1954	3,278	28,305	361	65,671	108,557	142,368
1955	17,073	40,713	1,200	71,735	149,026	147,800
1956	10,395	87,552	10,097	75,632	207,631	137,171
1957	10,552	114,974	7,653	78,882	236,010	105,723
1958	3,947	72,469	10,511	57,453	157,800	97,659
1959	4,083	64,259	28,394	82,532	192,843	75,647
1960	4,915	58,624	100,514	128,257	309,876	74,032
1961	3,152	49,188	114,012	142,114	329,597	57,526
1962	3,141	34,911	117,427	143,054	315,795	49,816
1963	1,626	20,264	81,261	122,018	235,134	42,477
1964	2,876	15,782	75,210	111,863	216,498	41,984
1965	4,537	20,050	90,853	103,159	232,421	50,222
1966	3,885	18,370	78,843	104,899	219,353	77,141
1967	3,939	15,517	47,178	89,407	166,697	62,567
1968	3,300	11,000	65,000	86,000	175,000	57,251

It is the industrial sectors of the host countries that benefit most from the availability of Italian labour, absorbing almost 80 per cent of the migrants.

TABLE 19.6

SECTORAL DISTRIBUTION OF ITALIAN MIGRANT WORKERS
(in selected host countries)

	Agriculture			Industry			Other sectors		
	1964	1966	1968	1964	1966	1968	1964	1966	1968
France	10·0	10·0	11·1	80·0	82·1	77·8	10·0	7·2	11·1
Switzerland	7·4	5·2	5·9	80·0	82·4	78·4	12·6	12·4	15·7
Germany	6·0	6·0	8·9	86·9	83·2	81·0	7·0	10·8	10·1
Europe, total	7·7	5·9	7·5	80·4	81·4	78·1	11·9	12·7	14·4

In the light of the example presented by Italy, it seems that the migration of workers from southern to northern Europe can be said to fulfil two functions for the countries of origin:

(1) Using industrial Europe as a training ground, it helps to produce, in a very short space of time, an experienced industrial labour force which may subsequently be used by the developing agricultural countries.

(2) In so doing, it sets up strong pressures for the industrialisation of these agricultural zones, as well as being a major asset in the industrialisation process itself.

It would seem that Italy, having for many years been industrial Europe's principal source of unskilled labour reserves, will soon be in a position to draw herself on these valuable manpower reserves that have been created beyond her frontiers. Industrialised northern Europe will thus have to go further afield in order to satisfy its additional manpower requirements.

III. GREECE

Up to 1960, Greek emigration was mainly directed towards America and Australia. In that year the pattern changed in two ways. Firstly, emigration grew quite considerably, from an annual average of 28,700 before 1960 to some 47,800 in that year. Secondly, a large proportion of the emigrants went to the countries of northern Europe. This pattern was subsequently maintained and emigration continued to grow up to 1965, in which year it reached a figure of more than 117,000. Since that date, however, emigration has declined and is now running at an annual rate of between 40,000 and 50,000.

Since the conclusion of the co-operation agreement between West Germany and Greece on 30 March 1960, Germany has absorbed the vast majority of Greek migrant workers (92·5 per cent in 1965). The reduction in the rate of Greek emigration noted above is thus in considerable measure due to the slowing-down of the German economy.

Greek emigration has come primarily from the poor rural departments on the western frontiers of the country – Epirus, Macedonia, Thrace. Over 84 per cent of the migrants are aged between 15 and 39. Owing to this age-distribution and to the relatively low birth rate (18·3 per cent in 1968), the Greek population is ageing. However, it has been estimated that between 20 and 25 per cent of migrants in any one year return to the country within a few years. They will then have acquired some training which may be of use to the Greek economy, providing, of course, that they can find an industry capable of employing their skills.

In fact, government measures attracted some $470 million worth of foreign investment between 1953 and 1967, of which $390 million went into manufacturing industry and the rest to the development of the industrial infrastructure and the transport system. The growth of technologically advanced industries in Greece, the fact that all these projects are carried out in the less industrialised regions, and the greater degree of information on the part of emigrants concerning job opportunities in Greece, are all tending to bring about an increase in the number of workers returning from abroad.

IV. TURKEY

Turkey has all the characteristics that we expect of a country with a high rate of emigration: in a total population of 32 million, the working population amounts to about 13 million; 75 per cent of these are employed in the primary sector, which in addition accounts for more than 1·5 million fully unemployed workers and 7·8 million seasonably employed. With the highest natural population growth in Europe (2·6 per cent per annum), a high rate of unemployment and an economy which is only just beginning to get off the ground, Turkey has immense reserves of unskilled labour.

Emigration from Turkey began in about 1961–2 and at present some 200,000 Turks are employed abroad: of these nearly 140,000 are in West Germany and 13,650 in the Netherlands.

V. YUGOSLAVIA

It seems likely that Yugoslavia will provide considerable amounts of manpower for the industrial countries of northern Europe in the future. It has a total population of 20 million, a primary sector which accounts for 56 per cent of the working population, a considerable problem of underemployment and a fairly low level of industrialisation. To date, some 300,000 Yugoslav nationals have gone abroad in search of employment. The largest number have gone to West Germany, which in 1968 had nearly 100,000 Yugoslav workers compared with only 5,000 seven years previously. France has 54,000 Yugoslav workers, but aims to increase its annual quota. About 22,000 Yugoslav nationals are resident in Sweden.

VI. SPAIN

Up to 1959, Spain existed in a state of economic semi-autarky which, as a consequence, meant that its agriculture and its industry were maintained at fairly autarkic levels of development. From 1960 onwards an enormous effort has been made to restructure and modernise the economy. Some degree of success has been achieved and Spain has at present the highest rate of growth of gross industrial production in Europe.

The programme of modernisation also embraced a fundamental reconstruction of agriculture which implied a considerable reduction in the rural population. The proportion of the total working population accounted for by the agricultural labour force has fallen from 45·2 per cent in 1954–6 to 30·5 per cent in 1964–6. Since the industrial sector was unable to absorb the large numbers of workers leaving the land, emigration has here again fulfilled the role of a safety valve.

More than 4 million Spaniards (12 per cent of the population) live abroad; 1·5 million of these are in other European countries. The largest number live in France (some 700,000); Germany has 120,000, and Switzerland 88,000.

Slightly fewer than half the migrants are aged between 25 and 35. They generally stay abroad no more than two or three years. The rate of emigration declined appreciably after 1965, and from 1966 onwards the number of workers returning to Spain was actually greater than the

TABLE 19.7

MIGRATION FROM SPAIN

(000's)

	1964	1965	1966	1967	1968
Emigration to European countries	182·8	181·3	130·7	59·9	88·0
To: France	69·6	55·9	42·6	26·8	
Germany	47·4	65·1	38·6	3·9	
Switzerland	49·1	28·1	30·7	26·6	
Numbers returning from European countries	99·0	120·7	131·7	85·9	100·0
From: France	40·6	29·9	18·4	1·8	
Germany	25·9	33·5	60·3	43·9	
Switzerland	27·1	31·0	31·3	27·9	
Net emigration to European countries	83·8	60·6	−1·0	−26·0	−12·0
Net emigration overseas	−1·4	−4·3	−4·0	−4·7	

Source: O.E.C.D., *Economic Studies* (*Spain*) (Paris, Jan 1969) p. 61.

number leaving. The return of these workers creates a problem of reintegration into the Spanish economy. Despite the creation of some 300,000 new jobs annually since 1964, there is still a considerable gap between the number of vacancies and the number of workers seeking jobs, due to the growth of the working population, the increasing female participation in the labour force and the continuing 'flight from the land'. Emigration – although somewhat reduced in numbers – will remain a fundamental economic fact of life in Spain.

VII. PORTUGAL

There have been four distinct types of emigration from Portugal:

(1) Emigration to Portugal's overseas possessions. The number of migrants in this category has remained relatively stable at about 12,000.
(2) Legal emigration. From 1951 to 1963, some 35,000 workers on average left Portugal each year. From 1964 onwards, the number has been growing: it reached 89,000 in 1965 and 120,000 in 1966.
(3) Clandestine emigration – mainly into France. It has been estimated that about 25 per cent of the total annual emigration is due to this type of departure. The workers concerned are mainly from the northern provinces of the country.
(4) Seasonal movements. Although they have grown steadily over time, seasonal migratory movements are of little quantitative significance, since fewer than 10,000 workers are concerned. They go principally to North Germany (fishing) and to France (harvesting of fruit, grain or grapes).

About half the emigrants are aged between 15 and 55. They come mainly from the primary sector, but increasingly also from the secondary sector. The phenomenon is thus somewhat similar to that which was observed for Spain.

With emigration concentrated in the younger age groups, the Portuguese population is also ageing. The 45–65-year-old age group accounts for over 20 per cent of the total population as against 16·2 per cent in 1950, while the share of the 0–20 age group has declined from 38·9 per cent to 36·6 per cent in the same period. Since net emigration has been greater than the natural population growth, the total population has declined since 1964. The number of workers returning to Portugal averages only 1,700 per annum.

The departure of some 600,000 people since 1960 has helped to cut the size of the agricultural sector considerably and has led to a better balance between the different sectors of the economy. The proportion of the total working population engaged in agriculture declined from 47 per cent in 1954–6 to 38·1 per cent in 1964–6. Portugal should take advantage of this situation to complete the restructuring of her agriculture and to achieve a more rapid rate of industrialisation.

VIII. THE HOST COUNTRIES: SWITZERLAND

The resident population of Switzerland stood at 6,115,000 in 1968. With a declining birth rate (17·7 per cent in 1968 against 18·7 per cent in 1965) and a high life-expectancy, the population is ageing. The proportion of persons over the age of 60 in the population was 17 per cent in 1968 against 15 per cent in 1960. The total number of foreigners resident in Switzerland has been increasing more slowly since 1967. It stands now at 952,000; of these 67 per cent are in possession of an annually renewable residence permit, 31 per cent have *permis d'établissement* (long-term work permits) and 2 per cent are international civil servants. The proportion of total births accounted for by foreign residents (28 per cent in 1968) is considerably greater than the proportion of these residents in the total population (16 per cent).

TABLE 19.8

STRUCTURE OF THE SWISS POPULATION, 1965–8

(000's)

	1968	1967	1966	1965
Total population	6,115	6,036	5,953	5,880
Swiss citizens	5,163	5,128	5,093	5,055
Foreign residents	952	908	860	825
Seasonal workers	144	154	165	184
Foreign workers resident in border areas of neighbouring countries	63	59	48	46
Total number of foreign workers	1,159	1,121	1,073	1,055

Since the end of the war, the Swiss labour market has been characterised by a severe shortage of labour. The slight falls in the level of employment that occurred in 1949, 1952–3 and 1958 led to no long-term easing of the situation. The employment of foreign labour has thus been a factor of increasing importance, since the manpower potential of the native Swiss population was exhausted at the end of the 1940s. The working population of Switzerland increased from 2·9 million in 1966 to 3,025,000 in 1969; the proportions of foreign manpower were respectively 27·1 per cent and 27·2 per cent, having reached 27·4 per cent in 1968.

In the course of its history, Switzerland has lost more than a million of its citizens through emigration. Even today, 297,000 Swiss subjects are resident abroad. Towards the end of the last century, in the period when Switzerland was taking part in the second phase of the industrial revolution, net migration became favourable: the industrial centres of that time – Geneva, Basle and Zürich – drew additional manpower from neighbouring French and Austro-German territories.

From 1945 onwards, Switzerland was closely concerned with the economic reconstruction of the belligerent nations of the Second World War. Domestic demand reached such heights that recourse to foreign manpower became indispensable. Up to 1955, Switzerland was able to call on the services of workers from the border regions of neighbouring countries: 21 per cent of the foreign labour force came from Germany and 10 per cent from Austria. After 1955, however, the domestic growth of these neighbouring countries absorbed increasing proportions of their native manpower resources, and Switzerland was thus obliged to go further south in search of the workers she required. Italians from the South took the place of Italians from the North, the number of Spaniards increased steadily and the first contingents of Greeks, Turks and Yugoslavs arrived. In 1950, for example, 96 per cent of Italian workers in Switzerland were from the North; by 1967 the North accounted for only 22·7 per cent and the South for 66 per cent.

TABLE 19.9

FOREIGNERS RESIDENT IN SWITZERLAND
(000's)

	1968	1966
Italians	523	484
Germans	115	108
Spaniards	88	78
French	47	42
Austrians	42	39
Yugoslavs	16	7
Greeks	8	7
Turks	8	6
All others	87	73

Three-quarters of these foreign workers are under 30 years of age and they generally stay no more than one or two years. The majority of them are employed in the industrial cantons of Zürich (124,000 in 1968), Berne (66,000), Geneva and Vaud (53,000). The building and hotel and catering industries have the highest proportion of foreign labour, followed by the metal-working sector, textiles, chemicals and clocks. These latter can be said to roughly correspond to the principal export sectors.

The distribution of foreign manpower is connected with the differences in the levels of qualification of Swiss and foreign workers. What has in fact happened is that the foreigners have replaced Swiss nationals in the secondary sector and the latter have 'emigrated' to the tertiary. Between 1950 and 1964, approximately 116,000 Swiss left the primary sector, 78,000 more native Swiss were employed in the secondary sector (as against an increase of 445,000 in the number of foreign workers employed), and 206,000 more Swiss were employed in the tertiary sector (as against 95,000 more foreigners).

The economic development of the countries from which Switzerland has drawn its supplementary manpower will enable them to provide employment for a growing proportion of their population. If, therefore, Switzerland wishes to retain at least some proportion of the foreign workers whose services she now enjoys, she will have to make certain modifications to her employment and immigration regulations and will have to embark upon an active integration policy.

IX. THE HOST COUNTRIES: WEST GERMANY

The post-war reconstruction of the German economy was considerably facilitated by the influx of some 10 million refugees and by the existence of massive unemployment. The economy thus had a large reservoir of manpower to hand, characterised by its high quality and a high degree of geographical and inter-sectoral mobility. From 1961 on, with the unemployment pool eliminated and the integration of the refugees into the West German economy accomplished, the problem changed to one of excess demand for labour. From as early as 1955, West Germany made agreements with Italy, Spain, Greece and Turkey for the provision of additional manpower, and a similar agreement was later reached with Portugal.

Germany has, however, a long tradition of employing foreign labour: in 1910 about 1·3 million foreigners were employed in the country, amounting to 1·9 per cent of the total population. In 1966, they accounted for a marginally higher proportion of the population than in 1910 (2·3 per cent). Since the recession of 1966–7 the number of foreign workers seems to have settled at about the million mark.

More than half the immigrants are under 35; they come from the physically most able-bodied section of their native countries and, contrary to what was seen above to be the case in Switzerland, the length of their stay tends to be relatively long, 83 per cent of the men and 74 per cent of the women staying at least two years in West Germany. The major part of the foreign labour force is employed in the metal-working and intermediate-goods industries, and in construction and services. The Greeks, Turks, Spaniards and Portuguese work principally in the metal trades, while the Italians and the Yugoslavs are employed in the construction industry.

In the report of the E.E.C. study group of the medium-term economic prospects of member countries,[1] it was estimated that the West German

[1] E.E.C., *Perspectives de développement économique dans la C.E.E. jusqu'en 1970* (Brussels, 1966) pp. 6–8 of the annex.

TABLE 19.10

FOREIGN WORKERS IN WEST GERMANY

(000's)

	1961	1966	1967	1968	1969
Total	476	1,314	1,024	1,015	1,924
Italians	208	339	274	287	454
Turks	5	158	137	139	205
Greeks	41	196	147	136	212
Spaniards	48	185	129	112	175
Yugoslavs	13	97	98	100	169
Austrians	41	63	56	56	
Dutch	45	59	45	45	
Portuguese			19	19	27

economy would lose about 350,000 people in the period 1966–70. The loss could only be made up by increased immigration; but according to the same report, attempts to boost immigration would run up against certain obstacles, not only on the supply side, but also from the nature of the demand. Relatively high costs are attached to the employment of inexperienced foreign labour and it can only be used for a limited range of tasks. Its utility is therefore limited. To increase present numbers by 350,000 would be a task of very considerable difficulty in its own right.

Two possible courses of action are thus open to West Germany:
 (1) to invest massively in the nationalisation of production processes;
 (2) to invest in the countries from which immigrants have been coming, in order to take advantage of the reserves of local manpower.

For the present, West Germany has been pursuing the first of these possible policies. But as closer links are gradually forged between the countries of Europe and if a strong economic community is created, the second may come to assume a growing importance.

X. THE HOST COUNTRIES: FRANCE

Unlike West Germany, France had no large reserves of labour at her disposal at the end of the Second World War. This was due partly to war losses and to the repatriation of the workers who had come to France from the countries of Eastern Europe, and partly to the effect of the very low birth rate in the second decade of the century. Immigration began to assume quite considerable proportions from about the middle of the 1950s at the time of the general European economic expansion. Today, there are 3·1 million foreigners living in France, in addition to 1·2 million naturalised French citizens.

Large-scale immigration and the positive measures taken by successive French Governments to assimilate these workers have been due less to economic factors than to France's very special demographic characteristics. Even in the nineteenth century, the French birth rate was the lowest among the main European nations; in 1946–50 it was estimated to be 20·9 per cent; in 1965, 17·7 per cent; and in 1968, only 16·9 per cent. In addition, the low concentration of her population makes it difficult to achieve a balanced distribution of economic activity. Immigration, in fact, accounts for almost a half (four-ninths) of the annual population growth at the present time.

Up to 1960, the Italians were the most numerous of the immigrant groups; after that date, the Spaniards overtook the Italians, and the Portuguese became more numerous than either of these other two groups. In 1967, nearly 35,000 Portuguese, 22,000 Spaniards and only 10,600 Italians entered France. Of the 3·1 million foreign workers, some 2·2 million are of European origin, about 880,000 come from Africa and 70,000 from the Overseas Departments (D.O.M.) and the French dependencies (T.O.M.).

TABLE 19.11

IMMIGRATION INTO FRANCE

Number of Workers

Year	Permanent	Seasonal	Total	Dependants	Total
1946	30,171	11,542	41,713		41,713
1947	68,223	19,442	87,665	4,930	92,595
1948	57,039	21,801	78,840	25,822	104,662
1949	58,782	20,050	78,832	26,597	105,429
1950	10,525	15,915	26,440	8,782	35,222
1951	20,996	25,713	46,709	5,283	51,992
1952	32,750	33,787	66,534	6,616	73,150
1953	15,361	34,175	49,536	4,982	54,418
1954	12,292	29,874	42,166	4,101	46,267
1955	19,029	35,276	54,305	4,647	58,952
1956	65,428	48,731	114,159	5,951	120,110
1957	111,693	56,769	168,662	8,851	177,513
1958	82,818	63,529	146,347	11,510	157,857
1959	44,179	63,797	107,976	8,832	116,808
1960	48,914	109,798	158,712	23,693	182,405
1961	78,927	96,956	175,883	43,454	219,337
1962	113,069	95,093	208,162	47,028	255,190
1963	115,523	101,274	216,797	43,580	260,377
1964	153,731	120,950	274,681	47,293	321,974
1965	152,063	131,571	283,634	55,429	339,063
1966	131,725	124,270	255,995	64,145	310,140
1967	107,833	113,971	221,804	54,479	276,293
Total	1,531,071	1,374,481	2,905,552	495,905	3,401,457

Source: Office National d'Immigration, *Statistiques de l'Immigration*, 1967, p. 8.

TABLE 19.12
ORIGINS OF FOREIGN WORKERS IN FRANCE
(000's)

Spain	695	Algeria	600
Italy	660	Morocco	100
Portugal	330	Tunisia	60
Poland	144	Africa (south of the Sahara)	40
Belgium	75		
Yugoslavia	54	Overseas Departments and Dependencies	70–80
Germany	46		

Approximately 25 per cent of construction workers are foreign, and on public works projects they account for about 50 per cent of the labour force. Foreign labour also makes up half the work force at the principal Renault factory at Boulogne-Billancourt. Immigration thus is certainly playing an important role in the current development of the Frnech economy.

France occupies a central position in the creation of a new European equilibrium; and, in particular, the successful development of her southern coastal provinces could be exceptionally important in bringing the industrial countries and the countries of the Mediterranean littoral closer together.

XI. THE HOST COUNTRIES: BENELUX

Belgium has traditionally been a country into which considerable immigration has taken place. Even at the end of the nineteenth century, the foreign population of more than 170,000 people accounted for 2·8 per cent of the total population. Leaving aside the war years, the number of immigrants has grown continually: it was 319,230 in 1930 (3·9 per cent), 453,486 in 1961 (4·9 per cent), and 600,000 (6·3 per cent) in 1966.

Net emigration has for many years been negative in the Netherlands. The rapid development of the economy and the country's demographic structure (the birth rate, at 18·9 per cent, is among the highest in Europe and the 0–14 age group constitutes 28 per cent of the population) have led to an increasing demand for foreign labour.

TABLE 19.13
FOREIGN WORKERS IN THE NETHERLANDS

Year	Total	Turks	Spaniards	Italians	Germans
1961	27,990	72	1,296	5,638	7,993
1963	38,033	693	7,158	6,767	7,653
1965	63,204	7,286	16,528	8,100	8,328
1966	76,272	12,165	17,054	8,477	9,057
1967	72,141	10,161	12,908	8,705	10,739
1968	80,339	13,643	12,139	9,506	11,652

Luxembourg is a special case, similar in many ways to Switzerland. As a small but highly industrialised country, Luxembourg has for a long time past had to make use of foreign manpower. In 1966 foreign workers accounted for the high proportion of 16·9 per cent of the total population. In 1968, the economy of the Grand Duchy employed 106,500 workers of whom 27 per cent were foreign. Amongst the immigrant groups, the Italians were the most numerous (11,262 in 1968), followed by the Belgians (4,845), the French (4,331), the Germans (3,881) and the Portuguese (1,143).

XII. THE HOST COUNTRIES: SCANDINAVIA

Since 1955 there has been a common market in labour between the Nordic countries (Sweden, Denmark, Norway and Finland), which allowed citizens of these countries to move freely from one to the other. This accounts for the relative insignificance of 'foreign' labour in these countries.

Since 1966 there has been a certain degree of tightness in the Swedish labour market, leading to a rapid increase in the number of immigrants from southern Europe.

TABLE 19.14

IMMIGRATION INTO SWEDEN FROM
SOUTHERN EUROPE, 1964-8

	1964	1965	1966	1967	1968
Italians	4,231	4,283	5,324	5,909	5,325
Spaniards	2,289	2,492	2,979	3,182	3,184
Yugoslavs	2,594	3,660	7,569	13,069	14,016
Greeks	834	1,621	4,066	5,894	5,942
Turks	312	482	937	1,641	1,785
Portuguese	201	275	356	540	678
Total	10,461	12,813	21,231	30,229	30,930

Source: Secrétariat Général de la Commission Internationale Catholique pour les Migrations (C.I.C.M.), *Travailleurs migrants*, 1102, (Geneva, Apr-June 1964).

The majority of these workers are employed in industry: they remain, however, of only minor importance, not only in relation to the indigenous Swedish labour force but also to the 'immigrants' from other Nordic countries. These latter compose two-thirds of the foreign labour force in Sweden.

About 29,000 foreigners were employed in Norway in 1968, of whom 40-45 per cent were in the merchant marine. They represented 2 per cent of the working population. As in Sweden, most of the immigrant workers are union members. Both these countries, it may be noted, pursue exemplary policies for immigrant integration.

XII. THE HOST COUNTRIES: GREAT BRITAIN

From the beginning of the nineteenth century up to about 1930, emigration from Great Britain to the countries of the Commonwealth and to the United States surpassed by far the amount of migration inward. The net loss amounted to more than 4 million people between 1871 and 1931. Since then, the flow has generally speaking been in the reverse direction; in the period 1931–51 net immigration into England and Wales was 755,000, while Scotland and Ireland experienced net emigration of 249,000 and 73,000 people respectively.

Immigration from the Continent to Britain started at the beginning of the century. Initially, it consisted mainly of Russian refugees and Polish Jews, who between them accounted for 40 per cent of all immigration. From 1906 onwards, Italians also began to arrive, in rather greater numbers – nearly 60,000 of them came between 1906 and 1925.

In the 1930s Great Britain took in some 250,000 European refugees, a large quota of Irish and a number of British subjects returning from the colonies and from the United States. Since 1958, the number of immigrants from the Commonwealth has grown considerably. Between 1960 and 1962, three-quarters of the total number of immigrants were Commonwealth citizens and nearly a half were from the West Indies alone. Following restrictive Government measures in 1962, net Commonwealth immigration fell from about 290,000 in 1960–2, to 66,000 in 1967 and to 57,000 in 1965.

In view of Britain's demographic structure – the proportion of young people below the age of 15 in the total population rose from 22·7 per cent to 23·4 per cent between 1956 and 1966, implying a further increase in the working population in a few years' time – and the economic difficulties which she faces (the unemployment rate dropped to 1·7 per cent in 1960 but rose again to 2·4 per cent in 1969), another reversal in the flow of migration might be expected. Between 1951 and 1961, England and Wales had a net gain of 352,000, while there was a net outflow of 255,000 from Scotland and one of 29,000 from Northern Ireland. Since that date, the expected reversal has in fact been taking place; emigration has surpassed immigration by a steadily widening margin. Net emigration rose from 30,600 in 1964 to 37,650 in 1965 and 84,000 in 1967.

In 1966–7, nearly 2½ million foreigners were resident in Great Britain, of whom about 162,000 were from the countries of southern Europe.

With the growth of racial tension inspired by the demands of Enoch Powell for a 'white England', a progressive increase can be expected in the numbers of immigrants coming from the Continent to replace the coloured immigrants from the Commonwealth.

TABLE 19.15

IMMIGRATION AND EMIGRATION IN THE
UNITED KINGDOM IN 1964-5

	1964	1965
Commonwealth immigrants	55,900	57,062
Foreign immigrants	71,911	80,863
Total immigration	127,811	137,925
Immigration from:		
Italy	6,778	10,430
Spain	7,106	6,912
Portugal	846	1,135
Greece	738	830
Yugoslavia	334	661
Turkey	254	527
Total immigration from Mediterranean countries	16,056	20,495
Total emigration	158,411	175,577
Net loss	−30,600	−37,652

TABLE 19.16

ORIGINS OF FOREIGNERS RESIDENT
IN GREAT BRITAIN, 1966-7

Ireland	647,560	Italy	96,660
West Indies	267,850	Spain	34,510
India and Ceylon	232,210	Yugoslavia	12,290
Germany	134,050	Greece	8,520
Poland	110,450	Portugal	5,420
Pakistan	73,130	Turkey	4,310
Cyprus	59,190	All others	740,870

XII. CONCLUSION

We have seen that migration occurs because of the differences in the stages of development of the economies concerned and the decisions of individuals who do not wish to accept passively the prospects offered in their home countries; depending on the circumstances, such movements can either be a dangerous haemorrhage or the beginning of a positive transformation.

It is important to determine the precise significance of the phenomenon discussed here, for it has taken place against a background of tariff disarmament both within Europe and internationally. And economic history has adequately demonstrated that enterprises of this type are properly effective only to the extent that the participants are strengthened and revitalised by them: where such benefits are not reaped, the initial liberalisation is followed sooner or later by reaction and decline, unless the weaker partner resigns itself to a sort of vassal status or is prepared to accept stagnation behind re-established tariff barriers.

The examples of the gap between North and South in Italy, the re-establishment of protection in Russia after the attempted liberalisation in the years immediately following the Napoleonic Wars, the gradual disintegration of the Hapsburg Empire after its initial attempt to oppose the Zollverein and its subsequent exclusion by Prussia, all have important lessons to teach today. In each case, it may be noted, the difficulties experienced by the less developed region or country in matching the rate of growth of the more dynamic zone or country have derived from a lack of the two fundamental socio-economic forces involved in economic development – an entrepreneurial class and an industrial working class – and from the absence of an internal 'dynamism', transforming external pressures and internal impulses alike in a process of ongoing development and growth.

In the light of the intra-European migration that has been described above, it is very pertinent to ask whether, with a similar absence of the forces required for development, we have not given very insufficient weight to the possible risk of turning the Mediterranean basin into a manpower reservoir for the overdeveloped industrial regions of north-west Europe.

The economic objectives of these northern industrial regions, which may be considered as the spearhead for Europe taken as a whole, would appear to be quite clear. In a continent lacking in raw materials but richly endowed with human and intellectual resources, they must aim to promote both a high level of general education and the effective deployment and development of the skilled manpower so created within a dynamic and modern economic system. It is Europe's educational and economic assets which will enable her to meet the challenge of competition from outside and to contribute to the improvement of the quality of human life and the progress of civilisation.

It would seem, moreover, from an analysis of the examples cited above, that the flow of immigrants to the industrial countries has constituted (and still does constitute) a particularly beneficial transfusion of resources. The inflow has in fact prevented the strains created by the conjunction of, on the one hand, an ageing indigenous population and, on the other, the desire to increase the time spent in full-time education, to lower the age of retirement, to shorten the length of the working week and to raise continuously the level of economic activity, from reaching crisis-point.

Let us take three significant examples: France, Germany and Switzerland. In the absence of the vital contribution made to these countries' economies by immigrant labour, it may well be the case that:

> (*a*) France would be in danger of experiencing an 'involution' of the sort which, unhappily, she lived through during the nineteenth century, involving both her demographic structure and her industrial structure. It is unnecessary to add that, as in the nineteenth century,

an 'involution' of this type would be catastrophic both for France herself and for Europe as a whole.

(b) Germany (where immigration is taking the place of the influx of workers from the East) would not have been able to construct one of the most powerful and efficient economies in the world. For, with a population with a relatively high average age, and an agricultural sector that is among the least modern – not to say the most archaic – in Western Europe, there may well have come a point at which the growth process would have seized up for lack of the necessary resources.

(c) Switzerland, with a population only one-tenth of Germany's, and an equally high average age, would not have been able to carry out such a large-scale and fruitful transfer of her indigenous working population to the upper strata of manufacturing industry and, above all, to the service sector.

To put this point of view in its most extreme form – although, clearly, this involves some degree of exaggeration – it could be said that, considering the age of the arteries, the fluidity of the life-blood and the level of activity to which industrial northern Europe has subjected its organism, the migratory flow has helped to eliminate or, at least, to reduce substantially the risk of economic paralysis or arteriosclerosis in the various parts of the European body.

But, it may be objected, if this process continues at the same rate in the future, is there not a very strong possibility that northern Europe will turn the Mediterranean basin into a reservoir of unskilled manpower and that, by creaming off the younger elements of the population, a process of senescence and sclerosis will be precipitated in those regions?

This is certainly a very real danger: but other, more optimistic, suggestions and hypotheses have been advanced. The first of these concerns the course of migration itself. In their studies of the possible development of the population structure of Europe over the next century, both Doxiadis in Athens and Jérome Monod in Paris have come to the conclusion that, of the immigration to Europe, which might amount to anything between 50 and 100 million people, 60 per cent would go to the regions of the Mediterranean littoral, 30 per cent to the northern coastal region comprising Benelux, northern Germany and the zones of influence of Paris and London and 10 per cent to the rest of Europe.

This sort of hypothesis is, of course, based on the presumption that in the future man will come to attach increasing importance to the quality of the environment and his conditions of life. If it is assumed that the sunshine and natural beauty with which the countries of the Mediterranean are blessed will, in fact, exercise such powers of attraction in the future, the question then arises whether these regions that are favoured by the climate and by nature will also be capable of providing the necessary conditions for industry to establish itself; and, further, whether the implantation of the industries required to provide a livelihood for the increased population is not likely to lead to a deterioration of the countryside and to the pollution of the natural environment.

The most important factors after labour would appear to be the supply of energy and the means of transport and communication. The economies of the Ancient World were based on the utilisation of wood and water, and it was upon this basis that the organising ability of the Romans, fertilised by the Greeks' sense of proportion, made the Mediterranean the heart and centre of the civilised world. However, the techniques and tools that had been conceived for use in the terrain and climate of the Mediterranean could not be directly transferred to the less clement conditions of northern Europe. They had to be re-thought and adapted for use in more difficult climates and terrains.

Thus the machines of the first Industrial Revolution were invented in the North by the descendants of those same Normans who, in the South, in Apulia and in Sicily, had created the basis for a huge Italo-Germanic political confederation with Frederick of Hohenstauffen. We have seen how Europe's centre of gravity was thus located on top of the supplies of the new source of energy and in the proximity of the forges which created the new tools and the new machines. In addition, we have seen elsewhere how the differences in the geographical distribution of the raw materials upon which the first Industrial Revolution was based, added to the different capacities of the socio-economic forces to exploit them effectively, fixed the new centres of gravity of modern Europe and the modern world upon the Rhine and the Atlantic littoral – where, moreover, they were to remain for a long while to come.[1]

Are we not witnessing at this very moment, however, a transformation of the scale of values which characterises our way of life, *at the same time* as a profound transformation is taking place in the Mediterranean region in the methods of production? In the field of energy, we have witnessed the prodigious growth in the use of oil and natural gas, for which the principal sources for Europe are the Middle East and North Africa. The newest form of energy – atomic power, which will be supplying a quarter of our needs in thirty years' time – requires exceptionally large quantities of water for cooling purposes, thereby making it necessary to have recourse to the waters of the Mediterranean owing to the inadequacy of inland water resources. At the same time, the introduction of giant oil-tankers and ore-carriers puts practically any factory built on the coast within easy reach of both the best sources of energy and raw materials and the most

[1] Henri Rieben, Jacques Schenchzer, Georges Domeyer, Jean-Marc Mattinger and Martin Nathasiers, *Un centre de gravité européen*, vol. 1 (Centre de Recherches Européennes, Lausanne, 1969).

attractive outlets throughout the world. This revolution in the transportation of heavy materials over long distances implies a radical change in our ideas about industrial location.

Some four decades ago, the Italian, Oscar Sinigaglia, had a clear vision of the benefits which would accrue from this transport revolution. Centred on Cornigliano, Piombino, Bagnoli and Taranto, the Italian steel industry was a model for the future. The Japanese have followed their example, and at the present moment, in the Mediterranean region, the French are planning to set up a very large-scale, ultra-modern integrated steel complex at Fos (near Marseilles) and the Spanish intend to do the same at Sagunto.

Encouraging developments are taking place in Greece and Turkey, while along the whole coast, marine construction and ship-repairing, and the merchant fleets themselves, are gradually developing on a scale commensurate with the size of the revolution that is occurring. To quote just one case among many, the spectacular example of Lisnave at Lisbon gives some idea of the scale of what has so far been achieved and what can be expected in the future.

But at a time when the Japanese, with their coastal-situated and fully integrated plants, are launching an offensive to capture half the world market in bulk exports, complexes of these dimensions only make economic sense to the extent that as large a proportion as possible of the metal produced eventually incorporates a very high value-added. In other words, this basic industry, an industrialising force *par excellence*, must serve to diffuse towards the hinterland a range of metal-using industries of an increasingly sophisticated type.

With their combined transport infrastructure on both sea and land, the countries of Europe, as they move gradually closer together, have it within their power to develop a series of modern industrial centres along the Mediterranean littoral, with a high capacity for generating further growth. This growth will take place along the natural 'corridors' of expansion, and the growth axis so created will eventually meet the axis which runs from Scandinavia, and which makes that industrial belt one of the most powerful in the world. A few decades only will be enough to bring about this all-important junction between the growth axes of the Rhine and the Rhone.

But in achieving this, do we not run the risk of ruining some wonderful countryside? To avoid this otherwise inevitable result, production techniques which combine efficiency with the control of harmful side-effects must be chosen with rigorous care. In fact, the range of such techniques is rapidly expanding due to the pressure of those people who are attempting to protect the balance of the environment and to the work being done at Pittsburgh and elsewhere by the disciples of Richard King Mellor and David L. Lawrence.

But in the light of these technological developments and the changes in the organisation of production which make so many things possible today, we have still to ask whether the Mediterranean countries have the internal dynamism capable of using these opportunities to the full. By internal dynamism, we mean the capacity of the socio-economic forces of the country concerned to turn external and internal pressures into a policy of ongoing and self-maintaining growth.

The industrial nations of northern Europe have provided a great service to the countries of the Mediterranean by creating in their factories, in just two decades, an industrial labour force whose members will be ready to return to their countries of origin as soon as they know that they will be able to put their new-found skills to use there. In any case, this new labour force will exercise a direct or indirect pressure on the countries from which emigration is taking place to step up the rate of their economic and industrial development. There are already some important industrial centres on the Mediterranean coast which show the sort of performance which can be reached. Others will follow. International co-operation, either between Mediterranean countries or between the countries of northern and southern Europe, or on an even larger scale still, will multiply the effects of the strategy that is just being embarked upon.

However, impressive as some of the individual or national achievements quoted here may appear, they do not yet match up to the far-reaching implications of the three phenomena which make up their background – the reduction of tariffs both within and between continents, European integration and the intra-European migration of unskilled labour. In short, the gap between industrial northern Europe and Mediterranean Europe remains wide and is probably getting wider; integration is aimed at closing this gap, but there still remains considerable tension between these two very divergent areas.

But in economics, as in electricity or in psychology, a well-managed tension can become a source of beneficial energy. On the other hand, if it is badly managed it produces an explosion which burns, disrupts and destroys. This metaphorical diversion brings us back to the central problem from which we started: that is, to the socio-economic forces of the Mediterranean countries.

The transformation of a part of the southern peasantry into an industrial labour force in the factories of northern Europe will facilitate a rather more rapid industrialisation of the Mediterranean littoral than would otherwise have been the case. But if the industrialisation process is to take place in a balanced and harmonious fashion, the state and the entrepreneurial classes must be able and willing to keep in step.

We have seen the far-reaching nature of the technological developments that can help them achieve this objective; but the onus remains squarely on them to reverse the secular trend that began when the men of northern Europe adapted the technology of the Normans to their own climate and terrain. In other words, the men of southern Europe must today attempt to graft the technology of the North on to the style and conditions of life that are proper to the cradle of Mediterranean civilisation. It is an exhilarating challenge to the peoples of southern Europe; but the capacity to respond adequately has yet to be acquired.

In the face of this challenge, they would do well to remember the piece of cautionary advice which Seneca gave to the people of those same regions at the dawn of our modern era, and adapt it to their own situation. 'A favourable wind,' he said, 'can only blow for the man who knows where he wants to go.'

Discussion of the Papers by Professors Scott and Rieben

Mr Lundgren said that he had learned a lot from the papers. The most widely used international trade models assumed that factors of production were immobile. In fact, they were mobile enough to make the use of such theories dangerous. The theory of international labour migration had received very little attention. He could see two ways of approaching the problem. First, one could work out a theory of international exchange with limited labour mobility, and full mobility of capital. Or one might look at data, and test hypotheses as to why labour moved. The two papers both took the latter route. Professor Scott also discussed the effect of labour migration on income per head and capital formation. Perhaps income per head would be reduced a little in the receiving country; the contribution to capital formation in that country by immigrants was not great. They mainly brought human capital.

There were very different emphasis in the two papers. Professor Scott dealt mainly with estimates and explanations of migration from Europe to North America, and not much with immigration within North America. Professor Rieben dealt mainly with migration within Europe, and only scantily with emigration from Europe to North America. Clearly, this Conference was interested mainly in emigration from Europe to North America, but this was not to say that intra-European migration was unimportant to this question. In particular, it threw light on the interplay between the absorption capacity of North American and European industry.

Two questions arose in this connection. Had the earlier emigration from backward European areas been diverted from North American to European industry? This might emerge from the discussion. If so, did this imply that the 'pull' effect from European centres was becoming greater? Professor Scott pointed to the low immigration from Europe since 1945. One could also ask whether there was an intra-European brain drain?

The different emphasis in the two papers was also shown by the fact that while Professor Scott was concerned with lower immigration to North America since 1945, Professor Rieben talked of the high mobility of professional people. Professor Scott explained these different movements. He thought that the importance of the brain drain to the United States was marginal, though it might be significant from the European end. He pointed out that the share of skilled and professional people had risen to one-third of the flow leaving Europe.

On the effect of the new immigration laws of the 1960s in North America, Professor Scott held that they increased discrimination against the unskilled and uneducated. In the near future, the percentage of skilled and professional workers would therefore be boosted by new legislation. This was not a market-guided change, but a politically-guided one.

Professor Scott looked at hypotheses about emigration trends. He asked why there were certain kinds of fluctuation, and went on to look at welfare aspects. It was a pity that Professor Rieben passed over an analysis of the welfare effects and contented himself with assuming that the brain drain had a negative effect on Europe, and could be stopped without loss. It seemed very important to know the truth.

There was much literature on this, and he would like to hear Professors Scott and Kindleberger say something about the effects of immigration. If we left out the issue of the individual's freedom to move and the political independence argument (Canada and Australia, for example, wanted bigger populations), there seemed to be two general approaches. The first was the neo-classical type of estimate of gains, touched on by Professor Scott. This analysis was based on the market-guided tendency for marginal products of factors to equalise between countries. There was so much land in North America that there was a relative shortage of skilled labour and capital. This approach had been used by Harry Johnson. The other approach was to use theories of agglomeration, large-scale economies and other externalities, along the lines of regional analysis. He wondered what kind of result one got from proceeding one way rather than the other. Could one explain the role of Norrland in Sweden or the Appalachians in the United States by the use of theories which also had some explanatory value in an analysis of the relations between Europe and the United States? In the very long period, it seemed that the former areas might be emptied of nearly all resources. Which was the best method of analysis to use?

Professor Kindleberger said that his first contact with this problem was when Per Jacobssen had told him that all the lazy Swedes emigrated, and all the good ones stayed. Similarly, in eighteenth-century Germany, all the lazy Germans had stayed behind. The problem was cleared up later, by Mrs Dorothy Swaine Thomas and then by Brinley Thomas. It turned out to have been a cyclic problem. In periods of high activity, people moved to the cities; when low activity returned, they emigrated to the United States.

He had been impressed by Professor Rieben's characterisation of the classic argument between Professors Patinkin and Johnson. The former took a nationalist view; the latter was cosmopolitan. Each threw light on economic theory, and perhaps on his own position and attitudes as well. There were many economic, social and political issues.

At the moment, Europeans moving to North America could get citizenship after five years. Therefore politicians organised the movement. But in Europe it was not possible to obtain citizenship in this way. Foreigners remained beyond the pale. Even if they were already citizens, as Pakistanis, West Indians, etc., were in the United Kingdom, the result was political and social turmoil when they came. So they were kept out. He thought that perhaps Professor Lundgren had been too ready to leave out movement from the Mediterranean to the North of Europe. The American multinational corporation was more a European than a French, German or Dutch firm, in that it belonged in no one country and was prepared to move to another location when that was clearly more profitable, and more efficient. Similar Mediterranean labour provided mobility and efficiency to the E.E.C. because it had no roots attaching it to one country. E.E.C. labour did not move about the Common Market in this way. There was, of course, some border commuting, and a considerable number of Dutch citizens worked regularly and lived in the Ruhr. The Italians were both Mediterraneans and members of the Common Market, but the South Italians had little advantage over other Mediterraneans. Because of the competitive situation, the same benefits they received had had to be extended to the Portuguese, Spanish, Greeks and Turks.

On movement back, Professor Kindleberger had talked to the Australian expert, Borrie, who explained that Australia was looking for immigrants who had returned to Greece from Germany. They had learned about modern society, but had become rootless in the process. This was sad if they liked their own Greek culture. Similarly, it was claimed that immigrants from England only became real Australians after their first trip back to the United Kingdom.

On agglomerations, Professor Kindleberger thought there was an important literature in France, mainly from geographers, on how difficult it was to move industry to people. In fact, the Peugeot factory at Socheaux mainly employed Algerians. Similarly, Michelin had decided not to expand their plant at Clermont-Ferrand. Cities like Paris, London, Boston and New York were there because they did give economic benefits.

Professor Khachaturov had raised what was effectively a game-theory aspect. He thought that America should keep immigrants out. It was hard to know what to do. One could feel a good deal for Greece; and one sympathised with Professor Patinkin. If all the good people went, one worried about those who were left. In English literature, there was a poem about the Deserted Village and Professor Kindleberger worried about the last to leave. This was a serious question. Should the United States work to the public good by keeping Greeks out, if it was to the private good that Greeks should be allowed to enter.

Dr de Mello gave some reasons which, in his opinion, accounted for Portuguese emigration. A major motive was that young people grew up more quickly because of conscription. The country had to respond and the entrepreneurs were in a better position than anyone else to do it. He was afraid that the majority of the entrepreneurs lacked the necessary aggressiveness. The industrial and financial group he belonged to was interested in well-trained men. His plants had to compete internationally, and Portugal had been, up to now, more used to commerce than to industry. A great deal of money was being spent on management training, with the collaboration of the Stanford Research Institute. Some industries, such as ship-repairing – especially of tankers – proved to be suitable for Portugal. In fact, Portugal had a privileged geographical situation for this.

The country also had natural conditions for the chemical industry based on pyrites, sulphur and copper, iron and non-ferrous metals. Very much depended on the vision of the entrepreneurs, who were bound to take risks. Of course, foreign capital and know-how were favourable.

Professor Scott said he had welcomed the opportunity to write his paper. He had earlier worked only on the brain drain, and was glad to look now at the larger subject of mass emigration. The major difficulty about doing this lay in obtaining adequate data. On the broad issues of international migration, one had to use sample studies, which might not be very adequate. For the brain drain, study was much more simple and sample surveys often covered a large proportion of those moving.

He had explained on p. 448 that he was not sure whether the figure of 4 per cent for the addition from post-war immigration to the 1967 native-born human stock in the labour-force age group was a big or small number. He had done the same kinds of calculation as Denison had, and shared the doubts expressed in earlier sessions about these methods. But at least one could look at neo-classical ideas as they related to this. Professor de Mello and Mr Lundgren had referred to movements within Europe and Professor Kindleberger has suggested that labour might be more mobile in Europe than capital was. Educated labour was certainly very mobile between the South and the North of Europe. So, for example, one found fragmentary evidence like the report that 95 per cent of a graduating class in engineering in Turkey had left the country within one year.

Professor Kindleberger had referred to Borrie's remark that the most contented immigrant was one who had migrated once before and who moved finally, Professor Kindleberger said, to Australia. But a difficulty was that in each generation we did not know whether this was the final move or not. Certainly, there had been very high rates of return of Italians to southern Europe in the nineteenth century. They did so, even though the Italian standard of living was much lower than that in the United States. They went to America to acquire capital, not to live there permanently. Could one really say that the recent waves of migration were any more permanent? Would most emigrants (now in their twenties) stay where they were? Just as mortality rates changed during one's life, so did return rates.

Several people had referred to the cosmopolitan versus the nationalistic approach. They had mentioned the argument between Professors Johnson and Patinkin. The Appalachian or Norrland exodus was what one got if one followed a cosmopolitan approach which said that one must allow free movement to areas with high marginal productivity of labour. Professor Johnson would go on to say that this was good from *everyone*'s point of view. If workers went where the marginal productivity was highest, production of all goods would gradually be centred where efficiency was greatest. Therefore all would eventually gain, wherever they lived. It was true that all might get traded goods cheaply; but what about non-traded services? Those remaining in backward areas which had lost doctors would hardly be happy with that situation, even though other kinds of goods and services were now cheaper.

One answer was that countries with stable and low incomes could produce their own doctors cheaply. But would they stay? One would then be led either to stop doctors from moving or to train low-level doctors who could not migrate to treat patients with higher standards of living.

The basic conclusion of the paper was that intra-North American migration was now *very* important. Professor Rieben showed how important migration within Europe was. Similarly, he argued that the brain drain from Europe to North America might have a major impact on the losing country – but not much on the receiver. The flow of untrained people was not now very important.

Professor Rasmussen wanted to add a footnote about the brain drain. So far we had treated Western Europe as though it was a homogeneous whole. For the brain drain, this was not true. There was a lot of movement out of Norway, but not much from Denmark. There was a lot of movement from the United Kingdom, but not much from France. One had to look at the problems of individual European countries, because not all these countries were similar.

Professor Campbell wanted to raise the question of remittances. He knew that in some countries these could be very important. For example, Jordan's main source of foreign exchange was foreign aid; the next most important source was remittances from those who had gone abroad. The actual situation depended a good deal on whether these were really extended families, or whether emigrants intended to settle permanently abroad, or only remain temporarily.

Living as he did in Toronto where there were a quarter of a million Italians and 60,000 Portuguese, he was impressed by the large number of immigrants always in his bank sending money back home.

He also wanted to re-raise the issue Professor Robinson had mentioned about the agriculture of low-income farms in Germany. Workers stayed on the farms while Spaniards, Portuguese and Italians moved into urban employment. This was also true on the other side of the Atlantic. The flow of immigrants tended to restrict the rural–urban flow.

Professor Robinson wondered whether the statistics on the brain drain were gross or net figures. In the United Kingdom, one had statistics showing the percentage of all students who had obtained Ph.D.s who went abroad. Of their students at Cambridge, about two-thirds were foreigners. It was only natural that they should go home. But British students often wanted to go to the United States for at least part of their period of graduate work. Momentarily, this appeared to be a brain drain. But the same people reappeared three years later and gross figures were therefore very misleading.

On the brain drain argument itself, he wondered what were the real issues. He found it hard to accept the position of Professor Johnson, at any rate as expressed at the I.E.A.'s Montreal Conference a year earlier, when he had assumed that all incomes everywhere were equal to the net productivity of the person concerned. He would like to think about this in an actual case. For example, in Pakistan, there were probably ten or a dozen really good economists. He wondered what was their value. They were paid a conventional civil service wage. This was a reasonable estimate of what a civil servant ought to be paid, compared with average incomes. They were therefore paid much less than if they worked for an international organisation or a British or American university. There was a great temptation to move abroad. He would say that the net productivity of those who stayed and did work on the national plan was much greater than the conventional wage. The loss to Pakistan of three of their ten best economists to America was immensely greater than the wage they earned. It followed that one simply could not say whether the world was being benefited by movements of trained people if one simply looked at their income in the place where they worked. One was not really looking at the relative values of people in different countries and occupations. For example, he did not think that the marginal productivity of top industrialists in the United Kingdom was exactly equal to £25,000 per annum.

What mattered was the relationship of wages and salaries to average incomes in given countries. Should European countries pay higher salaries to stop particular highly mobile people moving to the United States? This was happening at the moment with British airline pilots. Should the airline pilots be paid a salary similar to men in the same kind of job in the United Kingdom? Or should they be paid enough to keep them from joining T.W.A.?

Professor Robinson wondered how many of the problems of the world were best put right by migration. How many were better solved in other ways? In an I.E.A. Conference at Varenna, in 1967, they had looked at backward areas in advanced countries. It had been shown that backward-area problems in most European countries were due to the fact that there were cultural groups where people preferred to live. A cultural group was a reality. One could not solve all the problems of Sicily or Greece by migration. One would then be left with an older, less mobile nucleus that was incapable of dealing with local problems. If anything, the Italians had solved too many problems by migration to the North, and to other countries. They had left a hard core of older, less adaptable people in this way.

Professor Ashton said he wanted to look at the agricultural side of the problem, because he had no special knowledge of population movements. He had, however, looked at the effect of emigration on agriculture in Turkey and Greece. He had once been told by an official in Brussels that there was no longer an agricultural problem in Greece. Eighty thousand workers a year were leaving Greece for the E.E.C. In a stark, cynical way, this was true, but it left Greek villages with the old and infirm. Professor Zolotas, who had written a good deal on this subject, saw this continuation of immigration as a proof of the total failure of the Government's economic policy. The modern industry which had been introduced into Greece was very capital-intensive and did not use enough labour.

Professor Ashton made two other specific points about Greece and Turkey. First, the flow of population from remote areas tended to be to towns, and then to industrial areas in northern Europe. The loss of local employment opportunities was felt in the mountains and remote areas. In the past, workers from these areas moved seasonally to the plains for harvest and to bring cash back home. So, for instance, in the plain of Thessaly, agriculture was very labour-intensive. As the labour supply fell off, one had the paradox of labour shortage.

Second, many emigrants retained their ownership of land in Greece. Greeks were great fragmenters of land and emigrants kept their titles to particular parts of the country. This greatly impeded a rational layout of farms. Professor Ashton wanted to emphasise the point made by Professor Campbell that remittances were of great importance for a country like Greece.

On definitions, he had never been able to make out why the Greek statistics had two entries for remittances. One was from emigrants – in Australia, the United States, etc.; the other was the much bigger item of remittances from workers abroad – especially in Germany. This was, optimistically perhaps, not looked upon as permanent emigration.

Professor Lebedev said that he had been fascinated in reading Professor Rieben's paper to find a passage about Yugoslavia. He was not asking for recipes, but here was a case study on the migration of the labour force. There was no detail on the economic development of Yugoslavia, but in any underdeveloped country he thought that emigration was not beneficial in the long run. He thought rather that emigration was a net loss. He knew that people left the country because they had no gainful occupation, but perhaps the problem of providing a job was simply shifted to the receiving country. If the emigrant moved to a country with a higher standard of living, perhaps he would stay at a lower level in the labour structure.

Labour was the main productive force and, when a country lost labour, its production force diminished. It was no help to the economic problems of that country. The benefits went to the receiving country. We had heard a good deal about the remittances which emigrants sent from, for example, Toronto. This obviously helped the family and the economy back home; but was it not better to try to use the labour at home to begin with?

Professor Robinson had said that emigrants liked their own country and culture. He did not think that emigration was a positive thing for such underdeveloped countries. These issues occurred again even in the brain drain in advanced countries.

In discussing Yugoslavia, Professor Rieben had described this as 'almost a capitalist economy'. He was orthodox enough to think that perhaps emigration was almost a direct result of this.

Professor Scott had one line in his paper which said that 'people and empty land without capital and enterprise can produce a Siberia'. He did not want to make a political argument, and he knew that this was a British figure of speech, but he thought that the remark was a little unfair on Siberia.

Mr Merigó was worried about the effect of the brain drain on income distribution in Europe. If a man had been to the right kind of business school, he was paid a good deal more than an older man, or a manual worker. What effect would this have in the long run on the distribution of salaries?

Professor Scott had said that the fact that immigration added to human rather than physical capital had tended to reduce the welfare of the receiving country. He was puzzled by this. One could take Germany as an example. This country had a stagnant active population and, because of the small size of the agricultural labour force, very little possibility of transfer of labour from agriculture to industry. Nevertheless, given German income levels and propensities to save, rather more savings could be generated than were required to depreciate the existing capital stock. Surplus savings could thus take the form either of capital exports or increased domestic capital stock. German entrepreneurs had been notoriously reluctant to invest abroad. But when they tried to satisfy their preference for domestic investment they found they did not have enough labour for the increased capital stock. They could have chosen a different combination of factors of production (labour-saving investment) but this clearly did not maximise their profits. Thus, recourse to immigration had the following results for Germany:

(i) it maximised entrepreneurial profits;
(ii) it gave German labour the opportunity to increase its welfare by holding the better-paid or more pleasant jobs, and leaving the badly-paid or unpleasant jobs to immigrants;
(iii) a more subtle, but still important, factor which applied to all countries with tight labour conditions was decreased labour hoarding if free immigration was available. This increased labour mobility and productivity.

Mr Merigó also said that the situation of countries like Canada or Australia was quite different because of the natural growth of the labour force. One could assume that Canadians could not generate more savings than were required to increase capital stock *pari passu* with the natural growth of the labour force. In this case, the capital stock required to employ the immigrants had to be supplied from foreign savings. Thus, extra profits went to foreign residents and salaries to immigrants. Even then, there could be thought to be increased welfare for the native population if only from the economies of scale. These could be quite important in sparsely populated countries such as Canada or Australia.

Professor Eastman said that years ago there had been a lot of discussion on where the loss fell in educating those who then emigrated. One could ask the same kind of question about immigrants in relation to the native-born. This took us back to what Mr Merigó had said about who got what kind of job. The coming of immigrants who were skilled could, by depressing the price for those jobs, reduce the gains from investment in training of the less educated in the native population.

Mr Lundgren turned to the question of why there were depressed areas such as Sicily. A theoretical analysis could run in the following terms. Sicily had certain disadvantages in industrial production compared to northern Italy, because of transport costs, absence of the positive external effects of an industrial environment, etc. To attract investments on a scale necessary to achieve full employment, wage levels must therefore be lower in Sicily. These lower wage levels would not create mass emigration to the North, because in their calculations Sicilians added the psychic income they derived from living in Sicily rather than in the North. Many then found themselves better off in Sicily.

However, because of collective bargaining and characteristics of a national labour market, wage levels in Sicily became too high to maintain full employment there. The area was depressed and the unemployment stimulated emigration to northern Italy and other parts of Europe. He thought it likely that the psychic income derived from living in one's native region was high in relation to money wages for unskilled and semi-skilled workers in Europe. The use of full employment policies, the possibilities of selecting exchange rates and the fact that collective bargaining was restricted to the national economy, combined to keep down the international migration of such workers today. If we learn to handle regional depressions more efficiently, much of the remaining stimulus to such migration would be gone as well. This connection between regional policy and international migration might be of considerable interest.

Professor Kindleberger said that he had been amused and frustrated for twenty years by the question 'Is 4 per cent big?' The Marshall Plan had been drawn up on the basis that all the Europeans lacked was 2 per cent of national income. He had tried to work out how much de Gaulle had spent on 'gloire' from the French national income. He thought it was about $2\frac{1}{2}$ per cent. He had then asked whether that was big. He had decided that it was big or small, depending on how useful it was and how capable of being applied in different ways.

What about 4 per cent of capital stock? Canada had enough farms; 4 per cent more would not help. However, if she was about to expand her metallurgical industry, 4 per cent more scientists of the right kind was big.

He wondered whether many Greek workers who went abroad were involved in 'target' work. That was to say, did they aim at amassing a given sum of capital? If such Greek workers went back and built boats, this was of no use, because Greece was already over-fished. If the returning emigrant bought a farm, the question was, what did the selling farmer do with the money? A young economist in the A.I.D. office in Turkey had prepared recommendations for a special exchange rate for emigrant remittances which had halted the return of earnings in the form of second-hand cars, television sets, etc., and produced highly useful foreign exchange.

Mr Grogan recalled that Professor Scott had asked how far the immigration of labour and of capital were substitutes. At the end of the war, economic thinking in Australia had been dominated by fear of another world recession. Estimates were made, at the time, of the social costs involved for Australia in respect of each immigrant. It was thought that a migrant intake at an annual rate greater than 1–2 per cent of the population would necessitate enough investment to result in inflation. This cautious attitude over immigration was supported by the trade unions who feared competition for scarce jobs if, in fact, a recession should develop. Subsequent experience suggested that if immigration had been faster, and accompanied by appropriate domestic policies, overseas investment might have come in and offset any added strain on the balance of payments. Mr Grogan said he did not know to what extent the actual rate of immigration had meant any sacrifice in economic growth, especially if one thought in terms of growth in real per capita incomes. For the period 1947–63, the rate of population increase had been 2·3 per cent per annum, second only to Canada among the countries with high living standards. In the early part of this period immigration had contributed about half of this increase and, more recently, about one-third.

Replying to the discussion on his paper, *Professor Rieben* said that he had had certain preoccupations when writing his paper. In the nineteenth century, with the Zollverein, Austria at one moment under Metternich had tried to join. Though this was a correct calculation, Austria had neither the industry nor the working class to enable it to take its place alongside Prussia, etc. Austria had improved both militarily and economically by 1870. Russia had faced the same problem. With most-favoured-nation treatment, Russia had tried to export steel products in competition with German industry. Competition had forced her to return to agricultural and pre-industrial activities. These were two examples of how disintegration could occur. We should take the counsel of Gunnar Myrdal, when he went to the E.C.E., that if one opened the frontier, but gave no support to industry, trenches would be dug between agriculture and industry very quickly. But in the eighteenth and nineteenth centuries, it had taken something like fifty years for any country to catch up with the United Kingdom. The problem was training the working class. It had now been possible to create in northern Europe, in about twenty years, a working class fron the South.

So he accepted Professor Lebedev's first proposition. The human factor was the vital force. However, Professor Kindleberger was right. One needs to work sector by sector and look at each's strong points. Industrial strategy had allowed the Mediterranean basin to transform itself. There were two levels to the problem. One was the need for private entrepreneurship. The other was the need for the state to co-operate. The I.R.I. and the Cassa per il Mezzogiorno had done good work. In Greece, too, the U.S.S.R. was supplying refinery capacity, and America an aluminium plant.

To Professor de Mello, Professor Rieben said that the question was how one could stimulate the development of an entrepreneurial class which would transform the Mediterranean basin into a unit which was strong enough to live alongside the economy of northern Europe. Where men were concerned, he was a liberal. They were responsible for their own decisions. At the European level, the surplus energy from the South could help the North to reach a level where it could compete with America.

Professor Scott also replied to the discussion. He said that on the 4 per cent question, what Professor Kindleberger had said threw attention on to the time dimension. All the calculations that had been made were backward-looking; we needed to look forward. We certainly also needed to look at the versatility of capital. Professor Eastman had talked about the debt owed by emigrants to the country of their birth, education, rearing, etc.; Professor Robinson had distinguished net and gross emigration.

He himself had worked on the brain drain of economists between Canada and the United States. Some Canadian economists worked in the United States; some Americans worked in Canada. Canadians often moved after training in Canada to train further in the United States, and then returned. Americans did the opposite. The net/gross calculation therefore arose again. 89 Canadian economists were now in the United States; 35 Americans were in Canada. Canada was also 'indebted' to America for $750,000 which had been embodied in Canadians during training given in the United States. (When discussing these issues, he always wanted to put the words 'owed' and 'debt' in quotation marks.) On balance, Canada owed more than it gave.

He agreed with Mr Merigó, though he would point to the fact that on the world-wide scale immigrants did not always enter the labour force at the bottom of the scale. (As for his remark on Siberia, he could only apologise for it.)

What Professor Robinson had said about Pakistan was not the same as his own reference to internationally non-traded goods. This kind of output by 'brains' deserved further study.

Professor Scott said he wanted to conclude by saying again that, in rural depopulation, the 'best' people did *not* always leave first. He had read studies of two centuries, and for many countries, and he thought that the relative qualification of emigrants depended on the size of emigration. In a small emigration, it was unlikely that the best would go first. The best would probably be very well established early in their lives. But if there were mass emigration, as had happened in Sicily, the best would certainly not leave last. The only people left behind then, would be those who were unemployable elsewhere.

Part 5

The Search for Solutions

20 Optimal Economic Interdependence

Charles P. Kindleberger
MASSACHUSETTS INSTITUTE OF TECHNOLOGY

I. THE CONFLICT BETWEEN ECONOMICS AND POLITICS
Practically all technical questions of international economic arrangements for trade, money, capital flows and payments adjustment reduce to one general issue: should these arrangements be revised to facilitate linking the developed countries into a single integrated system? If so, what should be the nature of the system? If not, what are the optimal arrangements for giving or preserving the necessary national independence of economic policy with mixed negative repercussions of one country's policies on other countries?

The case for integration is largely economic. Reduced barriers to transport and communication, wider horizons, broader markets produce efficient specialisation and economies of scale – up to some optimum point which has probably not been reached in goods markets nor in the international market for capital, management and technology.

The case against adopting world common policies for freedom of movement of goods and factors, a single money and a single monetary policy, plus co-ordinated or harmonised policies in fiscal matters and in such questions as the regulation of monopoly, is largely political. National preferences differ. Few countries are willing to cede sovereignty or the power of decision-making to bodies of representatives in which their national views can be overruled. International machinery for developing and applying international economic policies lags because of the absence of effective international political authority. A democratic international system has yet to be developed; one imposed by an imperial or economically dominant leader is effectively resisted.

This uneven development on the economic and political fronts is the heart of the issue. Much economic debate over what appear to be technical questions of, say, fixed versus floating exchange rates or the benefits and dangers of the international corporation are implicitly political debates over whether an international polity can be developed to manage the international economy. Those who adopt the solutions of *laissez-faire*, free trade, absence of controls over capital movements and international corporations, fixed exchange rates, an attempt to replicate the conditions of the internal national market on an international scale, believe either that appropriate international institutions can be developed or (less likely) that one country's policies can be imposed on the world trading system. The opponents of the 'cosmopolitan' solution, who argue, say, for flexible exchange rates and control of foreign corporations within a national economy, are both sceptical that international policies can be devised or 'imperial' solutions resisted and conscious of the necessity to adapt economic policies to the special requirements of local conditions.

Clash between economies of scale and political diseconomies is not new. In *The Great Transformation*, Karl Polanyi pointed to social diseconomies of the specialisation and technological change induced by widening the market. At the same time, the alternative of resisting the economic potentiality of scale and technological advance is historically unattractive. National policies in France sought to protect the peasant from competition, but succeeded mainly in delaying the inevitable change and making it convulsive.

The choice is whether to accept the trend to wider world scale in economics and build the political machinery that would be needed to harmonise purposes that would otherwise diverge, to provide for necessary exceptions or special transitional arrangements, or to accept the difficulties of political institution-making and adapt economic policy to the realities of national policies.

II. THE COSMOPOLITAN ECONOMIC SOLUTION

The efficiency of a cosmopolitan economic solution is not self-evident or even capable of establishment in all aspects of economic life. The infant-industry argument provides one major exception, largely ignored in this paper which deals with the developed countries. Maximising national solutions of the optimum tariff or optimum lending or borrowing are also ignored because they depend on the absence of retaliation in the optimum interest of another nation, and because co-operation to escape optimal restrictions on the national level, if necessary with transfers to the country which might otherwise gain, is a superior international solution. There are clearly diseconomies of scale to agglomeration beyond certain sizes, and perhaps these are encountered in some fields. There is doubt whether a world market for labour increases welfare when migration takes place from countries which have not begun family limitation, and whose migrants are rapidly replaced by increased survivals. None the less, there is a presumption that wider markets for goods, for capital, and for the activities of corporations beyond national frontiers increase the potential for economic welfare.

The case is most readily made and most readily accepted with regard to goods. Theorists prefer trade with tax-cum-subsidy to free trade in order to offset distortions of market prices from social values, and contemplate cases where effective tariff rates may be reduced by raising market rates. Most economists at this stage of the development of our science, however, are prepared to put this counsel of perfection into the class with lump-sum progressive taxation as unattainable, and establish a broad presumption for lower tariffs and for free trade. The theory of the second-best argues for intervention in the market, but we know too little about the divergences between private and social costs and between private and social returns, and measurement of effective tariff rates is too rudimentary, to do more than establish a presumption as to which tariffs should be reduced first if they cannot be reduced as a group.

About factor movements and the operation of the international corporation there is less agreement. It is generally accepted that the international movement of ordinary labour from countries of high net reproduction rates is likely to reduce world welfare by lowering per capita income in the country of immigration without raising it in the country of emigration. For skilled and educated labour, national and cosmopolitan solutions conflict. The cosmopolitan view states that a unit of labour is best employed where it can earn the highest return; the national approach emphasises the interactions between various kinds of labour, and between emigrating labour and other factors, holding that the gain for the migrating units may be more than offset by external negative effects. This analysis, of course, is no different from that applied to movements within countries. When local populations acquire opportunities to earn higher incomes in more rapidly developing parts of the country, the more energetic and more skilled units of entrepreneurship and labour leave first, imposing stagnation on those remaining.

Where there are family limitations and no externalities in the country of emigration, there is a presumption that migration benefits growth. Under the Lewis model of growth with unlimited supplies of labour, moreover, migration can stimulate growth in both receiving and sending countries. In the receiving industrial country, wages are held down, and profits up, stimulating capital formation and growth. In the sending agricultural country, removal of the dead weight of redundant labour may raise the marginal product of labour to the real wage, which increases the incentive to invest, redistributes income in favour of landowners which adds to savings, and leads to an increase in agricultural productivity. Unlimited supplies of labour cannot initiate growth but can sustain it. The dynamic path is non-linear, however. On the economic side, the initial immigrants are content to work hard, save a great deal of their earnings, and add more to supply than to demand. Later, as migrants are joined by their families and overcrowding reaches limits, a need is felt for social overhead capital – housing, hospitals, schools. Continued migration may aid the private sector, but impose a burden on public investment. In addition, to the extent that the labour is unskilled, the amount that can be absorbed is limited because the amount of skilled labour required to work with more than limited amounts of unskilled labour may not be available.

Also operative is a social limit, which varies from country to country, and with the racial, cultural and class distance between immigrants and the local population, and the latter's capacity to empathise.

The externalities associated with labour migration – absence of family limitation, fixed requirements in the receiving country, need for social overhead capital, and cultural barriers – set limits to the desirability of building a world market for labour. A classical world in which goods move and factors do not, and one where obstacles to the movement of goods are so low that factor-price equalisation can be approached – is in some respects a solution superior to factor-price equalisation through migration. In the long run, where education alters skill-mixes and depreciation allowances make possible the transfer of social overhead capital, migration is a good solution save for the loss of cultural identity.

The presumption in favour of freedom of international capital movement lies between that for goods and that for labour. Many economists are concerned that destabilising speculation, differences in taxation, the presence or absence of complementary factors, and non-economic factors (at certain levels of analysis) such as revolution, confiscation, etc., are so widespread that any randomly selected capital movement is likely to be in the wrong direction from the point of view of cosmopolitan economic welfare. International rules provide for the ready imposition of restrictions on capital movements and inhibit restriction on goods.

There is a danger that the desirability of two-way capital movements and the economies of scale in broader capital markets are ignored in this analysis. Canada borrows on balance from the United States, as is appropriate between the relatively capital-scarce and capital-abundant countries, but many Canadians hold United States securities. The suggestion that Canada requisition all private Canadian holdings of United States dollar securities and use them to buy up United States direct investment holdings in Canada, but not debt, appealed to virtually no one in Canadian financial circles or in government. It was evident that large gross two-way investments increased the welfare not only of individual Canadians, but the aggregate welfare of the country, as it enabled Canada to share in the gains from rapid growth of new industries such as computers and copiers which it could not have done if gross capital outflows had been prohibited.

Capital flight from developing countries and investment in hiding in developed countries are undesirable from a cosmopolitan point of view, and especially where they reduce investment and growth in capital-scarce economies. But gross international capital movements which facilitate diversification and investment in securities preferred by investors fulfil an economic function. It should be recalled that European investors bought European securities issued in New York prior to the Interest Equalisation Tax, accepting a lower yield than that available on securities issued in Europe in return for a more marketable and hence more liquid security. The New York market provides economies of scale not available in Europe. And one means of stimulating the interest of capitalists in developing economies in investment in their own country is for the country to issue securities abroad and permit its nationals to buy them. There is no net capital movement, to be sure, but possibly the beginnings of a learning process. When gross borrowing and lending through an external market have gone some distance and established confidence in the credit of the country in the minds of its own citizens, the operations can be brought home to develop a local capital market.

In my judgement, the economists have underrated the contribution to economic development of an international capital market. The visible hand of foreign aid and even of international loan funds may be a less sure road to development in less developed countries than the arms-length bargaining between borrowers who have to establish their credit-worthiness and lenders who have to be convinced. The scholarly presumption against free capital movements, while that in favour of free trade remains, is an unfortunate heritage from pathological experience from 1928 to the Second World War.

The clash between economic and political goals is nowhere more evident than in attitudes towards the international corporation with its capacity to transfer readily about the world management skill and technology, and in some instances capital. The corporation is welcomed for its contribution to economic growth, but disliked for its foreign control of domestic resources. Economic reasons to restrict the entrance of foreign corporations exist: infant-industry, the second-best and monopoly. In no case is restriction optimal. For the infant industry, the answer is not exclusion of the foreign firm, but subsidy to domestic resources, provided that the ultimately higher return of the domestic over foreign resources can cover the subsidy and interest on it. A second-best case based on, say, inability to transfer profits on direct investment by way of the balance of payments, or refusal to allow foreigners to invest in non-essential goods – cosmetics, soft drinks, milk bars – calls for the first-best solution, in these cases improved capacity to transform the economy between the foreign trade and the domestic sector to effect remittance of profits abroad – assuming that the balance of payments difficulties are not due to overvaluation – and taxes in those cases where consumer sovereignty is subversive of the national long-run interest. The monopoly question is more difficult and two-sided. Much resentment of foreign investment is a result of its breaking up local monopoly. In this case it should be welcomed. Where it takes over or establishes a local monopoly, it should perhaps be resisted, or perhaps be embraced and then controlled by inviting still more entrants. What is difficult to accept is the complaint that foreign investment is monopolistic, or expensive because it takes high profits out of the country when the domestic market is protected by tariffs and practices such as retail price maintenance are condoned.

The political argument against foreign investment remains: 'We want our assets controlled by us, not by them.' The economists cannot argue against non-economic goals. His task is to remind the politicians that benefits must be weighed and costed. 'National independence' which the Watkins Report in Canada included in four of its five stated separate targets has its economic cost which may or may not be worth paying. All economic intercourse with the world economy has a cost in loss of independence, and even the economy with no contacts in trade, capital movements, migration, tourism or investments across its frontier may have its national independence threatened militarily as Commodore Perry threatened the Japanese. Foreign corporate interest in Japan is regarded as a second coming of 'the black ships', but where scarce technology is available only in combination with foreign equity ownership of an enterprise, the price may be worth paying, as the Japanese have finally decided in some cases.

An asymmetry exists in direct investment in that the government of the parent company can control the activities of the subsidiary company abroad more fully than the host government can affect the parent company through pressure on the subsidiary. But the host country is not wholly without influence, which varies directly with the volume of assets under its jurisdiction. The extent to which direct investment constitutes a substitute for colonialism or imperialism is a moot question. The host government has the option of forbidding foreign investment and marginally increasing its national independence at some cost in access to technology, management and perhaps capital and markets.

In the writer's opinion, the intrusive features of direct investment which gain political power for one country over another can be eliminated by international agreement; and the monopoly features could be handled by international machinery. Unhappily the machinery would have to address itself to separate cases, since in the anti-trust field small differences in fact lead to different decisions. For General Electric to buy Machines Bull makes for more competition in the computer industry internationally; for International Business Machines to buy it, less.

III. A SINGLE MONETARY SYSTEM

If the developed world is to operate with free trade, functioning international capital markets, constrained migration, and international corporations operating within harmonised policies regarding taxation, balances of payments and anti-trust policies, supervised by international machinery, it requires one money. One market means one money which means one monetary policy. This could be a single money – gold, sterling, the dollar, or a new international unit, although most on the list are non-starters. Or it could be a fixed exchange-rate system. Where the price of any two items is fixed, they can be regarded as one commodity, according to the theorem of Hicks, and the same is true of money. A single money, supervised by a single world central bank, is a more efficient economic instrument, but its demands on political goodwill may be excessive.

The need for a single money for joined markets is simply the argument for money instead of barter. The emphasis is less on the medium of exchange than on the unit of account, the store of value and the standard of deferred payment. Exchange risks inhibit trade, capital movements and the international corporation. The extent of such inhibition is a matter of some debate.

In trade, it is often claimed that the risk can be hedged through forward markets. This statement makes three errors. First, a formal error, which does not affect the substance; forward markets are unnecessary to hedging which can take place with spot exchange through borrowing in one market and lending in the other. Second, the trader with his own exchange risk covered is still exposed to the risk that his competition may be able to buy foreign exchange cheap or sell it dear. Third, as Anthony Lanyi states, exchange risks inhibit not the transaction so much as the activity. With exchange rates flexible, it is less interesting for the normal risk-averter to engage in exports or in import-competing activity, or to lend or borrow abroad, and world allocative efficiency is thereby diminished.

Exchange-rate flexibility may or may not decrease capital movements, depending upon the type of capital and the detailed circumstances. It is difficult to generalise, but the net effect is almost certainly to reduce desirable net movements from countries where savings are abundant to those where they are scarce. Short-term movements under stabilising speculation as in the Canadian case from 1950 to 1961 are probably stimulated. The long-term movement of capital to Canada through bonds appears to have ignored the exchange risk and focused on the wide difference in interest rates; but this may be a special case affected by the historic integration of the Canadian and New York capital markets, and the hysteresis effect which made it likely that the Canadian and the United States dollar would not get far apart in the long run.

In direct investment one might expect fear of long-run changes in exchange rates to have no effect because of the long-run expectation that the internal and external appreciation or depreciation of a currency would be offsetting. If the currency depreciates, internal prices and profits will rise, to leave the rate of return in the investor's currency unchanged. But investments are made and wound up in the short run, and at any single point in time the rate, whether appreciated or depreciated, may be under- or overvalued relative to domestic price levels and profits rates overall, and those for the particular industry and firm in particular. If this be the case, flexible exchange rates increase risks of investment and probably reduce it.

This is not to deny the argument of proponents of flexible exchange systems that there are other risks in a world of fixed exchange rates, risks of inflation and deflation, over- and undervaluation, of exchange controls, price controls, confiscation, and so on. The fixed exchange system is of little use without co-ordination of macro-economic targets and policies. The point is rather that in a world of fixed exchange rates and co-ordinated targets and policies, if that world is politically attainable, the risks of trade, migration, capital movements and direct investment are less than in a world of flexible rates and uncoordinated policies. In consequence, there will be more trade, capital movement, direct investment, economies of scale and more efficient resource allocation.

The economic requirements of the fixed exchange-rate system are widely understood from the discussion of the optimum currency area of Mundell and McKinnon. Mundell's emphasis was on factor mobility: factors were mobile within a single currency area, but not between. McKinnon's criterion was the openness of an economy: economies which traded widely with each other belonged in the same currency area, while those with limited outside trade could operate a flexible exchange-rate system.

Beyond factor mobility and openness, however, an optimum currency area must have common or co-ordinated economic policies. Under the gold standard, a surplus was supposed to lead to expansion, a deficit to contraction; to the extent that this actually occurred, it involved co-ordination. Today it is important that parts of a common currency area pursue parallel policies with regard to price stability. If such parts have different trade-offs between price stability and unemployment, they must choose the same rate of price increase with whatever that implies for unemployment.

One market implies one price, which implies one money and one monetary policy. One price and one money imply one price level. Where markets are closely connected for money and for capital, there will emerge one rate of interest, and if there is international financial intermediation, with gross as well as net flows, one interest-rate structure for the total spectrum. This means the loss of independence of monetary policy for the single country locked into a fixed exchange-rate system, unless it dominates the aggregate of the others or unless doubt that the fixed rate can be maintained inhibits people from taking exchange positions in the currency. Independence of monetary policy ultimately requires breaking up money and capital markets by introducing exchange risks.

The theory of economic policy suggests that there must be as many policy variables as there are targets. It is sometimes suggested that with three targets – price stability, growth or full employment, and balance of payments equilibrium – there must be three policy variables – monetary policy, fiscal policy, and exchange-rate policy. With the fixed exchange-rate system one lacks both independence of monetary policy and a weapon to cope with the balance of payments. But the view that exchange-rate policy is a policy variable for all countries is illusory, except in the unrealistic circumstance of a small country operating to vary its exchange rate in a world of fixed rates. With two countries, only one has freedom to manipulate its rate, since the rate of the second is the reciprocal of that of the first. One country can give up its freedom to alter its rate; with n countries there can be at most $n-1$ countries free to adjust their rates, and since cross-rates are important, the one country without the freedom had better be the largest whose currency is used as numéraire; or exchange rates must be co-ordinated among countries, so that the flexible exchange-rate system gains little independence of policy. The argument is somewhat extended and cannot be developed here, but I favour one monetary policy for the North Atlantic (plus Japan) community, separate fiscal policies in each country, and capacity to establish interest differentials from the general level of rates for all countries but the United States. The modal country would have three targets – stability, growth and balance of payments equilibrium – and three policy variables – general monetary policy, local fiscal policy and the interest-rate differential. The United States would have two targets – stability and growth – and two weapons – general monetary policy and local fiscal policy. This assumes that general monetary policy and fiscal policy in the separate countries suffice to enable all the countries of the trading world to achieve a common rate of inflation, preferably very low, and political willingness to accept the rate of unemployment which this implies. If this proves not to be the case, there is need for incomes policies – not heretofore known for their effectiveness – or reluctantly exchange-rate changes. The problem is to change exchange rates in the long run to equalise the world rate of inflation in terms of a common money, without breaking up goods and factor markets by short run exchange flexibility.

If the system works, and other countries have three weapons and three targets while the United States has two of each, the target the United States would let go would be its balance of payments. The United States balance of payments would be residual of the balances of payments of all other countries. This assumes that United States monetary policy would be dominant. If this were the case, there would be a need for representation of other countries on the board determining United States (general) monetary policy. In the long run, the Euro-dollar market is likely to become sufficiently strong, independently of the United States money market, so that it can serve as the '*n*th' of the *n* - 1 countries, the focus of general monetary policy, from which the United States along with other countries could establish differentials for balance of payments purposes. At this point, of course, there must be no worry about the balance of payments position of the Euro-dollar market, as there is not now.

Is it easier to co-ordinate monetary policies or exchange policies? The question doubtless is unanswerable except perhaps in a stipulated context. In the 1930s, it was exchange policies which needed co-ordination. Today, it is monetary policies. I am not disposed to accept the view that co-ordination of exchange policies can be evaded by policies of non-intervention. To agree on non-intervention in the exchange market is likely to prove the most difficult type of co-ordination, since it requires a country suffering inflation or deflation from an undervalued or overvalued rate produced by market forces to submit to outside force. The argument that a floating rate in which intervention is not permitted will always keep to the equilibrium level is unconvincing. Even if speculation were generally stabilising, it is not always so. When the rate does track to one or the other side of equilibrium, there is pressure to intervene which is hardly proof against the self-denial implied by the freely floating system.

A dollar system, or better a Euro-dollar system, of fixed exchange rates, a common monetary policy and co-ordinated fiscal policies may need infusions of liquidity if most countries want to add to reserves each year and the United States, or the Euro-dollar market, is not to run large deficits. The technical details are unimportant and need not detain us. It is worth insisting, however, that two types of liquidity are needed: that which grows every year, through gold production, S.D.R.s, international financial intermediation (i.e. borrowing long and lending short), and is somehow stabilised against Gresham's law runs of the kind that Triffin has worried about; and crisis liquidity, such as may be needed when a given currency is under pressure. The latter is now provided by swaps under the Basle arrangements of March 1961 carried out through the Bank for International Settlements. The International Monetary Fund proved unable to cope with crises because its quotas were based on trade patterns, not financial responsibility, and are limited in the amounts that can be provided at any one time. In crisis, funds must be made available freely. The problem is afterwards to mop up the extra liquidity thus poured into the economy and to get back on trend. In due course, the B.I.S. should be converted into an international central bank with powers to rediscount in crisis, and perhaps to undertake open-market operations to furnish trend liquidity. The grant of sovereignty to an international body to perform in this fashion, with unlimited amounts, and in the absence of political surveillance, makes clear that an act of faith is required. Such an act was not performed at Bretton Woods when the United States took the lead in hobbling the I.M.F. It is unclear how far we have advanced politically since 1944.

Given a fixed exchange rate, common and co-ordinated policies, and a central bank, would the North Atlantic (plus Japan) community be geared up to the necessary to cope with problems of adjustment and growth? In trying to answer this question it may be useful to compare trade and payments within and between countries. This takes us back to a literature on the difference between interregional and international payments which flourished in the early 1950s, and is in process of revival today.

The basic difference between the interregional system and that proposed is the absence of a sharing mechanism working through an overall government which taxes and spends without regard to state boundaries. A progressive tax system and benefits which are skewed in favour of the poorer classes in society effects a degree of income redistribution which is likely to assist in balancing regional payments. The effect is achieved unconsciously, as contrasted with the tortured special arrangements for compensating the balance of payments outcome of the United States troops in Germany. Central governments act as to a considerable degree as a collection agency for taxes which are returned to the location where they are raised; this is to improve efficiency and to avoid gaps and overlaps in taxation at the local level which distort resource allocation (such as exist internationally today). It also serves to furnish aid from richer to poorer regions and fill the payments deficits of the latter.

International burden-sharing effects a modicum of redistribution and balance of payments assistance of the sort which is routine interregionally, but the development has not gone far. The World Bank, European Social Fund, Investment Bank, sharing in the budgets of the United Nations and its specialised agencies, foreign aid represent the beginnings. Occasionally an effort to contribute to an international project on a shared basis will break down as in the 'juste retour' of Euratom which required funds to be expended in the country which contributed them, rather than in the cheapest market. Like tied loans and tied aid, these nationalistic measures taken for balance of payments reasons, although practised also by countries with surpluses, are subversive of specialisation and sharing which exist within countries but are lacking between.

IV. THE MINIMAL POLITICAL REQUIREMENTS

Neither economists nor political scientists have a clear view of the minimal political requirements which must be met to convert foreign into internal transactions in an optimum currency area embracing the world, or the world less the Soviet–Chinese bloc and the developing countries. Embryonic agencies of economic government exist like the Bank for International Settlements, the Group of Ten, the Organisation of Economic

Co-operation and Development, and especially Working Parties Nos. 2 and 3, and the Development Assistance Committee, the North Atlantic Treaty Organisation, the General Agreement on Tariffs and Trade, and the more highly structured and limited International Monetary Fund and International Bank for Reconstruction and Development. Some United Nations organisations with a wider membership may also develop into more nearly sovereign agencies, notably the Economic and Social Council, the regional Economic Commissions, the Food and Agriculture Organisation.

There can be little doubt, however, that hysteresis is stronger in the political than in the economic field. Political power is clung to long after economic power has been yielded – by the agricultural sector, by state or provincial governments, prefectures, counties, municipalities, etc. Sovereignty is the last asset to be pawned. State governments in the United States have only limited functions between the national and the local levels – road building, higher education, utility regulation, police and correction of criminals – most of which could be transferred up or down. State lines interfere with the efficient management of urban and productive agglomerations. But like county governments they hang on. How much less likely is it that national states will yield sovereignty to intergovernmental bodies to the extent needed to function?

This is not a plea for world government. A vital principle of administration is that decision-making should be decentralised as widely and as far down the line as possible, consonant with taking into account repercussions, spillovers, feedbacks, externalities running outside the unit. The argument for international decision-making rests on foreign repercussions, so that no big country's macro-economic policies, balance of payments, tax levels, exchange rate, commercial policy, etc., can be set in isolation. The question, however, is whether functional decisions can be taken on a series of separate issues such as exchange rate, monetary policy, tariff reduction, corporate taxation, anti-trust, balance of payments, foreign aid without the provision of sufficient fused political authority to exercise authority over the experts.

This was the issue in the European Economic Community before which the France of President de Gaulle drew back. Nationality won over efficiency in coal, atomic energy, corporate mergers, agriculture (where a complex compromise was evolved), and even in monetary policy. In the view of some, the setbacks represent a pause from which further advances will be made. But can improved international economic institutions be devised in the absence of a high degree of political community, a degree so high, in fact, as to produce political organs to supervise the economic institutions? I do not know, but this is where major forces in trade, transport, communications, capital movements, foreign exchange, and especially the international corporation are pushing.

Discussion of the Paper by Professor Kindleberger

Professor Sohmen said that in the first part of his paper Professor Kindleberger held that arguments for 'cosmopolitan' policy solutions were economic; arguments against were mostly political. Many countries and their inhabitants had different preferences. There was a case for allowing them to pursue these to some extent, even if this led to non-optimal results in purely economic terms.

In the second part, Professor Kindleberger discussed some purely economic arguments against cosmopolitan policies. On the movement of goods, he said that cosmopolitan arguments were strongest. Most economists would agree that even if it were possible to estimate an 'optimal' tariff, its realisation was only a satisfactory proposal, even from a single country's point of view, if there were no retaliation. It might be defensible for a relatively poor country to gain at the expense of the rest of the world, but there were other, better ways of reaching the same result. As for the infant-industry argument, other policies could do the job of the tariff better, and interfere less with trade in doing so. Subsidies or loans could be used.

As to the existence of distortions, say external economies and diseconomies, in theory at least there were other and better solutions than interference with free trade. In practice, it was hard to apply the policies that theory suggested because it was difficult to quantify the relevant factors.

On the advantages of free migration, Professor Kindleberger was less sanguine. Economically it appeared desirable for labour to move from where it had low to where it would have higher marginal productivity. While his liberal convictions resisted interference with people's freedom of movement, Professor Kindleberger conceded that, while lowering wages in the recipient countries, emigration from overpopulated areas might not raise incomes there because, for example, of reduced mortality. One could also have divergences between private and social returns. Roads, bridges, hospitals, etc., were available to new immigrants who did not have to bear their cost. There were also social considerations. If immigrants could not be absorbed ethnically or socially by the recipient population, this could lead to social unrest. There were therefore external costs arising from new immigration. The conclusions flowing from this were not appealing, but it was difficult not to accept many of them.

On p. 494 of his paper, Professor Kindleberger summarised his conclusions on this score: 'A classical world in which goods move and factors do not, and one where obstacles to the movement of goods are so low that factor-price equalisation can be approached – is in some respects a solution superior to factor-price equalisation through migration.' Few economists would, of course, expect complete equalisation of factor prices by movements of goods alone. They would expect that at least substantial capital movements could be necessary for this to happen.

On capital movements, Professor Kindleberger spoke of a 'scholarly presumption against free capital movements . . ., an unfortunate heritage from pathological experience from 1928 to the Second World War' (p. 495). At the end of the war, many people had indeed been convinced that there could no longer be free movement of capital. The situation was now very different and no 'scholarly presumption against free capital movements' could be said to exist in Continental Europe at least. The objections came mainly from outside the scholarly community. Differences in taxation and the existence of tax havens had, of course, distorted capital flows, and he agreed with Professor Kindleberger that they should be abolished. Were free capital movements distorted by agglomeration effects? There was certainly considerable evidence of this. For example, in France, capital was heavily concentrated around Paris. On the world scale, one often had movements of capital from underdeveloped to developed countries where the opposite movement might be more desirable. We needed more incentives for lending to backward countries. Professor Kindleberger put particular emphasis on the advantages of two-way capital movements. A country could profitably float bonds abroad where capital markets were better developed, even if these were bought by its own residents. Also, risk was reduced by portfolio diversification, and this factor also favoured simultaneous capital movements in opposite directions.

Professor Kindleberger saw the multinational corporation as an important carrier of managerial and technological skills, and as a transmission for capital which would not flow if it did not go to a subsidiary of the parent firm. Turning to economic objections to multinational corporations, Professor Kindleberger dismissed infant-industry and second-best arguments. On the monopoly question, Professor Sohmen agreed with Professor Kindleberger when he said that the argument was, paradoxically, often used to oppose the entry of multinational corporations by monopolists in receiving countries who feared its competition. However, there was a legitimate argument that the multinational corporation often strengthened monopoly power in the world as a whole. A handful of companies operating on a world scale could more easily agree to restrain competition. Even in the E.E.C., he thought most mergers were guided by attempts to control markets rather than by the desire to exchange knowledge on production methods, etc. Professor Kindleberger would prefer to use international mechanisms to control the monopolistic tendencies of the multinational corporation. He himself thought one had to put more faith in national controls in the foreseeable future. Even in the E.E.C. there was no real co-ordination of anti-trust policies at the moment.

Professor Sohmen said he disagreed most strongly with Professor Kindleberger on monetary issues. On p. 492, Professor Kindleberger referred to 'the opponents of the "cosmopolitan" solution, who argue, say, for flexible exchange rates'. Was this a correct description? Professor Sohmen saw flexible exchange rates mainly as a substitute for exchange controls, which were hardly a cosmopolitan device.

On p. 497, Professor Kindleberger said 'exchange risks inhibit trade, capital movements and the international corporation'. However, Professor Sohmen agreed more with the qualification that 'the extent of such inhibition is a matter of some debate'.

Also on p. 497, Professor Kindleberger referred to forward markets. He said 'In trade it is often claimed that the risk can be hedged through forward markets. This statement makes three errors.' The first error was that forward markets were unnecessary because traders could use credit transactions instead. This did not involve an error; it just pointed out one alternative. The very fact that forward markets existed and were used by business showed that they played an independent and useful role. It was less costly to cover forward than to obtain a loan abroad.

The hedging of exchange risks was also important for capital movements, and in his case there was no alternative. One could not cover against the exchange risk involved in a capital movement except by forward cover. Well-developed forward markets were therefore perhaps the most important factor unifying the capital markets of different countries. If one could lend abroad while covering the exchange risk forward, one had in principle, even with flexible exchange rates, the same conditions as in a common currency area, except for the trivial fact that the exchange rate at which one transferred back did not, as a rule, coincide with the one at which money was transferred outside. But what really counted was that both rates were known in advance. Even under the present system, exchange rates might change, so the cosmopolitan solution needed forward covering facilities under all circumstances.

There was, it was true, still the risk that 'competition may be able to buy foreign exchange cheap or sell it dear', as Professor Kindleberger pointed out. However, this merely confirmed that it was often possible to make more money by speculating than by playing it straight. The argument criticised by Professor Kindleberger merely held that it was *possible* to cover against exchange risks without paying a risk premium in a regime of flexible rates, not that this was always the most profitable behaviour.

Professor Kindleberger went on to argue that 'exchange risks inhibit not the transaction so much as the activity'. Exchange risks might indeed be increased by floating rates, but Professor Sohmen pointed out that greater flexibility of this variable tended to reduce the risks presented by the variability of other economic phenomena such as exchange controls, deflation, etc. He did not agree that overall risk was necessarily increased by exchange-rate flexibility. The opposite might normally just as well be claimed.

On p. 498, Professor Kindleberger contrasted the combination of fixed exchange rates and co-ordinated policy with the combination of floating exchange rates and uncoordinated policies. Professor Kindleberger found the first better than the second alternative. But this could tell us nothing about the relative advantages of fixed and flexible rates. One could, in addition, have floating exchange rates together with co-ordination, and fixed exchange rates without co-ordination of policy. Professor Kindleberger's comparison had left out the latter case, the one we actually found in the real world.

After p. 498, Professor Kindleberger discussed international liquidity, distinguishing between needs for liquidity under normal conditions and on a crisis basis. There was, in his view, too little machinery for providing crisis liquidity at present. Therefore arrangements such as the *ad hoc* Basle agreement and swaps among the Group of Ten had to be made.

While it asked many more questions than it answered – or perhaps because of this – he had found Professor Kindleberger's paper most suggestive and stimulating.

Professor Kindleberger said he would not take up the issue of floating exchange rates. He and Professor Sohmen had now argued over it for twelve years. He would simply say: 'we differ'. On whether floating exchange rates gave autonomy rather than the co-ordination of policy, he would refer Professor Sohmen to a paper by Professor Harry Johnson, which made exactly this case. Professor Johnson said floating rates were desired to give countries autonomy.

Professor Robinson said he agreed inevitably with a lot of what Professor Kindleberger said. He would argue on a fraction of the total. He did not think it true that economic problems were simple, and all residual problems were political. All economists might agree on what was the first best solution. But economists had different degrees of optimism as to whether this could be achieved. Professor Kindleberger was simply an outstanding optimist. The big question was not whether first best is first best. The big dangers arose in an oversimplified working out of what the best long-run equilibrium would be, and then saying that all who wanted less than this were obscurantists believing in fourth-best solutions.

One major issue was whether ordinary people really wanted the economists' first-best solution if the condition for getting it was to make one treat the world as a unitary state, with perfect mobility. This was especially true if one asked people not just to allow migration to where incomes were higher, but to accept the obligation to migrate themselves.

On the bigger issues, he would go back to the paper by Professor Svennilson to the I.E.A. Conference in Lisbon in 1957. They had there discussed the economic consequences of the size of nations. Svennilson had asked the question: what makes nations important? He said that the nation-state was not a wholly political concept, but much more. The nation was the unit for welfare services; the area within which people had welfare rights; the unit for social policy-making. It was the unit where people were unified enough to agree on what they wanted the welfare state to do and not to do. In a broader sense, it was the area where, because of a common language, culture, and human relationships, one could look for a high degree of labour mobility. The frontier was not just an obsolete political phenomenon; it had reality, perhaps an increasing reality. Because of all this it was the unit with a uniform fiscal policy.

The reason why Professor Kindleberger was over-optimistic was that he assumed that full employment would be achieved in all individual nation-states – without going into the big problems of policy-making that this masked.

To achieve high employment consistently with free international trade, one had to solve the question of how countries could attract enough activity to give each a high level of employment. One would therefore need different real wages in different countries. If the world were one where comparative advantage stood still for ever, this would not be too difficult. In fact, of course, comparative advantages changed over time. For example, the United Kingdom once had a unique comparative advantage in textiles. This was now dead. The United Kingdom had been forced to acquire different comparative advantages. The same was happening in most European countries. If one then tried to get a high level of activity in each separate administrative area, one would need different rates of change of real income and different levels of real income in different countries. This was why one needed to be able to change relative wage rates. One could not depend solely on deflation to force down real incomes in some countries. One would also have both rich and poor countries. In a world with changing comparative advantages, one would need to have different currencies whose relative values could be changed.

Professor Robinson wondered how far all this would affect the desirability of moving in the short run in Europe to something like the unitary state that existed in the United States.

Mr Brittan said that his reaction to the paper was a mixture of strong agreement and strong disagreement. The paper repeated, for the world scene, one of the questions the Round Table had asked about the E.E.C.: Would the whole organisation work better with more centralised policy, whether with fixed or flexible exchange rates?

First, he wanted to raise some technical points. On p. 499 of his paper, Professor Kindleberger said 'the modal country would have three targets – stability, growth and balance of payments equilibrium – and three policy variables – general monetary policy, local fiscal policy and the interest-rate differentials'. How could all these variables and targets exist in a world of one money and one market price? Even if they could, there were grave objections to using fiscal or monetary measures as the main weapon for adjusting the balance of payments. On the welfare side, if one used the rate of interest, capital would move to a country not because of a high rate of return, but because there was a current-account deficit. The reason for the deficit could be nothing more fundamental than an above-average rate of inflation. This would be even more serious where funds moved to meet a long-run deficit, because the investment flows would strengthen disequilibrium on current account. If a country with a current deficit attracted a capital inflow by having a high rate of interest, everything might be well for a time, but in the end this would increase the current deficit through the servicing of the investment. These flows would also increase the surpluses of the surplus countries. Therefore current deficits would grow, and ever-bigger capital flows and ever-increasing interest differentials would be needed to offset them. But perhaps Professor Kindleberger's main instrument was the co-ordination of national policies and his instruments were mainly a short-run expedient.

Mr Brittan said that his basic misgivings started on p. 491. It was unwise to point to an ideological divide between those who did and those who did not want a cosmopolitan solution. Professor Kindleberger seemed to believe in an army of the virtuous who believed in free capital movements, fixed exchange rates, etc. On the other side, he saw narrow-minded people who did not like the multinational corporation and who wanted independent national currencies. This was just as harmful a division as the misleading polarisation of national politics into the left and the right.

Professor Kindleberger in fact saw a distinction between a sinister coalition of the *dirigiste* left and the nationalist right on the one hand, against the liberal world traders allied (strangely) with central bankers on the other. It was true that floating exchange rates did attract chauvinistic nationalists, but Professor Kindleberger should not use guilt by association to discredit other advocates of floating exchange rates. Oswald Mosley had, for example, been a pioneer of Keynes's ideas at a time when even Mundell would agree that they were relevant. It would have been wrong to have changed one's economic views in the 1930s just because Mosley was an advocate of extreme nationalism as well.

On most of the issues between free movement and national control, Mr Brittan said he came down on Professor Kindleberger's side and would choose the more cosmopolitan solution. Oddly enough, in many cases control was better in theory than freedom in practice. One example was the monopoly argument for allowing in foreign capital. A domestic monopoly was often supported by tariffs, overvalued currency, etc. It was more important to improve domestic anti-monopoly policy than to keep out overseas investment.

Mr Brittan wanted to stress the extreme importance of two-way investment, which was often neglected in the balance of payments approach. There were only two real arguments against the free flow of overseas investment. First cause the claims of the government of the parent company for jurisdiction over its overseas subsidiary. This was most obvious when the American Government tried to ban trade with Communist countries.

Second, an argument he had not seen refuted was that the profits of home companies at home were taxed by home governments: the profits of subsidiaries abroad were taxed by overseas governments. There was therefore an offset to overseas investment because of a difference between private and social returns. The only solution seemed to be a tacit convention between governments to ignore this – because if all countries ignored it, world welfare would probably be increased.

Mr Brittan said the main division between himself and Professor Kindleberger was on fixed exchange rates. Mr Brittan saw fixed exchange rates as the biggest real obstacle to a cosmopolitan world. One could argue endlessly whether the developed Western world was one optimum currency area. An optimal currency area was not necessarily the same as an optimal nation-state. In the theoretical discussions, the extent of factor mobility was often given as the criterion. But perhaps one should add the trade-off between different political goals in different countries. Even if Phillips curves were in line in various countries, could one have an optimum currency area involving countries with different policy preferences? France and the United Kingdom might be a better currency area than France and Germany.

But even if the Western world were an optimal currency area, differences of policy now existing would make fixed exchange rates not the best but the worst possible approach to the common ideals Professor Kindleberger shared with him. We lived in a world where exchange rates were fixed in theory but could change overnight in practice. The insistence of governments on postponing changes and then allowing big single jumps made it hard to state the argument for liberal economic policies.

Mr Brittan could not agree that trade liberalisation had no effect on full employment, with such clear connection between increased imports and deflation. There would be a multitude of illiberal policies so long as there were fixed exchange rates. One could always argue that if, five years ago, a better government had pursued a better policy for regulating the supply of money, these restrictions would not be needed. But this was irrelevant. Far from freeing capital movements, we were moving backwards. He thought that we should see many more such restrictions while there were fixed exchange rates.

He did hope for a world with not too much movement of exchange rates, since these hindered trade. However, he wondered whether we would not best approach our goal by accepting that equilibrium exchange rates did vary over time. It would be less disturbing to trade to allow gradual adjustments. One would then hope to reduce the need for movement over the years.

Professor Izzo asked whether, when Professor Kindleberger talked of one money and one price level, he would allow any choice in the distribution of the money supply between countries. Would liquidity preference at full employment differ between countries? If it did, and no provision was made for it, one would probably have different unemployment rates in different countries.

Second, what of the transfer of real resources implied by this system? Even with equal rates of inflation, disequilibria on the balance of payments on current account were possible; there would therefore be transfers of real resources from one country to another.

Professor Scott was concerned that Professor Robinson and Mr Brittan assumed a North American predilection for international rather than regional or national arrangements, because Professor Kindleberger pointed this way. He had himself been over-excited by the Kindleberger paper, simply because he thought it had argued the other way and was far too attracted by the argument for fragmentation. One difficulty of analysis was that descriptions of factor movements were often made against a cosmopolitan background, because the cosmopolitan would accept this, and sometimes against a local background where only 'non-economic' arguments needed to be made. One wanted some presuppositions about the desirability of a cosmopolitan world, or it would be clear that economists were wasting their time in talking of removing the barriers to movement of goods. If we were predisposed to a cosmopolitan world, with labour and capital movements, the impact on individual countries would be equal to the impact on geographical units caused by the mobility of labour and capital. In the long run, one would have conurbations, wherever labour was mobile. Then what role did capital play? This sounded like science fiction but showed what might happen. In a fully mobile world, states would not be built only on a common culture, history and language. They would also depend on common tastes for public goods and agreement about what should be done collectively.

With agglomerations of people and capital, caused by mobility, it did not follow that nation-states would disappear. Units like today's nations were fully consistent with continuing labour and capital mobility. This was the kind of issue that Stigler and Breton had discussed in their writings on various kinds of federalism. The resulting agglomerations might have high homogeneity and unity.

Professor Kindleberger said that very big agglomerations of people and capital could not continue indefinitely. Rising rents, air pollution, etc., would stop their growth in the end. The fact was that, while some people might want to crowd together in this way, others might want to go elsewhere. One could only hope for 'optimum agglomeration' by free trial and error.

Professor Kindleberger's second difficulty was that perhaps all the poor might want to be in one country and all the rich in another, so that mobility could accentuate the separation of underdeveloped and developed areas. But why *would* the mobile poor move to poor regions? Anyway, perhaps international fiscal measures could offset this alleged tendency.

Professor Robinson had emphasised the changing comparative advantages of countries, in part due to changing ratios between labour and capital.

Professor Lundberg said Professor Kindleberger's paper was good in spirit, but he objected to its assumptions and analysis. There had been much good discussion in the Round Table, and he agreed with what Professor Robinson had said about nation-states. He could not see why the cosmopolitan view of a cosmopolitan world did not take seriously income distribution between countries. Then one could understand why economists were unhappy with free capital movements, without regarding it (as Professor Kindleberger said on p. 495) as 'an unfortunate heritage from pathological experience from 1928 to the Second World War'. One could see why economists objected to free capital movements and were hostile to increasing gaps between underdeveloped and developed countries.

Perhaps there was a vicious circle here. We agree that rapidly expanding big companies, big cities, etc., tended to increase differences of wages. We were sceptical about free capital movements, because these were in danger of increasing differences between underdeveloped and developed countries, or between middle-rich and very rich countries. The prosperous became even more prosperous. Economists reacted to this by wanting to interfere with free capital movements. This raised the whole issue of income distribution within and between countries, and partly explained why there was so much interference with capital movements. Perhaps a cosmopolitan world with a lot of regulation of capital flows, in ways that would help to equalise incomes internationally, would also be a world with some kind of solidarity.

What would be the functional interplay between free capital movements in developed areas and targets for rapid income equalisation between countries? He could not see much being done without considerable free capital movement, and a good deal of steering and selection by governments. There would be a lot of co-operation like this. He was looking at the world as it was, with countries with different ambitions.

On p. 499 of his paper, Professor Kindleberger used the device of specifying as many equations as targets, and policy and other variables. This was a good device for teaching students, but it could not even hint at the complexities of monetary policy – even less of fiscal policy. How many variables were there? How should one use such analyses to understand monetary and trade policy?

Professor Houssiaux agreed with much of what Professor Kindleberger said. On p. 501 he discussed the fair return ('juste retour') from Euratom. One could not really say that in the E.E.C. it was possible to calculate a fair return. This was a technique of analysis used by civil servants in attempting to avoid perverse results, say, in the effects of aid to Euratom. They did not want this to oppose the creation of wealth. Some distributions of capital would actually reduce income.

On p. 502, Professor Kindleberger suggested that nationalism had won over efficiency. One could not think of nationalism as an entity: it was a variable. There were differing degrees of it. One could have action which seemed nationalistic but had international effects. An example was mergers. National mergers prepared the way for international penetration. One should see it this way rather than as a victory for nationalism.

On the optimum size of a currency area, he would refer back to Professor Mundell's paper. Mundell agreed that its political acceptability was basic; this was especially true for Germany. For example, Professor Houssiaux thought a monetary zone, including Germany, would require transfers from richer to poorer parts of Europe; i.e. from Germany to elsewhere. This would have to be politically acceptable to the country. Even this could be done for any given country, but with difficulties. For example, if the chosen area were to include the two parts of a divided Germany, it would be politically impossible.

In petroleum, French firms were always trying to see what the final situation would be. This needed a dynamic analysis – some elaborate form of dynamic programming. While this was useful, one needed an intermediate stage – regional integration. Despite the inefficiency of monetary, industrial and agricultural policy in the E.E.C., this was not due to governments but to inadequate information flows in Europe.

He wondered on what time-scale Professor Kindleberger saw his international integration being achieved and what accidents he feared on the way. We had international organisations and agreements already: how did they help?

Professor Campbell wanted to refer to the case of Canada, and particularly of direct investment by the United States. Professor Kindleberger relied on the profit motive of large corporations. The issue was not the present location of investment, but which plant should supply which markets, etc. He challenged this. Professor Kindleberger was now saying that what was good for General Motors was not only good for America but excellent for Canada, Portugal and indeed everyone else. We had seen offensive aspects of this kind of policy where decisions in Washington had stopped firms sending trucks to China and flour to Cuba. These cold-war influences were limited, but one would expect other examples of a less publicised kind. The same thing could well happen through specialisation and the multinational corporation.

Mr Shonfield took up Professor Lundberg's reference to cumulative disequilibrating forces. He would ask: would we get a better distribution of capital resources from the point of view of underdeveloped countries if there were no government foreign aid, cuts in taxes and if we left everything to the capital market? The answer was no.

If one looked at the political aims and motives of individual countries so far as the capital market was concerned, one could compare the results with those of Professor Kindleberger. The notion that there were rational capital movements by which the world capital market would provide the optimal amount of capital for underdeveloped countries was an idea in the realm of fantasy.

With high rates of interest in the Western world heavily discounting the future, and the economic problems of the United States, the rate of return demanded of underdeveloped countries was too high. They had to show dramatic results over, say, four years to take funds from activities like amusement arcades in developed countries. It followed that movements of interest rates reduced the welfare possibilities of movements of capital, and we were in a particularly bad period for this at present. We had both high rates of interest and a general impatience with the failure of underdeveloped countries to grow.

However, the main issue in Professor Kindleberger's paper was raised on p. 491, where he said that the way to proceed was to 'an attempt to replicate the conditions of the internal market on an international scale'. The idea also appeared in the last paragraph of p. 502, where Professor Kindleberger asked 'can improved international economic institutions be devised in the absence of a high degree of political community'? This had been a constant theme in the Round Table. He wanted to put the question this way: How big a package of bargains must the big package be? It had been made clear in Professor Albert's paper that the E.E.C. now suffered through the diminution of its package.

But could one imagine sectoral trade bargaining on a very extensive scale? He was optimistic about this. We had enlarged negotiating packages impressively in the 1960s. One did not need a cosmic package for there to be useful bargaining – so long as the underlying understanding was that the countries concerned would go on to make further bargains in a fairly generous spirit. They had to agree that they were committed to one another politically and that their objectives were similar enough for them to bargain usefully over a long period. One needed a Group of Ten rather than a group of seventy-seven in UNCTAD.

Mr Shonfield referred to the question of free movements of capital and their relationship to free trade. Professor Mundell had said that we should not bother excessively about trade; capital would be sure to move, and resource endowments would automatically adjust. He rejected this view of the inevitability of the outcome.

He also thought that Mr Lamfalussy was wrong in arguing that any control of capital movements necessarily led to the control of trade. It was true that to control capital movements one must split capital and current elements in trading. Those paying for imports must show the customs authorities evidence of the nature of the transaction; but this was different from imposing controls on trade. If the United Kingdom moved from capital controls to devices like import deposits, this was because the United Kingdom had failed to solve its balance of payments problem. Consequently, controls had escalated. But this kind of escalation was not in the nature of things.

The Mundell line was that freedom of movement was important, and that free capital movement was the most important of all. It made free trade otiose. But for some of us, entirely free capital movements had enormous social implications. He feared that a new Gresham's law was operating on tax systems, and that more and more people had an eye on the tax system when deciding where to invest. A country with no tax attracted a lot of funds. With free capital movements, the welfare states would be starved of capital for the benefit of the anti-welfare states. In that case, the social welfare of populations would be decided by a small capital-owning class. The movement of goods did not have these implications. So one came back in the end to the fact that whether one was freeing capital movements or freeing trade had political implications and decisions were needed on the kind of distribution of resources one was after.

In deciding how much freedom of movement was appropriate, one had to take account not only of Professor Robinson's point that the nation-state was today the chief instrument of welfare policies; there also was the objection to putting so much power over these policies into the hands of capital-owners.

Professor Kindleberger commented on the discussion, saying that most speakers had said that they sympathised with the tone of his paper and then went on to fire big cannons into the middle of it. He would just observe that sympathy was cheap!

Professor Kindleberger said that he would not talk about floating exchange rates at length. It was hard to defeat Professor Robinson's point about the need for real wage adjustments, or indeed what Professor Sohmen and Mr Brittan had said. Mundell, McKinnan and he believed that floating exchange rates were ineffective because there was no longer a money illusion. Professor Robinson wanted to protect real incomes during moves toward new comparative advantages. With no money illusion, the only way to do this was to reduce real incomes more directly than could be done by fiddling with prices. Professor Johnson's article said that floating exchange rates were not a panacea. There was no free lunch any more than there was perpetual motion.

Professor *Sohmen* retorted that there was nevertheless a cheaper lunch!

Professor *Kindleberger* went on to say that support for floating exchange rates was a notion derived from partial equilibrium analysis and could not be used, because altering exchange rates constituted a general equilibrium problem. Devaluation implied the need to redistribute national income. If one could do this, devaluation would succeed. General de Gaulle had made it work; would the French people allow Pompidou to do so?

On the multinational corporation, Professor Robinson said three things. First, it was closing the technological gap; second, it was closing the managerial gap; third, it was bringing a foreign ownership. Professor Robinson was happy about one and two, but was not sure about three. Professor Samuelson's elementary textbook said 'every child knows you cannot have both'. One could not separate these things. One could not say: we will take the technology but not the ownership. For example, Japan had rules for foreign corporations, but these did not apply to I.B.M. Negotiations between governments and the multinational corporations were bilateral monopoly problems. To the extent that the multinational corporations were oligopolistic, they were a feature of the world that one had either to lump or accept. One could use multinational corporations to develop one's industry, but one could not then complain at the price they demanded. Perhaps one could hire technology, but if one could not one should not weep.

Professor *Kindleberger* agreed with Professor Campbell that America's policy with regard to foreign subsidiaries was not always desirable, but where people moved across borders, governments would pursue them. International law allowed hot pursuit: these were problems of hot pursuit, as on Cuba. But while he did not like his own country's policy on Cuba, the United States was surely allowed one.

Obviously, multinational corporations would try to avoid taxes by using tax havens like the Bahamas or Liechtenstein. The way to correct this was through tax agreements. For example, fifty years ago Delaware had cheap incorporation. Nowadays no one knew of the existence of Delaware. In the long run, present tax havens would go too.

But the multinational corporation in the United States had increased welfare by moving capital to labour. After some uneasiness, it was now accepted by the American public. Europe was at present in the position of America at the time of the Sherman and the Clayton Acts; it had the Robinson–Patman period still to go through. Europe would have to emulate communities in the American South which, after defending the local store, now loved the A. & P. supermarket.

On agglomerations, his critics had a real point. There was market failure here. Sometimes the multinational corporation was bigger than the market. With agglomerations it was not, and governments should deal with this problem. We needed more shared expenditure on the problem – perhaps organised by the I.B.R.D. We wanted all countries to provide more foreign aid and the cost should be shared. However, one should not get so worried over external diseconomies in agglomerations that one stopped accepting the *economies*. The international capital market helped everyone because of economies of scale. While one needed more research on external diseconomies, they did exist.

On perverse capital movements, he would like an international convention on the registration of bonds. He wanted to see countries not stopping capital movements from, say, Mexico, but more borrowing. Sometimes the capital market seemed to move funds in the wrong direction; public institutions must move funds the other way.

Professor Kindleberger said that a workable system of competition was only possible when there was a desire to help its occasional unfortunate victims. One should not eliminate competition instead. If one were helping those who suffered from it, one could tolerate competition a great deal better.

Professor Scott said we should deal with countries as they were, or might be. Should one shuffle resources around? As a theorist, he had no judgement. One should become an empiricist and look at individual cases.

Professor Houssiaux had spoken of a dynamic pattern in French petroleum. In any short-run situation it was hard to see how one would get to the long-run position. To add to what Keynes had said, we were dead, too, if we merely applied long-run solutions.

Where should we be going? There would be detours – stops for lunch. But we should get on the turnpike to obtain the benefits of scale.

On the politics of the problem, he thought the best line in his paper was that sovereignty was the last asset to be pawned. He was not sure if this remark was original, but he knew Canadians understood it. Here, there was the dynamic problem with the regions. How could Canada get the provinces to give up power? He had recently had an excellent seminar paper by a professor on the multinational corporation, which contained the pregnant question: Which will be here in seventy-five years' time, General Motors or France? The nation-state, the multinational corporation, foreign capital, and foreign trade were all at war in the short run. He thought economic forces would win in the long run.

Professor Rasmussen was fascinated by Professor Kindleberger's picture of the world, though it was an abstract one. Taking the paper at its face value, he thought that on p. 499 Professor Kindleberger had forgotten the crucial policy variable which would be needed – namely, wage rates. One must either control these, or assume that the Phillips curve for individual countries moved easily. If one did not assume control over wage rates, what room was there for manœuvre in general monetary policy?

Professor van Meerhaeghe thought that since Mr Lamfalussy had had to leave the Round Table, he should say for him that if one imposed controls on capital movements, this would lead to controls on trade. Lamfalussy had claimed that the multinational corporation could disguise capital movements as current movements.

Professor van Meerhaeghe also said that he agreed with Professor Kindleberger on fixed exchange rates. Professor Kindleberger had given theoretical reasons for them. However, Professor van Meerhaeghe thought many economists liked to be in opposition to whatever was the normal or 'operational' view. This was why they opposed fixed exchange rates. On p. 494, Professor Kindleberger said 'capital flight from developing countries . . . [is] undesirable from a cosmopolitan point of view', but added 'international capital movements which facilitate diversification and investment in securities preferred by investors fulfil an economic function'. Did Professor Kindleberger want such movements or not? Did he approve of African heads of state who transferred their funds to Switzerland? Should such movements be controlled?

Professor Eastman said that he understood that Professor Kindleberger recommended certain policies of adjustment for countries with balance of payments disequilibria, but from today's and earlier comments by Professor Kindleberger, it seemed that there was no possibility of disequilibrium existing in the United States balance of payments, only in those of other countries. What would Professor Kindleberger take as evidence of disequilibrium in the United States balance of payments?

Professor Wallich made a comment on the asymmetry of size between countries and its effect on the possibility of integration. The existence of different economic weights between countries favoured the emergence of leadership. There was the problem of whether the leader was acceptable, and of conflict between developed and underdeveloped countries too. Integration was the way to development – but sacrifices would be required of underdeveloped countries.

On regional as against national arrangements, he would take it for granted that overall control of monetary policy would give a better situation. However, if such policy decisions were more like a random walk (as often seemed to be the case), perhaps the mistakes by the one group of countries needed cancelling out by the mistakes of other countries in the opposite direction.

A good argument for two-way capital flows was based on distributing risks more widely. Just as one should invest in a firm one did not work for, so one could spread risk by investing in a different country.

Professor Yamamoto thought it was necessary for advanced countries to try to change the basis of their common economic policies. Even the E.E.C. needed stronger central control over its political machinery. Was it possible for the E.E.C. or North America to achieve this soon? There had been a movement towards European political integration in the 1950s, but this had faded away. Why had Europe not harmonised national economic policies on a regional basis? To develop South-east Asia, economic unity was also desirable, but this too was held back by nationalism. Underdeveloped countries needed 'economic development communities' to co-ordinate planning. But why could not advanced countries find a way of doing this and set an example to all underdeveloped countries?

Professor Kindleberger had referred to Japan at various points in his paper, especially on p. 496 when he said 'Foreign corporate interest in Japan is regarded as a second coming of 'the black ships''.' However, there was no fear of importing foreign capital now. Japan wanted to co-operate from a cosmopolitan point of view.

Professor Mundell said this was a disturbing paper, partly because it was right and because nothing much could be done about it. Its general theme was the idea that technological progress was pushing us to a world of interdependences we did not care for or really like. The configuration of sizes of countries was important, and the United States made up half the world economy. So the eighteenth- and nineteenth-century options no longer existed. The world would not collapse if the pound or the mark changed its foreign exchange price. So, while Mr Brittan wanted flexible exchange rates, he did not think the issue was important for the world economy, even if it was crucial to a particular country.

Perhaps the United Kingdom would be the first to leave fixed exchange rates, because the idea of living under the umbrella of the United States was unpleasant, but he was not inclined to recommend this course to any country. He thought that the effects of the franc devaluation would be disappointing.

Professor Mundell thought that perhaps the United States needed to set in motion centripetal forces leading to economic fusion in Europe, and to currency regionalism. Even the non-sovereign part of some alternatives was worse than pawning it. After more changes in exchange rates, Professor Mundell thought European countries would see the enormous costs of not forming a currency area as a coalition against the dollar.

Professor Mundell said he would not go into a discussion of optimal political, trading and currency areas. As with Professor Scott, this simply brought us back to the complicated question of what defined a nation.

Professor Ashton commented on the possibility of obtaining technology without sacrificing ownership. Apart from Coca-Cola franchises, a good example was the operation of Conrad Hilton in several countries, before he sold out to T.W.A. Hilton had introduced advanced hotel technologies to each country, without bringing capital. Only Switzerland thought it could do better.

Professor Ashton thought it unfair of Professor Kindleberger to go out on a theoretical limb and pay lip-service to the problems, but say the show must go on. For example, in Turkey, the World Bank said they would lend, but Turkey must sort out its position first. The same had probably been said by a recent agricultural mission to Portugal. One trod on so many toes trying to remove distortions. Borrowing countries resented the leverage used on them by lenders. In Turkey, for example, no agricultural issue was unaffected by the overvaluation of the Turkish currency. One should tackle fixed ideas, but the main need in this case was to change the exchange rate.

Professor Ashton saw a danger of polarising the issue between what was desirable in the long run and the inescapability of short-run decision-making.

Professor Kindleberger said to Professor Rasmussen that the world must first decide on an inflation rate. This would be a hard process. As Henry Wallich had said, if the United States was forced to reduce output, it would be hard to agree on a world-wide inflation rate. But the problem should be attacked by world monetary policy, through the Euro-dollar market or international institutions like the B.I.S.

Professor Izzo had asked how one should divide up the money supply between countries. Under a gold standard, things were rather chaotic. A change in the price of gold was equivalent to a change in the supply of dollars. This was not the way to fix the dollar supply. It should be done rationally. Perhaps economic policy-makers did produce a random walk. For example, Milton Friedman wanted to establish two simple policy rules, and then throw the key away. In fact, Milton Friedman now said he had been unclear on the floating exchange rates because he did not deal with the n-1 country problem. But the world supply of money could be regulated through the Euro-dollar market, and its distribution between countries by international lending – by changes in the rate of interest. Professor Kindleberger said he would offer one generalisation. We should be guided by how national monetary systems worked and look at parallels between national and international operations and markets. One might ignore sovereignty, but it was important from an economic point of view.

To Professor van Meerhaeghe, Professor Kindleberger said he wanted *net* movements in the right direction, but really was making a plea for balanced portfolios for individuals holding international assets.

To Professor Wallich, he said that if citizens lent to their own country abroad, buying, in foreign markets, the bonds issued by their own government, this might be a beginning of developing domestic capital institutions.

Professor Kindleberger agreed there was a fear that the multinational corporation might obliterate the local capital market. He had an answer to this, but suggested that we should wait for a full study by McKinnan. As for floating exchange rates, we should look at Israel. There was no money illusion there. Therefore money was not a store of value or a standard of deferred payments. We should keep an eye on Israel, which would move from floating exchange rates. Recently, in Bologna, Lord Robbins had said that if there were a floating exchange rate in the United Kingdom, he would want to be paid in dollars. Professor Meade said he believed in the money illusion and wanted pounds. Who would do best in the long run?

Professor Yamamoto had asked about O.E.C.D. opening up the Japanese market. Professor Kindleberger found American efforts here very offensive. He preferred Japanese attempts to open up the Japanese market. This was happening because Japan wanted to carry out overseas investment, for example, in Australia. Japan also wanted to import the technology of the multinational corporation, but put restrictions on it. Heinz was originally permitted only about 40 per cent of a Japanese firm; but its Japanese partner was short of cash and Heinz was increasing its share.

Professor Kindleberger said he always agreed with Professor Mundell where he could, but two years ago Mundell had a theory of crisis in foreign exchange. Now he had a theory of non-crisis. The theory of crisis had been that changes in national exchange rates could lead to serious problems. We were moving back in the direction of the 1930s. Professor Kindleberger was glad that Professor Mundell did not see this happening now. Recent devaluations had been restrained. Devaluing to equilibrium rather than to an undervalued rate was the rule.

Professor Kindleberger agreed with Professor Ashton that if one could get technology without sacrificing ownership, one should acquire it. But perhaps the franchise was being overdone in the United States now. There were franchises to sell fried chicken being marketed by famous sportsmen.

21 Regionalism in International Trade[1]

Andrew Shonfield
SOCIAL SCIENCE RESEARCH COUNCIL, ENGLAND

I. THE PROBLEMS

The major influences which have shaped the institutional framework of world trade during the 1960s have been the emergence of two powerful regional trading blocs in Europe. Even the world-wide trading initiative of the Kennedy Round can reasonably be regarded as being, in large measure, a consequence of the regional development in Europe: at any rate it is unlikely that the United States Government would have proposed its scheme for a massive across-the-board tariff cut and got it through Congress in this form without the European Common Market to supply America with a motive. By the late 1960s some 40 per cent of total world exports came from the two regional blocs in Western Europe, E.E.C. and EFTA. If the Soviet trading bloc is added, the total comes to just over 50 per cent. The question that I am going to examine in this paper is whether the regional pattern established in the 1960s is likely to continue during the next decade, and if so how it is likely to affect the structure of international trade.

The first step is to try to establish how far the regional trend has exerted an influence on the actual pattern of international trading so far. As soon as one examines the record, one is struck by the remarkable paucity of hard evidence on this subject. There is plenty of good theoretical work on what *ought* to happen if tariffs are moved in various ways, but very little which satisfactorily isolates and identifies the effect of regional integration on which actually did happen to international trade in the 1960s. The practical difficulties of tracing this particular current, separating it from all the other forces, known and unknown, which influenced the movement of international trade, and then estimating precisely by how much and in what direction it affected the performance of an individual country over a succession of years, are in fact enormous. There are, however, certain incidental rewards in at least trying. One discovers for a start the very limited usefulness of the elaborate calculations of price elasticities of imports which figure so largely in the arguments about the advantages or disadvantages of one or another of the various designs of free-trade area.

[1] I am grateful to Professor Sidney Wells, who read and commented on this paper in draft.

II. ATTEMPTS TO MEASURE THE EFFECTS OF E.E.C. AND EFTA

Both GATT and EFTA have made studies of the effect of regional integration up to 1965.[1] These are concerned only with the static effects of reducing tariff barriers. Plainly the more important economic consequence of a regional free-trade system is potentially the way in which it affects resource allocation in the member countries. If, as a result of increased competitition at home and enlarged market opportunities abroad, there is a general shift of resources towards activities where factors of production are more efficiently employed, the result would eventually show up not only in a faster rate of growth of G.N.P. but also in the performance of exports to third markets outside the regional bloc. However, to unravel the detail of such a causal sequence, to isolate the effect of one particular trend in international trade from the other factors which might bring about changes in resource allocation and then to measure it represents an exceptionally formidable task. Indeed, even the methodology that would be appropriate to such an enterprise is obscure.

The GATT study proceeds cautiously by way of identifying those factors in intra-bloc trade which are *not* the result of the process of integration, measuring these, and leaving us with a 'residual deviation' which includes the integration effect. What the calculation does in effect is to set an upper limit to the influence exerted by the latter on the trade of members of the regional bloc. In practice it would almost certainly be less than the 'residual deviation', since other factors, notably the effect of changes in the relative competitiveness of export suppliers both inside and outside the bloc concerned, are included in it. For the E.E.C. the 'residual deviation' in trade in manufactured goods over the period 1960–5 worked out at 10 per cent of intra-bloc trade in 1965. This was the value of the increase in the trade among member countries during the five years which could not be accounted for by other readily identifiable factors, these factors being the 'normal' geographical distribution of each member's trade and its commodity composition. That provides some indication of the response to a reduction of 50 per cent in the tariffs on trade inside the Common Market between the years 1960 and 1965. In EFTA, where there was a tariff cut of the same magnitude over the period, the calculated 'residual deviation' was equal to 11 per cent of intra-bloc trade in manufactures in 1965. Another way of putting the result is to say that in 1965 some nine-tenths of the exports of members of each bloc to one another would have been sold even if they had not been members. It is worth observing in passing that a large part of the residual gain made by E.E.C. and EFTA members on their intra-regional trade

---

[1] GATT, *International Trade 1966* (Geneva, 1967); *The Effects of EFTA on the Economies of Member States* (EFTA, Geneva, 1969).

was offset by the residual loss of exports from one bloc to another, according to GATT's calculations.

The study by the EFTA Secretariat, which is confined to EFTA alone, is a more detailed and elaborate analysis of demand patterns in the individual member countries, and is rather more confident that it has successfully identified what it calls the 'EFTA effect'. It is based on an analysis of 1959–65 – 1959 is chosen as a base year in preference to 1960 because it is more closely akin to 1965 in terms of its place in the business cycle – and compares trade trends during these years with the period before integration, 1954–9. The answer at which it arrives is that the 'EFTA effect', over a period of six years during which tariffs came down by 70 per cent, accounted for 12 per cent of intra-bloc trade in manufactures in 1965. This indicates a somewhat weaker leverage of tariff cuts on trade than the GATT result.[1]

The EFTA study calculates that slightly over half of this gain in intra-bloc trade caused by integration was attributable to the diversion of exports from traditional suppliers of EFTA outside the bloc. No comparable estimate of the effect of trade diversion is available for E.E.C. However, the general evidence is that the price elasticity of substitution of imports between different suppliers is higher than straight import demand elasticity[2] – and this accords with ordinary expectations, since purchasers of some products at least may well be more resistant to changing from a home supplier to a foreign source than to switching between foreign suppliers of a product that they are accustomed to buy from abroad. So that it would be reasonable to suppose that a substantial part of the E.E.C. 'residual deviation' was the effect of trade diversion. If the proportion were similar to that estimated for EFTA, the trade-creation effect of E.E.C. would have been around 5 per cent of intra-bloc trade.

The calculated elasticities of import demand, on which so much of the recent arguments about the relative effects of membership of various trade blocs have been based, would have led one to anticipate results of a different order of magnitude. Balassa's estimates, which have been widely used, put the import elasticity of demand for manufactures (S.I.T.C. 5–8) at some 3 per cent for E.E.C. and 2½ per cent for EFTA (2·7 per cent for the United Kingdom and 2·3 per cent for Continental EFTA). This, it is

[1] There are certain differences in the method of calculation adopted in these two studies which make it difficult to compare the results. For example, the GATT study includes negative movements in intra-bloc trade, which have occurred in particular commodity groups, in its calculation of the net 'residual deviation', while EFTA leaves out of account reductions in trade flows within the bloc below the trend line in calculating the 'EFTA effect'. It does this on the ground that the process of integration 'could not generally have the effect of reducing imports from an EFTA country below what they otherwise might have been'.

[2] See Bela Balassa, *Trade Liberalisation among Industrial Countries* (New York, 1967).

to be observed, measures the trade-creation effect only; it allows nothing for the effect on intra-bloc trade of the diversion of exports from outside suppliers. In E.E.C. the weighted average of the external tariff of the six countries on manufactured goods was, according to Balsassa, 12·2 per cent; the reduction of internal Common Market tariffs for the period 1960–5 applied to this figure amounts to 6 per cent. Its effect should have been to increase the volume of imports of E.E.C. countries by 16·5 per cent, on the assumption of no rise in the relative prices of the products concerned inside the bloc compared with those charged by outside suppliers, and by some 11 per cent on Balassa's formula, allowing for a price rise inside equivalent to one-third of the cut in tariffs.[1] Using the same coefficient of elasticity to measure the trade diversion effect, but applying it only to the share of imports of manufactures which was derived from inside the E.E.C. at the start of the period – it was rather more than half in 1960 – the combined result of the tariff change should have been around 25 per cent on the assumption of no price change and 17 per cent on the other assumption. It should be noted that these are volume figures and would need to be adjusted upwards for the rise in export prices in order to be made comparable with the actual 10 per cent increase in the value of intra-E.E.C. trade shown in the GATT analysis.

There are, of course, supply constraints which are likely to limit the effect of changes on the side of demand: the capacity of producers inside a regional bloc is neither infinite in extent nor infinitely prompt in responding to market opportunities. The assumed increase in the prices of export products subject to the new forces of demand inside the bloc is to some extent an allowance for this factor: it reflects the expectation that additional supplies of some of these products by members of the bloc will be sticky at the former low prices. Plainly this is a very rough-and-ready adjustment to a calculation which is itself based on a heroic averaging of the tariffs of the different members of the Common Market. Between 1960 and 1965 two movements were in progress: while tariffs between member countries were being cut, their external tariffs against the rest of the world were being realigned by steps towards a common level. On the whole, however, the latter movement seems unlikely to have had a significant effect on the outcome. The E.E.C.'s common external tariff is itself the product of a process of averaging individual national tariffs; the average of national tariffs weighted by the combined E.E.C. imports of various commodity groups, which is used here, should not, therefore, distort the picture. The actual process of moving individual tariffs up or

[1] The percentage change in imports is the coefficient of import elasticity multiplied by $\frac{ts}{1+t}$, where t is the starting tariff rate (as a fraction of the c.i.f. cost of the import without the tariff) and s the reduction in the tariff rate. To allow for the rise in prices, this is reduced by one-third.

down in different countries in the course of the steps towards a single external tariff may, of course, affect the flow of trade in particular commodities. Wells[1] examined the trade between Britain and the E.E.C. in a number of groups of manufactured products during the early 1960s, in order to see whether it was possible to identify such an 'alignment effect independently of the general effect of trade discrimination'. His evidence from the examination of a variety of British exports which for various reasons should have been sensitive to this influence was that the 'alignment effect' was 'relatively weak or non-existent'.

It is more difficult to make a meaningful comparison in EFTA between the overall effects of tariff changes and the anticipated results based on calculated elasticities. But a rough estimate[2] suggests an order of magnitude for the anticipated increase in import demand of the bloc, exclusive of the diversion effect on existing imports, of 20 per cent against an actual figure for the period 1959–65 (as calculated in the EFTA study cited above) of 6 per cent. Even when all allowances are made for the approximate character of these calculations, the results of the two western European regional blocs in terms of the additional trade generated for the benefit of their members seem meagre.

III. NORTH ATLANTIC FREE TRADE AREA

It is this, among other things, which makes one approach with some reserve the bold calculations by the proponents of a North Atlantic Free Trade Area of the probable trading results of their profferred solution: these lean heavily on estimates of import elasticities.[3] The central estimate of the alleged gain to British exports in the United States market that will result from NAFTA made by Stamp and Cowie in their contribution to the Atlantic Trade Study is so startlingly favourable – a volume increase of nearly 70 per cent[4] – that it prompts a closer look at the figures underlying it. There are qualifications – though they tend to get lost in the mainstream of the argument. For a start, there is a recognition of the probability that British exporters will not use the fall in United States tariffs solely to increase the volume of their exports to that market but

---

[1] *Scottish Journal of Political Economy*, Feb 1966.
[2] Based on the mean of the United Kingdom tariff and of Continental EFTA combined, 16·5 per cent and 9 per cent respectively according to Balassa's weighted averages.
[3] See H. G. Johnson (ed.), *New Trade Strategy for the World Economy* (London, 1969).
[4] Ibid., Table 3 of Part IV by Stamp and Cowie (p. 251) which shows a rise in British exports to the United States of $730 million at 1965 prices, on the assumption that British export prices do not rise as a result of the favourable tariff situation. This figure relates to the total of United Kingdom actual exports of manufactures in 1965, shown in Table 4 (p. 252) of $1,060 million.

will also raise their prices. In that case it is calculated (on the assumption that British prices may go up by a quarter of the amount of tariff reduction and the export be reduced correspondingly) that the net additional exports of manufactures to the United States – the 'trade creation' effect – will just about balance the extra British imports from there, induced by a fall in British tariffs. The final effect on the balance of trade will then depend exclusively on the benefits of the trade diversion brought about by NAFTA. This crucial element in the story, which provides an estimated gain to Britain of some $487 million in the United States market and of $552 million in North America as a whole, seems to have been calculated on the basis of some curiously implausible assumptions.

The detailed arithmetic of the calculation is not spelt out, but the two main elements in the anticipated diversion of United States business to British suppliers are a block of exports from the E.E.C. and from Japan. In each case some 10 per cent of their existing exports to North America is expected to be lost. Why 10 per cent? The answer is that average United States tariffs over the range of manufactures which comprise this trade work out at that percentage, or more strictly will do so by 1972 when the Kennedy Round cuts take full effect, and the elasticity of substitution between United Kingdom exports and E.E.C.–Japanese exports is estimated to be 1. The odd thing is that no part of these winnings derived from the failure of E.E.C. and Japan to hold their own in North America is supposed to be shared by any other member of NAFTA. Britain scoops the lot. It is not clear why.[1] After all, NAFTA will contain some quite effective industrial exporting countries, like Sweden and Switzerland. They will surely claim their share of the outlets opened up in North America by the weakening of the competitive power of some of the E.E.C. and Japanese exporters to that market. The experience of EFTA to date suggests that when it comes to opportunities offered by trade diversion, the other members of this group are at least as quick off the mark as Britain.[2]

Then there is the problem of Japan. Stamp and Cowie concede that it is on the cards that Japan will join NAFTA. A more plausible judgement would be that if such an organisation were ever set up, the Japanese Government would use every resource at its disposal and not rest until it had been given full rights of membership in it. It surely is quite unrealistic to suppose that the Japanese would quietly sit it out while their main export market became part of someone else's preferential trading system.

[1] Ibid. Something is said in a footnote (p. 211) about a decision deliberately to underestimate the elasticity of substitution between imports, i.e. to understate the diversion effect of NAFTA, in order to allow for certain factors which the authors 'have not been able to quantify'; the effect of United States competition in the EFTA import markets is mentioned. But there is no reference to other EFTA competition against Britain in the United States or Canada.

If Japan joins, the authors of the NAFTA study calculate that Britain's benefit from the trade-diversion effect in the North American market would be reduced by $248 million, i.e. by the value of the sales of Japanese goods to North America that we were going to win away from them if they stayed outside NAFTA. But what this implies is that Japan, too, like the other members of EFTA, would obligingly refrain from competing for any of the existing E.E.C. business in North America, which could be diverted to members of the new Free Trade Area. The more realistic assumption, surely, is that the Japanese economy with its wonderful capacity for the rapid expansion of output in response to market opportunities would capture a substantial part of the trade diverted from the E.E.C. To suppose otherwise is to fall victim to the fallacy that Britain will somehow exercise a monopoly over what was formerly E.E.C. trade with the United States, as a 'dominant supplier' of the particular range of products in question.[1] Of course the Japanese market will also be opened to British exporters on a tariff-free basis and there should be some additional gains there; however, the authors of the Atlantic Trade Study estimate that these will just about be offset by the increase in Japanese exports to Britain.

To recapitulate the arithmetic (as shown in Table 21.1 below), the original net figure of $552 million of additional British exports derived from trade diversion should first of all be reduced to $304 million, because Japan will not allow itself to be diverted. Next, this $304 million, which is the sum total of trade diversion from the European Common Market, should be shared with other members of EFTA: the other members of this group already have important outlets in the United States and would be well placed to enlarge them. Finally, there is Japan's formidable competitive power. How much of the benefits of trade diversion in NAFTA would eventually come Britain's way? It is impossible to do more than guess; but surely it would be very sanguine indeed to suppose that Japan and the other EFTA countries would leave the British with much more than half of the total of $304 million of exports diverted from the European Common Market. To round off the story, this balance of

TABLE 21.1

UNITED KINGDOM EXPORT GAINS IN NAFTA AND E.E.C.

	$m.
Total trade diversion	552
less existing Japanese exports to North America	248
Remainder	304
less share of this trade captured by Japan and other EFTA countries (say one-half)	152
Net additional British export earnings in North America	152
E.E.C. alternative: net additional British export earnings	221

[1] See Balassa, op. cit., p. 194.

payments effect of NAFTA is to be compared with the Stamp and Cowie estimate of the effect on the British trade balance of the alternative course of joining the E.E.C., which they calculate would produce a net gain of $221 million. It is not by any means clear even on the basis of their own figures, adjusted in the light of the qualifications made above, that this would be the worse bargain of the two.

IV. A 'THRESHOLD EFFECT'

These particular calculations are worth pursuing in detail chiefly because they provide a potent illustration of the pitfalls of a favoured analytical method. There is, in fact, no simple predictive device which will allow one to distribute the trade resulting from the diversion of exports from the non-members of a regional bloc among the individual members in advance of the event. Balassa has made some rough estimates on the basis of a close and detailed examination of each nation's recent trading record, and has come up with the plausible conclusion that the Japanese would do much better than anyone else in a free-trade area. But the straight application of coefficients of import elasticity to a hypothetical situation such as a free-trade area involves a wide range of assumptions about relative costs of those competing for the market which are most unlikely to be true. To begin with, the assumption that a tariff cut of 1 per cent in the United States tariff for manufactured goods will actually allow exporters to push up their sales by an additional 4·12 per cent (as Balassa's elasticity calculations indicate) is to take the view that the prices charged by domestic suppliers are currently equal to marginal costs. It is only if this is so that it will prove impossible for them to reduce their own prices by the required 1 per cent in response to the challenge. If they have any room for manœuvre at all, they will not respond to the challenge from abroad by promptly going out of business. The same argument applies to the effects of trade diversion inside a regional bloc. There is by now plenty of familiar experience of the pricing behaviour of exporters which shows that in the face of a sudden pressure on their prices, caused for instance by a devaluation of the currency of the country in which they are selling, they will absorb the additional costs or the reduction in profits, rather than sacrifice volume. Of course, if the required cut in their prices is large enough, they will reconsider their market strategy and may even in the last resort leave the field. But how big is enough? The preliminary evidence suggests that, at any rate in the short and medium term, price movements in a range of, say, up to 5 per cent, caused by tariff changes, may have a disproportionately weak effect in relation to the calculated elasticities of import demand.

In other words, there is likely to be a discontinuity, a marked 'threshold effect', in the influence exerted by the establishment of regional trading blocs, customs unions or free-trade areas on international trade. Why should this be? To provide the answer one would need to have a lot more data about the nature of this phenomenon spread over a longer period. In default of this empirical data one can only guess at possible explanations. It is likely that some part of the result is due to the special attitude of entrepreneurs to certain types of export trade. The problem of maintaining customer goodwill, which derives from a continuous presence in the market, may be regarded as more than usually important. 'Les absents ont toujours tort' is a saying which an exporter is likely to have very much in mind. Indeed, the input of resources required to create the confidence that there will be continuity of supplies in a foreign market – where it is often necessary to make a particular effort to overcome the suspicion that deliveries from abroad are more liable to the risk of interruption or likely to be more difficult to come by than from a local supplier – may represent a considerable investment by the individual firm. It would not be surprising if such a firm were reluctant to throw away the capital asset that it had created because of a marginal cut in the rate of profit. (Of course the effect of tariff changes on the rate of profit will depend on the 'effective rate' of the tariff, i.e. its relationship to the value added to imported materials or parts, rather than on the 'nominal rate'.)[1] The exporter with an established outlet in a foreign market may think of his business abroad in a spirit analogous to that of an owner of a mine in a period when the price of his product deteriorates; he will be moved by the consideration that he cannot close down his enterprise without incurring some very high costs when he wishes to resume sales.

This argument is likely to apply only where the export trade in question is being conducted by substantial enterprises, rather than by small firms operating very near the margin of profitability. Perhaps, indeed, the important point is that a high proportion of trade in manufactures between advanced industrial countries nowadays is conducted by fairly large entrepreneurial units. Again one needs more precise data on this, but the evidence available does suggest that the large firms account for an increasing proportion of manufactured exports. It may also be relevant that a substantial part of the export trade of advanced countries consists of the transfer of products between the affiliates of big international companies; the most recent surveys suggest that these accounts for as much as one-fifth to one-quarter of manufactured exports from the United States and Britain.[2] It is possible that there may be a delayed action effect in international trade, as such firms as these establish productive facilities inside regional trade blocs to replace supplies previously sent from branches of the firm abroad. In that case the trend which we

[1] See Balassa, op. cit.
[2] *Survey of Current Business*, Nov 1965, United States Dept of Commerce; *Board of Trade Journal*, 15 Aug 1968.

have identified in EFTA and E.E.C. might change and a larger share of trade in manufactures might be diverted to exporters inside the bloc. Again it is much too early to say. There is certainly no evidence so far to suggest that any such development is a significant influence on the direction of trade.

Assuming that it is not, one might perhaps hazard a hypothesis about the probable further effects of regionalism in international trade in the 1970s after the Kennedy Round tariff cuts have taken effect. By that time many of the tariffs on manufactured goods will be low. Even if these tariffs are eliminated altogether inside new or enlarged regional blocs, the pattern of international trade will not necessarily change in any marked fashion in consequence. That is, of course, not a reason for avoiding such tariff cuts. Indeed, if they result in reducing the prices charged by exporters outside the regional bloc, rather than in diverting trade to suppliers inside, the net effect on the welfare of the region will be that much greater.

V. E.E.C. AND EFTA

If we are about to enter a period of low tariffs in the advanced industrial world during the 1970s, does it follow that the influence of regionalism on the direction and volume of international trade may be expected to be slight? I am assuming for the moment that we are unlikely to be faced with the emergence of new and significant regional economic blocs in the underdeveloped world in the period under consideration. This judgement is, admittedly, based on a simple extrapolation of the political experience of the recent past. It could be falsified in the event – and many of us hope that it will be. But in a calculation of the probable factors shaping international trade in the 1970s, it is not unreasonable to concentrate on the existing regional blocs in the developed world. In the remaining argument of this paper I shall concentrate chiefly on the European Economic Community, since it provides us with a model of an advanced type of regional economic union. I do not go so far as to assert that there is a principle of convergence here which will necessarily make the other two important economic blocs, EFTA and COMECON, approximate to the structure of the E.E.C. But at least the E.E.C. supplies us with an unusual accumulation of data on the kinds of problem which other regional organisations are likely to face, if they pursue the objective of achieving the maximum freedom of movement of goods and services across the frontiers of member states.

This is the first point to be observed: a common market is not merely a device for reducing the visible obstacles to existing trade, in the form of tariffs and quantitative restrictions – its aim is to free from the trammels of a national protectionist system all items which are capable of being the objects of commercial transactions. Thus the particular concern of the E.E.C. is with non-tariff barriers to trade among its members. It may be argued that this does not mark the European Common Market out in a very special way, since its preoccupation with non-tariff barriers is now shared by the other countries of the advanced industrial world and is reflected clearly in the current work programme of GATT. It is also true that EFTA has begun to make a systematic effort to remove some of the obstructions to trade within the group which are caused by varying national standards and technical specifications of electrical products. What makes the E.E.C. distinctive is the range and the intensity of its activity in the non-tariff field. In order to cope with the problems which it has set itself it has to formulate doctrines – and that, apart from anything else, makes it an easier object of study.

The most obvious, indeed notorious, example of its concern with non-tariff obstacles is agriculture. This is the subject of another paper. All that I wish to do here is to draw attention to two general points about the E.E.C.'s agricultural policy which are germane to the broader argument about the future pattern of international trade. First, there is the wholly rational point that is made by the E.E.C. about the nature of international bargaining on trade in agricultural products – and in a subject so heavily infused with the irrational it is a pleasure to be able to identify another element – that viable arrangements can only be made on the basis of a negotiation about the *total* support accorded by each individual country to its agriculture. This, of course, means that all the multifarious subsidies to farmers, open and hidden, deliberate or merely accidental, have to be identified and at least approximately quantified. The E.E.C. had to do this for its own members in order to induce them to adopt a system which is supposed to lead to free trade in agriculture; and it insisted when it came to negotiate on agriculture in the Kennedy Round that the same principle of bargaining about the overall financial support to agriculture was the only way in which to conduct a serious negotiation on the subject. That leads to the second point which is that if a group of countries purports to be able to negotiate with outsiders about possible reductions in the degree of agricultural support provided by the regional bloc as a whole, it will almost inevitably have to establish some measure of centralised control over agricultural prices and output. This is a political fact which derives from an established relationship between the governments of the Western world and the farming community lasting over several decades. When the advanced nations bargain with one another about agriculture they are generally bargaining in reality about the volume of welfare payments to be made to their respective farming communities. If, in addition, they try to establish equal conditions of competitition for their farmers, in order to give them a free run of a common market, they must face the need to agree on a common set of criteria about the proper standard of human welfare to be applied to this section of the community.

VI. THE NECESSITY FOR COMMON SOCIAL OBJECTIVES

The significance of this conclusion for our present argument about international trade is the following. Since a decision on a matter of this kind is profoundly based on political and social considerations, it is most unlikely that a uniform answer would be arrived at by a group of nations with very disparate views on social objectives or indeed on politics at large. This is one reason why a regional form of negotiation among nations of broadly similar character offers more promise in the sphere of agricultural trade than a world-wide negotiation. Secondly, even a piecemeal negotiation on individual commodities, between any Western European group of nations and the United States, is likely to require as a preliminary a complex series of bargains among the Europeans on non-tariff barriers to trade based on some over-view of the interests of the whole agricultural community. Thirdly, it may well be that the Europeans in their negotiations on a common set of arrangements governing the subsidies and the other forms of public support for a particular economic sector, whether agriculture or some other, will make bargains at the expense of the interests of outsiders.

It is in this last sense that the accusation commonly levelled at the European Common Market by those outside it, that it is 'inward-looking', is justified. If EFTA is less inward-looking, it is because it is less concerned with the wholesale removal of non-tariff barriers standing in the way of the possible enlargement of the range of goods and services that could be traded among members of the bloc. In consequence, the EFTA group of countries is a much more responsive and adaptable bargaining partner in a world-wide negotiation like the Kennedy Round than the E.E.C. However, what the proponents of the common market principle would argue is that the short-run convenience is purchased at the expense of the surrender of a longer-term and more ambitious objective, which is the decisive enlargement of the *content* of international trade. Even though the intra-regional arrangements of a common market in new fields of trade may initially show a high degree of indifference to the interests of non-member nations, their effect in the longer run will probably be to induce the latter in turn to engage in novel forms of bargaining. On this argument the pattern of the Kennedy Round, where the challenge of the E.E.C.'s prospective customs union elicited the United States response of a proposal for a 50 per cent all-round tariff cut, stands a good chance of being repeated in other fields of international negotiation in the future. The claim may seem to be a large one, in view of the comparative meagreness of the E.E.C.'s performance to date in creating novel or unconventional opportunities for international commercial transactions, not available elsewhere. But this is the test of its long-term significance as a positive factor in international trade.

VII. PUBLIC AUTHORITY PURCHASING

Perhaps the most promising area for the expansion of international trade, largely untapped hitherto, is public authority purchasing. The volume of purchases made by central and local governments combined, including publicly-owned enterprises, is already large and is almost certainly destined to grow as a proportion of G.N.P. in developed countries. Much of the expenditure consists of straight salary payments to employees, but there is also a substantial amount of outside purchases of equipment and services. These have very largely escaped from the sphere of international trade. Buying is either restricted explicitly by devices like the Buy American Act or, more usually, by various informal though no less powerful devices. The E.E.C. has so far made no noticeable progress on this front.[1] It was only in June 1969 that the European Commission issued a first series of tentative proposals, in a report by one of its Committees of Experts, on a method of concerting action on public contracts for high-technology industries – computers, telecommunications equipment and scientific instruments – among member countries. This made it very clear that there is a long way to go before the E.E.C. establishes a system of free competitive tendering among its members for public contracts.

But the significant fact is, in my view, that it feels under a compulsion to make a beginning. No one has yet seriously tried to subject the placing of public contracts to an agreed set of rules on a fully international basis. However, EFTA has adopted a set of measures designed to eliminate preferential purchasing (of goods; EFTA is not concerned with services) by governments of member states in favour of their own nationals: there are guidelines for tendering by public authorities and arrangements for publicity.[2] These have been in operation since the end of 1966, and go further than anything so far proposed by E.E.C. The evidence suggests that the issue itself is one that belongs naturally on the agenda of regional blocs, regardless of whether they take the common market or free-trade area form. This seems to derive from the essence of the relationship that is established among the members of a group which engage themselves to reach a series of agreements on a wide range of matters over a stated period of time; they tend to find that the many small conflicts of interest which arise in the process can be more readily settled if they have started by agreeing to a big package deal of mutual commitments. Thus the principle of equality of advantage is built into the scheme, and has to

---

[1] A report in 1965 stated that 'in all member states almost all public work contracts have so far been assigned to national contractors since there is a universal tendency to keep public funds within the country'. European Parliament Document, 1965–6 session, quoted by Balassa, op. cit.

[2] See H. Liesner, in *Economic Integration in Europe*, ed. G. R. Denton (London, 1969).

include cases such as that of a country with a big electrical equipment industry capable of exporting equipment for public authority contracts at highly competitive prices but which does not have the same competitive power in the market for articles of private consumption. It would be too obviously anomalous if its partners in a regional bloc had all the benefits of free trade in manufactured consumer goods, while international trade in equipment for public contracts were completely blocked. In this sense a late-twentieth-century trading bloc implies a degree of mutual inspection of government activities, which is far beyond anything imagined by List or the other early proponents of customs unions.

VIII. INTERNATIONAL TRADE IN SERVICES

So it seems a reasonable expectation that the market in public contracts will be progressively absorbed into international trade during the period ahead. Part of the explanation for the E.E.C.'s poor performance in this field is, no doubt, that it has been in a state of intermittent political crisis ever since the conflict with France came to a head in 1965. This situation has produced a kind of built-in lag in its whole programme of integration. It has, besides, confined the main initiatives to those subjects which are clearly set out with a detailed programme and a timetable in the Treaty of Rome. The Treaty lays down a detailed programme on three subjects only: the first of these is, of course, the conduct of foreign trade in ordinary manufactured goods, and the other two are agriculture and transport. It is here that one should look for guidance about methods of securing an expansion of international commerce in untraditional fields – if and when the political climate in the European Common Market is favourable to new initiatives.

The arguments about establishing a common market for transport took longer than those over agriculture, and the results to date are very modest. Still, the five regulations on a common market in transport services issued by the Council of Ministers of the E.E.C. in the second half of 1968 and in early 1969 serve to indicate the type of problem that has to be tackled before a virtually closed area can be opened up to international trade. Indeed, in view of the trouble involved the whole issue may well be felt by those outside the E.E.C. to have been given disproportionate attention. It has been pointed out that the unequal conditions in the fixing of transport rates in the different countries of the Common Market are unlikely to have much quantitative effect on the delivery prices of goods moving across the frontiers.[1] But the fact is that transport services are regarded by the members of the Common Market as a commercial item which should be open to competition on equal terms from any member country, regardless of the place of origin or destination of the cargo or passengers

[1] See H. Liesner, *Atlantic Harmonisation* (Atlantic Trade Study, 1968).

concerned. It is a market whose value is in total at least as great as that of many industries about which more fuss is made. I have the impression that there may be an unconscious bias among economists of the Anglo-American school, who tend to underrate this issue because they are used to thinking of international transport as taking place chiefly by sea and air, where the markets are either closely regulated by international cartels or subject to free international bargaining through institutions such as the Baltic Exchange. There is the further difference from sea and airways that the infrastructure costs of land highways, whether road or rail, are heavy and have to be paid for by somebody – so that there is a natural dispute about who should have the right to use them if the taxpayers of the nation in which they are situated pay for their capital cost and upkeep. Discrimination in favour of national carriers is in fact the rule in international road and rail transport.

It would be unnecessarily laborious to go through the detail of the new legislation on transport. My purpose is, in any case, only to use it to illustrate the broad character of the problem of creating competitive conditions which are regarded as giving equal treatment to all the members of a regional bloc. The first point which is worth attention is the granting of the right to act as a carrier anywhere in the European Common Market. The issuing of licences to carriers is, in any case, restricted inside the national territory of each of the members, and so the 'freeing' of transport services really amounts to a decision to issue a limited number of licences to operate as carriers anywhere in the Community, on equal terms with local carriers. The initial number agreed is 1,200. But it is not just a question of bargaining about a number; the market will only work fairly if the regulations for road transport haulage are the same in all countries – the same minimum age (twenty-one years for heavy vehicles and passenger coaches), uniform qualifications and licence fees, and uniform penalties for infringements of the highway code. The last is required in order to make sure that all carriers receive, and are seen to receive, equal treatment at the hands of the law in each of the six countries.

Apart from the penal laws, there are the social regulations applied to long-distance lorry drivers engaged in intra-Community trade. Again, if the conditions of competition are to be equal, then arrangements must be made to ensure that no national group of carriers has an unfair advantage in bidding for freight, because it is less strict in the rules that it applies about the hours of work, the rest periods and the welfare of drivers. These matters are, therefore, subjected to a new set of rules on a uniform basis throughout the Community. Even a standard log-book has been designed in which drivers and their mates make compulsory entries on a uniform basis recording work and rest periods, mileage, etc. All these regulations will also apply to lorry drivers from countries outside the Common Market who bring their loads into any one of the member countries. And there is now a further proposal by the European Commission to make the instalment of a tachometer of standard design compulsory in all vehicles with a Community licence. This device, which provides an automatic record of time at the wheel, speeds and so on, is regarded as an important additional means of checking that the lorry drivers really do stick to the health and welfare regulations.

Thus something which begins as a device for opening a new area of commercial activity to international competition among a group of nations ends up by handing over the authority to make rules about the working conditions and legal rights of half a dozen different societies to a central agency – and the latter then goes on to introduce a standard piece of vehicle equipment of a kind which has been the subject of sharp dispute by British trade unions in the haulage business. (The drivers regard it as an automatic spy on their personal lives.) The general conclusion which emerges from this illustrative study of the first steps in the establishment of a common market in transport services is that in the course of opening up new areas to international commerce, regional blocs will tend to find themselves faced with the need to centralise authority previously exercised by national governments and to engage in new forms of regulation of a social and economic character. These are the factors which tend to endow a regional bloc among advanced industrial countries, whether it wills it or not, with a distinctive political character. And if nations outside the bloc wish to share in the enlargement of international trading, they too will have to engage in negotiations of a political and social character, which will involve aspects of government that have traditionally been regarded as matters for exclusively domestic control. Some aspects of these arrangements, as the E.E.C. transport agreements indicate, are likely to have a *dirigiste* appearance, since they will tend to substitute for existing informal rules and compromises on social and economic matters operating inside nations a more explicit, formal type of international regulation.

IX. THE FUTURE OF REGIONAL BLOCS

All this, it need hardly be said, is not intended as a prediction about what *will* happen in the 1970s. It is, however, an indication of what may very well happen if the regional blocs which have established themselves in Western Europe in the 1960s continue to evolve during the period ahead. There is a tendency, at present, after a period in which these regional organisations have failed to make any dramatic advances that have caught the public eye, to write them down as being of very little account for the future of international trade. In part, no doubt, that is because they have proved in the event less disruptive to outside interests than was earlier feared. I have suggested above some reasons when they are unlikely to be a source of disruption in world trade in the future either.

It is arguable that if the regional blocs are to continue to exist, they will have to make an effort to extend the range of economic activities in which member states are assured of equal access to the whole regional market. Member states are unlikely in the long run to accept the practice of non-discrimination in one field, where they may be at a disadvantage, without demanding that the principle be extended to others where they feel that their chances are better. Since the services sector is where the growth of expenditure is likely to be especially rapid during the period ahead, the opportunities for removing the restrictions on international transactions in this sphere are unlikely to be overlooked. It is hard to predict precisely where the openings will come. Apart from the public authority contracts, to which reference has already been made, there is the large and growing area of what has been labelled the 'knowledge industries'. Exchanges of services in higher education, for instance, could in time, especially among societies bent on promoting closer communication with one another, have a significant impact on the blaance of payments. A country with good universities, coupled with correspondence courses and an industry supplying educational books or programmed learning kits, might find itself with an important source of foreign exchange earnings. As already indicated, the problems to be overcome before nations engage in the large-scale exchange of educational and other services are largely of an institutional and political character. They have to develop new techniques of compromise amongst themselves. No doubt this might be done on a univeral scale, but it is more likely to happen in practice among more limited groups of nations sharing similar cultures and political assumptions.

At worst, then, the regional blocs may make some internal bargains in what are largely new fields of international commerce among developed countries which will pay little heed to the economic interests of nations outside. At best they will prompt these outsiders to bargain with them on subjects and on methods of conducting their intergovernmental relations which have hitherto had no place in negotiations on international trade. They could be the pace-setters. Which of the two is the more probable outcome depends chiefly on two factors. The first is the continuing expansion of international trade of a conventional kind. In any future negotiations on a world-wide scale involving the services sector, which will surely be of a complexity and *longueur* at least as great as the Kennedy Round, the chances of success will be greater if conditions for the exports of the industrial countries are as favourable as they were in the mid-1960s. The second condition is that the international political environment inside the existing European regional blocs, or in some future North Atlantic grouping continues favourable. These experiments in novel forms of collaboration across national frontiers involve political risks – and politicians have to be in the right mood in order to take them.

Discussion of the Paper by Mr Shonfield

Professor Wallich said the paper began with sceptical observations about the efficiency of regional blocs, but did not conclude that no further attempts should be made to set them up. Instead, Mr Shonfield suggested where regional groups could make a contribution.

The paper looked at studies which had been made to measure the trade effects of the establishment of EFTA and the E.E.C. They were smaller than import price elasticities would lead one to believe. Professor Wallich was not convinced, but there might well have been no great results from the E.E.C. However, one should not fall into the trap of being sceptical of elasticities. We had seen, in the case of recent devaluations that long-run elasticities were greater than short-run ones. Also, the average tariff cut in Europe during the period of study had been only 25 to 30 per cent. This was what led to such small results. Mr Shonfield speculated on whether there was a threshold effect. Perhaps only a big tariff change would lead large firms (which were now important) to take advantage of new arrangements.

Mr Shonfield also looked at NAFTA. He assumed that this would not include Japan. He assumed that a disproportionate share of the benefits would go to the United Kingdom. Only then would there be big gains for the United Kingdom. Professor Wallich did not see America entering NAFTA and exposing her industry to Japanese competition. Mr Shonfield regarded this line of advance as closed. Mr Shonfield said that much had been accomplished but asked what the E.E.C. and EFTA could now do that was novel. He suggested three areas for development: agriculture; public authority purchasing; and transport.

Agriculture raised new problems, and perhaps a small group like the E.E.C. could get a unified policy, and then negotiate with outsiders to systematise or reduce barriers to trade. This was possible. The existing, and probably the present, agricultural policy was not moving in that direction but perhaps the rest of the world could negotiate with the E.E.C. as a bloc. Second, Mr Shonfield said that the percentage of public authority purchases would rise. Third, Mr Shonfield thought it might be hard to do much in transport, but attempts should be made.

The paper emphasised the basic issue that there were two ways to reach a unified world. First, there were universally reciprocal tariff bargains; second, regional approaches. Mr Shonfield would go for situations where countries had a national affinity. He hoped, from then on, to move towards a universalist solution. During the Kennedy Round, there would probably have been less world-wide tariff cutting had there been no E.E.C. There were other effects beside those on trade. There was the restructuring of industry, and there were the political issues which were the whole basis of the E.E.C. The same was true of the formation of groups elsewhere. For example, there was more point in attempting Latin American integration than in setting up NAFTA.

Professor Wallich said one was concerned about underdeveloped countries, where each tried to develop its own steel industry. These countries had inefficient structures and needed to co-ordinate their industrialisation. Monetary integration had been spoken of and a lot could be done. In so far as one was saying that the membership of monetary groups should be increased, he wondered if there were optimal currency areas. If all countries wanted to inflate, then it might be better to have floating rates. One needed blocs where currencies could float.

Mr Lundgren returned to the question of long-run versus short-run elasticities in the E.E.C. and whether the long-run had yet arrived. Mr Shonfield gave a number of reasons why perhaps there would be more change in the future. One reason might be the existence of sunk costs of marketing abroad. In the European case, an important factor was that all European firms had to calculate with the possibility of a wider European market solution. There was therefore a good deal of uncertainty and firms might be exporting with a suboptimal geographic pattern, and even making losses, in the hope that some kind of closer link between EFTA and the E.E.C. would develop in the near future. This was one reason why Mr Lundgren thought the results from integration observed so far were so small.

On the question of international negotiations over non-tariff barriers, the American Secretary of Commerce had recently hinted, when in Europe, that the Administration might propose negotiations, perhaps in 1971, on non-tariff barriers. However, in agriculture there were so many ways of giving protection that it seemed almost impossible to have negotiations. Every country could give loose promises, but it would take decades to identify all protectionist measures. If one could quantify what agricultural protection was worth to each country, this could be done before negotiations. Could one quantify non-tariff barriers to agriculture? This was important, because non-tariff barriers might be the most important type of protection.

On procurement, Mr Lundgren understood that America had a 6 per cent rule; if a tender of a foreign firm was more than 6 per cent cheaper than that from the American firm, it would get the business. This might be one way of quantifying the degree of protection existing now. One could then start by an agreement not to raise this level which would correspond to the freezing of tariffs that occurred when GATT was started.

Professor Houssiaux also commented on the role of public procurement in the E.E.C. He was not so pessimistic as Mr Shonfield, but there was a general rule of national non-discrimination in the Rome treaty (Article 7), which might be broken by international agreements over procurement.

Professor Houssiaux said there was development in each country on the attitude towards central purchasing. There was a tendency to move towards buying only within the E.E.C. The invitation of tenders on an internationally competitive basis had been given up for more flexible arrangements. Thus, one Dutch firm did only harbour building. Italian firms were given contracts to build natural-gas pipelines, despite the fact that the traditional rules of Gaz de France gave an advantage to French industry. Some of this business was financed by the European investment bank. No national discrimination was allowed. What was needed most now was an improvement in state purchasing arrangements.

Professor Fauvel said that, on agriculture, Mr Lundgren had said it was hard to measure the extent of back-door support. But governments, including Ministries of Finance, were anxious to show what was being paid to agriculture. Within the E.E.C., governments wanted to tell the truth about agriculture, certainly as compared with the United States and the United Kingdom. Of course, the Ministry of Finance was glad to obtain funds from other countries in the form of agricultural subventions, but there was enthusiasm for moving towards a less protected situation. An evolution in protection was what the technocrats were suggesting. These changes should be borne in mind.

Mr Lundgren pointed out the risk that Ministers of Finance looked only at costs to themselves. They were quite willing to reveal these; yet other farm protection might still be there.

Professor Ashton wanted to suggest a general proposition. The more one discussed individual measures of protection internationally, the less likely one was to do anything about it. In the negotiations of the United Kingdom with the E.E.C. on agriculture, the more one looked the more interesting the situation became, but the outcome was negative. He was not against measuring the effects of non-tariff barriers, but he wondered whether their disentanglement could really form the basis for a package deal. Non-tariff barriers tended to freeze the situation, often to the disadvantage of the countries which had these barriers. For example, the American milk industry had been overtaken by a technological revolution and its location would have responded to changing technology if only milk production on the eastern seaboard had not been so heavily protected by such factors as price and transport restrictions. Non-tariff barriers were the first stage of a rundown rather than part of an active, or ongoing, policy.

Professor Ashton said that Mr Shonfield had led us back to the right size of the package on protection – and to getting a *rapprochement*. However, he wondered, if there were too much calculation of benefits, whether anything would happen at all. He thought this could be said of the Ottawa agreement. No one was very sure what the pros and cons were. Nor perhaps should Britain have repealed the Corn Laws. He liked what Mr Shonfield had said about a calculated risk in the last paragraph of his paper. If the United Kingdom resumed negotiations with the E.E.C., agriculture would have to be part of a much larger general package – including, for example, science and technology.

Professor Kindleberger retorted that Mr Shonfield meant 'uncalculated risk'. Professor Kindleberger said he always told a young man choosing a wife to list all the qualities he desired – and then marry the girl he loved! At some point an act of faith was needed. This was true of countries as well as people.

To Mr Lundgren, Professor Kindleberger said the United States had had a 25 per cent rule; then a 6 per cent rule; and then went back to 25 per cent. Now, under an outrageous policy, it had gone to 50 per cent. There was, however, strong Pentagon pressure to eliminate the rule because the United States was paying too much in sending Wisconsin milk to Germany near the Danish border.

It would be useful to think over the 6 per cent rule. He recalled that General Motors in Australia had a similar rule that it should buy from Detroit unless the Australian product was 10 per cent cheaper. The policy had then been reversed: buy in Australia, unless the product is 10 per cent cheaper in Detroit. The aim was clearly to try to cut the cost of decision-taking. There was therefore a rule of thumb saying: only make cost comparisons if the differences are important. It was a mistake to ask for extensive calculation for every decision.

Mr Grogan said that he wished to make clear that, as for the possibility of international action to modify non-tariff barriers, he inclined towards Professor Fauvel's view. A working party of GATT had looked at this matter in the early 1960s but had failed to make much progress. Personally, he thought that, given goodwill and some supervisory body with 'teeth', the technical problems might not be insuperable. He also shared Professor Fauvel's views on the dominance of officials in this field; he thought there was something to be gained by widening the debate to include more non-official, expert participation.

Professor Sohmen pointed out that, ten years before, Professor Scitovsky had concluded that pure trade effects of trade liberalisation were moderate. The really important effects came from greater competition. Professor Sohmen was struck by the fact that not only was the latter hard to measure; often it was not even mentioned at all nowadays. He thought that informal agreements restricting competition were being intensified in the E.E.C. and that too little was being done about it. That was why he was also sceptical about the advantages of multinational corporations. The most important reason for international mergers might be not to transfer technology but to control the market better. The Fiat–Citroën merger, for example, did not give much to Fiat except increased opportunity for market domination. Economists should therefore pay more attention to anti-trust policy in the larger market.

Mr Brittan said that in the first part of his paper Mr Shonfield spoke of the calculations on NAFTA. Mr Brittan thought that Mr Shonfield had conceded too much. He was right to doubt the figures on the effect on the British balance of payments. In any case, that was the wrong way to assess this kind of case. Unless the international adjustment process was clogged up, one should look at effects on real income, assuming payments equilibrium and full employment. Working too much in balance of payments terms was often a fault.

On non-tariff barriers, Mr Brittan was sceptical whether one could measure the amount of agricultural protection by Finance Ministry-type calculations. Quite apart from the Common Market, the United Kingdom was probably moving from deficiency payments to levies. The attraction of the latter was that they were deceptive. Governments thought that since the costs were not shown in the budget they were not costs to its citizens.

On the general issue, Mr Brittan wondered whether there was anything to say for expressing non-tariff barriers and back-door protection in general, in terms of tariff equivalents. How feasible was this?

On the Common Agricultural Policy, Mr Brittan wondered what kind of bargain it was? If one took Germany and France without the Common Market, it would pay a German Government to combine heavy support for domestic farmers with a policy of buying its residual imports as cheaply as it could. French farmers would need more moderate support, but had more interest in keeping imports out. The E.E.C. bargain was a French-type system, but with the level of prices that was required by the inefficiency of German farmers. The welfare results were interesting. There was a loss to German consumers; German farmers probably did well. The net effect of extending the Common Market to agriculture was to increase the level of farm protection. It would have been better to have kept agriculture out of the E.E.C. until more progress had been made in moving farmers to other jobs.

Professor Robinson said he was worried by the relationship of international trade to other things. Free-trade policy was only one aspect of a whole set of policies. The most desirable thing was clearly to have first-best solutions all round. If not, what were the best second-bests? Perhaps participants had been putting too much stress on the perfection of international trade, and so got out of line with the whole of economic policy.

If one took countries with populations of 50 million (France, the United Kingdom, Italy and Germany), exports were about 20 per cent of G.N.P. If one asked how much more trade could be brought about by closer economic relations, the answer was probably 25 per cent of present trade at best. One would therefore get a rise in the percentage of exports to G.N.P. from 20 per cent to 25 per cent. What was the gain from trade? Certainly not more than 100 per cent of this increase. In European agriculture, that was about the relationship of the costs of the worst of the E.E.C. producers to world prices. But, of course, much international trade took place on the basis of smaller advantages of exchange than this. If one therefore took an average of 50 per cent, and asked how much gain there would be from a 25 per cent addition to existing trade, the answer was $2\frac{1}{2}$–5 per cent. If this could be achieved with no frictions, let us have it. But if one was in a country like the United Kingdom, struggling all the time with balance of payments difficulties, what price was being paid for liberalisation?

In the United Kingdom, since 1964, restrictions imposed to protect the balance of payments had lost about 1–$1\frac{1}{2}$ per cent of G.N.P. per annum. So, he thought that there had been a negative gain from additional trade since 1964; the United Kingdom had lost about $7\frac{1}{2}$ per cent of G.N.P. Growth had been put back continually to protect international trade arrangements.

This led him back to the big issue at the I.E.A.'s Lisbon Conference. How far was it really necessary for countries to be big in order to obtain important economies of scale? It was true then, and he thought it was still true, that more than half the world's industrial production came from plants employing less than two hundred people. The number of industries where one needed very big plants was limited. They included aircraft, automobiles, computers and some spearhead industries. While not underrating these, even in such industries most economies of scale were obtainable in a plant in a 50 million national market. A lot of the spearhead firms were in electronics, and were not large-scale. How big they were depended on how much research and development they had to do, but they were not essentially very large-scale plants.

One should not underrate, however, the importance of getting these technologies to Europe. In the United Kingdom, one problem of increasing investment was the high import content of the equipment that spearhead firms wished to install. For example, the automobile industry had to buy a lot of plant abroad. It was easiest to provide for such imports if the problems of the balance of payments were not acute. It was true that for nearly all countries the period of greatest growth was when they had a favourable balance of payments. For example, the Rostow 'take-off' periods for almost all countries were periods of favourable balances of payment when it was not necessary to put on the brakes.

Nevertheless, the periods of most rapid growth were not in all countries periods of liberal free-trade orthodoxy. The countries which grew fastest had often applied unorthodox policies. They gained more from internal expansion than they lost on trade. Professor Robinson wondered whether we were over-emphasising one aspect of economic policy? Or should we, on the other hand, stress external relations as the dynamic which brought about growth?

Mr Lundgren recalled Mr Brittan's statement that we should look at gains in real income rather than balance of payments effects. However, one was judging United Kingdom policy now, and there *were* balance of payments problems. There was the threat, even in Mr Brittan's paper, of more protection. One could not, accordingly, leave out balance of payments considerations.

However, he joined those who thought that the gains from further cuts in industrial tariffs were small. He would go further. If gains were much bigger than an *ad valorem* tariff, then trade should be profitable in spite of the tariff. Only marginal trade was stopped. 5, 10 or 15 per cent was the usual rate of protection. Perhaps one should not divide this by 2, but certainly one had to multiply it by a coefficient smaller than 1.

Dynamic effects of trade liberalisation were probably impossible to measure, but surely one could identify them conceptually. Economists did not often work with imperfect knowledge, though they knew it was imperfect. For example, there might be advertisement effects of tariff cuts on small firms not yet exporting. All firms associated higher risks with overseas sales than with domestic sales. If tariffs were cut, the feeling might spread that they would not be raised again soon. Therefore, tariff cuts might reduce the risk connected with trading in foreign markets.

Mr Lundgren added that firms may also look at the machinery set up for tariff reductions. The reduction in risks would probably be greater if there was a very bureaucratic customs union secretariat. This was the one case for having one!

Even allowing for these points, he thought there was not much to be gained from further cuts in industrial tariffs. It seemed that with tariff reductions in EFTA, E.E.C. and GATT, most industrial tariff protection was now removed between advanced countries. The major tariff barriers were now directed against underdeveloped countries and a large number of social and regional problems in the developed countries were connected with these barriers.

Professor Campbell wanted to refer especially to agricultural protection given to countries with comparative disadvantages. For example, Canada protected dairy products. For industrial commodities, too, if one ended protection, firms that had built businesses with existing tariff structures needed help in dealing with the adverse effects of their elimination. This was in the general interest.

The automobile agreement with the United States had an Adjustment Board to train labour, etc., in firms that suffered from the agreement. The same kind of thing would be needed in future with Canadian agricultural products. Or, indeed, for any area, because it would make changes in protection more acceptable to those who were hurt.

Professor Campbell still had doubts on Professor Kindleberger's view of the multinational corporation. He did not agree that there was necessarily a co-incidence between profitability and the interests of those buying from multinational corporations.

There was free trade in farm machinery between Canada and the United States. No tractors were produced in Canada, only harvesting equipment. Trade generally was in balance. Nor were there any tariffs on imports from the United Kingdom. In Ontario, the Federation of Agriculture had found it could buy

British tractors cheaper than those in Ontario. Therefore it imported two hundred tractors. It saved 25 per cent of the price – perhaps a net $1,000 on each tractor. However, the Federation of Agriculture could not buy from Ford or Massey-Ferguson in the United Kingdom. Nor could they buy from dealers, nor from farmers who had bought tractors and promised not to resell equipment. They had to buy from a farmer, who had got the tractor from another farmer, who had got it from a dealer indirectly. This was not in the best interests of farmers, because multinational corporations could manipulate markets.

Professor Kindleberger went back to Professor Robinson's claim that import restrictions in the United Kingdom would have given an extra $7\frac{1}{2}$ per cent of growth over the last four years. He had done historical work on the relationships between trade and growth. One could have export-led growth, as in the United Kingdom in the 1780s, or Germany and Japan today. One could also obtain growth from falling exports, if these led to a stimulus to change. Indeed, one could have them from rises in imports, as had happened in France after the Cobden–Chevalier Treaty of 1860. No simple relationship existed.

One needed other variables. In the United Kingdom, if labour were available and imports cut, it was supposed that more income was saved. He could see nothing in the British economy to show that savings on imports would be invested. If there were a fall in imports, then people would save more, and they might invest more. All this was true; but he did not see it happening. He thought Professor Robinson's was a simple-minded, partial-equilibrium view that an improved balance of payments would always help growth. One could not go straight from the balance of payments to growth at all. Other evidence about the United Kingdom was needed, and the evidence he had led him to doubt what Professor Robinson said.

One was back to the public versus private goods issue, where an optimal tariff helped if there were no retaliation. But GATT was trying to get all countries to cut tariffs and improve efficiency. If the United Kingdom could get its full monopoly/monoposony benefits from an optimal tariff, she would gain. But this was not possible in the kind of world we were trying to build today.

Professor Wallich was intrigued by what Professor Robinson had said about trade and growth. Much of the answer had come already from Professor Kindleberger. But perhaps one should look at the point in other contexts. If a country suddenly decided to control imports and ignore the balance of payments, and had capacity available, it could increase investment for a while. It would accelerate growth from existing resources. This would not affect the rate of growth permanently. For example, in Germany in the late 1930s, growth had been very rapid. But tight controls were needed and this was not tolerable in a modern economy. Looking at a much longer period, would countries have grown more if there had been less trade over the last fifty years? Suppose we substitute for trade and communication in general. Without the present supply of technology, travel, etc., could small, isolated economies have made much progress?

If one tried to quantify the effects of the E.E.C., in the short run it was clear that there was acceleration of growth. What was not clear was whether this was due to increased E.E.C. trade, or to a diversion of trade from outside, or expanded aims when countries found that they had improved balances of payments, or a general inflationary push. Whatever one thought, trade did not seem to bear very strongly on E.E.C. growth.

Professor Rasmussen said that Mr Lundgren had reminded the Round Table that we needed to distinguish the gain from having trade at all from the gain from tariff reduction. This was true, but he would like to underline the point that there were a number of types of commodity or service with no trade at all in the present, but which in future may be traded a good deal. One was education, and the other housing. In the University of Copenhagen, for example, they used a well-known British economics textbook. While not perfect, it was better than the Danish book used before. One now had better-educated Danish students, but it was hard to measure how much better.

In Denmark, productivity in house building was low and perhaps even falling. This was a sector where we should certainly see much more trade, for example in prefabricated houses. That would squeeze Danish home production.

The area for home-produced goods would therefore probably diminish in future, and one could use services as an example of this. Hotels in Spain, Portugal and Italy competed with each other for custom, though in different countries.

To Professor Robinson he would say 'yes, perhaps', but while countries like the United Kingdom had increasing imports, they could also hope to increase exports by even more. He did not see that this Mercantilist argument proved very much.

Professor Dunning wondered if the discussion had taken enough account of the medium-term effects of integration on trade, via the initial impact on investment flows. He was struck by the contribution of foreign-owned firms in Europe to the growth of activity in research-intensive products. Over the life of the E.E.C., he estimated that the contribution of subsidiaries of American and British companies to the growth of trade in the E.E.C. was between 12 and 15 per cent. One should not imagine that this investment resulted only from European integration; much would have happened anyway. But because of the common external tariff and growth prospects, American and British firms had moved to the E.E.C. and had contributed to the increased output and exports of European countries, especially in the research-intensive sectors.

This was partly because of the increase in trade within the E.E.C., and partly because of its changing composition. There had been a good deal of substitution working against United States and United Kingdom firms in Europe. This was linked to the interesting fact that the income elasticity of demand for American exports to Europe had fallen. One reason was that local manufacture had been stimulated. This, in turn, had raised European incomes, but less of any increased income was now spent on imports from the United States.

As for the impact of the E.E.C. on other countries, he had researched tentative conclusions for the United Kingdom, which suggested that if it had joined the E.E.C. at the beginning, the British balance of payments deficit may well have now been well below its current dimensions. There would have been substantially more American capital flowing in the United Kingdom, and increased United Kingdom exports to the Continent. Not joining the E.E.C. had diverted capital and trade to Europe. This had probably helped Continental Europe to improve its trading position versus the rest of the world and also within Europe. But this had probably been to the disadvantage of Britain and perhaps America as well. However, the United Kingdom was getting some gain from interest in dividends from its subsidiaries in Europe. In fact, the multinational corporation was likely in future to be the main agent steering trade between countries. At present the United States got a quarter of its imports from its own subsidiaries all round the world and sent the same proportion of its manufacturing exports to its subsidiaries.

Professor Lundberg said that Sweden, facing E.E.C. tariffs, found the extent to which its firms had set up subsidiaries in the E.E.C. a problem. Profits would come back to Sweden only to a very limited extent. Most were being reinvested.

Professor Sohmen said to Professor Robinson that he did not see how a country could escape the balance of payments constraint on employment and growth policy by increasing protection. Even if the United Kingdom cut trade from 25 per cent of G.N.P. to 10 per cent, an expansionary policy would run into trouble in the end if it had done so before. The country would lose exchange reserves and, with fixed exchange rates, return sooner or later to balance of payments problems. The only alternative would be a continual increase in protection. Only complete autarky would really work.

Professor Sohmen said that, with high growth rates as a goal, one should not forget the adverse allocative effects of protection. More resources were often wasted in keeping out imports than were lost by letting them in. He did not think that more liberal trade policies would harm United Kingdom growth, not least because the United Kingdom was already more protectionist than most other European countries.

Professor Robinson said he must have explained himself badly. The Round Table was discussing proposals to increase the ratio of trade to G.N.P. He had not said that the best way to close the existing balance of payments gap of the United Kingdom was to reduce trade. He was just saying that he wondered what gain there would be from an attempt to achieve an even higher level of trade in the United Kingdom. Was such a policy not going to involve such difficulties that one would have to put the brakes on other aspects of policy to expand internal production? He was therefore disturbed by the optimism which participants were expressing that the effects of further trade liberalisation would quickly and easily increase total welfare.

Professor Scott said Professor Dunning had opened a Pandora's box by his remarks on the diversion of capital movements by domestic policy. One could think of non-traded services, other than transport, open to possible foreign investment. Examples were storage, communications, construction, banking, tourism, domestic service, etc. If one thought of these, then, apart from prefabricated buildings, all implied direct local investment or migration of executives. The industry's output could not be moved to more efficient countries.

Professor Scott was interested in what Mr Shonfield had said about the adverse impact of free international capital movements on declining or stagnating cities and countries. He wondered if Mr Shonfield could say how he thought the similar movement of capital would affect such regions *within* the proposed trading regions. Was an intra-regional capital market more humane than a completely free international one?

Mr Shonfield said that he had intended the E.E.C.'s transport policy, which he had described in his paper, to stand merely as an illustration of the kind of services that he would expect to see liberated from national protection as a result of the process of regional integration. He had in mind the more general point that, in the advanced industrial economies, services constituted an increasing proportion of total consumption, and that there would be growing pressure inside a regional bloc from the suppliers of these services to bring them within the scope of the free-trade system. There were special difficulties which applied to trade in services which did not apply to trade in goods. For instance, it was characteristic of many of them that they had to be consumed, like tourism, in the place where they were produced. But this was not uniformly so. The services associated with higher education, which might well be a growth area during the period ahead, could be supplied increasingly in other places than lecture halls – via the use of television, audio-visual recordings, and correspondence courses backed by computer-assisted learning techniques. Educational goods and services were already a significant element in international trade. With cultural convergence among the advanced countries, there was a likelihood of growing convergence in professional qualifications – and so there would be more scope for the international exchange of educational services. His point was that in order to expand international trade in services of this kind, certain political and cultural preconditions would have to be met among the nations concerned. For instance, there would have to be agreement on minimum professional and intellectual standards.

On agriculture, the question had been raised how far it was possible or useful to subject the international trade effects to rational calculation. The answer was that people were bound to attempt to do it. This had been true – *pace* Professor Ashton – even of the Ottawa Agreement. The evidence was (see *Survey of British Commonwealth Affairs* by W. K. Hancock, vol. II) that Britain had been finally persuaded in favour of the scheme by statistical evidence the extent to which it had become, by the early 1930s, dependent on export markets in the Empire and Commonwealth. The instinct of the E.E.C. to set out to make a comprehensive list of national measures of agricultural protection, direct and indirect, was surely right. In order to establish a basis for international negotiation on this subject, each side had to convince itself that no obscure bit of subsidisation or protection was being hidden by the other.

To Professor Houssiaux, Mr Shonfield would say that if the French were now being as generous to the Italians about public authority contracts as he averred, it was good news – but it was very recent news. The effort was belated. EFTA had taken earlier measures aimed at securing equality of treatment for all member countries in public authority tendering. But the main point he was trying to make was that it was the essence of a regional bloc, whether a Common Market or a Free Trade Area, that it could not exclude these areas of potentially profitable trade from the scope of its arrangements.

Professor Dunning had raised an interesting point about the balance of payments effects of the transactions of international companies. An analysis of United Kingdom experience in the *Board of Trade Journal*, 16 Aug 1968, included some quantitative estimates of the extent to which British export trade consisted of the transfer of goods by foreign-controlled companies to their subsidiaries or affiliates overseas. In the British motor industry, as much as 80 per cent of the exports of the United States-owned companies went to their overseas affiliates. This tended to bear out Professor Dunning's thesis.

On Mr Lundgren's point, he agreed that regional economic blocs among advanced countries were unlikely to bring about a reduction in their tariffs on imports from underdeveloped countries; if anything regional arrangements tended to work the other way, because the most protectionist members of a regional bloc were sometimes placated at the expense of outsiders. The question was: what happened next? There was the example of the United States response to the establishment of the E.E.C.: this could be seen not merely as an attempt to reduce tariffs but also as an effort to secure a tighter set of international rules governing the conduct of international trade, in the face of the challenge of the regional blocs. (Hence the new emphasis on non-tariff barriers.) We needed this sort of healthy pressure on the regional blocs, on behalf of the underdeveloped countries. He thought that there was an important place for international law in the field of commercial relationships between the regional groups established by the rich nations and the underdeveloped world. No doubt the international rules would sometimes be overridden, if some regional bloc felt that it was greatly in its interest to do so. But if there were proper backing from articulate international institutions, it was reasonable to anticipate that the pressure of world opinion would have an increasing effect on how governments behaved. He reminded the Round Table that it had taken the United States about a hundred years, from the Civil War, to convert the laws which expressed the norms that ought to apply to the treatment of the black population into realities. But the fact that the laws existed and were codified helped to give force to the pressure on people to conform.

To Professor Robinson's fundamental query about the gains to welfare from the pursuit of more and more international trade, part of the answer seemed to Mr Shonfield to be that we were in any case the kind of societies which, at the present phase of our development, tended to devote an increasing proportion of our consumption of goods to imports. It was not therefore a question of whether it was worth our while, in some ultimate welfare sense, to put so much effort into increasing the opportunities for exports, but of what it would cost, in terms of the sacrifice of political and social freedom, to compel people to spend less on imports. If it were true that the United Kingdom balance of payments problem was the result of a special feature of British society which made it have an exceptionally high propensity to import, then one might have to accept that the welfare argument pointed to the wisdom of imposing restrictions. But since the whole of the developed world seemed to have the same high propensity to import, there was a strong case for trying to exploit the opportunities for enlarging international trade more systematically. Professor Robinson had asked whether there were further large benefits obtainable from improved resource allocation as a result of international trade. Mr Shonfield had mentioned international trade in services and in public authority purchases as promising fields for development; he could not say whether the result would show large gains to the national products of the countries concerned, but there would surely be some gains. The main argument, however, was not that, but that it was impossible to halt on the course that we had already undertaken without accepting its reversal, and this would have other deleterious consequences.

Finally, on the subject of regional development policy inside an economic community or trading bloc, Mr Shonfield thought that the E.E.C.'s experience was relevant to Professor Scott's argument. The Rome Treaty included a commitment among the member countries to treat assistance to backward or disadvantaged areas in the Community as a collective responsibility. This meant that fiscal factors came into play as an offset to the market forces that would otherwise tend to reinforce many of the disadvantages of poor regions. This was, of course, moving an economic problem on to the plane of political decision. If German taxpayers were prepared to accept an additional burden in order to finance investments supporting regional development in the South of Italy, this implied a view about the nature of the long-term common interests of the inhabitants of the Community as a whole. The notion of belonging together, which this sort of decision was supposed to reflect, might be real or mythical; or the practice of the myth might in turn make it more real. In that case he would be inclined to say: 'Long live the myth.'

Index

Entries in the Index in black type under the names of participants in the conference indicate their papers or discussions of their papers. Entries in italic indicate contributions by participants to the discussions

Adams, W. (ed.), 449 n.
Adler, F. M., and Hufbauer, G., 395, 397 n., 400 n.
Agricultural policies, mutual repercussions of Western European and North American, xix–xxiv, 283–97, 298–320, 321–36, 337–50
Albert, M., xi, xxi, **57–86**
Aldcroft, D., 373 n.
Aliber, R., 244 n.
Allais, M., 240 n.
Allen, H. C., 369 n.
Amzalak, M. B., *159*
Andrén, N., 105 n.
Antonsen, K., 454 n.
Armstrong, Sir William, 90 n.
Arrow, K. J., 364 n.
Ashton, J., xii, *50–1*, *129–30*, **322–36**, **337–50**, *483*, *516*, *537*
Automotive agreement, Canada–U.S.A., 37–41, 48–56

Bagehot, W., 238
Bailey, J., 240 n.
Balassa, B., 14, 36 n., 37, 166, 167 n., 168 n., 520 n., 521, 522 n., 524 n., 525, 526 n., 530 n.
Bandera, V. N., and White, J. T., 391 n.
Baranson, J., 39 n.
Behrman, J., 393 n., 398 n.
Bernstein, E. M., 268 n.
Berthoff, R. T., 371 n., 372
Bertrand, R., 166
Beveridge, W., 68
Blume, S., 449 n.
Borts, G. H., and Stein, J. L., 449 n.
Brittan, S., xiii, *20*, *77–8*, *83*, **87–102**, **124–139**, *179*, *235*, *270–3*, *414–15*, *507–8*, *538*
Bruggman, C., 117 n.
Buckley, K. A., and Urquhart, M. C., 451 n.

Cagan, D., 240 n.
Campbell, D. R., xii, xx, xxi, *51*, *188–9*, **283–97**, **337–50**, *415*, *481–8*, *512*, *540–1*

Canada, essential elements in foreign economic policies of, xxi, 31–47, 48–56
Capital market, international relation of U.S. to, xi–xix, 192–208, 209–222, 223–226
Carrothers, W. A., 449 n.
Caves, R. E., 130
Chorafas, D. N., 377 n.
Clapham, J., 371 n.
Colonna di Paliano, G., 351 n., 352 n.
Commercial policy and comparative advantage in U.S.A., 13–15, 17–30
Comparative advantage and commercial policy in U.S.A., 13–15, 17–30
Competitiveness of Europe with North America, 60–4, 75–86
Complementarity of Europe with North America, 57–64, 75–86
Cooper, R. N., xii, xvi, xxii, 7, **29–30**, 89 n., 119 n., *176–7*, **192–208**, **223–36**, *277–8*, *344*
Coram, T. C., 367 n., 368 n., 370 n., 371 n., 372 n.
Corbet, H., 116 n.
Corbett, D. C., 450 n.
Cosmopolitanism and regionalism, xv–xix
Curzon, G. and V., 118 n.

Dales, J. H., 35 n., 437, 438, 450 n.
Daly, D. J., Keys, B. A., and Spence, E. J., 33 n.
Davis, N. H. W., and Gupta, M. L., 447 n., 450 n.
de Gaulle, C., xiv
Denison, E. F., 60, 165 n., 166, 167, 391 n., 445; and Poullier, J.-P., 32, 33
Denton, G. R. (ed.)., 530 n.
Despres, E., Kindleberger, C. P., and Salant, W. S., 209
Dewhurst, J. F. (ed.), 454 n.
Dormeyer, G., Mattinger, J.-M., Nathasiers, M., Rieben, H., and Schenchzer, J., 474 n.

Douglass, G. K., 365 n.
Dovring, F., 454 n.
Duncan, D. D., and Spengler, J. J., 450 n.
Dunning, J., *364–403, 407–421, 542*

Eastman, H. C., xi, *20*, **31–56**, *232, 340, 416, 484–5, 515*; and Stykolt, S., 33 n.
Economic policies, co-ordination of Canadian and foreign, 42–7, 48–56
English, H. E., 33 n., 123 n.
Erickson, C., 372 n.
Europe and North America, monetary relations between, xi–xix, 237–55, 256–269, 270–9
European Economic Community, common agricultural policy of, xix–xxiv, 298–320, 337–50; economic and commercial policies of, xi–xxiv, 64–9, 75–86; effects of U.S. policies on, 57–74, 75–86; industrial policies of, 351–63, 407–21
Evans, J. W., 120 n.

Factor endowments, and Canadian trade, 32–4, 48–56; and U.S. trade, 13–15, 17–30
Farley, A., 425 n.
Fauvel, L., xii, xix, **298–320, 337–50**, *536–7*
Fein, R., 450 n.
Ferras, G., xiii, *20, 78, 130–1, 178–9, 226,* **256–79**
Fisher, I., 250
Foreign investment, U.S. problems arising from, xiii–xv, 12–13, 17–30
Foreign trade sector, smallness of, in U.S.A., 6–7
Fullerton, D. H., and Hampson, H. A., 33 n.
Freeman, G., and Young, J., 395 n.
Friedman, M., 240 n., 265

Galbraith, V., 322 n.
Gallman, R. A., 368 n.
Garland, S. W., and Hudson, S. C., 292 n.
Gates, T. R., and Linden, F., 62 n.
Gilbert, M., 263 n.
Gilkey, G. R., 450 n.
Girard, L., 355 n.
Grogan, F., *54, 179, 343–4, 485–6, 538*
Grubel, H. G., and Scott, A., 447, 450 n.

Gruber, W., Mehta, D., and Vernon, R., 364 n., 379 n.
Gupta, M. L., and Davies, N. H. W., 447 n. 450 n.

Haas, E. B., 105 n.
Hague, D., *18–19, 413–14*
Hamilton, E., 229
Hampson, H. A., and Fullerton, D. H., 33 n.
Hansen, A., 444
Harrod, R. F., 130
Hathaway, D. E., and Sorenson, V. L., 289, 293, 294, 295 n., 328, 330
Heckscher-Ohlin model, 34
Hicks, Sir John, xii, *132, 177–8, 223–4, 278,* 497
Hirsch, S., 365 n.
Houssiaux, J. R., *52, 75–6, 84–5, 131, 137, 342–3, 345,* **351–63, 407–21**, *510–11, 536*
Houthakker, H. S., and Magee, D., 95
Hudson, S. C., and Garland, S. W., 292 n.
Hufbauer, G. C., 364 n., 365 n.; and Adler, F. M., 395, 400 n.
Hume, D., 238, 239
Hurd, R. M., 429

Industrial policy in Western Europe, American influence on, 351–63, 364–406, 407–21
Interdependence, optimal, xi–xxiv, 491–502, 503–17
International trade, regionalism in, xi–xxiv, 518–34, 535–46
Isaac, J., 450 n.
Izzo, L., *22, 27–8, 53, 78, 84, 131, 189, 278, 407–9, 508–9*

Jackson, W. T., 370 n.
James, E., *24, 28, 79–80, 131, 224–5, 342*
Johnson, H. G., 36 n., 45 n., 89, 100, 402 n., 448, 450 n., 522 n.

Keesing, D., 364 n., 404 n.
Keynes, J. M., 68, 167, 237, 238
Keynes-Hicks model, 240 n.
Keys, B. A., Spence, E. J., and Daly, D. J., 33 n.
Khachaturov, T. S., *187–8, 415–16*
Kindleberger, C. P., **xi–xxiv**, *17–18, 19, 20, 22, 52, 54, 83, 135, 176, 177, 227–9, 234–5,* 373 n., 401 n., 402 n., *411–12,*

Index

429, 450 n., *479–80*, **492–517**, *509–10*,
537, *541*; Salant, W. S., and Despres,
E., 209
Kock, K., 118 n., 120 n.
Komiya, R., 240 n.
Krause, L. B., 395 n.
Kuznets, S., 373 n., 437, 444; and
Rubin, E., 450 n.

Ladinsky, J., 450 n.
Laffer, A., 240 n.
Lamfalussy, A., xiii, xiv, *78*, *83*, *130*, *174*,
176, *179*, **209–32**, *273*, *339–40*
La Tourette, J. E., 450 n.
Lawrence, D. L., 474
Layton, C., 364 n., 398 n.
Lebedev, I. A., *84*, *136*, *483–4*
Leontieff, W. W., 15, 33
Lewis, A., 493
Lierde, J. van, 330 n., 332 n.
Liesner, H. H., 530 n., 531 n.
Linden, F., and Gates, T. R., 62 n.
Lithwick, N. H., and Wilson, T. A., 437,
451 n.
Lundberg, E., xii, *19*, *21*, *22*, *23*, *125–7*,
174–5, *188*, *232–3*, *410–11*, *543*
Lundgren, N., xii, xviii, **87–138**, *176*,
478–9, *485*, *536*, *537*, *540*

McCrone, G., 130
Machlup, F., 72
McKinnon, D., 240 n., 498
Maddison, A., xi, *23–4*, *53*, *132–3*,
163–79, *188*
Magee, D., and Houthakker, H. S., 95
Marchal, Mme A., *135*
Marchal, J., *52*, *174*
Mason, F. R., 371 n.
Mattinger, J.-M., Nathasiers, M., Rieben,
H., Schenchzer, J., and Domeyer, G.,
474 n.
Meerhaeghe, M. A. G., van, *21*, *76*, *130*,
188, *225*, *341*, *409*, *412–13*, *514–15*
Mehta, D., Vernon, R., and Gruber, W.,
364 n., 379 n.
Mello, J. de, *189*, *480*
Mellor, R. K., 475
Melvin, J. R., and Wilkinson, B. W., 36 n.
Merigo, E., *83*, *232*, *343*, *484*
Metzler–Patinkin model, 240 n.
Michalopoulos, C., 450 n.
Migration, intra-European, 452–78,
479–87; transatlantic, 426–51, 479–87
Mikesell, R., 370 n.

Mill, J. S., 239
Mishan, E. J., and Needleman, L., 450 n.
Molitor, B., *26*, *81*, *82–3*
Monetary relations between Europe and
America, xi–xix, 237–55, 256–69, 270–9
Mundell, R. A., xiii, *178*, *229*, **237–55**,
270–9, *498*, *515–16*

Nathasiers, M., Rieben, H., Schenchzer,
J., Domeyer, G., and Mattinger, J.-M.,
474 n.
Needleman, L., and Mishan, E. J., 450 n.
Nordic group, foreign economic
policies of, 103–23, 124–39
North American agricultural policies,
xix–xxiv, 283–97, 337–50
North America and Europe, monetary
relations between, xi–xix, 237–55, 256–
269, 270–9
North Atlantic area, trade and payments
of, 163–7, 172–9
North, D. C., 367 n., 370 n.
Nunes, M. J., *159*, *411*
Nurkse, R., 367 n.

Optimal interdependence, xi–xxiv,
491–502, 503–17
Overstone, Lord, 238

Paish, G., 370 n.
Pankhurst, K. V., 450 n.
Parai, L., 450 n.
Patinkin, D., *18*, *28*, *175*, *177*
Perlmutter, K., 362 n.
Petersen, W., 436, 450 n.
Phelps, E., *24*, *273–5*
Pinto Barbosa, A., xi, **140–60**
Plotnikov, K., *23*, **180–91**
Polanyi, K., 492
Pollard, S., 371 n.
Portugal, development of, as affected by
U.S. policies, 140–58, 159–60
Posner, M. V., 364 n.
Potter, J., 369 n.
Poullier, J.-P., and Denison, E. F., 32,
33
Presnell, L., 369 n.
Prink, M., 370 n.

Quinn, J. B., 374 n.

Rabaeus, B., 117 n.
Rasmussen, P. N., *23*, *28*, *135*, *172–4*,
175, *178*, *278*, *421*, *481*, *514*, *542*

Reddaway, W. B., 401 n.
Regionalism, and cosmopolitanism, xv–xix; in international trade, xi–xxiv, 518–34, 535–46
Reserve currency, problems of, in U.S.A., xiii–xv, 10–12, 17–30
Resnick, S. A., 70
Ricardo, D., 238, 239
Richmond, A. H., 429, 450 n.
Rieben, H., xii, *54–5, 82, 345,* **452–87**; Schenchzer, J., Domeyer, G., Mattinger, J.-M., and Nathasiers, M., 474 n.
Robinson, E. A. G., *17, 19, 20, 50, 54, 128–9, 278,* 328 n., *337–9, 344–5, 416–7, 538–40, 543*
Rostow, W. W., 367 n.
Rubin, E., and Kuznets, S., 450 n.
Russo, G., 457 n.

Safarian, A., 401 n.
Salant, W. S., Despres, E., and Kindleberger, C. P., 209
Scandinavian countries, foreign economic policies of, 103–23, 124–39
Schenchzer, J., Domeyer, G., Mattinger, J.-M., Nathasiers, M., and Rieben, H., 474 n.
Scitovsky, T., 166, 167
Scott, A., xii, xxiii, *48–9, 54, 55, 136–7, 234,* **425–51**, **478–87**, *509, 543*; and Grubel, H. G., 447, 450 n.
Scott, F. D. (ed.), 450 n.
Shonfield, A., **xi–xxiv**, *19, 21, 26–7, 51, 52, 55, 82, 124–5, 135–6, 230–1, 341–2, 409, 421, 511–12,* **518–46**
Šik, O., 417–18
Size and efficiency of the Canadian economy, policies to increase, 34–7, 48–56
Sjaastad, L., 450 n.
Slater, D. W., 32 n.
Smith, Adam, xxiii
Socialist countries, European, relation of, with N. America and W. Europe, 180–6, 187–91
Sohmen, E., xiii, **30**, *79, 83, 177, 189, 226, 233, 340–1, 415, 503–5, 513, 538, 543*
Sorenson, V. L., and Hathaway, D. E., 289, 293, 294, 295 n., 328, 330
Spence, C., 370 n.
Spence, E. J., Daly, D. J., and Keys, B. A., 33 n.
Spengler, J. J., and Duncan, D. D., 450 n.

Stein, J. L., 240 n.; and Borts, G. H., 449 n.
Stobaugh, R. B., 365 n.
Stokes, H., 250 n.
Strassman, P., 372
Stykolt, S., and Eastman, H. C., 33 n.
Supple, B., 373 n.

Technological gap, U.S. foreign investment and the, 351–63, 364–406, 407–21
Timlin, M. F., 444, 451 n.
Thomas, B., 437, 444, 449, 451 n.
Thomas, D. S., 451 n.
Thornton, M., 238
Tobin, J., 240 n.
Tolpekin, S. Z., *132*
Tontz, R. L., 322 n.
Trade and payments of North Atlantic area, 163–71, 172–9
Triffin, R., 210 n., 500

United Kingdom, agricultural policies of, 321-36, 337–50; external economic policies of, xviii–xix, 87–102, 124–39
United States, essential elements in foreign economic policies of, xi, xii–xv, 3–16, 17–30; foreign investment and the technological gap, 351–63, 364–406, 407–21
Uri, P., 60
Urquhart, M. C., and Buckley, K. A., 451 n.

Vanderkamp, J., 425 n.
Verdoorn, P. J., 166
Vergeot, J. B., 355 n.
Vernon, R., 15, 365 n.; Gruber, W., and Mehta, D., 364 n., 379 n.

Wahl, D., 33 n.
Walker, F. A., 429
Wallich, H. C., xii, **3–30**, *131–2, 159, 177, 189, 225–6, 233, 515, 535–6, 541*
Walters, D., 32 n., 445, 451 n.
Warley, T. K., 283 n.
Weir, T. R., 442 n.
Wells, L. T., 365 n., 383 n., 403 n.
Wells, S., 518 n., 522
West, Q. M., 329
White, E. W., 120 n.
White, J. T., and Bandera, V. N., 391 n.
Wiklund, K., 121 n.

Wilkinson, B. W., 32 n., 33 n., 34, 365 n. 451 n.; and Melvin, J. R., 36 n.
Williams, D., 194 n.
Wilson, T. A., and Lithwick, N. H., 437, 451 n.

Wonnacot, R. J. and P., 33 n., 38 n., 166
Worthington, H. L., 323 n.

Yamamoto, N., *24*, *84*, *137*, *188*, *341*
Young, J., and Freeman, G., 395 n.

LIBRARY OF DAVIDSON COLLEGE

Books on regular loan may be checked out for **two weeks**. Books must be presented at the Circulation Desk in order to be renewed.

A fine is charged after date due.

Special books are subject to special regulations at the discretion of the library staff.